From Reich to Revolution

European History in Perspective
General Editor: Jeremy Black

Benjamin Arnold   *Medieval Germany*
Ronald Asch   *The Thirty Years' War*
Christopher Bartlett   *Peace, War and the European Powers, 1814–1914*
Robert Bireley   *The Refashioning of Catholicism, 1450–1700*
Donna Bohanan   *Crown and Nobility in Early Modern France*
Arden Bucholz   *Moltke and the German Wars, 1864–1871*
Patricia Clavin   *The Great Depression, 1929–1939*
Paula Sutter Fichtner   *The Habsburg Monarchy, 1490–1848*
Mark Galeotti   *Gorbachev and his Revolution*
David Gates   *Warfare in the Nineteenth Century*
Alexander Grab   *Napoleon and the Transformation of Europe*
Martin P. Johnson   *The Dreyfus Affair*
Paul Douglas Lockhart   *Sweden in the Seventeenth Century*
Peter Musgrave   *The Early Modern European Economy*
J. L. Price   *The Dutch Republic in the Seventeenth Century*
A. W. Purdue   *The Second World War*
Christopher Read   *The Making and Breaking of the Soviet System*
Francisco J. Romero-Salvado   *Twentieth-Century Spain*
Matthew S. Seligmann and Roderick R. McLean
Germany from Reich to Republic, 1871–1918
Brendan Simms   *The Struggle for Mastery in Germany, 1779–1850*
David J. Sturdy   *Louis XIV*
David J. Sturdy   *Richelieu and Mazarin*
Hunt Tooley   *The Western Front*
Peter Waldron   *The End of Imperial Russia, 1855–1917*
Peter G. Wallace   *The Long European Reformation*
James D. White   *Lenin*
Patrick Williams   *Philip II*
Peter H. Wilson   *From Reich to Revolution*

European History in Perspective
Series Standing Order
ISBN 0–333–71694–9 hardcover
ISBN 0–333–69336–1 paperback
(outside North America only)

You can receive future titles in this series as they are published by placing
a standing order. Please contact your bookseller or, in the case of difficulty,
write to us at the address below with your name and address, the title of the
series and the ISBN quoted above.

Customer Services Department, Palgrave Ltd
Houndmills, Basingstoke, Hampshire RG21 6XS, England

From Reich to Revolution

German History, 1558–1806

PETER H. WILSON

First published 2004 by
PALGRAVE MACMILLAN
Houndmills, Basingstoke, Hampshire RG21 6XS and
175 Fifth Avenue, New York, N.Y. 10010
Companies and representatives throughout the world

PALGRAVE MACMILLAN is the global academic imprint of the Palgrave
Macmillan division of St. Martin's Press LLC and of Palgrave Macmillan Ltd.
Macmillan® is a registered trademark in the United States, United Kingdom
and other countries. Palgrave is a registered trademark in the European
Union and other countries.

ISBN 0–333–65243–6 hardback
ISBN 0–333–65244–4 paperback

This book is printed on paper suitable for recycling and made from fully
managed and sustained forest sources.

A catalogue record for this book is available from the British Library.

Library of Congress Cataloging-in-Publication Data

Wilson, Peter H. (Peter Hamish)
    From Reich to revolution : German history, 1558–1806 / Peter H. Wilson
        p. cm. – (European history in perspective)
    Includes bibliographical references and index.
    ISBN 0-333-65243-6 (cloth) – ISBN 0-333-65244-4 (paper)
1. Germany-History-1517–1871. I. Title. II. Series.

DD175.W54 2004   2004044502
943-dc22

10   9   8   7   6   5   4   3   2   1
13 12 11 10 09 08 07 06 05 04

Typeset in Great Britain by
Aarontype Ltd, Easton, Bristol

Printed in China

For Nina

Contents

List of Maps   ix

List of Tables   x

Preface   xii

List of Abbreviations   xiv

1   The Peculiarities of German History   1
1.1   Writing the German Past   1
1.2   Three Directions in German Politics   7

2   Reich and Territories   18
2.1   The Political Geography of Central Europe   18
2.2   Imperial and Territorial Government   29

3   Fundamentals   50
3.1   The Parameters of Life   50
3.2   Society   63
3.3   Economy   78
3.4   Community   96

4   The Great War (1618–48)   103
4.1   Causes   103
4.2   Conflict   117
4.3   The Long Road to Peace   136
4.4   Legacy   144

5   The Reich in Action   157
5.1   Taxation and Defence   157
5.2   Justice and Conflict Resolution   175
5.3   The Kreise   183
5.4   The *Reichskirche*   198

6   Territorial Absolutism   208
6.1   The Rise of Absolutism   208
6.2   The Territorial State   218
6.3   The Territorial Estates   247
6.4   Public and Private Finance   253

7   State and Society   264
7.1   Regulation and Reform   264
7.2   Conflict and Collaboration   289

8   Imperial and European Politics   305
8.1   The Imperial Recovery   305
8.2   The Rise of Prussia   319
8.3   Germany and the French Revolution   332
8.4   The End of the Old Reich   338

Conclusion   343

Glossary   346

Appendix 1   Major rulers   351
Appendix 2   Territories, by Kreise, *c*.1800   364
Appendix 3   The imperial cities, *c*.1800   378
Appendix 4   The ecclesiastical territories, 1792 380

Guide to Further Reading   382

Notes   387

Index   417

List of Maps

1 The Reich in the Thirty Years War   xvi
2 The Reich in 1745   xviii
3 The Kreise   xx

List of Tables

2.1	The imperial princes	43
3.1	Population of the Reich and associated lands	50
3.2	Wealth distribution in selected early seventeenth-century German cities	72
3.3	Jewish communities in the Reich and associated lands, 1795	77
3.4	Factories employing over ten workers, c.1790	82
3.5	Proportion of the population sustained by agriculture, c.1650	83
3.6	Western and eastern German agrarian models	84
3.7	Imposition of *Schollenpflichtigkeit* and *Gesindezwangdienst*	87
4.1	Leading German opera and theatre houses	155
5.1	Imperial defence	172
5.2	Kreis convenors	184
6.1	German palace construction	219
6.2	Size of selected German courts	220
6.3	German military strength, 1650–1790	226
6.4	Growth of the Prussian army	227
6.5	Numbers of personnel in selected administrations	241
7.1	Foundation of workhouses in the Reich	276
7.2	Introduction of compulsory elementary education	287
7.3	Abolition of judicial torture	294
7.4	Incidence of serious protest in minor German territories after 1648	298
7.5	Major constitutional disputes in imperial cities after 1648	301
8.1	Territorial shares of the Reich	307
8.2	Growth of the Habsburg monarchy	308
8.3	Overview of gains and losses of the Habsburgs	309

LIST OF TABLES   xi

8.4 Population of the Habsburg monarchy   310
8.5 Growth of the Hohenzollern monarchy   322
8.6 Overview of Hohenzollern gains   323
8.7 Hohenzollern lands and peoples   323
8.8 The Hohenzollern monarchy as a proportion of total
     'German' power   324
8.9 Strength of the other secular electors   325

Preface

German history after the Reformation is often passed over quickly as a confusing period of political failures before the emergence of powerful states like Prussia give some coherence to the national narrative. Emperor Charles V's failure to solve Germany's political and religious problems by 1558 seems to condemn the country to an inevitable descent into the chaos of the Thirty Years War and the subsequent partition of the Reich, or Holy Roman Empire, into virtually independent states until its final collapse in 1806.

This book treats the period 1558–1806 as something more than a precursor to the Napoleonic era and the rise of Bismarck's second Reich. It weaves insights from new research into a comprehensive account of German social, political, economic and cultural development, addressing fundamental questions such as how the apparently fragile structure of the Reich survived the trauma of the Thirty Years War and why, despite gross social inequality, Germany did not experience a mass French-style revolution.

The first chapter explains the importance of this period to the broader debate on Germany's historical development. The second examines the country's complex political and religious structure, including the key institutions developed between 1480 and 1550 that shaped German life until the end of the Reich. The material and social conditions affecting ordinary Germans are explained in Chapter 3, which also addresses issues of gender, home and community. The next two chapters examine the causes, conduct and consequences of political and religious strife in the century after 1550, and indicate the continued flexibility and vitality of imperial institutions after 1648. The interaction between ordinary people and wider political, social and economic change forms the subject of the next two chapters, before the last examines major developments of the century preceding the Reich's dissolution in 1806.

While the Reich provided a measure of political unity to central Europe, it was not synonymous with Germany, and many of its inhabitants spoke other languages. It is hoped that the following pages acknowledge this diversity by paying proper attention to these other cultures and lands both within the Reich and associated with German rulers, including Hungary, Switzerland, the Netherlands and parts of Italy. Where place names have different forms, the German version has generally been used, simply because this is usually the one most familiar to Anglophone readers. Individuals are referred to by their original German names, except where Anglicised versions have been established in the wider literature. Technical terms are italicised and explained when first mentioned in the text, and the more important are also included in a glossary. Notes have been kept to a minimum, concentrating on important recent works and those that guide the general reader to the more specialist literature. Additional material can be accessed through the suggested further reading.

This book has taken shape over several years, during which I have benefited from the advice of many good people. I would particularly like to thank Karin Friedrich and an unnamed American reader for helpful comments on the entire typescript, as well as the participants of conferences and symposia at Birmingham, Essen, and Oxford Universities and the Institute for Historical Research, London, where parts of the argument were rehearsed. Cohorts of students at both Newcastle and Sunderland have posed searching questions, forcing me to rethink my presentation of German history. Staff at Sunderland's Murray Library have performed their customary miracles in locating obscure material. Series editor Jeremy Black, together with Terka Acton and her colleagues at Palgrave Macmillan, have stuck with this project and provided constant encouragement. Finally, Eliane, Alec, Tom and now Nina have tolerated my prolonged absences in front of the word processor with more than their fair share of good humour.

List of Abbreviations

BDLG	*Blätter für deutsche Landesgeschichte*
CEH	*Central European History*
EHR	*English Historical Review*
FBPG	*Forschungen zur brandenburgisch- und preußischen Geschichte*
fl.	florin, or Gulden
GH	*German History*
HJ	*Historical Journal*
HJb	*Historisches Jahrbuch*
HZ	*Historische Zeitschrift*
IHR	*International History Review*
IPM	*Instrumentum Pacis Monasteriense* – Peace of Münster, 1648
IPO	*Instrumentum Pacis Osnabrugense* – Peace of Osnabrück, 1648
JMH	*Journal of Modern History*
JGMOD	*Jahrbuch für die Geschichte Mittel- und Ostdeutschlands*
MIÖG	*Mitteilungen des Instituts für Österreichische Geschichtsforschung*
MÖSA	*Mitteilungen des Österreichischen Staatsarchivs*
P&P	*Past and Present*
tlr	taler
VSWG	*Vierteljahreshefte für Sozial- und Wirtschaftsgeschichte*
ZBLG	*Zeitschrift für bayerische Landesgeschichte*
ZGO	*Zeitschrift für die Geschichte des Oberrheins*
ZHF	*Zeitschrift für historische Forschung*
ZNRG	*Zeitschrift für neuere Rechtsgeschichte*

ZSRG GA	*Zeitschrift der Savigny-Stiftung für Rechtsgeschichte*
	Germanistische Abteilung
ZWLG	*Zeitschrift für württembergische Landesgeschichte*
ZSRG KA	*Zeitschrift der Savigny-Stiftung für Rechtsgeschichte*
	Kanonistische Abteilung

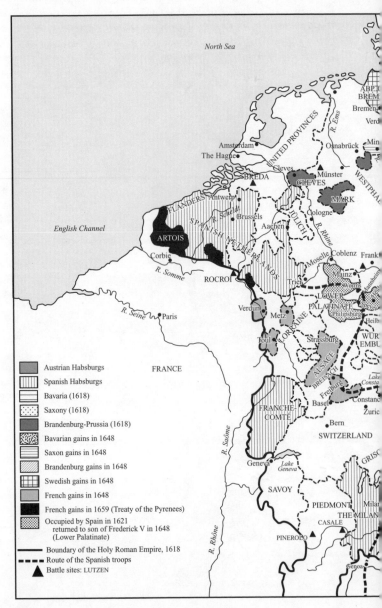

Map 1   The Reich in the Thirty Years War

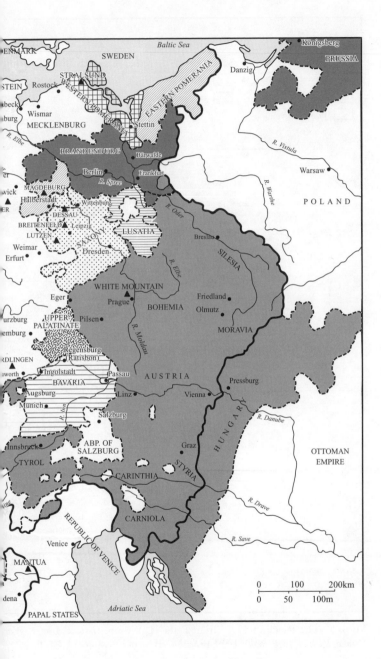

Map 2   The Reich in 1745 (from Peter H. Wilson, *German Armies: War*
German Politics, 1648–1806 (1998; reproduced by permission of UCL Press)

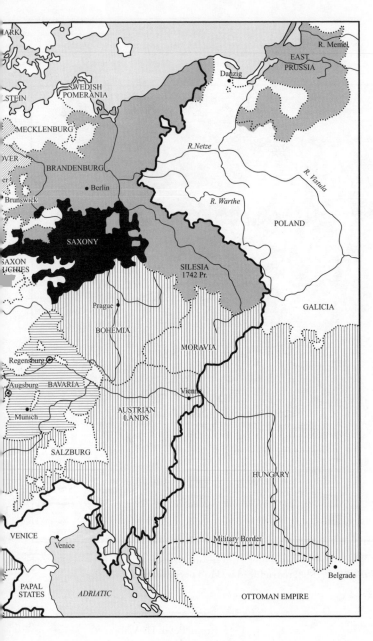

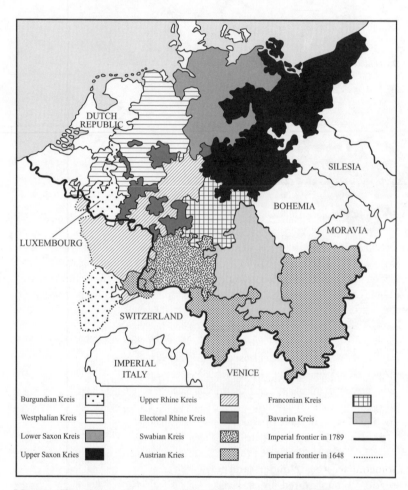

Map 3 The Kreise (from Peter H. Wilson, *German Armies: War and German Politics, 1648–1806* (1998; reproduced by kind permission of UCL Press)

Chapter 1: The Peculiarities of German History

1.1 Writing the German Past

Germany's special path?

Hitler cast a long shadow over German history. The horrors of the Holocaust demanded an explanation and subsequent generations have reached deep into the German past to find one. While they concentrated primarily on Germany's involvement in the two world wars, their writing shaped interpretations of that country's earlier development. Since the reunification of the two post-war German states in 1991, there has been an understandable impatience within Germany to close this page of history and move on. Those born before Hitler's seizure of power are now well into their seventies at least and it is largely their grandchildren who have the main say in government, business and culture. History has also changed as an academic discipline. New approaches, together with further research, have opened other questions that require answers.

It is entirely appropriate that current research should reflect these changes. Yet, the legacy of the recent past cannot be easily dismissed by someone wishing to understand early modern German history. First, the reader is confronted by a large body of literature published since the 1940s that reflects the concerns of those decades. This literature in turn drew on existing debates about German development in the nineteenth century, particularly the process of unification that produced the Prussian-dominated Second Reich in 1871. The nature of the Holy Roman Empire, or first Reich, which ended in 1806, was addressed at least indirectly in these discussions. Secondly, the debate on the course of German history cannot be dissociated from the more general explanations of European development, particularly as it is used as a prominent example by historical sociologists and political scientists. The purpose of this chapter is to outline these different approaches to the German past and to explain their significance for our understanding of the period 1558–1806.

Explanations for the rise of Nazism took two broad directions after 1945. One line of argument was rapidly subsumed by the Cold War division of Europe after Hitler's defeat and interpreted the recent German past through the lens of post-war ideological struggles. Those on the left generally saw Nazism as a product of the crisis affecting western capitalism in the late 1920s. Their liberal critics defined it as another variant of the 'totalitarianism' they saw gripping Soviet-dominated eastern Europe beyond the Iron Curtain. The other approach focused more narrowly on the German experience and questioned whether Hitler was simply a short-term aberration, or a sign that Germany had deviated from the 'normal' pattern of European development and headed down its own 'special path' (*Sonderweg*). It is this latter interpretation that concerns us most, because it raised the question of when this fatal step was first made. Most historians concentrated on the mid-nineteenth century, arguing that the origins of later problems were to be found in the process of unification in the 1860s and 1870s. The political structure created by Bismarck in 1871 was criticised as a sham that allowed an essentially feudal aristocracy and their upper-middle-class collaborators to dominate the country. This structure came under increasing strain as Germany rapidly industrialised in the later nineteenth century, forcing the controlling elite to adopt a series of increasingly reckless measures to hold on to power, including plunging the country into the First World War in 1914, and later, assisting Hitler's rise to power in the mistaken belief they could manipulate him.[1]

These arguments naturally affected how the eighteenth and seventeenth centuries were interpreted, since this period saw both the rise of Prussia as the leading German state, and the consolidation of a significant landowning aristocracy. Historians wanted to know why this group survived in Germany, whereas elsewhere in Europe it was swept away by revolution or gradually replaced by liberal parliamentary democracy after 1789. The answer appeared to lie in the nature of earlier German political development, which fostered a peculiar subservience to authoritarian rule. This seemed entirely plausible because it accorded with what many nineteenth-century Germans themselves had written, and also matched more general explanations of European political development.

The authoritarian state

Most political science and historical writing assumes that state structure, military organisation, political culture and economic activity are closely related. It is believed that certain types of state will be dominated by particular kinds of people with definite attitudes about political organisation, social life and other activity. As there are only a finite number of basic different forms of political organisation, there are only a limited number of paths from the past to modernity. German history is regarded as exemplifying one of these routes, based on the creation of an authoritarian, centralised 'power state' (*Machtstaat*). In this form of organisation, political authority rests on a strong coercive power, usually a large and efficient permanent army that can be deployed to enforce domestic obedience as well as defending against external attack. Political culture is characterised by subservience to this authority, as both state and society are dominated by men of violence who lead by martial example and expect obedience to their commands. Most people are only partly integrated within this system, which offers few avenues for popular political participation, but none the less fulfils minimum essential functions.

Some Germans regarded this type of state as positively desirable, while others merely saw it as an unavoidable necessity. They pointed to their country's central European location, noting how seventeenth- and eighteenth-century Prussia was threatened by powerful neighbours and only survived a series of violent international struggles by intensifying its mobilisation of war-making resources. Unlike Britain or other maritime nations, Prussia derived little benefit from the first phase of European colonisation after the sixteenth century. Its economy remained predominantly agrarian and under-developed in comparison. Political power and military muscle developed as substitutes for economic strength to ensure the country's survival.

It became customary well before 1900 to contrast the authoritarian model of Prussia's development with what was generally labelled a liberal, constitutional alternative, apparently exemplified by Britain, the United States and, to a lesser extent, France. These countries seemed to have representative forms of government with high levels of popular participation. They were led by men of dialogue who governed by debate, persuasion and compromise. Their military structures were more decentralised, relying on navies, militias or citizens-in-arms who were ill-suited to repressing their own people. Geography and economics were likewise used to explain these advantages. Located in splendid isolation far from immediate danger and with good access to world markets, these countries had developed more advanced, commercialised economies that sustained their vibrant political cultures.

The national question

Many nineteenth-century Germans rejected this positive gloss on the western, liberal model of political development, arguing that the Prussian-led unification heralded a unique solution to the unsettling aspects of modernisation, like the social alienation stemming from rapid industrialisation and urban growth. Influenced by a conservative reading of Hegelianism and other contemporary philosophies emphasising the state, historians like Johann Gustav Droysen (1808–86), Heinrich von Sybel (1817–95) and Heinrich von Treitschke (1834–96) presented German history as exemplifying the benefits of strong, centralised government. They interpreted European history in Darwinian terms as a struggle in a hostile international environment in which only the fittest nations could survive. A strong central government was essential to provide leadership, mobilise resources and prevent internal conflict that could open the country to foreign attack. Culture and economics would benefit too as the government channelled creative and entrepreneurial energies towards greater achievements.

This present-minded use of the past was common in the nineteenth and early twentieth centuries and was not restricted to Germany. Nor were all German historians conservative apologists for authoritarianism. Some singled out liberal elements in Prussian development, such as municipal self-government and a respect for the rule of law. However, all those who reflected on their country's long-term development had to confront the question of German political unity and national identity. The more strident, like Treitschke, became active participants in the process of mid-nineteenth-century political unification, advocating Bismarck's 'Little German' (*Kleindeutsch*) solution to the national problem, which involved the defeat and ejection of the multi-ethnic Habsburg Austro-Hungarian monarchy from what became the German Second Reich by 1871. They sought historical foundation from this process, contributing to what has become known as the Borussian, or Prusso-centric, school of German history. Prussia's emergence after 1640 was interpreted as the first stage in its mission to unite Germans in a single state. This process frequently acquired religious overtones as Prussia's victory over Austria seemed to confirm the cultural and economic superiority of Protestants over Catholics.

The chief victim in this approach was the old Reich, which was condemned for failing to provide the strong leadership Prussia seemed destined to give. To most nineteenth-century historians, the first Reich symbolised national disunity and international impotence. Germany's historical 'wrong turn' was not a rejection of liberalism in the nineteenth century, but its much earlier 'failure' to create a single national monarchy like those that had united the English, French and Spanish. Some medieval German emperors were portrayed as struggling valiantly to do this, but all were defeated by the practical problems of distance and too few resources, together with unwelcome external interference and the perpetual feuding between the local lords and princes who ruled the individual territories. Further attempts at centralisation became compromised when the imperial title passed to the Habsburg dynasty in the fifteenth century, because this family allegedly put their own cosmopolitan interests before their national duty as German rulers.

Internal disputes between the emperor and princes became overlaid by confessional strife between Protestants and Catholics after 1517, creating constitutional paralysis by 1618. The subsequent Thirty Years War was treated as a general disaster that reduced the German population by a third or more, and left the Reich an empty shell by 1648. The concluding Peace of Westphalia froze the imperial constitution, emasculating the emperor in an intricate web of legal restrictions that reduced him to little more than an ineffectual figurehead. The political vacuum was filled by a host of competing secular lords, each ruling their own dukedoms and counties, alongside other fossilised relics of the medieval past like the prince-bishops and prelates governing the ecclesiastical territories still associated with the Catholic Church, or the numerous, but tiny, urban republics of the imperial cities. Few of these 300 or so governments could see beyond their own immediate frontiers. Mired in the myopia of this petty particularism (*Kleinstaaterei*), national interests were neglected and Germany became a battleground for France, Russia and other powers. As Habsburg Austria became a distinct European power, it fell to Prussia to pick up the vacant mantel of German leadership. Austria used its remaining powers in the Reich to confront Prussia, notably summoning the imperial army against Frederick the

Great during the Seven Years War (1756–63). As a barrier to national unity, the Reich had to be destroyed. The onset of the Revolutionary Wars against France after 1792 exposed the weakness of the arthritic imperial structure, which was finally swept away by Napoleon's victory over Austria in 1805–6. The French triumph represented another national humiliation, not least since it also involved Napoleon's defeat of old Prussia later in 1806. None the less, it was broadly welcomed by German nationalists as an essential step in clearing the way for unification later in the nineteenth century.

The experience of National Socialism between 1933 and 1945 discredited the earlier approval of the authoritarian state, but did little to change this basic interpretation of the old Reich. Instead of representing it as a unique solution to the problems of modernity, many historians now depicted the nineteenth-century Second Reich as a device for perpetuating the economic and political pre-eminence of an essentially early modern social elite. The old Reich remained condemned as both the birthplace of this elite and of the Prussian state they controlled, as well as the main reason why national unity was fatally delayed into the nineteenth century. Unable to develop 'naturally' over several centuries, national unification had to be forced artificially by Bismarck and others, pushing German development down the wrong path towards the horrors of two world wars.

New views of the old Reich

This interpretation of German history never found universal acceptance. The Second Reich was not as illiberal or 'feudalised' as it was sometimes depicted in the 1960s and 1970s, nor were Britain, France and other western states as progressive as often thought. More importantly, new research reconsidered the Borussian approach to the era before 1806. The imperial framework re-emerged as a flawed, but none the less functioning system that provided a measure of security and political coordination to the numerous German territories prior to the creation of a more centralised state. The individual histories of these territories were woven back into the narrative of German history. Given that Prussia had contained less than a ninth of all German-speakers prior to the later eighteenth century, it no longer seemed appropriate to write all German history from the Prussian perspective alone. A better appreciation of social and economic history also widened the focus beyond royal courts and central governments to examine the experience from below. It was recognised that there were other ways that ordinary people could contribute to political development than just violent protest or through the ballot box. This new research has gathered pace since the 1970s, producing a vast range of specialist literature. Opinion remains divided on the character of early modern German state and society. Yet, most scholars now present the old Reich as a relatively viable, flexible and resilient structure, that continued to develop after 1648 having survived the traumas of the Reformation and the Thirty Years War.

These findings inform this book, but there are signs that the recent revisionism now risks replacing an unduly negative interpretation with an overly positive one. The petty particularism that was once condemned has been celebrated recently by one historian as evidence of the 'multi-ethnic' character of the old Reich, which constituted a 'central Europe of the regions' where the multitude of territorial governments embodied the 'principle of subsidiarity' alongside coordinating imperial institutions.[2] Such language deliberately adopts that of the European Commission in Brussels, transforming what was once dismissed as a medieval anachronism into a state that looks more progressive than its European neighbours. Taking a different approach, another recent writer reclaims a positive national past, presenting the Reich as the first German nation state, because it bound the different German-speaking regions within a single political framework.[3] Others have detected parallels between imperial institutions and the federal government of modern Germany, or between local popular representative assemblies in some of the German territories and modern republicanism. These historians are careful not to present early modern Germany as a utopian society, yet their conclusions contrast sharply with earlier findings, indicating some confusion as to how this period should be presented.

1.2 Three Directions in German Politics

The dualist model

The lack of consensus is not surprising given the complexity of the subject matter. Political history is generally used as a framework to relate other aspects of human development within a common chronology. We are used to having history built around the stories of states and nations, kings and revolutionaries. These things are not easily identifiable for early modern Germany. Political power was shared between the emperor and a multitude of minor princes and governments. Their combined territory stretched well beyond the borders of the modern Federal Republic and included millions of people speaking languages other than German.

The usual solution is to see German political development as a set of two overlapping struggles between centralisers and those who resist them. One conflict affected the entire Reich as the princes contested the emperor's authority. The general conclusion is that this contest ended in the failure of national monarchy. The emperor was unable to create an infrastructure to make his formal authority effective across the entire Reich. The Habsburgs were the last imperial dynasty to attempt this, but their efforts were compromised by their partisan support for Catholicism in the sixteenth and seventeenth centuries, and by the distraction of their other interests elsewhere in Europe. Moves to more direct rule by Emperor Charles V (r. 1519–58) and particularly by Ferdinand II (r. 1619–37) were criticised as the imposition of an alien, Catholic-Habsburg 'imperial absolutism'. As the emperor's authority crumbled, the initiative passed to the princes, who were able to widen their own powers at his expense. The Reich was eaten away from within as real power passed to those princes who ruled the larger, more compact territories like Brandenburg-Prussia, Saxony and Bavaria.

The second struggle occurred inside these territories, with the opposite result. Whereas the emperor's authority was devolved to the princes, the trend within the larger territories was towards the centralisation of power at the expense of the local nobility, clergy and leading towns. Here the princes consolidated their authority as absolutism by the mid-seventeenth century, enabling them to develop their own fiscal and military infrastructures and play a growing part in international affairs. Many general accounts treat these territories as independent states after 1648 and trace their individual development as a distinct 'territorial history' (*Landesgeschichte*) with little further reference to imperial institutions.

This perspective has been labelled the dualist model since it reduces political development to a two-way struggle between centripetal and centrifugal forces and portrays the centralised state as the only possible outcome: either the emperor would be successful and create a single superstate, or the princes would triumph and divide Germany into a series of mini-states. Such arguments allow German history to be written as a single narrative, but oversimplify what was a more complex process. As the Reich was never a centralised national monarchy, the emperor's problems cannot be interpreted as a 'decline' of central authority. Equally, the territorial states did not emerge simply through the transfer of former imperial rights to the princes, nor as a perpetual struggle against entrenched local interests. Instead of the Reich declining while the territories rose, political development moved forward at both levels simultaneously, creating common imperial institutions that acquired their own internal dynamic.

The imperial hierarchy

This process appears so confusing because it contained three parallel, partially contradictory trends, which evolved concurrently. Overall, political developments since the fifteenth century consolidated the Reich as a hierarchical structure under the emperor's overlordship, but not his direct control. This interlocking framework of territories and imperial institutions existed during the middle ages, but assumed a more definite shape in the four decades after 1480. It was consolidated by constitutional changes in the mid-sixteenth century, enabling it to survive the Thirty Years War. Rather than freezing the existing structure, the Peace of Westphalia left many areas still ill-defined and capable of further development (see Chapters 2 and 5). As new institutions were developed and old ones revived, the hierarchy became more complex, assigning the emperor, rulers and peoples of the Reich different positions within a web of corporate rights, legal immunities and overlapping jurisdictions (see Figure 1.1). This structure came under increasing strain during the eighteenth century with the onset of Austro-Prussian rivalry.

This struggle is also generally viewed in dualist terms, ignoring the continued role of imperial institutions and consigning the other territories to the role of a passive 'Third Germany' that was being fought over by the two giants. While the disproportionate growth of Austria and Prussia as European powers loosened the imperial hierarchy, it did not demolish it altogether and the Reich remained the preferred framework for the political organisation of central Europe. However, in the longer term it proved impossible to contain these tensions, particularly when they coincided with new international crises in the west with the onset of the French Revolutionary Wars after 1792 and the implosion of Poland in the east and its partition between Austria, Prussia and

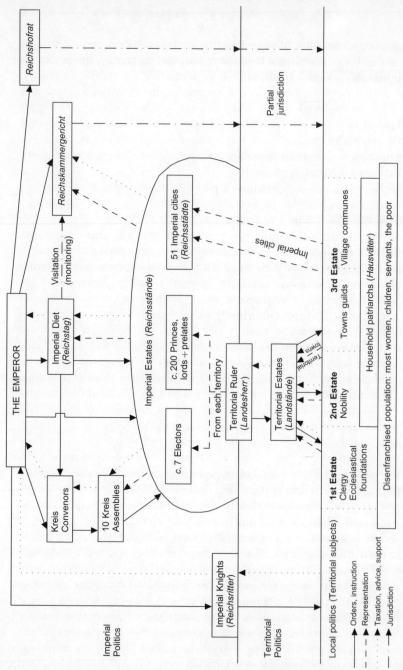

Figure 1.1 The imperial constitution.

Russia (see Chapter 8). The Reich was dismantled between 1801 and 1806 as the medium-sized German territories joined Austria and Prussia in seizing the lands of the lesser territories.

Monarchism

Attempts to strengthen imperial authority represent a second, monarchical trend, which was generally more latent than active. The spectre of 'imperial absolutism' remained a propaganda device of the emperor's opponents, rather than his actual objective. No emperor tried to transform the Reich into a centralised national monarchy. Instead, they periodically tried adjusting its constitution to enhance their personal authority and make the complex hierarchy easier to manage. They were least successful when their own dynastic interests diverged from the broader imperial interests of the Reich's constituent territories and their rulers. Few princes were prepared to risk their subjects' lives and money in external wars of aggression intended to extend the personal possessions of the imperial family. Such reluctance reduced political consensus to the lowest common denominator of defence against foreign attack, reinforcing the Reich's largely passive role in European affairs, in pointed contrast to the aggressive stance of subsequent German states (see section 8.1).

Federalism

The third trend can be labelled federalism and is rather more complex. The foundation of the western, Federal Republic of Germany in 1949 revived interest in earlier forms of federalism and led some writers to describe the Reich or its institutions in these terms.[4] In some respects this is appropriate. The Confederation of the Rhine grew out of the Reich in 1806 as a federation of the larger states that had annexed their neighbours. Following Napoleon's defeat in 1814–15, central Europe was reorganised as the German Confederation, grouping the surviving 35 or so states within a common framework. Austria was ejected from this organisation following its defeat by Prussia in 1866. The Prussian-dominated northern states were briefly regrouped in another, smaller confederation, before being merged with their remaining southern neighbours in the Second Reich, founded in 1871. While Prussia annexed

much of the north and had a controlling stake in the new empire's institutions, the Second Reich retained some federal elements by leaving the
surviving states with considerable autonomy over their own affairs.
The subsequent Weimar Republic, which replaced the Second Reich in
1919, embodied a strongly federal structure and Germany was only sub-
jected to truly centralised rule with the Nazi seizure of power in 1933.

Unfortunately, attempts to depict the early modern Reich in federal
terms rather underestimate the levelling tendency within federalism,
which was inimical to the basic hierarchical imperial structure. A federation is a state composed of regions sharing equal rights, some of
which they surrender to a central government charged with general
oversight, especially of foreign relations. While this is an appropriate
definition of what came after 1806, it cannot be applied before then.
Moreover, interest in the later federal structure often implies a false continuity, across the centuries, between imperial and modern institutions,
and between the old territories and the *Bundesländer* that comprise the
present Federal Republic.

Princely federalism

Early modern federalism had its origins in the medieval principle of association between corporate social groups, communities or territories.
This could range from simple agreements to cooperate over immediate
goals, towards more integrated structures capable of lasting institutional
development. Rather than constituting a federation itself, the complex
imperial hierarchy offered three levels of subsidiary federal development. Princely federalism proved ultimately the most corrosive form
since it pushed the Reich towards a genuine federation of sovereign states.
Cooperation amongst the princes was encouraged by imperial law,
which required them to uphold the internal public peace (*Landfrieden*)
and defend the Reich against invasion. In addition to formal collaboration through imperial institutions, the princes were free to make alliances
amongst themselves or with other Christian rulers long before the Peace
of Westphalia confirmed these rights in 1648.[5] However, they were not
yet independent sovereigns for they remained under the emperor's overall authority and they were forbidden from conspiring against the
common good. Many princes broke these laws and took up arms against
the emperor, particularly at times of religious tension during the sixteenth and seventeenth centuries. However, none of these anti-imperial
alliances represented a viable alternative to the Reich.

The Protestant princes faced particular problems in the sixteenth century when they claimed that loyalty to the 'true religion' overrode that to the emperor. When this was put to the test in the Schmalkaldic War (1546–7) against Charles V, many Protestants remained loyal to the emperor, even though he clearly favoured the Catholics. The same problem arose during the Thirty Years War when the dissident Protestant Union opposed the Habsburgs (see Chapter 4). Catholics did not face the same conflict of religious and political loyalties, but still suffered from the more general problem of competing princely dynastic interests. Doubt over the legitimacy of princely leagues fostered uncertainty whether their decisions were legally binding on all members. The more hesitant princes frequently abandoned their allies in times of crisis. All were reluctant to invest time and money in developing their leagues into more permanent federations, restricting most alliances to loose agreements on collaboration within existing imperial institutions. This tended to reinforce the traditional hierarchy since the Reich retained its relevance as a convenient forum in which to advance dynastic interests.

The corrosive element of princely federalism was not the loose cooperation between principalities, but the political developments within them. The hierarchical structure of the Reich fostered competition amongst the princes for titles and influence. Each princely dynasty sought to improve its relative position within the Reich, whilst keeping its rivals firmly in their place. Those holding more prestigious lands and titles also tried to join the ranks of European royalty and play a role in affairs beyond the Reich. Such ambitions required considerable resources, encouraging rulers to develop political, military and fiscal infrastructures within their own territories. Christian theology and various secular philosophies gave this additional impetus, transforming personal princely rule into more abstract state authority (see Chapter 7). As these material and intellectual foundations solidified, they lessened each territory's dependence on the wider imperial structure. This process varied across the Reich with only Austria and Prussia becoming truly viable states in their own right before the late eighteenth century, while most of the others still relied on imperial institutions to resolve conflicts, and to provide external security and other vital functions. Between these two extremes lay a group of middling territories like Bavaria, Saxony, Württemberg, Hessen-Kassel and the Palatinate. While none of these sought to leave the Reich, their rulers none the less often chafed against the hierarchical imperial framework that prevented them from improving their dynastic position at the expense of their neighbours. The Reich's collapse during the Revolutionary Wars cast these territories adrift, enabling those that were better placed to emerge as fully sovereign states by 1806.

Aristocratic federalism

The emergence of these sovereign states has obscured the presence of two other federal traditions with the potential to create more decentralised forms of government through combinations of aristocratic corporations or more direct popular action. The aristocratic federal tradition took two forms, depending on whether its main sphere of activity was within imperial or territorial institutions. Federal cooperation through imperial institutions was restricted to those aristocrats who aspired to join the princes as rulers of territories with a clearly defined place in the Reich's hierarchy. These lords formed regional alliances from the late fifteenth century that secured them a position as the princes' junior partners by the mid-seventeenth century (see section 2.1). This type of aristocratic federalism strengthened the imperial hierarchy by inserting additional strata of lesser rulers holding small counties and ecclesiastical lordships which thereby escaped incorporation within the larger duchies and principalities. By contrast, collaboration through territorial institutions offered a route to new types of state formation from below.

Estates as social and political institutions

Such collaboration drew on a distinctly late medieval form of political representation that differed fundamentally from modern democracy. Modern democracy rests on the principle of equality, irrespective of whether elections are decided by direct votes for individual candidates, or proportional representation. People either elect leaders to act on their behalf in a national parliament, or decide matters more directly by voting in a plebiscite. Most modern states use some combination of these methods. All enfranchised citizens can participate and constituencies are determined proportionately by the size of their populations. Late medieval representation followed different principles in deciding who could sit in an assembly to negotiate with a monarch, or represent that country if the assembly itself constituted the government, as in the case of the imperial cities, or republics elsewhere in Europe. Representation was guided primarily by social status, not by the size or distribution of the population. Society was composed not of equal citizens, but of distinct orders, or 'Estates' (*Stände*), each distinguished by corporate privileges based on their original function (see section 3.2).

Estates-based representation in Germany originated in the twelfth century with the growth of cathedral and abbey chapters in the ecclesiastical territories (see section 5.4). Other representative institutions developed in many secular lordships by the fifteenth century. Unlike the chapters, these institutions, called territorial Estates (*Landstände*), were rarely involved in choosing their immediate lord, who ruled instead by hereditary right. Only those in Bohemia and Hungary claimed the right to choose their own king, whereas the others merely asked to participate in regencies for under-age or incapacitated rulers. None the less, the Estates assumed growing importance because of the lords' inability to cope with the mounting social, economic and political problems from the resources of their own direct possessions. Increasingly they were obliged to ask their subjects to provide additional assistance in the form of taxes and soldiers. The Estates emerged during the fifteenth century as the forum for these requests to be debated. As the ecclesiastical lords encountered similar difficulties, Estates often emerged alongside the existing chapters in their territories (see section 6.3).

While the exact composition of the Estates varied between the territories, all represented corporate social groups rather than individuals. Representatives were selected not by popular vote, but by virtue of the special privileges they shared with others of similar backgrounds. When assembled, they sat segregated by corporate status rather than party affiliation and adhered to a strict order of precedence when speaking or voting. Nobles generally predominated, representing their peers and, indirectly, their dependent peasant tenants. Abbots, priors and the heads of major ecclesiastical foundations usually represented the clergy, while those speaking for the townsfolk were mainly limited to the mayors of the important territorial towns. More popular representation remained sealed off at local, communal level in the widespread self-management of villages and small towns by peasants and citizens possessing at least modest property. Here people could elect town councillors and other municipal officials, or decided matters themselves by attending meetings in their village hall.

The formation of the Estates followed that of German lordship in that it was territorial. Each territory in the Reich developed its own Estates to represent its population in negotiations with its ruler in an assembly known as a 'diet' (*Landtag*). Each of the Estates tended to preserve its own unique identity even when its lord acquired new land elsewhere. Major dynasties like the Habsburgs, who accumulated land across the Reich, thus found themselves confronted by different assemblies in each of their provinces. This reinforced the composite character of German rule. Territories were patched together from different lands both within the Reich and beyond, each of which preserved its own laws and identity.

Princely centralisation offered one way to forge these elements into a single state. Estates-based aristocratic federalism provided another, developing through a network of alliances between territorial diets. Since princes almost invariably opposed such alliances, aristocratic federalism was generally a protest movement directed at preserving or extending local autonomy by forcing rulers to confirm or extend Estates' privileges in return for taxes and other cooperation. This severely restricted its political potential, because each diet was reluctant to submerge its own historic identity within a wider framework. The spread of religious tension partially counteracted this from the early sixteenth century, since it could place rulers in opposition to their subjects if each embraced different faiths. Linguistic divisions could also create common bonds between nobles in different provinces, whilst distancing them from their ruler. Both these factors worked in the Habsburg monarchy to produce major revolts, particularly in the Netherlands against the Spanish branch of the family after 1568, and in Bohemia against the Austrian line in 1618. In both cases, Habsburg rule was opposed by federations between different provincial diets, dominated by the local aristocracy and drawn together by a common Protestant faith and resentment against a dynasty associated with an alien language and culture. Such federations had the potential to develop into independent states where they could create common institutions, as occurred in the Netherlands, where the northern parts broke away to form the United Provinces, or Dutch Republic, by the early seventeenth century. As we shall see, the Bohemian and Austrian provinces failed to achieve the same degree of cohesion and were defeated during the Thirty Years War (see Chapter 4).

Popular federalism

Communal representative institutions in towns and villages offered a third, broader form of federalism within German politics. Like the Estates, the strength of communal representation varied greatly between the territories and tended to be most pronounced in the south and west, particularly Switzerland, which was part of the medieval Reich and had been governed by the Habsburgs. Swiss opposition to Habsburg rule rested on a pact between three mountain valleys, in 1291, that spread into a network of alliances binding rural and urban communities into a single Confederation. Repeated military incursions failed to reverse this process and the Habsburgs were forced to accept defeat by 1499. The Confederation remained nominally part of the Reich, but suspicions of Habsburg intentions deterred the Swiss from participating in the imperial institutions that were then assuming permanent shape. Like the Dutch they opted out of the Reich and secured international recognition for their independence by 1648. The progressive consolidation of the imperial hierarchy discouraged other southern and western communities from 'turning Swiss' by the mid-sixteenth century, but communal institutions continued to offer other ways in which ordinary people could shape politics into the eighteenth century.[6]

Chapter 2:   Reich and Territories

2.1   The Political Geography of Central Europe

The Reich and Europe

Sixteenth-century Germans lived under political institutions that had existed for up to seven centuries and which claimed a direct descent from those of ancient Rome. Many looked back with pride to this earlier imperial heritage, which shaped political activity and identity till the very end of the Reich. The Reich emerged during the Frankish conquests of the Germanic tribes after 774. Charlemagne, the greatest of the Frankish kings, decided to revive the ancient Roman imperial title and was crowned Holy Roman Emperor on Christmas Day 800, with papal blessing.[1] Though Frankish rule lasted only a few generations, the Reich retained key elements of its early medieval foundation throughout its existence.

The political organisation of medieval Europe was characterised by the universal and the particular. Christianity and the legacy of ancient Rome fostered a sense of a single Christendom under papal spiritual guidance and imperial secular leadership. There was a general acceptance of a common religion, some agreement on law, and the limited use of Latin as a means of intellectual and political communication. Yet these universal sentiments failed to translate into firm political structures, because of the considerable practical difficulties of coordinating human activity across the vast, under-populated expanse of Europe. Political organisation and, for the most part, identity as well, remained localised in small counties, lordships and kingdoms. The modern concept of the nation state emerged as an intermediary level between the vague notion of a single Christendom and the vast patchwork of localised rule. Some

18

modern states developed from below, either through the alliance of smaller communities, as in Switzerland, or by the gradual accumulation of power by one authority at its rivals' expense, as in the case of the great western monarchies of England, France and Spain. Other states emerged from the fragmentation of more widely flung authority, such as the Spanish Habsburg monarchy, which lost control of large parts of western and southern Europe in the seventeenth century.

The creation of this new, intermediary level of political organisation eroded both the universal and the particular, pushing Europe towards the system of independent, sovereign states. The Peace of Westphalia is generally regarded as a milestone in this process, not least because it restricted the emperor's power. In fact, it only gave qualified support to the new principle of sovereignty and it remained unclear whether European states would interact as equals, regardless of size, or be arranged in some kind of hierarchy according to military potential and the status of their rulers. The numerous wars, between the mid-1650s and 1815, were waged primarily to determine this, and particularly to defeat repeated French attempts to assert hegemony over other states.

The gradual transition towards a system of sovereign states had profound repercussions for the Reich, because it undermined the emperor's international position. Just as religious schisms restricted papal influence by dividing Europeans into different confessional groups, political coalescence around more distinct national states confined the emperor increasingly to central Europe. This also raised important questions about the position of the German princes who were his direct vassals. If German politics followed the monarchical trend, the princes would be firmly confined to the sphere of domestic politics, like the aristocracies of France, Spain and other kingdoms. If federalism became more pronounced, the better placed princes would emerge as sovereigns over their own distinct states. Both of these possibilities threatened the traditional imperial hierarchy, which still combined the medieval characteristics of the universal and the particular.

The great imperial dynasties

Early medieval German history was dominated by three great royal dynasties after the demise of the Franks in 911: the Ottonians (919–1024), Salians (1024–1125) and Staufer (1138–1254).[2] The collapse of the Staufer was followed by a prolonged interregnum till 1273, during which rival royal claimants fought for supremacy. The situation was exacerbated by the absence of clear rules governing the succession. Initially, little distinction was made between hereditary and elective monarchy, since all new kings had to seek homage from their vassals after their accession. It remained open whether this implied an active element of choice, or the simple acceptance of a rightful ruler. Even election could be reconciled with hereditary right, since it was possible to chose a king's son as his direct successor. However, the principle of election became entrenched after 1273, because the leading German lords chose each new king from a different dynasty until 1347. The Luxembourg family then secured re-election on two occasions thereafter, to rule until 1437 as the last medieval dynasty. The Luxembourgs consolidated their position by defining electoral procedure in the famous Golden Bull of 1356, restricting it to seven leading princes, now called electors (*Kurfürsten*), who were partly chosen from their own immediate supporters. The choice of Archduke Albrecht to succeed the last of the Luxembourgs in 1438 heralded the start of Habsburg imperial rule, since all future emperors were chosen from this dynasty, with the single exception of the Bavarian Wittelsbach, Charles VII (1742–5).

A Holy Roman Empire

Charlemagne's original resurrection of the ancient imperial title was reaffirmed in 962 and continued thereafter by all future emperors. It imparted unique characteristics, setting the emperor above other European kings. Medieval emperors fostered a belief in the 'imperial translation' (*translatio imperii*), interpreting world history according to the Book of Daniel in the Bible. This prophesied that the ancient Roman Empire would be the last of four great world civilisations before the Day of Judgement. Far from creating a new title, they argued that Charlemagne had simply assumed the existing Roman one, implying an unbroken continuity between the Reich and the ancient empire. By exercising this imperial title, the German kings placed themselves at the head of a divinely sanctioned European order. The German word for emperor, *Kaiser*, derived directly from the ancient title *Caesar*.

Papal participation in the imperial coronation imparted another important universal element as the emperor was anointed as defender of the faith and the secular protector of all Christendom. Many medieval emperors clashed with the papacy over this role, forcing a greater distinction between the imperial title and that of German king.[3] The royal title was clearly associated with those lands inhabited by peoples that already called themselves Teutons (*Teutonici*). The German king only needed the approval of his own vassals to assume office, whereas he had to be crowned by the pope before he could call himself emperor. Growing resentment at papal interference prompted Maximilian I (r.1493–1519) to assume the new title of 'elected emperor' in 1508. His successor, Charles V, was the last emperor to be crowned personally by the pope and thereafter papal involvement lost much of its significance, with future coronations being conducted in Germany by the archbishop of Cologne.

This made the old royal title effectively redundant since the emperor could assume his imperial prerogatives immediately. The title of king was now associated with the position of successor designate, formally called King of the Romans (*Römischer König*). This title could be conferred by the electors during an emperor's lifetime to ensure the smooth transition of power on his death. If an emperor died before these arrangements had been made, his prerogatives devolved temporarily to the rulers of Saxony and the Palatinate as the two leading secular electors. They exercised these powers as imperial vicars (*Reichsvikare*), with Saxony having responsibility for northern Germany and Westphalia, and the elector Palatine overseeing the south and Rhineland. Though not an elector himself, the duke of Savoy assumed imperial authority over the parts of northern Italy that still fell under the emperor's jurisdiction. The archbishop of Mainz, as the most senior elector, held important powers to prevent the three vicars from becoming too independent. Mainz was to summon his colleagues to the city of Frankfurt within three months of an emperor's death and give them no more than thirty days to decide on a successor.[4]

The imperial title was initially associated with both land and prerogatives. Whoever became German king had direct access to the crown lands, as well as political and legal jurisdiction over all the other feudal lords. Over time, these lords evolved into the electors, princes and other rulers governing the individual territories. Most of these lands became the hereditary possessions of the German princely and aristocratic families, but a significant proportion remained the lands of the 'imperial church' (*Reichskirche*), governed by ecclesiastical rulers elected by their cathedral and abbey chapters. The actual crown lands were never very extensive and were dissipated, especially in the thirteenth century, as individual emperors mortgaged them to their creditors or supporters.

The emperor's real power lay in his prerogatives, the most important of which allowed him to act as supreme judge and to summon the other lords to assist in military campaigns. Other powers included the right to confer titles, including those of nobility and university degrees, as well as to mint coin, grant economic concessions and levy certain taxes.

Early medieval emperors relied heavily on the support of key lords, particularly those controlling church lands. This became more difficult with papal interference, forcing emperors after 1273 to exploit their imperial prerogatives, many of which were transferred as rewards to relations and other supporters. The Luxembourg dynasty shifted the basis of imperial authority back to land, but instead of trying to recover the earlier crown lands, they enlarged their own dynastic possessions within the Reich, particularly Bohemia, as well as acquiring the separate Hungarian royal title. They continued to see their imperial mission in largely traditional terms, as defenders of Christendom against the Ottoman Turks, and as guardians of order within the Reich. However, they created new institutions to extract the necessary resources from their hereditary power base. A permanent royal court and administrative chancery were established in Prague, distinct from the old imperial court that followed the emperor on his personal travels around the Reich. The Habsburgs continued this practice when they acquired the title in 1438, using their own expanding hereditary possessions to support a reinvigorated imperial mission to bring peace to Europe and defeat the Ottomans. The growing distinction between the emperor's hereditary power base and his elective title became a fundamental structural feature of imperial politics, establishing tensions between the centralising drive inherent in the monarchical tendency and the Reich's traditional hierarchical character.

Overall size

Though the Reich lost considerable land during the middle ages, more was gained by eastward expansion after 1147 across the river Elbe into the lands of the Slavs. By 1600 the emperor's jurisdiction extended over 750,000 km^2, an area that was about 40 per cent larger than Bismarck's Second Reich and which took thirty days to cross on horseback. The original Frankish empire had been partitioned into three kingdoms in the ninth century. The western part eventually became France, while the central area split into a collection of smaller territories stretching from the North Sea, through modern Belgium, Luxembourg, Lorraine, Alsace and into Savoy and Piedmont in what was then loosely known as Italy. The imperial title remained associated with the third, Germanic kingdom, which lay largely east of the Rhine. The medieval struggles with the papacy were partly to determine the southern extent of this kingdom and resulted in the emperor establishing jurisdiction over northern 'imperial Italy' (*Reichsitalien*), which stretched for 65,000 km^2 and included Savoy, Milan, Parma and Tuscany, but not Venice which became an independent republic.

The central European core

The mid-sixteenth-century Reich is best considered as a central core in southern and western Germany surrounded by a series of more peripheral regions. The core had been settled first, and remained the most heavily populated part of the Reich throughout the middle ages. It was characterised by a greater degree of territorial fragmentation than the peripheral regions that were incorporated later and contained fewer, more compact territories (see Map 1).

The western part lay along the Rhine and was subdivided into three regions. The Upper, or southern, Rhine extended west into Alsace and the duchy of Lorraine, as well as eastwards into the central part of Germany around the city of Frankfurt. This eastern area contained the relatively compact territories of Hessen and Nassau, as well as numerous, much smaller counties such as Solms, Königstein, Isenburg, Leiningen, Wittgenstein and Falkenstein. These territories were frequently partitioned into even smaller parcels by their ruling families, particularly the counties in the Wetterau region north and west of Frankfurt. The heart of the Upper Rhine was controlled by a series of prince bishops based in Speyer, Worms and Strasbourg, whose lands straddled the river.[5] The Middle Rhine lay immediately to the north and was dominated by the three ecclesiastical electors of Mainz, Cologne and Trier, and their secular colleague governing the Palatinate around the modern towns of Heidelberg and Mannheim. The presence of these important princes lent the area its other name of Electoral Rhine. The Lower Rhine stretched from Cologne to the exit of the river in the North Sea. Much of this region lay more on the Reich's periphery since it fell under the control of the dukes of Burgundy, who succeeded to the old Frankish middle kingdom in the later middle ages. The bishopric of

Liège remained firmly part of the Reich, as did the numerous small territories covering Westphalia stretching north from the Rhine and east of
what is now the modern Netherlands. Westphalia contained the relatively large secular duchies of Cleves, Mark, Jülich and Berg clustered
around the Rhine near Cologne, as well as the principalities of Oldenburg and East Frisia to the north-east. Between them lay the important
bishoprics of Münster, Paderborn, Osnabrück and Verden, as well as
numerous smaller counties and abbeys.[6]

The south was also divided into three regions by 1550. Swabia in the
south-west contained only one substantial territory, the duchy of Württemberg, which covered a third of the entire region. The area between it
and the Rhine was split between the Austrian Habsburgs, who ruled the
Breisgau, and the two margraves of Baden, based respectively in Baden,
and Durlach. The remainder of Swabia was divided into around 90 different spiritual and secular lordships, including the majority of the
imperial cities.[7] Franconia to the north-east was only slightly less fragmented, with the bulk of its land shared between the secular margraves
of Ansbach and Bayreuth, the bishops of Bamberg and Würzburg, and
the city of Nuremberg, while the remainder was split between various
lordships and lesser cities. The third southern region was called Bavaria
and lay immediately east of Swabia and south of Franconia. Bavaria was
dominated by the duchy (later electorate) of that name, but contained a
number of other distinct territories, including the large archbishopric of
Salzburg and the important city of Regensburg.[8]

The northern periphery

Between these southern and western core regions, lay a third, smaller
and more central zone called Thuringia. This heavily forested region
between the rivers Werta and Saale had been conquered relatively early
by the Franks and played an important part in the medieval Reich. Like
the other core areas, it was also split into numerous, small territories,
including Gotha, Weimar, Jena, Anhalt, Schwarzenberg, Stolberg and
Reuss. These were frequently partitioned by their ruling families into
still smaller units, complicated by a quirk of history in the case of Reuss,
which broke into five branches, each of which insisted on choosing the
name Heinrich for every prince between 1132 and 1918. Thuringia was
subsumed within the Saxon lands along the northern periphery, which
were only incorporated within the Reich with the Germanic expansion

across the river Elbe in the twelfth century. As a region, Saxony had evolved into two halves by 1550. Upper Saxony lay to the east, between Bavaria and Bohemia to the south and the Baltic Sea to the north. Apart from Thuringia, Upper Saxony retained its later medieval characteristics of large, compact territories. The two secular electorates of Saxony and Brandenburg covered most of the region. Their rulers converted to Protestantism during the sixteenth century and incorporated most of the Upper Saxon church lands into their territories. However, Brandenburg's access to the Baltic Sea was blocked by the smaller duchies of Pomerania and Mecklenburg.[9]

The latter belonged to the Lower Saxon region, which stretched from Brandenburg in the east to Westphalia in the west, and from the Upper Rhine in the south to Denmark in the north. Its principal lands had been controlled since the twelfth century by the Guelph (*Welf*) family, who rose to prominence thanks to the patronage of medieval emperors. Their main territory of Brunswick (*Braunschweig*) had split into three duchies by the later sixteenth century. The two northern ones of Lüneburg and Calenberg were often known after their respective capitals of Celle and Hanover, and were combined under the latter name in 1705. The technically senior line ruled the other, smaller duchy of Brunswick-Wolfenbüttel. The rest of Lower Saxony was composed of modest-sized territories, like the bishoprics of Magdeburg, Halberstadt, Hildesheim and Bremen, and the duchies of Holstein and Schleswig, as well as smaller counties and the five cities of Hamburg, Bremen, Lübeck, Goslar and Nordhausen.

The Habsburg lands

Bohemia and Austria were incorporated in the Reich during the tenth and eleventh centuries, but grew more distinct through their long association with the Habsburg dynasty. Bohemia included the dependencies of Moravia, the Lausitz (Lusatia) and (from 1335) Silesia, and was confirmed as a separate kingdom in 1158, buttressed by a vibrant economy and distinct language and culture. Its king enjoyed considerable privileges, including an electoral vote, but was largely exempt from imperial jurisdiction and required to provide relatively few soldiers or taxes. The Habsburgs were keen to preserve this autonomy when they inherited the kingdom in 1526, since it prevented the other German princes from interfering in its affairs.[10] They also kept Bohemia's internal administration separate from that of their Austrian lands, which they acquired much earlier in 1278. Like Bohemia, Austria was another composite territory composed of different provinces held together by common allegiance to the same lord. Knitting these parts together took several centuries and was far from complete by 1550, when Austria still consisted of three distinct regions. Lower Austria contained two provinces called Upper and Lower Austria, as well as the dynastic capital of Vienna. Inner Austria comprised the provinces of Styria, Carinthia and Carniola and was governed from the town of Graz. Further Austria, governed from Innsbruck, consisted of the Tirol and the area known as Outer Austria (*Vorderösterreich*), composed of enclaves in Swabia, including the Breisgau, as well as most of Alsace. Collectively, these regions provided the Habsburg monarchy with its own core, since these were hereditary possessions independent of the imperial title.[11]

In addition to these lands within the Reich, the Habsburgs inherited the kingdom of Hungary immediately to the east, in 1526. Unfortunately, this coincided with the Ottoman invasion, resulting in the partition of the country by 1541 into three, roughly equal parts. The Ottomans held the south and east, restricting Habsburg rule to a narrow western strip that included the autonomous kingdom of Croatia. Northeastern Hungary maintained a precarious existence as an independent principality of Transylvania, which was a constant flash-point for Habsburg–Ottoman tension. Habsburg Hungary remained a narrow buffer between the Reich and the Ottomans until the Great Turkish War of 1683–99 when Emperor Leopold I (1658–1705) conquered the entire kingdom (see section 8.1). The combination of Hungary and Austria survived till the collapse of the Habsburg monarchy in 1918, whereas ties to Spain proved less durable. Spain was also acquired by inheritance and came with both European dependencies in Naples, Sicily and Sardinia, as well as a growing collection of New World colonies. It was joined to the other Habsburg possessions by the personal rule of Emperor Charles V, who became king of Spain in 1516. Management of this far-flung empire proved too much and Charles partitioned his lands in 1556, creating separate Spanish and Austrian branches. The former only survived until 1700, but was initially more powerful since it had access to Spain's considerable resources and colonial wealth.

The Habsburgs also ruled much of the land along the western and southern periphery of the Reich, where their authority was often disputed by entrenched local interests and jealous foreign powers. The western periphery, known as Burgundy, remained a constant source of tension between France and the Reich until the Napoleonic era. France seized the actual duchy of Burgundy early on, splitting the region into two parts. The northern area encompassed modern Belgium, Luxembourg and the Netherlands and was separated by Alsace and Lorraine from the more southerly Franche Comté, immediately west of Switzerland. The entire area formally remained part of the Reich, but was granted considerable autonomy in 1548. This increased when Charles V partitioned his possessions in 1556, assigning the Burgundian lands to the Spanish branch, which governed them through a viceroy based in Brussels. Opposition to these arrangements was one factor behind the Dutch Revolt (1568–1648), which resulted in a new republic in the northern Netherlands.[12] The other Burgundian lands remained part of the Reich, but were eaten away by France, which seized the border areas in the long wars of the later seventeenth century. The remnants, together with most of the Italian possessions, passed to Austria on the extinction of the Spanish Habsburgs in 1700.

The Hohenzollern lands

The Habsburg's great rivals, the Hohenzollerns, originated in the Swabian and Franconian heartlands of the Reich. They remained a comparatively minor German dynasty, even after one branch acquired the electorate of Brandenburg in 1415. Their association with Prussia stems from the collapse of the Teutonic Order in early sixteenth century. The Order had established an aristocratic religious state in Prussia and the surrounding region during the thirteenth century. This collapsed following a series of defeats by the Poles, who seized control of western, Royal Prussia by 1466. Eastern Prussia only escaped this when the Order's grand master, Albrecht von Hohenzollern, secularised it as a hereditary duchy under Polish overlordship in 1525. In 1618 Prussia passed to the Brandenburg branch, who joined the Habsburgs in the select group of German princes ruling land outside imperial jurisdiction (see section 8.2).

German dynasties and European politics

The rest of the Order's lands, in Livonia, Courland and Estonia, passed to Polish, Swedish and ultimately Russian control. Despite the claims of later German nationalists, these had little connection to the Reich or its subsequent history and of the 1.2 million inhabitants of this region in 1800, less than 8 per cent spoke German. Whilst remaining a separate state, Poland-Lithuania was tied to the Reich by a dynastic union with Saxony (1697–1763) as the Poles chose the Saxon electors as their kings.[13] Tracing these dynastic connections can seem an arcane exercise, but they became an important feature of German politics from the seventeenth century. Perhaps the most influential example is that of the Hanoverian Guelphs who were chosen to succeed the defunct Protestant Stuart line in Britain in 1714. This union lasted until 1837 when Hanover became, albeit briefly, a separate kingdom.[14] In both cases, the complexity of their new kingdoms distracted the Saxon and Hanoverian rulers from German politics.

However, such connections could catapult minor dynasties into the front rank of European royalty. One case was Denmark's complex ties to various north German duchies. The Danish kings asserted overlordship over Schleswig and Holstein at the southern end of the Jutland peninsula. Schleswig was only partly German-speaking and left the Reich in 1027, but Holstein remained within it and secured representation in the imperial institutions created from the late fifteenth century. By then, the north German dukes of Oldenburg had become the Danish royal family, reinforcing the connection to the Reich. This family ruled Denmark until 1863, but generally assigned Oldenburg to a junior branch, who exercised the family's rights as imperial princes, except from 1667 to 1773, when the king himself assumed this. Holstein was entrusted to another junior branch after 1533. This subsequently split, with the Holstein-Gottorp line asserting their independence in defiance of the Danish king, who continued to regard all Holstein as his possession.

The Gottorps sought their own connections to Denmark's Baltic rivals, Sweden and Russia. The Vasa dynasty that ruled Sweden (1533–1654) was replaced by a new king selected from their German relatives in Zweibrücken-Kleeburg, a tiny principality in the Rhineland. This line ended in turn when Queen Ulrike Eleonora abdicated in favour of her husband, Frederick of Hessen-Kassel, in 1720. This new German connection did not survive Frederick's death in 1751 and Sweden passed to a branch of the Holstein-Gottorps, who ruled until deposed by Napoleon's marshal, Jean Baptiste Bernadotte, in 1818, the founder of the present Swedish royal family. On each occasion, the German principality was too small to exert any influence on its new royal partner and instead risked being drawn into its wars. This is illustrated by the fate of Holstein itself. Carl Friedrich of Holstein-Gottorp (1700–39) forged a new alliance with

Russia by marrying the Tsar's daughter Anna Petrovna. Their son, Carl Peter Ulrich, was designated as heir to all Russia, becoming Tsar Peter III in 1762. He was only able to enjoy his new power for seven months before being murdered in a palace coup engineered by his own wife, another German, Princess Sophia Augusta of Anhalt-Zerbst, better known as Catherine the Great.[15]

The repercussions of this brutal act were settled in 1773 after long negotiations. Holstein was transferred fully to Denmark, in return for Oldenburg passing to other relations of the Russian imperial family. The German Confederation of 1815 repeated the earlier arrangements of including Holstein within its frontiers, but acknowledging Danish rule over both it and Schleswig. Nationalist agitation and Prussian expansionism terminated this connection by 1864.[16] Thanks to their ties to Russia, the families ruling Oldenburg and Anhalt survived the vicissitudes of nineteenth-century German politics and were not displaced until the socialist revolution of 1918.

2.2 Imperial and Territorial Government

Territorialisation

Seventeenth- and eighteenth-century German political history is complicated by the fragmentation of authority amongst the Reich's different territories. In order to understand this territorialisation of political power, it is necessary to return briefly to its medieval origins.[17] The early emperors had been warrior kings, who parcelled out authority to 300 or so loyal followers and local collaborators. These agents gradually evolved into the German aristocracy though, contrary to the claims of their genealogists, few of the later princes could genuinely claim direct descent from Charlemagne's knights.

The early royal agents were responsible for defence and public order. The emperor assigned specific lands and peoples to support each knight and enable him to carry out these functions. Over time, these arrangements became a more permanent feudal system as rising production supported a growing hierarchy of lords. These lords became hereditary aristocrats by the twelfth century, taking their name from their family's principal castle and exercising authority over the surrounding area. As their numbers grew, they assumed different titles that increasingly denoted status rather than political function. A fundamental division emerged by the fourteenth century, delineating a superior imperial aristocracy (*Reichsadel*) above an inferior territorial nobility (*Landadel*). The former were distinguished by their status of immediacy (*Reichsunmittelbarkeit*), indicating no overlord other than the emperor himself. They assumed superior titles in an ascending scale of baron, count, burgrave, landgrave, margrave and duke. The lesser territorial nobility usually only had the title of lord (*Herr*) or knight (*Ritter*), lay under the jurisdiction of one or more imperial aristocrats and were only indirectly subject to the emperor.

Despite their different titles, the imperial aristocrats coalesced as a distinct group of territorial lords (*Landesherren*) between the thirteenth and sixteenth centuries. Initially, jurisdiction over people had been more important than that over land, since much of medieval Germany was uninhabited forest. Population growth put pressure on land, increasing its importance and linking lordship more directly with jurisdiction over a given area. The emperor codified these territorial rights for ecclesiastical and secular lords respectively in 1220 and 1231. The latter decree made the first use of the term *domini terrae*, or territorial lordship (*Landesherrschaft*), and provided the basis of all future derivations from the term 'territory' (*Land*): territorial law (*Landrecht*), territorial subjects (*Landeskinder* or *Landesuntertanen*) and territorial ruler (*Landesherr*). It was not inevitable that such rulers would invariably be aristocrats, since medieval politics also recognised incorporated rural communities (*Landschaften*) and cities as capable of exercising authority. However, the senior aristocrats emerged as the dominant force, assuming the general status of princes (*Fürsten*), irrespective of their precise title.

The growth of territorial lordship related political power to specific localities. As these became more distinct, they were subdivided into districts (*Ämter*), overseen by officials chosen from the ranks of the territorial nobility, or governed by local towns or monasteries. Lords increasingly saw themselves as rulers rather than the emperor's agents, regarding their territories as public trusts to be preserved, enhanced and passed on to future generations.

Confessionalisation

Religious change accelerated the territorialisation of political power from the early sixteenth century by restricting the jurisdiction of the Catholic Church. This process fundamentally altered German history, but it was not entirely a sudden or complete break from the past. Secular lords had exploited earlier periods of papal weakness to assert claims to supervise spiritual activity and property in their own territories. For example, the Habsburgs secured considerable control over clerical appointments in Austria in their concordat with the pope in 1448. The intention of such agreements was the harmonisation temporal and spiritual interests, rather than outright secularisation of church property. Territorial lords offered protection to local ecclesiastical institutions and encouraged spiritual renewal by supervising 'visitations', or inspections of the parish clergy. In return, the church allowed the ruler to appoint his clients to senior positions and assisted in maintaining public order, particularly by enforcing morality.

The Protestant Reformation profoundly altered these church–state relations by shifting the spiritual basis of Christianity to personal faith. Good works, including donating wealth to the church, now took second place to individual conviction and belief. Significantly, Protestantism developed differently in each territory as it spread through parts of southern, central and north-eastern Germany from the early 1520s. Protestant theologians did write common statements of faith, notably the Lutheran Confession of Augsburg in 1530, which was expanded as the Book of Concord in 1580, and served as a theological benchmark for believers across Germany. However, they failed to establish a matching church structure equivalent to that of the Catholics. This reflected their distinction between the secular material world (*Externa*), and the personal spiritual one (*Interna*). The secular authorities should assume greater supervision of church property to allow the clergy to concentrate on spiritual welfare. This division of responsibility greatly increased secular oversight of ecclesiastical affairs, encouraging the formation of distinct territorial churches (*Landeskirchen*) in the Protestant principalities and imperial cities. Protestant rulers placed themselves at the head of their own church, assuming episcopalian powers, and issuing comprehensive ordinances for their territories. Some regarded this as a sanction for direct secularisation and dissolved monasteries and other religious institutions, incorporating them within their own private domains. More frequently, they reorganised former Catholic property into a public trust supervised by a new management board, called a church council (*Kirchenrat*). Staffed by lay administrators, this used the property to pay the pastors' salaries, and to support schools and other welfare measures. Overseeing of spiritual matters was entrusted to a separate consistory (*Konsistorium*) composed primarily of clerics, who enforced theological orthodoxy and discipline amongst the pastors.

Catholics bitterly opposed these changes, making disagreements over the purposes of ecclesiastical wealth one of the most explosive political issues of the sixteenth century. The papacy was determined to preserve its influence and, where possible, recover areas that had converted to Protestantism. It presided over the Council of Trent (1545–63), which issued definitive doctrinal statements of Catholicism and new guidelines for ecclesiastical management. Despite the creation of reforming religious orders like the Jesuits (1534), this Catholic or Counter Reformation could make little headway without the cooperation of rulers throughout Europe. Within the Reich, this included the territorial rulers as well as the emperor. Political opposition to Charles V's plans to strengthen his imperial authority combined with Protestant resistance to his continued adherence to Catholicism. Charles was defeated in the so-called 'Princes' Revolt' of 1552, and left his brother and eventual successor, Ferdinand I, to negotiate a compromise in the Peace of Augsburg in 1555.[18] This settlement entrenched the territorialisation of religious confession by allowing most princes to accept either Catholicism or Lutheranism in their territories. Summed up later by the famous formula, 'He who rules, decides the religion' (*cuius regio, eius religio*), this sanctioned political supervision of the church in each territory by granting rulers the power of reformation (*ius reformandi*).

Despite their deep doctrinal divisions, all Catholic and Lutheran rulers regarded religious conformity as an essential prerequisite for political stability. They collaborated with their local clergy to enforce their chosen faith within their territory, expelling dissenters or encouraging them to convert. Catholic rulers refrained from creating new secular management boards for their clergy and continued to recognise the spiritual jurisdiction of the German bishops and archbishops, most of whom were territorial rulers in their own right, still governing the lands of the imperial church. However, they generally used similar methods to enforce lay and clerical discipline, and to extend their patronage over ecclesiastical appointments within their own territories. These broad similarities have encouraged many historians to discuss church–state relations, regardless of denomination, as a common process of 'confessionalisation' whereby the ruler and clergy collaborated to ensure clerical education and discipline, a theologically appropriate use of church resources, and the morality and obedience of parishioners.[19] While the intent and effectiveness of such measures remain controversial, there is evidence for the hardening of confessional boundaries between the different German territories by 1600 (see section 4.1).

Territorial sovereignty

The growth of more distinct boundaries encouraged the consolidation of territorial authority. Territorial lordship gradually lost its medieval character of feudal ties of personal loyalty between lords and vassals, and assumed the early modern character of an institutionally and territorially closed state. New attitudes towards sovereignty encouraged this. The French political theorist Jean Bodin argued in 1576 that each country could only have one sovereign and a monarch could not share his powers with his subjects. This posed considerable problems for the Reich where authority was still divided along medieval lines between the different levels in the imperial hierarchy. Most Germans rejected Bodin's theory since to realise it in practice, the Reich, would have to be transformed into a single, unitary monarchy, or split into smaller separate principalities. They also rejected his description of their country as an aristocracy where the emperor was simply the first among equals, with few distinguishing powers. Instead, they struggled to explain the imperial hierarchy more clearly. The emperor remained supreme overlord and monarch over the entire Reich. His power was not absolute, however, because he shared authority with the territorial rulers. Their lordship was increasingly redefined as 'territorial sovereignty' (*superioritas territorialis*, or *Landeshoheit*) by the mid-seventeenth century.

This set them apart from the mass of territorial nobles and other authorities like town councils, whose power was restricted to the local level within individual territories. These authorities were now more clearly subordinated as territorial subjects, and denied a direct say in imperial affairs. The territorial sovereigns exercised their rights not merely as the emperor's direct vassals, but also as their own subjects' guardians. The latter aspect became increasingly important, implying powers to change social and economic relations within their territories, as well as to represent their subjects in all dealings with outsiders, including foreign governments. These powers were confirmed as territorial rights (*ius territoriale*) in Article VIII of the Treaty of Osnabrück (*Instrumentum Pacis Osnabrugense* or IPO): the part of the Peace of Westphalia that dealt directly with the imperial constitution.

However, this did not mean that the princes and other territorial rulers were now fully independent sovereigns. The IPO made no attempt to list all territorial rights, or even offer precise definitions for those it did include. The *ius reformandi* was re-stated, but in a more restricted form than that granted by the Peace of Augsburg. Rulers were still charged with supervising spiritual affairs and church management, but were forbidden to change the religion of their subjects, which had to remain as it had been in 1624 (see section 4.3). The right to make alliances (*ius foederis*) was not specifically mentioned, though the IPO did confirm the imperial legislation of 1495–1570 empowering the princes to cooperate in upholding the public peace. This was understood as extending to alliances with foreign powers, but all were subject to the restriction that such collaboration was not to harm the general good of the emperor and Reich. Similarly, the right to maintain troops and military installations (*ius armorum*) was also omitted since it was covered already in the public-peace legislation. Other judicial, legislative, fiscal and police powers were also left out, or only indirectly referred to.

Many historians have criticised this lack of precision as a major flaw that allowed the princes to escape the emperor's authority. In fact, it left room for further constitutional development. The new understanding of territorial sovereignty implied that rulers exercised their own permanent dominion over their subjects, reversing the medieval relationship between power and office. It was no longer the exercise of power that distinguished a particular lord as an imperial prince. Rather, the position of territorial sovereign automatically granted him a monopoly of key political powers and the exercise of government. This important development could be reconciled with the persistence of the imperial hierarchy precisely because territorial sovereignty was not clearly defined. The powers of individual rulers varied considerably across the Reich, depending not only on the original functions associated with their various princely titles, but also on the historic development of the individual territories. Not only was it impossible to list all these variations in the IPO, but no ruler wanted all his powers clearly defined since this would also spell out what he could not do. The imperial constitution retained its primacy, since all princely rights derived their legitimacy from it. Moreover, the same also applied to the emperor, whose powers were also left vague, implying that he too had the capacity to expand his practical authority. The IPO reserved a special category of superior sovereignty exclusively for him, identifying him as the Reich's 'supreme head' (*Reichsoberhaupt*).

The emergence of territorial sovereigns was thus not necessarily a threat to imperial authority. Contrary to the implications of the dualist model of German politics, princes and emperors were not inveterate opponents, but partners in a collaborative enterprise of constructing the Reich. Their relationship varied across the centuries. Territorial power derived neither exclusively from above as a gift from the emperor, nor from below as a seizure of former imperial prerogatives. Both these processes certainly happened during the middle ages, but emperors and lords also developed new powers together in common response to changing circumstances.

The Reichstag

The most important example of this was the creation of new imperial institutions from the later fifteenth century to coordinate a response to the mounting problems of internal disorder and external threats. These institutions gave the Reich its early modern shape, which it retained until 1806. Most were established between the 1490s and 1520s, including the *Reichstag*, or imperial diet, which provided the main forum for negotiation between the emperor and the territorial sovereigns. The Reichstag emerged from the earlier, intermittent meetings of the emperor's own royal court.[20] These became more frequent in the later fifteenth century as the Habsburg emperors requested military aid. Territorial lords had to choose between gaining a voice in decision-making by paying their share, or avoiding the new burdens, but losing political influence. The responses to this dilemma determined which lords and cities became full 'imperial estates' (*Reichsstände*) with representation in institutions like the Reichstag, and which slipped back into the ranks of the territorial nobility and towns. These choices were made across a relatively short period as the new Reichstag met 22 times between 1486 and 1518. The 1521 meeting in the city of Worms drew up a list of all eligible territories and computed their obligations in terms of cavalry and infantrymen and their cash equivalents. This 'matricular list' (*Matrikel*) became the benchmark for all subsequent arrangements, even if some territories later lost their status as imperial estates, while others acquired it.

   The frequency of the early meetings also established basic structures and procedures that remained essentially unchanged for the next 300 years. The imperial estates were divided into a hierarchy of three *corpora* or colleges, in ascending order of seniority from cities, to princes, to electors. The archbishop-elector of Mainz acted as chairman and set the agenda, but the emperor retained the right of proposition, meaning he determined the order in which matters were discussed. Each corpus debated separately and then conferred, taking decisions internally by majority vote.[21] Once all three reached a consensus, the verdict was summarised as an imperial recommendation (*Reichsgutachten*) and pre-sented to the emperor. If he agreed, the decision became law and was included in the concluding document (recess or *Reichsabschied*) of that meeting of the Reichstag. The emperor retained considerable authority, since he could veto any decision and his approval was necessary for the Reichstag to assemble.

Later historians have criticised this cumbersome process and many contemporaries recognised its faults. Constitutional amendments wid-ened the potential for obstruction by 1648. However, comparisons with democratic parliaments and other modern regimes are misleading. The Reichstag embodied a political culture that placed unanimity and respect for privilege above speed and ruthless efficiency. The priority was to reach a compromise that was both practical and acceptable to all. The appearance of the new imperial institutions during the transi-tion from the late medieval to the early modern world left a lasting impression on German political thought. The purpose of politics was not to safeguard *liberty* in the modern sense of individual rights and freedoms, but to protect the medieval notion of *liberties*, or corporate pri-vileges possessed and exercised collectively by the legally-recognised social Estates. German society was not divided into a privileged elite and a subordinate, powerless mass. Instead, it was composed of a com-plex hierarchy of corporate groups in which no one was totally with-out rights. Each group regarded its rights as part of a wider 'German Liberty' (*Teutsche Freiheit*), which distinguished the inhabitants of the Reich from those of other European monarchies, who were thought to live in slavish servitude to their kings.[22]

Early modern Germans did not view politics in abstract terms, but as the transient activities of mere mortals within a divinely ordained Christian order. It was not their business to construct a constitution by blueprint, in which everything was neatly defined. The spread of written culture since the fourteenth century did encourage the recording of rights and privileges, especially those associated with the exploitation of land and resources. This process was detrimental to the peasants, whose access to land became more restricted by new notions of property ownership. It also encouraged the fixation with status amongst nobles and princes, who insisted on listing all their titles in formal documents, lest any omission implied their ownership of a particular piece of land had lapsed. However, they were less keen to define their other liberties, since this might preclude the later acquisition of new powers.

The civic corpus

The tripartite division of the Reichstag reflected this corporate character of German society. The imperial cities remained the junior partners
of the princes and electors, because they were governed by commoners,
rather than aristocrats or clergy. None the less, the cities displayed a far
higher degree of political organisation than most lords prior to the mid-
sixteenth century. Medieval emperors had sponsored urban growth
during the twelfth century, protecting many cities from neighbouring lords and founding new ones under direct imperial overlordship.
These free and imperial cities (*Freie- und Reichsstädte*) developed their
own territorial lordships, often extending no further than their own
walls, but sometimes covering the surrounding countryside as well (see
Appendix 3). The often volatile internal politics of such towns made
them appear dangerously subversive to neighbouring princes, who also
feared they would take trade away from their own territories. Yet, most
princes recognised that cities offered dynamic concentrations of people,
wealth and talent, and founded their own territorial towns (*Landstädte*).
These were far more numerous, numbering around 2,200 by 1500, compared with 80 or so imperial cities. Their lack of imperial immediacy
restricted their political activity to the territorial Estates, whereas the
imperial cities gained voting rights in the Reichstag by 1582.

The consolidation of the civic corpus accounts for the decline of the
urban leagues that characterised medieval politics. The Hansa was
the largest of these, developing from a merchants' association in 1160 to
become an umbrella organisation for a network of civic alliances stretching across northern Europe from Flanders to Finland. Its core membership of 70 imperial and larger territorial towns was concentrated along
the north German rivers and coast, including cities like Hamburg,
Bremen and Lübeck. Another 100 cities were associate members and
participated in an annual congress, or *Hansatag*, that coordinated trading and diplomatic relations with other powers. Other, smaller leagues
existed periodically during the middle ages as a means of defending
urban autonomy against aggressive princes who wished to assert their
authority over towns. However, none of these organisations succeeded
in fully harmonising the disparate interests of its membership, severely
restricting the potential of this form of federal politics. As the imperial
hierarchy assumed a more permanent form, it became increasingly
attractive to cities, such as the Hansa founder-member Lübeck, which

secured recognition as an imperial city in 1226. The formation of the civic corpus at the Reichstag made these earlier leagues largely redundant and attempts to revive the Hansa after the Thirty Years War attracted little support, and the venerable organisation was wound up in 1671.

Of the 86 cities recorded in the 1521 matricular list, only 51 remained as members of the civic corpus by the start of the French Revolutionary Wars in 1792. This decline has been interpreted as a sign of the Reich's inability to defend the integrity of its weaker components. In fact, only nine cities disappeared through annexation by neighbouring princes. Of these, only Constance (1548) and Donauwörth (1608) were substantial towns, while the others (Soest, Brakel, Warburg, Lemgo, Verden, Düren, Herford) were hardly greater than walled villages incapable of bearing the burdens placed on them by the status of imperial estate. Seventeen western cities were lost to French encroachment, starting with the annexation of Metz, Toul and Verdun along with the bishoprics of those names in 1552. Louis XIV took Saarburg (1661), Besançon, Cambrai, Strasbourg and the ten Alsatian towns known as the Decapolis (all 1679–81). Another three left voluntarily, joining the Swiss Confederation in the early sixteenth century to preserve their autonomy: Basel, Schaffhausen and the Alsatian town of Mulhouse. The remainder disappeared because they lacked any firm foundations for their privileges. Most, like Göttingen, were incorporated into neighbouring territories in the sixteenth century, leaving only three to be forcibly suppressed shortly after the Thirty Years War: Münster, Erfurt and Brunswick (see section 6.2). The emperor acquiesced in these cases, but he defended the others, particularly the former Hansa towns of Hamburg and Bremen, which were recognised as imperial cities to preserve them from Danish and Swedish annexation.

The majority of the losses occurred in the north and far west, restricting the imperial cities to the old core zones of Swabia and Franconia, which together contained 37 of the survivors after 1648. These formed the Swabian bench in the civic corpus, while the other 14 constituted the Rhenish bench, including the Bavarian city of Regensburg and the remaining north German cities. Attendance at the Reichstag declined in the later eighteenth century, but mainly because the poorer cities economised on diplomatic representation by empowering richer neighbours to act as proxies. The Reich offered the best guarantee for civic autonomy and its disintegration signalled the end of urban freedom.

The electoral college

The smallest and most prestigious college in the Reichstag was that of the electors. It was also the oldest, taking shape in the absence of a powerful royal dynasty after 1254. The Golden Bull of 1356 fixed the identity of the electors and territorialised their powers. There were now three ecclesiastical electors, in Mainz, Cologne and Trier, and four secular ones, in Bohemia, the Palatinate, Saxony and Brandenburg. These lands were defined as 'electorates' (*Kurfürstentümer*), which could not be subdivided to create new electoral votes, but could be inherited or transferred to other lords.[23] Charles V repaid a political debt by switching the Saxon title from the Ernestine branch of the Wettins to the Albertine line in 1547. Ferdinand II (1619–37), attempted the same in 1623 when he rewarded the duke of Bavaria by giving him the electoral status of his Palatine relations. Widespread opposition to this forced his successor, Ferdinand III (1637–57), to create a new eighth title to compensate the Palatinate. As the even number of titles raised the possibility of a tie in imperial elections, the Bohemian vote was suspended. None the less, creation of a new title set a precedent that encouraged other princes to hope for similar preferment. Leopold I created a ninth title for Duke Ernst August of Calenberg (Hanover) in 1692 in return for strong military and financial support. Other princes felt aggrieved and blocked recognition until 1708 when Joseph I (1705–11) skilfully secured not only acceptance of the new Hanoverian elector, but re-admission of the Bohemian vote held by the Habsburgs.

Competition for additional titles grew during the eighteenth century. None the less, princes continued to respect the basic assumptions of the imperial hierarchy, believing that any new titles should only go to old, established dynasties ruling substantial territories. This left Württemberg and Hessen-Kassel as the only realistic candidates as the others lacked either the resources or inclination to pursue such expensive ambitions. The extinction of the Bavarian Wittelsbachs in 1777 made the college more exclusive, as their title was suspended so that the Palatine elector who inherited Bavaria would not have two votes. Both Württemberg and Hessen-Kassel hoped this 'vacant' title might now pass to them, but their aspirations were blocked by Habsburg intransigence and the controversy surrounding the admission of another Protestant to the largely Catholic college. Movement came only in the wake of the French Revolutionary Wars and the increased penetration of imperial

politics by France and Russia, each of whom sponsored their own candidates. The Cologne and Trier votes were abolished in 1803 when
all the ecclesiastical territories were secularised and annexed by other
princes. The Mainz title was transferred to the new composite territory
of Regensburg-Aschaffenburg, while new titles were created for Salzburg, Baden, Württemberg and Hessen-Kassel. When Salzburg was
incorporated into Austria in 1805, its title was transferred to the (by
then) grand duchy of Würzburg, which had only six months of its new
status before the entire Reich collapsed in 1806.[24] The old titles retained
their allure, however, and the rulers of Hessen-Kassel styled their land
Kurhessen between 1815 and 1866 to distinguish it from that of their
Darmstadt cousins who were 'merely' grand dukes.

The Golden Bull firmly entrenched imperial elections in the Reich.
Though the electors did negotiate with foreign powers over their choice
of candidate, they generally placed wider imperial interests above
immediate personal or pecuniary gain. While they were keen to receive
political favours from powerful allies, they did not want to endanger their
own status by appearing the slaves of external interests. For instance,
they resisted French pressure in 1648 to introduce a constitutional prohibition on the election of two successive emperors from the same dynasty.
They appreciated the need to reconcile their right to select any prince as
emperor with the need for political continuity within the Reich. While
diplomatic wrangling preceded each election, the outcome was never
contested, sparing the early modern Reich the crises of disputed suc-
cessions that plagued other European monarchies. The Habsburgs did
oppose Charles VII, the Bavarian Wittelsbach who was elected in
1742, but fought him as a rival claimant to Austria rather than as an
illegitimate emperor (see section 8.2).

The electors enjoyed the privilege of self-assembly since it was necessary for them to meet in the event of an emperor's death to decide his successor, or to exercise imperial prerogatives if an incumbent monarch was
absent from the Reich. Such assemblies offered a potential alternative to
the Reichstag. The electors had viewed the Reichstag with suspicion
in the early sixteenth century since it threatened to erode their superior
status amongst the princes. The abdication of Charles V gave them an
opportunity to assert their own distinctive role when they assembled to
confirm the accession of Ferdinand I as the next emperor in 1558.
Whereas the Reichstag had met 19 times during Charles' reign (1519–
58), it only assembled on another 11 occasions between then and the
Thirty Years War, whereas separate electoral assemblies (*Kurfürstentage*)

became more common.[25] Free from the interference of the princes and cities, the electors could act decisively, notably in 1630 when they compelled Ferdinand II to dismiss the famous imperial general Wallenstein (see section 4.2). However, religious divisions opened a serious split amongst the electors as Saxony, Brandenburg and the Palatinate became Lutheran. A new rift opened when the latter converted to Calvinism in 1561, since it now competed with Saxony for leadership amongst the German Protestants. The Catholics were also divided since the three ecclesiastical electors resented the power and influence of their parvenu Bavarian colleague from the 1620s. The electors' inability to solve the considerable problems facing the Reich encouraged them to accept closer cooperation with the lesser princes and cities. The emperor also now appreciated the value of the other two colleges as a potential counterweight to the electoral oligarchy. The Reichstag reconvened in 1640–1 and 1653–4. All parties found it convenient to prolong the meeting that opened in 1663, so that the Reichstag remained permanently in session thereafter as the 'eternal diet' (*Immerwährender Reichstag*) (see section 1).

The college of princes

Whereas the cities and electors preserved their corporate unity by forming two distinct colleges, the other princes remained undecided how to proceed. Most held aloof from the earlier meetings of the royal court and only joined the Reichstag after 1485. They resented the additional burdens associated with political representation, particularly after 1495 when the Reichstag introduced permanent taxation from all imperial estates to fund the new institutions. A considerable number of lesser lords and knights remained on the margins, outside the new institutions, yet struggling to avoid incorporation within the princely territories and electorates. A group of aggressive princes became increasingly impatient, forcing the knights to make a definite choice. When the Rhenish and south German free knights resorted to violence in defence of their liberties, the princes blasted them into submission by bombarding their castles in 1522–3. Eventually, only 350 families preserved their autonomy by agreeing to pay special taxes directly to the emperor in return for his recognition of their status as 'imperial knights' (*Reichsritter*).

Collectively these knights ruled 1,500 separate aristocratic landed estates (*Rittergüter*), covering 10,455 km^2 with a population of 450,000 in the later eighteenth century, or less than 2 per cent of the Reich's inhabitants. These were grouped regionally into 14 'cantons', each with an elected captain and coordinating council, whose main function was to ensure that all knights paid their share of the special taxes on which their collective autonomy depended. They remained distinct from the other 50,000 noble families who were directly subject to territorial princes. Yet, the knights remained a minor force in imperial politics, particularly as they were excluded from all the key institutions. Campaigns for Reichstag representation failed after 1648, leaving the knights wholly dependent on the emperor's continued protection.[26]

The knights' experience encouraged the other minor lords to seek closer involvement in the Reich. However, the princes refused to grant them equal status in their new college, and they had to accept shares in collective votes (*Kurialstimmen*), whereas each principality enjoyed a full individual vote (*Virilstimme*). The minor ecclesiastical and secular lords were eventually admitted on a regional basis as six regional 'benches', each with a single collective vote. The prelates secured two votes, with the larger Swabian bench being recognised in 1575, followed by the smaller, more disparate Rhenish one later. The well-organised Swabian and Wetterau counts received votes during the sixteenth century, followed by the Franconians (1641) and Westphalians (1654).[27]

The presence of the prelates indicates a division within the Reichstag between secular and spiritual rulers, alongside the partition into three colleges (see Table 2.1). The importance of the imperial church to the medieval emperors resulted in a disproportionate number of spiritual rulers, whose combined lands only covered a sixth of the Reich. Not only were the three most senior electoral titles held by ecclesiastics, but the spiritual princes held a clear majority in the college of princes in the early sixteenth century. This situation had been transformed by the later eighteenth century, when the secular princes outnumbered their ecclesiastical colleagues by nearly three to one.

Secularisation only accounts for a quarter of the ecclesiastical losses. The first wave of secularisation removed relatively few spiritual territories and these were often enclaves in larger, secular principalities. The Peace of Augsburg attempted to preserve the Catholic character of the imperial church by fixing the distribution of clerical property as it had been in 1552, and denying spiritual rulers the right to change the religion of their territories: they were still free to accept Lutheranism themselves, but had to step down in favour of another Catholic. This

Table 2.1 The Imperial Princes

General category	Ecclesiastical			Secular		
	Titles	Numbers in 1521	Numbers in 1792	Titles	Numbers in 1521	Numbers in 1792
Electors	Elector	3	3	Elector	4	5
Princes	Prince-archbishop Prince-bishop	50	24	duke margrave landgrave	33	61
Lords	abbot/abbess prior/prioress	83	40	counts	143	99
		136	67		180	165

'ecclesiastical reservation' (*geistlicher Vorbehalt*) was ignored from the 1580s, particularly in northern Germany where several important bishoprics passed into Protestant 'administration'. Catholic objections to this contributed to the outbreak of the Thirty Years War, during which further church land was seized (see section 4.2). Some of these changes were sanctioned by the Peace of Westphalia, bringing the total number of bishoprics secularised since 1521 to 15. Six of these retained their distinct territorial identity when they passed to neighbouring Protestant princes, who could now exercise their votes in imperial institutions.[28] The other nine were simply annexed, with six directly incorporated within other Protestant territories,[29] and the other three remaining Catholic, but being absorbed into Habsburg territory.[30] A further bishopric (Chiemsee) lost its own identity, but remained part of the imperial church by being incorporated into the archbishopric of Salzburg. Rather fewer of the 83 imperial abbeys and priories disappeared this way. Seven were secularised, while three convents simply became Protestant parts of the imperial church.[31] A few others were absorbed by Catholic princes, notably the two Austrian 'commanderies' of the Teutonic Order.

Foreign annexations accounted for a further six bishoprics, of which Cambrai, Metz, Toul and Verdun went to France, Utrecht to the Dutch Republic and Schleswig to Denmark. Other external losses were largely voluntary and reflect the ill-defined character of the imperial frontier in the sixteenth century. Three bishoprics and nine abbeys opted for incorporation within the Swiss Confederation, indicating that 'turning Swiss' was not merely a popular movement favoured by peasant and urban communes.[32]

Likewise, the contraction of the Reich accounted for only a fraction of the losses among the secular lords and princes. The substantial western principalities of Alsace, Lorraine and the Franche Comté were lost to France during the seventeenth and eighteenth centuries, but this made only a slight impression on the total number of princes. Some small counties were taken by their German neighbours, but in most cases when a prince bought or inherited a county, he kept it as a distinct possession in order to exercise its rights in imperial institutions. Rather more counties and abbeys disappeared from the matricular list because they were unwilling or unable to pay their share of imperial burdens, and they accepted 'mediatisation', or incorporation within a neighbouring principality. Natural causes removed around half of the 94 counts who disappeared after 1521, as their lands passed to princely relations on the extinction of the native ruling line.

Altogether, secularisation, annexation and mediatisation account for only half of the changes, while the remainder simply moved position through their elevation to a higher rank. While the emperor rarely created new electoral titles, he frequently promoted loyal prelates and counts, giving them new individual votes in the college of princes. This was noticeable during the sixteenth century when the impact of secularisation was reduced by promoting 11 lesser ecclesiastics to princely rank.[33] A number of comital families were also elevated,[34] while the emperor also rewarded his own Habsburg nobility with imperial titles, particularly families that remained loyal during the turmoil of the Thirty Years War.[35] An even larger group were made imperial counts.[36] These Habsburg nobles only became *Personalisten*, or titular imperial princes and counts, since their possessions within the emperor's hereditary lands remained under his territorial jurisdiction. These newcomers spent large sums buying territories from the existing comital families outside the Habsburg lands to underpin their new status, indicating the continuing significance of the imperial hierarchy to aristocratic prestige and identity.

The older princes remained suspicious of these parvenus, rightly suspecting the emperor of wanting to pack the Reichstag with his cronies. They compelled Ferdinand III to agree in 1654 that all future elevations required their approval. Whereas 160 counts and other individuals were given princely rank after 1582, only 19 of these elevations occurred after 1654. These changes stabilised the overall numbers in the college of princes. Though 27 spiritual principalities lost their representation between 1521 and 1792, 10 others became new permanent members, bringing the total to 33. Similarly, the drastic decline amongst the counts was off-set by the creation of 50 new titles, either as *Personalisten*, or by promoting imperial knights.[37]

These changes help explain why the number of secular princes more than doubled across this period. The final factor in this was the tendency of the major families to divide into distinct branches, each identified by a series of additional hyphenated names attached to the original title. For example, when Landgrave Philipp of Hessen died in 1567, he partitioned his lands amongst his four sons, creating new branches named after their territorial capitals: Hessen-Kassel, Hessen-Darmstadt, Hessen-Marburg and Hessen-Rheinfels. As was customary, the first named was designated the senior line and got the lion's share of the land. Detailed inheritance arrangements were made to decide who should receive what land if any of these new branches died out. In this case, Marburg fell to Kassel in 1604 and Rheinfels to Darmstadt in 1583. However, it proved impossible to cover every eventuality, creating numerous dynastic inheritance disputes, especially if some of the new branches subsequently subdivided, as was the case with the Darmstadt line, which had broken into three by 1596. Disputes over the Marburg inheritance, as well as another parallel conflict over the four Westphalian duchies of Jülich, Cleves, Berg and Mark, were contributory factors in the outbreak of the Thirty Years War.

A major factor in these disputes was the question of who should exercise the rights associated with the land. Many princes hoped that partition would create additional votes for their family in imperial institutions, without bringing additional financial or military obligations. This proved possible during the sixteenth century when, in addition to the creating of new Kassel and Darmstadt votes, others were added by two-way splits in the Pomeranian, Mecklenburg, and Holstein ducal families, as well as the Franconian branch of the Hohenzollerns. More came with the tripartite division of Baden, a quadruple split amongst the Guelphs, and quintuple partitions within both the Saxons and the Palatine Wittelsbachs! The emperor and other princes combined to curb this practice, ruling in 1582 that political rights were henceforth permanently tied to distinct territories and could not be created by new partitions. Families now had to decide which branch could exercise imperial rights, or agree to share these together.

The territorialisation of representation

This decision encouraged the general territorialisation of representation, tying political rights to pieces of land, rather than princely dynasties or their subject populations. Whoever legally held the land, could exercise its associated rights. This also applied to the regional grouping of the territories into ten imperial circles, or *Kreise*, that was established in 1500–12 (see section 5.3). Each Kreis had its own assembly (*Kreistag*) to coordinate regional security and public order. Those territories that qualified as imperial estates were also represented in the Kreis assemblies. However, the minor rulers enjoyed greater weight at this level, because each territory enjoyed a full vote, regardless of the college it belonged to in the Reichstag.

The electors and more powerful princes distrusted the Kreise for this reason, though some later appreciated the advantages of active participation. The territorialisation of representation encouraged this, because it enabled powerful dynasties to increase their influence in different regions by acquiring qualifying territory there. For example, the Hohenzollerns had three votes in the Upper Saxon Kreis because they held part of Pomerania and the secularised bishopric of Kammin, in addition to the electorate of Brandenburg. Their influence spread into other regions during the seventeenth and early eighteenth centuries, thanks to the acquisition of additional land – matched only by the Wittelsbachs, who were represented in four Kreise (see Appendix 2).

This accumulation of votes was even more pronounced in the Reichstag, where the secular electorates acquired a growing number of princely votes. Already by 1653 the 94 individual votes in that college were exercised by only 60 different rulers. The six secular electors held 28 votes there by the early eighteenth century, while Austria, Baden, Hessen and Mecklenburg each had three.[38] The electors also possessed significant shares in the four collective votes of the counts, particularly in Westphalia where most of the indigenous families had died out. The territorial redistribution in 1802–3 shifted power even more decisively in their favour as the (now 10) electors collectively held 78 of the remaining 131 full individual votes. Even without Napoleon's victory over Austria two years later, it was clear that the Reich was moving inexorably towards a federation of sovereign states, though the Habsburgs still entertained plans to revive the Reichstag.[39]

The emperor's powers

The development of the Reichstag consolidated the Reich as a 'mixed monarchy', defined by contemporary theorists as a state governed by a king in collaboration with his Estates. As imperial estates, the territorial rulers participated in all key decisions. Yet, the Reich remained a monarchy, because the emperor possessed exclusive, superior or 'reserve' powers (*jura caesarae reservata*). Like princely rights, these were still ill-defined, allowing the emperor to maintain his aura of supremacy. The princes restricted this by defining which powers he had to share with the Reichstag, creating two other categories of imperial prerogatives.

The narrower *jura caesarae reservata limitata* were shared only with the electors and included the right to summon the Reichstag, deciding who could inherit vacant territories, and arbitrating in conflicts between imperial estates. The electors' exclusive role in these decisions rested on their privileges in the Golden Bull and their ability to extract further concessions from the emperor. These concessions were codified after 1519 in a written document, known as an electoral capitulation (*Wahl-kapitulation*), which negotiated with each new emperor.[40] The electors' intention was not to weaken the Reich, but to curb any tendency towards imperial absolutism. They regarded themselves as the 'pillars of the Reich' (*Säulen des Reiches*), acting as trustees for German Liberty. Charles V was obliged to sign the first electoral capitulation, because the electors wanted to ensure he did not squander imperial resources in his dynastic wars against France. The process became entrenched when they obliged his successor, Ferdinand I, to accept a similar undertaking in 1558. The terms were tightened in 1612, because of Rudolf II's obvious neglect of imperial affairs and his refusal to nominate a successor. The electors consolidated their powers during the Thirty Years War to prevent the emperor disregarding constitutional propriety.

The electors' behaviour aroused the princes' suspicions, because it threatened to erode the Reichstag's role in key decisions. The Protestants were particularly concerned because they were outnumbered in both the electoral college and the college of princes. They led a campaign for all princes to be included in drafting a permanent capitulation (*Capitulatio perpetua*) that would fix imperial prerogatives and prevent the electors widening their own powers. The electors naturally rejected this and the matter was postponed as too controversial in 1648. A draft text was completed in 1711, but never sanctioned and the princes gave up their demands in 1751. The electors retained their privileged position, but though they obliged Leopold I to include confirmation of the IPO in 1658, they refrained from adding further significant restrictions thereafter.[41]

In addition to preventing the emperor rewarding his supporters with new titles, the electors were primarily concerned to stop him using his reserve powers to punish princes he did not like. The emperor's main sanction was the imperial ban (*Reichsacht*), which deprived an individual of all lands, titles and rights, including that of assistance from fellow rulers. In seeking to restrict this punishment, the electors wanted to make it more effective as to well as to curb its potential misuse. They wanted to introduce more time to allow a wayward ruler to see the error of his ways, before soldiers were despatched to seize his possessions. The 1519 capitulation bound all subsequent emperors to consult the electors and institute formal legal proceedings before using the ban. Later emperors did not contest the validity of this restriction, but developed a new category of 'notorious rebellion' (*notorium crimen rebellionis et laesae majestatis*). The emperor could dispense with a trial if a ruler had taken up arms or otherwise demonstrably broken the public peace. The need for swift action in such cases was obvious to all and no objections were made to this new arrangement until Ferdinand II started using it against his opponents during the Thirty Years War (see section 4.2). The electors closed ranks and imposed new restrictions in Ferdinand III's capitulation of 1636, obliging him to consult them before acting against other 'rebels'. However, they still appreciated the need for an effective sanction and resisted Swedish proposals to make the ban dependent on the agreement of the entire Reichstag.[42]

The emperor was still free to act when he had good grounds, and made careful diplomatic preparations. For example, Joseph I imposed a ban on the electors of Bavaria and Cologne in 1705–6 after they had taken up arms against him during the War of the Spanish Succession (1701–14). The other electors were now sufficiently alarmed to compel his successor, Charles VI, to agree in 1711 to involve the Reichstag in future cases. This did not prevent Charles from deposing Duke Carl Leopold of Mecklenburg-Schwerin for tyrannical rule, in 1727. The loophole was finally closed in 1742, when Charles VII was obliged to agree that all future bans were dependent on the Reichstag's consent. The ban none the less remained a sanction of great symbolic importance, and Austria compelled the Reichstag to impose it on Prussia during the Seven Years War. Mentally unstable or wayward rulers could still be deposed with the agreement of their relatives.[43]

The involvement of the Reichstag widened the range of broader *jura comitialia*, which the emperor could only exercise in conjunction with all imperial estates. These powers encompassed a wide range of legislative, judicial, fiscal, military and diplomatic prerogatives. None the less, the emperor retained the initiative in the Reichstag, particularly through his retention of an absolute veto. Seventeenth- and eighteenth-century emperors cooperated with the Reichstag, not necessarily because they had to, but to lend greater legitimacy to their actions. War-making provides the most important example. Leopold I consulted the Reichstag to sanction military action against France in 1689 and 1702, because the formal declaration of war (*Reichskrieg*) added moral force to his policies. He was not obliged to do this, because the public peace legislation already empowered him to summon forces against foreign invasion.[44]

Chapter 3:   Fundamentals

3.1   The Parameters of Life

Population

The Reich had well over 28 million inhabitants by the late eighteenth century, making it the most populous state in Europe, alongside France and Russia. This represented a considerable increase on earlier levels, which followed wider European trends (see Table 3.1). The Black Death reduced the Reich's population by a third in the mid-fourteenth century. Numbers recovered from around 1470, and then rose sharply after 1530, putting increased pressure on land. The Thirty Years War interrupted this, though the exact extent of the decline is in dispute (see section 4.4). Overall numbers slowly returned to their pre-war level by 1714, and

Table 3.1   Population of the Reich and associated lands (in millions)

Date	'Germany'*	Prussia**	Habsburg	'Burgundy'	Reich total	Overall
1560	14.0	–	6.2	3.0	21.1	23.2
1618	17.0	0.3	8.7	1.1	23.1	26.1
1650	12.0	0.25	7.0	0.7	16.0	20.15
1700	14.0	0.4	8.2	0.9	19.9	24.5
1750	16.2	0.6	14.97	1.2	23.17	31.77
1800	18.56	3.66	24.08	1.89	29.24	48.19

* Includes Prussian Silesia for 1750 (1.2) and 1800 (1.78). Prior to this, Silesia is included within the Habsburg Monarchy.

** I.e. Ducal Prussia, plus later Polish acquisitions. Brandenburg and the other Hohenzollern lands are included within the 'Germany' total.

began rising sharply between 1730 and 1750, placing renewed pressure on resources by 1770.

These overall figures obscure more subtle fluctuations, or 'crises'. Some of these crises were due to food shortages, mostly related to the general climatic changes known as the Little Ice Age that affected much of Europe between 1520 and 1720, with a peak in the 1690s. Rainfall increased by 10 per cent, while temperatures fell by between 1° and 1.5°C, shortening the growing season by a month, substantially reducing yields and magnifying the danger of a bad harvest by up to twelve times that of the middle ages. Settlement contracted as Germans abandoned the higher ground after 1580. It became more difficult to grow some traditional crops, such as grapes in central Germany. As people drifted to warmer areas, the terraced hillsides fell into disrepair and were frequently washed away by the heavy rain, leaving only barren rock. Social and political arrangements made matters worse. Custom dictated what crops should be sown, discouraging a search for more viable alternatives. Taxes and tithes increased as yields fell, adding to the misery. Conflict intensified the difficulties, notably in the so-called *Kipper und Wipperzeit* of 1618–22, a period of wild price fluctuations and inflation, caused by war profiteering, coinage devaluation, and trade disruption. These problems intersected with the rise in population in the later sixteenth century, inflating food prices. Per capita meat consumption fell from 50 kg in the fifteenth century to only 20 kg by 1800, with the shortfall only being partly made good with more grain. Malnutrition reduced female fertility and doubled infant mortality.

However, hunger itself was rarely a direct killer. Usually, malnutrition contributed to a second type of demographic crisis brought by plague and other epidemics. Poor nutrition and hygiene left people susceptible to typhoid and dysentery, while the bubonic plague returned periodically until 1709–12 when the last major outbreak killed a third of ducal Prussians and others across northern Germany. Subsistence crises resumed with renewed population growth during the eighteenth century, causing major problems in 1770–1, 1816–17 and 1846–7.

Life expectancy

Despite these later problems, life expectancy improved from the mid-seventeenth century after four centuries of decline. Most Germans died as infants or toddlers until well into the nineteenth century. Only half of those born alive reached their fifteenth birthday. Boys who survived that far could expect to live another 42 years in 1600, whereas girls had only 23 more left; a figure depressed by high female mortality in child-birth. Around a third of the survivors at 15 lived through adulthood, with a fifth reaching their fifties, compared with an average lifespan of 77 for German women and 73 for men in the 1990s. It was not uncommon for parents to outlive all their children and find themselves alone in old age.

Boys were most likely to die before they reached their first birthday, with girls more frequently succumbing in subsequent years. The principal child killer was diarrhoea in summer, caused by contaminated water or cow's milk that turned sour. The plague was also a major threat, taking 10% to 30% of adults, but 90% of babies and small children. Immunisation programmes against smallpox in the eighteenth century reduced deaths, but children still remained at risk, particularly of accidents in the frequent absence of adult supervision. Adults were most vulnerable in winter and spring because of the higher incidence of chills and influenza.

Social inequality in death

While death claimed all, it affected social groups differently. However, this was not simply a case of the rich living longer. 'Social differences in mortality were ... overwhelmingly differences in child mortality'.[1] Child mortality was highest amongst those groups with greater marriage and fertility rates. Those who practised birth control, or married later, produced fewer children, more of whom tended to survive. Religious conviction was instrumental in this. Protestants and Catholics married around the same age, of 26 for men or 23 for women, after 1650. However, Protestant couples generally had between five and nine children, whereas Catholics produced more than ten. Calvinists were the most likely to practise birth control, but their midwives were also generally better trained, increasing the likelihood of survival for both mother and child.

Breastfeeding, either by the mother or by a wet nurse, was another factor and it was considered exceptional for a baby raised on pap or cow's milk to survive. Wet nursing was restricted to the urban upper classes. Social taboos gave poorer women some relief. It was widely believed that a woman who had just given birth was 'unclean', inducing employers to grant them six weeks' maternity leave. They were still expected to return immediately thereafter and the high child mortality in parts of Swabia and Bavaria was due in part to the presence of the textile industry, which employed large numbers of female workers. Evidence suggests that infant mortality was also inversely proportional to income within each confessional group. For example, over 57% of journeymen's children died in eighteenth-century Berlin, compared with less than 11% of those of aristocrats. Contemporaries were aware of such inequalities, but largely accepted them as 'normal'.

Mortality was generally higher in towns than in the countryside, because peasants had better access to food and more hygienic accommodation. While 50% of Brandenburg peasants died by their fifteenth birthday, 25% lived beyond their sixtieth year, with a respectable average lifespan of 72. Burghers often survived longer than nobles, while clerics lived the longest, because of better food and minimal manual labour. The life expectancy of German princes actually declined between 1500 and 1699, though the overall numbers of those surviving beyond 15 increased. By the later seventeenth century it had become common for princes to be outlived by their sons, reducing the incidence of dynastic crisis. However, intermarriage did affect the gene pool. Habsburg power was endangered when Ferdinand III's son, Ferdinand IV, died unexpectedly in 1654, and it proved difficult to persuade the electors to chose his younger brother as Leopold I four years later. A second, far more serious crisis occurred in the eighteenth century when Charles VI's only son, Leopold Johann, lived less than six months, leaving his daughter Maria Theresa as his successor (see section 8.1).

Resilience and recovery

Despite these losses, the German population proved extremely resilient. Given the high infant mortality, each couple needed at least five children to sustain stable numbers. Losses from plague or war could be made good by lowering the marriage age by an average of four years, increasing the number of child-bearing years and adding another two children per couple. Wartime casualties created new opportunities. Land became vacant and more children survived as food prices fell because of reduced demands and state bans on exports. These factors assisted the recovery after the Thirty Years War and travellers in the 1660s noted Germany as a land of children. The birth rate levelled off in the 1670s, but remained high as the baby boomers of the 1650s reached marriageable age. The recovery slowed in the 1680s as the growing numbers put more pressure on resources, coinciding with increased taxes and renewed warfare after 1672. The bad weather of 1691–8 and 1709 caused severe problems, but births still exceeded deaths. Gender differences narrowed as life expectancy improved after 1650, and by 1700 teenage girls could expect to reach 60, or five years longer than their brothers.

Population levels stabilised in the early eighteenth century, as the marriage age rose, reducing the number of new births. The situation began to change, starting in northern Germany after 1725, and accelerating from mid-century. Hessen achieved an annual growth rate of over 12%, four times that in Saxony, though some areas experienced a decline, like Bavaria where a local agrarian crisis caused the population to fall by up to 6% each year from 1771 to 1794. None the less, the overall growth of 30% added up to 6 million additional inhabitants in the Reich during the second half of the eighteenth century. Opinion is divided as to the reasons behind this impressive growth. German historians have tended to stress the impact of state action, notably the immunisation programmes, agrarian reform and other welfare measures. While these certainly made a difference, they were probably less important than improvements in food production and the prolonged absence of war from 1714 to 1733 and from 1763 to 1792.[2]

Childhood

Children assumed legal status at birth and were protected in law, especially by the dire penalties imposed for infanticide. They were considered legally competent at 7 and at 14 could be held responsible and punished. This associated childhood with only the first seven years, leaving the rest indeterminate. Many Germans had only a rough knowledge of their own age, and people were judged by appearances, being accepted as adults if they looked old enough. Work started early, with girls as young as 8 hiring themselves as babysitters. Many trades accepted apprentices from 11, and all children were given a multitude of household tasks and were often 'lent' to help childless couples.

Puberty occurred later than today, delayed until the late teens by poor diet and hard work. However, the difficulty of amassing sufficient wealth prolonged adolescence, because material independence was a criterion for marriage. The age of maturity varied, but was gradually standardised at 25 by the spread of Roman Law, adopted by most territorial governments in their marriage legislation. Parental control remained stricter in wealthier families, with female adolescence shorter and more closely supervised. Many aristocratic women were destined by their families for unmarried life in a convent. While peasant girls had more freedom, this was related to work outside the home, which gave them the chance to meet other young people, whereas burgher and aristocratic daughters generally only met relations or their father's colleagues.

Marriage

Marriage was an ancient institution, but did not became a milestone in the life cycle of most Germans until the sixteenth century. Restrictions on consanguinity, and social and economic factors, combined to limit marriages during the middle ages. This explains the prevailing attitude to prostitution, which was intended to protect the daughters of the rich from male aggression. The medieval church had pushed a new model of consensual marriage between two adults, but met with strong opposition from all sections of society, who preferred arranged marriages. The clergy also resisted, adopting elements of the lifestyle of the communities they served, including concubinage, while clandestine marriages without clerical consent persisted. The population recovery in the later fifteenth century shifted attitudes as the richer sections of society saw publicly sanctioned marriage as a way of controlling access to scarcer resources. Such demands were well received by clerics, who wanted to reconcile actual custom with the medieval theological ideal.

Changes introduced during the sixteenth century radically altered marriage practices, with profound consequences for relations between German men and women after 1600. Protestant theologians in particular backed the laity's demands for secular controls on marriage and an end to clandestine unions. Marriage was to be celebrated publicly in a church and required parental consent. The territorial governments stepped in, requiring written registration and establishing courts to judge divorce and adultery.[3] Children who were conceived prior to marriage were now considered illegitimate. Combined with growing restrictions on marriages amongst the poor, this contributed to a rise in illegitimacy from 2% of births in the sixteenth century, to 5% by the late eighteenth. Rates were higher in Catholic areas, and in garrison towns, where they reached 8% to 14%, because of the widespread prohibition on soldiers' marriages.

Such restrictions reflected a wider effort to control sexuality. Brothels had been intended for single men. Since it was obvious they were frequented by married men, Protestant theologians demanded their closure to protect the new status of marriage as a unique union of two adults. 'Whore' now became an insult for any woman suspected of sexual relations outside marriage, and an imperial decree banned concubinage in 1577.

Catholics still defended clerical celibacy, regarded marriage as a sacrament, and left its regulation to the ecclesiastical courts, but otherwise adopted measures similar to those of the Protestants. Regardless of confession, however, all theologians found the secular authorities reluctant to enforce what they preached, and even the parish clergy resisted the new official norms. For example, concubinage amongst Bavarian priests rose from 10% prior to 1517 to 90% by 1583 when the duke finally ordered the papal and imperial prohibitions to be enforced. This took until the mid-seventeenth century and was only successful when popular attitudes changed. Whereas late medieval critics saw 'strong' women preying on easily-led priests, eighteenth-century society called for the state to protect 'weak' women from men.[4]

Old age

Despite the restrictions, marriage became very common with around 85% of adults marrying at least once in their lifetime. Widowers remained attractive potential partners because of their status as masters of a house, and often remarried, many finding younger brides to look after their children. Widows' prospects were more limited, particularly as they usually had to share their inheritance with any children. Fewer men were willing to take on the responsibility of a ready-made family and those widows who remarried generally took much poorer second husbands. Some trades permitted widows to continue a family business and those without a family could buy a place in a city hospital. Peasants devised inheritance strategies that included retirement shares for parents, though their sons often bought them out.

Professional pensions and other welfare measures remained restricted. The church already offered limited provision for retired clergy prior to 1600. Territorial governments introduced measures from the 1680s, but restricted these to their own servants, particularly soldiers, who had invalidity and retirement benefit schemes funded by pay deductions.

These were barely adequate, and threatened by the perennial shortage of cash – the duke of Württemberg raided his soldiers' pension fund in the later eighteenth century to meet other military expenditure!

Professional groups established their own funds after 1700, which represented a transitional stage between earlier arrangements made by urban guilds to look after their members and modern life insurance schemes. Some of the new funds had state backing, like the Württemberg 'widows and orphans chest', but many were initiatives by merchants and other professional groups seeking to consolidate their collective identity. Traditional welfare relied on large endowments that generated the income needed to pay pensions and other benefits. The new mutual societies expanded this by allowing members to buy annuities, including husbands making provision for their wives, but often extended their liabilities beyond their income in a desire to recruit new members. After a wave of spectacular failures, the Hamburgische Allgemeine Versorgungs Anstalt was founded in 1774. As Germany's first modern life assurance company, this was no longer a charity judging applicants by their morals, but a purely commercial venture assessing them by their health and ability to pay premiums.[5] However, the high mortality drastically reduced the numbers of old people and, contrary to popular nostalgia, it was rare to find three generations under one roof.

Gender

Sixteenth-century German intellectuals already discussed gender stereotypes, contrasting manly strength with womanly weakness. However, such distinctions were far from clear to the rest of society which defined status in more complex terms. For instance, the standard modern paradigm of warlike men and pacific women was far from universal. Martial virtues were largely appropriated by the aristocracy, and ordinary soldiers were despised and feared. This changed across the seventeenth century as war became desacralised, shifting responsibility for the outcome away from divine favour and towards the affairs of men. As a larger proportion of the adult male population was called to serve, rulers tried to improve soldiers' status, whilst simultaneously excluding women from active involvement, reclassifying female dependants and ancillary personnel as 'civilians'.[6]

Work remained the primary element in male identity and was linked to associations of honesty, physical strength and respect for craft traditions. It encompassed both horizontal relations between school or work mates, as well as hierarchical ones between father and son, master and apprentice. Such distinctions were expressed through dress. The few surviving male autobiographies from this period all note the significance of the first pair of breeches, usually given to boys aged five, which marked both a progression toward adulthood, as well as a distinction from female siblings. Marriage represented maturity and independence, as symbolised by the ritual of parents dressing their son for the last time on his wedding day.

Marriage also represented independence for women, with the ideal of a wife complementing that of a husband as the joint heads of a separate household. It was a partnership in which both had different, but roughly equal roles. Women represented households, not as substitutes for absent husbands, but in their own capacity as mistresses of the house. The role of mother was only one element of this, and was esteemed as a further symbol of the wife's status. Despite the risks of pregnancy, most women's fear was barrenness, not conception, because children represented continuation of the lineage and potential security in old age. Contraception was mainly a concern for unmarried women and prostitutes. Wives had their own sphere of authority and carried out their tasks without male supervision. The husband did hold the purse strings, but many women had property in their own right, particularly in areas of partiable inheritance (see 3.2), as well as amassing hidden savings. Housewives oversaw the children or maids, who did much of the work in the home, though they were also expected to help in major tasks.

Female labour was an essential part of life, adding flexibility to a relatively inelastic economic structure. Women stepped in when male labour was scarce, or new processes developed, such as the putting-out system of textile production involving piece work done at home. However, this offered little chance for the kind of corporate rights enjoyed by the predominantly male craft organisations. It was difficult for female workers to organise, particularly as their employment depended on the existing guild structure. For instance, the new textile companies employing women were backed by the local territorial governments, who had little interest in pushing for better conditions that might cut into their share of the profits.[7] Women were generally forced out once male labour became available, or once their task acquired higher social status.

None the less, the growth of wage labour in sixteenth-century Germany provided growing opportunities for women, particularly in areas of impartiable inheritance where it was otherwise difficult to accumulate wealth. It created a new, distinct period of youth as a time of financial semi-dependency between childhood and married adulthood – a period that had lasted a lifetime for most medieval Germans who had been unable to marry.

The distinction between married and single women was reflected by their different status in law. In civil cases, including disputes over property, women had to be represented by their male relations, unless they were widows, or the contention was between husband and wife. Criminal law treated both sexes as equally competent. Though special penalties were reserved for specifically 'female' crimes, such as death for infanticide, women were generally punished less severely. They paid fines at half rate, while special rules applied if they were pregnant. Men did not necessarily escape justice more easily. The great imperial law code, the *Carolina* of 1532, stipulated equal penalties for adultery. There were wide variations, because the imperial code was interpreted differently in each territory. However, women could have their sentence for 'fornication' reduced if they denounced their male partner, since territorial governments were keen to ensure that fathers took responsibility for any children.

Regardless of gender, the courts treated spouses with more respect than those who were unmarried. Married women could use the courts to obtain legal redress because their position as mistress of the house lent credibility to their statements. They could initiate cases and act on behalf of unmarried women, such as their daughters or maids. Single women could still prosecute employers for unpaid wages, or initiate paternity or alimony suits.[8] The authorities willingly accepted such cases, particularly those involving violent or abusive husbands. However, their concern was to preserve the household as a stable social and economic unit and they sided with the party whose behaviour corresponded closest to the official norms of thrift, honesty and duty.[9] Women who played by these rules were often successful, while those who transgressed failed. This situation compared relatively favourably with that elsewhere in Europe, particularly with the legal reforms initiated by eighteenth-century territorial governments. Women's right to divorce was introduced in Prussia, Württemberg and other territories a century before it was granted in France or Britain, and the legal status of women under the German absolutist governments was better than under the French revolutionary republic.[10]

Other changes were less favourable as the ideal of the 'bourgeois' family gradually displaced the earlier concept of marriage as an equal partnership. To divide the household into separate, more clearly gendered spheres, offered new space for emotional warmth as the role of mother assumed greater prominence. Yet, such an ideal still depended on proletarian households and female servants to sustain it. It emerged as some opportunities for female work declined, particularly as certain activities, such as medicine, were professionalised, while the growing population increased the availability of male labour. Many female tasks were no longer considered 'work', eroding women's public status. Changes in political theory reinforced this. Married women and widows had been eligible for citizenship in some German towns and could participate in communal politics in the sixteenth century. During the seventeenth century these rights became increasingly associated with wealth and the capacity to bear arms. In the meantime, Protestant theologians promoted the alternative sphere of female domesticity in the home. These economic, political and moral norms were entrenched by the early nineteenth century, so that when German liberals campaigned for broader rights, they claimed these for men only.[11]

Geographical and intellectual horizons

The rapid pace of modern life races in apparent contrast to the seemingly static pre-industrial world, regulated by the seasons and bounded by the narrow confines of the home and the parish. Yet, the lives of early modern Germans were full of uncertainty, and death was a constant companion. The two centuries after 1550 saw regular periods of economic and demographic crisis. Nearly everyone who survived till adulthood experienced at least one period of abnormally high mortality, and most families lost at least one child. Attitudes to life display a lack of care for the future. Most people spent three-quarters of their income on food and drink, gorging themselves on the few occasions when this was widely available. Uncertainty prompted a search for answers, with people turning to magic and other beliefs, either to to empower the powerless, or to explain the inexplicable.

Many took a more practical response to their difficulties and went in search of sustenance and a better life elsewhere. Seasonal migration was particularly pronounced in northern Germany with the practice of 'going to Holland' (*Hollandsgehen*) as people regularly crossed the frontier to cut hay, dig peat, catch herring, or make bricks. Drovers went several hundred miles on round trips taking livestock to Dutch markets.

Throughout Germany, journeymen travelled to find work and complete their craft training. Many became permanent migrants, settling in other areas (see section 7.1). Immigrants formed between a third and half the population of most medium and large towns. People also moved frequently within their community. Roughly half the inhabitants of most towns changed their address within ten years, while others left it altogether, indicating a greater degree of mobility than was experienced in nineteenth-century German cities.

Most left because they were unable to find work. Over half the journeymen bookbinders arriving in eighteenth-century Frankfurt left because they were unable to find a position – and this was the capital of the German book trade! The economic stagnation and decline suffered by many towns during the seventeenth century made them less attractive destinations. For example, short-distance migration to Schwäbisch-Hall from its immediate hinterland increased, but far fewer long-distance migrants arrived, giving the town a provincial character. The same occurred in Augsburg, Ulm, Nördlingen and other formerly important cities, though busy seaports like Hamburg continued to draw newcomers from far and wide. Rural households were less mobile, but their younger children often had to leave as urban migrants, seasonal workers or soldiers.[12]

Mobility widened horizons, partly counteracting what one historian has described as the self-absorbed 'home town' mentality of many small German communities.[13] The degree of popular participation in the dissemination of information and political communication has been interpreted differently. The general conclusion was that the rise of absolutism suppressed popular political discourse and presented a carefully crafted message of divinely-ordained princely authority to a largely passive audience. The official view was only challenged as the growth of market networks opened new channels of 'bourgeois' communication, transforming the 'public sphere' by giving rise to the force of public opinion. More recent research reveals that absolutist communication was not entirely one-way and subjects were expected to play an active role in certain circumstances. Not only did governments fail to suppress traditional forms of communication, but public discussion of politics and current affairs was widespread much earlier than previously thought. Attempts to restrict information were not merely a form of political control, but reflected the deep-rooted belief that powers of discernment and critical awareness were directly related to social status. Placed next to beasts in the divinely-ordained social hierarchy, peasants were judged incapable of rational thought and were supposedly seduced by appearances rather than arguments. These prejudices persisted long after absolutism had been displaced by more liberal forms of rule.[14]

Rumours were regarded with suspicion as the first sign of sedition, but were rife in all sections of society, particularly in the world of court intrigue. Folk songs and popular theatre remained one way of obtaining information, but rarely reached a wide audience. The printed word was more effective and was often brought by 'news singers' peddling single sheets with a rhymed text that could be sung for a fee to the illiterate. The authorities used these for official propaganda, notably during the Thirty Years War, but switched to the regular press, which grew from the early eighteenth century. There were already 60 newspaper publishers in the Reich by 1700, rising to 90 by mid-century and up to 300 by the end. Many produced official news sheets reporting the doings of the local ruling dynasty, its decrees and regulations. Others were commercial enterprises, printing international news, as well as economic, literary and political discussion. Circulation of the *Allgemeine Deutsche Bibliothek* reached 2,500 each issue between 1765 and 1805, but most averaged only 500. None the less, the number of new books and journals published each year rose from 1,000 in 1720 to 3,560 by 1790 when there were an estimated 10,000 writers in German, a third of whom were professionals, or three times the number in France. The number of novels published in Germany leapt from 73 in the decade 1750–9, to 1,623 in 1791–1800, or twice as many as in France. Theological works represented 38.5% of the books for sale at the Leipzig trade fair in 1740, but only 13.5% sixty years later as the demand for political science, economics and literature boomed.

These publications reached a surprisingly wide audience. At least 15% of Germans could read in 1700 and the proportion probably doubled over the century. The literacy rate was much higher in some areas and reaching 80% for adult males and 40–60% for women in Oldenburg and Koblenz in 1800. In more rural areas, such as East Prussia, the proportion still topped 40% at that point, or four times the figure in mid-century. Even amongst the poor, rates were comparatively high, with 47% of male and 28% of female day labourers having minimum literacy in eighteenth-century Koblenz. The few books in such households were generally religious works, but most major towns had lending libraries by the late eighteenth century, while newspapers and other publications were often passed around villages or read aloud to a larger audience.

3.2 Society

Estates society

Early modern Germans lived in a society characterised by orders, or Estates (*Stände*), which had their origins in functional divisions that had emerged since the eleventh century. Their role in praying for common salvation placed the clergy as society's first Estate. The nobility formed a second Estate of warriors, who defended society and offered political leadership. The rest of the population constituted a third, nourishing Estate that provided for everyone's material well-being. All observers acknowledged that the reality was far more complex than this basic tripartite division suggested. Each Estate had its own internal hierarchy and was composed of distinct groups with their own identities and corporate privileges.

Social differences were marked by modes of speech, forms of address, segregated seating at public functions and distinctive clothing. The latter was specified in sumptuary ordinances issued by municipal and territorial governments. That of Strasbourg from 1660 identified 256 different groups amongst the city's inhabitants, divided into six grades, each with specific dress. Osnabrück's first law, issued in 1618, was revised thirty years later and remained in force until 1788, identifying four grades. Such measures were still being issued in the later eighteenth century. A Weimar ordinance from 1778 specified that the cheap cotton dresses produced by the state factory in Eisenach had to be stamped by the police before sale, so that it would be possible to distinguish mistress from maid in the street.[15]

The division of society into these distinct groups was widely accepted as reflecting a natural inequality in human energies and talents, dating back to the fall from grace and the flight from the Garden of Eden. It also reflected observation of both the natural environment and economic activity as relatively static. Change seemed possible, but only within narrow limits. The notion of full equality was rejected as incompatible with a developed, sophisticated society. Privileges were corporate, not individual, and no group was totally without rights. Collective well-being took precedence over individual freedom, which seemed a licence to harm others. Each person had a defined role to play in promoting the common good, and received rewards allegedly commensurate with their own efforts and abilities. Such thinking attempted to reconcile human diversity with collective good. It presented the outward appearance of social harmony, whilst masking deep contradictions. There were considerable variations in wealth across all three Estates, whilst corporate rights did not sever other ties of kinship, marriage, gender, religious confession or local identity.

Some historians interpret these contradictions as indications that German society was developing along class lines. Social position in a class society is determined primarily by each individual's relationship to the productive process. Economic change is commonly seen as the driving force behind class formation, and the emergence of a distinct proletariat and bourgeoisie alongside a landowning aristocracy is generally attributed to the growth of capitalism. This analytical model was developed by Karl Marx and others to explain industrialisation and, unlike the categories of Estates, does not date from the period before the mid-nineteenth century. This poses problems for those who have applied it to seventeenth- and eighteenth-century Germany, and the identification of classes in this period depends very much on the criteria used to interpret evidence like tax registers, court records, wills and domestic inventories.

None the less, elements of class formation were clearly taking place, most obviously amongst those who fell outside the three recognised Estates; particularly the day labourers and others who depended on the growing market economy in both town and countryside. However, this early proletariat emerged whilst corporate estate society expanded to recognise new groups, indicating that the state was an additional motor of social change. The state's role is confusing, since its regulations pushed society in two different directions. Government-sponsored social mobility was directed at giving previously disadvantaged groups new privileges in return for their assistance in achieving state objectives. Yet, other measures eroded corporate distinctions, levelling society as a common body of subjects. As political power became more concentrated and defined, territorial governments assumed more definite and uniform relations with their subjects. Legal codification, fiscal reform and other measures gradually reordered social relations. Old obligations within and between Estates declined and were replaced by new, individual duties owed directly to the state. Distinct economic and political spheres emerged. Corporate privileges, such as those enjoyed by the craft guilds, were regulated by territorial law, depriving them of much of their autonomy and forcing them into a more uniform legal framework.

Combined with the economic changes, this process pushed society beyond that of subjects and towards one composed of citizens. The

German term *bürgerliche Gesellschaft* captures the ambiguities inherent in this transformation more successfully than any English equivalent. The term *bürgerlich* implies political rights and participation (citizenship), and a *bourgeois* society relating more closely to capitalism and market forces. This transformation was under way in the late eighteenth century, and was not completed until well into the nineteenth. It was driven by the continued population growth and economic expansion, as well as by reform-minded governments seeking not so much to create a new social order, but to respond to the problems of a fading one. These changes had little to do with the collapse of the old Reich, but did encourage the revolutionary activity that swept Germany in 1830–48.[16]

The clergy

We can trace these developments by examining the main Estates in more detail. The clergy comprised less than 2% of the total population and were split along both confessional and territorial lines. The first generation of Protestant pastors were overwhelmingly Catholic priests who embraced the new faith in the 1520s and 1530s. Thereafter, the Protestant clergy diverged sharply thanks to the acceptance of clerical marriage by theologians. Though it remained a vocation, as it was for Catholics, the priesthood became substantially self-recruiting as sons followed fathers. Nearly two-thirds of sixteenth-century Württemberg pastors came from clerical families and though the proportion declined, it was still 44% in the eighteenth century. The difference was made good by the sons of territorial and municipal officials, who contributed more than a quarter of all Württemberg pastors after 1700. In contrast with the Catholic Church, very few peasants entered the Protestant clergy, which rapidly assumed a position equivalent to the middling sections of the privileged urban burghers.

Much of this was due to the dominant role played by territorial governments in the management of the Lutheran and Calvinist churches. Lutheran princes and city councils used former Catholic assets to endow scholarships to train their clergy at the local territorial university. While the tithe was abolished or modified, parish clergy lived relatively comfortably from land or grain rents attached to their church, or from stipends paid by the central government. Calls for the popular election of local clergy were suppressed after 1525, permitting town councils and noble landlords to recover much of their former patronage over parish appointments. The management bureaux established from the 1530s to manage the Lutheran church in each territory generally accepted the local patrons' choice of candidates provided these were suitably qualified. None the less, central control was imposed through regular visitations to ensure conformity with official orthodoxy. This supervisory structure retained many of the higher clerical posts established by the Catholic Church, though episcopal rights were now exercised by the prince or his representatives. The Lutheran Church thus offered a relatively clear and well-funded career structure to educated commoners drawn from much the same social backgrounds as the officials of the burgeoning territorial administrations. The Calvinist clergy largely shared these characteristics because of the nature of the so-called 'second Reformation' in Germany, which saw the spread of the Reformed faith through the conversion of Lutheran princes and counts after 1561. These simply modified existing Lutheran institutions to serve the new theology, and the presbytery system found elsewhere in Calvinist or Puritan Europe was restricted to a few isolated communities in north-west Germany, notably Emden in East Frisia.

The territorial character of the Protestant churches was reflected in the geographic origins of their clergy, who were overwhelmingly from the same area as their parishioners. By contrast, the Catholic clergy remained more cosmopolitan, with up to half of those in the bishopric of Speyer coming from outside the territory. This was partly a consequence of the political distribution of the Christian confessions in the Reich. Protestantism predominated in the larger territories, like Brandenburg, Hanover, Saxony, Hessen, Württemberg and the Palatinate, as well as the smaller, but still comparatively populous imperial cities. Apart from Bavaria and the Austrian lands, Catholicism was concentrated in the smaller, more fragmented principalities, counties and ecclesiastical territories. The structure of the Catholic Church also contributed to the more varied origins of its clergy. The jurisdiction of the German prince-bishops extended into the lands of neighbouring Catholic rulers, where they had considerable powers to appoint parish and other clergy. For example, prior to the later eighteenth century the diocese of the prince-bishop of Passau extended far beyond his own small territory to encompass the Habsburg provinces of Upper and Lower Austria, and he was represented in Vienna by his own special official with powers to supervise and appoint parish priests.

While Catholic rulers progressively curbed such extra-territorial jurisdiction, they none the less professed a universal faith that looked to Rome for spiritual guidance and education. Protestant criticism in the early sixteenth century stimulated existing demands within the Catholic Church to improve clerical morality and education, which gained momentum with the Tridentine decrees of 1563 stipulating new standards throughout the Catholic world. Some German rulers had already begun to found seminaries before the Jesuits became established as the leading Catholic educators by 1600. None the less, Catholic Germany continued to suffer a shortage of trained priests into the later seventeenth century and it was not uncommon for two-thirds of a territory's clergy to be without a seminary education. Turnover remained high because Catholic parishes were often poorly endowed and because peasants, through either conviction or opportunity, stopped paying the tithe during periods of religious tension. Though the church offered the chance for talented men of humble origins to rise to high positions, the German nobility entrenched its hold over the well-endowed benefices of the imperial church during the later sixteenth century (see section 5.4). Both the fortunes of the parish clergy and their total numbers only improved significantly as demographic and economic growth improved church finances from the early eighteenth century.

The nobility

Whereas moralists placed the clergy as the First Estate, society generally gave this distinction to the nobility. These were even more exclusive, numbering no more than 50,000 families in 1800, or perhaps 250,000 individuals representing less than 1% of the population. This proportion was roughly comparable to that in France or England, and indicated a decline since 1500 when there had been around 375,000 German nobles. New nobles came under German rule as Prussia and Austria expanded into Poland, where about 7% of the population claimed aristocratic status. By 1800 there were 34,000 noble families in the new Polish provinces of the Hohenzollern monarchy, compared with 20,000 in the older parts. The Habsburgs also governed significant numbers of Hungarian nobles, who constituted around 5% of that kingdom's population.

Only a tiny minority enjoyed the status of imperial immediacy and its associated representation in imperial institutions. The rest were territorial nobles, subject to their prince or lord (see section 2.2). They were distinguished from commoners by their hereditary political, judicial and fiscal privileges. Many had a political voice through their membership of

the territorial Estates. While territorial governments curbed independent aristocratic jurisdictions, they largely left other judicial privileges
intact. These were supplemented by social prejudice. Courts showed a
greater willingness to accept a nobleman's 'word of honour' rather than
resort to torture to extract a confession. While most nobles enjoyed some
tax exemption, they did not escape the tightening fiscal net entirely. For
example, the Saxon knights were exempt from their elector's land tax,
but they still had to pay the personal levy introduced in the eighteenth
century to maintain the state workhouse. These privileges attracted criticism, though mainly because some nobles used them to force other groups
to shoulder more of the burden.

   Nobles were expected to conform to a certain lifestyle centred around
landownership and an honourable career. The expansion of territorial
armies and bureaucracies opened new possibilities in the seventeenth
century, compensating for the decline in senior clerical positions following the Reformation. However, many nobles found it hard to keep up
appearances, particularly with the spread of primogeniture, introduced
to preserve the viability of the family estate. Though aristocratic titles
derived from the ancestral castle, few nobles actually possessed one.
Around half the nobles living in the Leipzig area of Saxony left after
one generation, and only five of the 206 families owning land there
between 1681 and 1844 held the same estate throughout.[17]

   Such evidence contradicts the stock image of German nobles as reac-
tionaries opposed to all change. Some individuals did correspond to this
stereotype, but the nobility was not a monolithic class with uniform interests and outlook. As later chapters will indicate, some nobles fought the
territorial state, while others served it. Equally, some embraced economic and social changes that their neighbours bitterly opposed. Not
only were there significant regional variations, but the nobility was
highly stratified. Those with higher titles, though not necessarily more
money, found it easier to gain employment and influence across Germany, while the lesser nobility were bound more closely to their own territory. True magnates with huge estates were only found in the Habsburg
and Hohenzollern monarchies, since their equivalent elsewhere in the
Reich had joined the ranks of the lesser lords and counts, ruling distinct
territories. Around a quarter of Brandenburg-Prussian nobles could be
considered prosperous, while a half were moderately well-off and the
remainder comparatively poor.[18] The latter were attracted to state
employment, but there were never enough positions to go round, particularly as many were given to commoners (see section 6.2).

Peasants

Peasants formed the majority of the Third Estate, numbering over 20 million or around three-quarters of the Reich's population in 1800. The term 'peasant' (*Bauer*) was used indiscriminately for all rural inhabitants, masking considerable diversity. The common characteristic was that all were able to support themselves to some extent from their own food production. This placed land at the centre of the rural world and made it a key factor in defining status and access to resources, along with gender, legal and feudal arrangements, and the physical environment.

Most land was acquired through inheritance. The most common form was impartiable inheritance, where all property devolved on the eldest male heir. This practice spread during the middle ages and was consolidated in the sixteenth century as population growth put pressure on land. Territorial governments stepped in to regulate this, prohibiting the subdivision of peasant farms, as in Brunswick-Wolfenbüttel in 1597. Impartiable inheritance had far-reaching implications. It strengthened both patriarchy and hierarchy, since communities were dominated by property-owning male heads of household. Passage to adulthood was abrupt, with relatively few males inheriting sufficient property to permit marriage and a family. The rest remained dependent labourers, or emigrated to employment elsewhere. The alternative of partiable inheritance persisted in the Rhineland, Württemberg, Baden, Lower Franconia, south-west Westphalia, Thuringia and southern Hanover. It divided property among a wider group of relatives, including women, giving a stronger basis for communal life since more people had access to resources. Transition to adulthood was more gradual, since property could be acquired in stages from different relatives. This also reduced the barriers to marriage and gave greater opportunities to remain in the community. It risked impoverishment if population growth forced continual subdivision into uneconomic plots. This could stimulate innovation, as peasants were compelled to make better use of the available land. However, governments generally responded by encouraging the use of impartiable inheritance, by specifying minimum sizes for farms, as in Hessen in the eighteenth century.

Access to land combined with feudal obligations to divide peasants into different groups. Around 92% of German peasants owed some sort of obligation to a feudal lord, or to others such as municipal corporations or religious institutions that exercised jurisdiction over land. However, this did not necessarily imply full serfdom, and the majority of peasants owned or rented land (see section 3.3). Around 20% had substantial plots in 1800, but these were not found everywhere, and fell into two subgroups. Less than half were completely free peasants producing for the market. In Westphalia, these were called *Schulten*, and were found only in Mark, Münster and Paderborn. The others were full peasants (*Vollbauern*, *Huber*, or *Meier*) who owned or rented at least one *Hufe* (44 hectares) of ploughland, and often employed other peasants as labourers. Many of these came from the ranks of the smallholders, called *Gärtner* in Saxony, *Kossäten* in Brandenburg, *Kotter* in Westphalia, and *Seldner* in Swabia. They held small parcels of land outside the main fields in each village, and formed around a third of the rural population. This proportion rose as population growth put pressure on land. Many were reduced to 'cottagers' (*Häusler*, *Büdner*, *Hüttner*, or *Neusiedler*), with only their dwelling, and forced to work for others. Their numbers rose in Saxony from 20,000 in 1550 to 310,000 by 1750, or more than eight times the overall rate of population growth. Many lost their homes altogether, or had no property to inherit. These landless adults worked as servants and labourers (*Gesinde*, *Einlieger*) for their landlord or richer peasants. These were the ones generally subject to the restrictions of full serfdom, particularly east of the river Elbe, and they collectively comprised a fifth of the rural population.

Peasants possessed only limited rights, yet were essential for society's survival. Their role had been recognised by German intellectuals in the sixteenth century, some of whom argued that peasants were closer to god than even the clergy, because Adam had been the first to till the soil and all men were his descendants. Peasants embodied the Christian virtues of labour, patience, subordination, duty and piety, in pointed contrast to the sinfulness of cities, and the idleness of the aristocratic 'leisure classes'. These attitudes reflected how peasants themselves thought, and formed the mainstay of popular and intellectual opposition to the spread of commerce and capitalism. This positive image was gradually displaced by urban prejudice during the seventeenth century. Writers drew on existing stereotypes of boorish peasants to depict all rural inhabitants as lazy, ignorant louts who, in the words of one eighteenth-century Bavarian, stood 'between the unreasoning beasts and man'.[19] Many territorial governments tried to dispel such views, deliberately fostering more positive images as a way of promoting their agrarian reforms. These had some impact, particularly when linked to military conscription and new ideas of nationhood as encompassing all inhabitants. Gothic revivalism in the decades after 1815 encouraged this, presenting the medieval past as a

rustic idyll in contrast to the incipient mass urbanisation and industrialisation that was already transforming the German countryside.

Burghers

The urban burghers (*Bürger*) formed the other main segment of the
Third Estate. Germany was comparatively highly urbanised compared
with other European countries thanks to the numerous territorial towns
and imperial cities founded since the twelfth century (see section 2.2).
Urban inhabitants already constituted over 13% of the Reich's population by 1450. This proportion remained roughly constant until 1700 and
then doubled across the eighteenth century. Only 17.5% of the French
population lived in settlements of 2,000 or more in 1806, and only two
of these (Paris and Lyon) had over 100,000 inhabitants. The majority of
German towns were equally small, and only a fifth of the total urban
population lived in cities of more than 10,000 inhabitants in 1800. Such
cities were comparatively numerous, none the less. Though no German
city compared to London, which contained a tenth of the English population, there were only two other English towns with more than 15,000
inhabitants, the size of most German territorial capitals.[20]

Less than half these town-dwellers were full burghers, or citizens of the
place where they lived. Despite the walls and municipal privileges,
the urban world had strong ties to the countryside on which it depended
for food, markets and migrants. Many burghers owned fields beyond the
walls and engaged in rural industries like winemaking. Both they and
richer peasants employed people from the same lower stratum of proletarian workers as day labourers, messengers, servants and others outside
the guild structures. None the less, each town had a distinct identity and
relations with its rural hinterland could be difficult, particularly when it
was an imperial city with its own dependent villages.

Burghers were distinguished from mere 'residents' (*Einwohner*, or *Bei-
sassen*) by their possession of specific civic rights. Citizenship had lost its
original egalitarian character as an association of free-born inhabitants
of the same town, and had become a privilege dependent upon successful
application and the acceptance of associated burdens, including paying
taxes and serving in the civic militia (*Bürgerwehr*). The latter had largely
lost its military function, even in imperial cities, since these maintained
their own small regular forces (*Stadtgarden*) for internal policing and
to discharge their obligations towards the Reich. Like the guilds, the

militia became another element in each town's corporate structure, dividing its inhabitants into distinctive groups.

Inequalities amongst the burghers were marked by the commanding position of the patricians, who rarely numbered more that 5% of a town's population, yet usually controlled its government. Charles V rewrote the constitutions of 30 imperial cities after 1548, strengthening the already oligarchical character of their governments. Territorial rulers similarly intervened to curb what they saw as urban radicalism following the Reformation. Such measures consolidated the patricians, who increasingly assumed the character of an urban nobility, complete with hereditary titles. Renewed constitutional conflicts arose where this group clung tenaciously to power in the face of further social and economic change. One challenge came from a growing group of *Honoratioren*, or notability, comprising rich merchants, senior municipal officials, lawyers, doctors and other professionals. Other distinguished residents, such as clergy or nobles, belonged to this group, even if they lacked formal burgher status. Urban wealth was concentrated in their hands, particularly in the bigger cities (see Table 3.2). However, this alone did not guarantee their status, which only became tangible when it received outward recognition in the form of appropriate deference and respect from their fellow citizens.

The majority of burghers belonged to a broad, middle layer of craftsmen, traders, small-scale entrepreneurs, junior officials and shopkeepers. This group was still quite large in 1600 and constituted the bulk of the guild membership. The guilds functioned as more than craft organisations. They provided a forum for sectional interests to lobby the city council, as well as serving as social networks, religious congregations and welfare organisations. This middle layer remained large in the

Table 3.2   Wealth distribution in selected early seventeenth-century German cities

City	Population	Proportion of wealth in the hands of top 2%	Proportion of wealth in the hands of top 10%
Augsburg	45,000	61%	92%
Nördlingen	11,000	30%	60 to 70%
Schwäbisch-Hall	6,000	25%	55 to 60%
Kitzingen	3,400	?	50%

smaller and medium towns into the nineteenth century. The proliferation of 'residence towns' (*Residenzstädte*) housing the court, government
and major garrison in each territory also sustained this middling sort by
providing new markets for specialist goods and services.

This group faired less well in larger towns, while the numbers of poorer
residents rose generally across the Reich, usually numbering half the
inhabitants of any town. This lower strata was headed by a broad group
of urban poor, who usually lacked burgher status and were employed as
unskilled workers outside the guild structure. Many were first-generation
migrants who, for instance, formed 93% of all apprentices in Würzburg
in 1675 and 62% of those in eighteenth-century Durlach. The proportion
among servants was generally the same and together these two occupations accounted for 20% of most towns' inhabitants. They were joined in
garrison towns by soldiers, who represented an equally impoverished
group, forming about 10% of the population of most residence towns, or
up to a third of that in more heavily militarised Brandenburg-Prussia.
The military and their dependants constituted a fifth of all Berliners
between 1680 and 1800, compared with only 2.8% in 1871. At least
10% to 15% of urban inhabitants were too poor to pay tax. Many were
destitute and lived by a mixture of casual labour, begging, and crime.
Up to a fifth might be on some form of municipal or church welfare,
though this proportion was lower in commercially active cities and residence towns, where work was more available.

The growing stratification of urban society was fuelled by a combination of economic change and state regulation. The guild system remained
flexible into the sixteenth century, offering artisans considerable opportunities for wealth mobility. Wealth and occupation were not invariably
tied together as there were both rich and poor practising the same trade.
Competition from other urban craftsmen was only one factor transforming this over the next two centuries. As towns were integrated into market
networks, they suffered competition from craftsmen elsewhere who could
offer their wares at the same regional fairs. However, rural tradesmen
appeared as additional competitors in some crafts, particularly as population growth forced villagers to diversify their activities. This tended
to affect the poorer trades like shoemaking, weaving, clothing and pot-
tery, but it soaked up local demand and increasingly penetrated urban
markets. Innkeepers, bakers and others who supplied their own urban
market directly escaped this competition, as did those engaged in highly
capitalised ventures requiring specialised training unavailable to rural
craftsmen.[21]

Proto-industrialisation also affected towns and their hinterlands where these supplied regional and distant markets. The usual case was the textile industry, which spread through the introduction of piece work organised by richer merchants. Artisans and other workers often found this system initially attractive, because it offered access to both markets and capital. However, they invariably fell into debt-peonage as market fluctuations forced them to borrow money and materials which they found hard to repay. Established guilds reacted defensively towards these new forms of competition by restricting opportunities for others to rise within the same trade. The middling groups of craftsmen, shopkeepers, and petty traders were squeezed, with a few escaping upwards to join the notability, but most forced downwards into the ranks of the proletarian poor.

From burghers to bourgeoisie

There were clear signs by 1800 that the corporate structure of society was being replaced by one more closely characterised by a correlation between wealth and occupation. This was also fostered by political debates that attacked the old concept of the burgher as synonymous with the privileged patriciate and guild elite. Many historians identify a 'new', progressive middle class emerging alongside 'old', conservative burgher groups and eventually replacing them by the mid-nineteenth century. This new group indeed appeared in the larger, commercial centres and residence towns, and was united by a common emphasis on talent and individualism. However, the new bourgeoisie remained a tiny minority amidst a still complex urban society. It was still overshadowed in mining and commercial activity by established burgher groups and the nobility. For example, commoners owned only 2 of the 243 mines operating in Upper Silesia in 1785, while nobles and the Prussian king controlled the rest.

Older burgher groups remained dynamic elements of German society, contributing to the formation of the new bourgeoisie. New groups joined them through state patronage. In addition to the expanding civil bureaucracy (see section 6.2), these included the educated 'learned' commoners (*Gelehrten*) who had emerged during the sixteenth century. They represented a largely progressive element, encouraging the replacement of a privileged birth with education (*Bildung*) as a criterion for social respectability. Entrance into this select group of intellectuals was open to men of talent, regardless of nationality or background. Personal reputation was based on pursuit of the truth in this self-styled 'republic of letters', which manifested itself in patriotic societies, reading clubs and other groups that mushroomed in the later eighteenth century. Such societies propagated the ideal of the engaged patriot who transcended social status and privilege to work for the good of the entire community. The reality fell far short of these lofty aspirations. Many clubs retained segregation based on privilege and their political direction remained ambivalent. Some welcomed the French Revolution, seeing the declaration of the rights of man and citizen as an endorsement of their own programme. Certainly, the French equation of active citizenship with property ownership accorded closely to the language of many German patriotic societies. Yet, most rejected French egalitarianism in favour of the alternative vision of Germanic Liberty rooted in a mythical Gothic medieval past interpreted through a romanticised reading of classical Greece. Talent replaced privilege as a new form of social distinction. The learned remained a narrow 'intellectual aristocracy', numbering no more than 80,000, who distinguished themselves from what they saw as the formless, ignorant masses (*Pöbel*).[22] These elitist sentiments spread throughout the new German bourgeoisie in the nineteenth century, particularly when it felt its property under threat.

Outcasts

Many Germans fell outside the ordered categories of Estates society, through social prejudice as much as poverty. It would be wrong to lump these marginal groups together as a single underclass, or underworld, since they were also stratified. Many were marginalised for reasons other than birth, and for some it represented only a temporary state, blurring the lines between these outcasts and the nascent urban and rural proletariat forming within the Third Estate.[23] Social prejudice consigned some occupations to the semi-respectable fringe of ordered society, such as soldiers, cottagers, industrial workers and many wage labourers. Others were placed there by physical circumstances, like orphans, widows with children, the sick, disabled and mentally ill.

The dishonoured (*unehrliche Leute*) formed a second category of outcasts that fell roughly into three recognisable subgroups, who were tolerated with varying degrees of unease by their more fortunate neighbours. Honour was defined socially rather than morally, relating it to the hierarchy of corporate Estates. Some trades were considered dishonour-able, because they involved dirty, smelly tasks, or contact with 'polluting' animals. These included many whose work was essential for public health, like grave diggers, skinners, knackers, tanners, mole catchers and barber surgeons, yet their mere touch was often considered shameful by respectable society. Others were despised because their work took them into the wild, like shepherds on the rough hillside, or charcoal burners in the forest. The reordering of marriage placed prostitutes in this category, but they continued to be tolerated in many areas, particularly garrison towns like Berlin, where there were 100 brothels employing 1,000 women in 1780.

A wide range of public officials formed a second subgroup, because their work brought them into contact with criminals. Hangmen and executioners were the most notorious, particularly as they were charged with other disagreeable functions, such as driving lepers from the com-munity or disposing of the bodies of suicides, who were denied a Christian burial. However, a whiff of dishonesty also surrounded night watchmen, bailiffs, gaolers and many other public officials.

The third group were stigmatised by illegitimate birth, or by ethnicity and religion. Gypsies were particularly distrusted since the sixteenth cen-tury when they were accused of spying for the Ottomans. The Reichstag ordered their expulsion in 1498 and this was repeated in later imperial and territorial decrees. There were only around 1,000 Sinthi and Roma in the Reich in the early seventeenth century, yet they loomed large in the popular consciousness as a dangerous group. The later seventeenth century saw the start of renewed persecution as all major territories branded them footloose criminals who would be hung without trial if they ever recrossed the frontier.

The Jews were more numerous, but also suffered from the prevailing Christian prejudice that stigmatised them as Christ's killers. They had been subject to growing restrictions in the Reich since 1240 and were required by an imperial decree of 1530 to wear a yellow badge. Protes-tant reformers initially showed some interest in Judaism, but turned hostile from the 1540s as attempts at conversion failed. The polarisation among Christian confessions towards the later sixteenth century found one expression in growing anti-Semitism. Cities like Speyer and Worms tightened restrictions on their Jewish minorities, while Jews were expelled from Wetzlar (1609). The worst case occurred in Frankfurt where Vincenz Fettmilch, a pastry cook, enflamed anti-Semitism as a means of mobilising the artisans against the city council after 1612. The disturbances culminated in the pogrom of August 1614 when Christian workers herded the Jews into the cemetery, plundered their homes and then expelled around half of them. The emperor intervened and Fett-milch was executed two years later. However, Jews were excluded when the Peace of Westphalia widened religious toleration in the Reich. Their right to remain still depended on the emperor, who only sanctioned communities in six imperial cities, whilst expelling Vienna's 4,000 Jews in 1670.

By the early eighteenth century, however, more princes appreciated the services offered by Jewish financiers and merchants. Some of these 'court Jews' used their position to secure limited toleration for small communities that were established in the leading residence towns (see Table 3.3). Most Jews lived in the Habsburg monarchy, particularly in Prague, home to Europe's largest Ashkenazi community, numbering 11,000, despite their temporary expulsion in 1745 when they were

Table 3.3 Jewish communities in the Reich and associated lands, 1795

Prague and Bohemia	68,800
Hungary	80,000
Berlin	4,150
Prussian Silesia	9,000
Electorate of Mainz	6,000
Electorate of Cologne	6,000
Electorate of Trier	2,000
Palatinate	1,000
Saxony	500
Württemberg	500
Würzburg	3,600
Bamberg	4,000
Osnabrück	50
Ansbach	3,000
Bayreuth	2,400
Hanau	1,000
Frankfurt	6,600
Hamburg	3,800
Bremen	1,700
Worms	500
Speyer, Wetzlar, Gelnhausen	7,000
Imperial knights	20,000

accused of collaborating with the Prussians. The annexation of Polish territory brought additional Jews within the Habsburg and Hohenzollern monarchies, bringing the totals there to around 300,000, compared with 100,000 elsewhere in the Reich.[24] Many earlier restrictions were lifted, but official policy remained inconsistent. For example, Jews were expelled from Württemberg at the request of the Estates in 1739, but were later re-admitted by the duke, though public worship was not permitted until 1832. Popular prejudice persisted into the 1860s and was whipped up again within a few decades by more politicised anti-Semitism.

Many outcasts belonged to the wider itinerant population. Only a few of these were considered semi-respectable, such as travelling players, pedlars and demobilised soldiers. The latter were often numerous and formed a significant number of the beggars who crowded the larger towns, particularly in the ecclesiastical territories. Like many civilians, soldiers resorted to begging once an injury had rendered them incapable of earning a regular living. However, chronic under-employment was the major cause and unemployed craftsmen and other workers generally accounted for up to half of those arrested for vagrancy. Most were men, though women and children were also found among those on the road, who numbered around 3 per cent of the total population, even in times without war or poor harvests.[25]

3.3 Economy

General characteristics

Agrarian activity formed the mainstay of economic life, accounting for up to three-quarters of the German gross national product in the mid-eighteenth century.[26] However, modern distinctions between agricultural and industrial sectors have little meaning for this period, since the latter depended heavily on the former, yet agriculture alone could not support more than half the population. Industrial and agrarian production relied on human and animal muscle power as their primary motive force, while the exploitation of the soil and inland waters was essential to both. Around 55% of the Reich was under cultivation by 1800, leaving 25% as forest and the rest as settlements and wasteland. Mining was important, but was yet to reach the scale achieved in the following century. Coal production stood at 800,000 tons and was concentrated in the Harz mountains and the north-western areas of Mark,

Aachen, and the Mosel and Saar river valleys. Iron output was higher at 2 million tons, but was more scattered, with the largest centre, Bohemia, producing only 50,000 tons. Salt mining was significant in Bavaria, Salzburg and north-west Saxony, but more was made from brine than dug from the ground.

Wood remained the principal natural resource, vital for construction, energy and manufacture. Forests also contributed additional food, such as berries, fruit, mushrooms, honey and game, as well as serving as a source for medicines, and fertiliser from the rotting leaves peasants transported to their fields. However, population growth placed a premium on agricultural land. Whereas half of Ducal Prussia had been covered by forest in 1570, this proportion fell to 45% by 1700 and 33% a century later. Lords and princes converted their earlier jurisdiction into absolute ownership, commercialising forestry and denying villagers access. This was already a major grievance in the great Peasants War of 1524–6 and remained a constant source of friction for the next two centuries. Cities also experienced problems as their expanding populations required greater quantities of firewood, building lumber and pine torches. The cost of firewood rose by 300% in Berlin between 1700 and 1787, when the municipal authorities had to shut down production in the city's glass and iron factories in order to divert urgent supplies to householders. England had experienced a similar energy crisis in the late seventeenth century, but switched to coal instead, whereas Germany remained heavily reliant on wood, and as late as 1850, three-quarters of its iron production was still wood-fired.[27]

Capitalism and market networks

The commercialisation of forestry was one aspect of a wider expansion of market networks that spread throughout the Reich from the late fourteenth century as economic activity shifted from subsistence production to regional specialisation and exchange. Market networks expanded at three levels simultaneously. Local exchange between town and country through weekly markets established clear regional centres, providing access to inter-regional markets served in turn by major cities holding specialised trade fairs, such as those of Leipzig and Frankfurt. These arrangements established a hierarchy, with lesser towns acting as gateways to wider networks. However, commercialisation also spread through the extension of credit to rural communities by landlords and merchants, creating new networks of dependency.

As these networks were far from integrated by 1800, it is not possible to speak of a single German economy. A distinct south-eastern network developed within the Habsburg monarchy, centred on Vienna, with branches extending to Prague, Passau, and through Graz and Trieste to the Adriatic. It was linked by the Danube to south-west Germany. A largely separate north-east trade route emerged within the Hohenzollern monarchy from Breslau in Silesia, through Frankfurt/Oder to Berlin and thence by the canal and river routes to the Baltic and North Sea. A spur ran southwards through Magdeburg to the central German trading area centred on the great fairs in Leipzig and Frankfurt/Main. Other connections ran north from the central area along the Weser through Bremen to the North Sea and down the Rhine via Cologne to the Dutch Republic and English Channel. Further routes linked the south in Franconia, or followed the Rhine up to Basel and access to the Alpine passes.

These routes provided limited access to the world markets that developed with the general shift of European trade to the Atlantic seaboard, and the onset of colonisation in the sixteenth century. Most 'foreign' trade remained inter-territorial, rather than international, but long-distance markets were already important with trade beyond the Reich's frontiers accounting for 20 per cent of the total in 1800, or roughly similar to the proportion in France. The Reich was also important for international transit trade, particularly grain from Poland and the Ukraine, which was shipped through German ports, but also oxen and cattle, which were driven 1,000 miles from Hungary through Germany to markets in Denmark, the Netherlands and elsewhere in western Europe. Manufactured goods formed a significant proportion, by value, of German exports, but there were considerable regional variations, and such items, along with colonial produce, also featured prominently amongst imports to the Reich.

Industrialisation

The relatively low importance of a manufacturing sector points to the under-developed character of German industry, which lagged behind that of Britain and other parts of western Europe. German industry remained largely decentralised in small workshops and did not make the transition to mechanised factory production until the 1830s, or seventy years after Britain. The reasons for this are to be found in the general character of economic activity as it developed away from regional self-sufficiency and towards specialisation and inter-regional trade in non-luxury items. Industry had grown to serve these trading networks, appearing wherever specialised craft skills were concentrated in areas with good access to resources and markets. Germany had remained at the forefront of European industrialisation until the seventeenth century. The area around Nuremberg and Ulm was one of the three leading manufacturing centres of late sixteenth-century Europe, alongside the Netherlands and northern Italy. This position had been lost by 1800 and the country appeared relatively backward.

The standard explanation blames the Thirty Years War, the adverse impact of foreign competition and the restrictive practices of German territorial governments. Recent research rejects these explanations as insufficient, pointing instead to a more diverse regional pattern of development. Two-thirds of German industrialising regions were monostructural, meaning they were dominated by a single activity. This was generally some form of textile production, of which linen was the most important business, employing up to 99 per cent of all industrial workers in parts of Westphalia. Though the remaining regions were polystructural, textiles still played a major role in most cases (see also section 7.1).

The predominance of textiles points to the continued significance of agriculture to German industrial development. Outside Saxony and the Rhineland, most industrialising regions were urban–rural conglomerations where peasants supplied raw materials, such as wool, for decentralised production. Much of this was through the putting-out system (*Verlagswesen*), which is generally seen as a first step, or proto-industrialisation, integrating rural workers into market-orientated export production that later became more concentrated in factories using machinery. However, this system did not develop throughout Germany, nor was it essential for later industrial development. It did enable existing corporate groups to retain control while developing new forms of production. A good example is the merchants' consortium known as the Calwer Company, which operated in the Black Forest from the 1590s and eventually employed around 7,000 people, of whom only 168 worked in a factory, the rest mainly in their own homes. The company was controlled by a small group of families who dominated its board and bargained concessions with the duke of Württemberg to protect their interests. The duke's role in sustaining these restrictive practices is an important reminder not to overestimate the role of the state in promoting economic change (see section 7.1). The company

Table 3.4 Factories employing over ten workers *c*.1790

Hohenzollern Monarchy	220
Saxony	170
Wittelsbach lands	150
Rest of the Reich	450

exported 70 per cent of its production, supplying garments to the Catholic clergy throughout Europe, despite the solidly Lutheran convictions of its management. It was already in decline before the French Revolutionary Wars disrupted trade routes, and it folded in 1797.

The putting-out system employed by businesses like the Calwer Company retarded other forms of industrialisation since it offered substantial profits, without requiring direct supervision of the workforce. There was no need to invest in expensive plant, and entrepreneurs were free to play an active role in public life. Production remained decentralised, in small and medium towns with rural hinterlands: there were six times as many rural weavers as urban ones in the major textile area of Westphalia in 1800. Factory production was limited to high-value specialist items where the greater danger of pilfering encouraged entrepreneurs to develop a more supervised work environment. Cloth dying and other textile processing still accounted for one-third of all factories employing more than 10 workers (Table 3.4). Few had over 500 workers, though the 19 based in Leipzig employed 2,000 artisans and 10,550 workers in mid-century. The putting-out system failed to soak up all the underemployed, particularly as population growth accelerated in the later eighteenth century, creating a labour reserve ready for Germany's industrial take-off after 1850.

Agriculture

Additional labour came from the rural world, where less than half the population lived from agriculture alone (Table 3.5). Productivity remained low, with an average seed-yield ratio of under 1:5. Southwestern peasants tried to minimise the risks of crop failure by planting spelt and rye. These were both hardy strains of cereals that could grow on poor soils and were resistant to the frosts and heavy rainfall characterising seventeenth-century weather. Other mixed systems were

Table 3.5 Proportion of the population sustained by agriculture, *c.*1650

Saar region	50%
Ducal Prussia	44%
Electoral Saxony	42%
Bavaria	38%
Hanover	33%
Baden	30%
Brandenburg	28%
Upper Swabia	27%
Paderborn	21%
Eastern Swabia	20%

introduced where possible, such as the combination of grain and animal husbandry practised in parts of northern Germany.

However, most farms were too small to permit greater diversification. Peasants with less than 10 hectares rarely had any surplus for sale. Those with between 10 and 16 hectares might be able to offer 20% of their crop for the market, while the few, larger farmers with more land could sell 40% of their produce. The brutal logic of these figures drove an enclosure movement in parts of western Germany after the Seven Years War that brought most of the common land in Westphalia into private ownership by 1800, adding to the ranks of the landless.[28]

The trend to large-scale farming was already well under way east of the river Elbe much earlier, prompting historians to speak of an 'East Elbian' economic structure that spread from the Danish peninsula, through Brandenburg, Saxony, Bohemia and into parts of Austria and Hungary, as well as to Poland and Russia by the mid-seventeenth century. The analytical model to explain this divergence in European agriculture was first devised in the 1880s by Georg Friedrich Knapp and Georg von Below, who contrasted eastern lordship over manors and serfs (*Gutsherrschaft*) with western lordship over land and tenants (*Grundherrschaft*) (Table 3.6). This model has been refined by recent research, notably for Brandenburg, by the American historian William Hagen, Germans like Liselott Enders, Heinrich Kaak and Hartmut Harnisch, and a major project coordinated by Jan Peters at Potsdam University.[29] Their principal conclusion is to reject the earlier idea of two fundamentally different economic and social systems, on the grounds that full serfdom only affected a small proportion of those living east of the Elbe.

Table 3.6   Western and eastern German agrarian models

Characteristic	Grundherrschaft	Gutsherrschaft
Private estates	few/none	large
Landlords' income	rents in money or kind	labour service/robot
Peasants' legal status	free	serfs
Peasants' property rights	good	poor
Settlement pattern	large villages	fewer, smaller villages
Lordship	fragmented	concentrated

Moreover, elements of eastern serfdom could also be found in the west where general conditions were not necessarily milder or more progressive. There were considerable variations on both sides of the traditional divide and agrarian relations changed quite significantly over time, making it hard to generalise. Provided these qualifications are borne in mind, it remains helpful to compare eastern and western developments using the older analytical model as a point of departure.

Western Grundherrschaft

Western conditions were created by the Black Death and prolonged agrarian depression between 1315 and 1351. As the population contracted, prices fell and labour value rose as the survivors found more land and work. They were able to extract better conditions from landlords, who broke up their estates and devolved management of daily life to peasant communities (see section 3.4). Fields were split into plots and leased to peasant families in return for rent. Hereditary leaseholds (*Erbpacht*) developed in regions like Bavaria, enabling peasants to pass on their farms to their children. Fixed-term contracts (*Zeitpacht*) emerged in more commercialised regions, like the Middle and Lower Rhine, and the north German coast. Lords favoured these agreements, because they commuted earlier feudal obligations into cash at a time when territorial rulers increasingly demanded taxes in lieu of military service from their vassals. They also offered lords ways of extending new forms of dependency, particularly debt peonage. Lords loaned grain, tools and livestock to their tenants, but demanded repayment in cash, forcing peasants to commercialise agriculture to repay their obligations. Western German lords already relied heavily on rents by 1500 and their remaining domains provided only a small proportion of their incomes.

These arrangements were still feudal, because lords retained other forms of jurisdiction. The most important were judicial authority (*Gerichtsherrschaft*) over minor offences, and control of labour (*Dienstherrschaft*), which enabled them to summon peasants to perform specific tasks (*Fronen*), such as transporting goods, mending roads, or repairing their mansions. However, these rights were rarely concentrated in the hands of a single individual. It was common for peasants to be tenants of one lord, but under the judicial authority of a second, and to owe labour service to a third. This fragmentation of lordship offered western peasants further opportunities to bargain for better conditions, by playing one master against another. At the same time, however, the transition to rents forced them onto the market, since they had to pay both their rents and, increasingly, territorial and imperial taxes as well (see section 5.1).

Eastern Gutsherrschaft

Economic relations were broadly different east of the Elbe, where lords created large estates worked by serfs or hired labourers. The main problem with the older analytical model is that it generalised from the condition of serfdom, which only applied to a small proportion of the East Elbian population, whilst neglecting the significance of wage labour for estate farming. Serfs paid little or no rent and had free access to small plots to grow their own food to sustain their families. They also, initially, paid no taxes, since their lord met any obligations to the territorial ruler. In return, serfs had to work a specified number of days each week on the lord's estate. They were legally tied to the land (*Schollenpflichtig*), unable to leave without permission, which was only granted on payment of large fees. Their lord exercised direct legal mastery over them (*Leibherrschaft*). His permission was necessary for key events in their lives, including marriage and inheritance, all of which were associated with further fees and obligations. Other feudal rights tended to be concentrated in his hands as well, reducing the opportunities for appeal against increased burdens.

The result in areas where serfdom was pronounced was a commercialisation of lordly estates, rather than peasant farms. The lord received little rent, yet he was obliged to pay taxes to the ruler and often the tithes associated with any peasant land he incorporated into his estate. His income depended on selling the produce on the international market, particularly grain exported to western Europe. This commercialised the eastern 'manorial economy' (*Gutswirtschaft*), turning feudal landlords into what some historians call 'agrarian capitalists'. Peasants could not enter the market because labour service on the lord's estates left too little time and energy to produce their own crops for sale. Lords and peasants became locked into the same system. Lords could not follow the western example and commute labour service into rent, because peasants had no way of raising the money.

The trend towards the manorial economy was already under way in the later fourteenth century following the Black Death. Eastern lords seized the opportunity to consolidate their hold over land and its inhabitants and prevent the surviving workers fleeing to the towns. They already owned half of the land east of the Elbe, following the Germanic conquests of the region after 1120. Their rule was also more recent than that in the west, where time had fragmented lordship through the partible inheritance strategies practised by the early medieval nobility. Under-population enabled eastern lords to establish larger manors than in the west. The demographic recovery after 1470 stimulated the demand for food, particularly in the west where population growth outstripped production after 1530. This demand was met by increasing the capacity of the grain-producing regions in the east. Rye was already a favoured crop, since the region was less suited to other food production, such as animal husbandry or wine, and alternatives, like mining, offered little employment. There were few immediate markets for eastern grain as there were few towns. Western peasants lived in more densely populated areas where nearby towns offered local markets for their produce. Bulk production was the only commercially viable way eastern producers could reach these western markets.

Bulk production placed a premium on both land and labour. Eastern lords had already incorporated waste or abandoned land during the consolidation of their manorial lordship during the later fourteenth and fifteenth centuries. Their drive for the manorial economy forced the expropriation of additional land from free peasants and tenant farmers in a process known as *Bauernlegen*, or eviction, which was mainly confined to Brandenburg, Prussia and the Baltic coastal region. For example, lords in the Uckermark district of northern Brandenburg increased their share of the arable land from one-eighth to a third between 1500 and 1620. Where possible, they sought to prevent peasants from fleeing or demanding wages since this would reduce their labour force and profits. Lords appealed to territorial rulers to legislate in their favour. Brandenburg had already passed laws limiting peasants' inheritance rights in 1518,

Table 3.7 Imposition of *Schollenpflichtigkeit* and *Gesindezwangdienst*

Territory	Schollenpflichtigkeit	Gesindezwangdienst
Ducal Prussia	1577	
Holstein	1614	1614
Pomerania	1616	
Lausitz	1651	
Silesia	1652	1623
Brandenburg	1653 (confirmed)	1620
Mecklenburg	1654	1654
Osnabrück		1648
Saxony		1651
Anhalt		1653
Baden	1678	1622

followed by Ducal Prussia in 1526. *Schollenpflichtigkeit* was imposed from
the later sixteenth century, transforming peasants into serfs by legally
tying them to the land (see Table 3.7). None the less, this process was
mainly confined to Mecklenburg, Pomerania and the Uckermark and
Neumark districts in the north and east of Brandenburg. Even here,
lords relied heavily on hired labour to work their estates, recruiting
workers from their tenant farmers or the landless, who already formed a
significant proportion of the rural population.

This process was interrupted by the Thirty Years War, which brought
both problems and opportunities for the lords. The drop in population
reduced the available workforce, prompting the survivors to exploit the
labour scarcity by demanding better conditions. Lords could expand
their estates by seizing further abandoned land, expropriating 42 per
cent of Pomeranian peasant farms between 1628 and 1717, for example.
Their main problem remained insufficient labour, particularly in Brandenburg, Mecklenburg and Pomerania, which suffered heavily during
the war. Later settlers and colonists were often reluctant to take over
abandoned farms that required considerable capital investment to
restart production. This reduced the number of workers available for
hire, encouraging lords to increase feudal labour service from those who
were under their more direct control. This had already risen from an
average of one day a week in 1530 to two days by 1600 and was intensified
during the first half of the seventeenth century through the introduction of *Gesindezwangdienst* (see Table 3.7). Under these arrangements,

peasants' sons were obliged to work for three to seven years on the lord's estate, for little or no money. Meanwhile, the labour service of cottagers and other peasants was increased to three days a week within the Hohen-zollern monarchy, or, in extreme cases, up to five days.

The manorial economy was firmly established in eastern Schleswig, Mecklenburg, Pomerania, Ducal Prussia and Silesia by 1650. It attracted lords further south and west, who found that price rises from 1570 eroded the value of the cash rents from their tenants. Bohemian and Hungarian lords began intensifying labour service and adopting other elements of the manorial economy for this reason during the sixteenth century. How-ever, it developed differently than in Brandenburg and other parts of the north. Bohemian lords derived up to 40 per cent of their income from selling beer brewed on their estates to their tenants, and so they were keen to preserve peasant purchasing power by allowing them limited commercialised farming. Bohemia also escaped the severe depopulation that occurred in fifteenth-century Brandenburg and so had a ready supply of landless and semi-landless peasants available for paid work on the lords' estates, either in the fields, or in fish farming, brewing and other commercial enterprises. It was only where parts of rural Bohemia had lost up to 40 per cent of their population that demands for forced labour approached Brandenburg's levels following the Thirty Years War. The political redistribution of land by the Habsburgs to Catholic loyalists after 1620 assisted in the consolidation of estates that were far larger than those to the north. Whereas the Boitzenburg estate, the largest in Brandenburg, had 189 dependent peasant farmsteads in 1730, Bohemia was divided into around 300 estates each with an average of 715 dependent farmsteads. By contrast, Austrian landowners preferred rents, compensating for falling values in the sixteenth century by exploiting their better market networks and diversifying into forestry and other commercial activities.

Despite the spread of the manorial economy, Brandenburg and Saxony remained mixed areas with many free peasants. Though two-thirds of Brandenburg land was held by only 260 noble families in 1650, they only used 10% for estate farming and leased the rest to rent-paying tenants. Only about 11% of agricultural land within the entire Hohen-zollern monarchy was farmed through the manorial economy and this was concentrated in Ducal Prussia and Silesia, bastions of the local *Junker* nobility. Another 4.5% was farmed as domains belonging to the crown, again mainly in the east, with a similar proportion owned by cities and other corporations. Peasants still had access to the remaining

80%, even though they owned little of it directly and most lay under some form of lordly jurisdiction.[30]

A typical *Junker* or crown estate thus consisted primarily of rent-paying tenants and a substantial number of smallholding cottagers. Whilst all were subject to the lord's authority, their subordinate status derived from occupying his tenancies, which entailed services and dues. These tenancies were either hereditary, or short-term contracts, which were also not unfavourable to peasants since they were free to go elsewhere when the lease was up. Only a small proportion of the population was actually under personal servitude (*Leibeigenschaft*) and they were concentrated in the Uckermark and Neumark, as well as beyond Brandenburg in Prussia, Pomerania, Mecklenburg and parts of Holstein. Even in the Uckermark, only one-fifth of peasants owed two or more days' service a week in the mid-eighteenth century, while about half had to perform less than two and the remaining third were free of such obligations. Forced labour through *Gesindezwangdienst* affected only the younger sons for a limited part of their lives and most went on to marry and hold their own cottages or full farms. Thus, wage labour remained the backbone of the manorial economy, with both the lord and his richer tenants employing the substantial number of cottagers and landless peasants to work their fields.

The fragmentation of lordship inhibited the spread of the manorial economy to lands further west, but mixed forms still developed where lords exploited their command of labour (*Dienstherrschaft*) to force peasants to work their remaining domains or act as unpaid forestry workers. They buttressed this by expressing old feudal jurisdictions in the language of the east, referring to their dependent peasants as serfs. Westphalian lords introduced a form of *Schollenpflichtigkeit* to restrict peasant movement. The codification of property law assisted this during the eighteenth century, by reinforcing lordly jurisdictions. These restrictions covered one-fifth of the rural population of Paderborn, a third of that in Recklinghausen, and most in Münster. A similar situation developed in Hessen and Franconia, and parts of the south-west, like Baden.

Economic incentives were not necessarily foremost in these western developments. The imposition of new forms of serfdom frequently brought very little additional income for the lords, who were often more interested in its symbolic importance in reinforcing their supremacy over an often truculent rural population. Given the fragmentation of lordship, exploitation of old feudal rights also offered a way of extending political influence into neighbouring territories by claiming jurisdiction over some of their inhabitants. The Abbey of St Blasien tried to extend its authority over the peasant communities of Hauenstein in the Black Forest by claiming they were its serfs in the later seventeenth century. The Palatine and Mainz electors clashed over the same issue in the so-called *Wildfang* dispute in the Rhineland in the 1660s.[31]

The presence of serfdom in these regions indicates that the manorial economy and western landlordship were not mutually exclusive agrarian forms. Neither were conditions for eastern serfs necessarily worse than those of western free peasants. Legal institutions were not absent in the east, since territorial law bound both lord and peasant in a common system regulated by the ruler. Agrarian reforms offered serfs limited formal protection, compensating for the relative inability of the imperial courts to intervene in eastern territories to defend subjects' rights (see section 5.2). Despite the famous Recess of 1653, confirming lordly rights over serfs, Brandenburg peasants continued to use the electors' courts to challenge their lords into the eighteenth century and successfully curbed the consolidation of manorial estates through further evictions. They were also prepared to take collective action to give force to their demands, such as the protest by 100 villages in the Prignitz district against rent increases in 1700–2. Such evidence dispels the cliché of the downtrodden serf whose life was little better than that of a colonial slave. In fact, Brandenburg peasants enjoyed a diet comparable to that of the middling sort of farmer in western Europe or the New England colonies. They had access to considerable land and were allowed to pass this on by inheritance, despite the lords' formal right to reassign farms on the death of the head of the household. For example, on the Stavenow estate 150 km west of Berlin, 83 per cent of farms were passed on this way to children or step-children. Serf families thus had incentives to improve their land and acquired horses, cows and other valuable assets. Village welfare arrangements safeguarded these rights, protecting women and orphans, as well as retirement plots for the elderly. None the less, individual lives were full of uncertainty, subject to the vagaries of the weather and heavy tax demands related to wars and other political events beyond their control. Lords were prepared to tolerate rent arrears and other acts to sustain an image of paternal benevolence, but relations with their peasants were primarily dictated by practical necessity, not sentiment. They depended on minimum compliance with their demands from a rural population whose reverence and deference stemmed from self-preservation and who were ready to escape its burdens whenever possible.

Agrarian reform

The spread of the manorial economy was facilitated by the relative weakness of eastern territorial rulers, who depended on their lords for political and military assistance. However, there was no wholesale pact between them at the peasants' expense (see also section 6.1). As the cost of warfare increased, rulers started protecting the remaining free peasants as viable taxpayers. At first, this 'peasant protection' (*Bauernschutz*) aimed largely at stabilising existing arrangements to safeguard revenue and discourage revolt. Rulers decreed limits to labour demands and preserved opportunities for peasants to earn money through market exchange. For instance, the elector of Brandenburg confirmed the right of his peasants to engage in the territory's internal grain trade as early as 1536. Policies became more innovative as rulers became convinced that the relative in-elasticity of the East Elbian economy could be overcome by altering the forms of production along more capitalist lines. They hoped to transform serfs into independent farmers, whose greater efficiency would yield both higher taxes and rents.

Many nobles resisted because it was clear that the ruler's main intention was to redistribute existing agrarian profits by reducing their share and diverting the rest into the treasury as additional taxes (see section 6.4). Moreover, tax demands rose from the later sixteenth century precisely when lordly incomes declined, with rising labour costs and the disruption of the Thirty Years War. The spread of new forms of aristocratic culture also ate into lordly wealth by encouraging extravagant lifestyles and expensive new mansions. However, the lack of market opportunities hindered peasant protectionism, since there was little alternative to the bulk grain trade. These problems restricted innovation primarily to the ruler's own domains, since here he was his own master and could implement changes without recourse to the Estates. The domains of East Elbian rulers provided a significant share of territorial revenue and constituted a major economic sector in their own right since they were generally more extensive than those in the west. Rulers hoped that reforms on their domains would stimulate aristocratic landowners to follow their example and so spearhead more general change. Such reforms have been associated with the spread of enlightened thought in the later eighteenth century and the rule of Frederick II in Prussia (1740–86) and Joseph II in the Habsburg monarchy (1765–90). In fact, they began much earlier and were driven by the need to raise taxes and respond to peasants agitating for change.

Serfdom was resented not simply as a material burden, but as incompatible with personal and collective honour, particularly as Roman Law equated it with slavery.

Reforms started on the margins of the East Elbian zone, which had better access to markets. The duke of Holstein-Gottorp and the king of Denmark commuted labour service into rents in stages between 1597 and 1661 in the north and west of their shared jurisdiction across Holstein and Schleswig. This arrested the spread of the manorial economy, but failed to prevent its intensification in those areas where it was already established. The spread of textile manufacture, mining and other alternatives slowed its development in Bohemia from the later seventeenth century, but Habsburg reforms were stimulated mainly by popular pressure. The Bohemian revolt of 1679 against rising labour demands prompted Leopold I to fix limits in 1680. Similar measures were decreed for Moravia (1713), Hungary (1715) and Slavonia (1737), also partly in response to further protests. However, this merely regulated rather than reformed the situation. The rudimentary nature of Habsburg administration forced the authorities to rely on the landlords to police themselves until enforcement was tightened by additional reforms in the 1750s.

The fiscal pressures of the Seven Years War revealed the inadequacy of these measures, prompting more innovative reforms after 1763. These addressed technical aspects of production by encouraging new crops like potatoes, as well as pushing deeper, structural change by dismantling serfdom and encouraging the commercialisation of peasant farms. The earlier concern for productivity and public order was joined by a new moral tone as Empress Maria Theresa and especially her chief minister, Anton Wenzel von Kaunitz, became convinced that serfdom represented a fundamental human injustice. Emperor Joseph II also embraced reform, but for largely different reasons since he wanted to introduce Prussian-style conscription into the Habsburg monarchy. A preliminary study by the high command in 1771 revealed that many Bohemian peasants were unfit for military service. The army blamed labour-service abuses and urged the division of the manorial estates into tenancies farmed by sturdy, independent peasants, citing the example of leading aristocrats connected with the government who were already doing this on their own estates.[32]

The government forged ahead. Already in 1767 it issued the *Urbarium*, restricting labour service in Hungary to one day a week in a move intended to win popular support for a wider assault on the political autonomy of the Hungarian nobility. Landlords' resistance delayed full implementation of this until 1775, but the government signalled its intent in 1770 when it temporarily deprived Prince Heinrich Mansfeld of his estates at Dobris and ordered him to pay compensation to his serfs following ill-treatment. The *Urbarium* was extended to the newly annexed province of Galicia in 1772, where the nobles also lost their previous exemption from taxation. Further decrees restricting labour service followed for Habsburg Silesia (1771), Lower Austria (1772), Moravia (1775), Styria and Carinthia (1778), and Carniola (1782).

While the concern of Kaunitz and many Habsburg officers was genuine, these measures should not been regarded as gifts from a benevolent government. Popular pressure forced the pace of change, particularly in Bohemia and Hungary. Bohemia received its equivalent of the *Urbarium* in April 1774. Kaunitz and Maria Theresa had wanted to fix a definite limit to demands, but Joseph intervened and ruled that the lords could ask their peasants to work more than three days a week if they agreed. This opened the door to widespread abuse, prompting a massive rising that secured a revised decree on 13 August 1775 that did fix upper limits. Joseph now swung behind more radical measures and formally abolished serfdom in Bohemia on 1 November 1781. This was extended to Lower Austria and Galicia the following year, permitting peasants to acquire hereditary tenancies. They were now free to leave the land, but still owed labour service where this had not yet been commuted to rent. These reforms restricted serfdom to Hungary and Transylvania. Impatient, the Transylvanian serfs rebelled in October 1784, killing hundreds of their landlords. Joseph had the rebel leaders executed, but none the less sympathised with their objectives and abolished serfdom across Hungary on 22 August 1785.

The rapid pace of change alienated many aristocrats, particularly as sweeping tax and land reforms decreed in 1789 imposed limits to what lords could demand in rent. Joseph II's successor, Leopold II, reversed this new reform in 1792, halting the official programme of commuting labour service. The government retreated to a more passive role of simply adjudicating landlord–peasant disputes, recovering aristocratic support at home when the regime was threatened abroad by the French Revolutionary Wars. Attitudes hardened despite official attempts in 1798 to revive agrarian reform, and full emancipation in the Habsburg monarchy had to wait until 1848.

Brandenburg had a long history of peasant protectionism dating to the sixteenth century when the elector confirmed the right of his subjects to appeal to his law courts. These often ruled in the peasants' favour, ensuring that the *Junkers* did not abuse their authority, or push demands beyond the 'pain threshold'.[33] Effective arbitration dampened popular protest and kept Brandenburg free of large-scale peasant risings. As tensions mounted during the Thirty Years War, the elector again intervened to limit the *Junkers*' demands and divert more of their profits into his treasury. More innovative measures had to wait until 1702 when King Frederick I announced his intention to abolish serfdom in return for cash compensation to the lords. This programme had been devised by a royal official, Christian Friedrich Luben, who was rewarded with ennoblement as von Wulffen in 1704. Luben's plan was implemented on the royal domains, where temporary leases were converted into hereditary tenancies to encourage the spread of commercialised smallholding. Unfortunately, this project became enmeshed in the internal dispute between Crown Prince Frederick William and his father's advisors. Reforms were suspended in 1711 and the royal domains were leased in large blocks to entrepreneurs instead.[34]

Frederick William continued the transfer of domains to non-noble estate managers after 1713. Since the managers had to pay rent to the crown, they had an incentive to develop more productive farming methods. Attempts to implement the promised abolition of serfdom in 1719–23 failed, because the peasants had few opportunities to raise the money expected as compensation, and because Frederick William still insisted they perform labour service. His son Frederick II renewed these efforts after 1763 on his own lands, but otherwise subsidised inefficient *Junker* landlords by extending loans through new land banks. This failed to stem the spread of commoner landownership as nobles sold up. A tenth of all noble estates were in bourgeois hands by 1800 and the proportion in the *Junker* bastion of Ducal Prussia was even higher at 15%. The growth in population caused food prices to rise in the later eighteenth century, improving returns to peasant producers and enabling some villages to buy out their own landlords. Peasants also benefited from the growth of the internal market, supplying large military and political centres like Berlin and Potsdam. Government reforms after 1807 abolished serfdom on all private estates by 1848. Combined with the collapse in land values after 1807, this accelerated the transfer of aristocratic land so that by 1857, commoners owned over 42% of all 12,399 Prussian noble estates.

This trend was general and was facilitated by much earlier changes in imperial law, which already recognised the right of commoners to hold aristocratic fiefs in the fourteenth century. Most territorial rulers had accepted this by 1600, permitting such landowners to enjoy the privileges associated with aristocratic land, including hunting rights, though not political representation in the Estates. The proportion of noble estates in commoner hands by the later eighteenth century varied from 4% in Bavaria, 16% in Hessen-Kassel, to 35% in north-west Saxony. While aristocratic landownership was declining, commoners still needed their rulers' permission to acquire noble estates and there is little evidence for a rural invasion by a wealthy bourgeoisie before 1806.[35] Moreover, aristocratic landowners were not necessarily against change. Many Prussian *Junkers* were ahead of their king in regarding wage labour as more efficient than unenthusiastic serfs. They began commuting *Gesindezwangdienst* into a cash substitute (called *Dienstgeld*) in the early eighteenth century, as well as subdividing their estates into tenancies. The considerable rise in productivity during the eighteenth century was little short of an agricultural revolution and derived not from intensified feudal exploitation, but from capital investment and a rapid expansion of wage labour. While individual landowners lost out and sold up, the group overall was strengthened because it consolidated its ownership of land, which was now worked by landless labourers. Cottagers constituted 40% of Brandenburg rural inhabitants in 1618, but declined to 30% by 1800 when there were at least twice as many landless, who formed the growing rural proletariat.

Such changes were not restricted to the large Habsburg and Hohenzollern monarchies. The prince of Hohenlohe-Langenburg emancipated his serfs in 1765, as did the elector of Hanover for his own domains. Peasants were prepared to pay high manumission fees to be free of relatively light, but highly derogatory obligations, and negotiated their own freedom in Hauenstein in 1738 and St Gallen in 1795. The margrave of Baden implemented manumission without compensation to lords in 1783 and serfs were also freed in Mainz (1787), Holstein (1805) and Darmstadt (1811). As with the Habsburg monarchy, the French Revolution slowed rather than accelerated the pace of change, as governments became less confident in promoting progressive reform.

The importance of the state in these changes can be gauged by Mecklenburg's experience, where princely authority collapsed in the early eighteenth century. Like other East Elbian rulers, the duke had extensive domains that covered 38% of the available land. His nobles controlled 47% directly and another 3% indirectly through their influence within the duchy's Lutheran Church. The remainder was held by the towns, but the largest of these, Rostock, sided with the nobles because it depended, as a major port, on the bulk grain trade for its livelihood.

Responding to the general pressures of war, the duke tried to protect peasants as a means of improving his own revenue from the 1690s. The nobles combined with Rostock in the duchy's Estates to appeal to the emperor when the impulsive Duke Carl Leopold (1713–47) tried to break their opposition by quartering soldiers on their land. The emperor sanctioned military intervention in 1719, forcing the duke to flee to his castle of Schwerin while the duchy was placed under imperial administration. Carl Leopold tried to regain control with the aid of a peasant rising in 1733, but was defeated by renewed military intervention. He spent the rest of his life concocting ever more fanciful schemes to recover his land. Prussia finally imposed a new constitution on his successor in 1755, which confirmed the aristocratic ascendancy and prevented any meaningful reform until it was abolished in the 1918 revolution.[36]

3.4 Community

Size and numbers

Outside the household, the community was the focal point in German life. It embodied political as well as social organisation, extending beyond simply designating a settlement, to embrace all forums for dealing with common concerns. The corporate structure of German society created different levels of community, ranging from the village and urban commune, through specialist bodies like monastic orders and universities, upwards to include Estates and entire territories. The commune was by far the most significant of these and has been the subject of a fierce historical controversy.

There were around 2,400 towns and 100,000 villages in the Reich, as well as 30,000–40,000 aristocratic castles and mansions in the eighteenth century. This represented a decline from 170,000 settlements prior to the Black Death, but though relatively few new towns or villages were founded after 1500, the existing ones expanded considerably in size. This increase fluctuated in line with the general population movements. For example, around three-quarters of Württemberg's population lived in the duchy's 1,200 villages, which had an average of 1,000 inhabitants by 1560, or twice as many as in 1490. The population remained stable until 1620, when the average size fell to 400 during the Thirty Years War. Numbers recovered to 1,000 by 1720 and remained at this level for forty years, before doubling again by 1800. As these figures indicate, most settlements were small by modern standards and few German cities had over 10,000 inhabitants.[37]

Basis

The nucleated pattern of settlement became the most common after the thirteenth century with the spread of so-called 'cluster villages' (*Haufendörfer*), where the houses were grouped round a visible focal point such as a church. Such villages were especially common in Bavaria, Swabia and Franconia and provided a strong basis for common identity and autonomy. However, more scattered, non-nucleated settlements were not necessarily a barrier to communal political organisation, since supralocal institutions could develop to bind them together, as occurred in the Black Forest, Tirol and Voralberg, where each hamlet sent elected officials to a valley council.

Economic activity forged one common bond. Without machines to assist them, villagers had to work together at harvest time, and to protect their fields and homes from scavengers and wild animals. This required the delegation of authority for coordination, as well as a division of labour, such as when peasants collectively paid communal shepherds. Defence against external attack was a further factor reinforcing communal identity. The village and urban parish formed the basic recruiting districts for all territorial militia organisations, as well as the conscription systems introduced after 1650 to support regular armies (see section 6.2). Villagers and townsfolk combined against internal disorder, using their own legal systems (*Dorf* or *Stadtrecht*), which replaced the earlier feudal law (*Hofrecht*) of the aristocratic manor. Participation in religious ritual offered a third focal point, heightened since the Reformation with the Protestants' greater involvement of parishioners and by the Catholics' renewed emphasis on the Mass. Finally, the need to negotiate with outsiders over the distribution of burdens like rents, tithes and taxes fostered the growth of communal institutions.

Emergence

Modern research rejects the once influential thesis of Otto von Gierke (1841–1921) that these institutions had their roots in the fellowship (*Genossenschaft*) of the ancient Germanic tribes. In fact, the public character of German communities (*Gemeinde*) was more recent and rested on the powers of villagers and townsfolk to control their own affairs. These powers did not spring spontaneously from earlier associations of peasants as individual producers, but were the outcome of negotiations between them and their lords. Urban communes emerged first, securing autonomy after 1100 by assuming the supervisory functions previously entrusted to aristocratic or ecclesiastical bailiffs. Village communes appeared in the twelfth century in the wake of the Germanic colonisation east of the Elbe and were firmly established there by 1500. In the west, similar structures appeared later as the medieval manorial system declined and management of daily life was devolved to those tenants who held full farms.

Communal institutions administered resources attached to their settlement, such as common land, meadows, forests and, increasingly, other essential facilities like halls, taverns, breweries, mills, smithies, shepherds' huts, and poorhouses. Enfranchised householders could participate in a communal assembly that convened at least once a year. These assemblies were displaced in the towns by the growth of narrower, governing councils from 1200, but remained central to village life. Some had the right of self-assembly, but most required their lord's permission to meet. Those in the east were generally convened by the lord or his representative, who presided over the session and chose the village headmen and other key officials. In the west, these posts were generally filled by election. The commune thus combined the individual management of labour through the household with the collective administration of common resources and regulation of internal disputes through village courts.

Despite the greater powers of their lords, peasants east of the Elbe still possessed effective communal institutions. The bailiff or judge (*Schulze*), appointed by the lord to represent his interests, resided in the village and belonged to its community. Similar figures also existed in north German villages alongside elected headmen. Many *Schulzen* identified more closely with other villagers than with their lord, while in Brandenburg and Saxony, assemblies enjoyed the right of self-assembly like some in the west.[38]

Communalism

These institutions provided the basis for common action to achieve popular goals, in what Peter Blickle has termed 'communalism'. Clearly distancing himself from Gierke's romanticised view of the folk community, Blickle sets out to rewrite German history by stressing the positive contribution of ordinary people to its political development, tracing a direct line from early modern communalism to modern parliamentary democracy and republicanism.[39] Communal identity, he argues, represented a horizontal political plane diametrically opposed to the vertical hierarchy of feudal lordship that provided the origins of the German territorial states. Villagers shared a belief in communal liberty, equality and justice, symbolised in their annual collective oath to their community. The small-scale and often agrarian basis of most towns overcame the barriers between the urban and rural worlds, widening horizontal solidarity between communities. Communal institutions rested on the consent of their members. Power was shared, with leaders acting as delegates, not rulers. Towns were particularly innovative, pioneering administrative and fiscal techniques considerably in advance of those in princely territories during the later middle ages. Blickle believes that such developments demonstrate communalism's potential as Germany's 'third way' between the Reich and princely territorial states, offering the chance to build political organisation from below and create a different kind of egalitarianism and democracy than that offered by the French Revolutionaries of 1789.

These arguments have proved controversial. Critics suggest that Blickle unintentionally back-projects a Cold War division of Germany into a democratic west and authoritarian east by arguing that the manorial economy prevented communalism from taking root across the Elbe.[40] Ironically, the recently discovered evidence of the vitality of eastern communes potentially strengthens his case. A more serious criticism is the charge that the communalism thesis exaggerates the strength of horizontal solidarity both within communities and between them, minimising the problems of conflict and exclusion. Much of the debate centres on the contested nature of the contemporary term 'common' (*gemein*) and its derivatives.[41]

Early modern Germans distinguished between 'common good' (*Gemeinnutz*) and private self-interest (*Eigennutz*), celebrating the former and condemning the latter. The purpose of any government should be the promotion of the common good. The difficulty lay in defining what constituted both the common good and the ideal community. The rhetoric of community was claimed by lords, as well as peasants and burghers. It operated on several levels and could exclude as well as include. The powerful sense of local space and home reinforced solidarity between neighbours whilst fostering hostility toward outsiders, including other towns and villages. An individual was member a of a unique legal corporation and his or her communal rights were not valid in another community. However, people identified with the wider community of the Reich, as this offered legal protection for their rights. The growth of the larger principalities as distinct political and legal spaces cut popular ties to the Reich and eroded local particularism by integrating settlements within a more uniform framework of territorial law. The dynasty offered a more immediate focal point for loyalty than the distant emperor, substituting for religion, which was split into different confessions, and for language and culture, which did not match political boundaries.

Not only were there alternative communities along the vertical hierarchy of lordship, but the horizontal plane of communal solidarity was more fractured than the rhetoric of the 'common man' might suggest. First, the term was gender specific, and its positive attributes were primarily male, since 'common woman' meant a prostitute belonging 'to all men'.[42] While women could be represented in village assemblies and have burgher rights, this was not the norm and they were disbarred from holding office. Secondly, the unique character of each community discouraged permanent association with neighbouring settlements, which could be economic competitors, or otherwise separated by confessional or territorial boundaries. Town–country alliances were particularly precarious, since townsfolk were often numbered amongst those exploiting the rural hinterland. Rifts also existed within communities, as well as between them. Fundamentally, communal spirit envisaged a society not of each according to his or her needs, but of each according to contribution. Those who bore the heaviest burdens, should exercise the greatest power. Since householders produced more and paid higher taxes, they were enfranchised, while the poor, who contributed far less, were denied a voice.

Communes displayed another key characteristic of the corporate society to which they belonged. All early modern assemblies from the Reichstag to the village hall embraced the belief that majority decisions reflected the general will. This could justify oppression, since collective interest overrode individual interest. The pressure to conform not only came from authorities higher up the vertical hierarchy, but was exerted within the horizontal plane of communal life. Neighbourliness included not only a willingness to help those next door, but the expectation that they would keep their own house in order, and not disturb the peace or endanger other dwellings through careless behaviour. Expressions of disapproval for those who failed to conform ranged from banging pots and pans and other 'rough music', up to fines and denial of communal resources.

The intrusion of the state

Territorial governments gradually stepped in to regulate both landlord–commune relations and internal communal life. This had begun before 1500, but accelerated after the Peasants War of 1525, eroding communalism as a potential alternative path for political development. However, such intrusion was not entirely a measure of control, but also developed in response to pressures from below (see section 7.2).

One aspect involved integrating each community within a wider framework of territorial law. Rulers required each community to adopt written law and administrative procedures during the seventeenth century. These village and municipal codes were increasingly standardised for all communes within the territory after 1700. The authorities used this opportunity to assert greater central supervision, taking control of all communal forests in Hessen-Kassel in 1711, for instance. A second strategy was to co-opt village and municipal officials as the lowest echelon of the territorial civil administration. Communal institutions, like the village headmen and councils, retained their names but assumed new functions and were subject to tighter supervision from above. They served as brokers between rulers and their subjects, rather than as agents of a repressive state.

The political penetration of the communal level was part of a general process enmeshing communities within wider economic networks through the spread of money as a uniform medium of exchange. This medium was also used by the state, since its taxes were to be paid in cash, forcing communes to restructure their internal public economy by, for example, commuting punishments into fines to raise additional income. The process became mutually reinforcing, since communities joined the expanding market networks by seeking new opportunities to sell their produce and raise money. State economic regulation was intended to encourage this by favouring productive, viable households over other members of each community (see section 7.1).

The intrusion of the state combined with demographic and economic problems to erode the commune across the sixteenth and seventeenth centuries. Population growth after 1530 increased the numbers of rural landless and urban propertyless, who soon outnumbered the enfranchised members of most communities. This process was repeated as the population recovered after the Thirty Years War, and worsened again as demographic growth accelerated from the 1730s. Some communities were totally destroyed, like those in the Allgäu and Lake Constance region, which were abandoned in the sixteenth century as people left to find better conditions elsewhere. More generally, social stratification and internal tensions increased with the growing numbers of poor. Attempts by the enfranchised property owners to defend their position could reaffirm communal solidarity where the threat appeared to come from outside in the form of increased tax or labour service demands, or was expressed in religious terms as confessional strife between rulers and ruled. Communities could serve as powerful platforms for popular mobilisation in such cases. More usually, however, enfranchised householders closed ranks, forming an oligarchy intent on denying marginal groups access to scarce communal resources.

Such tensions produced not only conflicts between the haves and have-nots, but also infighting amongst householders. Despite sharing the franchise, these were rarely a homogenous group, but divided into a comparatively rich minority, several substrata of varying wealth and a substantial group who risked slipping into the ranks of the poor. Arguments over tactics split communities into factions that cannot be analysed solely in terms of wealth or class, since they were cut across by generational rifts and could even divide individual families.[43] Around a third to a half of all villagers generally refused to join protests or rebellions, further undermining solidarity. Internal divisions often opened communities to external penetration as factions sought allies outside. Lords did not automatically ally with the urban or rural elite, but often sponsored marginal groups as new forms of dependent labour. Such groups were shunned by the established householders, who rarely accepted them as marriage partners and feared them as a potential drain on communal resources.

Whilst state intrusion eroded late medieval communalism, it unwittingly fostered new forms of popular political action. By expanding their responsibilities and seeking to regulate wider areas of activity, the authorities extended the possibilities for appeal to their courts and administrations, raising popular expectations for redress and improvement. Peasants took advantage of these facilities to press their own demands and so became more closely integrated within the territorial state.[44]

Chapter 4: The Great War (1618–48)

4.1 Causes

The debates

The Thirty Years War appeared to subsequent generations as a deep chasm, scarring German history by wrecking the country's social, economic and cultural fabric and stunting its political growth. To those who lived through the conflict, it was simply 'the Great War'. Yet, they were as concerned to explain its causes as later historians. The controversy was already well under way by 1643 when it became enmeshed in the long peace negotiations as the contending parties sought to improve their positions by blaming their opponents for starting hostilities. The only area of agreement was expressed in contemporary poetry that blamed the Germans for bringing the catastrophe upon themselves through their sinful lives, which had induced God to send foreign armies to ravage their land.

Later historians have favoured three alternative explanations.[1] The most common Anglophone interpretation sees the war as part of a longer, international struggle between the Habsburg dynasty and its rivals. This shifts the emphasis to Spain and its prolonged conflicts with the Dutch rebels (1568–1648) and France (1635–59), reducing events in central Europe to a side show after the suppression of the initial Bohemian revolt (1618–20), until Sweden's intervention in 1630. The most extreme version of this approach denies that the fighting between 1618 and 1648 constituted a distinct, coherent war, and subsumes it entirely within these wider European conflicts.[2] The term 'thirty years war' was already current by 1645, and though a myth, in that the conflict was not a single, uniform struggle across this time, none the less indicates that contemporaries believed its intensity and duration warranted distinguishing it from other, parallel wars.[3]

A second interpretation emphasises the social and economic problems encountered in the previous chapter, particularly the climatic changes of the Little Ice Age and the tensions stoked by population growth in the later sixteenth century. These problems climaxed in what is labelled the 'General Crisis of the seventeenth-century' as the underlying shift towards capitalism triggered a series of violent civil and international wars.[4] Like the first interpretation, this approach sees the central European struggles as part of a broader European phenomenon, but argues they were caused by socio-economic rather than political or religious problems. Contemporaries did blame arms manufacturers and soldiers for prolonging the war, and the need to secure resources certainly propelled Sweden to invade the southern Baltic shore. However, it is difficult to draw a direct connection between the wider socio-economic tensions and the outbreak of war in 1618. It is even harder to find evidence to support the theory that the conflict can be interpreted in class terms. Corporate groups like the aristocracy did pursue sectional interests, but they were riven like the rest of society by confessional, dynastic and other loyalties.

The role of belief gives rise to the third explanation, which sees the conflict as a 'religious war'. The Dutch and Bohemian revolts represented popular challenges to rulers' claims to religious as well as political sovereignty over their subjects and imparted a sectarian character to the main civil wars. These were linked by the alliances forged between the major belligerents, dividing Europe into large armed coalitions that appeared defined by the religious agendas of the Reformation and Counter Reformation. The war was prolonged by the fear that defeat would entail the loss of religious identity and the imposition of the opposing side's beliefs. Those who subscribe to this interpretation note that the religious element was not present evenly throughout the struggle, particularly after the alliance between Catholic France and Lutheran Sweden in 1635 signalled a move to more pragmatic, secular concerns.[5]

Regardless whether this religious war is seen as a general international struggle, or a narrower central European one, its origins are usually located in the unsatisfactory nature of the Peace of Augsburg of 1555. This conviction was possibly reinforced by twentieth-century experience of a second 'thirty years war' as the Peace of Versailles of 1919 failed to resolve the problems of the First World War, making the outbreak of the Second apparently inevitable in 1939. Closer examination suggests that the seventeenth-century conflict was only a religious war in so far as issues of faith were inseparable from a struggle over the imperial constitution.

The Augsburgian settlement and its consequences

It is misleading to view the Peace of Augsburg as an armistice that merely temporarily delayed the resumption of sectarian violence. The settlement proved remarkably durable and only faltered when later problems compounded an underlying disagreement over the true nature of earthly peace. The medieval vision of peace rested on universal harmony within a single Christendom headed by pope and emperor. Many clung to this after 1517, hoping that reconciliation between the theologians would restore the lost unity. Confessional peace offered a more immediate remedy to the growing religious divide. It looked back to the belief that political stability required religious uniformity, but recognised that it was currently impossible to re-establish this across Europe and sought instead to ensure its implementation within individual countries. Most European monarchs favoured this solution, imposing religious conformity on their subjects with varying degrees of violence. The alternative, secular civil peace was first advocated by Jean Bodin in response to the French Wars of Religion after 1562. He proposed a monarchy that remained broadly Christian, but that disociated itself from any particular confession in order to take religion out of politics.[6]

Charles V failed to restore the lost universal peace. His defeat also reduced the applicability of the two alternatives to the Reich, since both confessional and civil peace required a strong central state to uphold them. This was impossible in the Reich, where greater monarchical authority impinged on German Liberty and was compromised by the Habsburgs' partisan support for Catholicism. The idea of civil peace also conflicted with the Reich's medieval roots as a Holy Roman Empire, because it entailed disassociating law and theology. Religious plurality implied a variety of competing claims to the truth, yet early modern law relied on theology for its moral force. Protestants and Catholics still clung to the universalist notion that there could only be one law and one faith, because there was only one truth. They believed their current problems stemmed from a faulty interpretation of timeless, divine laws, and the theological arguments centred on finding the 'correct' interpretation of Holy Scripture. The Protestants had not rejected the Bible, only the Catholic interpretation of it. In short, both sides claimed to be right and believed that if they could prove their interpretation was correct, they could challenge the validity of their opponents' entire position.

Given these circumstances, the prospects for compromise appeared slight by the mid-sixteenth century. However, Germans were saved by the flexibility of the imperial constitution, which allowed elements of all three concepts of peace to be accommodated within the Augsburgian settlement.[7] This was a universal peace in that it bound both Protestants and Catholics within a common system. The text deliberately used ambiguous words like 'peace', 'religion' and 'reformation', which were universal values that all subscribed to but defined very differently. An element of confessional peace was introduced to minimise the consequences of such ambiguity. By granting the right of reformation to the princes, the settlement rejected the usual European model of confessional peace at national level, displacing this to the territories where it could be implemented with less violence (see section 2.2). The inclusion of limited rights of emigration and freedom of conscience softened the impact of these terms and reduced the likelihood of popular discontent. Finally, the entire settlement rested on the secular framework of the imperial public peace that had been developed since 1495 to maintain order and arbitrate disputes through the *Reichskammergericht*, or supreme court (see section 5.2).

The court informally embraced the principle of religious parity, because judges were appointed from candidates proposed by the territories, which were free to select their own co-religionists. Around a third of the judges were Protestants in the later sixteenth-century, including a minority of Calvinists, even though this confession was not officially recognised in 1555.[8] The court acted swiftly to resolve the numerous disputes over the possession of ecclesiastical property and only received seven formal complaints against its verdicts between 1559 and 1589. This represents a remarkable success, compared with the violence engulfing both France and the Netherlands from the 1560s, and there was no German equivalent of the notorious massacre of St Bartholomew in Paris in 1572. The Reich's relative tranquillity rested in part on a coincidence of interest amongst its rulers. Princes were reluctant to disturb a settlement that had greatly increased their powers to oversee spiritual affairs. The external threat posed by the Ottomans encouraged even the Protestants to collaborate with the emperor in maintaining collective security.[9] Irenicist sentiment underpinned the collaborative spirit, by encouraging hopes that mutual understanding would lead to peaceful reconciliation between the confessions.[10]

Growing confessional tension

These hopes faded as the century wore on. Calvinism gained ground when the conversion of the elector Palatine in 1561 was followed by that of the count of Nassau (1578), the landgrave of Hessen-Kassel (1603) and the elector of Brandenburg (1613), as well as numerous minor lords and aristocrats. A rift opened as the Palatinate challenged Saxony's leadership, splitting the German Protestants into two groups by 1600. The Palatinate led the more radical group of primarily Calvinist princes and counts, who demanded constitutional change in their favour. The moderate, predominantly Lutheran majority under Saxony was thrown onto the defensive, yet hesitated to side firmly with the Catholics. The latter were growing more hostile as the spread of Calvinism appeared to confirm that the Protestants could not be trusted since they could no longer agree on the definition of their own faith.

Confessional lines hardened as leadership passed during the 1570s into the hands of a generation that had only known religious schism. Educated in segregated schools, they regarded the more tolerant policies of their elders as a sell-out. Theologians produced definitive doctrinal statements to distinguish their faith more clearly from its competitors. Catholics believed that the Protestants had been given their hearing by the pope at the Council of Trent and had been pronounced guilty of heresy in its concluding decrees in 1563. Calvinists devised their first authoritative statement in the Heidelberg catechism in the same year, while Lutherans issued the Book of Concord in 1580, which signalled a lasting break with other reformed faiths.

The growing influence of militant Catholics in education is one important example of these sharper distinctions. The papacy had already established the *Collegium Germanicum* in 1552 to train German, and later Hungarian, senior clergy. Nearly a fifth of all German prince-bishops were graduates of this college between 1560 and 1803, as were 30% of Austrian bishops and 25% of the canons in the imperial church. Alumni included Franz Wilhelm von Wartenberg who, as bishop of Osnabrück from 1627, was a leading zealot during the Thirty Years War, as well as Christoph Bernhard von Galen, the martial bishop of

Münster from 1650 to 1678. The Jesuits established their first mission in Cologne in 1544 and by 1630 had 3,000 members active in the Reich.

The militants were more prepared to use force to resolve problems, because they believed the other side had already broken the peace. Though initially resented as papal interference, Catholic rulers swung behind the pope's verdict on the Augsburgian settlement, seeing it as a tactical concession that simply tolerated heretics out of political expediency. The emperor's ability to restrain the militants decreased during the later sixteenth century. Maximilian II (r.1564–76) still favoured reconciliation, but became disillusioned by the spread of Calvinism. His successor, Rudolph II (r.1576–1612), was more openly partisan. Though prepared to cooperate with Calvinists on political matters, he consistently opposed them in matters of religion. He still sought negotiated settlements, but his ability to secure these was lessened by wider shifts in European politics. France's internal collapse after 1562 removed it as a counterweight to Spain, which had resolved on a military solution to its problems in the Netherlands. German Protestants expected the emperor to mediate, because the Netherlands had once belonged to the Burgundian Kreis and were still associated with the Reich. They seriously overestimated the Austrian Habsburgs' influence in Madrid and mistook diplomatic failure for covert Catholic collusion.

Spain became increasingly drawn into imperial politics as its position crumbled in the Netherlands. It relied on the route known as the Spanish Road along the Rhine to send reinforcements from its possessions in northern Italy to its forces operating against the Dutch rebels. It feared German Protestants might cut this and suspected them of secretly assisting the Dutch. Spain backed the Catholic candidate in the disputed election to the archbishopric of Cologne in 1583 as it feared Protestant success here would sever the crucial supply route. Madrid also encouraged the Catholic duke of Lorraine to intervene in both the French Wars of Religion and the disputed election to the bishopric of Strasbourg in 1593–1604. Further intervention followed when it appeared that the strategic duchies of Jülich, Cleves, Berg and Mark would be inherited by Protestant Brandenburg in 1609.

Habsburg weakness

The emperor's inability to master these difficulties points to a more serious, underlying cause for the war that started in 1618. The dynastic partition of the Habsburg lands in 1556–64 broke the Austrian branch into three lines. These inherited earlier debts, but lost the previous economies of scale. All were forced to raise taxes, leading to renewed disputes with their provincial Estates who seized the chance to demand new concessions, including freedom of worship as many Habsburg aristocrats embraced Protestantism.

As head of the senior Austrian line, Rudolph II initially received his family's backing as emperor after 1576. He was filled with a sense of mission to preserve European peace and repel the Ottomans. His deep interest in astronomy, astrology and the occult inclined him towards the irenicists, who likewise put faith in obscure solutions to complex problems. However, his time at the Spanish court had given him an inflated sense of majesty, making him reluctant to delegate power and convinced that Catholicism was proof of political loyalty. Any chance of imposing his authority was undermined by his personal flaws. His awkwardness in public worsened as he got older, preventing him from cultivating the personal friendships amongst the princes that were essential for effective imperial rule. His removal of his court to Prague in 1582 heightened Protestant anxieties and raised general suspicions that he was neglecting the Reich.

His brother Matthias tried to fill the growing political vacuum. His period as Habsburg governor of the Netherlands (1577–81) had been a failure, but had emboldened him to think of himself as a statesman. He travelled widely, visiting Lutheran Denmark, and recruiting Calvinists as well as Catholics as his advisors. He re-emerged as governor of Austria after 1595, but was essentially a dilettante and fell under the influence of the strong-willed Catholic Melchior Khlesl (1552–1630) three years later. Matthias began conspiring with other disaffected relations in what became known as the 'Brothers' Quarrel' (*Bruderzwist*).[11] Archduke Ferdinand of the Styrian branch was the most important of the co-conspirators and was altogether a more forceful character. His mother was Maria Anna, sister of the influential Duke Maximilian of Bavaria, and like his brother-in-law, he had been educated by the Jesuits.

Ferdinand is often misrepresented as a Catholic bigot. He was deeply convinced of the dignity of the Reich and that he was serving the higher cause of true religion. For him, the continued toleration of Protestants within the Reich was an affront to God and undermined the legitimacy of Habsburg authority because the family was failing to fulfil the divine will. Mundane objectives thus acquired the force of religious conviction as he resolved to make Catholicism a test of political loyalty. None the less, arrogance was tinged with uncertainty as he could never be sure that God remained on his side. His concern for the Reich encouraged a legalistic approach to political problems and he was by no means opposed to Lutherans who respected his interpretation of the Augsburgian settlement. His Jesuit upbringing also imparted an element of pragmatism and he accepted their belief that clemency was the mark of a just king. He aimed to restore the imperial constitution to its 'true' form, rather than subject the Reich to absolute authority.[12]

Like many Catholic princes, his father, Archduke Charles II (r.1564–90), had initially refused to enforce the Tridentine decrees in Styria and had granted wide freedom of conscience even to his peasants in 1572. He reversed this five years later as confessional lines hardened across the Reich and Ferdinand intensified this Counter Reformation drive after 1596. A reform commission under Bishop Martin Brenner of Seckau toured the country with the protection of 300 soldiers, demolishing Protestant churches and burning their books. Nobles were permitted to worship in their own homes, but others were given a month to convert or be expelled. Around 2,500 left, including the famous astronomer Johannes Kepler. However, though Ferdinand curtailed the Styrian Estates' rights, he believed they remained an integral part of his territory and, in practice, he tempered Brenner's militancy, frequently extending the deadline for conversion and rarely expelling the peasants and poor. Tensions persisted, but Ferdinand's firm rule stabilised Habsburg authority in Styria while it was crumbling elsewhere.

War and revolt, 1593–1606

Rudolph II squared up to his imperial role in 1593 when the sultan attacked Habsburg Hungary in what became known as the Thirteen Years War. Habsburg operations began with high hopes as the Reichstag voted substantial financial aid, while the Ottomans' Christian vassals rebelled in Transylvania, Wallachia and Moldavia and sided with the emperor by 1597. Rudolph might have realised his dream of defeating the sultan had he not both widened the war to include the reincorporation of Transylvania into Hungary, and used the presence of his forces to promote re-Catholicisation. Leading Hungarian and Transylvanian nobles like Stephen Bocskay and Bethlen Gabor were Calvinists and resented Habsburg encroachment as a threat to their religious and political liberties. Many thought the Ottomans were preferable and turned against their former allies in 1604 after Archduke Matthias ordered

General Belgiojoso to seize the town of Kassa (Košice) in Upper Hungary, which was the centre of Protestant discontent.

The Hungarian revolt is significant as the first manifestation of wider trouble throughout the Habsburg monarchy. The disturbances that started in 1604 never fully subsided, but fused with similar problems elsewhere in a broader movement of provincial protest and religious discontent, reaching its climax in the Bohemian revolt of 1618. It was the most potent expression of aristocratic federalism in the Reich and rested on the cultural affinity shared by Austrian, Bohemian, Hungarian, Transylvanian and even Polish nobles, who became radicalised by confessional strife. Provincial autonomy now seemed necessary not only to preserve aristocratic privileges against Habsburg centralism, but to defend religious freedoms against Catholic repression. Bohemian and Hungarian aristocrats were ready to accept more radical resistance theories because they already believed they possessed the right to elect their kings, and could reject monarchs who failed to observe constitutional agreements. Faced by a common enemy, provincial Estates were prepared to forgo some of their distinctiveness in order to forge federal alliances with like-minded partners elsewhere. This search was eventually to link the problems in the Habsburgs' hereditary lands with those in the Reich when the Bohemians accepted the elector Palatine as alternative king in 1619.

Rudolph seemed powerless in the face of these mounting problems. He already left many key documents unsigned after 1598, while his refusal to marry created uncertainty over the succession. By April 1606, Matthias was determined to have him declared mentally ill as a first step to forcing his abdication. Backed by other disaffected relations, Matthias opened negotiations with the rebels, leading to the Treaty of Vienna on 23 September 1606. This introduced formal toleration for Lutheran and Calvinist Hungarian nobles and royal towns, as well as recognising Transylvanian autonomy and the privileges of the Hungarian Estates. Conservative Catholic Hungarians accepted Matthias's sweeping concessions to the radicals, because they did not want to exchange Habsburg for Ottoman rule and feared that a continuation of the revolt would stir popular discontent amongst the peasants. The Treaty greatly enhanced the role of the Estates in the Habsburg monarchy, since those of Austria and Bohemia served as guarantors for the new peace. Bocskay repaid Matthias by mediating a relatively favourable treaty with the sultan at Zsitva Torok on 11 November 1606, stabilising the frontier in Hungary with relatively few concessions.

Habsburg civil war, 1606–12

Rudolph had been sidelined and refused to recognise the Treaty of Vienna. Imperial troops remained in Hungary, while others enforced a clumsy policy of confessionalisation in Lower Austria. Matthias believed he could use the mounting discontent to give his brother the final push and he joined the Austrian and Hungarian Estates in the Treaty of Pressburg (Bratislava) on 1 February 1608. He confirmed the Treaty of Vienna and sanctioned the spread of the manorial economy, in return for political backing against Rudolph. The Estates now held the upper hand, since Matthias's action legitimised their wider opposition to Habsburg centralisation and those of Moravia joined the Austrians and Hungarians in an agreement of 19 April to blackmail the archduke into improving his terms. The Bohemians had remained aloof, since they still jealously guarded their premier position and refused to see the Moravians, Silesians and Lausatians as their equals. They seized their chance when Matthias moved to capture Rudolph in Prague. The Bohemian Estates joined their Silesian and Lausatian counterparts in coming to the emperor's rescue in return for concessions of their own in June. Rudolph confirmed his allies' privileges and recognised the legality of the *Confessio Bohemica*, a synthesis of Hussite, Lutheran and Czech Brethren texts from 1575.

With the two sides evenly matched, the brothers were forced to compromise in the Treaty of Lieben (Stará Libená) on 25 June. Rudolph partitioned his lands along the lines of the existing alliances: Matthias received nominal control of Hungary, Austria and Moravia, along with the promise of succession to the imperial title, while the emperor retained Bohemia, Silesia and the Lausitz. Rudolph was now on the defensive and at the mercy of his Estates. The Bohemians compelled him to grant the famous Letter of Majesty on 9 July 1608, extending the treaty of Lieben, recognising Calvinism and guaranteeing religious freedoms even for serfs throughout the kingdom. Similar concessions were made to the Silesians on 20 August.

Rudolph resorted to desperate measures to escape these commitments. He summoned his cousin Leopold, Ferdinand's younger brother, who was bishop of Passau and then Strasbourg. Leopold had recruited 7,000 of the soldiers discharged after the Thirteen Years War with the intention of opposing French intervention in the Jülich-Cleves inheritance dispute in 1609. Rudolph promised to make him King of the Romans, thereby cutting Matthias out of the succession. After long preparations,

Leopold finally entered Bohemia from Passau intending to free Rudolph from his virtual captivity in Prague. The Bohemians appealed to Matthias when Leopold's troops arrived in January 1611. Fearing he would be caught in the middle, Rudolph back-tracked and ordered his cousin to leave. Refusing to settle for anything less than the Bohemian crown, Leopold continued his advance, occupying Prague in February. He had run out of money by this point and his troops pillaged the city, further undermining the dynasty's credibility and the Catholic cause. He finally pulled out on 11 March as Matthias approached with his own forces, entering the city that night and imprisoning Rudolph in the castle.

Matthias's largely bloodless victory paved the way for his coronation as Bohemian king on 27 May. Rudolph formally relinquished power to him on 18 August, but retained the imperial title, because Saxony refused to connive in Matthias's plan to depose him. This merely postponed the final act which followed the unhappy emperor's death on 20 January 1612 as the electors agreed to make Matthias emperor on 13 June.

The Brothers' Quarrel fuelled the centrifugal forces fragmenting the Habsburg monarchy since the partitions of 1556–64. Each faction made important concessions to the Estates, strengthening their autonomy and legitimising their federal alliances. By 1610 each of the Estates effectively controlled the government and military organisation of its own province or kingdom. All secured confirmation of religious freedoms, accelerating the spread of Protestantism, especially amongst the nobility. Hungary became effectively Protestant, while Lutherans and Calvinists enjoyed open toleration in Transylvania. Up to 90 per cent of the Austrian nobility were Protestant and only Croatia remained solidly Catholic. Bohemia was dangerously independent. It received authorisation to levy its own army under Count Heinrich Matthias von Thurn and had already begun negotiations with the German Protestant princes in 1606. Georg Erasmus Tschernembl, the radical leader of the Upper Austrian Estates, followed suit in 1608. Matthias's decision to shift the imperial court back to Vienna in 1612 fuelled Bohemian ambitions and within three years its Estates were considering a break-away federation.

Paralysis of the imperial government

The Habsburgs' domestic difficulties had such serious repercussions because they prevented an appropriate response to the mounting problems within the Reich. Rudolph devoted what little energy he possessed

to defending his crumbling position at home, and increasingly abandoned constitutional propriety in his management of imperial affairs.

The main crisis developed around the operation of the *Reichskammergericht* charged with upholding the Augsburgian settlement by arbitrating
religious disputes. This court was subject to an annual visitation by a
committee of princes on rotation from the Reichstag. The archbishop
of Magdeburg was next in line to fill a vacancy on this body when he
was vetoed by Rudolph in 1588 on the grounds that he had converted
to Lutheranism. Though it undermined faith in imperial justice, the
matter was not immediately fatal. However, the elector Palatine and
other radicals deliberately politicised the issue to wrest Protestant leadership from the more moderate Saxons. The elector saw his chance when
the court passed judgements in the so-called 'four monasteries' dispute'
(*Vierklösterstreit*), involving the management of four ecclesiastical properties. As with previous cases, the court assessed these on their individual
merits, reaching majority verdicts with the help of Protestant judges.
As all four were favourable to the Catholics, the Palatinate led Brandenburg and Brunswick in denouncing it as a mis-trial, sabotaging the entire
visitation process in 1601.

Even moderate Protestants began to have doubts about the impartial-
ity of an unregulated judiciary. These fears appeared to be justified when
Rudolph seriously mishandled another relatively minor dispute in the
imperial city of Donauwörth. This city had been officially bi-confessional
since 1555, but the local militants fought over rights of public worship.
Such cases would normally be handled by the *Reichskammergericht*, which
would appoint Catholic and Protestant judges to assess the case and, if
necessary, could commission a prince of each confession to impose a
settlement. Desperate for help against Matthias, Rudolph ignored these
rules and handed the matter over to the other imperial supreme court, the
Reichshofrat, which depended entirely on the emperor (see section 5.2).
This proceeded to name Maximilian of Bavaria as sole commissioner,
despite the fact that he was not a member of the Swabian Kreis to which
the city belonged. Bavarian troops occupied Donauwörth in December
1607 and with Rudolph's permission, formally annexed it in lieu of their
expenses seven months later.[13]

This action reinforced the Palatine arguments that the Catholics could
not be trusted, and the elector led the Protestants in a walk-out from the
Reichstag in 1608. Imperial politics now appeared to polarise along religious lines, beginning with the formation of the Protestant Union under
Palatine leadership. Fearing isolation after his action at Donauwörth,

Maximilian of Bavaria overcame his own antipathy to such alliances and established a rival Catholic organisation in July 1609. This was dubbed the 'Liga' by its opponents in deliberate reference to the Catholic League associated with many of the atrocities during the French Wars of Religion.[14] The two organisations appeared to square up over the Jülich-Cleves inheritance dispute, which erupted following the death of these duchies' last ruler in 1609. Local pragmatic toleration had defused confessional tensions in the area, despite their proximity to the fighting in the Netherlands.[15] Yet, this very proximity combined with a clash between a Catholic (Pfalz-Neuburg) and a Protestant (Brandenburg) claimant to make the dispute an international issue. The French monarchy, having recovered from its own civil war, decided to restore its international prestige by contesting Spanish interests in the region. The assassination of King Henry IV in 1610 averted this contest, but did not prevent the more local German dispute, which dragged on with intermittent fighting until Brandenburg and Pfalz-Neuburg finally agreed to partition the inheritance between them in 1666.

However, other factors were at work besides the murder of the French king, in containing confessionalised violence within the Reich. The failure of the Union's mobilisation during the Jülich-Cleves crisis revealed deep divisions within its ranks, which numbered only 25 principalities and cities and were split between the moderate, largely passive membership and a radical, increasingly conspiratorial leadership.[16] The Union's director, Elector Palatine Frederick V (r.1610–32), and his lieutenant, Christian von Anhalt-Bernburg, viewed imperial politics in confessional terms, regarding the emperor as party to an international Catholic conspiracy to exterminate Protestantism. Protestants could only survive the approaching Armageddon by forming an equally broad alliance, leading Frederick and Anhalt to negotiate secretly with the Bohemian, Austrian and Hungarian Estates after 1606, and to sign treaties with England (1612) and the Dutch rebels (1613). These views were not shared by the membership, creating an opportunity for Matthias and Khlesl to defuse tension within the Reich by isolating the radicals.

Tension subsides, 1612–17

Khlesl changed tack after Rudolph's death, abandoning his earlier confrontational policies and trying to rebuild Habsburg influence by regaining the middle ground between the major confessional groups.

This was extremely difficult, especially since Khlesl's ardent Catholicism precluded further concessions to the Protestants. He resumed the policy of the early 1590s by using the Ottoman threat to rally broad support for the emperor. The sultan had backed Bethlen Gabor, who had become prince of the effectively independent Transylvania in 1613. Khlesl presented this as evidence of a fresh Ottoman threat. The Protestants joined the Catholics at the Reichstag that year to vote a further two years of imperial taxes to strengthen Habsburg border defences, but rather than uniting behind the emperor in a new war, the German princes combined to compel Khlesl to keep the peace.

This cross-confessional cooperation signalled a general rejection of radical policies by the majority of the imperial Estates, who wanted above all to preserve domestic and international peace. Despite the *Reichskammergericht's* problems, imperial justice functioned well into the 1620s, because the *Reichshofrat* stepped in to take over the case load. Though radical Protestants criticised this as evidence of Habsburg imperial absolutism, they also appreciated peace and even the Union's leaders sent their cases to the emperor's court.[17]

As religious militancy lost ground, Khlesl tried to merge both the Union and the Liga into a broad cross-confessional alliance behind Matthias. First, he curtailed the Liga's autonomy by forcing Duke Maximilian to admit the Habsburg hereditary lands as members in 1615. As the organisation lost its utility as a platform for Bavarian interests, Maximilian resigned, enabling Khlesl to wind it up in 1617. The Union needed less attention, because it was already falling apart. Like the Liga, it was essentially a paper organisation, lacking either a permanent army or an executive. Doubts over the legality of such alliances within imperial law encouraged only relatively loose arrangements to collaborate politically and mobilise in an emergency. The Union's position was especially precarious, since it included Calvinists, whose faith was not recognised by the Augsburgian settlement. The elector Palatine felt that a loose alliance offered insufficient security and pressed after 1604 for a more coherent, autonomous Protestant block within the Reich. This was vehemently opposed by Saxony and the majority of Lutherans, who effectively derailed Palatine plans by refusing to join the Union after 1608. Even Union members distanced themselves from Palatine radicalism after 1610 and refused to join the elector in making further protests against Habsburg policy. By 1615 Frederick V had abandoned his wholesale opposition to the emperor and only made specific proposals. Within a year, he was calling for the dissolution of both the Union and the Liga

and the formation of a new cross-confessional alliance to back Duke Maximilian in challenging the Habsburgs in the next imperial election. There
was nothing inevitable about the outbreak of war two years later and
certainly it was impossible to predict that the Habsburgs' problems in
Bohemia would lead to such a prolonged and violent struggle.

4.2 Conflict

The Bohemian revolt, 1618

Ironically, the Bohemian revolt was triggered by the revival of Habsburg
fortunes after 1617. As the monarchy recovered its sense of direction, it
headed on a collision course towards its increasingly alarmed Estates.
The man behind the more assertive policy was Ferdinand of Styria, who
assumed the initiative from Matthias. The emperor was childless and all
his other relations had either renounced their claims, or discredited
themselves by their actions, like Leopold of Passau. Though Matthias
lived until 20 March 1619, it was Ferdinand who now took the important
decisions. The Bohemian Estates accepted him as their next king on
6 June 1617, followed by the Hungarians on 16 May 1618, in return for
his confirmation of their privileges, including those won in 1606–8.
Ferdinand granted this as a tactical concession, believing privately that
the religious freedoms were a licence to serve the devil. He had no intention of confronting the Estates directly, preferring to undermine their
autonomy by exploiting legal loopholes and promoting loyalists to influential positions.

Unfortunately, neither he nor Matthias were actually in Bohemia,
which was governed through a regency council in Prague castle. Concessions granted in 1609 permitted the Estates to maintain a committee,
called the Defensors, to ensure the regents did not infringe the new privileges. Ferdinand grew impatient with the Defensors' constant criticism
and ordered them to disband. Incensed, the committee marched into the
castle and threw two of the leading regents, together with their secretary
out of the window on 23 May 1618. This 'Defenestration of Prague' was
highly symbolic, mirroring the action that had started the Hussite
national and religious revival movement 200 years before. The Bohemian nobles under Count Thurn replaced the regency council with a
provisional government of 30 members of the Estates.

Khlesl sought a compromise, but Ferdinand had him arrested.
He believed he now had firm grounds for a military solution, since the

Bohemians had broken the law and God would expect them to be punished. Within two months of the Defenestration, Ferdinand had assembled an army of 14,200 men virtually from scratch, under Count Bucquoy, a professional soldier from the Spanish Netherlands. This impressive response masked fundamental weakness, as the monarchy had not yet recovered from the debilitating effects of dynastic partition, civil and foreign war. Bucquoy advanced boldly on Prague, but had to turn back half way when the money ran out. Having raised an army of 17,000 from provincial levies and mercenaries, under Count Ernst Mansfeld, the Bohemians set off in pursuit. By December Bucquoy was urging Ferdinand to make peace. Three months later, the Bohemian forces had risen to 50,000, enabling them to invade Lower Austria and trap the Habsburg troops in Vienna, Budweis and Krems.[18]

Thurn and Mansfeld concentrated on extending their political alliance while blockading their opponents. The first step was the *Confoederatio Bohemica* of 31 July 1619, which represented a genuine attempt to form a federal state based on the aristocrat-dominated Estates. Bohemia gave up its attempts to assert primacy over Silesia, Moravia and the Lausitz, accepting these as equal partners in the new state. In August, the Bohemians extended their confederation to include Upper and Lower Austria, annulled Ferdinand's election as king and chose Frederick V in his place. Another agreement persuaded Bethlen Gabor to attack Habsburg Hungary from Transylvania and by November 1620 his forces joined the Bohemians before Vienna. Finally, these arrangements were consolidated on 25 April 1620 when Frederick, Gabor and the Bohemian and Austrian Estates reaffirmed their alliance and agreed to send a joint mission to seek Ottoman help.[19] These moves considerably raised the stakes. The Bohemian revolt had thrust deep into the Habsburg heartlands and thrown out tentacles into the Reich and the Balkans.

Ferdinand's diplomats were also busy in widening the scope of the conflict. He already enjoyed the support of the Spanish ambassador, Don Balthasar Zúñiga, who had pushed for closer cooperation between the two main branches of the Habsburgs since 1613. Reacting to the Brothers' Quarrel, Zúñiga proposed that Madrid should throw its weight behind one Austrian candidate as next emperor, in return for imperial assistance against the Dutch, and territorial concessions to Spain in Italy. Zúñiga chose Ferdinand and reached a preliminary understanding with him along these lines on 31 January 1617. Though he was recalled, his successor, Count Oñate, cemented the alliance in a secret treaty on 20 March 1617, securing additional concessions for Spain, including the transfer of the emperor's rights in Alsace. In return, Spain offered money and military assistance, initially for Ferdinand's local dispute with the Venetian Republic, but also offering the prospect of more substantial help once he had been elected emperor. Back in Spain, Zúñiga, now a member of the Council of State, responded to the Bohemian crisis by urging King Philip III to honour this agreement.

Family loyalty and confessional solidarity were only secondary considerations behind Spain's involvement. The Spanish government knew that its costly war against the Dutch would resume once the Twelve Years' Truce expired in 1621. If the Austrian Habsburgs collapsed, they would be unable to prevent German Protestants from assisting the Dutch. Frederick V's involvement in Bohemia was of particular concern, because his Lower Palatinate straddled the Spanish road along the Rhine. While Spain sent reinforcements and money to help Ferdinand directly, it concentrated its main effort in securing its vital lines of communication. Detachments from its garrison in Milan moved into the Valtelline passes over the Alps to secure the southern end of the Spanish road, triggering a series of bitter local conflicts there, particularly once France became involved. Another Spanish army assembled in Luxembourg to secure the northern end by occupying the Lower Palatinate.

Spanish assistance stabilised the situation, but for victory Ferdinand needed German help. Matthias had died before Ferdinand could engineer his election as successor. Frederick V seized the opportunity to link his dispute with the wider future of the Reich. Although his enemies were closing on Vienna, Ferdinand went to Frankfurt to persuade the assembled electors to grant him the imperial title. Despite the Bohemian crisis, the majority believed that only a Habsburg could restore peace, and accepted Ferdinand as emperor on 28 August 1619. The election restored Habsburg prestige and ended the division within the Austrian branch, since Ferdinand now held both the imperial title and formal possession of the main hereditary lands. As emperor he could use the full sanction of imperial law against his enemies and stood a good chance of rallying Catholics and moderate Protestants to his cause.

Ferdinand's strategy indicates the continued relevance of imperial institutions throughout the war. He based his position on his interpretation of the constitution, summoning assistance within the framework of the public peace and legitimising his military operations as the pacification of disorderly territories. The Spanish units invading the Lower Palatinate were officially termed soldiers of the Burgundian Kreis, to which Luxemburg and the southern Netherlands still belonged.

However, this worked the other way, since it enabled Spain and Ferdinand's other allies to present themselves as the executors of imperial
law and to demand appropriate recompense for their actions. This was
already noticeable in Ferdinand's agreements with Bavaria and Saxony,
which were to be the Habsburgs' main allies throughout the war.

Bavaria was a large, compact territory with a model administration
and a relatively full treasury. Duke Maximilian was conscious of his
heritage as a Wittelsbach and was determined to play a more prominent
role in imperial politics. He shared Ferdinand's Catholic convictions,
but he was not a militant and remained more pragmatic than his Calvinist relation, Frederick V. He looked back to the 1540s when Emperor
Charles V had faced opposition from the Schmalkaldic League of Protestant princes and cities. Charles had rewarded the Albertine Saxons
for their help in his victory of 1547 by giving them the electoral title of
their Ernestine cousins. Maximilian wanted Ferdinand to repeat this
and transfer the Palatine title to him in return for his help in defeating
the Bohemian revolt. He realised such an act would arouse widespread
hostility within the Reich and so insisted that Ferdinand agree to the
revival of the Liga by the Treaty of Munich on 8 October 1619. Maximilian did not see the Liga in purely confessional terms and would have
been prepared to admit moderate Lutherans as members. Rather than
constituting the military arm of a papal Counter Reformation, the Liga
was primarily a platform for Bavarian interests. These were primarily
defensive, since once he had received the electoral title, Maximilian
had no desire to prolong the war.[20]

The re-established Liga comprised a firm core of four main territories
and a looser periphery of around 14 ecclesiastical principalities along
with most of the Catholic Swabian prelates and counts. Maximilian
held the coordinating role as commander and director of the southern
group around Bavaria. His brother, Elector Ferdinand of Cologne, was
director of the Rhenish group, which included Mainz and Trier. Though
the Liga established an advisory council and held regular meetings, it
depended on Bavaria, which provided the bulk of its 25,000-strong
army under Jean Tserclaus Baron Tilly. This was funded by contributions from the members, who expected the soldiers to defend their own
lands, rather than attack Protestant territories.[21] The need to respect his
partners' concerns stiffened Maximilian's resolve to avoid widening the
war and to secure formal peacekeeping mandates from Ferdinand before
starting any operation.

The Saxons were even more cautious. They feared the Bohemian revolt would destabilise the entire Augsburgian settlement, undermining both the Reich and their prominent position within it. Saxony's leadership of the German Protestants depended on the 1555 Treaty, which had recognised Lutheranism and sanctioned the elector's possession of the secularised bishoprics of Meissen, Merseberg and Naumburg. The elector naturally inclined towards Ferdinand as the defender of the constitutional status quo and as head of the dynasty that had raised the Albertines to political prominence. He initially tried to broker a compromise along with Hessen-Darmstadt, the other leading moderate, but the more radical north German Protestants rejected Ferdinand's interpretation of the Bohemian revolt as a breach of the public peace. Once it became obvious that the emperor's improving military position offered Saxony some protection, the elector swung behind the Habsburgs. Like Maximilian, he sought imperial mandates sanctioning his invasion of Silesia and the Lausitz in 1620 as part of a wider process of pacification.[22]

The Habsburg counter-attack started in May 1620 as the emperor's forces invaded Lower Austria, while Maximilian and the Liga army attacked Upper Austria. The two united in September and turned on Bohemia, while 24,000 Spaniards under Ambrosio Spinola advanced from Luxembourg into the Lower Palatinate, and the Saxons occupied Silesia and the Lausitz. Reinforced by a small Spanish contingent, the combined imperial–Liga army of 24,800 met Frederick V's 23,000 on White Mountain outside Prague on 8 November. In little more than an hour, 4,000 of Frederick's troops were dead, the rest scattered and his royal ambitions in ruins.[23]

However, the Bohemians' defeat had deeper causes than Tilly's astute generalship and the emperor's superior forces. First, the revolt lacked an accepted ideological platform. The majority of influential Bohemians refused to abandon the traditional mixed monarchy of ruler and Estates. This tempered their faith in new resistance theories, since loyalty to a king remained an indispensable part of their political thinking.[24] Secondly, reluctance to replace elitist liberties with a broader liberty restricted their wider appeal. Unlike the Dutch rebels, or the English and Scottish parliamentarians after 1637, the Estates' aristocratic leadership failed to mobilise genuine wider support. The peasants' revolt in Lower Austria of 1595–7 was still fresh in their minds and they feared arming the rural population at a time when they were intensifying manorial lordship. Thirdly, they failed to construct central institutions comparable to the Dutch States General or the English and Scottish parliaments, leaving the rebel federation without a clear political centre. It proved difficult to develop a common policy across provincial and linguistic boundaries, particularly as the Transylvanians and Hungarians remained preoccupied with the Ottoman presence, while the Bohemians and Austrians were more concerned with imperial politics. Finally, each province was riven by internal political and confessional divisions. There was always a substantial Catholic minority who feared that a complete victory for the Estates would signal the end of their religious rights. Even Protestants had their doubts about the radical course adopted by Thurn and his associates.

Only a tenth of the Bohemian nobility participated in Frederick's election in August 1619. It took the arrival of Bohemian troops before the Moravian Estates declared for the federation in May 1619, and their leader, Karel of Žerotin, remained loyal to Ferdinand. György Drugeth de Homona, a Catholic Hungarian aristocrat and personal enemy of Bethlen Gabor, raised 11,000 Poles to attack Transylvania in November 1619. Divisions extended beyond animosity between Lutherans and Calvinists, to split individual families, like the Waldsteins (Wallensteins), Dietrichsteins, Kinskys, Kaunitzs and Černins. These confessional divisions cut across ethnic and linguistic boundaries, indicating the futility of interpreting the revolt as a proto-nationalist rising. Some Protestant leaders were Czechs, but so were the Catholic Lobkovic, Martinic and Slavata families, who remained loyal to the Habsburgs.

The consolidation of Habsburg authority after 1620

Ferdinand claimed the right of conqueror after White Mountain, arguing that his opponents had forfeited their privileges by taking up arms against him. None the less, he remained within what he regarded as the law, and he only sought to modify traditional institutions, not abolish them. The defeated Upper Austrian Estates were required to kneel before him on 16 April 1625 and beg forgiveness, yet Ferdinand restored their provincial privileges with only mild revisions. He did curb their powers to act independently, in a further decree on 28 January 1627, but respected their other key rights, notably over taxation. Bohemia was placed under military rule after 1620 until Ferdinand issued a revised constitution for its Estates in 1627. The Estates retained a role, but the kingdom was transformed into a hereditary monarchy and the king alone now decided key matters, like foreign policy and admissions to the aristocracy. The Letter of Majesty was revoked, and the practice of all faiths other than Catholicism and Judaism was prohibited. Saxon influence ensured Silesia retained its former privileges.

Military ascendancy paved the way for a radical restructuring of the provincial nobility along confessional lines. Here, the militants gained the upper hand as the Jesuits defeated Capuchin plans for limited toleration and conversion by persuasion and good example. Instead, reform commissions were sent into Bohemia, and Upper and Lower Austria, to impose a stark choice of conversion or exile. Around 50,000 people left Austria and another 200,000 were driven out of Bohemia, creating a huge pool of land that could be redistributed to loyalists (see section 6.1). Some of these were Protestants, indicating that Ferdinand did not push confessionalisation to extremes. He was also cautious in his dealings with Hungary and Transylvania, since he did not want to upset the Ottomans. Fortunately, the sultan had no desire to break the 1606 peace, because he was distracted by his own domestic problems and a new war with Persia (1623–39). The Hungarian palatine, as Ferdinand's representative and leader of the Estates, dealt directly with his Ottoman counterpart, the pasha of Buda, to resolve local difficulties and renew the 1606 peace.[25] Religious persecution was only one factor behind the expulsions and many left for economic or political reasons. A significant number of crypto-Protestants remained, particularly in rural areas, where villagers outwardly conformed to Catholic ritual, but practised their own beliefs at home. Ferdinand's successor, Ferdinand III, renewed efforts to impose uniformity in Bohemia and Austria during the early 1650s. Though this was continued after 1658 by Leopold I and extended to Hungary two years later, it met with considerable resistance and was never completely successful (see section 8.1).

Why the war continued

White Mountain destroyed the Estates confederation, but it did not end the war. Habsburg and Bavarian troops pursued the fugitive Frederick V westwards into the Reich. The Bavarians occupied the Upper Palatinate, which formed the other half of the elector's possessions, and which was forcibly re-Catholicised in 1622. Ferdinand transferred this along with the electoral title to Maximilian in 1623, while allowing Saxony to retain the Lausitz in lieu of its expenses incurred in 1620. Opposition continued as Frederick tried to raise the Protestant Union to assist him, but the response was ill-cordinated and hampered by the disparate ambitions of his allies. Margrave Georg Friedrich of Baden-Durlach raised a small army in the south-west in Frederick's name, but largely with the intention of securing his own regional influence. Mansfeld led the remnants of Frederick's own army on a long trek north-west with the vague intention of cooperating with the Dutch, while a third force was assembled by Christian of Brunswick, who had become the Protestant administrator of the bishopric of Halberstadt and hoped to remain there as prince. Ferdinand responded to these threats by extending his programme of pacification to the affected areas. The Spanish and Liga forces were issued with imperial mandates authorising them to restore order and, together with the emperor's own small army, they had little difficulty in defeating their scattered opponents by 1624.

Danish intervention provided the most immediate reason why the war continued beyond then. King Christian IV viewed Ferdinand's success with alarm, because he had joined other north German dynasties in appropriating additional ecclesiastical land after 1555 in contravention of the Augsburgian settlement. This was vital to his dynastic and strategic interests. He coveted the bishoprics of Bremen and Verden as appropriate establishments for his younger sons and as an outer buffer to protect the Danish peninsula. His control of the Baltic tolls filled his treasury and enabled him to raise a private army of 28,000 men. However, like Ferdinand, he based his intervention on imperial law, rather than religion, moving into north Germany in 1625 in his capacity as duke of Holstein and captain of the Lower Saxon Kreis, where he claimed he was needed to maintain order. Though reinforced by the remnants of the three Union armies, Christian was repeatedly defeated by imperial and Liga troops and had been driven back to the Danish islands by October 1627, where he held out before finally agreeing peace in the Treaty of Lübeck on 22 May 1629.[26]

Religion had little to do with shifting the war northwards, though militants on both sides did see the war in apocalyptic terms as a struggle fought not just to advance their own version of Christianity, but directly at God's behest and with the promise of his assistance in crushing the unbelievers. Victories were interpreted as proof of divine favour, while defeats were blamed on lack of resolve, and were used to criticise moderates for their sinful toleration of the other side. However, most Protestants and Catholics took a more moderate view of the war as intended to restore peace by compelling the other side to accept their interpretation of the Augsburgian settlement. This opened the door to possible concessions to secure acceptable terms and, though the extent to which they were prepared to grant these varied with the current military situation, compromise remained a constant principle. This pragmatic approach was not necessarily a more secular one than the militant position. Many moderates abhorred any prolongation of violence as a breach of their Christian duty to live at peace with their neighbours. For example, the Saxon elector refused to aid the Union territories in 1622 and used his powers in the Upper Saxon Kreis to prevent them recruiting more soldiers there. He also tried to mediate a compromise when Christian IV entered Lower Saxony in 1625.

Unfortunately, the war was developing its own internal dynamic, which made it harder to stop. The internal development of most German territories had reached a rough equilibrium by 1600, where further growth was impossible without more radical change. All the larger principalities had established systems of regular taxation, and had revised earlier militia systems to provide local defence (see sections 5.1 and 6.2). Ordinary revenue barely covered expenditure, particularly as all governments now faced the problems of rising population levels and pressure on scarce resources. The scope, duration and scale of war after 1618 broke all previous bounds, shattering this delicate equilibrium. Costs rose as it became obvious that professional mercenaries were better suited than territorial militias to the new methods of war. The Liga members alone spent 58.8 million fl. on military operations between 1620 and 1648, or more than the entire Reich during Rudolph II's reign. Such expenditure could only be met by desperate expedients. Emergency taxes only covered part of the shortfall, whilst fuelling the possibilities of domestic discontent and objections from the Estates.

Increasingly, all belligerents moved over to a system of 'offensive logistics', by seeking to make their enemies bear the brunt of the cost. This involved two forms of extortion, both called 'contributions'.[27] Either raiding parties threatened to burn towns and villages unless they provided food, clothing, horses and other materials, or more permanent garrisons held wide areas and diverted their normal taxes directly for military use. Both methods increased the scale of war by requiring additional troops beyond the 20,000–30,000 needed for a field army to attack enemy positions. The spread of operations into new areas added further commitments, fuelling a vicious circle of military expansion so that by the 1630s there were 300,000 men under arms in the Reich.

Ferdinand instrumentalised imperial law to legitimise contributions as a way to punish those who had breached the peace. This started in January 1621 when he placed Frederick V under the imperial ban. As an outlaw, the elector's lands and titles were forfeit, enabling Ferdinand to transfer them to his ally Maximilian. The procedure was extended in 1622 to cover Baden, Württemberg and other Protestant Union territories that failed to make peace in time. The resumption of Spain's war with the Dutch in 1621 spelt the end of Spanish subsidies to Austria at a time when Ferdinand's own resources were exhausted. The distinction between punishing rebels and simply seizing resources became blurred as the emperor widened the confiscation policy to fund his military expansion after 1625.

The extensive concessions to Bavaria and Saxony convinced Ferdinand that he could not be politically independent without a powerful army. An ambitious and enterprising Bohemian nobleman, Albrecht von Wallenstein (1583–1634), was contracted to raise an army of 24,000 men in 1625. Wallenstein was convinced that more were necessary to contain the Danish incursion, and had already mustered 40,000 by the end of the year. He assigned contracts to form regiments to a growing clientele of nobles and professional officers, who in turn subcontracted to their own contacts to raise the component companies. This system rested on Wallenstein's ability to sustain his contractors' faith that they would be paid. Ferdinand was soon unable to meet the growing demands and quickly lost control over his general, who widened the scope of operations to bring fresh areas within his contributions network. The emperor was compelled to grant him lands and titles in lieu, first making him duke of Friedland, a duchy created partly from estates confiscated from Bohemian rebels. Then he took the unprecedented step of enfiefing him with the duchy of Mecklenburg, which his troops had occupied in 1628.[28]

Wallenstein's meteoric rise to be prince of one of the oldest German duchies symbolised a world turned upside down by the violent conflict. Yet, it was but one cause of the growing controversy. The rapid expansion of Wallenstein's imperial army opened a rift between Ferdinand and his allies in the Liga. Whereas Tilly and the Liga army had formed the mainstay of the emperor's forces before 1625, they were outnumbered four to one by Wallenstein's troops two years later. The Liga declined from the status of ally to that of auxiliary as the imperialists gradually squeezed its lifeline by occupying the best quarters. Taxes from the membership could not make up the shortfall, and Tilly found his men defecting to imperial regiments, which enjoyed better pay and prospects. Disquiet amongst the Liga membership added to the growing criticism of Ferdinand's manipulation of imperial law to seize property without trial by labelling the owners 'notorious rebels' (see p. 48).

The Edict of Restitution, 1629

The confiscation policy compromised Ferdinand's efforts to restore peace through the Edict of Restitution on 6 March 1629, based on his interpretation of the Augsburgian settlement. This ordered the return of all ecclesiastical land that had been appropriated by the Protestants since 1555. At stake were nine north German bishoprics, which had passed into Protestant administration, including Bremen, Verden, Magdeburg and Halberstadt, as well as 500 abbeys and other institutions that had been incorporated within Protestant territories. The Edict was immediately controversial, given Ferdinand's confessional and confiscation policies since 1620 and the use of Wallenstein's troops to enforce it. It raised the spectre of imperial absolutism, by creating an opportunity for Ferdinand to extend the restructuring of his territorial nobility into the Reich. The Edict created a patronage bonanza, as Ferdinand could appoint new abbots, bishops and canons to administer the restored property.

None the less, it was not universally condemned, even by the Protestants. Though not required to surrender any land, Saxony joined Brandenburg in lodging a formal complaint, not least because the Edict had been issued without consulting the electors. However, Saxony did not contest the validity of the process in principle. It argued that the emperor was right to order the return of Catholic land that had been seized illegally. What it objected to was the way this was done using the army rather than by asking the *Reichskammergericht* to judge each case individually. The controversy deepened as Ferdinand intervened in the Franco-Spanish dispute over the succession to the duchy of Mantua in Imperial Italy later in 1629. Ferdinand again failed to consult the electors, raising fears that he was simply ignoring the constitution. Far from welcoming the Edict as a Catholic victory, Spain urged moderation, hoping that concessions might secure a German peace and permit Austria to assist in the war against the Dutch.[29]

The Regensburg congress, 1630

Thus, though he had defeated his military opponents by 1630, Ferdinand faced serious political challenges from his own allies. Led by Maximilian, the electors used their congress at Regensburg to force Ferdinand to make concessions. He was obliged to seek a negotiated settlement to the Mantuan dispute, leading to peace there by October. Wallenstein was dismissed and his army cut by a third. However, Maximilian did not want to lose his autonomy and so refused to merge the Liga and imperial armies. Instead, Tilly was named commander of both in November.

The dispute over command condemned the combined imperial–Liga forces to inactivity at a critical juncture. King Gustavus Adolphus of Sweden landed in Pomerania on 6 July 1630, initiating a resumption of the war. Maximilian had no desire to fight the Swedes unless they attacked Liga members. Though Gustavus Adolphus had only 14,000 men, Maximilian ordered Tilly to retire to Magdeburg, permitting the Swedes to widen their bridgehead and seek German allies.

Like Bavaria, Saxony had no desire for further fighting. The elector rallied the moderate Protestants in a new alliance formed at Leipzig on 12 April 1631 in an attempt to hold the ring between Ferdinand and Sweden. Saxony offered to help Ferdinand expel the Swedes, but only if he annulled the Restitution Edict and stopped the contributions system.

Swedish intervention

The Saxon Third Party had little chance in the face of Swedish determination to drive into Germany. Calvinist Hessen-Kassel had already begun raising an army in support before its landgrave declared openly for Sweden on 27 August 1631. This threatened the rear of Tilly's army around Magdeburg, forcing him to detach troops to the south. However, Tilly's retreat exposed Brandenburg, which was compelled to side with the Swedes on 21 June. Ferdinand authorised Tilly to use force if Saxony followed suit. Caught between the two armies, the Saxon elector chose what seemed the lesser of two evils and changed sides on 12 September. The Saxons joined the Swedes in time for their crushing victory over Tilly's army at Breitenfeld on 17 September. The imperial–Liga position deteriorated rapidly. By 1632 the Swedes held Franconia, Swabia and much of the Rhineland.

Arriving during the centenary celebrations for the Confession of Augsburg, the main statement of Lutheran faith, Gustavus Adolphus appeared the Protestant saviour come to rescue his German co-religionists from Catholic tyranny. Yet the king had only been invited by the council of the port city of Stralsund, which hoped to avoid occupation by the imperialists. His initial public statements deliberately played down any confessional aspect to his arrival. He had no desire to unite the German Catholics against him or antagonise France. Instead, he followed the Danish example and portrayed his intervention as a police action to bring order to the Reich, which the emperor had failed to do. This argument carried little weight once Sweden became more heavily embroiled in the fighting, and was dropped in favour of more open trumpeting of the Protestant cause. Gustavus Adolphus regarded this as essentially identical to his own strategic interests, which centred on security for his Baltic empire. Swedish power was parasitic in that it depended on tapping the wealth of others to sustain it. The king had already captured large parts of the Baltic shore from Poland and Russia in order to tax the bulk grain trade. He now aimed to extend his control to the north German ports as well.[30]

Once involved in Germany, the king was compelled to rely on contributions to fund his operations. Lacking the sanction of imperial law, he developed his own alternative system to justify the expropriation of German resources. Catholic land was seized both to supply the Swedish army and to reward Germans who supported it. As this system expanded, it began to undermine the Reich's fabric. The redistributed land was given as Swedish fiefs, while allies like Brunswick and Mecklenburg were obliged to renounce imperial overlordship and accept that of Sweden instead. The ultimate objective remains unclear, since the king's statements are ambiguous. There is some speculation that he planned to make himself a Protestant emperor. At the very least, he intended to reorganise his German sphere of influence into some more permanent dependency. These plans clearly exceeded Sweden's capacity and the king's death at the battle of Lützen in 1632 exposed the fragility of its position.[31]

Policy devolved to Chancellor Axel Oxenstierna, who dropped the ambitious plans in favour of more realistic objectives that were to guide Sweden's involvement until the end of the war. Essentially, Oxenstierna sought a safe way to extricate his country from Germany. For this he required what was termed 'satisfaction', or territorial concessions around the north German ports, where he could levy tolls to sustain the empire and pay off the army's mounting pay arrears. In addition, he looked for 'security' as a safeguard against potential Habsburg interference in the Baltic. To this end he marshalled the Protestant territories within the Swedish sphere of influence into the Heilbronn League on 23 March 1633. League members were obliged to pay contributions to sustain an army under Bernhard von Weimar to assist the Swedes under Count Horn. Saxony refused to join and the League was swiftly undermined when Oxenstierna switched the Swedish veterans to secure the north German ports, leaving the less effective elements to be defeated at Nördlingen in 1634.

The imperial recovery

The imperial victory was the first fruit of the emperor's recovery, which started tentatively after the setbacks of 1631–2. Ferdinand adopted a three-point plan to revive Habsburg influence and end the war. He would unite all imperial estates behind him, achieve military superiority and then drive the foreigners from the Reich, paving the way for a full restoration of the imperial constitution to its 'proper' form.[32] The first two steps were pursued in parallel from November 1631 when Wallenstein was reinstated as imperial commander, with wide powers to raise a new army and negotiate to detach Saxony from its new Swedish alliance. Wallenstein invaded Saxony in 1632, intending to force the elector to change sides. Gustavus Adolphus returned from the Rhineland with the main Swedish army and attacked the imperialists at Lützen on 16 November. Wallenstein's battered forces held their own, but withdrew that night. It was a tactical victory for the Swedes, but purchased at the high price of the king's death.

Ferdinand was unable to exploit the temporary disarray amongst his enemies, because Oxenstierna managed to regroup Sweden's allies into the Heilbronn League. More ominously, Wallenstein ignored orders to leave his positions in Bohemia and Saxony and did nothing to aid the beleaguered imperial garrisons in south Germany, which remained under pressure throughout 1633. The emperor began to suspect his commander was negotiating with the Swedes, Saxons and Bohemian exiles and was alarmed in January 1634 when Wallenstein demanded that all officers swear unconditional loyalty to him. Later that month, Ferdinand signed a secret order dismissing Wallenstein, and then authorised the use of force to arrest him for treason. The general was caught in his

quarters by a group of loyalist officers and murdered on 25 February.[33]
To the emperor's critics, this brutal act seemed further proof of imperial
tyranny. Yet, Ferdinand believed he was acting within the same law that
he had used to justify the confiscations policy. Wallenstein's removal was
also politically expedient, since he had become an obstacle to the imperial recovery plan, which depended on winning over the moderates by
allaying their fears of harsh military rule.

Spanish policy

The prospect of renewed Spanish aid made it easier to dispense with
Wallenstein. The end of the Twelve Years' Truce in 1621 coincided
with a change in the Spanish government following the accession of
Philip IV, and the rise of his powerful advisor the count-duke Olivares
from 1622. Olivares turned to Austria when his initial plan for a broader
European alliance against the Dutch failed. Austro-Spanish relations
underwent a fundamental shift between 1622 and 1659, with long-term
repercussions for the emperor's international position in the later seventeenth and early eighteenth centuries (see section 8.1). Initially the
stronger partner, Spain was slowly bled white by its prolonged conflicts
against the Dutch (till 1648), France (1635–59) and the Portuguese
(1640–67). Olivares was compelled to abandon the previously haughty
attitude to the Reich and seek a new understanding with Spain's Austrian cousins. Increasingly, Spain presented its Netherlands and north
Italian possessions as subordinate elements of the Reich, seeking imperial aid on the basis of the 1548 treaty, which obliged the emperor to
protect the Burgundian Kreis.[34]

Neither Ferdinand nor his Bavarian allies had any desire to become
involved in Spain's problems and resisted these overtures until the crisis
of 1632–3, when the Swedes controlled much of Germany and Wallenstein refused to follow orders. Other circumstances made Spanish
assistance less of a liability. Olivares began to think that a close alliance
with Austria would be counter-productive as it might induce France to
side openly with the Dutch. These fears seemed justified when France
attacked Spain's ally the duke of Lorraine, in summer 1633. Spain
now decided simply to divert reinforcements collecting in north Italy
away from the more direct route down the Rhine and to move through
southern Germany instead. This would offer temporary aid to Ferdinand, whilst allowing the Spanish to live at German expense and collect

additional recruits en route. It was this force of 15,000 men that contributed to the imperial victory at Nördlingen on 6 September 1634.

The battle encouraged closer cooperation and an Austro-Spanish alliance was signed on 31 October. Ferdinand recognised Spain's right to imperial aid for Burgundy, both agreed to collaborate against their respective rebels, and Olivares promised a cash subsidy to support the imperial army. The arrangement did little to improve Ferdinand's position. Concern for the security of their communications along the Rhine prompted Spain to arrest the elector of Trier on 26 March 1635 after he appealed for French protection.[35] France then declared war on Spain on 19 May, greatly increasing the pressure since its navy joined the Dutch in cutting the sea route to the Netherlands. Olivares realised that Spain could not win, and only continued the war to force the Dutch to return Spanish colonies and grant an honourable peace. He appealed for Austrian aid, arguing that the French had infringed imperial jurisdiction by occupying the Valtelline passes that March. Ferdinand was determined to avoid an open breach with France since this would derail his recovery plan. Spain would also need to withdraw its troops, whose presence in the Reich was deterring the moderate Lutherans from rallying behind him. He allowed Spain to take part of the imperial army into its direct pay, but otherwise refused further assistance.

French intervention

The outbreak of open Franco-Spanish warfare seriously damaged Ferdinand's chances of restoring peace to the Reich. Nördlingen precipitated the collapse of the Heilbronn League, destroying much of Sweden's German power base. Oxenstierna was prepared to compromise, already dropping demands for a full restoration of the elector Palatine and ready to recognise the new Bavarian electoral title. Unfortunately, as Sweden edged towards peace, France advanced to war.

French policy was steered by Cardinal Richelieu, who wanted to consolidate royal authority by gradually removing the autonomy extended to the Huguenots, or French Calvinists, as the price of ending the Wars of Religion in 1598. This was a difficult course to steer, since Richelieu had to avoid either handing the initiative to the radical Catholic zealots, or provoking a popular Huguenot rising. He had little desire to involve France in the German turmoil and used his influence to dissuade the Protestant Union from aiding Frederick V in 1620. The situation shifted by the early 1630s as the Huguenots had been crushed and royal authority had stabilised. Richelieu had viewed Ferdinand's successes in the 1620s with some alarm and decided to promote a neutral party within the Reich, capable of restraining the Habsburgs. He reached an initial understanding with Bavaria in the Treaty of Fontainebleau on 8 May 1631 as Maximilian was also keen to end the war. However, only Trier openly allied with France. Other German princes remained suspicious, fearing that such alliances could easily reduce them to dependency. Most rallied to the emperor after his victory at Nördlingen as he now seemed a better chance for peace than any external power. Imperial politics polarised again as the Protestant radicals remained defiant and renewed their alliance with Sweden. Richelieu was left with no choice but to move with the tide, extending loose cooperation with the Swedes from 1633 into a firm military alliance by 1635.

The Peace of Prague, 1635

Ironically, it was the very success of Ferdinand's recovery plan that increased the odds against him. Ferdinand's removal of Wallenstein permitted him to rally moderates of all persuasions into a new cross-confessional alliance. Agreements with Bavaria and Saxony paved the way. Both had tried to steer a middle course as heads of their own alliance systems. The Saxon-led Leipzig group had crumbled quickly in 1631, and though the Liga struggled on, it was clearly falling apart by 1634. Alarmed by the growing internationalisation of the war, Maximilian accepted the dissolution of the Liga as the price for closer cooperation with the emperor, agreed at Stuttgart on 19 November 1634. Saxony had never been happy at being coerced into alliance with Sweden and used Gustavus Adolphus's death as an opportunity to loosen its ties. Experience in 1631 had demonstrated the futility of trying to organise a neutral third party, so the elector accepted the inevitability of returning to his former alliance with the emperor. Conscious of his status as nominal Protestant leader, he secured limited concessions on religion, as well as permission to keep the Lausitz, in his preliminary treaty of Pirna in November 1634.

With Bavaria and Saxony on his side, Ferdinand proclaimed the Peace of Prague on 30 May 1635. The Edict of Restitution was suspended for forty years and could only be re-imposed if the princes agreed. A new normative date of 12 November 1627 replaced that of 1552, stipulated in the Augsburgian settlement. Protestants could keep church land held before that date, except for 14 Württemberg abbeys, where restitution remained in force. An amnesty was extended to all Lutheran rulers except those of Württemberg and Baden. Brandenburg was also included, but all other Calvinists were still considered enemies. Transfer of the Palatine lands and titles to Bavaria was upheld. All separate alliances, including the Liga, were formally abolished and all rulers told to place their field forces under imperial command. These units were to be combined with the surviving imperial soldiers as a new *Reichsarmada*, to number 80,000 men. The emperor was to have overall direction, though the Bavarian and Saxon electors were permitted autonomous commands of 20,000 men each. Later, a further segment of the new army was entrusted to Ferdinand of Cologne, the only prince to object to the abolition of the Liga.[36]

Ferdinand II now stood on firm ground, unlike France and Sweden, whose interference in the Reich rested on bilateral treaties with outlawed princes. The Prague system integrated leading Catholics like Bavaria, Mainz and Cologne, alongside prominent Protestants such as Saxony, Brandenburg and Hessen-Darmstadt. Ferdinand appealed to German patriotism to cement the alliance, calling on soldiers serving France and Sweden to stop fighting their fatherland. The electors did rally round, making Ferdinand (III) King of the Romans on 22 December 1636, thereby ensuring continuity of Habsburg rule when Ferdinand II died, on 15 February 1637.

By then, however, the Prague system was beginning to unravel. The choice of 1627 as normative date was unsatisfactory as it was the year of the imperial victory of Lutter am Barenberge, which had restored the north German bishoprics to Catholic control. The limited suspension of the Edict raised suspicions that the emperor would resume his partisan Catholic stance as soon as circumstances permitted. The exclusion of Calvinists from the amnesty weakened attempts to place German patriotism above confessional loyalty. With nothing left to lose, the Calvinist princes fought on as Sweden's only German allies. When Bernhard von Weimar died in 1639, the remnants of the old Heilbronn League army passed into French service. Resenting the loss of their north German bishoprics, the Guelph dukes resisted until 1642, when they were compelled to disband their army. Landgrave Wilhelm V of Hessen-Kassel still pursued his private feud with Lutheran Hessen-Darmstadt until imperial troops drove him out in 1637. His widow, Amalia Elisabeth, continued the struggle from a network of small forts across north-west Germany, where she survived by extorting contributions.[37]

While these pockets of resistance distracted the emperor's forces, the main problem remained Sweden. The Habsburgs seriously underestimated Swedish resilience. Thrown onto the defensive in 1634–6, the Swedes recovered by defeating an imperial army at Wittstock and had stabilised their position in north-east Germany by 1638. That March, they renewed their French alliance, with both parties agreeing not to make peace without the other. Another victory, at Chemnitz in April 1639, cleared the way for renewed thrusts into Bohemia and south Germany in 1640–1. France also recovered from initial setbacks when the imperialists nearly took Dijon in 1636, and by 1640 French forces were able to assist the Swedes by invading south-west Germany.

The new emperor, Ferdinand III, was unable to honour the promise to liberate the Reich. The extensive network of Swedish, French and allied garrisons denied him access to much of Germany. In particular, the Swedish occupation of Brandenburg after 1637 forced its elector to abandon the Prague system and make his own peace in July 1641. These problems weakened the new imperial army and forced it to continue the unpopular contributions as its only means of subsistence. A new Swedish offensive knocked out Saxony at the second battle of Breitenbach, in November 1642. The Swedes remained in Saxony until 1650, compelling the elector to leave the war in September 1645 and make his own peace the following April. Meanwhile, the French had occupied Alsace in August 1644 and pushed across the Rhine, forcing Bavaria to agree a truce in March 1647. Finally, Transylvania joined Sweden and attacked Hungary in 1645, opening a new eastern front.

Spain offered little help, because it would not intervene in the Reich unless the emperor made common cause against the Dutch. Any prospect of aid faded after the serious Spanish defeat at Rocroi in May 1643. Sweden's revival did prompt Denmark to declare war in 1643, but it was defeated within two years, effectively destroying its 'great power' pretensions and removing it as a major influence in north German politics for good.[38] Ferdinand III scraped together an army for one last push in 1645, but was defeated at Jankau in Bohemia on 6 March. Vienna was only saved because the Swedes were unable to cross the Danube. It was not enough to destroy the Habsburgs, but it did convince them that only major concessions could secure peace. The emperor sent secret instructions to Maximilian Count Trauttmannsdorff to open negotiations in Osnabrück in October 1645. The net gradually tightened. The last imperial–Bavarian field army was defeated at Zusmarshausen on 17 May 1648, by which time French, Swedish and Hessen-Kassel troops occupied 200 strategic towns, confining the emperor to Westphalia, parts of the Rhineland, Bavaria and Prague.

4.3   The Long Road to Peace

The peace process

The emperor's hopes of ending the war on his own terms faded as the Prague system crumbled. However, it also became clear to France and Sweden that, despite their growing military superiority, decisive victory remained beyond their grasp. The delay in reaching a settlement was due to the complexity of the issues and because all sides still believed further campaigns might improve their bargaining position.

The distinct character of the different European struggles produced three parallel sets of negotiations.[39] Spain and the Dutch had seriously considered peace as early as 1628 and began talks on 13 May 1646. France and Spain were already negotiating prior to their hostilities in 1635 and opened their discussions on 21 March 1646, while the emperor was in contact with the Swedes from before 1635. The spread of discussions raised hopes for a general European congress not only to settle the issues in hand, but to secure definitive peace for the entire continent. Pope Urban VIII (r.1623–44) pushed this idea, intending his mediation as the prelude to restoring Catholic unity throughout Europe. Catholic powers could not reject this offer outright, but Richelieu was determined to thwart it. He wanted to deal with Spain and Austria separately and so insisted that France's Protestant allies be included in any general congress. As it was impossible for Urban to accept this, the planned congress collapsed and the papacy played no part in the final settlement.

Though this underlined the decline of papal influence in imperial politics, it proved impossible to end the German war without accepting other external interference. Tentative talks opened in Cologne in 1637 as it became obvious that the Peace of Prague could not be maintained. Discussions continued in Lübeck the following year, where Maximilian hoped Ferdinand III would end the war by making concessions. However, the emperor tried to avoid this by calling the Reichstag, which opened for the first time in 28 years in Regensburg on 13 September 1641. He still wanted to base a final settlement on the Peace of Prague and asked the Reichstag to grant new financial assistance to secure this. The lesser territories had been denied a voice by the emperor's preference for dealing exclusively with the electors since 1613. Once they had assembled, the princes were determined to remain part of the peace process and Ferdinand found it impossible to keep his German negotiations separate from those with his external foes. Though the Reichstag closed later in 1641, it appointed a committee, which met in Frankfurt in 1642–5 to prepare peace talks for the Reich. Once these started, the three colleges held separate discussions throughout 1645–9 in what was 'a Reichstag in all but name'.[40]

The Lübeck congress of 1638 had moved to Hamburg with Danish mediation and concluded an important preliminary treaty on 25 December 1641. Austria, Spain, France and Sweden agreed to send representatives to the two Westphalian cities of Münster and Osnabrück to discuss a *pax universalis*. The two venues were declared neutral ground by all parties, who kept their troops out of the area. The Catholic delegations convened in Münster, while the Protestants assembled in Osnabrück, keeping in touch by a regular courier service. The initial discussions decided the agenda and two sets of parallel talks began in earnest in 1643 to resolve problems between Spain, France and the Dutch on the one hand and France, Sweden and the Reich on the other. The scope of the conflict drew in other participants until there were 194 envoys representing 16 European countries, 140 imperial territories and 38 other interested parties, with only Russia, England and the Ottomans not present.

The Treaties of Münster and Osnabrück

The first group of talks dragged on inconclusively as France and Spain could not agree. Eventually, Spain settled its scores with the Dutch in the Treaty of Münster (*Instrumentum Pacis Monasteriense* – IPM) on 30 January 1648, formally renouncing its sovereignty over the seven northern provinces. The Dutch Republic was now effectively an independent state, though the Reichstag still formally regarded it as part of the Burgundian Kreis until 1728.[41] As the Franco-Spanish war continued, the IPM deliberately excluded Burgundy from its terms as it was still considered part of the war zone. The emperor was also forbidden to assist Spain, in order to preserve the German settlement and prevent a resumption of general warfare. Though Ferdinand III covertly sent some troops to assist the Spanish in northern Italy, he recognised the importance of keeping the peace and the Burgundian lands remained outside the German settlement until France and Spain made peace in 1659.

The other discussions were more fruitful and produced the Treaty of Osnabrück (*Instrumentum Pacis Osnabrugense* – IPO) on 24 October 1648, ending the war in Germany. The constitutional questions were decided surprisingly quickly. The Hamburg Peace Preliminaries had already removed the major obstacle in 1641 by ruling that the imperial estates were to participate in the negotiations. The emperor could no longer claim an exclusive right to represent the Reich and had to acknowledge that the estates shared in the exercise of imperial prerogatives. As these arrangements already implied recognition of territorial sovereignty (see section 2.1), even Catholics like Maximilian joined Sweden and France in forcing Ferdinand to accept this as Article VIII by 1645.

It took another three years to agree the other issues, because there was still little agreement over religion or the 'satisfaction' and 'security' demanded by Sweden and France. The latter problem was particularly serious, because France, Ferdinand and especially Sweden could not disengage without settling their armies' huge pay arrears.

The religious settlement

As imperial ambassador, Trauttmannsdorff sought a swift resolution to the religious questions in order to rally all Germans in a united front to reduce Franco-Swedish demands. The Protestant response depended as much on politics as on confession. Moderates, such as Saxony and Hessen-Darmstadt, generally supported Trauttmannsdorff, especially where they had already achieved their political goals and wanted to secure these in a definitive peace. Militants opposed him, but mainly because they had yet to capture their objectives and, like Hessen-Kassel and the Ernestine Saxons, hoped to delay matters and win foreign support. The Catholics were initially more united, until it became obvious that the emperor was prepared to make concessions on matters of faith, when they split into zealots and moderates. While the former were personally sincere in their defence of religion, Catholic objectives were central to their own political goals. The leading zealots were Franz Wilhelm von Wartenberg, who held four north German bishoprics that were likely to be returned to the Protestants, and Adam Adami, who was abbot of one of the re-Catholicised Württemberg abbeys. Though numerous, the zealots had little political weight and were marginalised by the moderates, who generally ruled larger territories. Some, like Bavaria and Cologne, accepted concessions as the price for securing their wartime gains. Others believed in more genuine reconciliation as the basis of a lasting peace. The election of Johann Philipp von Schönborn as elector of Mainz in 1647 signalled that the latter group was gaining ground. Schönborn was already bishop of Würzburg and so held some of the most important lands of the imperial church. Though he was determined to defend the Catholic character of the Reich, he recognised the Protestants as fellow Christians and sought a practical basis for collaboration.[42]

Ferdinand's willingness to give ground on the Edict of Restitution paved the way for the settlement of the religious issues in Article V. This extended the terms of the Peace of Prague by permanently suspending the Edict and shifting the normative date from 1627 to 1 January 1624, a period before the Catholic confiscations had begun to bite. Unlike the Augsburgian settlement, the new arrangements were clearly intended to be definitive. Paragraph I of Article V accepted that the religious schism was permanent, but also signalled an end to revanchism. There was to be no possibility of militants undermining the treaty by trying to convert others to their faith. Protestants were granted full rights, rather than mere recognition, and these were extended to Calvinists as well as Lutherans. Though Wartenberg and Adami protested to the pope, who lodged a formal protest, the treaty already pre-empted this by declaring that it remained valid whatever the papacy later decided.

The right of reformation introduced in 1555 was restricted, to safeguard the permanency of the new settlement. Territories were henceforth designated as Protestant or Catholic according to their predominant religion in 1624. Their rulers were still free to convert, but could no longer compel their subjects to follow suit. Minorities who had existed in 1624 received the formal protection of imperial law, breaking the earlier insistence that political stability required religious conformity. In addition to four bi-confessional imperial cities, there were substantial recognised minorities in the Palatinate, Osnabrück, Jülich, Berg, Cleves, Mark, Ravensberg, Minden, Erfurt and the bishopric of Lübeck. These arrangements were extended to the imperial cities and knights, whose position was ambiguous in the Augsburgian settlement. The only exception was the Habsburg monarchy, where the emperor was given a free hand to continue his Catholic confessionalisation, apart from in Silesia where a Protestant minority received legal safeguards.

Despite the more favourable normative year, Protestants remained a political minority because there were far more territories officially recognised as Catholic, particularly in the still numerous church lands. Additional safeguards were introduced to allay the feelings of Protestant insecurity that had helped undermine the Augsburgian settlement. Religious parity was introduced into imperial institutions, including the *Reichskammergericht*, charged with adjudicating confessional disputes, though not the emperor's *Reichshofrat*. It was expected that the Reichstag and Kreis assemblies would still take decisions by majority vote. However, to protect Protestants, a system known as *itio in partes* was introduced for the Reichstag to permit discussions in two confessional blocks, or *corpora*, rather than the three colleges, where the Catholics had a permanent majority. These arrangements were intended only for matters touching religion and were designed to encourage decisions by mutually acceptable compromise.

The right of emigration granted in 1555 was revised to introduce the degree of flexibility necessary to make the rest of the religious settlement work in practice. A range of personal freedoms was extended to dissenters, including those who had lacked formal minority rights in 1624. Religion could not serve as ground to exclude people from corporations, guilds, societies, inheritance, hospitals or burial. Dissenters were allowed to send their children to schools in neighbouring territories, if there were none available locally. People living in areas where their faith had not been recognised in 1624 could still be expelled, but now only after being given extensive notice and permission to take their possessions with them. They were also granted the right of voluntary emigration, without the obligation to pay special customs duties.[43]

Security and satisfaction

Opposition from the militants forced Trauttmannsdorff to start negotiations with France and Sweden before the religious settlement was complete. France seized the opportunity to extract territorial concessions, weakening the Habsburg presence along the Reich's western edge. Austria surrendered its hereditary possessions in Alsace, and the two strategic fortresses of Breisach and Philippsburg guarding the Upper Rhine. In addition, the emperor was obliged to confirm French possession of the cities and bishoprics of Metz, Toul and Verdun, originally taken in 1552. These terms assisted the French goal of dividing the Habsburgs, since Spain regarded Austria's concessions as a betrayal of its security interests along the Rhine.

Trauttmannsdorff was unable to effect a similar rift between France and Sweden and was obliged to make additional concessions to the latter as well. Sweden was permitted to convert its north German garrisons into permanent possessions, giving it most of Pomerania, the port of Wismar and the former church lands of Bremen and Verden, which were now secularised. Sweden repaid Brandenburg for having abandoned the emperor in 1641, by promoting its claims. Ferdinand was compelled to grant Brandenburg the rest of Pomerania, plus the secularised bishoprics of Minden, Halberstadt and Kammin, and the expectation of receiving Magdeburg as well once its current Protestant administrator died.[44] This was a major blow for the Saxons, who had hoped to retain Magdeburg and receive Halberstadt. The Hohenzollerns' rise was magnified by the failure of the Guelphs, the other great north German dynasty, to make comparable gains. However, it was impossible to predict that Brandenburg would emerge to challenge Habsburg power. Ferdinand's concessions made sense from the perspective of the 1640s. They were not enough to make Brandenburg the dominant regional power, but were sufficient to strengthen it as a bulwark against Sweden. In particular, the division of Pomerania ensured that Brandenburg and Sweden would be preoccupied with their own local rivalry and unable to disrupt the Habsburg sphere of influence in central and southern Germany.

Saxony could not object because it was still occupied by Swedish troops. Though it retained the Lausitz from the Habsburgs, it was denied any further territory. The religious terms represented another failure, since the elector had hoped to defend his traditional leadership of the German Protestants by opposing full recognition of Calvinism. The inclusion of Calvinism in the peace redoubled the impact of Brandenburg's territorial gains, since the Hohenzollerns were now the major Calvinist dynasty.

The Palatinate lost its position as the other Protestant leader. Though the elector recovered the Lower Palatinate from Spain, Bavaria retained the Upper Palatinate, thus cutting his territorial base by half. Bavaria also kept the Palatine electoral title that was ranked fifth, while a new eighth title was created to compensate the Palatinate (see section 2.2). The other fugitive Protestant princes were restored in Baden-Durlach, Württemberg and Hessen-Kassel.

Implementation

The peace negotiations reflected the causes and course of the war in that the separate conflicts were settled in parallel discussions in which religious issues remained subordinate to political concerns. There were no coherent confessional parties, and the zealots' hopes that the emperor would join France against the heretics proved as illusory as the militants' belief that the German Protestants would swing solidly behind Sweden. Furthermore, while foreign powers influenced both the fighting and its resolution, they did not dictate the final settlement, which remained fundamentally a German solution to a German problem.

France and Sweden regarded the Reich as simply an extension of the emperor's hereditary power base and accordingly tried to weaken imperial authority in the peace treaty. They promoted plans to forbid elections of successive emperors from the same dynasty and to end the practice of choosing a King of the Romans during the lifetime of an incumbent emperor. Regardless of confession, the princes joined the emperor in rejecting these proposals. They regarded the Reich as a wider political community, in which they had a stake. They had no wish to destabilise the process of succession, since this would only provide further opportunities for unwelcome foreign interference. They were determined to ensure the success of the settlement and agreed to postpone the remaining constitutional problems as 'unfinished business' (*negotia remissa*), to be decided by a future Reichstag. By accepting this, Ferdinand III restored some faith in Habsburg leadership and signalled the Reich's determination to shape its own future free of external interference.

Though France and Sweden were recognised as the guarantors of the Peace of Osnabrück, this gave them only limited formal rights to intervene. Any imperial estate was permitted to appeal to either of the guarantors if it had been denied justice by the emperor or imperial institutions, but could only do so after a delay of three years. The revival of the imperial supreme courts under Leopold I after 1658 reduced the likelihood of this clause being invoked (see section 5.2). External interference was also checked by the divergent interests and development of the two guarantors after 1648. French policy was now directed by Cardinal Mazarin, who was primarily concerned to prevent German affairs disrupting his domestic policy and the ongoing war with Spain.[45] He refused to accept the land obtained from Austria as imperial fiefs, since this would imply the emperor retained jurisdiction and remained superior to the king of France. In order to detach them from the Reich, Mazarin had to relinquish their associated imperial rights, including representation in the Reichstag. Subsequent French interference in the Reich rested on practical military and diplomatic power, rather than rights under the imperial constitution, reflecting France's ambitions to displace the Habsburgs as the pre-eminent European monarchy.

   This contrasted with Sweden, which, while remaining a major European power until 1721, was already over-stretched and beginning to decline. Sweden accepted its new German possessions as imperial fiefs, thereby gaining full constitutional rights, including representation in the Reichstag and Upper and Lower Saxon Kreise.[46] This appeared to strengthen Swedish influence, since it could play a direct role in imperial and regional politics. However, in contrast to Gustavus Adolphus's plans to reorganise the Reich, Sweden was now formally the emperor's vassal, and not the other way round. Sweden failed to secure full judicial autonomy for its new possessions, which remained under the jurisdiction of the imperial courts. As Sweden declined, its dependence on the Reich increased, and it relied on its constitutional rights to protect rather than extend its German possessions.

   Immediate external influence was stemmed by demobilisation and withdrawal of the foreign armies. The signatories of the Peace of Osnabrück met again at a special congress in Nuremberg in 1649–50 to 'execute' the peace. Their task was complicated by the ongoing Franco-Spanish war and the exclusion of the Burgundian Kreis from the Osnabrück settlement. The Spanish retained their garrisons in the Rhineland until 1659. Though the Dutch held on to some positions on their eastern flank until 1679, they did evacuate their major Westphalian garrisons during the early 1650s. The French also pulled back into their new possessions. The emperor still had two armies totalling 49,000 men. He withdrew these quickly into his own lands to demonstrate his intention to adhere to the peace. Most of the soldiers were paid off using Habsburg taxes, but around 25,000 were retained as the nucleus of a permanent army. Though smaller than Wallenstein's great host, this force was none the less larger than that maintained before the war and was far larger than the small bodyguards of the other German princes, who had also paid off their wartime forces (see section 6.2). Removal of the 60,000 Swedes was more difficult since they were still owed years of back pay and their government hoped to use their continued presence to improve its position in northern Germany. The delegates at Nuremberg approved a levy of 5 million tlr from all imperial estates, to settle the army's demands, and the troops had been withdrawn by 1652.[47] Swedish attempts to hold on to parts of Pomerania were rebuffed by the emperor in Brandenburg's favour, while the north German princes also rallied behind the Habsburgs to prevent the Swedes seizing the city of Bremen in 1654 and 1666.

   The condemnation of later nationalist historians was not reflected in contemporary celebrations of the Westphalian settlement as a 'German peace'. This response was not instantaneous, since many initially doubted that the treaty signed in Osnabrück would prove any more durable than that made in Prague. However, confidence grew by 1650 as the soldiers left and people returned to abandoned farms and houses. Of the 204 public festivities staged across Europe in 1648–50, 180 took place within the Reich, underlining that, for those who survived it, the Thirty Years War was essentially a German war.[48]

4.4 Legacy

Demographic and psychological impact

The rhetoric of death and destruction looms large in all assessments of the Thirty Years War. It was already present by the 1630s as territorial governments began to collect statistics recording depopulation, reduced livestock and abandoned land. For example, the district around Gotha in Thuringia reported in 1638 that the number of inhabitants had fallen by two-thirds since 1618, half the houses had been destroyed and only a quarter of the horses and less than a tenth of the cattle were left. The worst case was the city of Magdeburg, which had been stormed and pillaged by Tilly's imperialists on 10 May 1631. Contemporaries reported up to 20,000 civilian deaths and an official census recorded only 449 surviving inhabitants.[49] The standard assessment of the total losses is that made by the German historian Günther Franz in 1941, that Germany lost around a third of its inhabitants, with urban areas experiencing a 30% decline against 40% in the countryside, and some territories like Mecklenburg and Württemberg losing up to two-thirds of their pre-war population.[50]

These figures are still disputed, partly because they have been manipulated by later historians to present the war as a tragedy thrust upon an unfortunate Germany by evil foreigners. The fact that Franz was a member of the Nazi party has not inspired confidence in his calculations. A more fundamental problem is the genuinely ambiguous nature of the surviving evidence. Many of the contemporary reports were clearly exaggerated by communities eager to find excuses to have taxes and other burdens reduced. Not everyone who left an area necessarily died, since many fled to safety elsewhere, or joined the army and other itinerant populations. This is already reflected in Franz's figures, which record a smaller decline for the towns where many peasants sought refuge. Some cities, such as Hamburg, clearly profited from the conflict and experienced a net gain overall. However, few now accept the extreme revisionism of S. H. Steinberg, who claimed in 1966 that Germany's population actually continued to rise during the war. The best current estimates suggest a decline of 15% to 20% overall, with some regions experiencing heavier losses, while others had a net gain. Uncertainty still surrounds these figures because of the anachronistic national focus of much historical demography, which calculates populations for regions defined by their later political boundaries. The Reich contained major non-German areas like the Bohemian lands and the Netherlands, which saw heavy fighting and prolonged occupation, as did Ducal Prussia, which lay beyond the Reich, but was governed from within it.[51]

More recent research has shifted attention away from the calculation of casualties towards the psychological impact on participants and survivors. Material factors lay behind much of the violence and the long duration of the conflict. The system of contributions has been aptly labelled a 'tax of violence' since it involved extortion and intimidation to extract resources from friendly, neutral and enemy populations.[52] While soldiers generally plundered because they had no other means of subsistence, their actions were governed by more than mere material necessity. Plundering was a recognised part of warfare and used systematically to deny resources to the enemy. The accompanying violence was also often part of a deliberate strategy of terror to intimidate a hostile population. However, brutality was also fuelled by religious animosities and mutual hatred between peasants and soldiers.

The latter was neither inevitable, nor a sign of some supposed populist rejection of a conflict benefiting only kings and princes. Most soldiers were previously peasants and most returned to the rural world when demobilised. The nature of military requisitioning encouraged violence. Soldiers moved in large groups, whose numbers were swollen by attendant unarmed camp followers who provided essential support services, including medical care. They often appeared unannounced and needed immediate food, lodging and firewood. Given that an average regiment was as large as a single village, military demands threatened peasants' survival, especially as few families had substantial reserves. Linguistic difficulties could raise the tension, notably in the case of the Croats serving with the imperial armies, who were often accused of using force to take what they needed. However, contemporary accounts frequently describe how soldiers took obvious pleasure in torturing peasants to

reveal hidden stores of food and valuables. Such brutality was the soldiers' response to their own insecurity. Their social status had declined
steadily since 1570 as their pay was reduced and disciplinary codes
curtailed their personal freedoms and corporate autonomy. The authorities' inability to maintain even the reduced pay rates during the war
both undermined official control and reduced soldiers' status still
further. Violence was a way of asserting themselves over a society that
despised them.[53]

Despite the brutality, there was no widespread breakdown of social
order. Religion appears to have been a major factor in sustaining survival. All Christian confessions encouraged stoic resignation to the present
difficulties as a trial sent by God to test faith, whilst offering hope that
justice would eventually triumph and deliver Germany from its purga-
tory.[54] It also has to be stressed that the war affected most parts of the
Reich only intermittently. Even where troops were stationed for long
periods, there was not necessarily constant fighting. The existence of
real violence lent credibility to tales of destruction, but did not mean
that this was universal. The spread of official and popular forms of political communication ensured the dissemination of stories, both true and
false. Increasingly, descriptions of torture and other horrors assumed a
standardised form, incorporating elements of earlier accounts. While
these magnified the extent of the physical damage, they accurately
reflected the psychological impact. There was widespread acceptance,
including amongst those who ruled, that the war was a disaster that
had inflicted real damage. The task of post-war government would be
to prevent a return to such disorder.

Economic impact

Discussion of the war's economic impact mirrors the controversy surrounding the demographic effects. The traditional view was that the
war retarded German trade, especially industry, and deprived the country of the chance of participating in the contemporary colonial boom
that benefited western Europeans. This attempt to blame foreigners for
later economic difficulties is not sustained by more recent research.
There was no national economy and the war affected each region differently. Many areas were already experiencing difficulties before 1618,
while some of the hardest hit by the fighting, like Saxony, Silesia and
the Rhineland, were at the forefront of later industrial development
(see section 3.3).

The primary reason behind the earlier decline of some regions was the general shift in European trade towards the Atlantic seaboard. This had benefited Spain, Portugal, France, Britain and the Dutch, all of whom started their maritime and colonial activity in the late fifteenth or early sixteenth century. Geography placed the Reich at a disadvantage and Germans already had little scope for colonial ventures prior to 1618. The limited impact of the war in this respect is demonstrated by the experience of Courland, the other former Crusading Order state that joined Prussia in falling under Polish sovereignty in the sixteenth century. The conflict did not prevent Courland becoming a major player in West Indian trade after 1638, despite its location at the eastern end of the Baltic.[55]

Attempts by German rulers to follow suit foundered on local difficulties as much as on the hostility of established colonial powers. Duke Friedrich III of Holstein-Gottorp founded the new town of Friedrichstadt in 1621, hoping to attract enterprising Dutch settlers and engage in overseas trade. The project met resistance from other Gottorp towns, which feared for their own trade, and was abandoned after North Sea floods swept over Nordstrand island in 1634. Later ventures faired little better. The Great Elector joined the other European slave traders by establishing the Brandenburg African Company in 1682. The Company received powerful state backing, including the transfer of most of the elector's fledgling navy and the despatch of troops to protect its outposts in the Gold Coast, Mauritius, and St Thomas in the West Indies. Brandenburg marines also occupied Emden to secure a home base with access to the western seas. However, the Company never prospered, and sold its West African bases to the Dutch in 1718. Some efforts were made to restart it in 1752 as a trading and transport company, but like the Habsburg companies founded in Ostend and Trieste during the early eighteenth century, it never succeeded against better-established British, Dutch and French competitors.

The westward shift in European trade also contributed to the relative decline of many German towns and imperial cities during the seventeenth century. However, there were often other, more immediate reasons for this. German princes imposed tighter political control on their territorial towns and encroached on the autonomy of neighbouring imperial cities. The Thirty Years War indirectly assisted this by impairing the ability of the imperial courts to intervene. However, Donauwörth's experience remained an exceptional case and all the other cities retained their autonomy in the IPO. Their relative economic decline was due more to their own innate conservatism, compounded by often chaotic and inefficient financial management. Wartime demands for contributions added to this, but did not cause the basic problems. South German cities were poorly placed to respond to changing market forces and suffered competition not only from foreign goods, but from those produced in Saxony, Silesia, Westphalia, northern Bohemia and the Rhineland before the war disrupted trade routes. Many faced additional competition from their own rural hinterlands by the mid-seventeenth century with the spread of rural crafts. This relative stagnation was not peculiar to Germany, as continued rapid urban growth between 1600 and 1750 was restricted to Europe's 50 largest cities, while the population of the continent's other 600 medium towns remained static.[56]

The Reich experienced an economic depression from 1648 to 1720, the basic contours of which mirrored that following the fourteenth-century demographic crisis. The decline in population relaxed pressure on resources, resulting in falling grain and land prices at a time when the surviving workers could demand better wages. The poorer sections of society experienced real benefits as their access to land improved. However, this intensified the practice of partible inheritance in the south and west, storing up problems for when population levels rose again, while the manorial economy was consolidated in the east (see section 3.3). While agriculture recovered relatively quickly, trade had suffered. Renewed inflation followed in 1667–90, though this was not as damaging as that experienced in 1618–23, and trade picked up from the 1680s. Some cities were already recovering in the 1630s, either by specialising in high-value goods, such as jewellery and cotton-printing in Augsburg, or by reorienting towards major industries like textiles and hardware in Nuremberg, Fürth and Erlangen. Some regions profited from the misfortunes of others, while others expanded on the back of growth elsewhere. For example, the Dutch concentration on shipbuilding, maritime and colonial trade created demand for other goods that was met by neighbouring Westphalia, which supplied cattle, corn, wood, linen and increasingly iron and coal.

None the less, the recovery was slow, not only because of the deep impact of the war, but also through the persistence of other adverse factors. Climatic conditions remained unfavourable and indeed worsened in 1693–1709. War resumed, initially in the Baltic (1655–60), and then with prolonged struggles in the west (1672–1714) and east (1683–99). Military operations consumed valuable capital that could have been invested in development. Further problems followed the mid-eighteenth-century wars, particularly the Seven Years War of 1756–63. Often, it was not so much the problems themselves but the way governments responded with protectionist measures and the distribution of privileges to key social groups in order to retain their allegiance (see section 7.1).

Secularisation and reconfessionalisation

Most surveys conclude that the Peace of Westphalia signalled an end to Europe's religious wars and the beginnings of secular politics in the Reich. These conclusions rest largely on the writings of earlier German Protestants, who argued that the IPO resolved the causes of war by giving Lutherans and Calvinists full parity with Catholics. Protestant celebrations of the Peace initially concentrated on a ritualised confrontation with the horrors of a still recent past. Over time, their purpose shifted as they became fixed elements in civic consciousness and identity, particularly for the citizens of the Protestant imperial cities. These public ceremonies, with their processions of singing schoolchildren and speeches from local worthies, persisted long after the Reich: Augsburg's practice of celebrating on 8 August is still marked as a local public holiday today. Such festivities had become more consciously Protestant by the mid-eighteenth century, marking a confessionalised interpretation of the conflict as a struggle against Catholic tyranny. Gustavus Adolphus, who had till then been largely ignored, now became a Protestant folk hero who saved German liberty. These attributes were transferred to Frederick the Great, who became a new Protestant champion valiantly defending 'true' German interests against Catholic Habsburg oppression. For example, Catholics in Schwäbisch-Gmünd and Isny burnt straw effigies of the Prussian king, while Protestant schoolchildren fought street battles against their Catholic rivals in nearby bi-confessional Biberach.[57]

This confessional dimension to eighteenth-century Austro-Prussian rivalry has led some historians to question whether the IPO really took religion out of imperial politics.[58] Some evidence suggests that religious tensions resurfaced soon after the Peace. Like the Augsburgian settlement, the IPO failed to define what constituted a 'religious question', casting doubt on the efficiency of the new constitutional safeguards given to the Protestants. The Protestants claimed a unilateral right to invoke the mechanism of *itio in partes* at the Reichstag, but this was rejected by the Catholics, who insisted both parties had first to agree

whether a matter touched religion. The first test of the new arrangements came in 1685 when the Catholic Pfalz-Neuburg line inherited
the Protestant Palatinate. The Reich defended this succession against
French counter-claims during the Nine Years War (1688–97), but the
new elector, Johann Wilhelm, collaborated with the French to insert
Article IV into the concluding Peace of Rijswijk in 1697. This confirmed
the reintroduction of Catholicism in those areas that had been occupied
by French forces during the war. German Protestants reacted with
alarm, partly because the French king, Louis XIV, had already driven
the Huguenots from France in 1685, but primarily because the guarantor
power was conniving in the first breach of the normative year specified
in the IPO.[59] The controversy persisted, because the 1714 peace settlement ending the subsequent War of the Spanish Succession confirmed
the Rijswijk clause.

German Protestants felt increasingly beleaguered, particularly as
Sweden's decline by 1721 removed their traditional sponsor, while
31 leading princes converted to Catholicism between 1652 and 1769,
including the rulers of Saxony (1697), Württemberg (1733) and Hessen-
Kassel (1754). Each ruler was obliged to issue formal guarantees, known
as *Reversalien*, protecting his subjects' faith and religious institutions.
None the less, the changes tended to revive religion as a local political
issue, particularly if it became embroiled in renewed ruler–Estate conflicts as in Württemberg. The bi-centenary of the Reformation (1717)
heightened sensibilities and coincided with renewed Catholic confessionalisation in the Palatinate, where the new elector, Carl Philipp
(r.1716–44), converted the Calvinist court chapel in Heidelberg to
Catholic use.

The positions held during the decades immediately preceding the
Thirty Years War were now reversed. Whereas late sixteenth-century
German Protestantism was a confident, rising force, its early eighteenth-century adherents were on the defensive and sought to preserve
the status quo against Catholics, who extrapolated new rights from
existing laws to change the IPO in their favour. Article VII of the IPO
had been drawn up to regulate the possible coexistence of Calvinists and
Lutherans in the same territory. Some Catholics argued that this also
extended to Catholic minorities in Protestant territories, who should
enjoy equal rights, including public worship. The solidly Lutheran
Württemberg Estates suspected their new Catholic duke, Carl Alexander (r.1733–7), of trying to introduce this *Simultaneum*, which they
regarded as illegal. The prince of Hohenlohe-Waldenburg used his

small army to try and impose it on his own lands after his conversion to Catholicism in 1728.[60]

The Protestants responded by activating their rights under the IPO to unite as a single *corpus evangelicorum* for political action in the Reichstag and other imperial institutions after 1712. Catholics saw the new corpus as a direct threat to the Reichstag's traditional structure since it levelled the distinctions between electors, princes, lords and cities, by grouping them in a single body. The emperor saw it as an attack on his prerogatives, since the confession of his own lands implied he was simply a member of the Catholic corpus. The Habsburgs reacted with growing hostility as the Protestant corpus began intervening diplomatically in local disputes involving religion within the Reich.

The Habsburgs had struggled to recover their influence after 1648 by presenting their imperial policy as benevolent and impartial (see section 8.1). Emperor Charles VI continued this strategy after his accession in 1711, banning inflammatory religious tracts and relying on the imperial courts to arbitrate confessionalised disputes. For example, he supported the courts in deposing a Catholic prince, Wilhelm Hyacinth of Nassau-Siegen, who repressed his Protestant subjects and trained his artillery on the palace of his Calvinist relations. By presenting itself as an alternative to imperial arbitration, the Protestant corpus made Habsburg management of the Reich more difficult.

However, these problems fell well short of those of the later sixteenth century. It is significant that initial moves to establish the corpus quickly dissipated in the 1650s and only resumed in the wake of the Rijswijk clause controversy. Protestant political mobilisation indicates a degree of dissatisfaction with the constitutional arrangements of the IPO, which had left the Catholics with an in-built majority in the Reichstag. Protestants were far more likely than Catholics to raise religion as an issue in disputes they took to the imperial courts. However, politics not piety dictated the corpus's formation and its subsequent policy. Discussion of the Rijswijk clause became so heated because it coincided with the Saxon elector's personal conversion to Catholicism in order to secure his election as king of Poland. The birthplace of the Reformation was now governed by a Catholic. The elector was aware of the potential damage and entrusted his religious rights to his privy council, which he hoped could act on his behalf to maintain Saxony's traditional leadership. However, the conversion of the Saxon crown prince in 1718, followed by his marriage to the emperor's daughter the next year, confirmed the new Catholic orientation of the Wettin dynasty. With the

Palatinate now also ruled by a Catholic, Brandenburg was able to step into the vacuum and use religion as a way of rallying a clientele among the weaker German princes.

The Hohenzollerns' manipulation of religion grew in line with their rivalry with the Habsburgs and it is no coincidence that the periods when the corpus was most active, in 1712–25, 1750–69 and 1774–8, were also times of extreme Austro-Prussian tension. The mechanism of *itio in partes* was only used four times (1727, 1758, 1761, 1764) and threatened on a fifth (1774–5), each time by Prussia in order to frustrate Habsburg policy by paralysing imperial institutions.

Appeals to religious solidarity became less effective after 1750 when the corpus sanctioned military intervention to end the *Simultaneum* in Hohenlohe-Waldenburg. Such action had little foundation in imperial law and was seized on by the Habsburgs to discredit the corpus. The *Reichshofrat* formally annulled the corpus's decisions and arranged its own settlement of the case. While religion featured in other local disputes, it was always overlaid with other questions of property, privileges and political rights. Confessional antagonism did not prevent the Reich from mobilising to oppose external enemies in the Wars of Spanish (1701–14) and Polish Succession (1733–5). Prussian manipulation of the *itio in partes* during the Seven Years War only occurred once shifts in international alliances pitted the largely Protestant north German territories against the Habsburgs. In any case, practical power was always more significant than religious sentiment for Prussia's management of the corpus. Territorial gains by 1715 already concentrated a third of all Protestant votes in the hands of Prussia and Hanover, sharply reducing the opportunities for the weaker princes to influence policy.

Religion ceased to play such an important part in politics precisely when formal conformity was being achieved. The three decades following 1648 saw the zenith of the confessional state as religious observance finally matched theological orthodoxy. This was most obvious in the Catholic lands, where piety was exuberantly displayed through the construction of imposing baroque churches and popular pilgrimages to new local shrines. Confessionalisation continued by force in some of those areas not protected by the minority rights enshrined in the IPO, particularly Münster and the Habsburg lands. The authorities remained suspicious of links between the faiths even in bi-confessional territories. For example, partition walls were erected where two congregations had to share the same parish church. Cross-confessional marriages were widely thought to lack a stable basis since they combined two opposing confessions within a single household. Critics drew analogies between the problem of dissenting minorities within a state and the wife's freedom of worship in a bi-confessional household, which was thought to undermine her husband's authority, particularly over the children. There were cases of relatives abducting children to ensure they were brought up in the 'true' faith.

None the less, the incidence of mixed marriages was relatively high, reaching a quarter of all unions in some bi-confessional territories, suggesting a degree of informal toleration amongst the wider population even before rulers began dismantling the confessional state (see section 7.1). Imperial law played an important role, since by sanctioning parity between the confessions, the IPO contradicted theological claims to absolute truth. People could invoke legal rights to emigrate, and to private worship and freedom of conscience. Imperial and higher territorial courts generally upheld such claims, since they were all part of the Reich's wider judicial fabric. For example, there are cases of women successfully appealing to higher courts to defend their freedom of conscience when lesser officials had sided with their husbands.[61] Such cases illustrate how the very complexity of the Westphalian settlement ensured its remarkable success, since disputes were channelled away from clashes over fundamentals, like religious truth, and towards arguments over specific local rights, which could be settled by judicial arbitration.

The horrors of the war discouraged the use of violence to solve disputes. Whereas confessional lines had hardened with the passing of generations in the sixteenth century, they gradually softened with changes after 1648. The IPO was no longer regarded as an emergency measure, but was seen as an integral part of the imperial constitution, which safeguarded the rights of all parties. Theologians began to acknowledge each other as devout Christians, even if they disagreed on detail. Bigotry remained, but there is strong evidence suggesting its gradual decline, at least among Christians. Württemberg conscripts did sing religious songs during their mutiny, to avoid being sent to fight Protestant Prussia in 1757. However, equally unwilling Catholic Bavarian peasants hung pictures of Frederick the Great in their cottages.

Rather than dividing Germans into two hostile camps, religious sentiment became a factor reinforcing local identity. Catholics finally accepted official attempts to enforce orthodoxy around 1700, but only after these made significant concessions to local customs and traditions. The laity eventually internalised confessionalised culture and made it their own. Faith could still divide communities, acting as an 'invisible frontier' segregating people within even the same town, despite social and economic ties.[62] However, each community depended on its membership of the wider Reich for its own distinct status. The territorialised pattern of religion survived the collapse of the Reich, with Catholic areas retaining their faith despite the dissolution of the imperial church. In an echo of the sixteenth-century fear that dissent would undermine political stability, nineteenth-century nationalists saw such religious diversity as a barrier to national unity and supported the anti-Catholic and anti-Semitic policies of the Second Reich.

Culture

This later nationalist anxiety stemmed partly from a belief that German culture had been damaged by the Thirty Years War, which had stifled earlier creativity and opened the country to dangerous foreign influences. The only noted cultural product of the war was the semi-autobiographical account of its horrors by Johann Jacob Grimmelshausen, whose novel *Simplicissimus* was first published in 1669 and became the only German bestseller before the literary revival of the later eighteenth century. The apparent dearth of German culture was noted by French authors like Voltaire, who wrote from Berlin in 1750 that 'I find myself in France here. Our language is spoken ... German is only for soldiers and servants'.[63]

In fact, Voltaire's remark betrays a particular type of elitism that defines 'culture' in narrow terms of certain forms of art and literature, and ignores much of what would now be classed under that heading. The Thirty Years War did not destroy the vibrancy of local identities or customs, and even its impact on 'high' culture was relatively limited.[64] The war actually stimulated a nationalist cultural backlash. Societies like the *Tugendliche Gesellschaft*, established in Rudolstadt in 1619, expressed the hope that the creation of a truly national culture would restore peace by transcending confessional and social antagonisms. Growing external interference during the later stages of the conflict intensified this by associating foreign languages and culture with invasion and destruction, leaving a legacy lasting into the eighteenth century. One manifestation of this was widespread Protestant suspicion of Catholic cultural forms as a sign of papal interference in German affairs. Another was the spread of guarded criticism of the cosmopolitan world of the princely courts and the associated aristocratic lifestyle, where immorality, intrigue and deception contrasted with 'honest German' virtues.

The place of French influence is difficult to determine since it was not a homogeneous, national force, but a defuse series of impulses incorporating ideas and styles from other parts of Europe that had already made their way into Germany more directly. For example, the spread of opera and other Italian musical forms was transmitted directly through the Habsburg court, as well as through the presence of Italian composers at Louis XIV's court. Foreign influence always filtered through individual taste and general fashion, and never entirely displaced German styles, which it often incorporated in new, eclectic forms, for example by combining folk songs in new compositions. Moreover, this cultural exchange was already an integral part of German life well before the war. The Saxon elector visited Italy in 1601 and introduced elements of Catholic baroque culture that were combined with indigenous Lutheran forms in his own lands.[65] If anything, the war simply disrupted such exchanges, which resumed with the restoration of peace. Many German courts employed French experts in the later seventeenth century, while German musicians went to Paris or Italy for experience. A leading example was Heinrich Schütz, who trained in Italy and was an important transmitter of innovative Italian early baroque musical styles to Saxony and northern Germany. The political orientation of Bavaria

Table 4.1 Leading German opera and theatre houses

Opera houses		Court theatres		Civic theatres	
Munich	1654	Kassel	1605	Augsburg	1630
Vienna	1666	Vienna	1626	Ulm	1641
Dresden	1667	Innsbruck	1650	Nuremberg	1667
Nuremberg	1667	Munich	1657	Hamburg	1678
Hamburg	1678	Ludwigsburg	1728	Leipzig	1693
Brunswick	1685	Stuttgart	1779	Vienna	1708
Leipzig	1693			Frankfurt	1782
Naumburg	1705				
Berlin	1741				
Lübeck	1746				
Stuttgart	1750				
Ludwigsburg	1764				

and other important rulers towards France after 1672 further encouraged the dissemination of new styles and tastes.

Opera provides the leading example and also illustrates the waning influence of religion. Music was already an integral part of the rituals marking saints' days and other festivals, particularly in the Catholic courts. However, the religious element gradually receded as the presentation of the dynasty assumed greater importance under absolutism. Opera offered an ideal form since it could be readily adapted to glorify the ruling family through allegory and musical metaphor. Its staging also emphasised the hierarchical social order through the tiered seating arrangements in court theatres. Opera was already performed in Germany in the 1630s and spread as each dynasty felt obliged to stage its own spectacles (see Table 4.1). It was well established by the 1660s and soon found a wider public following. Commercialised opera for a fee-paying public opened in Hamburg in 1678, followed by Brunswick (1691) and Leipzig (1693), while other public concerts had already started in 1660, helping to sustain such famous composers as Telemann, Buxtehude and J. S. Bach, as well as lesser luminaries like Johann Joseph Fux, Johann Mattheson and Reinhard Keiser.

Chapter 5:   The Reich in Action

5.1   Taxation and Defence

Imperial taxation

The Peace of Westphalia stabilised the imperial constitution, but did not give it a definitive shape. Though some elements were defined more precisely, further change remained possible, prolonging the life of the traditional hierarchy into the eighteenth century, despite the centrifugal forces within German territorial absolutism (see Chapter 6). The principal constraint on constitutional development after 1648 was not the IPO, but the decisions taken in the late fifteenth and early sixteenth centuries that had already given most imperial institutions their basic form. This can be seen most clearly in the area of defence and taxation, where the structures established from the 1490s remained in place after 1648, yet retained sufficient flexibility to permit their adaptation to meet new challenges.

Imperial military and fiscal institutions offered collective security for the entire Reich. Territorial institutions, such as the different German armies and tax systems, evolved to support these broader imperial functions, as well as to serve narrower dynastic interests. The Reich functioned because its imperial and territorial elements remained interdependent for so long.

The medieval Reich made no distinction between the crown lands associated with the imperial title and the emperor's own hereditary possessions, which were also expected to support his imperial role. The crown lands and their associated rights were largely dissipated after 1254, leaving only three small elements by 1500. The largest was the Ortenau region containing thirty villages on the Upper Rhine. The Habsburgs had transformed into an Austrian dependency by the mid-sixteenth century and they recovered it in 1771 after it had been entrusted to Baden-Baden in 1707 as a reward for Margrave Ludwig Wilhelm's services against the French and Ottomans. Five 'imperial villages' scattered across Germany constituted the second portion, whose status was confirmed in 1648 and survived till the Reich's collapse. The final element comprised a bundle of rights and privileges collectively known as the bailiwick of Swabia. Together, these medieval remnants retained some symbolic value for the emperor's position at the head of the traditional hierarchy, but produced virtually no income.

The same could be said for the surviving medieval taxes that made up the rest of the imperial prerogatives. These *Reichscamerale* included the *Opferpfennig* tax, levied on the Jews in return for the emperor's continued protection, the *Urbarsteuer*, paid by the imperial cities for the same reason, plus tribute from some ecclesiastical institutions, fines, and fees from the emperor's vassals owed on his accession. Whereas these sources had produced 130,000 fl. annually in the mid-fourteenth century, receipts totalled only 5,000 fl a hundred years later. This sum was so insignificant that the Habsburg dynasty made little effort to collect most of these traditional taxes until their acute financial crisis during the War of the Spanish Succession. Charles VI intensified efforts to revive the taxes on Jews and the imperial cities after the war, but met with strong opposition and largely gave up after 1725. Renewed efforts by Joseph II later in the century proved equally unsuccessful. [1]

It was already clear by the late fifteenth century that the emperor would have to sustain his imperial role primarily from his own hereditary lands. The fact that this dynasty had the largest lands in the Reich was a major reason why it was repeatedly chosen to provide the emperor after 1438. However, inheritance and conquest expanded Habsburg possessions to an unprecedented extent by 1526, widening their political horizons and forcing them to divert their German resources to meet problems elsewhere. These external difficulties grew exponentially with the coincidence of dynastic competition with France to the west and Ottoman expansion into Hungary in the east. The emperor's need for additional assistance from the imperial estates was the main factor behind the formation of the Reichstag between 1486 and 1521. The electors, princes and cities insisted on constitutional safeguards in return for financial and military grants to support Habsburg imperial policies. The Habsburgs responded by trying to reorganise the Reich into two elements. The emperor would retain direct control over the family's possessions in Austria, Bohemia and Burgundy and alone decide what they should contribute to their common defence. The Reichstag would be allowed to determine how much the other territories should provide, but the emperor would still retain exclusive control over the money and soldiers. Charles V came close to realising this plan in 1548, but his subsequent defeat in the Princes' Revolt of 1552 forced the Habsburgs to choose between integrating their lands into the Reich, or opting out. They chose dynastic partition, detaching Spain and its possessions entirely, including effectively separating those in Burgundy and imperial Italy from the Reich. Deprived of Spanish wealth, the poorer Austrian branch was compelled to accept closer integration of the Austrian and Bohemian lands within collective imperial arrangements. Only Hungary remained outside, but most of this kingdom was then under Turkish or Transylvanian rule.

Fiscal and military development in the Reich followed the basic European pattern of a transition from occasional emergency levies to regular taxation and permanent armies. Whereas this produced centralised fiscal–military systems in other European monarchies, the Reich's hierarchical structure split these functions on three levels. Central coordination of fiscal and military policy remained a joint decision of the emperor and imperial estates, taken in the Reichstag, which defined the purpose, level and general organisation of taxes and military contingents. Provision of both men and money was devolved to the individual territories, which thereby acquired the right to raise soldiers and taxes for their own purposes, particularly the maintenance of public order. The Kreis structure interposed a secondary, intermediate level between Reich and territories, also receiving men and money from the territories, but deploying these for regional policy determined by the Kreis assemblies. Territorial institutions thus served a dual purpose. They raised the men and money required for collective action agreed by the Reichstag and Kreis assemblies, including peacekeeping and external defence. However, the same institutions could also raise soldiers and taxes for the territories themselves, to support their own administrations, courts and the dynastic ambitions of their rulers. The Habsburg lands were essentially no different. They could also be called upon by the Reichstag to provide contributions to collectively-agreed objectives, as well as more directly supporting dynastic policies.

The success of this system depended on how far each territory subscribed to the common goals and honoured its obligations. Unlike the

French, English or Spanish monarchies, the emperor did not develop an administrative reach that extended into all parts of his realm. The Reich briefly experimented with a direct tax on all inhabitants, known as the Common Penny (*Gemeiner Pfennig*), in 1427. This was levied again in 1495–7, 1512, 1542–4, 1548 and 1551, but each time there had been the practical problem of collection. The huge extent of the Reich inhibited the development of a single, centrally-controlled revenue service. Moreover, had it been possible to construct such an institution, it would have promoted greater royal authority as it did in western European monarchies. Accordingly, the Reichstag made collection the responsibility of the electors, princes and cities, thereby entrenching fiscal powers at territorial level.

Territorial rulers already had limited tax powers. Like the emperor, they relied primarily on their own property within their territories. These domains still generally formed a far bigger proportion of each territory than the crown lands did within the Reich as a whole. However, electors and princes also faced mounting costs associated with public order problems, new responsibilities of government, and dynastic ambition. They sought novel ways of compelling their subjects to contribute. Just as the emperor's demands for assistance promoted the growth of the Reichstag, princely demands encouraged the formation of territorial Estates (see section 6.3). While they accepted the need for consultation with key corporate groups, few rulers were prepared to create additional checks on their authority in return for taxes.

The spread of taxation remained controversial into the seventeenth century. Imperial and territorial taxes were primarily for war. Cash was demanded in lieu of the earlier obligations of free men to serve in person to defend their homeland. The changing nature and scale of warfare rendered these traditional military obligations less effective, as battles were decided by large formations of professional soldiers trained to use the new gunpowder weaponry. However, agrarian relations remained feudal, with peasant producers obliged to perform labour services and pay fees to sustain lords whose privileges rested ultimately on their function as society's warriors. Peasants understandably objected to paying new imperial taxes on top of existing rents and dues, arguing that these were sufficient to sustain their lords, whose duty it was to defend the Reich. Such grievances were a major factor in the bloody Peasants War of 1525 and rulers looked to the emperor to legitimise their new tax and military structures.

They had to tread carefully, since they did not want to establish precedents for the emperor to tax and recruit their subjects directly, whilst
they also wanted assurances that any assistance they provided would be
used for commonly-agreed objectives and not diverted for private Habsburg goals. Equally, the emperor did not want rulers to tax their subjects
as they pleased, yet he desperately needed men and money to fight the
French and Ottomans. The result was a compromise marked by three
Reichstag decisions. The basic structure was established in 1507 when
the Reichstag ordered that rulers were permitted to call upon their subjects' resources to meet imperial obligations. Subjects made their contributions to their immediate territorial ruler, who forwarded the money
or men either to the Kreis, or to the central Reich treasury. The public
peace legislation of 1555 widened this by ruling that subjects were also
obliged to contribute towards any forces raised by their rulers to uphold
domestic order or defend the Reich. Finally, Paragraph 180 of the 1654
Reichstag's recess extended this obligation to include 'necessary fortresses and garrisons', thereby providing a legal basis for the raising of
taxes to maintain territorial armies.

Peasants and townsfolk protested into the seventeenth century that
rulers should meet their military and private expenses from their own
domains. However, imperial obligations had the moral force of Christian duty, because they had been characterised as 'Turkish Aid' (*Türken-
hilfe*) to defend the eastern frontier against the Ottomans, since 1521.[2]
Despite their religious grievances, even Protestants hesitated to refuse
such demands. Armed with imperial legislation and moral arguments,
rulers broke popular resistance to taxation in two stages. First, they met
imperial demands from the late fifteenth century by introducing the new
'Common Penny' tax approved by the Reichstag. This involved a direct,
graduated tax on fixed and liquid assets, which had been copied from the
systems developed by the imperial cities to tax their own inhabitants.
Princes and lords applied this to their subjects as well by 1544.[3] Though
they often had to secure approval from their Estates to establish such
taxes, rulers enjoyed a decisive advantage in that only they knew how
much they were obliged to pay into the Kreis and Reich treasuries.
Moreover, the emperor had no insight into how much money had been
paid, and because each territory collected its own money, rulers could
hold some back for their own use.

Well before this practice became widespread after 1610, many
rulers developed their own taxes alongside imperial levies. Initially,

they simply claimed the emperor had demanded more from their land than was actually the case, and diverted the surplus for their own use. Increasingly, they developed more sophisticated strategies, arguing, with some justification, that territorial governments had an expanding range of responsibilities sanctioned by imperial law to tackle public order, welfare, vagrancy and other problems. Sixteenth-century religious renewal brought additional responsibilities to protect the church and promote morality.

The division of fiscal responsibility in the Reich reinforced its political hierarchy by distinguishing between the rulers who decided tax levels for both the Reich and their own lands, and subjects who paid both imperial and territorial levies. Territorial political development was boosted by the devolution of fiscal and military responsibility. Rulers had already established the basic range of direct and indirect taxes by the mid-sixteenth century, which remained in force till the early nineteenth. However, long-term development remained constrained by the corporate structure of both politics and society, and by the lack of transparency and accountability at all levels (see section 6.4).

The matricular system

The desire to shield territorial resources from the emperor's reach inhibited the development of uniform, direct taxes across the Reich. Instead, the Reichstag apportioned common burdens amongst the individual territories by assigning each a fixed quota of men and money. The basic rate (*Simplum*) could be summoned in fractions, or multiples (*Duplum*, *Triplum* etc.) as required. The obligations of each territory were first recorded in 1422. This 'matricular list' underwent seven revisions, before the Reichstag meeting in Worms approved a definitive version in 1521.

It represented a political solution to complex fiscal and military problems. It safeguarded the status of the imperial estates, since only those lordships and cities recorded on the list had recognised rights within imperial institutions (see section 2.2). The original quotas crudely reflected each territory's status and resources as they were in 1521. The electors were generally obliged to contribute more than the princes, but the inferior political position of the cities resulted in many of them being over-assessed in relation to many lords. Equally, the emperor was able to ensure that his own lands were given only modest obligations.

None the less, the system was comparatively flexible since it made military and fiscal obligations interchangeable, so that territories could be asked to contribute men, money, or a combination of both. The 1521 list assigned each territory a number of infantry and cavalrymen as part of Charles V's escort for his planned coronation journey to Rome. In fact, the first practical use was the despatch of troops to protect Croatia against possible Ottoman invasion the following year, and it became the basis for distributing all future burdens. Taxes were raised by converting this military assessment into cash equivalents, based on the monthly wage bill of one cavalryman at 12 fl. and a foot soldier at 4 fl. This gave rise to the term 'Roman Month' as the basic unit of imperial taxes, equivalent to the monthly pay of the original force of 4,000 cavalry and 20,000 infantry agreed in 1521.

In other respects, the system was very inflexible. It was difficult to change each territory's assessment unless it subsequently lost or acquired land recorded on the list. Many quickly claimed they had been unfairly assessed and sought to have their obligations reduced. The Reichstag claimed the right to oversee such decisions, but it was difficult to judge claims in an age lacking accurate economic or demographic statistics. Six major revisions were sanctioned by 1582, reducing many quotas, but also raising a few considered too low. Those adversely affected lodged appeals with the *Reichskammergericht*, which was unable to resolve the matter as confessional tension impaired its operation. In the meantime, the affected territories continued to make payments at the old, lower rates, while others unilaterally revised theirs downwards in a practice known as 'self-moderation'. The Reichstag banned this in 1582 when it reaffirmed the 1521 list as the benchmark, but even the approved changes reduced the official value of a Roman Month from 128,000 fl. in 1521 to 64,000 fl. by 1577.[4]

The reduction has been taken as evidence of imperial decline[5] In fact, the figures are as misleading as the changing number of imperial estates (see section 2.2). Three-quarters of the losses were due to lands and towns leaving the list, either because they lost their status of immediacy, or when they were annexed by other territories or foreign powers. The remaining quarter stemmed from Charles V's separation of Austria, Bohemia and Burgundy, which resulted in the Roman Month becoming a tax on the non-Habsburg parts of the Reich. Further reductions made little impression on the overall official figure, which remained around 60,000 fl. till the end of the Reich. Actual receipts were generally lower, but rarely by more than 20 per cent – a figure that compares favourably with the collection rates in other sixteenth- and seventeenth-century European countries.

Imperial defence

Defence remained the primary purpose of imperial taxation. Like other princes, the emperor had to rely on his own hereditary lands to support his family, court and administration. Equally, assistance from the Reich was never more than a subsidy, just as territorial taxes were supposed to supplement, not supplant the contribution from a ruler's domains. These different elements were not clearly distinguished before the nineteenth century. It was not until the 1820s that the maintenance of German princely families was 'privatised' and detached from 'public' state finance (see section 6.4). Similarly, defence of the Habsburg lands only became separate from that of the Reich as Austria emerged as a distinct 'great power' by the early eighteenth century (see section 8.1).

The Habsburgs lacked the resources to meet the combined Franco-Ottoman threat without the Reich's assistance. While the wars against France are better documented, those with the Ottomans were more significant for the development of imperial defence. The Reichstag gave little aid to the Habsburgs in their struggles against France in the early sixteenth century, regarding these wars as essentially a private dynastic matter. Christian rulers, the emperor included, were expected to remain at peace. By contrast, there could be no lasting settlement with the Ottomans, since these were infidels who had to be driven from the earth. Defence in the east was a Christian duty to which all should contribute, whereas that in the west remained a matter of individual conscience, unless France or some other power directly attacked the Reich.

The Habsburgs developed a three-line defence against the Ottomans. The outer perimeter was the Military Frontier (*Militärgrenze*), a militarised zone from the Adriatic coast along the Habsburgs' entire eastern border as far as Poland. Based on earlier Hungarian precedents, it began in Croatia in 1521 and already stretched 1,000 km, held by 17,000 men, by 1556. Refugees were settled on the frontier, and given land, religious freedoms and political autonomy in return for serving in the border militia, manning blockhouses and mounting patrols against Ottoman raids.[6] Larger forts with permanent garrisons represented the second line. These works were built from the early sixteenth century in the new, bastioned, *trace italienne* system of defence in depth against artillery and enemy mining operations. They were sited at key points, particularly the confluence of rivers, and held by paid professionals. Such fortifications were built elsewhere, including Vienna and Prague, but the partition of Charles V's empire removed the major western works in the Netherlands and Italy from Austrian control until the eighteenth century. Garrisons in the eastern fortifications rose from a few thousand in the mid-sixteenth century to 18,000 men by 1662. These professionals provided the basis for the Habsburgs' field army, which constituted the third element of their defence. Already a small number of units were retained after the Thirteen Years War ended in 1606 and these provided the cadre for Ferdinand II's army during the Thirty Years War. However, the constant danger from the Ottomans restricted the numbers that could be deployed elsewhere.

In any case, there was little money for such soldiers before the later seventeenth century. The annual cost of maintaining the border defences rose from 1.67 million fl. in 1576 to 3 million by 1607, representing a major strain when the total revenue of the Habsburg monarchy amounted to less than 2 million.[7] The frontier militia also demanded more money in the early seventeenth century as the men found it harder to sustain themselves and their families from their small plots of land. The situation was most acute on the Adriatic coast, where there was even less land, forcing the local Uskok population to resort to piracy. The Venetian Republic intervened when the Uskoks widened their attacks, from targeting only Ottoman vessels to include Christian shipping. The failure of both Rudolph II and Matthias to address the problem prompted the Venetians to attack the Habsburgs' Adriatic possessions, with English and Dutch support, in 1615. Archduke Ferdinand (II) of Styria was obliged to suppress Uskok autonomy in 1617 and impose tighter control over the frontier.[8] Habsburg authority needed money to make it effective, forcing the dynasty by the 1570s to turn to its provincial Estates for financial assistance. The Estates had used this as an opportunity to extract important concessions, including religious freedoms and greater autonomy, thereby further weakening the monarchy and contributing to its internal problems by the early seventeenth century.

None the less, the Habsburgs represented the only force in the region capable of offering the necessary central coordination for frontier defence. This received some institutional underpinning with the establishment of the *Hofkriegsrat*, or Court War Council, in Vienna in 1556, which provided administrative and logistical support for the entire monarchy. Moreover, the Habsburgs had access to additional funding through their influence in the Reich.

The Habsburgs found it much easier to obtain support against the Ottomans than against the French, resulting in imperial defence diverging into eastern and western systems by 1570. Western war-making was tightly controlled by the constitutional restrictions placed on imperial prerogatives since 1519 (see section 2.2). Offensive operations against Christians were only permitted in order to defend the Reich's integrity by recovering lost land. Though Charles V received support from individual princes, the Reichstag only once provided substantial taxes for operations against the French (in 1544). The partition of the Habsburg empire by 1558 removed much of the western periphery from the emperor's immediate concern, since Burgundy passed to the Spanish branch until 1700. While the emperor no longer had a direct personal interest in western wars, other German rulers became more fearful for their security. As first France and then the Netherlands were plunged into civil and religious strife in the 1560s, it looked as if the fighting would spill across the Rhine into western Germany. However, the situation was now very different from that in the first half of the sixteenth century when Charles V had fought the French king. It was no longer clear who the enemy was, since the immediate threat came from internal wars, in which both sides attracted German sympathisers.

A military solution was clearly inappropriate, and the Reich addressed western security through its public peace legislation passed in 1555–70.[9] The intention was not to mobilise an army but to prevent violence elsewhere disturbing the domestic peace, by prohibiting the French, Dutch and Spanish from recruiting German soldiers or operating inside the Reich. The electors and leading princes were reluctant to strengthen imperial prerogatives at a time when many suspected the emperor of secretly backing Spain and the French Catholics. None the less, his central coordinating role was recognised as indispensable. The emperor was given general oversight of military recruitment throughout the Reich, though it remained unclear whether he could veto any assembly of troops he deemed unconstitutional. Coordination of security measures, including the mobilisation of peacekeeping forces, was devolved to the Kreise, each of which was to appoint a military commander and was empowered to raise contingents from its member territories using the matricular quotas. Given the need to confront disorder immediately, the Kreise were authorised to mobilise without prior imperial approval, though they were obliged to notify the emperor of their actions. The emperor remained suspicious of these arrangements, and the mobilisation of the five western Kreise in 1599 failed to dislodge Spanish troops who were using parts of Westphalia as a base for operations against the Dutch.

Concern about the effectiveness of western imperial security encouraged the small Rhenish counties to establish their own territorial defence militias (*Landesdefensionen*) from the 1570s. These rested on an amalgam of feudal duties requiring subjects to assist their lord in maintaining the peace and help in emergencies, including fighting floods and fires. From the fifteenth century, some of these obligations had been commuted into cash payments to pay mercenaries. Knights and commoners accepted this, because cash payments could be less dangerous or irksome than appearing in person, and because military taxes increasingly received the sanction of imperial law. However, mercenaries were expensive and could be difficult to find quickly. Obligations of personal service offered a potentially cheaper and more efficient form of defence. Despite the commutation of some obligations, the general population remained theoretically liable if the territory was invaded. While this duty was reaffirmed in territorial decrees after 1500, only a select portion (*Auswahl*) would actually be summoned. The rest of the population were required to pay taxes to clothe, feed and equip those who served as militiamen. Rulers had in their hands a very flexible instrument: they could adapt it to call out additional manpower if necessary, or use the general obligation to serve as grounds to demand more taxes in lieu.[10]

The new territorial defence militias represented a refinement of these earlier measures. Starting in Nassau-Dillenburg in 1572, they spread by 1600 to the Palatinate, Baden, Württemberg, Hessen, Saxony, Brunswick, Brandenburg and Ducal Prussia, as well as many smaller territories. In each case, the rulers ordered their local authorities to muster all the available men in each parish and divide them into sections on the basis of age and occupation. A select portion was formed from single men, generally in their twenties, who had not yet inherited substantial property. They were drilled each Sunday by professional officers, who taught them how to manoeuvre in the large, tightly packed formations necessary to maximise the effectiveness of the prevailing weapons. The emphasis on discipline and subordination distinguished these 'regular' militias from their earlier counterparts and was supposed to prepare them to face professional mercenaries where necessary.[11] Such organisations were essentially defensive, reflecting the deep-rooted belief that war among Christians could only be waged with a just cause, and that its primary purpose was to restore peace by rectifying whatever 'injustice' had triggered the conflict.[12]

These sentiments did not prevail in the east, where imperial defence rested more directly on the three-tiered structure built by the Habsburgs. The Reichstag had summoned contingents according the matricular system to help fight the Ottomans, on several occasions before 1544. Thereafter, the princes found it more convenient to vote cash grants instead of sending soldiers, which were often more expensive to recruit and maintain than the nominal values assigned in a Roman Month. The emperor readily accepted this shift. Imperial taxes improved his credit with potential lenders and allowed him to recruit his own army under his direct control. Whereas Charles V had received 73.5 Roman Months during 1522–52, his successors obtained 409 in 1556–1606. Rudolph II's success in attracting such support indicates how the Reich continued to function despite the confessional and political problems of his reign. Moreover, imperial tax grants increased the Reich's importance to overall Habsburg defence. Rudolph obtained as much money from the Reich as he did from his own lands, receiving a further 12 million fl. directly from the Kreise, in addition to the 18.69 million he got as Roman Months. This enabled him to maintain around 25,000 garrison troops from 1576, of which around a third could be deployed as the nucleus of a field army. However, the establishment of a permanent army entailed additional expenses and the monarchy encountered serious difficulties from the 1590s as military costs rapidly exceeded even the generous tax grants. Soldiers expected to be paid all year round and not just in the spring and summer 'campaign season'. The Habsburgs recruited across the entire Reich, but stationed their men in Hungary where they were most needed. It was not possible to send them home in the winter, or when operations had ended, particularly as cash-flow problems resulted in the army being owed considerable arrears. The monarchy's annual revenue came to only 1.85 million fl., but the Thirteen Years War created 8 million in debts, while to maintain the frontier required 2.5 million and the field army was owed another 2 million. Around 6,000 disgruntled troops loitered in Vienna after the war, refusing to go home unless they were paid, adding to Rudolph's worries.[13]

Doubts over the emperor's erratic policies within the Reich made the Reichstag less willing to place further large sums in his hands. The disappointing outcome of the Thirteen Years War raised suspicions that the money had been squandered or misappropriated by the imperial treasurer, Zacharias Geitzkoffler, a charge that was certainly false. Though the Reichstag did vote another 1.8 million fl. in 1613, arrears on this and earlier grants reached 5.3 million by 1619. While the electors and princes were responsible for 42% of payments, they owed 61% of the arrears, indicating the extent of political discontent among the more powerful German rulers by the time of the outbreak of the Thirty Years War.

The nature and scope of that conflict made any return to the Rudolfine system of defence impossible after 1648. Having experienced Wallenstein, the German princes were not prepared to give future emperors the means to raise another large field army, which could be just as easily deployed against them as against the Ottomans. Defence was one of the issues postponed at Westphalia for a future Reichstag. By the time this met in 1653, some of the larger territories were already establishing their own small territorial armies (see section 6.2). The growth of these 'armed princes' (*Armierten*) greatly complicated imperial defence since they insisted their still unarmed neighbours should pay them to defend the Reich. Such a solution would have decentralised defence, entrusting it to the larger principalities and electorates, whose political influence would have risen accordingly. Organised in the Rhenish Alliance since 1658, several of these powerful armed princes played a significant role during the brief war against the Ottomans in 1663–4.[14]

The Dutch War, 1672–9

The princes' influence grew with the outbreak of the Dutch War in 1672 as Leopold I had to improvise a defence in the west against France while many of his own troops were tied down suppressing a Hungarian rebellion in the east. Even with cash subsidies from the emperor's allies, the armed princes could not pay the forces they had raised. They persuaded the emperor to assign them the resources of the smaller counties, bishoprics and cities that had no troops to send to the front. Many rightly saw this as the first step towards full annexation as the armed princes demanded far more money than they needed to pay their forces and refused to leave, even when the war ended in 1679. German military operations became as much a scramble for the best billets as a defence against enemy attacks. Hanover, Münster, Celle and Brandenburg nearly came to blows over possession of key Westphalian territories.

Their actions were not entirely selfish. From less than 3,000 men in 1673, their contribution to the war against France rose to over 60,000 by 1678, a number comparable to those the emperor himself had in the field. In addition, Brandenburg and other north German territories sent over 40,000 against Sweden, which had joined France at the end of 1674. The cost of these forces threatened to undermine the still shaky financial recovery from the Thirty Years War and the princes expected the emperor to provide adequate recompense for their patriotic assistance.

Though Leopold asserted his right to determine which lands the armed princes could use as bases, sudden reversals of fortune on the ground often made it impossible to enforce these arrangements. For example, the emperor intended that the main field army should live at the French expense by invading Alsace in 1674, but it was defeated at Türkheim on 5 January 1675 and forced to winter in Swabia instead. Armed princes made their own agreements with the emperor's allies, Spain, Denmark and the Dutch, diverting troops to assist them. Münster and Cologne had even joined France at the beginning of the war. Though both were forced to change sides by 1674, it proved impossible to make Bavaria and Hanover contribute to imperial defence, since these were still secretly allied with Louis XIV, who paid them to keep their large armies at home.

The war saw France make the largest territorial gains in the last 250 years of the Bourbon monarchy. These were largely at the Reich's expense and included the entire Franche Comté. Despite the peace in 1679, Louis continued to consolidate his eastern frontier through a policy known as the Reunions, whereby additional land was seized as dependencies of existing French territory. The French refused to leave Lorraine and went on to occupy Strasbourg in 1681 and take Luxembourg three years later.

Defence reform

Imperial defence was in urgent need of reform, but the Reich could not agree on how to do this. Leopold would have preferred a monarchical solution along the lines attempted by Ferdinand II in the Peace of Prague. This would have extended the eastern part of the old Rudolfine defence system to the entire Reich. The Reich would have a single army under the emperor's control and paid for by the princes. The armed princes proposed their own federal form of defence, with a common army from their own forces paid for by the unarmed territories. As this would have undermined his authority, Leopold swung behind the lesser territories' solution based on the public peace legislation. The weaker rulers had no interest in playing an active role in European warfare and simply wanted effective security against foreign aggression. They looked back to the western element of the Rudolfine system, which had offered protection against wars elsewhere without providing opportunities for a potentially reckless emperor or belligerent princes to use German resources in wars of their own.[15]

The Reichstag endorsed this option in a series of decisions in 1681–2, creating a flexible mobilisation structure that could be used for internal peacekeeping as well as external defence. As before, each territory had to provide a contingent to the common forces. This sustained the imperial hierarchy by ensuring that the lesser territories remained part of the system. The 1521 matricular list was revised, giving each territory a share of a new basic establishment (*Simplum*) of 12,000 cavalry and 28,000 infantry. This was not the actual size of the imperial army, since the reforms simply rehabilitated the existing mobilisation structure rather than creating a standing army. In 1679, before the reforms were complete, the Upper Rhine counties and cities had already decided to maintain their basic quotas in peace as well as war. The prolonged warfare after 1683 meant that many other territories maintained their own small permanent armies, and this became general by 1714. These contingents were grouped by Kreise so that the small lands of one region combined their soldiers to form individual regiments, while the larger ones fielded entire units of their own. These soldiers were designated *Kreistruppen* when serving under generals appointed by their local Kreis assembly. They became *Reichstruppen* when they passed under the command of senior officers chosen by the Reichstag.

Leopold accepted this decentralised system, because his own hereditary lands remained outside the Reichstag's jurisdiction. While the Austrian and Burgundian lands received nominal shares of the basic quotas, the emperor was free to designate a portion of his own army as *Kreistruppen* or *Reichstruppen* where necessary. He still had to rely on taxes from his own lands to pay for this Austrian army, but he now had a more reliable way of summoning additional assistance from the Reich. Since the Austrian army remained by far the largest single German force, the Reichstag usually appointed Habsburg officers as imperial generals. The emperor was able to use the imperial army as an auxiliary force to take over the protection of the Rhine while his own troops pursued Habsburg

Table 5.1 Imperial defence

War	Kreis Contingents	Auxiliaries	Total
Turkish War			
1663–4	15,100	16,600	31,700
Dutch War			
1673	6,900	2,800	9,700
1674	11,150	56,600	67,750
1675	16,600	54,100	70,700
1676	17,200	64,600	81,800
1677	17,200	70,760	87,960
1678	7,000	74,100	81,100
Great Turkish War			
1683	14,700	24,400	39,100
1684	12,100	12,100	24,200
1685	31,900	10,000	41,900
1686	12,360	21,000	33,360
1687	9,260	8,000	17,260
1688	14,210	8,500	22,710
1689	3,100	2,500	5,600
1690	–	2,500	2,500
1691	–	9,820	9,820
1692	9,900	4,500	14,400
1693	6,400	7,500	13,900
1694	6,400	7,500	13,900
1695	–	14,000	14,000
1696	–	15,000	15,000
1697	3,600	15,000	18,600
1698	8,600	15,000	23,600
1699	7,600	–	7,600
Nine Years War			
1688	–	14,300	14,300
1689	30,000	13,000	43,000
1690	23,300	14,800	38,100
1691	26,400	19,900	46,300
1692	38,000	26,350	64,350
1693	38,000	27,500	65,500
1694	40,700	32,100	72,800
1695	42,700	36,100	78,800
1696	40,800	38,300	79,100
1697	33,500	38,300	71,800

Table 5.1 (*continued*)

War	Kreis Contingents	Auxiliaries	Total
Spanish Succession			
1701	22,680	33,400	56,080
1702	27,400	76,000	103,400
1703	40,400	83,600	124,000
1704	39,700	90,200	129,900
1705	41,200	103,500	144,700
1706	39,600	107,000	146,600
1707	41,700	110,500	152,200
1708	41,300	110,500	151,800
1709	41,300	113,300	154,600
1710	37,900	118,800	156,700
1711	37,900	118,300	156,200
1712	37,900	117,700	155,600
1713	44,400	30,000	74,400
Polish Succession			
1735	34,200	54,300	88,500

NB: All figures are effective strengths. Auxiliaries include those German troops hired by the emperor or his European allies. Since the Nine Years War ran in parallel with the second phase of the Great Turkish War of 1683–99, the figures under both from 1688 should be added together to produce the total German forces in the field. A further 10,000 or so auxiliaries served the Venetians against the Ottomans each year between 1685 and 1689. Habsburg forces, including those nominally serving as the Austrian Kreis contingent, are excluded from the above figures. The Habsburgs fielded around 51,000 in the 1663–4 Turkish War. Their army averaged around 60,000 in the 1670s and 80,000 in the 1680s, rising to 95,000 by the later 1690s. Maximum effective strength during the War of the Spanish Succession reached about 137,300, rising to 205,700 for 1735 (see also Table 6.3). Also omitted are the additional garrison troops maintained by the individual territories, as well as other small forces used in independent operations, particularly during the Dutch War. German princes provided another 25,000 auxiliaries for the Habsburgs during the 1716–18 Turkish war.

objectives elsewhere. Though the Reichstag had to agree the size and extent of any mobilisation, the emperor retained the initiative to declare war or peace.

The armed princes could no longer exploit their unarmed neighbours, but they were reconciled to the new system by the special favour shown to them by Leopold after 1681. The emperor allowed powerful rulers, like the secular electors, to field their contingents separately under their own generals, rather than integrating them with the forces organised by the Kreise. He permitted them to make local arrangements with weaker territories to provide soldiers on their behalf in return for payment. He also hired additional forces to augment his own troops, under special bilateral treaties that often held out the promise of political favours. Hanover acquired its electoral title this way in 1692, while Brandenburg got its Prussian crown in return for sending more auxiliaries in 1700. The armed princes thus retained their military autonomy and their forces remained 'household troops' (*Haustruppen*) under their own command and jurisdiction.

Imperial defence reform created a structure that was undoubtedly cumbersome in practice, but ideally suited to the Reich's complex political hierarchy. It provided a minimum measure of security to the weaker territories without unduly strengthening either the armed princes or the emperor. Maintenance of territorial armies received imperial sanction, permitting even minor counts and dukes to compel their subjects to pay for the small forces they believed necessary to uphold their status and maintain order. The more powerful larger territories remained within the common framework and still contributed their share to collective defence. Mobilisation could take place at regional level through decisions taken by the Kreis assemblies, or across the Reich with the agreement of the Reichstag.

Imperial defence after 1682

The Kreis structure had already demonstrated its value in coordinating the contributions of the weaker territories in the partial mobilisations of 1663–4 and 1673–8 (see Table 5.1). This continued as the Reich mobilised to relieve Vienna from Ottoman attack in 1683. The Kreis contingents remained with the Habsburgs in Hungary until the outbreak of the Nine Years War in 1688, when they were withdrawn to defend the Rhine against renewed French aggression. Leopold accepted this redeployment because it enabled him to discharge his duty to defend the Reich without having to detach substantial Austrian forces. Further bilateral treaties with the powerful armed princes secured additional auxiliaries to make up the shortfall in Hungary and assisted in the Habsburgs' total victory on this front by 1699. While the forces on the Rhine were never sufficient for an offensive to recover Alsace, they did prevent serious French incursions after 1689 and contributed to the relatively favourable Peace of Rijswijk in 1697, which forced France to surrender Luxembourg and some of the other lands taken under the Reunions.[16]

The Reich mobilised again during the subsequent wars of the Spanish and Polish succession. Each time, an imperial army composed largely of Kreis contingents held the Rhine while Habsburg and other German forces operated more offensively elsewhere. Though the French broke through in 1703–4 and 1707 to raid southern Germany, the military situation stabilised, particularly after the battle of Blenheim knocked out Bavaria, which had now openly joined Louis XIV. Operations were less spectacular in 1733–5 when the imperial army failed to retake the key fortresses of Kehl and Philippsburg. However, the mobilisation structure worked fairly well, producing a large army that had even assumed the offensive by the time peace was made. France also returned the two forts, which were then garrisoned by Swabian and Franconian Kreis soldiers. The mobilisation system continued to function after 1735, but its effectiveness declined with the Habsburgs' growing problems and the start of open Austro-Prussian rivalry (see Chapter 8).

Justice and Conflict Resolution

Juridification

The public peace framework used to support external security had been originally developed to address the problem of violence within the Reich. Just as discussions of German military history generally ignore imperial institutions, those of its legal development also focus primarily on the individual territorial judiciaries. However, order did not rest on a unitary, centralised state, but was maintained by the complex imperial hierarchy, which offered plentiful opportunities to defuse conflict and popular grievances.

Like the individual German standing armies, territorial justice evolved along with imperial moves to replace violent self-help with respect for the rule of law and peaceful arbitration. This process has been labelled the juridification (*Verrechtlichung*) of German politics, as disputes were channelled away from feuds and rebellion into judicial review and administrative reform.[17] It developed in response to the public order problems of the later fifteenth and early sixteenth centuries and created a legal framework that served until 1806.

Medieval emperors had been primarily arbiters rather than law makers, intervening to mediate between feuding lords and princes. The early modern system of imperial justice inherited and developed this basic function of preserving the peace between the different territories of the Reich. Territorial justice stemmed from lordly jurisdictions that had emerged in the twelfth and thirteenth centuries. These settled disputes amongst the inhabitants and communities of each territory by reference to written, rather than customary law. Written law was codified under the influence of revived interest in ancient Roman Law that spread throughout Germany from the late fifteenth century and culminated in a series of territorial legal codes (*Landrecht*) issued by the princes and cities during the sixteenth century and renewed and revised by their successors after 1600. These codes gradually displaced the older, still largely unwritten laws used by the autonomous municipal and village courts to judge disputes at local level within territorial towns and villages. Such courts dealt with lesser civil and criminal cases, imposing fines, but rarely using severe corporal punishment, which was reserved for the higher courts of lords and ecclesiastical foundations.

The growth of imperial justice from 1495 shaped these territorial developments in two fundamental ways. First, it sanctioned the emergence of a distinct territorial judiciary as mediator between the different local and lordly jurisdictions. The violence and destruction wrought by popular protests, particularly the Peasants War of 1525, convinced both peasants and lords to settle their differences more peacefully. Backed by imperial law, princes stepped in as mediators, breaking the lords' exclusive jurisdictions and integrating them with the other local courts within a common legal framework. In doing so, princes pursued their own interests of promoting stable peasant households as a bulwark against further rebellion, and as the basis for increased taxes (see section 7.2).

Secondly, a separate system of imperial courts developed to regulate the territorial judiciaries, stepping in where these broke down or failed to resolve local problems, as well as mediating disputes between princes and other imperial Estates. Attempts to establish such a system dated back to the eleventh century and were related to the medieval public peace movement. Backed by the church, this called for the voluntary renunciation of violence by lords and princes and their common subordination to a single system of arbitration. The major stumbling block had been disputes over who should be the supreme arbiter. Whilst no one questioned the emperor's premier status, many were reluctant to permit him to be both judge and jury. They were determined to end personalised, political justice, which had allowed medieval emperors to use legal sanctions against their dynastic opponents.

The public peace and the Reichskammergericht

Working through the Reichstag, a group of reform-minded princes compelled Maximilian I to accept a compromise on imperial justice in 1495 in return for financial aid against his external enemies. The emperor declared a perpetual public peace (*Ewige Landfriede*), marking a significant break with medieval practice since all imperial estates agreed to renounce violent self-help and submit disputes to arbitration. Peace was equated with the rule of law, and the courts alone would decide where justice lay. The system was overseen by a new supreme court, called the *Reichskammergericht*, which was charged with judging all breaches of the public peace, supervising territorial justice and, from 1524, judging religious disputes as well. Given the principle that imperial justice remained superior to territorial law (*Reichsrecht bricht Landrecht*), the *Reichskammergericht* also functioned as a supreme court of appeal for cases from the individual territories.[18]

The court's independence from the emperor was ensured by a new levy imposed on all imperial estates to sustain it. Initially, the Common Penny tax was used (1495–9), but this was replaced in 1507 by regular taxes distributed, like defence burdens, according to the matricular system. These *Kammerzieler* levies became permanent and were collected in six-monthly instalments until the end of the Reich. The court was initially itinerant, moving to whichever city the Reichstag was meeting in. From 1527 it stayed in Speyer until a French attack forced it out in 1689 during the Nine Years War. It reopened in Wetzlar four years later and remained there until 1806. This anchored the court firmly in the south-west of the Reich where the majority of minor territories were. Its independence was further underpinned by arrangements for appointing the judges. While the emperor was allowed to name the presiding *Kammerrichter*, the assistant *Assessoren* were selected by the territories on a regional basis through the Kreise. Moreover, the territories only proposed candidates, who had to pass an exam. The court then selected one candidate to fill each vacancy. The new judge had to renounce ties to any former master and swear exclusive loyalty to the court. While there is evidence of covert collaboration between judges and individual territories in sensitive cases, recent research indicates that the court attained a high degree of genuine independence. The Reichstag provided overall supervision, issuing an ordinance governing procedure and regularly reviewing verdicts through the annual visitation.[19]

The breakdown of the visitation process after 1588 was only one problem facing the court. Its jurisdiction was curtailed by the 'privilege of not appealing' (*Privilegium de non appellando*) granted by the Golden Bull of 1356 to the electors and later extended to other princes. This theoretically closed their lands to the court by preventing their subjects from appealing to courts elsewhere. Older accounts have claimed this seriously impaired imperial justice, but the privilege's significance has been greatly exaggerated. Only the Habsburg lands were truly exempt. Elsewhere, serious cases involving substantial property could still be appealed against, even from the electorates. The electors slowly bargained 'unlimited' privileges for their lands. Saxony acquired this in 1559, followed by Brandenburg in 1586, but the Palatinate did not obtain it until 1652, Mainz in 1654 and Trier in 1721. Resistance from the Cologne Estates delayed it there until 1782. In each case, the exemption only covered those lands then in the elector's possession, compelling him to seek extensions when he acquired new land. The Hohenzollerns only secured full exemption for their possessions in 1750, while it took until 1762 before the Palatinate obtained it for Jülich-Berg. Lesser princes had to go through the same process when they acquired the privilege. For example, Hessen-Darmstadt and Hessen-Kassel received it in the limited form in 1631 and 1650, but had to wait until 1747 and 1743 respectively to have it extended to full exemption. Apart from these, only Mecklenburg acquired full exemption in 1724, but the local Estates prevented this from taking effect. Nassau and Baden obtained it in 1803, when it was already losing its significance. Even where rulers did secure greater judicial autonomy, the court could still intervene if they denied their subjects justice or broke imperial law.

Moreover, the exemptions assisted imperial justice by preventing the *Reichskammergericht* from being swamped by minor cases. Already, the Reichstag had ruled in 1530 that ordinary criminal cases were not to be appealed to it. While appeals from territorial courts made up four-fifths of its case load before 1600, the proportion fell to half thereafter, allowing it to concentrate on its primary function of upholding the public peace. Extension of the privilege also promoted the growth of territorial justice, since rulers only received exemption if they established their own judiciary, complete with an appeals court. The *Reichskammergericht* consistently rejected all claims to exemption that lacked firm foundation and reasserted jurisdiction over exempt areas if a ruler subsequently closed his appeals court.[20] This supervisory role encouraged standardisation of legal practice across the German territories, which generally based their own legal codes on imperial legislation, such as the *Carolina* criminal code of 1532. Imperial judges proceeded carefully, for instance rejecting witchcraft confessions extracted under torture, that had been accepted by their territorial counterparts. They also encouraged other avenues for appeal through the practice of *Aktenversendung* approved by the Reichstag in 1570. This upheld the principle that no one who was party to a suit against their ruler should be judged in his courts. These and other difficult cases could be sent to a university law faculty in another territory for an independent opinion. Some princes tried to restrict this in the eighteenth century and Prussia prohibited it entirely in 1746. None the less, it persisted and was revived in the 1790s and accepted again by the German Confederation in 1815.[21]

The Reichshofrat

Maximilian I recognised the new court only reluctantly and reasserted his judicial prerogatives by creating his own *Reichshofrat* in 1498. Based in Vienna, this was funded by Habsburg taxation and staffed by judges appointed exclusively by the emperor. The presence of this second supreme court was a potential source of tension between the emperor and the princes, though the latter were not invariably opposed to it. The Reichshofrat initially concentrated on safeguarding the emperor's traditional feudal prerogatives and providing legal advice to the Habsburg government. Ferdinand I issued new instructions in 1559, empowering it to deal with breaches of the public peace and hear appeals from territorial courts. Though this made it a potential competitor to the *Reichskammergericht*, the arrangement ensured the continuation of a functioning system of justice when the latter experienced difficulties after 1588. Protestant criticism compelled the emperor to agree in 1648 to appoint at least some Lutherans to the Reichshofrat. However, despite the court's role in legitimising the confiscations policy during the Thirty Years War, there is little evidence that the emperor directly interfered in its decisions in less politicised cases.[22]

Effectiveness

The presence of two supreme courts did create opportunities for delay as litigants could shift cases between them in the hope of more favourable verdicts. There was always a degree of tension between the *Reichskammer-gericht* as the 'princes' court' and the emperor's *Reichshofrat*. Rudolph II clearly blocked reform of the *Reichskammergericht* for political reasons in the 1590s, while Leopold I's interference compelled the elector of Mainz to close it temporarily in 1703. In each case, the *Reichshofrat* stepped into the vacuum, further delaying the revival of the *Reichskammergericht*. The secular electors also lost interest in the *Reichskammergericht*, because they wanted neighbouring territories to accept their own courts as alternative venues for appeal. The German writer Goethe, who briefly served as a legal trainee in Wetzlar in 1771, left an unflattering portrait of the court in his famous autobiography, giving the widely quoted figure of 20,000 cases pending and 50,000 unresolved.[23]

Such evidence is both inaccurate and misleading. Rivalry between the two courts encouraged reforms to enable one to match improvements in the other. The emperor's periodic hostility to the *Reichskammergericht* stemmed from political contingency, not principled opposition, since he appreciated the need for a functioning system of justice. For instance, Joseph I collaborated with Mainz in reviving the *Reichskammergericht* after 1707, as did Charles VI and, later, Joseph II in a renewed visitation in 1767–77.[24] Many of the court's problems stemmed from the territories' failure to pay their contributions towards its upkeep, especially during the Thirty Years War. Arrears totalled 880,000 tlr by 1711, seriously impairing operations. Even at the height of late sixteenth-century confessional tension, the court was never more than two judges below its official establishment of 38. This was increased to 50 in 1648, but shortage of money meant that only 13 were in post by 1704. Charles VI's reforms revised the complement to a more realistic 25, whilst doubling their pay to attract more competent candidates. Annual operating costs were now 50,000 tlr, but territorial levies produced only 21,000. This dire situation actually improved over the eighteenth century, in complete contrast to the standard picture of imperial decline. Despite preventing its own subjects from using the court, Prussia resumed its payments after 1713 and made up all its arrears in 1791. Other territories also responded so that annual income rose to over 100,000 tlr by the 1790s, producing a surplus of around 20,000. A full bench of judges was in post after Joseph II's intervention, whilst total staff was always much higher at around 150–180, including a large number of legal trainees whose presence reflects the court's continued prestige as the centre of German justice.[25]

The *Reichskammergericht* handled an impressive 77,500 cases with an annual peak of 700 in the 1590s at the height of the confessional tension that is widely supposed to have paralysed the entire Reich. The number did decline between 1620 and 1660, but rose again to 100 after the court reopened in Wetzlar in 1693 and averaged 230 to 250 a year throughout the eighteenth century. Goethe's figures are misleading, since he cites only 60 new cases, when the court actually received 227 in 1771. There was a backlog, though not nearly as large as he believed, and it was cleared entirely by 1785 following the reforms of 1775. All judicial systems were characterised by delay and there were, for instance, 11,500 unresolved cases still pending in Prussia in 1745. The rapid growth of the *Reichshofrat* enabled it to more than take up the slack. Its total case load reached 100,000 by 1806, rising from an average of 700 a year in the 1590s to 2,000–3,000 in the eighteenth century, include a small, but significant proportion from imperial Italy.

Many cases were protracted, but serious complaints at delay only surfaced in the late sixteenth century when 11% of the cases before the *Reichshofrat* took up to 40 years to resolve, while 4% had lasted a century. These statistics also need to be set in their context. In fact, Goethe's assessment of the true value of imperial justice is much more apt than his better-known criticism of its shortcomings:

> The affairs of great weight, the actual lawsuits, remained behind schedule and that was no misfortune. The state's only concern is to make possessions certain and secure; it can pay less heed to someone's legal right to possessions. Therefore no harm could come to the empire from the enormous, constantly swelling number of delayed lawsuits. Measures had been taken against people who used violence, and such people could be dealt with conclusively. As for the others, who were fighting legal battles for their possessions, they lived and enjoyed themselves, or suffered want as the case might be. They died, they were ruined, they were reconciled. All of that, however, was merely the happiness or misery of individual families, while the empire itself was gradually made tranquil.[26]

Like their territorial counterparts, the imperial courts were not concerned with absolute justice, but with workable compromises to sustain peace. German judicial opinion remained stuck in the late middle ages. The courts' purpose was to restore harmony, not to identify clear winners or losers. Cases took so long, because the courts engaged in an ongoing process of arbitration, adjusting verdicts according to changing circumstances.

Implementation

Both imperial courts depended on the territories to gather information, interview witnesses and enforce decisions. In most cases this was not a problem, since litigants usually provided voluminous documentation supporting their claims and paid their own lawyers to represent them in Wetzlar or Vienna. Most also accepted the eventual verdict. However, problems could arise in high-profile, politicised cases, particularly inter-territorial disputes between rulers. These generally concerned disagreements over borders and jurisdictions, or conflicting claims of inheritance. The division of the Ernestine Wettins in 1680–1 resulted in 61 cases before the *Reichshofrat* by 1739 to untangle the claims to Coburg-Eisenach-Römhild alone. Some rulers took matters into their own hands, particularly in Meiningen, which periodically sent troops to seize land its prince felt belonged to it, culminating in the Wasungen War of 1747–51. Mainz and Würzburg mobilised their armies in a dispute over forestry rights in 1749–50. Mainz and the Palatinate came to blows over conflicting jurisdictions in the Wildfang dispute of 1651–68, and Pfalz-Neuburg and Brandenburg fought periodic skirmishes over the Jülich-Cleves inheritance until 1651.[27] Along with a similar dispute between Darmstadt and Kassel, such problems could became more serious if they became enmeshed in wider conflicts like the Thirty Years War.

The public peace legislation was intended to eliminate these problems. The courts were empowered to appoint princes to act as their commissioners, to collect evidence and, where necessary, deploy troops to keep the peace or enforce a verdict. The Donauwörth case of 1607 demonstrated the political sensitivity of this role (see section 4.1). The IPO addressed this by making the Kreis convenors automatically responsible in breaches of the peace within their jurisdiction. However, the courts retained flexibility since they could revoke commissions from princes who failed to act properly.[28] Concern for their prestige encouraged most princes to stick to the rules. None of the rulers mentioned in the previous paragraph obtained their goals by violence alone. The open use of force remained very rare, since few princes were prepared to jeopardise their chance of securing a favourable court verdict by taking up arms. Those that did were dealt with firmly. Hessen-Kassel's invasion of tiny Schaumburg-Lippe in 1787 is an important example. The landgrave's 2,300-strong task force soon chased the few Lippe soldiers into their miniature fortress on an artificial island in Steinhuder Lake. However, the *Reichshofrat*, backed by diplomatic pressure from Prussia, Hanover and Cologne, compelled the landgrave to withdraw without bloodshed. The public humiliation was compounded by the obligation to pay reparations, seriously retarding the landgrave's hopes of being made an elector.[29] Only Prussia openly abused its commissioner's powers, using them to quarter part of its army at Mecklenburg's expense (1719–55) and to oppose Habsburg policy during 1789–90.[30] None the less, across the entire eighteenth century, contemporary critics counted only 100 cases where imperial court verdicts remained unenforced.

5.3 The Kreise

Origins and organisation

The Kreise played a key role in imperial defence and justice. They had been established in 1500–12 when the territories were grouped into ten regions to propose judges to the *Reichskammergericht* and enforce its verdicts.[31] They quickly assumed wider responsibilities for political, military and fiscal coordination. Each was empowered to establish an assembly, or *Kreistag*, in which member territories had equal votes, unlike representation in the Reichstag. In addition, the public peace legislation of 1555 gave the *Kreistage* the right of self-assembly as part of the decentralised security arrangements. This imparted a different character to regional politics, where the lesser counties, bishoprics and imperial cities had proportionately more weight.

The collective will of the assembly in each Kreis balanced the powers of the one or two princes chosen as *Kreisausschreibenden Fürsten*, or convenors, who acted as the conduit for all official communication between the region and imperial institutions (see Figure 1.1). The convenors also set the assembly's agenda, asked each member to speak in turn, compiled the final recess and maintained the regional archive. To prevent a single ruler monopolising this position, the Reichstag ruled in 1559 that there should be two convenors in each Kreis, one of whom should be an ecclesiastical prince. Regional politics ensured this pattern was not universally adopted, but it did result in Protestants securing the secular post in those Kreise where they formed a substantial proportion of the membership (see Table 5.2).

The Kreise's relationship to the Reich was ambiguous. They could strengthen the traditional hierarchy by providing regional coordination, assisting in the implementation of Reichstag decisions and court

Table 5.2 Kreis convenors

Kreis	Convenor	Confession
Austrian	Archduke of Austria	Catholic
Burgundian	Duke of Burgundy (i.e. Spain, then Austria)	Catholic
Bavarian	Elector of Bavaria Archbishop of Salzburg	Catholic Catholic
Electoral Rhenish	Elector of Mainz	Catholic
Franconian	Bishop of Bamberg Margraves of Ansbach and Bayreuth*	Catholic Protestant
Lower Saxon	Duke of Brunswick Bishops of Madgeburg and Bremen* (held by Prussia and Hanover by 1715)	Protestant Originally Catholic, de facto Protestant by 1648
Upper Saxon	Elector of Saxony	Protestant
Westphalian (Lower Rhenish)	Bishop of Münster Duke of Jülich (claimed by Brandenburg and Pfalz-Neuburg in 1609 with both exercising a function from 1666)	Catholic Catholic/Protestant
Upper Rhenish	Bishop of Worms Prince of Pfalz-Simmern (Palatinate)	Catholic Protestant till 1685, then Catholic
Swabian	Bishop of Constance Duke of Württemberg	Catholic Protestant

* Alternately.

verdicts, and in the mobilisation of men and money from the member
territories. They safeguarded the place of the lesser territories, providing
valuable services and ensuring they retained a voice in regional affairs.
However, the Kreise could be made to support stronger monarchical
rule if the emperor cultivated good relations with the convening princes,
who could marshal the others behind imperial policy. This offered a way
of governing the Reich without recourse to the Reichstag, where the
emperor might meet more concerted opposition. Finally, the Kreise
might serve as platforms for more federal politics, either when the convenors or other large territories used them to assert their influence over
neighbouring lands, or if the weaker members used the assemblies as
platforms for inter-regional collaboration.

Austria, Burgundy and Bohemia

The varied composition of the Kreise tended to dictate which of these
routes their development followed. The Habsburg monarchy enjoyed a
privileged position within the Kreis structure, with its Austrian and Burgundian lands grouped into distinct regions and Bohemia omitted
entirely. The decision to exclude the Bohemians had been taken by the
German princes before the Habsburgs acquired the kingdom. Memories
of the Hussite insurrection of 1419–34 were still fresh and the princes
regarded the Bohemians with suspicion. The Habsburgs were happy to
maintain this arrangement after 1526 and it was confirmed by Charles V
in 1548, although Bohemia was still assessed for imperial obligations
under the matricular system. Exclusion of Bohemia and its dependencies
kept over 17 per cent of the Reich's territory outside the Kreis structure,
considerably enhancing Habsburg autonomy within the imperial constitution. Realising their mistake, the princes lobbied to have Bohemia
included as an eleventh Kreis in 1646 to ensure the Habsburgs would be
more accountable for their contributions to common expenses. This
failed, as did an attempt in 1706–7 to have the kingdom added to the
Upper Rhenish Kreis.

Switzerland also remained outside the Kreis structure, but this was
largely irrelevant since that country had left the Reich. Omission of the
imperial knights only affected a small area, but the exclusion of imperial
Italy, while in line with that region's generally loose association with the
Reich, none the less benefited the Habsburgs by keeping their Italian
lands beyond the Reichstag's reach.

The other Habsburg possessions also enjoyed considerable autonomy. They were the sole member of Burgundy, which was the least defined Kreis: there was considerable doubt whether it covered the entire Netherlands, or only Franche Comté, Luxembourg and the eastern part of modern-day Belgium. The northern Dutch provinces claimed membership of the Reich in the 1590s as a device to enlist German support against Spain. This fell on largely deaf ears and the entire United Provinces opted out by 1648. The exclusion of Burgundy from the Westphalian settlement, by the IPM, also weakened its association with the Reich, and French diplomats persuaded the Reichstag that it lay beyond imperial jurisdiction when Louis XIV invaded the Spanish Netherlands in 1667. Spain contested this, reactivating the region's association with the Reich in order to secure German military assistance. Though Franche Comté was lost by 1679, the remnants were now recognised as part of the Reich and remained so when Burgundy passed to the Austrian Habsburgs after 1700.

The Austrian lands were grouped into their own Kreis, which contained few other members, and were in no position to challenge Habsburg leadership (see Appendix 2). As in Burgundy, the Kreis structure remained a useful device by which they could participate within imperial politics when necessary. As archduke of Austria, the emperor could act in the name of the Kreis when he did not want to use his imperial prerogatives. None the less, incorporation of the Austrian and Burgundian lands did anchor the monarchy within the Reich, and ensure it paid some respect to the imperial constitution.[32]

The Saxon Kreise

All of north-eastern Germany was initially combined as a single Saxon Kreis, but this split into Upper and Lower sections by the mid-sixteenth century. The former was dominated by electoral Saxony as sole convenor, alongside Brandenburg as the other major member. Swedish membership on behalf of Pomerania was recognised in 1648 and confirmed the overwhelmingly Protestant character of the region. Sweden also held Wismar and Bremen in Lower Saxony, as well as Verden in Westphalia. The Guelph dukes held most of Lower Saxony, where they gradually consolidated their holdings into two main blocks around Brunswick and Hanover by 1705. Brandenburg acquired representation here as well through its gains in 1648, which gave it a claim to convenor status.

Regional politics after 1648 were characterised by two four-cornered tussles for influence. Upper Saxony was split between the two electorates, which soon marginalised both Sweden and the lesser territories. The growth of Brandenburg power eventually eclipsed Saxony's influence and the Upper Saxon Kreis assembly was not reconvened after 1683 as the Hohenzollerns saw no need for it. The rival Guelph factions tended to cancel each other out in Lower Saxony, with neither Hanover nor Brunswick being able to displace Sweden or the remaining lesser members. No further assemblies were held after 1682 but, as with Burgundy and Austria, the Kreis structure remained on paper as a convenient arena for political action by the larger regional powers in both Upper and Lower Saxony.

Westphalia

The Westphalian, or Lower Rhenish, Kreis had a more mixed membership and, accordingly, a more vibrant institutional life. Its politics were shaped by the Jülich-Cleves inheritance dispute after 1609 between Calvinist Brandenburg and Catholic Pfalz-Neuburg. While the decision of these two powers to share both the lands and associated convenor's rights removed the threat of violence after 1666, it also signalled the intrusion of external influence in the region. This continued as the major Westphalian bishoprics tended to be held by rulers from outside the area, usually the elector of Cologne, whose main lands were in the Electoral Rhenish Kreis. Other counties and duchies passed by inheritance or purchase to rulers elsewhere, notably East Frisia to Prussia in 1744, which increased Hohenzollern influence, and the smaller counties to Habsburg aristocrats, like the Kaunitz family, later in the eighteenth century.[33] Their intrusion displaced Dutch influence, which had been important despite the formal separation of the Netherlands from Westphalia in 1548. The Dutch maintained garrisons in several Westphalian towns to secure their eastern frontier. The bishop of Münster removed them from his lands by 1660, while Brandenburg intervention in Emden after 1682 displaced Dutch influence in East Frisian politics by the 1720s.

Problems were most acute after the Thirty Years War and resulted in the suspension of assembly meetings between 1671 and 1697. However, the three-way split in convenors' rights between Brandenburg-Prussia, Pfalz-Neuburg and Münster prevented any one power dominating the region. As Münster gave up its pretensions to regional dominance, it became the spokesman for Westphalian interests against external interference. The assembly reopened in 1697 and by 1715 the weaker members felt sufficiently confident to reject further Prussian attempts to dictate regional policy.

Electoral Rhine

The four Rhenish electors in Mainz, Cologne, Trier and the Palatinate were only brought within the Kreis structure in 1512 by being allowed to group all their lands within their own region. This fragmented the Kreis geographically into the main area on the Middle Rhine and two large enclaves: one in Westphalia belonging to Cologne, the other around Erfurt in Thuringia belonging to Mainz. However, politically the region remained a compact group with the four electors completely overshadowing the other six members. The Kreis structure enabled the electors to cooperate with their neighbours, both in Westphalia and in the still more fragmented Upper Rhine. However, Palatine resentment at Mainz's exclusive leadership triggered a debilitating regional dispute that became enmeshed in French machinations to paralyse imperial politics after 1651. No assemblies were held between 1667 and 1697, when renewed fears of France caused the electors to close ranks and join the wider framework for regional security.

Bavaria

The other four Kreise lay in the south and were characterised by varying degrees of equilibrium between a few leading territories and the broader membership. The Bavarian Kreis was solidly Catholic after 1622. This and the dominant presence of the Wittelsbachs gave it a strong degree of internal cohesion. Not only did Bavaria cover two-thirds of the total surface area with three-quarters of the population, but its electors' relations usually governed the neighbouring bishoprics like Freising, Passau and Regensburg. However, Salzburg offered an entry-point for Habsburg influence through the election of pro-Austrian archbishops. Even when these were not in post, Salzburg had sufficient weight to ensure that Bavaria had to take some account of wider views. The Bavarian Kreis assembly met regularly and provided a convenient venue for resolving local problems and representing the region in imperial politics.[34]

Upper Rhine

The Upper Rhenish Kreis technically included the duchy of Savoy, the only part of imperial Italy to have formal membership of imperial institutions. However, the dukes chose not to exercise their rights, while those in Lorraine also failed to participate. The rest of the region fell into two unequal parts, with a belt of mainly Catholic minor principalities and bishoprics along the Rhine and an interior collection of largely Protestant lands around Hessen to the east. Dynastic partition of Hessen in 1567 removed the chance that it would dominate the entire region, but did not prevent the landgraves of the Kassel branch from seeking such control. The presence of the elector Palatine in the principality of Simmern caused additional problems since this gave him convenor's rights. The Mainz–Palatine dispute in Electoral Rhine was transported here when Elector Johann Philipp von Schönborn of Mainz became bishop of Worms in 1663 and thus also acquired Upper Rhenish convenor's rights. Hessen-Kassel intervened once the Catholic Pfalz-Neuburg family inherited the Palatinate, including Simmern, in 1685. Arguing that both convenors' powers were now exercised by Catholics, Kassel fanned religious fears as a means of promoting its own claims to regional leadership. This paralysed the assembly until 1697, but the lesser members were determined not to let political rivalry wreck regional organisation and established their own Upper Rhenish Union as a substitute in 1679. Though Kassel tried to assert control over this as well, it never succeeded, while fear of French attack prompted a minimum of collaboration. Relations improved after 1697 and the region became one of the more effective organisations during the early eighteenth century, particularly as Lutheran Hessen-Darmstadt was willing to collaborate with the largely Catholic Electoral Rhine.[35]

Swabia and Franconia

The most vibrant Kreise were also amongst the most politically fragmented. Swabia had 97 different members, yet probably functioned best of all. Though Württemberg comprised roughly a third of its area, it was counterbalanced by the presence of Baden-Durlach as an alternative focus for Protestant sympathies, as well as by the host of other small territories meeting regularly in the assembly. Franconia was also balanced between the two Protestant margraviates of Ansbach and

Bayreuth and the Catholic bishoprics of Bamberg and Würzburg. Like Swabia, this raised the possibility of paralysis along confessional lines, yet the practical need to collaborate always overcame religious tension in the end, and the Franconian Kreis assembly met no less than 322 times between 1517 and 1791.[36]

The Kreise in imperial politics

Recent research has revised the earlier view that the Kreise lost momentum after the mid-sixteenth century.[37] Confessional tensions certainly caused problems, but the Kreise remained useful forums for regional collaboration even into the Thirty Years War. Both the Liga and the Protestant Union based their organisation on the Kreis structure as a legitimate constitutional framework. The Saxon attempt to create a neutral third party of moderate Protestants at Leipzig in 1631 did the same, while Ferdinand of Cologne used the Westphalian Kreis to sustain his political and military autonomy within the Prague system in 1637–42.[38] However, no one managed to subordinate the Kreise entirely to their objectives and they remained the refuge of those who wished to preserve the Reich's traditional hierarchical order. For example, Franconians resisted Sweden's attempts to compel them to renounce imperial overlordship by uniting in their Kreis assembly in the 1630s. The princes also successfully used the Kreise as a platform to lobby for inclusion in the Westphalian peace talks in 1644–5. The IPO recognised them as integral parts of the constitution and signalled their role in political renewal after 1648.

The Kreise offered a viable basis for cross-regional collaboration, because hesitant territories were more likely to cooperate through them than by informal alliances. The public peace legislation also offered sanctions against the free-rider problem bedevilling most princely alliances, since the Kreis assemblies and convenors could take punitive action against members who failed to support the majority line. The Thirty Years War revealed how weak most territories were on their own. There was strong support for alliances, or Associations, between Kreise as a way of offering safety in numbers in what still seemed an uncertain international situation after 1648.

Some believed that such Associations could give the lesser rulers a louder voice in imperial politics and help them influence Habsburg policy. As one of the architects of the Westphalian settlement, Johann Philipp von Schönborn was determined to keep the Reich out of future wars. He saw collaboration through the Kreise as a way of compelling both the emperor and foreign powers to keep the peace, by denying them access to German resources. He was particularly concerned about the ongoing Franco-Spanish conflict, since his own possessions in Mainz, and later Worms, lay close to the fighting. He hoped that regional alliances would not only prevent war spreading to Germany, but enable the smaller rulers to interpose themselves as a neutral third party between the belligerents, and mediate lasting peace.

Schönborn had to battle against persistent confessional tension and regional rivalries, to which he also contributed. He also had to contend with hostile Swedish influence in the northern Kreise and with powerful rulers like the Great Elector of Brandenburg, who pursued their own objectives. Brandenburg sponsored its own, more overtly Protestant alliance, which undermined Schönborn's projected Association of the Upper and Electoral Rhenish Kreise. However, he received help from an unexpected quarter when France threw its weight behind him in 1658. Mazarin was looking for a convenient way to marshal German support for France's strategy of emasculating the Austrian Habsburgs within the Reich to prevent them assisting their Spanish cousins.

The resulting Rhenish Alliance of 14 August 1658 was not a true Kreis Association since it only had ten members, but it did bring together the leading players from Westphalia, Lower Saxony and the Rhineland. In addition to Mainz, Cologne and Trier, it was joined by Münster, Brandenburg, Pfalz-Neuburg, Hessen-Kassel, the Guelphs, and Sweden on behalf of its German lands. France was also a member, agreeing to back Schönborn's plans to uphold the Westphalian settlement, and another eight German princes joined by 1665.[39] Initial results were promising, boosting Schönborn's reputation as the 'German Solomon', helping to negotiate an end to the Franco-Spanish war in 1659, keeping north-west Germany out of the Polish–Swedish war of 1655–60 and helping to resolve that conflict as well. The Alliance also had teeth, through a mutual assistance pact obliging each member, including France, to provide a fixed contingent of troops, as well as holding a congress in Frankfurt. The bishop of Münster received military assistance to suppress his recalcitrant capital city, whilst the Alliance helped Schönborn reduce Erfurt's autonomy in 1664. The allies also acted internationally, sending a large contingent outside the Kreis structure to help Leopold I beat off the Ottoman attacks in 1663–4.

By this point the Alliance was already crumbling through internal rivalry and French manipulation. Mazarin, and later Louis XIV directly, used Schönborn's group to prevent German opposition to French expansion. The Alliance's fragility was exposed when Schönborn was unable to prevent his ostensible ally from attacking the Spanish Netherlands in 1667. The Alliance charter was not renewed in 1668, by which time the indefatigable Schönborn had launched a host of other schemes, all intended to dissuade France from further aggression and foster cross-confessional support for the Westphalian settlement. However, he was marginalised as Leopold abandoned his earlier neutrality and swung behind the Dutch, Brandenburg and others in opposing France after 1672.

The new Dutch War threatened to engulf the Reich, prompting renewed interest in possible neutral third parties. France encouraged this once its own bilateral arrangements with key princes failed to keep the Germans out of the war. Leopold intervened by sanctioning mobilisation through the Kreis structure to defend imperial frontiers after 1673.[40] The reform of imperial defence in 1681–2 represented Leopold's version of the Kreis Associations since it bound regional organisation within the system of collective security. Leopold consolidated this in the Laxenburg Alliance of 10 June 1682, integrating a network of bilateral alliances with favourable princes in a wider system embracing agreements with collective organisations such as the Upper Rhine Union and the Bavarian Kreis. The Laxenburg system was revised as the League of Augsburg in 1686 to provide security for the Reich and western Habsburg lands while the emperor fought the Ottomans in the Great Turkish War.

The outbreak of the Nine Years War in the west in 1688 spread dissatisfaction at Leopold's imperial management. Though the Kreis contingents were sent back from Hungary to defend the Rhine, it was obvious that the Habsburg monarchy would make its main military effort in the east. To defend the west, Leopold resorted to the same expedients as in the Dutch War and sanctioned the exploitation of German resources by the major armed princes in return for their help against the French. The weaker princes resisted this through the Kreis structure, arguing that the 1681–2 reforms had authorised all territories to raise their own troops and participate in imperial defence. The Swabians and Franconians led the way, first by compelling the larger rulers to collaborate within the Kreis structure and field their share of the common contingents under Kreis command, rather than as separate corps. They then signed a two-year alliance on 29 May 1691, rejecting all further attempts to use their lands as free billets for other German auxiliaries, and raising their common forces to a respectable 19,000 men. Ratified by the Kreis assemblies, this Association was binding on all members and was declared permanent in 1694. The Kreise now assumed the prerogatives of the armed princes, negotiating their own subsidy treaties with other princes to hire additional troops, and joining the Grand Alliance against France in 1696, giving them a voice in the peace negotiations.

The strength of the Swabian–Franconian Association was demonstrated by the failure of more conventional forms of collaboration through bilateral treaties between princes. Duke Anton Ulrich of Brunswick was angered at the favour shown by Leopold to his cousin Ernst August of Calenberg, who had been made elector of Hanover in 1692. Anton Ulrich rallied other disgruntled middling rulers into the League of Corresponding Princes to collaborate in imperial institutions and open negotiations with France and Denmark. However, the organisation was far too disparate to act as an effective third party and had collapsed by 1695.

Meanwhile, the Swabian–Franconian Association expanded, thanks to the efforts of another Schönborn, Lothar Franz, who was a nephew of the earlier elector and became bishop of Bamberg in 1693 and then elector of Mainz two years later. This gave him convenor's rights in two Kreise and he was determined to use his influence to expand the Association as a major force within imperial politics. He wanted to take the initiative away from the Reichstag, where discussions were dominated by the bigger armed princes, and shift it to the Kreis assemblies, where the more numerous, but individually weaker rulers had greater influence. As elector of Mainz, he reversed his immediate predecessor's opposition to the Association and brought all Electoral Rhine into the south German group. Uncertainty over the flagging imperial war effort prompted other regions to attend a congress in Frankfurt at the end of 1696. This produced an Association between Franconia, Swabia, Westphalia, Bavaria, and Electoral and Upper Rhine on 23 January 1697. All agreed to maintain their matricular contingents permanently to give a peacetime total of about 40,000 men. This was envisaged as a temporary arrangement pending the inclusion of the two Saxon and two Habsburg Kreise. It was not intended to replace the Reich, but did raise the possibility that imperial politics might be revised along more federal lines in the interests of the weaker territories.

The Association movement stimulated the revival of Westphalia, and Electoral and Upper Rhine. It checked the influence of the armed princes, who were no longer able to off-load their military expenses on their weaker neighbours, or deny them a voice in collective decisions. Though Lothar Franz did not intend it, his initiative also challenged the emperor. The elector wanted to continue his uncle's policy of neutrality during international conflict and hoped the military potential of the extended Association would deter the major powers from troubling Germany. However, Leopold wanted German backing for his bid to secure the impending Spanish succession for the Austrian Habsburgs. Ultimately, Leopold's appeal to traditional loyalty proved stronger than Lothar Franz's somewhat precarious Association, particularly once Bavaria's pro-French orientation compromised its neutrality. French incursions into the Rhineland in 1701–2 convinced the elector that closer cooperation with the emperor was unavoidable and he agreed to a joint conference at Nördlingen in 1702. Bavaria abstained, but the other members of the 1697 Association renewed their organisation and extended membership to the Habsburgs in their capacity as the Austrian Kreis. The Association backed the imperial declaration of war on France and was admitted to the renewed Grand Alliance.[41]

Lothar Franz struggled to prevent Leopold reducing the Association to a mere adjunct of Habsburg imperial management. He did stop the armed princes recovering their former influence. For example, the Westphalians refused to subsidise Prussia and Münster and fielded their own regiments instead. The Association drew wider support as the disproportionate growth of major electorates, like Brandenburg, Hanover and Saxony, marginalised even formerly influential territories, including Hessen-Darmstadt, Holstein-Gottorp, Mecklenburg, Ansbach, Bayreuth and the Ernestine Saxons. Moreover, Bavaria's crushing defeat in 1704 exposed the dangers of unilateral independent action on the international stage. These medium territories rallied to Lothar Franz's efforts to hold the Habsburgs at arm's length and prevent them exploiting imperial resources for their own dynastic ambitions during the war. The elector entered into closer negotiations with the Dutch from 1710 to extend their plans for a defensive fortified barrier in the southern Netherlands to protect the entire Rhineland from future French aggression.

This project collapsed as Britain and the Dutch made a separate peace with France in 1713, leaving the elector no choice but to side with the emperor, who continued fighting for another year. The prolonged struggle left the territories more disillusioned with the Association than with the emperor. Though the 1702 Association was renewed in 1714, it was now firmly subordinated to Habsburg security interests as an organisation of the five western Kreise to protect the Rhine while Austrian troops were free for operations in Italy and the Balkans. The Swabians and Franconians cooperated to garrison Philippsburg and Kehl and to subsidise maintenance of the Austrian fortress of Alt-Breisach in the Breisgau. The Upper and Electoral Rhenish took over responsibility for the stretch further downstream, garrisoning the key stronghold of Mainz itself, while the Westphalians nominally had responsibility for the sector by the Dutch frontier.

The Kreise briefly displayed their potential during the crisis following the death of Emperor Charles VI in 1740. For the first time in three centuries, the Reich was no longer governed by a Habsburg, for, after a prolonged interregnum, the electors chose Carl Albrecht of Bavaria as Charles VII in 1742. Weak Bavarian imperial rule lasted until 1745, during which time the Reich was rocked by two Austro-Prussian wars and the international conflict over the Austrian succession, which lasted until 1748 (see section 8.2). The Kreis structure offered a legitimate refuge from the storm. Citing their rights under the public peace legislation, the five western Kreise mobilised their contingents to maintain a precarious armed neutrality. Though they were unable to prevent the belligerents from operating across their lands, they did contain the damage, and felt strong enough to reject demands from both sides for active assistance. The Habsburgs redoubled their diplomatic pressure once their candidate was selected to succeed the unhappy Charles VII in 1745, but the Kreise consistently refused to join the war. Austrian pressure forced them to renew the Association in 1748, but this was a largely empty victory and the organisation only existed on paper.

The Swabians and Franconians abandoned the crumbling fortresses of Philippsburg and Kehl, though the Rhinelanders still garrisoned Mainz. Defence of the Rhine was in any case less pressing once France became the emperor's ally in 1757. Austro-Prussian rivalry was now the main problem and left little room for autonomous action by the lesser territories through the Kreis structure. Prussia extended its influence southwards, gaining a major stake in Franconia through the acquisition of Ansbach and Bayreuth in 1792. Though the Kreise continued to provide a framework for military mobilisation, attempts to revive the Association as a political movement failed in 1790–2.

Westphalia held its last assembly in 1784, followed by Bavaria in 1793. French annexations irrevocably damaged the Electoral and Upper Rhine after the start of the Revolutionary Wars in 1792. None the less, the Kreise still played an important role in organising the defence of the Reich, and the Franconian assembly met in permanent session from 1791 to 1806, while that in Swabia also continued to function. Plans to reform the Kreise were actively considered after 1791 and resurfaced during the discussions over Germany's future at the Congress of Vienna in 1814–15, remaining on the agenda of the subsequent German Confederation until 1848.

The Kreise and economic coordination

The reason for this continued interest was that the Kreise offered more than a framework for political and military collaboration. They served as the main mechanism for implementing economic and fiscal decisions taken by the Reichstag. Imperial economic policy concentrated on regulation of the Reich's fragmented internal markets, rather than direct intervention at territorial or local level. Already in 1576, the Reichstag had abandoned central coordination of tolls and tariffs, devolving these decisions to the territories themselves. The Kreis assemblies offered a more viable forum for regional disagreements to be resolved, though much criticised by later historians as a sign of the Reich's weakness; it is worth remembering that Germany lacked a national customs system until 1904, well after the creation of the nineteenth-century 'nation state'.

The Reichstag used the Kreise to enforce those areas of economic policy that it continued to decide, primarily trade embargoes against wartime enemies.[42] They also offered limited help at regional level, for example maintaining quarantine during cattle plagues and epidemics, and assisting in road construction. However, their primary economic role remained currency regulation as territorial rulers acquired minting rights and issued their own money. By 1692 there were 1,200 different types of coin circulating in the Reich. This decentralised system was open to abuse, particularly where governments issued debased coins, undermining market confidence and fuelling inflation. People looked to the Reich to regulate exchange rates, end debasement, control inflation and prevent the influx of foreign coin into their markets. These were modest and realistic ambitions, given the still relatively unsophisticated monetary system, relying on base and precious metals rather than paper currency, which was not introduced into central Europe until 1762 when the Habsburg monarchy began issuing notes to cover its expenses during the Seven Years War.

The Reich responded with a series of coinage ordinances during the sixteenth century, establishing two basic coins of account: the silver taler in the north and Hohenzollern monarchy, and the gold florin in the south, west and Habsburg lands. All other coins were related to these according to their precious metal content, enabling exchange across the Reich. The Kreis assemblies held bilateral currency meetings to regulate inter-regional rates, while the *Reichskammergericht* prosecuted those who infringed the rules, imposing dire penalties, including death for counterfeiting.

The system was flawed, however, because it was initially biased towards the southern florin zone, undervaluing the silver taler. Larger territories also resented interference in their monetary policies and those Kreise dominated by just a few powerful rulers stopped holding currency meetings: Bavaria in 1560, Upper Saxony in 1680, Lower Saxony in 1681, Westphalia in 1715, Electoral Rhine in 1728, Franconia in 1736 and Upper Rhine in 1766. As a result, the exchange rate mechanism gradually collapsed after 1753 as major territories like Bavaria, Saxony and Wolfenbüttel abandoned the official rate and devalued the florin against the taler. The Reich could have overcome these problems had it not been for the growth of open Austro-Prussian rivalry. Prussia deliberately introduced its own competing system, based entirely on the taler, in 1750, intending to pull all north German territories out of the southern florin zone dominated by Austria. This was only a qualified success. Imperial currency regulation continued to function outside the north-east, with areas like the Electoral Rhine still participating, even if they no longer held separate currency meetings.[43]

The disruption of the formal exchange mechanism complicated business transactions, but did not prevent them. The failure to agree a common currency was a product of the princes' own fiscal conservatism, rather than inadequate imperial institutions. Rulers continued to expect the Reich to enforce currency regulations last revised in 1566, yet economic and demographic change inhibited definitive arrangements for a system based entirely on precious metals.

The problems of currency regulation appear to corroborate the general view that German political fragmentation inhibited economic growth. Imperial law did preserve both territorial autonomy and corporate social privilege, which were obstacles to commercial expansion. However, not only were national economies still incomplete even in supposedly united countries like France, but the Reich mitigated the adverse impact of German territorial fragmentation. The imperial hierarchy offered numerous opportunities for local, territorial, regional and inter-regional collaboration and regulation. It reduced transaction costs by maintaining peace and arbitrating disputes, including those over tariffs and other protectionist measures. The relatively high degree of decentralisation gave more people a stake in economic decisions in contrast to the more centrally-steered economic measures in unitary states like France and Spain, which had difficulty in overcoming internal tariff barriers and provincial particularism. The broad freedoms for emigration and religious worship permitted some movement of labour between territories. Finally, political fragmentation could foster innovation by placing competitors in close proximity, encouraging the dissemination of new techniques.[44]

5.4   The *Reichskirche*

Origins and size

The ecclesiastical territories, collectively known as the imperial church (*Reichskirche* or *Germania sacra*), were distinct parts of the Reich, in contrast to the territorial churches (*Landeskirchen*) within the secular territories (see section 2.2). Medieval emperors had rewarded loyal bishops with secular jurisdiction over lands to supplement their existing spiritual authority. In return, the senior clergy had been amongst the early royal dynasties' staunchest supporters, providing invaluable technical expertise and military assistance. However, the emperor lost control over clerical appointments in the long struggle with the papacy known as the Investiture Contest.[45] This weakened papal authority as well, and by the fourteenth century, the choice of each new bishop or abbot was firmly entrenched in the respective cathedral or abbey chapter.

Despite the impact of secularisation and other losses, the imperial church remained numerous, governing around an eighth of all Germans and holding a disproportionate share of Reichstag and Kreis assembly votes.[46] In addition, bishops' spiritual jurisdiction extended across neighbouring secular Catholic territories, where they often influenced the selection of parish clergy and held considerable property. The losses were heaviest in the north-east and western borderlands, leaving the remaining parts of the imperial church concentrated in the 'priests' ally' (*Pfaffengasse*) along the Rhine, where the ecclesiastical territories were the oldest and best established, including the three electorates of

Mainz, Cologne and Trier, the smaller bishoprics of Strasbourg, Basel, Speyer, Worms, Constance and Augsburg, as well as numerous abbeys. The other lands were distributed along two spokes from this central axis. One ran east up the river Main, through Würzburg, Bamberg and Fulda, while the other pointed north into Westphalia and included Münster, Paderborn, Osnabrück and Hildesheim. The remaining lands lay in three isolated groups. Liege was sandwiched between Habsburg territory in the Netherlands, while Brixen and Trent were enclaves in the otherwise predominantly Habsburg Austrian Kreis, and the rest were concentrated around Bavaria, including Salzburg, Passau, Regensburg, Freising and Berchtesgaden.

Social structure

The imperial church was overwhelmingly an aristocratic institution. Of 347 prince-bishops who reigned between 1500 and 1803, 332 were nobles, 5 foreigners and only 10 commoners. Only the abbeys remained relatively open, as most prelates were commoners, often sons of peasants. Convents were aristocratic and remained an important resource for the German nobility, who needed suitable accommodation for their unmarried daughters. The cathedral and abbey chapters offered further careers for aristocratic younger sons, who stood little chance of inheriting their family's possessions. There were around 900 such posts, falling to 720 with secularisation by 1648.

The Catholic imperial knights and territorial nobles tended to monopolise positions in their own region. Westphalian aristocrats predominated in Münster, Paderborn, Hildesheim and Osnabrück with, for example, 188 of the 223 canons serving in Münster between 1650 and 1802 coming from the region, including 89 from the bishopric itself. Local influence also prevailed in the main belt of territories along the Rhine and Main, while Swabians predominated in Augsburg, Basel and Constance, Bavarians in Regensburg and Freising, and Austrians in Salzburg, Passau, Trent and Brixen. Cologne and Strasbourg were exceptions to these general trends, as the exclusive status of their chapters restricted access mainly to the imperial counts, though around a third of the 24 posts in Cologne were reserved for educated commoners. Augsburg also admitted non-noble canons. The emperor controlled appointments to dioceses within the Habsburg monarchy following his concordat with the papacy in 1448, and he tended to favour aristocrats from the Reich to prevent these positions falling into the hands of the indigenous territorial nobility.

The majority of secularised bishoprics retained their chapters,[47] while the IPO protected five Catholic monasteries in Magdeburg, two in Hanover, and 50 parishes in Hildesheim. In addition, Osnabrück alternated between an elected Catholic bishop and a duke from the neighbouring Guelphs, while Lübeck remained part of the imperial church under a Lutheran administrator, as did three Protestant imperial convents. Protestants thus gained access to the wealthy network of ecclesiastical benefices. Those in the fully secularised areas simply increased the scope for princely patronage, but the two bishoprics and three convents still within the imperial church retained their corporate autonomy.

The ecclesiastical territories offered an important field of political activity to the otherwise marginalised imperial knights who dominated the chapters in Mainz, Trier, Speyer, Worms, Würzburg, Bamberg and Constance, in addition to holding significant shares in Fulda, Eichstätt and some of the Swabian bishoprics. Individual families could rise to prominence through their election to powerful sees, notably the Schönborns, who came from this milieu and provided two electors of Mainz in the seventeenth century (see Appendix 1).

However, the knights' influence was challenged from the later sixteenth century by the Protestant princes, who secured the elections of their younger sons as administrators in many northern bishoprics. Though secularisation ended this competition in 1648, the knights were also displaced by the Catholic Wittelsbachs, who held Cologne continuously between 1583 and 1761, as well as Freising 1566–1763, Regensburg 1668–1763 and sometimes Passau and Salzburg. The Pfalz-Neuburg branch pursued this systematically from the late seventeenth century, considerably increasing its political influence.[48] Other competition came from those Protestant dynasties that converted to Catholicism after 1652. For example, Clemens Wenzeslaus, the youngest son of the Saxon elector August III, tried his luck, with French and Habsburg backing, in Cologne, Münster, Paderborn, Liège, Hildesheim and Passau from 1760, before eventually securing Freising, Regensburg, Augsburg and Trier by 1767. By contrast, the Habsburgs were rarely contestants. They did target Passau, close to Austria, which was ruled by three consecutive Habsburg bishops from 1598 to 1664, as well as Augsburg in 1646–65. Otherwise, they concentrated on promoting candidates from friendly dynasties such as the house of Lorraine, for strategic sees like Mainz and Trier.[49] Apart from

Strasbourg, French influence was limited, except where it received the emperor's approval.

Political structure

The cathedral and abbey chapters dominated the political structure of the ecclesiastical territories. The canons entrenched their influence through the elective character of princely rule, and their position as regents during local interregna. They also monopolised senior positions in the territorial administration, where certain functions were often reserved for them. As the leading clergy (*clerus primarius*) of the territory, they were usually represented in the local Estates, particularly in the north-west German bishoprics and Salzburg, where the dean usually chaired both the chapter and the Estates' assembly. This could cause resentment from the secondary clergy (*clerus secundarius*), such as the priors and abbots of the collegiate churches and monasteries within the territory, who had been excluded from the chapter during the middle ages, but retained some jurisdiction over their own institutions and the ordinary priests serving them. In Cologne, Münster and Trier the secondary clergy remained outside the Estates, holding their own assemblies to negotiate taxes and other business with the ruler. Elsewhere, they were represented in the Estates alongside the chapter, secular nobility and towns, except in Fulda and Trier, where the local aristocracy had escaped territorial jurisdiction by becoming imperial knights. This did not prevent the Trier Estates remaining active into the eighteenth century, like those in Cologne, Liège, Münster, Paderborn, Osnabrück, Hildesheim and Salzburg.

The influence of chapter and Estates hindered the growth of absolute princely authority, especially as many clerical rulers were elderly when elected and had little time to stamp their mark on their lands (see Appendix 1). Like hereditary rulers, the spiritual princes were dynasts, but their sphere of activity was very different. Rulers were chosen from the ranks of the canons, whose property and kinship interests extended into other ecclesiastical lands. It was possible for one individual to hold benefices in several territories at once. Well over 50 of the 137 canons who held positions in seventeenth- and eighteenth-century Osnabrück simultaneously held posts in Münster and often Paderborn as well. They tended to choose men of their own kind as bishops, and once the successful candidate assumed office, he remained preoccupied with patronage, office and aristocratic lifestyle, using his new influence to advance the careers of his relations and friends.[50]

None the less, ecclesiastical territories were not immune to the pressures shaping development within their secular neighbours. Most were small, and all depended on the Reich for protection. They still had to provide men and money to collective imperial defence and some, notably Münster and to a lesser extent Würzburg and Mainz, raised larger forces to play a more active role as armed princes. Even once Würzburg had largely given up its political ambitions in the eighteenth century, military spending still accounted for 45% to 55% of its total budget.[51] The need for taxes and soldiers fuelled a process of gradual administrative centralisation and reform similar to that in the secular territories (see section 7.1).

Princely authority was also strengthened by greater continuity of rule from the later seventeenth century. Bishops became more prepared to accept co-adjutors chosen by their chapter in their own lifetime, rather in the manner of the King of the Romans as emperor elect. Co-adjutors were still viewed with suspicion, since they were often forced on unwilling bishops by canons seeking to restrict their power, but incumbent princes also promoted their protégés to these positions. Chapters sometimes welcomed this too, since it avoided the dangers of an interregnum. Bishops increasingly refused further concessions to their chapters. Following a test case in Würzburg, in 1695 the pope forbade chapters from forcing new bishops to agree electoral capitulations. Leopold I confirmed this three years later, and though they were still made, bishops could count on the backing of the imperial courts in the event of a dispute. Many canons appreciated the benefits of good working relations with their ruler. Some acted from self-interest, hoping to be his successor and not wanting to weaken powers they might one day exercise themselves. Others realised that perpetual feuding increased the opportunities for unwelcome external interference, including that of Protestant princes.

The accumulation of sees offered a further way to strengthen princely power. This was forbidden by the Tridentine decrees and a ruler seeking election in a second bishopric had to obtain a papal dispensation and secure two-thirds of the canons' votes, not the usual simply majority. It was difficult to resign from one bishopric in order to seek election in a more prestigious one elsewhere, while the pope generally opposed accumulation. This opened the door to imperial influence, since the emperor could throw his weight behind a friendly bishop to win papal backing and manage the election in the new see. Both Schön-born electors of Mainz managed to combine their main title with other bishoprics in Franconia and the Rhineland. The most extravagant case was the Wittelsbach Clemens August (1700–61), who was known as 'Mr Five Churches' on account of his successive elections in Münster (1719), Padernborn (1719), Cologne (1723), Hildesheim (1724) and the Grand Mastership of the Teutonic Order (1732). The papal decree *Quam invaluerit* limited all subsequent rulers to no more than two sees at once.[52]

Role in imperial politics

The imperial church was the Holy Roman part of the Reich and the heart of German Catholicism: the electorate of Mainz alone contained 96 monasteries and convents. Its fate lay at the centre of the confessionalised disputes of the sixteenth and seventeenth centuries and it is not surprising that ecclesiastical territories dominated the Liga's membership. Not all were governed by zealots, and militancy declined after 1648. The shift towards more openly secular politics has led one historian to dismiss the remaining church lands as 'curious constitutional fossils' left over from the middle ages.[53] Yet, collectively they continued to play an important part in imperial politics.

Their primary aim was to avoid further secularisation, encouraging them to support the political status quo, which guaranteed their existence. Their generally small size inclined them to rely on the Reich for security and they could be numbered amongst the emperor's staunchest supporters, provided he stuck to his traditional role of *defensor ecclesiae*. However, this stance was not necessarily passive, as Mainz's leadership of the Kreis Associations demonstrates, since the ecclesiastical rulers were keen to develop those imperial institutions that suited their needs (see section 5.3).

This conditional loyalty irritated the Habsburgs, who periodically hinted darkly at further secularisation to bring the spiritual princes into line. While secularisation was thus kept on the political agenda, it did not become a serious issue until Charles VII's reign. Faced with enormous political and military problems, Charles contemplated sanctioning widespread secularisation to attract allies, notably Prussia and Hessen-Kassel, in 1742–3. The pope strongly opposed this, while Austria obtained details of the plan and published it to discredit the emperor.[54]

Prussia refloated the scheme during the Seven Years War, this time as a possible carve-up of the Westphalian bishoprics between it and Hanover, but abandoned it as Britain lost interest. Fears were soon revived by the First Partition of Poland, in 1772, between Joseph II, Prussia and Russia. If the emperor could settle great-power enmity at Poland's expense, he might also use the imperial church for the same purpose. Austro-Prussian cooperation soon faltered after 1772, but Joseph remained alarming, particularly as he secularised monasteries within his own lands and pushed radical plans to redistribute territory within the Reich (see section 7.1). Not only did he pressure the Wittelsbachs to exchange Bavaria for the Habsburg Netherlands, but he proposed to swap Liège for Salzburg, which was to be annexed along with Berchtesgaden by Austria.

The Catholic Renewal Movement

The embattled position of the later eighteenth-century imperial church produced the Catholic Renewal Movement. This drew on the medieval conciliar movement, which argued that the best way to revive Catholicism was by the collective action of bishops, rather than through the papacy. It also incorporated more recent enlightened ideas that were not necessarily inherently anti-clerical, and reflected a broader feeling amongst Catholics that they were being overtaken materially by the Protestants.[55]

One aspect of renewal followed trends in France known as Jansenism, and concentrated on inner spirituality in place of sterile ritual observance. Another tried to redefine relations with the papacy, hoping to end the interference of the nuncios based in Vienna, Lucerne and Cologne. The suffragan bishop of Trier, Nikolaus von Hontheim, published this programme as *De statu ecclesiase* in 1763. This outlined a German equivalent to the French notion of Gallicanism: a nationalist rejection of the ultramontane influence of the papacy. Such ideas had existed before Hontheim's book, but he gave them clearer expression, particularly the aspiration that Catholics and Protestants could be reunited in a German National Church once all outstanding complaints with the papacy were settled. These ideas became known as Febronism, after the pseudonym Hontheim adopted to protect his identity.

The movement gathered pace as Mainz, Cologne and Trier met in Koblenz in 1767 and drew up a list of 31 complaints, including a protest against papal restrictions on the accumulation of sees and a call to end the nuncios' jurisdictions. However, the bishops feared the three electors were seeking to appropriate papal authority for themselves. They broke ranks and Febronism waned after 1772. It revived after 1783 as Joseph II began curtailing the spiritual jurisdiction of prince-bishops, who had traditionally exercised authority over the Austrian clergy. Having bullied the bishop of Passau into accepting this, Joseph proceeded to revoke the rights of Salzburg, Regensburg, Freising, Liège and Trier as well. Passau's spiritual jurisdiction had been twice as large as its actual territory, while that of Freising extended over 17,000 Austrian and Bavarians, as well as its own population of 25,000. With so much to loose, the bishops rallied behind Mainz's revival of Febronism in 1784. Charges that the emperor was breaking the imperial constitution raised the possibility that this ecclesiastical opposition would combine with the discontented secular rulers coalescing around Weimar, Baden and Anhalt-Dessau, who opposed the disproportionate growth of Austria and Prussia. When the secular rulers combined as the League of Princes (*Fürstenbund*) in 1785, it looked as if Mainz and the rest of the imperial church would abandon its traditionally pro-Habsburg stance and join this otherwise solidly Protestant group. The Habsburgs reacted by engineering the election of Joseph's brother Max Franz in Cologne and Münster in 1784, as well as his nephew Clemens Wenzeslaus in Trier. With these in place, they were able to expose Prussia's increasingly blatant manipulation of the League and by 1787 the bishops refused to follow Mainz's lead and ended their flirtation with the Protestant opposition.[56]

The renewal movement ended in political failure. First, it alienated the papacy, which had Hontheim's book placed on the Index. Some of the spiritual reforms also alarmed more conservative German Catholics, sparking a fierce debate that was further fuelled by the controversy surrounding the dissolution of the Jesuits in 1773. Papal pressure compelled Hontheim to acknowledge his book and issue a retraction in 1778. He became a martyr for episcopalianism, but the debate damaged Catholic unity. Many believed the archbishops and bishops were concerned more about their political rights than about their spiritual duties, thus providing an argument for secularisation as a beneficial separation of church and state.

Secondly, the flirtation with the anti-Habsburg forces in the Reich alienated the Habsburgs, who viewed Mainz with particular suspicion. There was no return to the medieval alliance of emperor and bishops. Instead, Joseph sought greater control over the Habsburg church, for which he needed papal approval. In return, he backed the papacy in its quarrel with the Febronists. He skilfully avoided a breach with the pope by making a personal visit to Rome in 1783, paving the way for a new concordat the following year that increased his authority over the church in his own lands. His two immediate successors increasingly saw the imperial church as a useful bargaining chip in the negotiations with Revolutionary and Napoleonic France on central European territorial redistribution (see section 8.4).

Thirdly, the movement alienated secular Catholic princes. The Wittelsbachs were already losing interest in the imperial church after 1763, because they were running out of sons even to inherit their own possessions. Carl Theodor followed Joseph and intensified efforts were begun in 1761 to exclude the prince-bishops' spiritual jurisdiction across Bavaria. Like Joseph, he sided with the pope against German episcopalianism in return for greater authority over the church in his own lands, accepting a new nuncio based in Munich to supervise relations with a distinct Wittelsbach diocese.

Finally, though Hontheim attracted some Protestant supporters, he failed to convince the princes to abandon plans for further secularisation. Ultimately, the moderately powerful princes preferred local aggrandisement at the expense of neighbouring ecclesiastical territories, than broader cooperation with them to reform the Reich. They looked across the Rhine to the example of France, where the revolutionaries nationalised all church property on 2 November 1789, and introduced a civil constitution on 12 July 1790, abolishing 50 bishops and all church offices that were not strictly spiritual. The French then annexed Avignon in 1792 and secularised the papal states six years later. The outbreak of the Revolutionary Wars in 1792 weakened the constitutional constraints against these changes in the Reich. As the French annexed German land west of the Rhine, the affected princes petitioned to be compensated to the east at the church's expense. The German ecclesiastical rulers contributed by implicitly recognising secularisation as a legitimate way of accumulating power. Clemens Wenzeslaus, who had lost most of Trier to the French, demanded Constance and Kempten as compensation, while Friedrich Carl von Erthal wanted Fulda to replace parts of Mainz.

Secularisation began in 1801 as the powerful secular rulers started to occupy neighbouring church land well before this was formally sanctioned in 1803. The Catholic Church continued as a spiritual organisation, but the nobles lost their benefices and political rights, which were appropriated by the enlarged secular states. The new rulers plundered their windfall for a quick profit. Over 50 churches and chapels were demolished in Cologne alone, Catholic universities were closed and art treasures were dispersed. Baden sold the cooper roof of St Blasien, melted its bells for cannons and turned the building into Germany's first mechanised arms factory, employing 800 workers, a quarter of them children, while Württemberg turned Zwiefalten abbey into a mental hospital. Regeneration was slow, especially as many of the church's remaining resources were tied up paying pensions for the former canons and clerics. The cause of renewal passed to a new generation of spiritual bishops and clergy appointed by the successor states.[57]

Chapter 6:   Territorial Absolutism

6.1   The Rise of Absolutism

Absolutism – a myth?

The term 'absolutism' dates from the liberal critique of monarchy after the Napoleonic Wars. It was later adopted by historians and political scientists to distinguish authoritarian royal rule from both constitutional monarchy and liberal republicanism. It is usually defined as unrestrained royal power, legitimised by divine and hereditary rights, and exercised through a centralised bureaucracy and permanent army. This form of government was rejected in Britain during the Civil War and later Glorious Revolution of 1688, as well as by the Dutch in their revolt against Spain. France is usually identified as the leading absolute monarchy, symbolised by the reign of Louis XIV (r.1643–1715), who is supposed to have served as a model for its introduction elsewhere. Absolutism is thought to have developed in central Europe as a result of the Thirty Years War and is epitomised here by Frederick William, the Great Elector of Brandenburg (r.1640–88), who crushed his Estates and reduced the *Junkers* to a 'service nobility' staffing his army and bureaucracy. These developments had far-reaching consequences, leading many historians to label the entire period 1648–1789 as the 'age of absolutism'.

Further research from the 1960s cast doubt on this interpretation, by identifying limits to supposedly absolute royal power. The Estates and other traditional institutions were not swept away. The new bureaucracies were corrupt and inefficient, and had limited reach into the localities. Reforms were piecemeal and often counter-productive. This critique broadened after 1992 to dismiss absolutism entirely, as a 'myth' fabricated by nineteenth-century political rhetoric and historians who were dazzled by the façade of royal power. All monarchies remained variants of 'consultative monarchy', ruling by placating key interest groups such as the aristocracy. There was no new ideology of royal authority, and constitutional monarchs, like those in Britain, could be more powerful than the absolutist Bourbons in France.[1]

There is merit in both strands of criticism: there were indeed practical limits to royal power, and there was certainly no blueprint for a radical new form of government. However, the recent revisionism raises more questions than answers. The character and style of rule changed across the early modern period. Authority was conceptualised, justified and projected in more personal, authoritarian ways. Rulers were less prepared to accept formal constraints on their power. Bargaining with corporate groups continued, but it was now less likely to take place through formal institutions like the Estates than by patronage, social regulation and responses to popular pressure. Meanwhile, the infrastructure of power assumed greater coherence as administrative and military institutions became permanent. Many of these changes were gradual, but none the less there was a significant shift in central Europe between the 1620s and 1660s. This seems sufficiently important to justify later seventeenth- and eighteenth-century German princely rule as absolutism, provided the historical reality is not measured against an anachronistic, abstract model.

However, German absolutism was not a singular form. 'Imperial absolutism' existed only as a propaganda device of the emperor's opponents, not as a Habsburg objective. Absolutism developed at territorial level and was characterised by its diversity. Most interpretations distinguish sharply between the allegedly modern, progressive and responsible governments of the larger territories like Prussia, and the 'petty particularism' (*Kleinstaaterei*) of their smaller neighbours, ruled by 'a host of little tyrants' with 'no limits to their power'.[2] More recently this relationship has been reversed, with the lesser princes appearing as enlightened, model rulers in contrast to the repressive, militaristic larger states. This chapter will test these views, first by exploring how and why princely power was reinterpreted in the mid-seventeenth century, before examining absolutism's key institutions.

Absolutist theory

Absolutism was not a coherent body of thought, but this is not sufficient grounds to claim it did not exist. Republicanism and constitutional monarchy also lacked clear, accepted definitions in this period. All early modern political ideas were an amalgam of classical models, Christian theology and practical experience, and absolutism was simply one of several currents.

German political theory distinguished between despotism (*monarchia herilis*) and limited monarchy (*monarchia limitata*). The former was roundly condemned, and even such ruthless monarchs as Frederick II hesitated to publicly endorse Machiavelli's 'reasons of state' arguments as a licence to do as they pleased.[3] This has not stopped later historians from applying the term 'despotism' to eighteenth-century German government. The phrase 'enlightened despotism' was coined by a French economist in 1767 to describe later, more reform-minded rulers. The historical record is also full of tyrannical outbursts, most notably from Frederick William I of Prussia:

> So long as God gives me breath, I shall assert my rule like a despot. . . .
> My subjects must dance to my tune or the devil take me: I'll treat
> them as rebels and have them hanged and roasted like the tsar does.
> . . . After all, we are lord and master and can do what we like.[4]

Some of Frederick William's actions matched his words. He was often seized by uncontrollable rage, and would beat anyone who came near him with his stick. However, this was an expression of his health, not a political philosophy. He suffered from the disorder of the metabolism known as porphyria and was fatally ill. Despite being only 1.65 m tall, he weighed over 136 kg and spent much of his later life in a wheelchair, drowning his sorrows in drink, tobacco and amateur art. In fact, he, not his son Frederick II, first stated that 'the king is the first servant of the state'.[5]

While absolutism was certainly a form of government no right-thinking person would condone, it was not the same as unrestrained despotism. Instead, it had its roots in late medieval ideas of constitutional monarchy, where the prince ruled within certain limits. Most sixteenth-century German theorists believed their rulers conformed to this, whereas the French and Italian potentates exercised an unrestricted *dominium regale* bordering on tyranny.[6] However, Germans disagreed on what the limits should be and how far a ruler was bound by them. One strand favoured mixed monarchy (*monarchia mixta*), where the ruler could only exercise his authority in conjunction with his subjects as constituted in the Estates. Agreements were binding on both parties and could not be renounced unilaterally. The leading proponents of these ideas, like Johannes Althusius and Hermann Conring, were dubbed 'monarchomachs' by their opponents, who accused them of favouring republicanism. While mixed monarchy did offer support for various resistance theories, its supporters remained monarchists. The Bohemian rebels still elected the Palatine elector as their replacement king. Even the Dutch were reluctant republicans who cast around for an alternative sovereign before evolving a highly complex constitution, retaining a strong monarchical element represented by the House of Orange.

The stigma of sedition helped discredit mixed monarchy by the mid-seventeenth century, reinforcing arguments for more absolute authority. This still recognised limits, including agreements with the Estates, but refused to accept them as binding in all circumstances. Princes could override these guidelines if necessary in the interests of the common good. Controversy centred on defining 'necessity' and 'common good'. Absolutism's apologists responded by distinguishing between natural and agreed limits. The latter were particularly complicated in the Reich, because they involved negotiations between emperor and princes, as well as princes and Estates. Princes generally pursued the monarchomach line in the Reichstag, insisting the emperor adhere to agreed limits, but rejected these arguments when dealing with their own Estates. Both territorial and imperial agreements were considered 'fundamental laws' (*leges fundamentales*), hallowed by time and tradition, that rulers were expected to confirm on their accession.

Such laws conflicted with the new understanding of natural limits emerging in the seventeenth century with natural law philosophy. This argued that a state was limited by its own functions and could not act in a manner that prevented it from discharging these. Legitimacy depended not on the form of government, but on its ability to carry out key tasks, like maintaining defence and internal order. Republics were not necessarily superior to monarchies. These arguments provided the basis for all contractual theories of government: people surrendered power to a ruler to enable him to govern on their behalf. Absolutism accepted this, but saw the contract as essentially one-sided, denying people the right to revoke it if the ruler failed in his duties.

These attitudes carried over into other aspects of absolutist thought. Rulers were also bound by their responsibility to God. While all authority was ultimately thought to derive from God's will, Germans rejected the strident 'divine right' arguments of the English and French kings, and saw princely power as a public trust, obliging the ruler to protect his subjects and foster their welfare.[7] This encouraged patrimonialism and patriarchalism. Lands were regarded as an asset to be nurtured and passed on to future generations. Subjects were children, whose care was entrusted by God to the ruler as 'father of his country' (*Landesvater*). Only the prince could truly understand the 'mysteries of state', whereas the Estates were simply a lobby for narrow, selfish corporate interests.

Ecclesiastical rulers shared these attitudes, even if they lacked the complementary emphasis on hereditary rights. Dynasticism was well entrenched before the seventeenth century and was not itself a uniquely absolutist characteristic, but it did assume different proportions from the 1620s as the internationalisation of imperial politics threw the princes' ambiguous status into sharper focus: they were not simply the Reich's aristocracy, yet they were not accepted as the equals of European royalty. Concern to define their position drove princes to emphasise their authority in their own lands, as well as their autonomy within the Reich.

Factors promoting the growth of absolutism

It is important not to see this as conscious state-building. Princes were driven by dynastic ambitions, not a desire to create new political and social arrangements. Certainly, force of personality played a role in individual cases, but people like the Great Elector and his erstwhile collaborator Georg Friedrich von Waldeck were not visionary modernisers.[8] They only changed existing structures where these proved obstructive, and had no pre-determined plan to eradicate entrenched interests.

Confessionalisation reinforced territorial authority, but it did not necessarily create absolutism. Only where religious differences reinforced latent opposition to centralisation did confessional strife encourage rulers to curb the power of Estates and other groups, as in the Habsburg monarchy after the 1580s, and in the Hohenzollern lands after the dynasty's conversion to Calvinism in 1613. The impact of war is widely acknowledged as a major factor, but the precise link between military and political change is disputed.[9] Older arguments that there was a single 'military revolution' between 1560 and 1660 now appear less convincing, and most recent research points to the later fifteenth and early sixteenth centuries as the crucial period of tactical and technological change.[10]

None the less, the warfare of the early seventeenth century was both quantitatively and qualitatively different. The earlier changes in warfare had affected developments at imperial level between the 1480s and 1540s, as the Reich was forced to develop new ways of mobilising men and money. These were consolidated with the growth of the Rudolfine system of eastern defence after 1576, but made their impact through the spread of imperial taxation rather than significant political change within the territories (see section 5.1). Regular taxation did not necessarily favour the consolidation of princely power, since rulers still lacked a developed administration and had to negotiate grants with their Estates, who supervised much of the collection. Rising population and productivity ensured relatively smooth ruler–Estate relations into the 1580s, provided these were not disrupted by confessional differences. Sixteenth-century princes could achieve their goals without having to break the conventions of mixed monarchy.

This became progressively harder as demographic growth out-stripped rising productivity in the later sixteenth century. The start of prolonged warfare removed much of the remaining common ground after 1618. Not only were taxes and troops required at unprecedented levels, but the fighting now took place within the Reich, unlike that in the sixteenth century. The associated destruction exacerbated the underlying socio-economic problems, because rulers were demanding more when resources were shrinking, and in desperation seized what they needed.

Some see this domestic background as having more significance for absolutism's growth than external factors like war and dynastic ambition. Marxist historians interpret absolutism as a necessary stage in the transition from feudalism to capitalism, since political centralisation facilitated the spread of commercialised production and exchange. There are fierce disagreements as to how and why this occurred, but the general starting point is usually that underlying economic changes disturbed late medieval feudal relations, producing two possible routes to absolutism.[11] Either the crown emancipated itself from aristocratic control through a temporary alliance with a rising 'bourgeoisie' in the so-called 'western model', or it forged a closer 'compromise' with the nobles at the expense of other social groups in the 'eastern' variant. Central European and Russian development is thought to have followed the latter course, because the 'stunted' economic development of these regions limited the crown's range of domestic allies. In return for confirming the aristocracy's socio-economic pre-eminence, the crown gained a free hand over fiscal and military policy. Nobles were reconciled to their loss of political influence through alternative careers in the army, and bureaucracy that also served to keep serfs and others in their place.

Absolute monarchy is thus a 'captured state', controlled by, or at least governing in the interests of, the aristocracy, in contrast to more liberal or conservative perspectives that see the crown as neutral, or even benign. Regardless of their ideological character, these interpretations reduce ordinary people to passive objects acted on from above, either protected and promoted by benevolent rulers, or exploited and repressed by rapacious lords. The broader population can either submit or protest, the latter action largely being dismissed as futile until the development of 'class consciousness' and a clear leadership with a revolutionary ideology. Recently, historians have begun to rescue ordinary people from this huge condescension of posterity, and interpret political development as the result of a wider bargaining process between rulers and wider social groups.[12] Revolts and other protests were integral to political development, compelling those in power to take account of broader opinion.

Political alliances did not split along class lines, since the economic, religious and other changes of the later sixteenth century lacked a uniform social impact. This can be illustrated by briefly analysing absolutism's emergence in the Habsburg monarchy, the Hohenzollern lands and Bavaria. The Bohemian and Austrian knights, or lesser nobility, were in decline by the late sixteenth century because of economic difficulties and the practice of dividing their property by inheritance. The Habsburgs promoted this shift by making Catholicism a test of political loyalty, excluding Protestants from ennoblement and the patronage they needed to supplement declining income from landed estates. Reductions in the ranks of the existing nobles created new openings for loyalists, and most of the 300 new families of knights were ennobled crown officials, doctors, and jurists. Initially, this merely fuelled resentment amongst the established nobility, who clung more tightly to existing institutions like the provincial Estates, to protect their interests and provide alternative careers. However, the Estates' defeat in 1618–20 paved the way for a more fundamental restructuring of the nobility as up to two-thirds of the knights' property was confiscated and redistributed to loyalists. These included a significant number of outsiders, notably army officers like Johann Sporck, a peasant from Paderborn. However, most land went to loyal Catholic loyalists and those from other provinces, who considerably increased their land. The Moravian Liechtenstein family, for instance, saw its number of dependent peasant households rise from 3,672 before 1618 to 15,459 by the 1640s. The Bohemian knights declined from 600 families in 1618 to only 100 by 1750, while the senior aristocracy was reorganised as 58 original and 95 new dynasties, dominated by ten magnates with huge estates. By the eighteenth century just 400 families owned a third of the land throughout the entire monarchy.[13]

The narrowing of the elite made it easier to manage, as it could be integrated into the Habsburg clientele through court, military and administrative posts, as well as new honours. The title of prince was first given to a Habsburg subject when Carl Liechtenstein received it in 1608. He remained loyal throughout the Bohemian crisis and served as the kingdom's military governor after 1620. Greater political integration permitted the Habsburgs to relax their earlier insistence on Catholicism and they granted freedom of conscience to 73 Protestant noble families who remained loyal during the Thirty Years War. Closer integration of the aristocracy in the Habsburg monarchy shifted political management away from formal institutions like the Estates and towards more informal bargaining, through patronage, to secure compliance on the ground. It did not mean that the aristocracy acted as a controlling class, since they were still fragmented by status, and by provincial and familiar interests. Instead, aristocrats used their positions at court and in the administration to reward their own clients, including lesser nobles outside the gilded circle of privilege, as well as non-noble groups. As we have seen (see section 3.3), the Habsburgs also responded to popular pressures from peasants and others, including interfering in landlord–tenant relations.

The situation was different in Hungary, where the magnates had also grown more powerful during the later sixteenth century but the lesser nobility were much more numerous, constituting up to 4% of the total population. Habsburg rule was always weaker owing to the presence of the Ottomans in much of the kingdom, and the continued Transylvanian autonomy. The Habsburgs had distributed the crown lands to retain support, and by 1600 the magnates, who formed about a third of all nobles, held 41% of Hungarian cultivated land. The spread of Calvinism reinforced their cultural and linguistic identity, further setting them apart from their Habsburg king. Integration in the Habsburg system was delayed until the reconquest of the rest of Hungary in the 1680s gave access to new land to reward supporters, plus a heavy military presence to repress dissent. Attempts to reverse this failed in the Rákóczi revolt of

1703–11, but Magyar strength compelled the Habsburgs to respect many of the Estates' privileges throughout the eighteenth century.

Consolidation of Hohenzollern power also followed a period of economic difficulty for the territorial aristocracy. Some exploited the crisis of the Thirty Years War to expropriate abandoned land and intensify the manorial economy (see section 3.3). However, most suffered as the demographic decline increased the bargaining power of the surviving workers, who demanded wages in place of labour service and even resorted to violence to press their demands in the 1640s. Rent and land values fell, reducing the *Junkers'* income by two-thirds between 1618 and 1670. The nobles were already in a weak position when the Brandenburg Estates met the Great Elector to negotiate their famous Recess in 1653. Far from cementing a compromise between crown and nobility at the peasants' expense, this merely stabilised the *Junkers'* crumbling position at the cost of giving the elector control of military and foreign policy.[14] The Estates were well aware that tax grants might free the elector from the need to consult them in future, and so limited theirs to only six years. However, the start of the Northern War (1655–60) enabled the elector to continue the levy as emergency taxation. By playing both sides against each other during the war, the elector secured full sovereignty for Ducal Prussia, ending opportunities for the Prussian Estates to appeal to the Polish king for protection. Similarly, an alliance with the House of Orange in 1655 curtailed Dutch backing for urban and aristocratic autonomy in the Hohenzollerns' Westphalian enclaves.

Opposition continued, not least because the elector was not prepared to abandon the peasants and towns entirely to aristocratic exploitation. He and his successor Frederick both relied heavily on other German nobles and Huguenot refugees; the latter made up one-third of the Brandenburg officer corps by 1688. Frederick William I met strong resistance when he tried to force the *Junkers* to send their sons to his cadet schools, and he relied considerably on commoners to staff his bureaucracy (see section 6.2). This trend was reversed by Frederick II, who openly favoured aristocrats, partly from personal inclination, but also from political necessity. It was already impossible to accommodate all *Junkers* in 1688 when there were 1,030 officer and 300 senior civil posts. The expansion of the state infrastructure widened opportunities, particularly in the army, which had 7,121 officers by 1806. Yet, there were at least 3,000 *Junker* families in Brandenburg, Pomerania and Ducal Prussia, while the Polish annexations after 1772 added another 17,000. Since the Hohenzollerns also used their patronage to extend their influence into other German territories, native nobles met stiff competition for posts. Only 10% of the court, bureaucratic and diplomatic elite were recruited from Brandenburg *Junkers* between 1640 and 1740, while 60% of the generals serving between 1730 and 1813 did not come from the traditional feudal aristocracy. At least two-thirds of native nobles stood no chance of an appointment. As in the Habsburg monarchy, the dynasty relied on cultivating the loyalty of key families.[15]

The nobility improved their socio-economic position thanks not to the crown, but to the demographic recovery, which restored population levels by 1713, providing more workers and reducing the peasants' bargaining power. The crown continued to assert its control and by 1733 had established a direct claim on peasant labour through new forms of conscription (see section 6.2).

Economic change also weakened the Bavarian nobility's resistance to absolutism. The richer nobles increased their overall share of land after 1590, while half the poorer families lost their membership of the Bavarian Estates by 1650, because they no longer owned the qualifying properties. Declining income forced many to seek a place at court, or in the Wittelsbach administration and army. Meanwhile, loyal servants were ennobled, bought property and so gained the right to sit in the Estates. The number of native-born noble families in Wittelsbach service rose from 155 in 1600 to 499 by 1679. However, as in the Hohenzollern lands, there were never enough places to go round, especially as grandees like the Törring and Preysing families monopolised the top positions. As the court, army and bureaucracy stopped expanding, they became a closed system, largely self-recruiting as son followed father, denying access to those still outside, who constituted at least a third of all Bavarian nobles. The outsiders' failure to break into the patronage system only served to further weaken the Estates in the 1660s.[16]

The experience of the Habsburgs, Hohenzollerns and Wittelsbachs was repeated with regional variations across much of Germany. In more western areas peasants suffered from the collapse in land values and food prices from the 1630s, making it harder to pay rents and taxes. Rulers acted forcefully to maintain their share as taxes at the expense of nobles and other landowners. This situation often became mutually reinforcing. As it became harder for nobles to live from agrarian profits alone, they had to seek alternative employment in princely courts, bureaucracies and armies.

6.2   The Territorial State

The court

The main elements of the absolutist state need to be seen as social and cultural systems, not just formal institutions. Often the informal connections between their members were more significant than their legal powers. This can be illustrated by studying the court, which reached a dazzling peak under absolutism. The absolutist court is often interpreted as consolidating political authority by conveying a message of princely omnipotence, and 'domesticating' the nobility. This functional explanation, advanced by Norbert Elias and Jürgen von Krüdener in the 1960s, has been criticised recently for exaggerating both the political dimension to court culture and the effectiveness of the court as an instrument of rule.[17] None the less, it remains useful provided it is not imposed rigidly on every aspect of court life. Moreover, it is important to remember that the German courts were not cheap imitations of Versailles, but drew on a variety of other influences that changed over time. The courts indeed presented only a façade of power, but this made a tangible contribution to the style and impact of absolutism.

The court originated in the ruler's household as a place for his family and servants to live. Other functions were attached or detached as territorial rule expanded, but the court always retained both private and public aspects. It usually contained several distinct households, plus courtiers and staff associated with the key members of the ruling dynasty. The principal household was that of the ruler, while others existed for any female consort, adult children, widows, or cadet branches of the main line. These sometimes resided in separate palaces, particularly in larger territories. This private dimension persisted into the nineteenth century, but the public aspect assumed much greater importance as the court became a political stage. Again, the timing of this shift is significant since it coincided with the establishment of absolutism in each territory. The Habsburg monarchy developed its representative baroque court between 1590 and 1630, while that in the Hohenzollern lands only emerged after 1640.

The baroque court

The baroque court was distinguished from earlier courts by its size, style and permanence. Princes built new palaces, generally removed from

Table 6.1 German palace construction

Territory	Old palace	New palace
Bavaria	Munich	Nymphenburg 1664, Schleissheim 1701
Hanover	Hanover	Herrenhausen 1679–94
Habsburgs	Hofburg (Vienna)	Schönbrunn 1695
Brandenburg	Berlin	Charlottenburg 1695
Waldeck	Korbach	Arolsen 1695
Palatinate	Heidelberg	Mannheim 1699
Baden-Baden	Baden-Baden	Rastatt 1699
Württemberg	Stuttgart	Ludwigsburg 1709
Baden-Durlach	Durlach	Karlsruhe 1715
Cologne	Cologne	Bonn
Trier	Trier	Koblenz 1784
France	*Paris*	*Versailles 1661–82*

their old territorial capitals, partly because of the need for a greenfield site, but also to symbolise a break with earlier, more limited forms of rule (see Table 6.1). Construction began well after other changes, having been delayed by the Thirty Years War and the cost involved. It is clear from earlier renovation of existing palaces, and limited new extensions, that princes were already moving towards a new style, and the greater fiscal stability after 1650 allowed this to flourish. The new buildings symbolised order through their coherent, rational and imposing designs. This extended to the surrounding countryside, politicising the landscape as formal gardens suggested that princes could tame nature itself.[18]

By moving out of their converted castles, German princes implied a return to stability, in which people no longer needed to live behind high walls. However, such buildings and their associated material culture always had multiple audiences. Princes could indulge their own interests and tastes, impress other rulers, aristocrats and subjects, and monumentalise their dynasty's lasting fame for posterity.

The Habsburg court and patronage

The Habsburg court was still itinerant under Rudolph II, who moved it to Prague, before it returned to Vienna under Matthias and expanded considerably under his successors (see Table 6.2). Expenditure rose

Table 6.2   Size of selected German courts

Court	Date	Size
Habsburg	16th century	average 450 to 530
	1630	600
	1672	1,966
	1704	1,840
	1720	2,000
	1730	2,500
Hohenzollern	16th/17th century	average 500 to 800
Bavarian	1508	162
	1556	486
	1571	866
	1573–1651	average 700
	1701	2,000
	1705	1,030
	1738	1,380
	1741	1,360
	1747	1,429
	1781	2,140
Württemberg	1709	354
	1717	404
	1745	c. 200
	1766	1,760
	1772	1,800
	1793	607
Wolfenbüttel	1747	381
	1748	389
	1749	400
Hessen-Kassel	1620	500
Hessen-Darmstadt	1630–1710	average 250
Weimar	1806	185
Gotha	1670	135
	1685	155
	1690	176
	1700	168
	1710	205
	1720	221
	1730	230

accordingly, increasing by 500 per cent under Leopold I and then more than doubling again, to reach 4.8 million fl. by 1736. While most of the personnel were menial servants, the number of senior posts reserved for aristocrats rose sharply: from 100 chamberlains under Ferdinand II, there were 423 by 1705. Expansion of court posts extended Habsburg patronage and assisted in a transformation of aristocratic behaviour, since only those who conformed could gain a place. Norbert Elias argued that previously independent warriors became cultivated courtiers, enmeshed in a system of favours and rewards that only the ruler could manipulate. This model of a 'court society' exaggerates rulers' freedom of action, but it is clear that the Habsburg court played a major role in concentrating patronage in their hands.

Patronage was the lubricant that enabled any early modern state to function 'at a time when the public and the private were not yet clearly separated'.[19] It involved reciprocal relationships between unequals. Clients looked to patrons for protection and reward. Though generally dependent on their patron, clients often displayed independence, and there are numerous examples of individuals who failed to support their benefactor, whether from necessity, conscience or opportunity. Moreover, individual relationships were woven into wider networks, so that one man's patron could be another's client.

Aristocratic patronage was detrimental to absolutism since it represented alternative focal points for loyalty. By establishing their court as the centre of honour and reward, the Habsburgs made it the hub for existing aristocratic networks. Though court life cost twice as much as remaining on a country estate, it became indispensable to maintain prestige and influence. The leading families built expensive town houses in and around Vienna to be close to the centre of power. This was a realistic policy, since there was no need to bring all the nobles to Vienna once the major players had been integrated in the system. The courtiers retained country estates, but rather than representing provincial interests, they became intermediary brokers, using their positions at court to advance their own local clients. This system extended into the Reich as other German aristocrats sought positions in Vienna, reinforcing Habsburg imperial influence.

Unlike other major dynasties, the Habsburgs eschewed large-scale palace construction prior to the 1730s, remaining in their relatively cramped Hofburg in the centre of Vienna. This was partly through financial stringency, but it served to underline their exalted European status. The medieval surroundings indicated their long heritage, in contrast to that of the parvenu monarchs elsewhere. It also suited Leopold I's severe, rather retiring character and dislike of public display. Significantly, when the monarchy's material foundations began to crumble in the 1730s, it began a new building programme to project an image of magnificence.

Other changes underscore the court's political role. For example, the dynasty deliberately avoided martial imagery in the artistic depiction of the emperor before 1683, presenting him instead as the restorer of peace after the Thirty Years War and re-emphasising his traditional imperial role at the head of Christendom to obscure his loss of practical influence. To allay Protestant fears, he was depicted as a Christian, not a Catholic. Ferdinand III and Leopold I were both portrayed as a new King Solomon, embodying virtue and wisdom, not zealotry. Images intended for domestic consumption had a more overtly confessional character, but none the less concentrated on the Ottomans rather than the Protestants as the main moral and military threat. The dynasty lost no time in celebrating its defeat of the Ottomans outside Vienna in 1683. At last it had a genuine military triumph, and moreover one that underscored its traditional imperial role. However, it avoided militarism. Leopold's victory was presented as virtuous rather than glorious, in an effort to assert moral superiority over the western enemy, Louis XIV. The continued stress on the dynasty's piety further contrasted with the more secular imagery of the French court. The emphasis on peace resurfaced under Charles VI after the prolonged warfare of 1683–1718, and the emperor was presented in art as the guardian of the common good and a hero of trade and commerce.[20]

The Wittelsbach courts

Vienna overshadowed all other German courts, though these also grew to incorporate native nobilities and project local dynastic ambition. As in Vienna, the periods of greatest expansion coincided with those of tense political competition. Once ambitions had been achieved, or abandoned, the court generally declined. The Wittelsbach experience illustrates this. As the Habsburgs' main German rivals before the mid-eighteenth century, the Bavarian Wittelsbachs maintained an establishment that equalled and occasionally exceeded that in Vienna (see Table 6.2). Expansion was particularly pronounced under Max Emanuel (1679–1726), who had ambitions to obtain a royal crown, and openly challenged the Habsburgs during the War of the Spanish Succession. Yet, this was an unequal contest. While the Munich court cost around the same as that in Vienna, it consumed 55% of Bavarian expenditure compared with only 5% to 8% in the Habsburg monarchy. Elector Carl Albrecht renewed the struggle to support his imperial ambitions, but the court was drastically scaled down soon after these collapsed in 1745. Though it revived under Carl Theodor (1777–99), this was partly through merger with the previously separate Palatine establishment in Mannheim.

Hanover and Saxony

The Hanoverian court also expanded in the 1680s as its dynasty strove first for the electoral title and then for the British crown. It was reduced once these goals had been attained, and the prolonged absence of the ruling family in England prevented a revival. The Saxon court was more stable, and was used to promote the elector's international image as Protestant leader. The family was presented as devout Christians, who patronised Lutheran church music and biblical drama. This shifted with the personal conversion of Augustus to Catholicism and his election as king of Poland in 1697. The Warsaw court was expanded to bolster his uncertain position in that kingdom, but a separate establishment remained in Dresden, and also grew in line with ambitions. The architect Matthäus Daniel Pöppelmann enlarged the Zwinger Palace (built 1708–28) and remodelled the city to celebrate the marriage of the Saxon crown prince to Joseph I's daughter in 1719.[21]

The Hohenzollern court

The Hohenzollern court often looked dowdy by comparison. It remained itinerant, following the elector on his travels around his scattered lands: the Great Elector spent only 12 of his 48-year reign in Berlin, with the rest in Königsberg, Cleve, Oranienburg, Potsdam and the Netherlands. However, both Berlin and Potsdam were enlarged as residence towns, particularly in the 1690s to support Frederick III's royal ambitions. Andreas Schlüchter built some of Germany's finest baroque buildings to prove Berlin was a worthy royal capital.[22]

Frederick William I drastically cut back after his accession in 1713, halting further building work and even giving away his father's lions, tigers and other exotic animals because they ate too much meat.[23] Court expenditure was slashed from 335,000 tlr in 1712 to 52,000 in 1713. This 'break in style' (*Stillbruch*) was celebrated by patriotic Prussian historians as an assertion of the country's 'proper' martial spirit over the previously 'decadent' regime. In fact, it revealed the Hohenzollerns' inability to compete with Habsburg, Wittelsbach and Wettin magnificence. There was also less need for show, now that the new royal title had received international recognition in the Treaty of Utrecht in 1713. The economies enabled Frederick William to impose his own will, purging his administration of all those he felt disloyal or incompetent. Money was diverted into military expansion, but the court still played an important role. Whereas his father had used 25 different sites across Brandenburg alone, Frederick William concentrated on the Berlin–Potsdam–Wusterhausen triangle. Potsdam became the main centre and the king's relocation there underlined his more autocratic style of rule by distancing him from the ministers who remained in Berlin. Wusterhausen was used as a personal retreat, while both Berlin and Potsdam sustained a representational role, accommodating important foreign visitors. Court expenditure soon rose, reaching 210,000 tlr by the mid-1730s. The king did not compete with Vienna, but maintained some parity with more immediate rivals like the Wettins.

Frederick II remodelled Berlin after 1741, possibly in order to match further lavish Saxon construction in Dresden. The Seven Years War gave him a chance to level the odds as a Prussian bombardment destroyed much of the Saxon capital in July 1760, and his troops deliberately vandalised the elector's favourite hunting lodge at Hubertusburg in 1761. To demonstrate that his own state was not bankrupt, Frederick built the huge Neues Palais outside Potsdam in 1763–9. Significantly, this was used only for guests, while the king himself preferred the smaller Sans Soucis palace built in the same park in 1745. This private retreat of the self-styled philosopher king reflected his misanthropic character, but was also a political statement. By residing in Potsdam, he not only kept his ministers at arm's length, but distanced himself from the court itself, which also stayed in Berlin. Again, this was for personal reasons, reflecting his difficult marriage to Queen Elisabethe Christine, who remained at court. However, it was also a strategy to deny his brothers August Wilhelm and Heinrich any influence on real decisions, effectively depoliticising the court by marginalising it.

The significance of this was revealed when Frederick William II moved back to Berlin and revived the court after 1786. Expenditure rose from an average of 300,000 tlr under Frederick II to reach 565,000 tlr by 1795, partly through the expensive renovation of the Berlin palaces. However, the king was now also surrounded by the court and open to its influences. The figure of the influential minister, absent since 1713, returned in the guise of Woellner, Bischoffwerder and Haugwitz.[24]

Standing armies

Like the court, the army was both a symbol and an instrument of power. German armies were an amalgam of the professional mercenaries and defence militias maintained since the late sixteenth century. To a certain extent, they sprang from the larger forces raised during the Thirty Years War that were 'left standing' in the peace after 1648.[25] Most German military history traces their development through the Prussian example, and regards regular forces as replacing earlier, less effective militias. However, this conventional picture only fits the Habsburg experience. The Habsburg monarchy already possessed a permanent army prior to 1618 and was the only German power not to disband its field forces in 1648. Though much reduced, the Habsburg army contained regiments that had existed for three decades or more by the 1650s.

Attempts by later German military genealogists to trace other units back to earlier formations are misleading, since even where these did survive, they existed only as individual bodyguard and garrison companies. For example, Bavaria and Hessen-Darmstadt disbanded all their troops by 1648, while Hessen-Kassel retained only 640 of its 16,000 men. The Hohenzollern establishment was scarcely larger and was split into three elements, each funded separately by provincial taxes in Brandenburg, Ducal Prussia and the Westphalian enclaves (see Tables 6.3 and 6.4). All of these forces, the Habsburgs included, lacked uniform regulations governing supply, discipline, appointment and promotion. The Habsburg army lacked a common tactical manual before 1749, while across the Reich the purchasing of uniforms, weapons and food remained in the hands of individual officers who ran the company and regimental 'economies'.[26]

Defence remained a priority given persistent international instability after 1648, but it was not possible to return to the territorial defence militias of the 1570–1618 era. These had proved disappointing during the war, which demonstrated the superiority of regular forces, whose advantage was cultural rather than technical. Apart from artillery, weaponry

Table 6.3   German military strength, 1650–1790

Date	Habsburg monarchy	Hohenzollern monarchy	Other territories	Total
1650	33,000	700	15,000	48,700
1660	30,000	12,000	20,000	62,000
1667	60,000	7,000	58,000	125,000
1670/2	60,000	25,700	60,000	145,700
1675/8	60,000	43,300	120,000	223,300
1682/3	80,000	25,000	87,000	192,000
1688/90	70,000	29,100	87,000	186,100
1695/7	95,000	31,000	150,000	276,000
1702/5	108,700	40,600	170,000	319,300
1710	129,500	43,800	170,000	343,300
1714	137,300	46,100	120,000	303,400
1730	130,000	66,900	85,000	281,900
1735	205,700	76,000	150,000	431,700
1740	108,000	77,000	115,000	300,000
1745	203,600	135,000	150,000	488,600
1756	156,800	137,000	120,000	413,800
1760/1	201,300	130,000	165,000	496,300
1770	151,600	160,000	110,000	421,600
1789/90	497,700	195,000	106,000	798,700

NB: The above figures are based as far as possible on effective, rather than establishment strengths. They exclude militia. Around a third of all soldiers were on extended leave during peacetime.

remained relatively unsophisticated and it was possible to train recruits and militiamen fairly quickly. However, regulars possessed a more developed military culture, conditioning them to accept authority and work together, and making them more effective than hastily-raised or part-time forces. Their presence added to the lustre of the new baroque courts and symbolised absolutism's claim to guarantee security, and order, and many rulers began augmenting their bodyguard and garrison companies from the mid-1650s. These were distinguished from the earlier 'rabble' (*Soldateska*) by princes who deliberately exaggerated the horror stories from the Thirty Years War to underline the need for powerful regular forces.[27] Such arguments were addressed to both soldiers and civilians, and accompanied efforts to discipline regular troops through tighter supervision and improved pay and conditions. Words

Table 6.4   Growth of the Prussian army

1640	4,650
1641	2,125
1650	692
1651	16,000
1653	1,800
1655	10,500 rising to 26,500 later that year
1661	4,800
1662	7,500
1665	13,500
1666	7,000
1672	15,000
1673	20,000
1679	30,000
1680	25,000
1688	29,154
1693	42,982
1697	22,876
1701	26,000
1704	40,604
1709	43,756
1713	39,963
1715	46,193
1720	56,575*
1725	64,203
1729	66,861*
1733	69,109*
1738	75,124*
1740	76,278 rising to 99,446 by December
1744	131,846
1746	134,910
1755	136,982
1756	158,000
1757	210,000
1762	168,198
1776	156,000
1786	195,000
1789	195,344
1792	217,469 (mobilised strength)
1806	217,664

* Excluding artillery and engineers. Around a quarter were on extended leave in peacetime from the 1680s, rising to over a third during the eighteenth century.

like *Knecht* (literally, 'servant') were no longer applied to soldiers, who were now referred to collectively as the 'military' (*Militär* – often spelt the French way, *Militair*) or 'troops' (*Truppen* or *Trouppen*). Frederick William's famous abolition of the word 'militia' (*Miliz*) should be seen in this context.

Armies and absolutism

The growth of these small German armies has been identified as a key factor consolidating absolutism. Many historians have assumed that most soldiers were 'foreign mercenaries', deliberately recruited so they would not sympathise with the peasants or domestic opposition. In fact, the violent confrontations during the birth of absolutism were already over by the time the new permanent forces were established. Apart from the Hungarians, aristocrats no longer confronted their rulers across battlefields after 1648, while other opponents were more likely to be neutralised by patronage or legal action than through direct coercion (see section 7.2).

The use of force within internal politics was largely restricted to the period 1655–72 and represented the completion of existing trends, rather than a new era of violence. Christoph Bernhard von Galen tried to force his capital city of Münster to relinquish its autonomy and Protestant sympathies. Two attacks in 1655 were followed by an equally unsuccessful assault in 1657, earning him the nicknames 'Bomber Bernhard' and the 'Cannon Bishop'. Schönborn also failed in his first attempt to suppress Erfurt's autonomy in 1663, but he eventually prevailed the next year, as did Galen in his fourth attempt against Münster in 1660–1. The Great Elector had more direct success with Magdeburg in 1666 as memories of the earlier sack induced the citizens to surrender once he brought his artillery to bear. The elector also deployed troops to intimidate the Cleves-Mark Estates, who accepted a revised constitution in 1661 to avert his imminent arrival at the head of 15 regiments. Another 3,000 men occupied Königsberg in 1663 to break resistance to taxation in Ducal Prussia, followed by further intervention eleven years later. Pfalz-Neuburg used troops to collect taxes when its peasants and Estates refused to pay in 1671. Its army grew from 900 unpaid men in 1668 to an efficient force of 2,600 by 1672, while Galen's initial 3,400, mobilised in 1654, periodically rose to over 20,000 and never fell again below 3,000.[28]

The princes set aside their numerous differences to collaborate against internal opposition. The Rhenish Alliance coordinated aid for Galen and Schönborn. Brandendurg and Pfalz-Neuburg combined to defeat appeals from their Estates to the imperial courts, and the Guelph dukes pooled their forces to suppress the city of Brunswick's autonomy in 1671. The collapse of the Rhenish Alliance in 1668 compelled them to develop an alternative framework the following September, joined by Bavaria, Brandenburg, Cologne, Pfalz-Neuburg and Mecklenburg-Schwerin. This group became known as the Extensionists because they wanted to widen the provisions of Paragraph 180 of the 1654 imperial recess, which restricted military taxation to only 'necessary' fortresses and garrisons.[29]

Their earlier experience already indicated that the emperor's attitude would prove crucial. Münster, Erfurt, Magdeburg and Brunswick all lost their autonomy not simply because their princes possessed superior military forces, but because the emperor ruled that their claims lacked foundation in imperial law. Backed by imperial mandates sanctioning a restoration of 'order', the princes were free to use force. They repaid the emperor by supplying part of their enlarged armies to assist him, particularly against the Transylvanians and Ottomans after 1657. The Hohenzollerns' alliance with the House of Orange and their sovereignty in Ducal Prussia after 1660 also made it easier to use force by inhibiting possible external intervention. In short, absolutism's use of force had to appear 'legal' to sustain its claim to guarantee order. This imposed limits on what rulers could do, as revealed by the failure of the Extensionists.

Though the Reichstag extended Paragraph 180 to grant princes unilateral powers to set tax levels, Leopold I vetoed the legislation on 13 February 1671. The Extensionists responded by forming a closer alliance on 6 June, agreeing to maintain a common army of 20,000 to crush domestic opposition.[30] Leopold soon outflanked this group through direct alliances with other key princes, such as the elector of Mainz and the Guelphs. Competition amongst the princes worked to the emperor's advantage and, paradoxically, encouraged greater respect for established rights. Few princes were prepared to see their regional rivals increase their influence. The Guelphs mobilised in 1670 to prevent Galen annexing the town of Höxter, and moved the following year to stop Elector Max Heinrich of Cologne suppressing the privileges of Hildesheim, capital of his secondary bishopric. Further cooperation through the Kreis structure enabled the imperial city of Cologne to resist incorporation in the electorate after 1671. Though Max Heinrich did suppress Liège in 1681–5, this was only after its citizens rebelled against his imposition of customs duties. By 1685 it had become very difficult to deprive communities or corporate groups of rights recognised in imperial law. There was nothing comparable in the Reich to the 'war of extermination' in Savoy, where the duke's troops, with French backing, killed over 2,000 Waldensian dissidents and expelled the survivors in 1685–7. Only the Habsburgs used repression on this scale and then only outside the Reich against the Hungarians.

Militias

There was little to distinguish the forces of the absolutist princes from those of the imperial cities, some of which also maintained substantial numbers of regular troops in the later seventeenth century.[31] The regiment was still the largest permanent formation. Administration remained largely in the hands of the officers, and strength fluctuated considerably in response to political and fiscal contingency. Despite the experience of the Thirty Years War, many territories still relied heavily on militias, issuing revised ordinances from the 1640s to muster and drill selected peasants. Performance remained disappointing, with the Würzburg militia proving hopeless against Erfurt in 1663. Peasants used militia systems to organise their own forces during revolts, notably in the great Bavarian rising of 1705–6. However, this did not make this form of military organisation any more 'democratic' than the standing army. Militia training was seen as an additional burden imposed from above and the Sunday drill sessions were frequently subverted as social events, characterised by heavy drinking and disorder. Local communities resented having to purchase weaponry and clothing for militiamen as well as paying regular taxes for permanent units. On top of the practical shortcomings, this resentment, rather than class solidarity with their opponents, accounts for the militias' failures in the field.

New model armies, 1680–1720

Princes sought an optimal combination of the militias' inexpensive larger numbers with the professionals' greater cohesion and effectiveness. Moves in this direction during the 1660s were disrupted by the Dutch War of 1672–9, when most territories found it hard to expand their small regular forces into large field armies. The economy had recovered sufficiently to soak up most of the under-employed, forcing princes to offer high bounties to attract volunteers. However, unlike 1648, there was no large-scale disbandment after 1679. Though reduced, the various territorial armies were retained and reorganised.

Larger electorates and principalities, like Saxony, Bavaria, Hanover and Hessen-Kassel, maintained forces of about 10,000 men apiece from the 1680s, while medium-sized duchies and bishoprics each had from 1,000 to 3,000. Previously independent companies were now grouped into infantry and cavalry regiments, while the artillery was given a more permanent organisation. Strength continued to fluctuate, but units were less likely to be entirely disbanded. The reorganisation coincided with a generational change amongst the officers. Those who had served during the Thirty Years War were now dead or retired, and their places were taken by new professionals more prepared to accept subordination to princely authority. The social composition also changed as the regular officer corps became increasingly aristocratic, confining commoners to the support services and militia. Greater permanence offered more opportunities for a career path as the hierarchy of ranks assumed a definite shape. Central supervision extended to the rank and file, whose pay and conditions were standardised through common regulations for all units. These were enforced at annual musters, which gave soldiers opportunities to complain about ill-treatment from their officers. Corruption continued, but not on the same level. The volume of new disciplinary and administrative regulations declined after 1720 as the basic procedures were accepted and further ordinances essentially revised existing systems rather than making radical innovations.

The new coherence rested on firmer financial foundations. Despite the Extensionists' defeat, imperial legislation still backed the princes' right to maintain troops, especially with the imperial defence reform of 1681–2. Prolonged warfare after 1683 denied the Estates a chance to reverse the new taxes. Foreign subsidies from France, Spain, Britain, the Dutch and elsewhere provided valuable additional funds, though they were not as lavish as some later commentators claimed.[32]

Funding remained a problem, however, because rulers were now seeking to maintain these larger forces all year round. There was little prospect of raising pay and recruitment bounties. Economic fluctuations and personal problems still drove men to enlist, but most armies needed to replace up to 10 per cent of their strength each year, lost through discharge, desertion and death in service.[33] The only way German rulers could afford to expand their forces was by partly civilianising them through the incorporation of elements of the militia within the standing army.

The new model armies established in the 1680s rested on a small core of professional officers and men, many of whom indeed came from outside the territory, though not beyond the Reich. It was rare for more than 20 per cent of soldiers not to be subjects of the prince they served, and most of these 'foreigners' came from neighbouring territories. They joined as volunteers, generally on short-term renewable contracts, and served for pay, around 4 fl. a month, of which about half was deducted for uniforms and food given in kind. Whether native or 'foreign', such volunteers formed the bulk of most armies into the 1690s, but were supplemented by growing numbers of conscripts selected through the old militia systems. Whereas earlier rulers had used their militias to mobilise additional regiments in wartime, they were now subordinated more directly to the new model armies to provide a regular flow of conscripts. The exact practice varied between the territories. Some, like Bavaria, still mobilised militiamen in separate units, but attached these as additional battalions to regular regiments. Others inducted men directly from the militia registers into line units, where they served until the emergency had passed. The militia thus became a reserve force, providing limited basic training to men who could be called up when needed.

Simultaneously, the professional element adopted some of the characteristics of a militia. To economise, the smaller territories began granting their soldiers extended leave – initially on half pay, later entirely unpaid. By 1700 it was common for a third or more of each army to be out of uniform for three to four days each week, working as day labourers, hawkers, porters and in other menial tasks. Attempts to prohibit soldiers from working in dangerous trades like construction usually failed, because the men desperately needed an income.

The Habsburg army only slowly followed these developments. While its generals felt they never had enough men, the monarchy's superior resources and political influence enabled it to maintain the largest regular force in the Reich without these expedients. Imperial privileges permitted the emperor to ask princes to recruit on his behalf in their territories. Charles VI obtained 100,000 recruits this way in 1733–9, compared with 120,000 from his own lands. The loss of the imperial title temporarily denied these resources to the Habsburgs in the 1740s, but another 122,200 men were recruited from the Reich between 1765 and 1790. Men were raised in the monarchy from volunteers and through impressment organised by the provincial Estates, who were assigned quotas to fill by the central command. Habsburg imperial commitments inhibited the introduction of the leave system. Regiments were frequently stationed far from where they had been raised, making it difficult to release men into the local economy. Militia service remained confined to the Military Frontier, where, into the nineteenth century, it performed a vital role in stemming Ottoman incursions, and the Tirol, which enjoyed special exemption from many military taxes.

Serious defeats between 1733 and 1763 forced the monarchy to reform its military organisation in 1771, replacing the ad hoc provision of men by the provincial Estates with a comprehensive system of conscription. Each unit was assigned a specific recruiting district and empowered to take men from a local register, selected by committees of officers and civil officials.

This system was consciously modelled on the Prussian canton system introduced by Frederick William I. Far from pioneering conscription, Prussia adopted it relatively late compared with the smaller territories. Like the Habsburgs, the Hohenzollerns had relied on their political influence to draw men and money from other German territories, particularly after 1672. This became more difficult as the previously unarmed rulers organised their own forces through imperial defence reform and the Kreis Associations. Their rejection of further Prussian exploitation coincided with the end of foreign cash subsidies to Prussia in 1713. Prussia's continued military expansion had to be sustained from its own resources. Professionals were now sought primarily in the other German territories, often by Prussian recruiting parties operating clandestinely from the imperial cities. The rest of the army was raised by conscription, with each regiment assigned its own district, or canton, from which it could draw men to keep it up to strength.[34]

Social militarisation?

Many see Prussian-style conscription as militarising state and society.[35] Contrary to popular belief, military jurisdiction did not reinforce the *Junkers*' feudal authority. Instead, the crown asserted its right to conscript ordinary Prussians over their lords' claims to their labour. Agrarian interests were mollified by releasing conscripts to work in the fields for up to ten months a year after their initial training. The system regularised recruitment, ending previous arbitrary impressment and making the process more predictable. Peasants developed strategies to cope with its demands and even manipulate them for their advantage. Conscripts remained subject to some elements of military jurisdiction, which they

could invoke to protect them from lordly exploitation, and they maintained contact with their families, unlike their counterparts in Russia,
who rarely saw their homes again. A far higher proportion of Prussian
soldiers were allowed to marry than was customary in eighteenth-
century armies – a factor contemporary Austrian planners believed
gave Hohenzollern conscription its social stability.

None the less, the system ultimately proved inflexible. Despite giving
up to half its personnel extended unpaid leave, the army still consumed
nearly 80 per cent of central government spending. Soldiers' pay
remained the same from 1713 to 1799, while their coats were cut so tight
by 1757 they could no longer be buttoned up at the front. The entire
system was 'front-loaded', dependent on a quick victory in the early
stages of any conflict, since it was difficult to dig too deep into the reserve
of cantonists without destabilising the economy.[36] The Seven Years War
clearly showed the army's limitations, but Frederick II had no answer
other than increasing his forces after the war in a hopeless bid to match
Austrian and Russian growth. Greater numbers could only be sustained
by extending leave at the expense of annual training, and increasing the
quota of foreign recruits, who were also allowed to work in the towns.
Distrust of Catholic Poles prevented the extension of the cantons to land
annexed after 1793, yet the army's commitments increased as it had to
suppress the Polish insurrection of 1794–5. The impossibility of fighting
a two-front war forced Prussia to make a separate peace with France in
1795, making north Germany into a neutral zone (see section 8.4). This
artificially prolonged the life of the Prussian military system by enabling
it to draw on north German recruits. Napoleon's reorganisation of the
Reich disrupted this, depriving Prussia of access to other German territories, and the army had to be thoroughly reorganised after its crushing
defeat in 1806.

The bureaucracy

Discussions of administrative developments under absolutism generally
concentrate on formal institutions and see Prussia as exemplifying wider
trends.[37] The sociologist Michael Mann has drawn attention to other
aspects of bureaucracy that must be considered to avoid imposing
anachronistic analytical models.[38] Mann distils Max Weber's classic
definition of bureaucracy to five key elements. The first two encompass
the formal institutional development that has been the principal focus of

most studies. First, modern bureaucracies are organised into distinct departments along functional lines for the entire area of the state, whereas medieval and early modern administration was mainly structured by geography, with a single body carrying out all tasks for each province. Secondly, modern functional departments are grouped in a centralised, hierarchical structure, and have their own internal chains of reporting and command. The next two characteristics concern the personnel staffing these institutions and define their professionalism. Bureaucrats are officials, not 'office-holders' who own the 'means of administration'. They derive their maintenance not from perks of office, but from uniform salary scales. Furthermore, appointment and promotion are according to impersonal criteria of experience and competence, not favouritism, blood-right or purchase. Lastly, the fifth element addresses the relationship between a modern bureaucracy and society. Officials are insulated from society's struggle over values; in short they are there to implement policies, not make politics.

Contrary to stock images of a 'modern' Prussian bureaucracy, no seventeenth- or eighteenth-century German administration met these criteria and most still fell short in some areas even after 1800. The following will examine German development against Mann's five points, starting with the decision-making process.

Executive power and the 'first minister'

Absolutism entailed both the centralisation of authority and personal princely direction at a time when governments were assuming new roles without having first completed administrative development. The changes placed a heavy burden on the ruler and a premium on his personal character and capacity for hard work. Consequently, actual developments ran partly counter to absolutism's theoretical emphasis on the centralisation of power. Leading, or 'first', ministers stepped into the vacuum, not only assisting the prince, but often determining policy as well.

Discussion of the Habsburg problems in the early seventeenth century has already demonstrated Khlesl's importance during Matthias's reign. Ferdinand II relied heavily on Prince Eggenburg, the head of his privy council, while Trauttmannsdorff assumed a leading role under Ferdinand III. Count Portia and Prince Auersperg shared this position under Leopold I. Such men came under attack from two directions.

There was the traditional critique of the 'favourite' from other aristocrats, jealous of being excluded from power, who accused ministers of creating personal tyrannies. Then there were complaints from the advocates of absolutism, who argued that the sovereign could not share his authority.[39] Criticism fuelled court intrigues, which displaced many favourites by the 1660s. Auersperg was banished from Vienna in December 1669 and Leopold deliberately widened his circle of advisors so as not to fall under the influence of one man.

However, the emperor's growing reliance on his confessor, Father Sinelli, indicates the persistence of powerful advisors. Prince Eugene of Savoy emerged as the dominant military and political figure in Vienna after 1703, but Charles VI's reign was characterised by the presence of a wider range of important ministers: Count Starhemberg at the head of finance (1703–45), chancellor Count Sinzendorf, and secretary of state Baron Bartenstein. Others exercised influence without holding high administrative office, notably Count Althann, who led the powerful Spanish émigré faction that accompanied the emperor back to Vienna in 1714.[40]

Developments in Brandenburg-Prussia followed a similar course. Count Schwarzenberg, the first minister under George William, lost power when the new elector, Frederick William, came to power in 1640. However, despite his more forceful personality, Frederick William also relied heavily on a few trusted advisors: first Georg Friedrich von Waldeck between 1651 and 1658, then Count Schwerin, who already exerted considerable influence from 1644. A succession of powerful ministers followed under Frederick III after 1688: General Schöning and Danckelmann until about 1697, then Ilgen and Wartenberg until 1711.

Ministerial influence detracted from princely authority and often impaired good government. Schöning was devious, while Danckelmann was dismissed and charged with treason. The corrupt Wartenberg was eventually forced out by the crown prince, the future Frederick William I. The Hohenzollerns were not alone in being deceived. Count Montmartin, chief minister to the duke of Württemberg in 1758–66, was a double agent planted by the Habsburgs to influence the duchy's policy during the Seven Years War.[41]

However, such figures were not necessarily incompatible with absolutism, since they allowed the ruler to remove himself from the growing business of government without loss of authority. Ministers were chosen by the prince and accountable only to him, not to a cabinet or the Estates.

The prince had the last word, but could avoid blame for failures by off-loading responsibility onto 'bad' advisors. A certain measure of delegation was necessary given the huge volume of business in even a minor territory. Carl Theodor, not noted for his hard work or dedication, received 100,000 petitions from his Palatine subjects between 1742 and 1777. Over the same period, he participated in 1,600 civil cabinet meetings, which made over a quarter of a million decisions, in addition to other meetings of his military council. He read the papers carefully, even if he did not scrawl notes across them like Frederick II, and he undertook numerous tours of inspection of his scattered domains.[42]

Ironically, only the Hohenzollerns, who ruled much larger lands, attempted extreme centralisation in what was called 'cabinet government'. This was not a ministerial meeting presided over by the prince, as in the smaller territories, but a system of written reporting to the monarch, who sat alone in his cabinet, or study, wrote his decisions and sent them back as orders. Prussian kings issued up to 400,000 of these orders between 1728 and 1795.[43] This practice was not in fact unique to Prussia, since other rulers also dealt with much business this way. What made the Prussian system so distinctive was that its monarchs carried it to extreme lengths, trying to be not just king, but commander-in-chief, and foreign, finance and interior minister simultaneously. Arguably, Joseph II went a step further and tried to be clerk as well. Like Frederick II, he was a man of exceptional ability with an extraordinary capacity for hard work. Yet, both were overwhelmed with paperwork, enmeshed in a system that left them heavily dependent on what their subordinates sent them. As Hubert Johnson has shown, Prussian officials were adept at dissembling, concealing, and influencing decisions by feeding only selected information.[44]

Joseph II was too clever to allow his obsession with detail to prevent his seeking alternative opinions, reopening space for influential ministers. This was already apparent in the 1740s when his mother, Maria Theresa, still controlled Habsburg domestic policy and promoted the career of Count Haugwitz, and then Wenzel Anton von Kaunitz, who rose through the diplomatic service to become the leading minister during the Seven Years War and into Joseph's personal rule after 1780. Baron Thugut and Johann Anton Pergen became increasingly important as Kaunitz aged in the 1790s.[45] Unlike the earlier favourites, who often lacked administrative office, or were associated with the court, the new ministers held senior positions in the formal institutions that had taken shape by the later eighteenth century.

The development of the central agencies

The central administration of the German territories had its origins, like the court, in the ruler's personal household. Court posts (*Hofämter*) developed to run the household and provide an inner circle of advisors, distinct from the other vassals, who largely lived elsewhere. This divergence of government and representation culminated in a distinction between princely administration and territorial Estates by the sixteenth century. The growing business of government was already forcing further subdivisions within the household, splitting this into a separate court and administration. The lines remained blurred into the seventeenth century as courtiers often simultaneously held administrative posts.

The court also remained more prestigious, an arena for both projecting power and striking deals between prince and vassals, whereas administration was initially mainly concerned with record-keeping. The position of chancellor (*Kanzler*) emerged by the thirteenth century to keep lists of princely rights, vassals' obligations, dues and rents. The chancellor had generally been supplemented by a larger court council (*Hofrat*) by the late fifteenth century. Despite its title, this had little connection with the court, but was staffed by other nobles and, increasingly, university-trained commoners with law degrees. It met regularly, with a set schedule, under the nominal presidency of the prince, who in practice was usually represented by the chancellor. Local administration was entrusted to castellans (*Burgvögte*) and bailiffs (*Vögte* or *Amtleute*) selected from the vassals for each district (*Amt*) to oversee the application of the law, public order and subjects' duties to the ruler. Communities were still largely self-governing and only loosely connected to the higher echelons (see section 3.4).

This structure developed in each territory, so that larger, composite lands like the Habsburg monarchy replicated it in each of their major provinces, which had their own chancery and dependent local administrations. Meanwhile, central government was facing more complex tasks, forcing a further subdivision along partly functional lines. The *Hofrat* delegated routine business to specialist subgroups. Legal matters were often jettisoned first, being passed to a court tribunal (*Hofgericht*), such as that established in Bavaria in 1480. While the judiciary did not become truly independent, functions were split between law courts passing judgements and a legal department (usually called *Regierungsrat*) that advised on the drafting and application of legislation. This separation was often in response to pressure from the imperial courts (see section 5.2), but was generally restricted to central government. Justice and administration were not separated at local level until much later: Hessen-Darmstadt in 1775, Württemberg in 1818, Bavaria in 1862 and Lippe-Detmold in 1879. Finance was detached to the treasury (*Hofkammer*), which grew from an audit office charged with checking actual collection to a major budget and economic planning agency after 1648. Military affairs were devolved to a war council (*Kriegsrat*), first in the Habsburg monarchy (1556), and elsewhere after the 1580s. These councils were reorganised with the establishment of the new model armies of the 1680s, and spawned specialist sub-agencies for the commissariat, military justice and fortifications. The rise of the confessional state encouraged new religious departments in the sixteenth century, especially church councils (*Kirchenrat*) to oversee secularised wealth and pay pastors in the Protestant lands. The latter also created consistories to advise on theology and morals, starting in Saxony in 1539 and spreading to the smaller Protestant territories from the early seventeenth century.

Privy councils and cabinets

The growth of specialist departments from 1480 created new problems of management and institutional inertia. Bureaucracy is often regarded as a modernising force in history, yet established institutions frequently resist change, as they develop collective hostility to innovations threatening their autonomy and prerogatives. This characterised the court council during the sixteenth century in many territories, where it often became too large, preventing swift decisions and creating opportunities for factionalism and opposition to princely authority. Rulers began selecting privy councillors (*Geheime Räte*) chosen for their ability and loyalty, from the council and subordinate agencies, to confer privately on important or urgent matters. This select group coalesced into a permanent institution in the Habsburg monarchy in 1526, followed in other territories between 1570 and 1630, including Saxony (1571), Bavaria (1581), Brandenburg (1604) and Württemberg (1629).

As it became institutionalised, the privy council eclipsed the older court council entirely in some territories, or reduced it to a largely honorific body. Concentration on finance and high politics encouraged the privy council to assert itself as the head of the central administration to ensure its business received appropriate support from the specialist agencies. In time, it acquired the same corporate outlook as the earlier court council, particularly as princes appointed additional councillors to handle growing business or simply reward trusted courtiers. The Habsburg privy council had swollen to over 150 people by 1700. Further splits followed, usually in the early eighteenth century, distinguishing between a larger group of essentially honorific councillors who met infrequently for ceremonial functions, and an inner circle of trusted advisors, often called a cabinet (*Kabinett*) or privy conference (*Geheimer Konferenz*).

The privy council and its successor organisation generally included the department chiefs, as well as other selected advisors. The later ministerial system certainly sprang from these roots, but eighteenth-century administration was still highly personalised. All central agencies, including the councils and cabinets, operated along collegiate lines that had their origins in the sixteenth century, and were advocated by seventeenth- and eighteenth-century administrative theorists known as cameralists (see section 7.1). Members of each council or department were roughly equal, regardless of social status, and took decisions by majority vote after debating written memoranda prepared by the specialist subordinate agencies. The prince or first minister presided, but decisions were collective, and those made by the junior agencies had to be signed by all present before being passed higher up the ladder. Ministers merely chaired discussions and only the prince was not bound by decisions. The collegiate system persisted into the nineteenth century until rulers delegated greater responsibility to ministers for key functions, as in Prussia and Württemberg in 1808, and Austria in 1848.

The lower echelons

It took equally long to integrate all administrative agencies within a single, centralised system, especially in the larger, composite territories like the Habsburg monarchy, where the court war council was the only common institution apart from the dynasty itself before the creation of a council of state in 1761. Prussian centralisation was equally restricted to high politics and military affairs, with much still delegated to the chamber (*Kammer*) in each province.

The collegiate system did not extend to the lower echelons of administration, which remained largely in the hands of district officials wielding considerable immediate authority, though subject increasingly to closer supervision and compelled to follow written procedure. Their accountability was always upwards towards the prince, rather than to the communities they served, except for local officials, who were still appointed by villagers and townsfolk. This permitted the aristocracy to retain considerable influence, despite the growth of absolutism. The Prussian *Landrat*, or district administrator, is a good example. His role resembled that of the English justice of the peace and he acted as intermediary between the provincial chambers and the local landowners. Frederick William I asserted his right to appoint *Landräte* in Ducal Prussia, Cleves, and Mark, but elsewhere the aristocracy still elected them from their

Table 6.5 Numbers of personnel in selected administrations

Territory	Senior officials and central agencies		Total	
	Date	Officials	Date	Officials
Habsburg monarchy	1749	1,386	1740	5,000
	1754	1,731	1763	10,000
	1756	4,956	1780	20,000
Hohenzollern lands	1680	300		
	1720	500		
	1740	386*		
	1754	641*	1754	3,100
	1794	2,499		
	1800	2,997	1800	50,000
	1806	3,271		
Palatinate	1750	273		
	1770	391	1777	860
Bavaria	1808	730		
Württemberg	1717	188		
	1728	240		
	1789	315	1789	1,641
	1821	1,116	1821	34,811
Gotha	1670	34		
	1730	72		
Weimar	–		1780	250
Lippe-Detmold	1721/48	35	1721/48	258
Basel (bishopric)	–		c. 1790	200

* Excluding judiciary and diplomats.

midst. Regardless of their method of appointment, *Landräte* were caught between obligations to the crown and entrenched local interests. Frederick II's attempt to supervise all appointments simply demonstrated the limits to his style of personal rule: he did not know all the *Junkers* personally and was forced to rely on local recommendation. The *Landräte* remained autonomous elements within the Prussian system and often provided poor service, particularly during the Seven Years War.

In an age without electronic communication and data storage, bureaucratic reach depended heavily on local presence, but most officials remained part-time, while those in the central agencies frequently worked in several departments at once. Estimates of the total number of officials vary widely, whether or not these are included along with clerks, messengers and other junior staff. Accordingly, the figures in Table 6.5 should be treated as a rough guide only. Moreover, larger numbers did not necessarily translate into greater efficiency, since the German population rose significantly after 1730, while the Habsburg and Hohenzollern monarchies greatly increased in size with the Partitions of Poland.

Social composition

Bureaucratic growth is often associated with the rise of a middle class, whose supposedly rational outlook encouraged the dissociation of public office from private interest that Mann identifies as a key criteria of a modern system. However, not only did aristocrats continue to serve in large numbers into the nineteenth century, but they were often better qualified than their more humble colleagues. Moreover, the gradual growth of professionalism fostered a common ethos that partly transcended social distinctions, while confession and family ties also shaped administrators' identity.

Administrative appointments were usually governed by 'indigenous law' (*Indigenatsrecht*), stipulating that officials had to be natives of the territory they served. Confessionalisation added further religious criteria in the sixteenth century, cutting across social divisions by ruling that all appointees had to profess the official faith. There were always exceptions to these restrictions. Certain posts were reserved in the ecclesiastical territories for the cathedral canons, who were often outsiders, while the court and army were usually entirely exempt as appointments depending solely on the prince. Protestant princes frequently employed Catholic artists, musicians and architects, much to the disgust of their orthodox consistories. The growing importance of university education provided other arguments to appoint foreign talent, while newly-created institutions often escaped the restrictions entirely.

Commoners already formed a significant presence in medieval administrations, especially clerics, who were valued for their literacy and education. Their numbers grew with the expansion of university education and the development of 'cameral science', a vocational mix of economics, business studies and policy management that was taught in the seventeenth century. The proportion of nobles among Württemberg councillors fell from 70% to 30% across the sixteenth century, and aristocrats constituted only a tenth of all officials by 1600.[46] The integration of aristocrats into absolutism reversed this trend from the mid-seventeenth century. Nobles exploited their social connections and status to force their way into princely administrations, but in doing so, accepted the obligation to study first at a university, unlike their counterparts in France and Spain, who still expected posts by right. Of 55 aristocratic south German privy councillors serving between 1660 and 1720, 30 had attended university and only three had no formal education, and they were all army officers with at least some practical experience. Commoners still held a significant proportion of senior posts in the later seventeenth century, particularly in the smaller territories, where they generally accounted for two-thirds of the privy councillors.[47]

The percentage of aristocrats rose again during the eighteenth century, notably in Prussia where it climbed from 17% of the main central agencies in 1740 to 61% by 1806. Commoners were restricted to the finance department, municipal posts and the lower ranks of the central agencies. Most junior ranks, such as clerks, were recruited from the peasants, many of whom had served as soldiers, though the secretariat of the major central agencies were predominantly more wealthy commoners, many with university degrees.

However, the aristocracy's commanding position in Prussia was exceptional and not a sign that German administrations were becoming generally more exclusive. Nobles tended to reach high office earlier and receive more money for the same job, but German administration remained more flexible than that in France and there was no equivalent of the privileged administrative aristocracy of the *noblesse de robe*. Commoners could be ennobled by grant of letters of nobility (*Briefadel*). This was one of the imperial reserve powers that had been delegated since the middle ages to the Austrian archdukes and the counts Palatine (*Pfalzgrafen*). Bavarian dukes claimed the same powers, but no other prince could ennoble unless he possessed sovereign territory. Acquisition of royal titles by Saxony, Prussia and Hanover thus greatly increased their rulers' powers of patronage. Those without such powers had to petition the emperor to elevate their favourites. Ennoblement did not automatically confer full aristocratic status, which only came when an individual secured the respect of his new peers. However, it could open access to advantageous marriages and higher pay, both of which could bring the new noble into closer proximity with the established aristocracy.

Ennoblement accounts for much of the growing aristocratic presence in the administration and demonstrates how patronage was used to consolidate absolutism. The Habsburgs regularly ennobled loyal servants from the sixteenth century, followed by medium-sized territories like Bavaria around 1650 and the lesser principalities after the 1680s. Ennoblement offered rapid social mobility to the favoured few. Khlesl was the son of a Moravian baker, but he rose in the traditional manner through the church. However, his successor Eggenberg was originally a Styrian merchant, who was made a prince by Ferdinand II. Georg Derfflinger, a peasant who fled Habsburg religious persecution, rose in Hohenzollern service to be an imperial baron, governor of Pomerania, and field-marshal with an annual salary of 18,000 tlr and the income from 20 manors. Such cases were exceptional, but ennoblement was widespread in many territories: 47 of 85 south German councillors were ennobled by the emperor in the course of their careers between 1660 and 1720.

Established aristocrats often opposed absolutism for this reason. In the north-western ecclesiastical territories they seem to have prevented their prince-bishops from promoting many commoners by insisting on lineage as proof of status and discouraging unequal marriages. It was this social conservatism that Voltaire ridiculed in *Candide*, where the hero's mother, a Westphalian noblewoman, refuses to marry his father 'because he could only claim seventy-one quarterings, the rest of his family tree having suffered from the ravages of time'. This did not prevent some commoners reaching high office without ennoblement. For example, three of the eleven ministers serving Carl Theodor between 1745 and 1777 were commoners, including Josef Anton Reibeld, a peasant's son, who became chancellor in 1765. Moreover, Frederick II's blatant prejudice was reversed by his successors and by 1800, 36% of senior Prussian posts were held by men of bourgeois origin, rising to 60% by 1829. Aristocrats only reasserted themselves in the conservative reaction following the 1830 and 1848 revolutions.[48]

The bureaucratic ethos

Regardless of social origins or status, German officials increasingly shared a common set of values. This was partly because they became largely self-recruiting, with sons following fathers into administrative careers. Newcomers also tended to marry into the families of existing officials. Approximately two-thirds of common-born councillors married noblewomen, while ennobled commoners and aristocratic high-flyers usually reinvested their salaries in land and joined the local elite.

This process of renewal and assimilation could be disrupted. Many territorial elites were small, inter-related networks of families susceptible to violent shifts, such as the conversion of their ruler to a new faith. As the discussion of the court has demonstrated, there were never enough posts to go round, especially in the larger territories. Small territories often lacked sufficient local talent where the local nobility had opted out as imperial knights, yet the restricted scope of their administrations often encouraged ambitious officials to leave for better positions elsewhere. Only one-third of non-noble south German councillors were natives of the territory they served. Half had worked somewhere else in a more junior capacity prior to their appointment. Mobility was higher still among aristocrats, three-quarters having served more than one master during their careers. Larger territories offered more opportunities for promotion, but also attracted ambitious men from outside, like the numerous Protestants prepared to convert in order to advance in Habsburg service.

Common outlook was reinforced by the close ties between higher education and administrative service. The first university in the Reich was founded in Prague in 1348. Fifteen more were established by 1448, followed by another 18 in 1502–1648. By 1795 there were 50 institutions, compared with 22 in France and 2 in England. These were primarily princely creations; only two German universities were located in imperial cities. The universities' primary purpose was to train public officials. Of 599 Frankfurt citizens who graduated in law between 1600 and 1800, a third became territorial officials, a fifth municipal councillors, 10 university lecturers and the rest lawyers, apart from only 8, who entered business.[49] Law increasingly displaced theology as the main subject. From a mere 50 law graduates in the 1650s, numbers reached over 300 in the 1700s, before settling down to between 110 and 200 each decade in the eighteenth century. They remained in short supply, but were supplemented by trained cameralists with the establishment of this subject in the Prussian universities of Halle and Frankfurt/Oder in 1727, followed by Rinteln in Hessen three years later and others soon after. Higher education's dependence on the territorial state is underlined by the closure of 19 universities after 1796 in the wake of the political reorganisation of the Reich.

Professional examinations had formed part of the appointment procedures for imperial lawyers since 1495. Prussia introduced this requirement for senior judges in 1693 and extended it to all in 1737. On-the-job training was introduced in most branches from 1723. Senior officials had to pass an exam after 1770 and this became a general criterion for all appointments in 1792. While financial expediency prompted some rulers to sell positions, most followed a similar pattern of encouraging appointment by merit. There were few hereditary administrative titles and generally German rulers were not faced by the entrenched corporations of office-holders that existed in Spain and France.

The patrimonial aspects of administration were restricted to the right to supplement often meagre incomes by charging fees for services rendered, and limited powers to pick subordinates. Private connection and public duty were blurred, but not necessarily permanently in conflict, and contemporaries made fine distinctions between justifiable and illegitimate use of influence. Patrimonial elements were eroded, not merely because rulers wished to assert their authority over their servants, but because administrators developed their own corporate professionalism.[50]

Habsburg administrative reforms, like those later in Prussia, fostered the ideal of the dedicated state servant (*Staatsdiener*). By improving pay and job security, they steered personal ambition along institutional lines. Already in the seventeenth century, governments assigned cash equivalents to the free accommodation, firewood, candles and other perks that were given in lieu of regular pay. These were increasingly converted into enhanced salaries in the eighteenth century. Pay scales were regularised, often minimising the previous social inequalities between noble and non-noble officials, and replacing these with higher rates for those with a university education. Employment contracts were no longer terminated automatically on the death of each ruler. Officials now served an increasingly impersonal state that transcended the lives of individual princes. This entailed the loss of some freedoms, as it became harder to resign and serve another government. Other employment also became incompatible with public office. Yet, job security improved and was extended by regular pension schemes that no longer depended on the whim of each ruler. In 1762, Maria Theresa introduced pensions at 50 per cent of the previous salary, and these there extended by her son in 1781. The dissolution of many smaller governments during the territorial reorganisation of 1801–15 spread these arrangements, because the successor states took responsibility for the former officials, who received alternative appointments or pensions.

Officials welcomed these reforms as strengthening their own corporate rights. The earlier critique against favourites was institutionalised as a campaign to secure transparency in promotions, and protection against unfair dismissal. The instrument of absolutism began dismantling the system from within. Rulers relinquished exclusive powers to dismiss officials, entrusting these instead to special commissions like those created in Württemberg in 1787 and Prussia in 1794. By 1800 most governments operated a system of formal notice of three to six months, consolidated in Bavaria as a comprehensive set of corporate privileges, the *Beamtenrecht* of 1 January 1805. This had been copied by all German states by 1850 and gave public officials job security for life, protecting them from dismissal except in cases of professional misconduct. Corporate privileges and outlook found tangible expression in the spread of civil service uniforms, such as that introduced in Bavaria in 1799, four years after similar measures in Revolutionary France, and copied by Prussia, Württemberg and Baden by 1804 and Austria ten years later.

German officials probably identified more firmly with an impersonal state than their counterparts in any other European country by 1800. Administrative structures met at least some of the criteria for a modern bureaucracy, but its officials were neither dynamic modernisers, nor impartial figures presiding over the maintenance of a benevolent status quo. They were partisan and self-serving, taking decisions which today often seem heartless and cruel. Some were corrupt even by their own standards. Yet, they displayed an extraordinary capacity for hard work and attention to detail in ill-lit, cold, cramped conditions, and made a major impact on the world around them.

6.3 The Territorial Estates

Origins

The Estates had their origins in the same 'crisis of the court' that saw the separation of administration from the ruler's household in the fifteenth century[51] While still claiming to advise the ruler and share in the exercise of his authority, the Estates also claimed to represent his subjects. The uniquely hierarchical character of the Reich ensured that this development occurred on two levels at roughly the same time: the imperial estates coalesced in the Reichstag to advise the emperor, while their own vassals and subjects combined in Estates in most territories. The presence of powerful cathedral chapters inhibited this in seven major bishoprics, but otherwise Estates also emerged in most ecclesiastical territories.[52]

Estates met either in plenary session, when all members attended, or as selected committees chosen according to rules that varied in each territory. Most had meeting halls close to the ruler's residence, such as the *Landschaftshaus* in Stuttgart a few blocks away from the duke of Württemberg's castle, or in the Bohemians' case, actually in the Hradschin castle above the river in Prague. Plenary diets were summoned to discuss major issues, such as new taxes and the amortisation of princely debts. Like the Reichstag they opened with an address from the prince or his leading councillor, who announced a list of demands. The Estates generally responded by presenting written *Gravamina*, or a list of complaints against their ruler, citing all his transgressions since the last diet. The Gravamina have often been misread as evidence of irreconcilable differences between ruler and ruled, but like the prince's demands they were essentially a bargaining position. Over the coming weeks both sides would trade concessions to secure their actual goals, with the prince generally agreeing to end various 'abuses' by his officials in return for (often much reduced) new taxes. In the sixteenth century, rulers generally attended a celebratory banquet to conclude the proceedings, but this became rare after 1620 as it was incompatible with absolutist pretensions. Standing committees met more frequently, usually at least twice a year, when the diet was not in session. Their meetings were used to compile *Gravamina* and to negotiate with princely officials and local communities over the actual collection of agreed taxes. Together with a small staff of salaried clerks and archivists, such committees gave the Estates a permanent place in their territory's political life.

Territorialisation of representation was deeply entrenched, with each province in composite monarchies, like the Habsburg lands, having its own institution. The classic form was a tricameral assembly reflecting the corporate representation of clergy, nobility and commons. This form was relatively rare, though it was found in some leading Catholic lands and persisted in some Protestant ones where former abbeys retained their role in the new territorial church.[53] Bi-cameral Estates existed where the nobility had opted out as imperial knights, leaving only the clergy and leading towns represented.[54] The nobility were sometimes split into lords and knights, particularly in the north-eastern territories,[55] while the towns were often dominated by a single major city.[56]

The German assemblies thus differed considerably from representative institutions in England, Poland and Hungary, which were also bi-cameral, but where representation in the upper and lower houses cut across the boundaries of the social estates: aristocrats and bishops sat together in England's House of Lords, while gentry and commoners intermingled in the Commons. The basis of representation was also different. English MPs and Hungarian dietines represented geographical constituencies, whereas Germans spoke for corporate groups. Nobles sat either by virtue of owning qualifying land, or through election by their peers. While commoners could purchase noble land, they were denied the associated political rights, thus undermining aristocratic representation in some areas.[57] Clerics were also chosen by election or by the right of important foundations to send a representative. Towns and cities sent their mayors, who were elected by the enfranchised citizens. Representation was indirect in all cases. Mayors represented disenfranchised residents alongside citizens, while clerics represented other clergy, and nobles claimed to speak for the 'country', meaning their tenants.

Ordinary people only had a more direct voice through the *Landschaften*, which, in its broadest sense, denoted Estates that contained deputies from rural as well as urban communities. The Tirol diet of 1720 was attended by representatives from 84 rural districts, alongside 10 mayors, 10 abbesses, 12 prelates, the bishops of Brixen and Trent, and 200 aristocratic families. Popular participation existed elsewhere, but it was only pronounced in Württemberg and East Frisia.[58] In its narrower sense, *Landschaften* meant a different form of representation, emerging from below without aristocratic or clerical participation. The most famous developed in the imperial abbey of Kempten, appearing briefly in 1496 and 1526–7, and then more permanently from 1660. Others existed in smaller Swabian and Rhenish counties and some imperial cities with substantial numbers of dependent villages.[59]

Their appearance raises the question of whether Estates can be seen as precursors to modern democracy. Many writers have drawn a direct connection between the early assemblies and modern parliaments, portraying the Estates as valiantly championing liberty in the face of princely despotism.[60] Marxists have condemned them as part of the same oligarchy as the prince, and see ruler–Estate disputes as internal struggles among the ruling class.[61] Peter Blickle has also rejected the liberal interpretation, arguing that the origins of modern democracy and republicanism lie in the true *Landschaften*, not the aristocratic-dominated Estates.[62] *Landschaften* embodied the democratic potential of communalism, offering an alternative route to modernity by building state and society from the bottom up, rather than imposing an authoritarian system from above (see section 3.4). This provocative interpretation has generated considerable controversy since the 1980s, but is best examined alongside the older liberal claims for the Estates' democratic roots.

Estates were intermediary bodies between rulers and subjects. Radical mixed monarchy arguments had been discredited by the Bohemians' defeat and the actions of the English regicides in the seventeenth century. Few Germans were prepared to advocate that Estates share power with their prince on equal terms, still less claim they should supplant him altogether. Instead, they based their rights on the theory of limited monarchy. The initiative lay with the prince, but the Estates were there as guardians of the fundamental laws. Their influence rested on the power of their purse, since princes had to negotiate over the exact scale and nature of new taxes. Advocates for the Estates claimed their presence ensured better government, since they offered more impartial advice than the servile flattery of courtiers. Their roots in the localities gave them access to information, enabling them to forward suggestions and complaints. They could offer administrative support through their own secretariat and small standing committees, which met when the full diet was not in session. But they also constituted part of the 'authorities', concerned to prevent popular anarchy as much as to curb tyranny.

They had some potential to create larger states through aristocratic federalism, though the Bohemian experience demonstrated that there were distinct limits to this (see section 4.2). They remained entrenched in corporate society, and even radicals like Althusius, thought by Blickle to advocate communal representation, were extremely reluctant to give ordinary people a role.[63] Peasants criticised those Estates that denied them representation and called for *Landschaften* instead.[64] These had more democratic potential, but were also limited by the divisions within communities, which restricted the franchise to a small proportion of largely male property-owners. Republicanism was not a timeless, abstract phenomenon, but one of many contested political terms. It was not indelibly linked to individual freedom, and in the seventeenth century was concerned more with liberties, than with liberty. Communalism's political character was demonstrated in Switzerland, the one part of central Europe where it succeeded in creating a state from below. The Swiss Confederation was a network of alliances between communities, each retaining its own privileges and rights. Its modernity lay in its commercial and financial institutions, not its creaking political structure, which was eventually destroyed by Revolutionary France in 1798.[65]

Lack of democratic potential did not mean that the Estates were entirely unresponsive to popular concerns. Mayors, clerics and aristocrats knew their local influence and prestige depended on defending broader interests against princely fiscal and military demands. The dualist model favoured by the liberal interpretation exaggerates the level of ruler–Estate conflict. Whilst not simply part of a homogenous ruling elite, both prince and Estates were none the less authorities embedded in territorial politics and obliged to work together. Cooperation depended on the degree of converging interests. External dangers and confessional solidarity generally fostered good relations, and the absence of these factors in the Habsburg lands after 1606 was a major factor in the Bohemian revolt (see section 4.1). Rulers could break Estates' opposition by cultivating loyalist groups through patronage or co-option.

Useful though these strategies were, they alone do not account for the decline of Estates after 1648. Full assemblies ceased to meet in Brandenburg after 1653, followed by Hessen-Kassel (1655), Bavaria (1669), Holstein (1675) and Baden-Durlach, while elsewhere they became more infrequent, such as Wolfenbüttel, where none was held between 1682 and 1768. As indicated above, the growth of a standing army had little to do with this. First, many Estates were already declining by the later sixteenth century as their ruler's financial position became more secure. The Bavarian assembly met 34 times between 1514 and 1579, but only six more diets were held by 1612 and then none until the last in 1669. War taxes effectively became permanent after the 1650s, removing the need for further negotiations. The Thirty Years War ruined the Estates' credit, because they defaulted on the repayment of princely debts they had assumed during the previous century. Princely finances were also battered, but the Reichstag enacted special protection against their creditors in 1654. The clarification of territorial sovereignty through the IPO and Paragraph 180 of the 1654 recess consolidated the absolutist interpretation of limited monarchy, confining Estates to a clearly subordinate role. Few Estates possessed the right of self-assembly, and those that did, saw this challenged by Leopold I's ruling in favour of the princes in 1658.

None the less, the Estates generally survived, even if plenary assemblies no longer met. Rulers still appreciated good advice and those in Westphalia continued to consult their Estates into the 1790s. The wave of conversions to Catholicism amongst Protestant dynasties from 1652 gave their Estates a new role as guardians of their territories' official religion, while those in Catholic ecclesiastical lands often survived because the prince was an absentee ruler. The revival of the imperial courts from the 1670s ensured that surviving rights could be defended, notably three celebrated cases in Mecklenburg, East Frisia and Württemberg, where rulers resorted to force to break opposition to tax increases. All three Estates obtained favourable court injunctions, with those in East Frisia and Mecklenburg being upheld by military intervention through the Kreis structure. In the latter case, the duke was deposed by the emperor, and his successor was compelled to accept a new constitution mediated by Prussia in 1755 that survived without significant modification until 1918. The East Frisian settlement also favoured the Estates and was confirmed when Prussia inherited the principality in 1744. The Württemberg Estates exploited the discontent following the conversion of the ruling dynasty to Catholicism and conspired with disaffected elements in the duchy's administration. They staged a coup with sympathetic army officers after the death of Duke Carl Alexander in 1737, overturning a Catholic regency and installing a more pliant government, which accepted tight fiscal limits two years later. After achieving his majority in 1744, the new duke, Carl Eugen, used the Seven Years War (1756–63) to break these restrictions by decreeing emergency taxation. The restoration of peace permitted the Estates to appeal to the *Reichshofrat* in 1764, culminating in a verdict six years later that confirmed the 1739 tax levels. These remained unchanged until the French Revolutionary Wars (1792–1802) gave a later duke, the ruthless Friedrich, the opportunity to suspend the duchy's constitution after 1797.

In each case, the Estates succeeded because they based their position on recognised law, whereas their rulers resorted to force. However, the imperial courts intervened to stabilise the internal political balance, not to favour one side or the other. Estates' appeals were rejected when they opposed rulers acting within recognised limits, as in Lippe-Detmold in 1746 when the *Reichskammergericht* upheld the prince's right to maintain an expensive, but tiny army, on the grounds that this was required to discharge imperial defence and public peace obligations.

Continued recognition in imperial law accounts for the Estates' partial revival in the later eighteenth century. The Bohemian, Styrian and especially Hungarian Estates became increasingly vocal in opposing Joseph II's reforms and the financial crisis of the Turkish War of 1787–92. This was a conservative protest, however, and subsided once Leopold II reversed many of the controversial measures. Development diverged, with the Habsburg and Hohenzollern monarchies retaining corporatist Estates representation, while those of the lesser German territories were replaced by more liberal parliaments by the 1830s. Criticism of the Estates as narrow oligarchies had been growing since the 1760s and by the 1790s radicals distinguished between them and 'popular representation'.[66] However, criticism remained in practice within traditional political boundaries and did not extend into a wholesale attack on privilege as in France. Liberals searched for an optimum balance between monarchy and corporate liberties, encouraging gradual rather than revolutionary change. Article 13 of the German Confederal Act of 1815 obliged all states to establish Estates (*Landständen*). Prussia, Austria and Hanover only created these at provincial level, but the others transformed existing institutions in stages by reducing corporate representation in favour of a wider, property-based franchise. For example, Saxon reforms eroded the aristocratic presence in the assembly from 1805 to 1820 and then replaced this with a bi-cameral parliament in 1831.

6.4 Public and Private Finance

The rise of the tax state

The public elements of government gradually separated from private life, despite the personalised nature of absolutist rule. This can be seen most clearly in the area of finance and involved a fundamental shift in attitudes. Corporate society expected each group to fend for itself, including lords, who were expected to 'live off their own' from the 'ordinary revenue' of their personal domains and feudal prerogatives. Additional assistance was only forthcoming in exceptional circumstances, like the charity given to the 'deserving poor', or the extraordinary taxes paid to a ruler faced by invasion or natural disaster. By centralising authority and making it more tangible, absolutism propelled development towards an impersonal state as an overarching public sphere, detached from and superior to all private bodies.

The impersonal state was not impartial, since it did not treat its inhabitants equally. However, government was no longer an extension of the ruler's patrimony. The state asserted control over taxation that was now permanent, but detached this from the ruler's own income, which became his 'private purse'. This process was far from complete by 1800, but it had transformed earlier forms of irregular feudal tribute into regular taxes legitimised by the state's sovereignty over its territory and inhabitants. This transition has been described as one from 'domain state' (*Domänenstaat*) to 'tax state' (*Steuerstaat*).[67] It was driven by the growing complexity of social, political and economic problems that accompanied the demographic recovery from the fourteenth century agrarian crisis. Changes in military technology from 1450, as well as the confessional strife after 1517, provided additional impetus. Finally, the commercialisation of the economy, either as western landlordship or eastern 'agrarian capitalism', facilitated the transition by enabling extraction in cash to replace earlier tribute in kind (see section 3.3).

Late medieval lords responded first by intensifying their exploitation of the farms, fisheries, mines and forests that constituted their domains. These remained important into the eighteenth century, particularly in the larger electorates, where they still provided up to a third of central government income. The prerogatives of territorial lordship were developed to provide additional money, chiefly through expedients like coinage debasement and the sale of public office and titles. Though still practised by some smaller territories into the 1740s, these were never as important in Germany as they were in France, Spain or England.

Forms of taxation

The development of regular imperial taxation from the 1480s increased the importance of extraordinary revenue negotiated with the Estates (see section 5.1 and Figure 6.1). This was usually collected through various direct taxes, chiefly poll taxes levied on individual subjects, or property and wealth taxes using systems like that of the Common Penny, or a combination of both. A ruler would agree an amount with his Estates, who would apportion quotas amongst the three main corporate groups of clergy, nobles and towns. The nobles passed their share on to the peasants, who constituted the majority of taxpayers, so that the usual direct tax, generally called the Contribution, was primarily a tax on rural inhabitants. As the grants became more frequent and prolonged, it became harder for the Estates to maintain their initial character as corporate tribute. The different corporations were no longer free to use

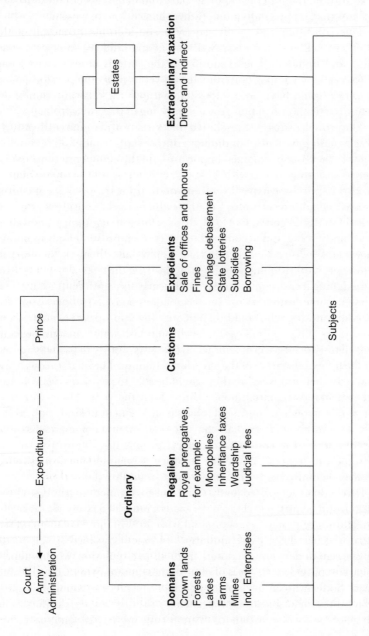

Figure 6.1 Structure of territorial finance

their own methods of raising their share and had to accept standardised systems that tapped individual, rather than collective wealth.

This transition was facilitated by a considerable extension of the ruler's surveillance powers as written tax and land registers were compiled and updated. The expansion of the state is often viewed as an alien, repressive imposition from above, yet its intrusion into local communities would have been impossible without the tacit and sometimes active participation of those it was depriving of their wealth.

The growth of direct taxes shifted the extraction of resources decisively over to cash payments, but did not entirely replace older obligations in kind. In fact, these remained important into the eighteenth century and were transformed in line with the state's expanding role. Cash was mainly needed to purchase expertise and manpower for the permanent courts, armies and administrations. Yet, these also required considerable quantities of material goods, like food, drink, clothing, equipment, as well as heating, lighting and accommodation. It often proved easier to obtain such items by direct extraction than to purchase them on the market. However, requisitioning was integrated within the system of direct taxes by assigning it cash equivalents from the early sixteenth century. By 1700 it had become customary to issue receipts for goods and services provided by communities, who could then deduct the appropriate amount from their taxes. This method eased the chronic cash-flow problems bedevilling all territorial governments when peasants' ability to pay was limited by the inflexible nature of the agrarian economy. They had to sow, grow and reap their crops before these could be sold to pay taxes, yet war and other demands required money throughout the year. Along with new forms of borrowing, continued reliance on payment in kind enabled the tax state to grow faster than the rate of economic commercialisation. Around a third of Habsburg ordinary revenue in 1790 was still in the form of salt, minerals and other produce, while most territories relied heavily on limited conscription systems to maintain their armies.

Direct taxes accounted for up to 50% of government revenue, with the proportion being the highest in the eastern lands of Saxony, Bavaria and the Habsburg monarchy, compared with 30% in more commercialised territories like the city of Hamburg.[68] Indirect taxes increasingly made up the remainder through duties on goods in circulation. Medieval prerogatives provided the basis of some of these, notably taxes on wine and beer. Sixteenth-century rulers developed these as monopoly rights, which they then sold to entrepreneurs in return for regular fees. The range of monopolies expanded dramatically after 1650, but apart from salt, generally affected only luxury items like lottery tickets, wigs, and playing cards. Though unpopular, they rarely brought significant returns and were abandoned in the later eighteenth century.

New excise taxes (*Akzise*) were far more significant. They emerged during the Thirty Years War as emergency measures and were retained after 1648. The form of collection ensured they mainly hit the urban population, as excise officials levied a percentage of the value of goods passing through city gates. The old Berlin fortifications were replaced in 1734–6 by a 14 km long 'tax wall' for this purpose.[69]

Like the rural contribution, the excise became a permanent tax in most territories from the 1630s. By the 1680s, renewed warfare and changes in imperial legislation ended any chance of the Estates reversing these developments. Even in the great eighteenth-century ruler–Estate conflicts in Mecklenburg, Württemberg and East Frisia, the Estates' victory did not end the tax state, but merely imposed limits to what it could collect. The political outcome was thus largely absolutist, unlike that in Britain and the Dutch Republic, where the growth of war finance assisted representative control.[70] The negative impact of warfare was offset in these countries by their commercial and colonial boom. Expanding wealth could be tapped through indirect taxation, which accounted for 70% to 80% of Britain's revenue, or twice the usual proportion in the German territories. Yet, there was no correlation between tax burdens, the form of government, and liberty. By both per capita and proportional burden, British taxes were heavier than those of most continental monarchies.[71]

Germans still faced heavy burdens. Payments to landlords consumed a third of agrarian produce in 1600, far more than taxes, which varied from 3% in Franconia to 20% in south-western Germany.[72] Tax burdens rose dramatically under absolutism, primarily by redistributing shares from landlords and the church in favour of the state. Bavarian taxes rose by 325% across 1621–91, while those in Wolfenbüttel made a roughly similar increase between 1618 and 1700. The burden in Brandenburg increased ten-fold in 1618–88, as did that in Hessen-Kassel in 1650–1702. The state's share changed in quality as well as quantity, since it appropriated the bulk of the peasants' cash payments, leaving lords and the church with contributions in kind and labour service. For example, tax as a proportion of Habsburg peasants' cash payments rose from 64% in 1681 to over 76% by 1758. Joseph II's famous 'physiocratic urbarium' of 1789 imposed fixed quotas, limiting lords to only 17.77% of peasants' gross income, while 12.22% was earmarked for taxes, leaving the remaining 70% in the hands of the producers, whereas they had often been lucky to keep a third before. Aristocratic pressure forced Leopold II to repeal this, but most German governments now took the lion's share of their subjects' payments.

Credit and debt

Rising taxation gave the state a more tangible presence in the lives of most Germans. Yet, the distinction between public and private finance remained blurred, while corporate interests persisted. As part of the authorities, the Estates had their own fiscal institutions, contracting debts and collecting taxes like the ruler in the name of the common good. Loans were raised from individuals and from corporations like municipalities and religious foundations. Princes saw their debts as personal liabilities and many felt no obligation to honour those contracted by their predecessor. Consequently, creditors only offered short-term, high-interest loans, greatly increasing the cost of borrowing. Cheaper, long-term loans only became available with the rise of more impersonal concepts of the state as transcending the lives of individual princes.

Seventeenth-century debts were still *Kammerschulden*, owed by the prince's patrimony, rather than by the state. Debts soared with the rising cost of princely ambition, and princes only maintained their credit by transferring their liabilities to their Estates in return for political concessions. For example, the Württemberg Estates assumed responsibility for over 5 million fl. of ducal debts between 1514 and 1618, in return for confirmation and extension of their privileges.[73] These debts became *Landschulden* and the Estates were authorised to raise their own taxes to pay them off.

The precariousness of princely credit left rulers vulnerable, especially in wartime. The Habsburg monarchy plunged into crisis when its main banker, Samuel Oppenheimer, died in 1703, as it could not pay the 18 million fl. owed to his heirs. The Saxon elector accumulated debts of over 45 million tlr by 1756 and was forced to reduce his army to 18,000 men in May 1756, three months before the Prussian invasion.[74] Deficit finance became the norm, because even emergency taxes failed to cover the cost of war. Habsburg annual revenue more than doubled from 1661 to reach 9 million fl. by 1705. It then fluctuated between 20 and 30 million before the reforms of the late 1740s pushed it to over 40 million, and it then climbed to over 100 million by the 1790s. Yet the monarchy spent

1,312 million on war between 1700 and 1740, of which the military budget covered less than a quarter. The shortfall was made good by diverting civil revenue at the cost of halting debt repayment, increasing total liabilities from 22 to 101 million by 1740. Debts rose to 285 million following the Seven Years War so that by 1763, 41% of net revenue went on interest, while the army took another 50%.[75]

The Bank of England, established in 1694, enabled Britain to avoid these problems by funding a consolidated national debt through cheaper long-term loans. The Habsburgs sponsored their own bank in 1703, followed by other rulers, such as the elector Palatine in 1705. German banks attempted to float new loans through bills of exchange that could be bought and sold. The Habsburg finance minister, Gundaker Starhemberg, founded the Viennese City Bank (*Stadtbank*) in 1706, attracting 90,000 private investors, who helped pay off 22 million of state debt. However, all these schemes failed, because the government demanded too much, undermining public confidence. The City Bank foundered after it was obliged to bail out the state's Universal Bank (*Universalbancalität*), established in 1714, which owed 32 million. By 1738, City Bank liabilities totalled 50 million and its Dutch backers pulled out, precipitating its total collapse within seven years. Ultimately, all these ventures were doomed by slow economic growth, whereas the Bank of England was boosted by rising trade and commercial expansion.

Smaller territories were also affected. Hessen-Darmstadt was crippled by debts accumulated through warfare and courtly extravagance. The landgrave resorted to desperate measures, including alchemy in the hope of making gold, as well as devious accounting that soon meant no one knew who was owed what. Revenue totalled 345,000 fl. whereas expenditure reached 465,000, of which 185,000 went on interest. Landgrave Ernst Ludwig became a virtual fugitive to hide from his Frankfurt creditors, until the Estates agreed to assume two-thirds of the 6 million he owed at his death in 1739. Poor accounting was widespread and compounded the underlying problems: no annual budgets were compiled in Ansbach-Bayreuth, where the figures from 1767 were not audited until 1790.

The wars between 1740 and 1763 encouraged limited reforms, which started merging princely and Estate finances into a single public sphere. Bavarian debts totalled 35 million fl. by 1749, when the elector agreed a joint commission with the Estates. This discovered that the territory's ambassador in Paris had not been required to keep proper accounts of the French subsidies paid since 1703 and was now suspected of having pocked over 1.4 million! The Estates assumed 63% of the total debt, but only modest reforms were made, including a new, and equally unsuccessful state bank in 1762. Like the Darmstadt landgrave, the Bavarian elector still put his faith in the traditional, but hopeless remedy of alchemy. Württemberg also accumulated huge debts through the reckless pursuit of princely ambition, adding around 12 million fl. by 1767 to the 3 million already owed in 1744. A joint ducal–Estates debt commission was created in 1768 to amortise 5 million using a fixed proportion of regular taxation. It took until April 1803 to clear all but 42,000 fl. of what was owed.[76] The Habsburgs were slightly more imaginative as finance minister Count Ludwig Zinzendorf abandoned narrow fiscalism after 1763 in favour of a consolidated national debt, assisted by Joseph II's gift of 19 million fl. inherited from his father in 1765. A stock exchange was established in 1771 to trade in government bonds, while greater efforts were made to commercialise agriculture (see section 3.3). However, the War of the Bavarian Succession precipitated another virtual bankruptcy by 1779.

Thus, only modest headway had been made before the outbreak of the French Revolutionary Wars in 1792 heralded another prolonged period of expensive warfare. Prussia's experience illustrates the heavy impact. Prussia was exceptional in having fought its eighteenth-century wars without accumulating huge debts, yet its enviable financial position lacked a firm footing. Hohenzollern finances had yet to shake off their late medieval character. Royal domains still accounted for one-third of central government revenue, and the crown attempted to live off its own by avoiding debt. Emergency expenditure was met by stringent economies rather than credit. By paring ordinary expenditure to the bone, Frederick William I accumulated a reserve of 7 million tlr in gold coins stored in barrels in his palace vaults. Though his son soon used this to finance his first two wars against Austria in 1740–5, he saved up another 20 million in time for the Seven Years War. This conflict cost Prussia 125 million, but most of the deficit was met by ruthlessly exploiting Saxony and other occupied land and Frederick managed to leave his successor 52 million in 1786, equivalent to two full years' revenue.[77] Though contemporaries marvelled at Prussia's apparent solvency, the Hohenzollern system was inherently inflexible, since it had no way of meeting rapidly rising expenditure once its reserves were exhausted. Military intervention in the Netherlands in 1787 cost 6 million, while another 7 million went on the mobilisation during the war scare of 1790–1. Annual revenue reached 24.5 million with the annexation of additional Polish land in 1793–5, but this failed to match rapidly escalating costs after 1792. The coincidence of war in the west against France and a Polish insurrection in the east not only consumed the remainder of the war treasury, but left debts of 48 million. Facing bankruptcy, Prussia made its own peace with France in April 1795 and retreated into ten years of neutrality. Reform discussions failed to produce significant results by the time Prussia faced France again in 1806. That defeat added another 5 million tlr of debt, along with the 35 million war indemnity. Renewed war pushed debts to 206 million by 1815.[78]

The Habsburg monarchy fared little better. Annual revenue in 1790 was 163.5 million fl., but 38% of this consisted of loans, the sale of government property and the issue of paper currency, while debts stood at over 390 million. Inability to balance the budget added debts of another 16 million by the time France declared war in 1792. The deficit of 4 million that year had risen to one of 80 million eight years later. Already 12 million fl. had been issued in paper currency in 1771 and the government made increasing use of this expedient under Joseph II's personal rule. The amount in circulation by 1811 totalled 1,060 million, yet with debts of 700 million, the government had no chance of honouring these.[79]

War likewise affected the medium and smaller German territories, who faced additional problems from the territorial reorganisation of 1801–6. The winners were obliged to assume the liabilities of the lands they annexed. These were often considerable. Württemberg acquired an additional 3.5 million fl. of debts from its annexations by 1803, while Bavaria assumed another 93 million, increasing its total, allowing for some interim repayment, from 20 million in 1793 to 105 million in 1818. The medium-sized states were generally the hardest hit. For example, Baden grew six-fold to 15,070 km^2 between 1801 and 1810 by acquiring parts of the Palatinate, Austrian Breisgau and a host of smaller territories. The land acquired by 1806 increased Baden's annual revenue by over 70%, but added a staggering 15 million fl. of debt to a pre-war total of only 65,000. Expenditure exceeded revenue by 1.4 million that year and by 1818 debts reached 31 million, of which half was due to war and the rest to the liabilities of the annexed lands.

Governments resorted to emergency taxes and forced loans to cope with the costs of territorial reorganisation and renewed warfare. Administrative and fiscal reform stabilised the situation after 1806 by establishing uniform structures throughout the enlarged states. However, further warfare interrupted this after 1809, particularly as Napoleon expected his German allies to contribute substantially to sustaining his empire.

Governments met this through further borrowing, which continued on a reduced scale after Napoleon's defeat, to cope with the legacy of the conflict, and the social and economic dislocation.

The war thus accelerated an existing reform process that lasted until 1820 and consolidated government finance into a single public sphere.[80] State finance was no longer an extension of the ruler's private patrimony, though German kings and princes remained very wealthy and retained some personal control until 1848, and in some cases beyond. Revenue and expenditure were subject to constitutional checks, while all debts were consolidated into a single public liability, funded by central government taxation, for interest and capital repayment. Creditors now lent to an impersonal state, not to individual rulers or corporations like the Estates. This enabled state finance to adapt to market conditions, commercialising public debt through the issue of government bonds. The cost of borrowing was reduced, because bonds were transferable and no longer attached to specific securities. Governments no longer had to mortgage particular assets to reassure creditors. Moreover, the state could tap previously inaccessible sources of wealth, because relatively poor citizens could purchase individual bonds that guaranteed them regular interest. Whereas private individuals held only 10% of Bavaria's debt in 1790, that proportion had risen to 41% by 1818. In this way, public finance promoted the growth of market capitalism. Bankers no longer dealt directly with monarchs, but, along with stock exchanges, acted as intermediaries between governments and a host of lenders. They also gave German governments access to international capital, which had previously been limited to foreign subsidies and loans arranged by allies.[81]

These changes profoundly changed German politics. Government remained monarchical, but it was no longer absolutist. Princes could no longer dispose of revenue or contract debts as they saw fit. This process dug deeper into German society with the 1830 and 1848 revolutions, which removed most of the remaining fiscal privileges of the territorial nobility. Though revolution accelerated the pace of change, it did not start it, in contrast to France. There, the monarchy's limited attempts to commercialise public debt failed by 1720, forcing it to continue an increasingly inadequate fiscal and credit system that left it bankrupt by 1789. Eighteenth-century reforms eased the situation in the Reich, paving the way for more radical measures after 1792. Yet, German states made this transition to modern government finance much later than in Britain, where the greater transparency of parliamentary scrutiny helped commercialise public debt in the 1690s, and more innovative measures could be adopted to meet new burdens. Germany remained relatively backward even after 1871, failing to adopt income tax, which had been introduced in Britain in 1797.

Chapter 7: State and Society

7.1 Regulation and Reform

Social discipline

Absolutism's wider consequences are usually interpreted as some kind of disciplining process, whereby growing state regulation transformed society and shaped individual behaviour. Gerhard Oestreich was the first to label this 'social discipline', drawing on other theories of rationalisation to suggest the state as a motor of historical change.[1] Standing Marx on his head, Oestreich argued that early modern social regulation paved the way for industrialisation by disciplining society, rather than modernity being the product of the rise of capitalism. The secular state stepped in as the church, lords and communes proved incapable of dealing with the social, economic and political problems arising from the fourteenth-century agrarian depression and later demographic recovery. Though it continued to emphasise Christian morality, the state borrowed solutions from ancient Greece and Rome that were disseminated by Renaissance Humanism.

Social discipline made its impact through two stages according to Oestreich. Initial 'social regulation' stabilised society and enabled it to overcome the traumatic changes of the fifteenth and sixteenth centuries. This gradually broadened into 'social discipline', beginning with 'staff disciplining' as all public agencies were integrated into a centralised state and their personnel professionalised. Equipped with a more efficient, extensive and effective infrastructure, the state moved from regulating existing society to promoting social change by modifying people's behaviour. Instead of simply punishing deviancy, it now tried to eradicate it altogether by transforming people into morally-upright, diligent, thrifty and obedient subjects. This 'fundamental disciplining'

eroded corporate distinctions and created a more equal 'society of subjects' (*Untertanengesellschaft*) characterised by a uniform relationship of
all inhabitants to state authority.

This process transformed the state as well, modernising it from within
by rationalising its administration and eroding the personal characteristics of patrimonial rule. Officials served an impersonal state, not an
individual prince, while merit and achievement replaced status and
privilege as the basis of both social and political relations. Those who
accept Oestreich's approach believe these changes paved 'the way for
the founding and triumph of a modern capitalist and industrial society'.[2]

Oestreich's model has been widely criticised, perhaps most fundamentally for implying that the absolutist state was essentially benevolent
and progressive.[3] Much regulation was counter-productive, repressive
or simply ineffective. However, the concept remains helpful, provided
it is recognised that the state was not simply acting upon society from
above, but responding to pressures and influences from below.

The ideal of social order

Social regulation had its origins in the late middle ages as a new sphere of
activity alongside secular justice and ecclesiastical jurisdiction. Secular
justice expanded with the territorialisation of political power in the
Reich (see section 2.2) and concentrated in the hands of princes and
other rulers. It dealt mainly with public order and property, followed
written procedure and could only impose penalties following an investi-
gation and trial. Ecclesiastical jurisdiction was more concerned with
morals and imposed fines for behaviour deviating from Christian
norms. Social regulation filled a growing gap between these two activities as it responded to the expansion and integration of market networks, and to demographic growth, especially urbanisation, which
created new problems of public health, fire safety and accommodation.

Rulers tried to police these problems by issuing written instructions.
These became known as *Polizei* (or in its originally spelling, *Policey*)
after the Latin and Greek concept of the polity, meaning both 'state'
and 'good order'.[4] New intellectual currents fused with existing secular and theological ideas to promote the belief that it was both necessary
and legitimate for rulers to do this. Humans were distinguished from
beasts by their capacity for reason. Yet, the divinely-ordained social
order was hierarchical. It followed that those at the highest positions
in society must have a greater capacity for rational thought than those

at the bottom, who were closer to animals. As 'god's bailiff' (*Gottes Amt-mann*), the prince was responsible for his subjects' welfare, like the father, who was responsible for his children. The Reformation encouraged this with its doctrine of eudenomism, arguing that the basis of all moral and rational action should be its capacity to promote personal well-being and happiness. It seemed logical that the prince should assume the duty of promoting the happiness of his subjects by paternally regulating their lives to preserve social harmony and resolve problems.

Secular action acquired ethical dignity, but remained controversial because police regulation implied an almost unlimited agenda for action. The state was elevated above all other corporate bodies previously charged with promoting the common good. The maintenance of law was no longer a common enterprise of ruler and ruled, but the unilateral responsibility of the sovereign, who alone issued laws that his subjects had to obey. There was no right of appeal. The state both issued regulations and judged infringements, blurring the distinction between administration and justice.

None the less, German princes generally enjoyed the support of both the church and the emperor. Confessionalisation encouraged closer collaboration between throne and altar, since clerics saw secular police measures as a way of enforcing religious orthodoxy. They reciprocated, not only by providing institutional support in disseminating regulations at parish level, but also fostering acceptance. War and natural disasters like plagues and floods were presented as divine punishment for sinful behaviour. Such dangers could only be avoided by adhering to the moral and social norms propagated by church and territorial authorities. Imperial legislation reinforced territorial authority through three imperial police ordinances (*Reichspolizeiordnungen*) in 1530, 1548 and 1577. The first two set guidelines for territorial police measures, while the third widened the scope for local adaptation. Over time, territorial legislation established its own precedents justifying further action, so that the process acquired its own internal dynamic, particularly as reforming officials tried to advance their careers by devising additional measures. Even the tiny county of Lippe-Detmold issued 986 separate ordinances between 1571 and 1814.[5]

Early police regulation

Four basic areas of activity were established by the 1570s, though it's worth remembering that individual laws often served multiple agendas.

One set of measures covered the urban environment, regulating public health, sanitation, traffic, building, and fire safety. Early social regulation aimed primarily at stabilising corporate distinctions and privileges through measures like sumptuary laws (see p. 63). Economic policies supported this by regulating inheritance, property ownership and welfare with the intention of preserving the material basis of each group. Lastly, secular and theological objectives coincided in sustaining the confessional state. By regulating marriage, morals, education and social behaviour, both church and state sought to stabilise society against religious dissent and economic change.

Police regulation encouraged certain forms of behaviour by criminalising some previously accepted practices, rewarding others and introducing new ones. The upheavals of the Peasants War of 1525 had demonstrated the significance of propertied householders as community leaders. If they could be persuaded to cooperate, the territorial state could acquire a stable bulwark against potential rebels like sectarians, vagrants and the landless. Police regulation attempted this by offering a new ideology of the stable household and practical measures to support it. Princes, especially Protestant ones, referred to themselves in their ordinances as the 'father of the people' (*Landesvater*) and even civic magistrates adopted much of this paternalist discourse. It helped integrate the household within a wider social and political hierarchy. The 'father of the house' (*Hausvater*) exercised both authority over, and responsibility for, the others living under his roof. By equating authority with benevolent paternalism, police regulation placed dissent and rebellion on a par with patricide.[6]

Marriage became the centre of the household and the transition to adulthood and responsibility. Householders' authority over children and other unmarried dependants was strengthened. The adverse impact of the sixteenth-century price revolution was addressed by condemning luxury as both sinful and expensive, and as contributing to other problems like debt. Regulation was supplemented from the early seventeenth century by a burgeoning 'housefather literature' of practical manuals intended to give householders the technical knowledge required to produce a surplus, which could be taxed by the state, whilst simultaneously encouraging self-discipline through the example of an upright life. These measures clearly achieved their objectives in some areas. For example, Lutheran peasant householders had formed the backbone of resistance to Catholic confessionalisation in Upper Austria. Some were killed and others fled, but most compromised with the Habsburgs by

1630, restricting later opposition to millenarian movements supported only by marginal groups like cottagers, labourers and disenfranchised younger children.[7]

Cameralism

As Oestreich's model indicates, social discipline broadened in the mid-seventeenth century as it acquired its own inner dynamism and responded to the Thirty Years War. Police regulation continued initially. The chiliastic view of the Thirty Years War as divine punishment for immorality encouraged a return to earlier, harsh moral codes that had been relaxed around 1600.[8] New ordinances widened the earlier agenda to include control of animals as well as people. Public health legislation regulated slaughter houses and identified certain species as dangerous to the common good. Whereas medieval Germans had occasionally instituted legal processes against individual animals believed to have caused harm, entire species were now targeted and urban pest control was extended into rural areas. For example, peasants were ordered to kill a certain number of sparrows or pay a fine, ostensibly to protect crops.[9] However, these measures gradually merged with the wider system of territorial justice as police regulation became concerned less with social control than with policing civil and criminal law and punishing those who broke it.

Social regulation meanwhile developed into social innovation under the influence of cameralist thought disseminated by Johann Joachim Becher, Veit Ludwig von Seckendorff, Philipp Wilhelm von Hörnigk and Wilhelm von Schröder.[10] Cameralism claimed to be a rational science of public administration. It shared much with earlier police regulation, as well as western European mercantilism including a strong dose of Christian morality, and early cameralist writers peppered their works with Old Testament examples. Its coherence and modernity should also not be overestimated. Cameralists were not progressive thinkers and their ideas were often expressed as poorly articulated practical advice rather than a comprehensive philosophy.

None the less, it is possible to identify a core of common ideas. Cameralists combined theory with practical experience as officials or entrepreneurs, and wrote integrated works encompassing politics, economics, finance, administration and morality. Their belief in systems was encouraged by parallel scientific discoveries suggesting that the universe

and natural world functioned like perfect machines and that human
society could be improved once its internal fundamental laws had been
revealed and explained. They shared the mercantilists' assumption that
the wealth of the world was finite, measured in land, inhabitants and
especially bullion, all of which appeared in limited supply. The key to
greater wealth was competition, not cooperation, and cameralists advocated protectionism. However, whereas mercantilists looked overseas to
colonies and maritime trade, cameralists concentrated on continental
Europe. Hörnigk, for example, advised the Habsburgs to seize French
experts and entrepreneurs to work for Austria, while the monarchy
should expand southwards into warmer regions better suited to the production of cotton goods that could be traded for gold.

Such belligerence is understandable given that cameralists wrote in a
post-war era characterised by depopulation and low productivity. They
were dimly conscious of the gradual demographic recovery, but were
more aware of abandoned farms and empty villages. In response, they
advocated full employment supplemented by immigration, and a ban
on emigration. Schröder suggested importing Turkish and African
slaves to reduce labour costs, and Ottoman prisoners of war were certainly put to work on construction projects in Vienna and Munich in
the late 1680s.

Agriculture seemed inflexible as fertilisers and hybrid strains of seed
and animal breeds were still poorly understood. The answer appeared
to lie in industry and all cameralists advocated the manufacture of
high-value products for export, and import-substitution to reduce the
outward flow of bullion. However, they placed higher value on extractive industries like mining and forestry than did mercantilists, reflecting
the Reich's relative under-development compared with more commercialised western European economies.

Cameralism's greater emphasis on the state also distinguished it from
mercantilism. The belief in the child-like condition of the general population inclined cameralists to regard the state as essential for all beneficial change. People would only become more productive if they were
shown how to or, if necessary, compelled to. Banning imports would
force people to develop new industries to make these goods themselves.
Higher taxes would compel them to work harder and more efficiently.
In the end, cameralism boiled down to harsh fiscalism. It equated
common good with state power, since only a strong, militarised government could protect its subjects in the hostile post-Westphalian order.
However, the state was only to take what was necessary. Communities

and households were to be guided towards better management, but not deprived of the right to regulate their own affairs.

This social conservatism contributed to cameralism's many contradictions. Cameralists became increasingly frustrated by their lack of progress and sought to change social relations in the interests of greater efficiency. Faith in rational systems thus conflicted with complex social reality, pushing cameralism away from conserving police regulation towards more ambitious projects for change.

Military and court spending

Cameralists dreamed of a virtuous circle whereby heavy taxation would fund high military and court spending, which would stimulate further productivity and in turn permit still higher taxes. Military spending increased as armies were maintained permanently from the later 1650s. Most money went on soldiers' wages and food, as payments for fort construction and armament purchases, though individually larger, were made less often. Garrisons could stimulate local industries by concentrating demand. The Potsdam tobacco factory established in 1737 survived largely thanks to the local garrison, which brought 30,000 tlr into circulation each month.[11] Armaments was one of the four main consumers of Austrian iron and steel production, alongside agriculture, transport and construction. Brandenburg's industrial development centred around Potsdam and Berlin, partly because of the canal and river system, but also because of the high concentration of troops. The Lagerhaus state textile factory in Berlin supplying army uniforms was the country's largest single industrial enterprise after 1714, while the Potsdam arms factory freed Prussia from foreign imports after 1722.

Soldiers were used to break strikes at iron works and other industrial installations around Berlin. The Austrian Mittermayer family operating the Steyr arms factory from 1655 was ennobled as 'von Waffenberg', while the Splitgerber-Daum consortium became Prussia's biggest industrial group with an annual turnover of 4 million tlr by 1762 from its armaments and heavy industrial plants. While this reflected the close association of important military and court suppliers with the crown, it did not constitute an eighteenth-century 'military-industrial complex'.[12] Splitgerber and Daum's Potsdam factory never employed more than 400 workers and maintained a precarious existence with few customers other than the Prussian army. Political fragmentation kept armaments production decentralised, most weapons were still produced by artisan corporations in Sühl and Essen, and Germany's total annual capacity of 20,000 muskets was less than half that of late eighteenth-century France. German armies made their main impact through the food purchased by soldiers and their dependants, which would have been scarcely different had these been out of uniform.

Court spending likewise made only a limited impact, but at least it was more visibly concentrated in specific residence towns, where growth generally outstripped that in the former manufacturing centres of the imperial cities after 1648. Mainz's population grew twice as fast as that in eighteenth-century Frankfurt or Cologne and by 1792 it was estimated that the court and nobility put 2.5 million fl. into circulation there each year. The flight of the court in 1792 outweighed the benefits of the French military and administrative presence in Mainz thereafter and the city's population fell by nearly 9,000 to 21,615 by 1801.[13] Frederick William's economies also interrupted Berlin's population growth in 1713 and caused several businesses to fail. Growth only resumed in the 1730s thanks to the larger garrison and armaments industries.

Population policies

It proved hard to encourage immigration after 1648, because few parts of the Reich were over-populated. Strangers were regarded with suspicion and rulers hesitated to abandon their earlier insistence on confessional uniformity. Lutherans were prepared to welcome other Protestants and Württemberg allowed 2,000 demobilised Swedish soldiers to settle after the war and later accepted 3,000 Waldensians fleeing persecution in Savoy in 1697. Rather more refugees came from France, where Louis XIV repressed the Huguenot minority, culminating in the revocation of the Edict of Nantes ending all toleration in 1685. At least 200,000 Huguenots fled, of whom over 60,000 went to the Reich. Around a third of these settled in Potsdam and Halle on the invitation of the Great Elector, but others went to the Rhineland and parts of southern Germany.

They were regarded as notably enterprising and were encouraged by minor princes to found special new towns, like Erlangen in Bayreuth in 1686. Like many baroque new towns, Erlangen was conceived as a model community laid out in a geometrical plan. Despite the opposition from the local Lutheran consistory, its population rose from an initial 700 settlers to 5,629 by 1787. Huguenots started new businesses, like a tapestry factory, hat and shoe manufacture, paper making, stockings and other mainly luxury items that had a total turn-over of 200,000 fl. by 1698, equivalent to a fifth of the territory's central government revenue.[14]

Later Hohenzollerns continued the Great Elector's open door policy, particularly in response to the plague, which reduced Ducal Prussia's inhabitants by a third in 1709. Protestant refugees were welcomed from Lorraine, Nassau and other Catholic lands, with tax breaks, subsidised land and temporary exemption from military conscription. As many as half a million new inhabitants arrived between 1640 and 1786, notably to settle land reclaimed from the marshes around the Oder, Warthe and Netze rivers under Frederick II. The Habsburgs also attracted around 200,000 immigrants in the century after 1683 to resettle Hungary after the expulsion of the Ottomans.

Many of Prussia's immigrants came from Salzburg, where Archbishop Firmian was horrified to discover large numbers of crypto-Protestants in the Alpine villages on his accession in 1727. Their forcible expulsion in November 1731 provoked immediate controversy throughout the Reich, but was motivated less by Firmian's religious convictions than by his fear that dissent presaged political disloyalty.[15] It was a disaster for all concerned. Firmian had no desire to lose valuable taxpayers, but his insistence on public displays of loyalty prompted his subjects to openly show their dissent. He could not formally expel them, since the IPO guaranteed refugees the right to leave with their property. Though his soldiers confiscated over 2,000 firearms, he hesitated to call the protest a rebellion, since imperial law forbade the expulsion of rebels into neighbouring lands. In need of Protestant support in imperial politics, Charles VI compelled Firmian to respect his subjects' right to emigrate. He lost around a tenth of his total population of 200,000, plus property worth 800,000 tlr, equivalent to an entire year's revenue. Around 6,000 emigrants failed to reach their destination, with many dying on the road. Their plight attracted widespread attention, most of it hostile to the Catholic princes. A special relief fund was established in Regensburg and received donations from the kings of England and Sweden, as well as ordinary Protestants. The survivors reached Ducal Prussia, where they had been invited by Frederick William I, keen both to make a propaganda coup and to repopulate his devastated province. Like colonists everywhere, they faced the huge task of rebuilding their lives in a hostile environment, and many failed.

The Salzburg incident demonstrated confessionalisation's redundancy by stirring unrest amongst Protestant minorities in neighbouring

Berchtesgaden and the Habsburg monarchy, where 6,000 Bohemians also petitioned to leave. While it did not lead immediately to greater tolerance, it did accelerate the dismantling of the confessional state under way since the 1650s. The territorial state assumed many functions previously entrusted to the church. Schooling passed to secular supervision in Gotha in 1651, for instance, while a Brandenburg ordinance of 1685 created a rudimentary health system centred on the Berlin medical college, replacing earlier provision through local pastors.

Pietism

Religious revivalism paradoxically encouraged this secular trend by mobilising activists to assist government initiatives. A new form of Protestant fundamentalism known as Pietism developed after 1670 in Frankfurt, Saxony, Württemberg and especially Brandenburg, around the influential theologian and social reformer Philipp Jakob Spener (1635–1705). Spener drew on an earlier Lutheran tradition that had been interrupted by the Thirty Years War, and that had its origins in the late sixteenth century. Publication of the Book of Concord as a definitive statement of faith in 1580 was taken by many as a sign that Luther's reformation of teaching was complete and it was now time to move on to a 'reformation of life'. Spener articulated this precisely when many Germans felt the need for moral and spiritual rejuvenation after the horrors of the war. Though rooted in Lutheran theology, Pietism had much in common with radical Calvinism and English Puritanism in advocating a more personalised spirituality outside a formal church structure. Pietists typically met in friends' houses to pray together and discuss devotional literature.

It seems at first unlikely that such a fundamentalist movement could support the secular welfare and social regulatory measures of an authoritarian state. Indeed, Pietism could take a subversive, anti-authoritarian direction if it won adherents amongst those already opposed to princely power, such as some members of the Württemberg Estates. However, orthodox Lutherans regarded the Pietists as 'dangerous enthusiasts' (*Schwärmer*) whose 'excesses' would undermine their established church. This blunted the radical potential of Württemberg Pietism as the orthodox majority in the Estates collaborated with the duke to bring most fundamentalists back into the official church by the 1740s. The situation was different in Brandenburg, where the Calvinist Hohenzollerns had little desire to strengthen their Lutheran Church establishment and personally sympathised with much of the Pietist agenda. Spener was invited to Berlin in 1691 and other Pietists became professors at the new university established at Halle a few years earlier.

What attracted Spener's new patrons was his social activism. Some Pietists tried to realise their dream of a more Christian life by founding their own separate communities, such as that associated with Count Nikolaus Zinzendorf of Herrnhuth at Ebersdorf in the principality of Reuss. By contrast, Spener and his protégés, like August Hermann Francke, addressed pressing social problems directly by creating new schools and orphanages to promote a new morality by good example. Their emphasis on thrift, sobriety, hard work and obedience fitted perfectly with the absolutist cameralist agenda. Individual Pietists still criticised Prussian militarism, but their association with many areas of Hohenzollern policy gave spiritual force to secular measures, particularly between 1713 and 1740.[16]

Poor relief and 'corrective welfare'

Secularisation was most pronounced in the area of poor relief as cameralism intensified trends under way since the Reformation. The 1530 Imperial Police Ordinance outlined a basic system of secular relief by making all communities responsible for their own poor. The needy could only be sent elsewhere if their own community lacked the means to look after them and provided them with proper documentation. State intrusion displaced earlier charity through the church, and redefined the poor as a burden on society. Increasingly, Germans distinguished between a small group of 'deserving', like orphans, widows and the sick, who were to be assisted, and the much larger mass of 'undeserving' poor. Cameralism sharpened this by classifying people according to their ability to contribute materially to the common good, creating a scale rising from 'poverty' through 'misery', 'need', 'adequacy', and 'property' to 'riches'. An individual's place in these categories was no longer thought to be purely the result of birth or divine will, but came about of their own volition. In short, the poor only had themselves to blame.

Begging had been regarded as a distinct lifestyle, part of the medieval social order fulfilling an essential role: the rich could discharge their Christian obligations by giving alms to the poor. Poverty was a misfortune, but could also symbolise Christian rejection of luxury. Cameralists reclassified it as refusal to work and began a prolonged assault on deeply-rooted social attitudes. Germans made little distinction between work and leisure before the eighteenth century. Craftsmen worked 14 to 17 hours a day, perhaps an average of three more than merchants, but this included three hours for meals, plus other breaks for prayers, reducing productive time to no more than nine hours. Numerous religious holidays kept the number of working days to 260 to 290 a year. Cameralists equated work only with productivity, condemning holidays and breaks as idleness and encouraging governments to increase the number of working days.

This was part of a wider process of assigning material rather than moral value to behaviour. Fiscalism required objects and actions to be expressed in monetary terms. For example, cameralists justified new tax registers as tailoring assessments according to each household's ability to pay. However, they objectified behaviour: households were judged good or bad according to their productivity, not their morals or religious convictions. As one cameralist put it, 'it is the duty of all people to make themselves useful to their state by their energy and work; no one can be permitted to be a useless member of the community'.[17]

Official policy accordingly took two directions. Benevolence was restricted to ensuring efficient use of local resources to help the narrow group of 'deserving' poor, while punitive measures targeted the 'loafers' (Müßigänger), who were to be compelled to work. The former did create new, albeit limited, welfare rights. A Prussian ordinance of March 1701 permitted the poor to protest to their district official if they had been refused aid by their community. Such measures culminated in rights under the Prussian General Civil Code (Algemeines Landrecht) of 1794 establishing that the state was to oversee all welfare measures. Welfare was also secularised in the Catholic ecclesiastical territories under the influence of the Italian reformer Lodovico Antonio Muratori, whose work Christian Charity was translated into German in 1761. For example, Mainz established a General Poverty Commission in 1786 to oversee all welfare measures, including a poor law (1787), a free maternity hospital for unmarried mothers (1784) and an institute for deaf mutes (1786).[18]

Punitive measures concentrated on the itinerant population, who were rounded up by military patrols (Streifen) and driven over the frontier or, ironically, often drafted into the army.[19] Governments also made increasing use of workhouses, copied from the original Dutch tuchthuizen, especially from the 1660s (see Table 7.1). These were concentrated in Protestant territories before the eighteenth century as Catholics hesitated

Table 7.1   Foundation of workhouses in the Reich

Location	Date
Bremen	1609
Lübeck	1613
Hamburg	1614
Danzig	1629
Breslau	1668
Vienna	1670
Leipzig	1671
Berlin	1671
Lüneburg	1676
Brunswick	1678
Frankfurt/Main	1679
Munich	1682 (re-established in 1790)
Spandau	1686
Magdeburg	1687
Königsberg	1691
Cologne	1696
Olmütz	1701
Weimar	1719
Innsbruck	1725
Ravensburg	1725 (maintained for the Swabian Kreis)
Celle	1731
Graz	1735
Ludwigsburg	1736
Prague	1737
Mainz	1743
Berlin	1744

to adopt the brutal cameralist logic. However, the authorities increasingly blurred the distinction between the deserving poor and the 'work shy', sending vagrants' children to be disciplined by the workhouse along with prostitutes, beggars, criminals and insubordinate servants. New inmates were 'welcomed' with a beating from the warders, who hit them with sticks; a process that was often repeated for those fortunate enough to be 'discharged'. While inside, they worked to produce poor-quality goods, usually clothing for soldiers and government officials. In the fashionable sociological interpretation pioneered by the French philosopher Michel Foucault, such institutions symbolise the all-pervasive power of the disciplinary state. In fact, even by the late eighteenth century, there were only 115 workhouses in the Reich, with no more than 10,000 inmates. The number of poor was much larger: an official survey of Upper Austria in 1727 alone reported 26,000 beggars in a population of only 400,000, because of a recession in the local cloth industry.[20]

Moreover, other measures were more in tune with the prevailing 'moral economy', which expected the authorities to regulate prices and ensure no one starved. The small scale of most territories placed rulers in relatively close proximity to those they ruled, and they shared many popular convictions. Price regulation and restrictions on the grain trade cushioned most Germans from the worst of the economic fluctuations before 1771 and there were fewer hunger riots than in France. Ironically, the reception of French physiocratic ideas of free trade encouraged partial deregulation in the later eighteenth century precisely when a growing population forced up prices. This transition to liberal economics undoubtedly contributed to the unrest after 1790, which persisted until 1850.

The age of the expert

Cameralism experienced its zenith in the two decades of peace after 1714. Population and productivity had been largely restored, opening the way for the more ambitious projects of a new generation of theorists like Christian Thomasius, Justus Christoph Dithmar and Georg Heinrich Zincke. They retained some Christian ethics and paternalistic language, but placed greater emphasis on a rational, 'scientific' approach to society's problems. This was related to cameralism becoming an academic subject by 1727 and the proliferation of specialist administrative departments to promote economic and social change. Württemberg had no less than 50 specialist committees by 1737. Many were concerned with fairly traditional matters like the maintenance of ducal palaces, but others were deliberately created to disseminate new ideas, like the commerce council of 1709.[21]

Further advice came from the self-proclaimed experts who clustered around the princely courts. Some of these were exceptional men, like Johann Jakob Moser, a prolific writer on imperial law who still found time to write 600 hymns and raise a large family. His career illustrates the relative ease with which such figures moved within the Reich, but equally the precariousness of their employment. He served in turn as a minor ducal official in his native Württemberg (1726–7, 1731–6), university professor in Tübingen (1727–31) and Frankfurt/Oder (1736–9), free-lance writer and legal consultant (1739–47), privy councillor and civil service chief in Hessen-Homberg (1747–8), principal of his own school of public administration in Hanau (1749) and finally as legal advisor to the Württemberg Estates (1751–70). His inability to confine himself to one area of activity raised the suspicions of his many employers and antagonised his colleagues. Ultimately he alienated the Württemberg Estates without winning the trust of Duke Carl Eugen, who imprisoned him in solitary confinement from 1759 to 1765 during the duchy's constitutional crisis.

Other experts lacked Moser's formal education, but had a wealth of practical experience. Joseph Süß Oppenheimer was not as well connected as Moser, and suffered additional discrimination as a Heidelberg Jew. None the less, he rose to prominence as a supplier of scarce items to various south German courts and armies. While he acquired a personal fortune, his real wealth lay in his reputation as a financial expert, which opened doors to further commercial opportunity and sources of credit. He was hired by Carl Alexander to operate the Württemberg mint in 1733 and rapidly became an indispensable figure in the ducal entourage. The duke valued Süß's advice, but also used him as a front man in his efforts to discipline the ducal administration, which traditionally sympathised with the Estates' opposition to absolutism. Süß paid a heavy price after Carl Alexander's sudden death when he became the scapegoat for all his master's controversial measures: he was eventually hanged in a grotesque public execution in 1739, in breach of both Württemberg and imperial law.[22]

These two examples demonstrate both the risks and the rewards of government service. Most experts had more humble careers and their proffered panaceas almost invariably failed. A few gained respectability and personal fortunes, such as another Jewish financier, Meyer Amshel Rothschild founder of the later banking dynasty.

Enlightened absolutism?

Considerable controversy surrounds the later direction of absolutist reforms. Some believe new ideas changed princely rule so fundamentally around the mid-eighteenth century that it is possible to speak of a distinct phase of 'enlightened' or 'reform' absolutism. Critics argue that these changes were superficial at best and that policies remained driven by existing fiscal–military concerns.[23]

Writers like Johann Heinrich Gottlob Justi and Joseph von Sonnenfels remained concerned with state power, but were more aware of the relative difference between countries and the discrepancy between façade and reality. The earlier stress on Christian morality was replaced by a passion for statistics, supplied with growing accuracy by writers like the geographer Anton Friedrich Büsching. Both they and their readership were also influenced by new ideas associated with the Enlightenment.

The later seventeenth century saw a restoration of calm and confidence after the intellectual turmoil and doubts of the earlier confessional strife and scientific discoveries. A new orthodoxy emerged from a synthesis of old and novel ideas and formed the basis of what is generally known as the pre- or early Enlightenment, associated in Germany with Descartes, Spinoza, Leibniz and Christian Wolff. Much of this synthesis was inherently contradictory and contained the seeds of ideas that were to overturn many of its precepts. The initial harmony and optimism gave way to greater scepticism and pessimism by the 1740s and by the 1770s Enlightened thought was being challenged by Romanticism, which remained influential into the 1830s.

The Enlightenment professed scepticism towards that which cannot be proved to be true by reason or practical observation. This attitude encouraged a suspicion of tradition and received wisdom, especially that of the established churches. Human reason replaced divine revelation as the source of knowledge. Early enlightened thinkers were confident that everything could be explained by rational, scientific laws, providing the basis for a philosophy of progress claiming that people would improve the world once they discovered how it worked. One of the most radical concepts was faith in utility as the yardstick for determining the value of institutions or behaviour. Utility challenged the sanction of tradition by questioning whether existing practices served any purpose in promoting human happiness.

Later eighteenth-century thinkers turned many of these concepts into a critique of mainstream enlightened thought. The earlier interest in natural science broadened into the conviction that true harmony was to be found in nature, not abstract theory. Reason became a barrier to personal development, which could only flourish if human passions were given full scope to express themselves. In stressing irrationality, Romanticism was less a coherent body of thought than a style of living and thinking. It inspired both political conservatism and revolutionary liberal nationalism in the 1790s, but generally found expression through religious mysticism, free masonry, secret societies and the exaggerated and extravagant lives of a generation of angry young men.

Such ideas flowed throughout Europe. There is little evidence to support earlier claims that French influence predominated, despite Frederick II's correspondence with philosophers like Voltaire. English, Scottish, Italian and other ideas were equally important, but all were mediated through existing German debates, including cameralism.

The absence of clear patterns makes it difficult to determine the influence of these ideas on political thought and action. The appearance of enlightened idioms in princely decrees cannot be dismissed as merely window-dressing to impress fellow monarchs or win 'bourgeois' support. Frederick II's much publicised cultivation of his image as *le roi philosophe* was certainly a deliberate act, but though his own prolific writings were hardly original, they were sufficient to place him in the front rank of the European intelligentsia. Rather than providing a blueprint for reform, the new ideas introduced alternative solutions into policy planning. There were often fierce disagreements within territorial administrations over what should be done, and these debates were reflected in the growing public discourse from the 1750s (see section 3.1).

The Habsburg monarchy offers a good example. The mid-eighteenth-century wars exposed serious weaknesses in German absolutism. Prussia's survival against seemingly impossible odds forced other governments to rethink their policies, either importing Hohenzollern measures, or introducing their own solutions. The Habsburgs responded with a series of classic cameralist reforms, devised by Haugwitz after 1744, which raised revenue by an impressive 50 per cent.[24] However, the renewed strain of the Seven Years War indicated that these measures had not gone far enough and by the 1760s cameralism appeared to many as rigid and even obsolete. Some, like Joseph II, wanted to take cameralist rationalisation to its logical extremes and advocated copying Prussian methods. Others around Kaunitz favoured more genuinely enlightened alternatives intended to boost productivity by giving greater scope to individualism, while conservative and clerical opponents of both approaches remained strong.[25]

The smaller territories

Recently there has been greater interest in the medium-sized and smaller territories, whose rulers are now often depicted as more enlightened than either Frederick II or Joseph II. This overturns the earlier conservative critique of German petty particularism that saw these territories as failing to match Austrian and Prussian progress.[26] It is suggested that the Reich protected the lesser territories from great-power politics, permitting them to concentrate on benevolent reform and cultural achievements.

In fact, political ambition and imperial legislation compelled most small territories to maintain disproportionately large armies until 1763 when it became obvious they were completely overshadowed by Austria and Prussia. Some did divert military spending into cultural and social reform, like Friedrich II of Hessen-Kassel. However, this prince, along with those in five other medium-sized territories, was a signatory of the notorious subsidy treaties with Britain that despatched 30,000 troops to fight the American revolutionaries after 1775. Foreign subsidies brought 45 million tlr to Hessen in 1702–84, representing more than half of its revenue. Other governments saw these as the ideal solution to the debts accumulated through war, ambition and mismanagement. Friederich II invested much of the 12.65 million tlr he received after 1776 with Meyer Rothschild, creating reserves that were so large by 1830 that the interest alone was more than Hessen's entire tax revenue.

His namesake in Prussia called this an 'auction' as princes traded in the blood of their subjects. Friedrich Karl von Moser, one of Johann Jacob's three sons and a Hessen official, joined the public outcry by writing a series of critical articles. There was widespread suspicion that the money was squandered on self-indulgence or, as in Schiller's play *Kabale und Liebe*, spent on presents for mistresses. Fuelled by skilful American propaganda, the episode came to epitomise the tyranny of German petty particularism and was used by pro-Prussian nationalists to rally support for unification during the nineteenth century. In fact, a large part of the money went on the sort of reforms advocated by the treaties' critics. The per capita tax burden in Hessen was reduced from 5.2 tlr (1760) to 2.2 (1784), while other initiatives included a fire insurance scheme (1767), an agricultural assistance bank (1774), a maternity hospital (1761), preservation of historic monuments (1780), Europe's first modern museum (1779), and academies for agriculture (1765), the arts (1773), and painters and sculptors (1775). Wilhelm IX continued these measures after his accession in 1785 and was the first ruler to pass legislation to protect his subjects from dangers in the skies, particularly the newly invented air balloons and the fires they could cause. Unlike Hessen, the other five signatories were heavily in debt and used their income to reduce their liabilities: in Ansbach-Bayreuth from 5 million to 1.5 million fl. and in Wolfenbüttel from 11 million to 4 million tlr. This enabled a reduction in taxes and a limited range of fairly unsuccessful cameralist schemes.[27]

Despite the military failure in America, German princes regarded the operation as a success and five other rulers signed further treaties with the Dutch after 1782 in order to subsidise their military costs and reduce debts.[28] As the range of Hessen reforms indicates, the medium and smaller territories implemented the same mix of enlightened and cameralist measures as the larger monarchies. Whilst not havens of progressive reform, equally they were not examples of reactionary despotism.

Many smaller territories were adversely affected by the great-power wars of the mid-eighteenth century that had ravaged Saxony, Bavaria, much of Westphalia and northern Germany. The constitutional restraints on violence appeared to be failing as first Charles VII and then his Habsburg successors made war on their German opponents and contemplated radical territorial reorganisation. This encouraged a particular small-state brand of enlightened reform intended to sway public opinion against annexation and secularisation, as well as to rejuvenate the imperial constitution. It rejected the monolithic, rationalising standardisation imposed from above in Austria and Prussia, arguing that strength and vitality lay in the Reich's territorial diversity. The landscape gardens at Wörlitz in Anhalt-Dessau symbolised this programme by eschewing the formal baroque pattern in favour of combining different features in a pleasing whole. Rather than celebrating nature's wild irrationality, the gardens suggested its enlightened harmony and contained agricultural experiments intended to encourage subjects to follow the prince's example of self-improvement. Other territories also tried to reconcile enlightened ideas to the diverse corporate structure of German politics and society by promoting practical measures tailored to local concerns.[29]

Population growth and emigration

In addition to renewed warfare and the impact of enlightened thought, demographic growth also compelled later eighteenth-century governments to change their policies. Cameralist population policies had addressed the problems of post-war depopulation, yet by the 1730s renewed demographic growth was putting pressure on resources. This injected new life into other cameralist measures, and rulers reissued their earlier punitive decrees against idleness and vagrancy. However, the European-wide hunger crisis of 1770–1 indicated that they were faced by a new problem of potential over-population and opened the eyes of the more genuinely enlightened to the fact that poverty had economic rather than moral causes. How they responded provides a measure of the distinctiveness of this phase of absolutism.

One sign of the growing problems was a rise in emigration. However, the decisions to leave an area were always personal and complex, and cannot be reduced exclusively to material considerations. Once emigration set in, it built up modest momentum through 'chain migration' as earlier pioneers sent back information and helped later migrants settle in their new homes.[30]

The bad winter, famine and plague of 1708–9 prompted the first large-scale population movement as people left the affected areas. Most went to other German lands, as did others who fled in subsequent years of acute crisis: 40,000 Saxon and Bohemian peasants crossed into Prussian Silesia to escape hunger in 1770–4. However, areas with steadily rising populations experienced sustained emigration. Württemberg's population grew from 340,000 to 659,000 across the eighteenth century, but another 150,000 left the duchy, many for Hungary or North America. Altogether, at least 200,000 people left central Europe entirely over the century. Around 75,000 went to Russia, especially during the reign of Catherine II, who made a concerted effort to attract them. Others went to England's North American colonies where there were already 100,000 German-speakers by 1750. Around 6,000 of the German mercenaries sent to fight the American revolution chose to remain there. The Spanish government also promoted emigration to the Sierra Morena in 1766–76, believing Germans to be more diligent and enlightened than its native subjects. Like many of those going to America, Spain's colonists were recruited by freelance former army officers, who duped peasants with false promises. The government expected them to establish their new towns in a virtual desert and many died.[31]

As emigration to Russia and Spain accelerated after the Seven Years War, many Rhenish princes feared they were losing valuable workers needed for domestic reconstruction and they petitioned Joseph II to curb the rights of free movement granted under the IPO. Joseph cleverly framed his Emigration Patent of July 1768 so as to reassert imperial claims to the right to veto military recruitment for foreign powers as well as civilian movement, whilst still permitting migration to Habsburg

Hungary. The notoriety of the Sierra Morena colony induced princes and imperial institutions to collaborate in suppressing further emigration to Spain. The emperor also prevented recruitment for foreign powers, though he did not interfere in that conducted for Britain during the American war.[32]

While restrictions on emigration show the continued vigour of imperial institutions, they offer little evidence of enlightened reform. Official attitudes remained rooted in the cameralist maxim that a large population was a wealthy one. None the less, the growing awareness of the economic roots of poverty did prompt new agrarian reforms leading towards the emancipation of the serfs (see section 3.3).

Anti-clericalism

German Enlightened thought was less anti-clerical than that in France, but still provided arguments for secular reform. Cameralism had already begun to dismantle the confessional state, while the toleration extended by Joseph II and Frederick II represented the continuation of earlier measures to attract new settlers. None the less, there were innovations in other areas. Protestant territories extended greater freedom to discuss religious ideas as alternative interpretations rather than insisting on only one valid truth. There was a growing movement for 'popular enlightenment' (*Volksaufklärung*), which maintained that religious instruction and civil education should promote individual development rather than instil orthodoxy and conformity.

Some of these elements could be found in Catholic territories, but here the principal effort was directed at closing a perceived gap with their Protestant neighbours. Prussia's victories in the 1740s and 1750s convinced many Catholics that the Protestants had gained a decisive material advantage with the Reformation, not just in the secularisation of church wealth, but in a more rational way of thinking. Action was delayed in the Habsburg monarchy by the devoutly Catholic Maria Theresa. She was prepared to embrace some changes where these accorded with her conservative, cameralist objectives. For example, she agreed to expel the Jesuits in 1773 in order to wrest control of education throughout the monarchy. However, she saw mass literacy as a way of enforcing Catholic orthodoxy by enabling her subjects to read devotional literature. Her son Joseph had very different ideas, along with other key advisors like Kaunitz, Pergen and Sonnenfels, who deliberately called themselves the 'Party of Enlightenment', dubbing their opponents 'Men of Darkness'. Though the enlightened group disagreed over the purpose of education, they were determined to free it from clerical influence.

Maria Theresa continued to resist, only granting limited toleration to Moravian Protestants when her son threatened to abdicate in 1777. She finally allowed the first Protestant student to receive a degree at Vienna University the following year, yet she continued to persecute the Jews and re-established the Viennese ghetto. Joseph's great chance came after his mother's death and he issued his famous toleration edict in 1781, permitting private Protestant and Orthodox worship throughout the monarchy. Dissenters could now also buy and sell land, study at university and hold public office – decades before such restrictions were lifted on British Catholics by their supposedly more liberal, constitutional government.

Joseph then turned his attention to Catholicism's 'dead hand', suppressing 738 of the monarchy's 2,047 religious houses, and forcing over 40 per cent of the 65,000 monks and nuns to chose between a more productive life or retirement on a limited pension. The resources were diverted into public education, while church schools were compelled to teach secular subjects like science, maths, history and even agriculture. Civil marriage was introduced and divorce made easier. The state now re-drew parish boundaries and set clerical salaries, using some of the money from the monasteries to raise the pay of parish priests, whilst cutting that of the bishops and senior clergy.

While Joseph's measures were often enlightened, his motives were frequently otherwise. The toleration edict was intended to boost immigration and was very successful in attracting a quarter of a million new Protestant settlers by the end of his reign. It was echoed across the Reich as governments responded to the problems left by the mid-eighteenth-century wars, though Joseph was considerably ahead of his contemporaries.[33] He was genuinely concerned for his subjects' welfare, but his outlook remained profoundly that of a cameralist, believing the way to foster the common good was by intrusive state regulation. He took this to obsessive lengths, even forbidding corsets for girls and insisting the Viennese street sweepers present their brooms like soldiers as he drove past.

The more progressive views of Joseph's advisors were also shared by some ecclesiastical princes, who embraced much of the small-state enlightened programme. While this was intended to save them from secularisation, it cannot be entirely explained by practical or material motives. Influenced by Muratori's writings, enlightened clerics attacked superstition and intolerance, seeing no conflict between Catholic theology and progressive reform. Mainz, the centre of German Catholicism, introduced private worship and full civil rights for Protestants in 1788, having reduced restrictions on the Jews five years earlier. By the end of the eighteenth century a ninth of Fulda's inhabitants were Protestant, as were a third of those in Basel and the lands of the Teutonic Order.

Education

Education was the other main area of enlightened reform. Its importance was grasped by theologians in the early sixteenth century and schooling became a major part of the disciplining process to instil orthodoxy and obedience. Most Protestant territories had Latin schools for older children by 1600, while in Catholic areas the Benedictines and Jesuits educated the rich and influential. Yet, the Reich's territorial fragmentation had always inhibited fully confessionalised systems. The IPO permitted dissenters to send their children to neighbouring territories, but even without such rights, sheer market logic forced schools to open their doors since most relied on fees for much of their income. The growing importance of a rounded education as a way to social advancement forced the church to broaden the curriculum or lose the faithful, who would send their children to better schools elsewhere.

The Protestants had an advantage in elementary schooling since their theology stressed access to the bible for all believers, and it is not surprising that they often took the lead in introducing compulsory primary education (see Table 7.2). However, some Catholic areas were notably advanced and many villages in Bavaria, Passau and Bamberg already had schools by the mid-sixteenth century. Protestant higher education was also generally more developed, particularly as Joseph II's utilitarian approach to learning actually retarded Habsburg universities. Protestants dominated the Leipzig book fair and often had the best libraries, like the spectacular collection at the Wolfenbüttel court.

German education was comparatively advanced compared with that elsewhere in Europe, though class sizes remained large, still averaging 60 in the nineteenth century, and there were considerable regional variations. Whereas every village in Brandenburg had a school teacher by 1800, less than half of those in Cleve and Mark were as fortunate. The proportion seems to have been higher in the smaller territories, as most villages in Saxony and Württemberg had a teacher, as did all

Table 7.2 Introduction of compulsory elementary education

Territory	Date
Weimar	1619
Württemberg	1649 (renewed in 1729)
Münster	1693
Waldeck	1704
Prussia	1717 (renewed in 1736 and 1763)
Saxony	1724 (renewed in 1763)
Hessen-Darmstadt	1733
Holstein-Gottorp	1733–4
Wolfenbüttel	1753

in Catholic Paderborn. This did not mean than all children were educated. Only 19% of children in the Tübingen district attended school in 1601, though the proportion grew considerably by the late eighteenth century when Württemberg had 1,460 teachers.[34] Even with patchy success, it was a remarkable achievement to introduce universal elementary education in societies that were overwhelmingly rural, and by 1780 there were already 6,000 schools in the Habsburg monarchy, with over 200,000 pupils. The spread of basic literacy encouraged limited social mobility. Over 7% of law students at Halle University in 1768–71 were peasants' or artisans' sons, compared with 13% who were young noblemen, while over 23% of those studying theology came from humble origins.[35]

Such opportunities were largely incidental to the main thrust of official educational policy, which remained part of cameralism's broader project to transform society by modifying behaviour. Johann Ignaz Felbiger, a Catholic Silesian, helped Frederick II adapt Protestant educational policy to improve schooling in his native province after its annexation by Prussia. He later worked for Joseph II and despite his dismissal in 1782, his ideas influenced reforms in other Catholic lands. He summed up the generally conservative objective of absolutist policy as turning out '(a) honest Christians; (b) good citizens, that is faithful and obedient subjects of the authorities and (c) useful people for the community'.[36]

Prussian education policy in Silesia was far from benevolent and it responded to the shortage of textile workers in the 1760s by encouraging child labour. Throughout the monarchy the daily routine divided children into three groups according to age and ability. The first group concentrated on basic literacy, practising two new letters each day. The second group worked on spelling and started to read, while the more advanced group read, wrote and did sums. All spent two and half hours each day singing hymns and reciting the catechism, while the bible was the principal text for all exercises. In short, education was there to teach peasants enough to make themselves useful, but not so much as to foster expectations of rising above their station. It remained a low priority even in the so-called enlightened monarchies. Frederick II spent 4,000 tlr on school subsidies in 1768, but 10.4 million on the army. Joseph II was rather more generous, increasing the education budget more than eight-fold in 1781–9, yet it still remained less than 1% of military spending.

Social discipline – a verdict

There is little to suggest that absolutist regulation and reform were intended to prepare people for capitalist production, or prevent revolution by currying favour with the bourgeoisie and other allegedly progressive forces. Any moves towards capitalism were unintended consequences of attempts to make existing forms of production more efficient. Response to popular grievances remained restricted to traditional methods of retaining loyalty and there was no sense of impending doom, even after 1789 (see section 8.3).

Despite the growing passion for systems, regulation remained strongly conservative. The confessional state was gradually dismantled, but government remained broadly Christian, guided by theology and morality, though these were subject to changing emphases and interpretation. Reforms targeted threats to social harmony and economic productivity. Many of these problems were consequences of princely ambition, not least the adverse impact of war. Much of cameralist and later enlightened discourse simply rationalised rulers' own mistakes, stigmatising victims as responsible for their own misfortune. None the less, the overriding aim remained the common good as this was the basis of absolutism's legitimacy. It was defined in paternalistic terms that contained a strong streak of dynastic self-interest. Yet, rulers and their advisors did not intend to create new problems; these were the unforeseen consequences of their measures.

Reforms remained piecemeal, more ad hoc responses to circumstances than carefully planned programmes. None the less, rulers and administrators drew on prevailing intellectual currents, even if these did not provide blueprints for change. There are sufficient differences in both inspiration and content to identify three broad phases in official policy, beginning with the conserving police regulation before 1648, followed by more innovative cameralism and finally measures that were at least partly enlightened.

In the process, government expanded from simple wardship over society, to radical interference in everyday life. Many measures failed, not because they were necessarily ill-conceived, but owing to the huge discrepancy between intent and the means to implement it. Often, it was the more progressive measures, like religious toleration, that encountered the greatest resistance, raising the question of how far social discipline can be characterised as state repression.

7.2 Conflict and Collaboration

The sinister state and the 'invention of crime'

Discussions of reform generally present one of two interpretations of the state. In the more traditional, conservative view, benevolent governments headed by enlightened rulers promoted far-sighted progressive reforms that foundered on the ignorance and superstition of an ungrateful population. More recent interpretations suggest a repressive state imposing unwanted change from above, disrupting previously harmonious social relationships and destroying 'authentic' popular culture, smothering individual creativity with soul-destroying uniformity. This process involved 'penetration' as bureaucrats and businessmen sought to dominate rural society, and was met by either 'resistance' or 'adjustment' as ordinary people changed their behaviour to protect themselves, or benefit from the changes. For all its stress on 'history from below', this sinister view of the state still sees government as the motor for change, while both models see state–societal relations as essentially conflictual.

The sinister view argues that the state created most of its own problems, including 'inventing' crime by criminalising previously accepted practices. Certainly, cameralism responded to growing pauperisation by reworking charity to compel people to work. By emphasising the stable household as the social ideal, it hardened attitudes to those who, by choice or circumstance, lived outside settled family units. Officials voiced growing concern at the 'masterless rabble' (*herrenlose Gesindel*) with no fixed abode. Seventeenth-century decrees widened the group falling within this category by using the terms 'gypsy' (*Zigeuner*) and 'rogue' (*Jauner*) interchangeably.

Having identified targets, legislators imposed brutal penalties. A 1689 Habsburg decree forbade gypsies from entering the hereditary lands on pain of a life sentence to hard labour. Those caught entering Coburg a second time were to be hanged without trial, while Bavaria also imposed the death penalty. The Kreise coordinated patrols to round up itinerants. Since there were few workhouses, most of those caught were branded and pushed over the frontier. Expulsion was imposed for begging and other previously lightly-punished offences, simply swelling the numbers of homeless.

'Counter-culture' and 'social bandits'

The dysfunctional character of much official policy has led some historians to interpret crime as a form of resistance. They make some bold claims. Bands of vagrants and robbers are presented as more than purely utilitarian associations formed for mutual protection, or to commit specific raids. They become a key part of a wider 'bent' society bound by shared egalitarian values, where position was determined not by birth or wealth, but according to meritocratic criteria like courage, ability and achievement. Vagrants and bandits operated with the covert support of the urban and rural poor, who allegedly saw them as class allies against the state and bourgeoisie. Supporters offered a network of safe houses, fences, corrupt officials, helpers and sympathisers bound by a common 'counter-culture' expressed in its own language, or cant (*Rotwelsch*), of around 200 specialised terms and expressions.

Bandits assume the central role in this interpretation, which clearly owes much to the British Marxist historian Eric Hobsbawm.[37] While German robbers lacked the theoretical basis or insight to become true revolutionaries, it is claimed that their rejection of poverty and subordination none the less made them 'social bandits', who targeted capitalists such as moneylenders and merchants, as well as officials and other authority figures.

The presence of numerous bandits certainly challenged absolutism's claim to guarantee order. Bandits appeared where territorial fragmentation or wooded, hilly terrain made them hard to catch, chiefly in parts of northern Germany, central areas like Hessen and Thuringia, and parts of the south like Franconia. The Saxon Nickel List roamed across Brunswick, Hamburg and Celle for five years before being caught and executed in 1699. Lips Tullian, also from Saxony, operated in central Germany and Bohemia before being beheaded in Dresden in 1715. Some bands were very large, numbering up to 200, though groups of 10 to 20 were more common. Many were violent, notably that of Krumm-finger Balthasar, who called himself 'the general' and led 20 armed men into Franconia and Thuringia in the 1750s. Friedrich Schwann, another Franconian, became the model for the central character in Schiller's play *The Robbers*, but the most notorious was Matthias Klostermayer. Known as the *Bayerische Hiesel*, Klostermayer was the son of an Augsburg day labourer who deserted from the Bavarian army and led a gang of poachers, before being cornered in an inn in the village of Osterzell by a special task force of 300 soldiers organised by the Swabian Kreis. He and his accomplices were finally overpowered after a shoot-out lasting 16 hours and he ended his days broken on the wheel in Dillingen.

It is easy to romanticise such figures. The Rhenish bandit Johannes Bückler, better known as Schinderhannes, fainted at the sight of blood and was accompanied on raids by his lover Julie Blasius, dressed as a man. Klostermayer became a folk hero by eluding capture for ten years. Bandits did target the rich, like Anton Lautner who specialised in holding up stage coaches in the 1780s. However, this is hardly surprising, since the rich had more worth taking. While there are cases of robbers returning goods stolen from the poor, there is little to suggest a broad alliance against the rich and powerful. Schinderhannes's popularity stemmed mainly from anti-Semitism, since he targeted Jews. Others attacked indiscriminately. The Prussian Johann Horst burnt farms and entire villages before being arrested and himself burnt alive with his mistress in Berlin. Most relied on the threat of violence rather than its actual use, but were just as likely to find valuables during break-ins by torturing the servants as by threatening their masters. Jewish and gypsy bandits stole from their own communities as well as from Christians. In short, their actions only indirectly challenged authority, by exposing the authorities' failure to maintain order.[38] Bandits and other itinerants represented a sub-culture, rather than a counter-culture. They shared many of settled society's values. Vagrants imitated the rituals and usages of craft guilds, a world to which many had formerly belonged and that they still hoped to re-enter.[39]

Criminals and crime

Poverty and homelessness were major factors in crime. Though no more than 5% of Germans lacked a home, half of all bandits were without a permanent address. Two-thirds of criminals arrested in Bavaria in 1729 came from backgrounds outside the guild structure, or from so-called dishonourable trades, yet this group accounted for no more than 40% of the population.[40] Banditry also grew in line with the social dislocation and pauperisation accompanying the population growth of the later eighteenth century, but it peaked during the Revolutionary and Napoleonic Wars when conflict exacerbated the underlying problems.

None the less, bandits remained exceptional and most operated alone or with a few accomplices, engaging in clandestine break-ins rather than armed robbery. Of 34,500 offences brought to trial in a 15-year period in Lippe-Detmold, only 13 involved highway robbery and 110 grievous bodily harm. The murder rate averaged one or two a year at a time when the county had 49,000 inhabitants, and it is clear that violent crime in general declined throughout Germany from the late seventeenth century. Most offences involved theft, followed by moral and social crimes like adultery, drunkenness and other indecent behaviour. Breaches of moral codes declined after the late seventeenth century, partly because the authorities decriminalised some forms of behaviour and stopped prosecuting others. These had constituted about a third of all prosecutions in Munich in 1600–50; they accounted for only 14% a century later, while property crime rose from 25% to 52% over the same period.[41]

Trial, execution and state power

Though rarely resulting in death, violent crime was deeply disturbing in a society still characterised by face-to-face relationships, where strangers were instantly recognisable. It was not only the wealthy who called for government action and though the authorities could manipulate such anxieties to justify an extension of their power, they also shared the basic fear of disorder and violence.

The process of trial and execution symbolised the state's claims to monopolise power. Political centralisation changed the exercise of justice. Trials had been open hearings where the judge sat as arbitrator, assisted by lay advisors selected from the affected community. The shift to written law, made mandatory for the *Reichskammergericht* in 1540, reduced popular involvement. Hearings were held behind closed doors and conducted by trained lawyers. This process was not necessarily one of rational modernisation, since it spawned what one legal historian calls 'a veritable writing mania'. Lawyers and judges insisted on lengthy, elaborate documents, rejecting submissions that used the wrong terms or forms of address, partly as a way of inflating their fees.[42] None the less, the state asserted exclusive control over establishing the truth, judging actions against laws it alone made.

Execution of bandits offered a good opportunity for exemplary justice; a swift, harsh response to a spectacular and disturbing crime. It reflected a deeper sense that the punishment must fit the crime by having a visible effect on the delinquent. Fines and imprisonment were options in some cases, but corporal punishment and death were all more visible. Questions of motive, or the reform of the criminal, remained secondary. Justice acted in God's name. By their actions, criminals disturbed a divine order that could only be restored once they had been punished. Great emphasis was placed on a public confession and signs of repentance, which had to be witnessed by the public so they could see that justice was being done.

Yet, executions were ambivalent occasions. The crowd could be reassured by a fitting punishment for an evil act, but might just as easily sympathise with the criminal as another poor sinner. The mood could swing if anything departed from the norm, such as the condemned refusing to repent, or the hangman's rope breaking, which could be interpreted as a sign from God that the state had reached the wrong verdict. Elements of the state's ritual were appropriated by popular practices, such as the belief that the act of execution cleansed the criminal, making his blood a tonic against evil.[43]

Penal reform

The growing unease at public executions was reflected in a greater military presence on such occasions and by penal reform that also drew on the rise of rational, later enlightened ideas. The spread of witchcraft prosecutions in 1580–1620 demonstrated that torture was a poor way to the truth, and merely fuelled the authorities' paranoia as ever more victims were forced to reveal their 'accomplices'. Frederick II's abolition of torture was proclaimed in 1740 to loud applause from the European intelligentsia, but was not in fact enacted. His father had already made its use dependent on royal permission in 1720, a measure that some other German territories had introduced ninety years before. Torture was already declining before formal restrictions. Bavaria began curtailing it in 1751, but its use had already fallen from 44% of criminal cases in 1650 to 16% by 1690. The 1770s proved a turning point, clearly influenced by the enlightened ideas of the Italian legal reformer Cesare Beccaria, whose work was published in German in 1778 (see Table 7.3). Formal abolition coincided with that in other European countries, like Scotland (1709), Sweden (1734), Denmark (1771) and France (1788).

Other enlightened measures tried to rationalise the scale of punishments by removing distinctions based on the delinquent's social status to make the penalty fit the crime more appropriately. Though not primarily humanitarian, this none the less had a humanising element. It reflected a belief that official regulation had civilised society, removing the need for cruel punishments from earlier, more barbarous ages. The dismantling of the confessional state severely reduced ecclesiastical jurisdiction and removed the penalties of expulsion and other forms of

Table 7.3   Abolition of judicial torture

Territory	Formal abolition	Last use
Prussia	1754	
Mecklenburg		1769
Saxony		1770
Wolfenbüttel		1770
Lippe-Detmold	1773	
Austria	1776	
Palatinate	1776	
Hessen-Kassel	1786	
Hamburg		1786
Austrian Netherlands	1787	
Bavaria	1803	
Württemberg	1809	1778
Weimar	1819	1783
Hanover	1822	1818
Coburg	1828	
Baden	1831	1767

disgrace from many moral offences. Some also thought corporal punishment counter-productive, though it is noteworthy that the abolition of torture was not made public in Austria, the Palatinate and many other territories, so that the law retained its deterrent affect.

The authorities began to show greater interest in the criminal's motives and considered the possibility of rehabilitation. The emphasis in atonement shifted from symbolic ritual to material recompense through fines and workhouse labour. Use of the death penalty declined in the seventeenth century, when 140 people were executed in Frankfurt compared with 248 in the previous hundred years. The number of executions briefly revived from 1720 to 1750 in response to the initial dislocation accompanying the start of population growth, but then declined as rulers narrowed the range of offences punishable by death. Frederick II criticised its use for theft and infanticide, urging greater understanding for the motives that drove people to commit such crimes. The number of civil executions in Prussia fell to an average of 15 a year by the 1770s, considerably fewer than in Britain. While military regulations stressed care and consideration as the keys to good discipline, they none the less retained a wide range of brutal punishments, including running the gauntlet for desertion. Moreover, some of the punishments substituted for death amounted to much the same: of the 1,100 prisoners sent to haul barges along the mosquito-infested banks of the Danube by Joseph II, 721 died.[44]

The enlightened desire to curb public executions also stemmed from a desire to end popular participation, particularly stamping out practices like drinking criminals' blood, which persisted in some parts of Germany into the 1860s. The removal of death for infanticide also reflected the growing importance of gender, rather than status distinctions, in determining the scale of punishments. Women were considered less rational than men, acting on impulse, so death was no deterrent.

Similar ambiguities can be found in the process of enlightened legal codification, which tried to remove the contradictions between the Roman, customary and ecclesiastical elements of existing laws. Bavaria was the first territory to formally abolish the great imperial Carolina criminal code of 1532, replacing it with its own *Codex Juris Bavarici Criminalis*, devised by Baron Kreittmayr in 1751 and adopted by five neighbouring territories. Bavarian judicial and civil codes soon followed, indicating a rapidity of reform not matched by Prussia, where codification begun in 1745 was not completed till 1794, while that started in Austria in 1753 was only finished in 1811. The new codes standardised norms and procedures throughout each territory, but were not entirely progressive. The Bavarian criminal code introduced legal equality for men and women, yet a decree of 1746 confirmed witchcraft as a recognised crime, encouraging a new wave of prosecutions and burnings until 1756. Reform remained gradual and the Bavarian civil code of 1756 remained in force until 1900.[45]

As the execution of Süß Oppenheimer in 1738 demonstrated, governments could break their own laws in politicised cases. However, German justice was not normally arbitrary and its personalised character reflected absolutism's centralisation of authority, rather than disrespect for the law. Princes retained an absolute right to clemency, like the modern US President and state governors, whose pardons also cannot be challenged.

Attitudes to crime and justice

The image of the criminal on the scaffold is a potent symbol of the state's repressive potential. However, Karl Wegert offers an important warning against unqualified acceptance of conflictual models of state–societal relations. 'In our haste to pillory the authorities . . . we have fashioned a populist martyrology based on the proposition that victims are necessarily saints.'[46] Not only were robbers not 'social bandits', but the wider population participated in stigmatising and labelling marginal groups, as well as exercising their own forms of social control. Popular attitudes to justice did not represent some supposedly more authentic, egalitarian alternative to a repressive state apparatus, but were themselves a synthesis of common concerns and external demands.

Elite and popular attitudes overlapped, agreeing broadly in identifying common problems, but often proposing different solutions. There was genuine popular antipathy to certain crimes, especially those involving violence and sexual offences like incest or rape. Villagers and townsfolk were prepared to report those who transgressed accepted norms, often forming their own judgement in these cases before they went to court. Witnesses influenced the official verdict, which often simply confirmed the popular view of who was guilty.[47]

This explains why the enforcement of social regulation varied rather than meeting wholesale failure. Some laws were swiftly implemented, others partially, and the rest not at all, despite being frequently reissued. These variations affected all forms of legislation, indicating that it was not simply a case of those imposed by force being more successful. Many laws were observed without pervasive state surveillance, because they embraced wider attitudes.[48]

Popular protest

Research since 1975 has dispelled earlier assumptions that absolutism crushed popular protest, reducing resistance to 'lower forms of class struggle' until the advent of new, revolutionary ideology and leadership in 1789.[49] There were two further cycles of protest after the German peasants' defeat in 1525. In contrast to late medieval unrest, which had been concentrated in the south-west, the renewed protest beginning in the 1560s occurred in the east, especially in the Habsburg monarchy and Bavaria, where it peaked between 1594 and 1634. The Lower Rhine, Hessen and Lower Saxony were also affected, though unrest dissipated after the 1620s. The next wave came at the end of the eighteenth century and was concentrated in the East Elbian areas of the manorial economy.

Though there were no trans-regional revolts between the 1620s and the 1780s, at least 66 serious disturbances occurred between 1525 and 1789, compared with 59 in the preceding two centuries. These were concentrated in the smaller territories of south-western, north-western and central Germany, which were hit by five waves of protest: 1650–60, 1700–16, 1725–33, 1752–6 and 1767–73 (see Table 7.4).[50] If non-violent demonstrations are included, the numbers rise dramatically, with Hessen alone experiencing 55 disturbances after 1648. These lesser forms are now recognised as very important, enabling peasants to change tactics or combine different types of protest as it suited them. It also explains the longevity of some unrest. That in Hohenzollern-Hechingen stretched from 1584 to 1798, but only saw three violent outbursts in 1584, 1609 and 1619.[51] Most of the time, peasants employed a variety of strategies, such as boycotting forced labour, hiding their property so it could not be confiscated, and refusing homage. The latter could be particularly effective since it reinforced solidarity among the protesters and encouraged the belief that existing laws were no longer binding. The formal ceremony of greeting a new ruler was a traditional time to present grievances and many protests started this way.

The rise of the tax state did not shift protest from anti-seigneurial to anti-fiscal attacks, since all action was partly against feudal lordship.

Table 7.4   Incidence of serious protest in minor German territories after 1648

Territory	Periods of protest
Anhalt-Bernberg	1752–3, 1766–6
Fugger	1770–1, 1784–5
Greiz	1714–30
Hauenstein	1725–45
Hohenlohe	1744–50
Hohenzollern-Hechingen	1584–1798
Illereichen*	1653–61
Isenburg-Meerholz	1718–73
Kempten	1666–7, 1721–31
Korneleimünster	1676–1751
Nassau-Siegen	1703–40
Nassau-Weilburg	1718–73
Neu-Wied	1660, 1715–23, 1789–91
Riedesel	1750–4
Rantzau	1705
Sayn-Wittgenstein	1697–1725, 1776–1806
Schaumburg-Lippe	1784–93
Schönburg	1650–81
Schwarzburg-Rudolstadt	1627, 1716–36
Solms-Braunfels	1650–1729
Solms-Greifenstein	1650–1729
Triberg*	1642–54

* Lands of imperial knights.

Moreover, peasants were perfectly able to identify their own concerns and devise strategies without having to be taught by educated bourgeois or socialist activists. Protest was invariably against 'innovations' (*Neuerungen*) in the form of new taxes and other demands, but this did not make it necessarily reactionary or 'traditional'. Popular aspirations were expressed in the flexible language of 'ancient rights', which were believed to pre-date written law and embodied the horizontal, associative ideals of the commune (see section 3.4). This was not a fading rural utopia, since many 'ancient rights' were recent inventions and their very vagueness made them flexible, capable of sustaining demands for new freedoms in response to changing circumstances.

Protest before 1525 was often anti-clerical, but ecclesiastical lords were only half as likely to be attacked thereafter and religion became more a means to express discontent than an actual cause. Upper Austrian Protestant peasants and nobles were persecuted by the Habsburgs, yet fought amongst themselves over the intensification of lordly exploitation in 1594–7. Religion remained a factor where confessional differences intensified existing disagreements between rulers and ruled, but could as easily provoke inter-communal sectarian or anti-Semitic rioting. None the less, the large number of princely conversions to Catholicism after 1652 did make Protestants more likely to cite religion in appeals to the imperial courts. Johann Jakob Moser diligently recorded 202 such complaints between 1720 and 1770.[52]

The great wave of protest in the 1590s–1620s was triggered by the adverse climatic conditions and growing demographic pressure on resources. Inflationary and fiscal policies exacerbated these problems and focused popular hostility on the territorial authorities, just as the intensification of the manorial economy prompted new anti-seigneurial protests. The burden of war after 1618 deepened the crisis in Bohemia, Upper Austria, Eichsfeld, Bavaria and parts of Brandenburg. Anti-seigneurial protests continued in a number of smaller counties after 1648 where rulers and lords imposed new feudal obligations. However, the main opposition to feudal lordship was in the east, where this weighed heaviest. Protests in Bohemia after 1679 and later in Hungary were instrumental in hastening government intervention in the manorial economy, leading to the partial abolition of serfdom by 1785 (see section 3.3). The massive uprisings in the Habsburg lands had no parallel in the Reich. Only Saxony was affected on a similar scale, when its peasants revolted against the slow pace of change: their long-standing grievances had accumulated 230 cases pending in the elector's courts on the eve of their rising in 1790.

Taxes formed the immediate basis of a quarter of all protests after 1648, but most of these occurred in the smaller German territories, which were more prone to unrest than their larger neighbours. They suffered a greater imbalance between resources and government expenditure, because imperial levies hit them disproportionately. Though their military and fiscal obligations were small, they lacked the economies of scale enjoyed by the larger, often more compact principalities and electorates. They had a greater need for imperial protection and tended to meet their duties in full to safeguard their status as imperial estates. Their rulers usually had smaller domains and passed on a larger proportion of the burden to their subjects. At the same time, many minor dynasties entertained delusions of grandeur, attempting to compete with their more prestigious neighbours, despite their more limited resources. In this sense, the traditional image of petty despotism is at least partially correct, but often the lesser counts had little choice if they wanted to preserve their precarious status during the prolonged warfare of 1672–1714.

The closer proximity of ruler to ruled could also prove a disadvantage. The ruler was often simultaneously the largest landowner, frequently controlling the only major indigenous resource, like the count of Wittgenstein who owned the forest, while his counterpart in Lippe owned 67% of the land and commanded 55% of all feudal income.[53] The distinction between public and private became even less clear as rulers intensified demands for rents as well as taxes. The absence of intervening administrative and judicial layers associated oppression still more exclusively with the ruler. Lack of resources made it harder to respond to major problems and it is significant that four of the five waves of protest affecting the lesser territories coincided with the hunger crises of the 1650s, 1698–9, 1709, 1756–7 and 1770–1.

Urban unrest

Imperial cities and territorial towns shared some of the problems of the smaller counties and lordships, notably a lack of resources and the close proximity of ruler and ruled. However, the representative character of their governments gave urban protest a distinctive character. The corporate basis of most urban governments meant that elections were not contests between rival candidates proposing alternative solutions to common problems. The limited franchise restricted participation through the guilds, who selected a proportion of councillors while others, often holding the senior positions, were co-opted by those already in power. Thus, when substantive issues arose affecting the inhabitants' material or psychological well-being, citizens were faced with the choice of either accepting the official solutions, or opposing the entire council.[54]

Constitutional conflicts developed as sectional interests sought greater influence, or the disenfranchised poor tried to break patrician oligarchy (see Table 7.5). The social structure of large municipalities was too complex for it to fragment along class lines, because individual citizens were members of different overlapping communities within the

Table 7.5 Major constitutional disputes in imperial cities
after 1648

City	Periods of dispute
Aachen	1789
Buchau	1748–9, 1787
Dortmund	1763–71
Frankfurt	1702–32
Hamburg	1685–6, 1693–1712
Giengen	1746
Mühlhausen	1639–1725, 1732–5
Nuremberg	1797–1806
Ulm	1794–1802
Wangen	1676–9, 1692–3, 1704–5, 1707–17
Zell	1766

wider framework of their home town. For example, regardless of wealth, most Frankfurt citizens closed ranks to preserve the Lutheran character of their city against its Catholic, Calvinist and Jewish minorities.[55] Smaller towns were less affected, because their internal structures were under-developed and usually allowed wider participation. Instead, they were more likely to be affected by the problems of the rural world, with which they often had much in common economically.

The juridification of popular protest

The judicial framework and systems of appeal developed after 1525 encouraged the juridification of protest, shifting it away from violent outbursts and towards peaceful arbitration and redress through the courts and territorial administrations (see section 5.2). That ordinary Germans accepted this is at first surprising. Above communal level, all courts were controlled by the authorities and were staffed by men who generally believed peasants to be naturally ignorant, obstinate and unruly. The judiciary relied on written law, requiring sophisticated, learned knowledge and documentary proof, yet the system was also open to favouritism, bribery and other forms of corruption.

However, violence was inherently risky. Changes to imperial law since 1526 banned violent protest as sedition, authorising the authorities to cooperate through the Kreise to suppress revolts. Improved military technology and the growth of professional armies tipped the scales still more decisively in the authorities' favour. Popular protest was rarely truly spontaneous. It progressed through a series of often carefully orchestrated phases, with the use of violence as the last resort. Disputes over tactics and objectives were common. Since all communities were internally stratified, attempts to mobilise them often simply reinforced existing tensions. Communal institutions could provide leadership, but equally could become venues for divisive debates, and often solidarity had to be enforced by threats to ostracise those who failed to back the majority line.[56] Such factionalism opened the door to negotiated settlements. This was not simply cynical 'divide and rule', because the authorities' legitimacy rested on their ability to preserve social harmony. They were prepared to work with those who favoured peace and were usually prepared to grant concessions to secure this. Real gains could be made, particularly if protesters avoided violence and framed their case in language likely to appeal to the authorities' own sense of benevolence and clemency.[57] More than a quarter of *Reichshofrat* cases after 1648 and up to a fifth of those before the *Reichskammergericht* were brought by subjects against their rulers.[58] Experience gained in one case assisted later protests, and communities often shared knowledge and pooled resources to pay lawyers to represent them.

Rulers accepted legal defeats, because armed repression was not a viable option. Policing remained a matter of local self-regulation in communal hands. Even large cities had few professional watchmen, such as Vienna with only 188 police for 175,000 inhabitants in 1753. Paramilitary units were maintained in rural areas, chiefly to patrol the highways on horseback, but these were hardly adequate to chase bandits, let alone confront entire communities. Small territories lacked large armies and were reluctant to call in external assistance, which was invariably expensive and might not leave when asked to. Having failed to come to terms with their subjects after decades of protests, the counts of Sayn-Wittgenstein relied on Hessen-Kassel's troops to collect taxes after 1794 in the first step to what became permanent annexation in 1803. Regular troops were neither trained nor equipped for internal security. They could guard palaces and grain stores, hold back crowds at public executions, or break tax strikes by occupying the protesters' homes. However, they had little alternative but to open fire if they met determined resistance. The results were disastrous, particularly in the Sendlingen Christmas massacre of 1705, when over 1,000 Bavarian peasants were killed. Repression also damaged political reputations and opened the door to unwelcome interference. The imperial courts frequently censured rulers for using force, or even exaggerating reports of unrest. A court injunction compelled Carl Eugen to abandon forcible collection of taxes in 1764, while Carl Leopold of Mecklenburg and Wilhelm Hyacinth of Nassau-Siegen were both deposed by the emperor after they turned their troops against their subjects.

The conservative character of German justice

The growing intervention of the imperial courts in the imperial cities and smaller territories after 1648 was a sign of the Reich's revival rather than of mounting political crisis. The courts stabilised the weaker elements of the Reich by resolving their internal problems and defusing popular tension. Oligarchy was curbed in Frankfurt and Hamburg through limited constitutional reform imposed by the *Reichshofrat*. The courts made growing use of debt commissions from the mid-eighteenth century to tackle the financial problems of imperial cities and counties, compelling their governments to cut back luxury and military expenditure and introduce greater fiscal transparency and accountability.[59]

Volker Press has questioned the effectiveness of these measures, arguing that they addressed symptoms rather than causes, simply propping up an already crumbling structure and inhibiting more fundamental modernising reform.[60] For example, Landgrave Ludwig VIII used his close ties to Maria Theresa to frustrate the *Reichshofrat* case brought by his creditors, who wanted to declare Hessen-Darmstadt bankrupt in 1772. However, the courts could act forcefully. The imperial debt commission in Sachsen-Hildburghausen called in military assistance from neighbouring territories when the prince refused to accept its reforms in 1769. The threat of intervention could encourage rulers to put their own house in order. Ludwig VIII began his own reform programme after 1772, which eventually cleared his 6 million fl. debt by 1814.[61] Other measures in the imperial cities also had respectable results.

Internal reforms made the larger territories less dependent on imperial institutions to resolve their difficulties. The authorities emerged as arbiters, forcing both lords and subjects to submit to their courts and administrations. However, like their lesser neighbours, they shared the same basic political and legal culture, which preferred workable compromises to absolute justice. As Ulinka Rublack aptly observes, early modern German government was about 'deals instead of discipline'.[62] The complex, multilayered social and political structure prevented sharp divisions along class or other lines. Interests overlapped and their were always numerous opportunities to appeal to external agencies or sympathisers to protect privileges and advance goals.

The overall result was to reinforce conservatism. The authorities believed that genuine grievances lay behind most protests, and saw radicalism as the work of a few hot-heads who duped the others. Judges and administrators intervened to restore social harmony, addressing specific issues, but equally punishing those pushing for more fundamental change, particularly if they used violence. The very success of popular appeals dampened enthusiasm for more radical action. The system facilitated certain forms of protest that could obtain limited goals. Violence could still erupt if wider hopes were frustrated, as in Saxony in 1790, but appeal through recognised and legitimate channels remained the preferred option. Ultimately, this had negative consequences for German political development. As the state guaranteed the rule of law, there seemed less need for alternative constitutional safeguards. With their interests and rights already protected by the law, people did not need representative or democratic government.

Chapter 8:   Imperial and European Politics

8.1   The Imperial Recovery

The constitutional debate

All major German writers before 1618 agreed the Reich was a monarchy, in which the emperor held exclusive supreme jurisdiction, while territorial rulers, acting through the Reichstag, merely assisted in the exercise of these powers. Outsiders disagreed and, under the influence of Bodin's theory of indivisible sovereignty, described the Reich as an aristocracy, in which the emperor, like the doge of Venice, was merely the first among equals. Later interpretations of the period after 1648 generally followed the foreigners' view, writing German history from the perspective of the larger, absolute principalities as if these were already independent states. Yet, the Reich survived for another 158 years and during most of that time displayed considerable vitality and continued development. This manifested itself most clearly in the ongoing debate on the imperial constitution and in the revival of imperial prestige and influence after 1648.

Bodin's interpretation was ill-received in Germany, even amongst Protestants, who still recognised the supremacy of the Catholic Habsburgs into the 1620s. However, German hostility to the Reich's monarchical character grew as Ferdinand II's successes threatened to reduce Protestant political influence and autonomy. Encouraged by Sweden, Protestant propagandists seized on Bodin's idea to denounce Habsburg policy as a general assault on 'German Liberty'. The most influential of these was Bogislaw Philipp von Chemnitz, who wrote under the pseudonym of Hippolithus à Lapide. He used the elective character of the

305

imperial title to assert the princes' supremacy over the emperor. In his version of the true form of the imperial constitution, the Reichstag supervised the emperor, who was merely there to coordinate defence and peacekeeping. The debate polarised as Habsburg supporters, such as Dietrich Reinkingk, defended the monarchist interpretation, stressing the emperor's superior role.

The Peace of Westphalia is often regarded as pushing political reality towards Chemnitz's federal interpretation, by dissolving imperial authority and granting near sovereignty to the territories. Further evidence appears from Samuel von Pufendorf, whose 1667 study of the imperial constitution made him the most influential of all seventeenth-century German political theorists. He described the Reich as degenerating from a regular kingdom with well-defined royal powers, into an irregular system of fragmented sovereignty that he famously labelled a 'monstrosity', because it did not fit any accepted categories of political science. Though widely cited, Pufendorf's assessment was partly flawed, because the Reich had never been a regular kingdom and instead evolved its unique political hierarchy through the interaction of emperor, princes and imperial institutions (see section 2.2). Moreover, he showed considerable sympathy for this structure as one appropriate for central Europeans, and far from seeing inevitable disintegration towards a lose confederation, believed the Reich capable of further development. Other, less well known writers like Seckendorff and Johann Limnaeus also continued to analyse the Reich as a hierarchical order headed by the emperor.[1]

Pufendorf's optimism was well founded, because imperial institutions experienced a significant revival after 1648. This trend was first identified as the 'imperial reaction' by the constitutional historian Erich Feine, who analysed the Habsburg response to the setbacks of the Thirty Years War.[2] 'Imperial recovery' is perhaps a more apt term since it recognises that reform and revival had broader roots and did more than just repair Habsburg dynastic influence. None the less, an examination of Habsburg policy still offers a good place to start analysis of the process of recovery and to assess its limits.

The methods of imperial recovery

Habsburg prestige had been severely damaged by the Thirty Years War, which saw land lost to France, the intrusion of Sweden into the Reich and a significant increase in princely power. The Reich remained fundamental to the dynasty's European status. Nearly three-quarters of Habsburg land lay within its frontiers, while possession of the imperial title brought authority over the multitude of other German territories, which combined, were still more than twice as big as the dynasty's own possessions (see Tables 8.1 to 8.4). The Habsburgs needed to hold on to the title and restore the emperor's influence as the basis of their own international standing. These goals did not necessarily conflict with the wider imperial interests of the territorial rulers. The war had convinced most Germans that a strong constitution was necessary for domestic peace and external security and they rejected Franco-Swedish efforts to weaken key institutions in the Peace of Westphalia (see section 4.4). The imperial patriotism of the Schönborn electors of Mainz was another expression of this conviction, as they mobilised the lesser territories through the Kreise to resolve common problems (see section 5.3). The Habsburgs could rebuild their influence provided their own objectives remained broadly in line with this sentiment. While the dynasty still favoured stronger monarchical authority, it saw this as a means to achieve its own goals rather than an objective in itself.

The Habsburgs abandoned the confrontational policies of the war years and tried to achieve their goals within the new constitutional

Table 8.1   Territorial shares of the Reich

	1648		1714		1748		1792	
	km^2	%	km^2	%	km^2	%	km^2	%
Habsburg monarchy	225,390	(32.8)	251,185	(36.5)	213,785	(31.1)	215,875	(31.4)
Hohenzollern monarchy	70,469	(10.2)	77,702	(11.3)	124,122	(18.1)	131,822	(19.2)
Other 4 secular electors	89,333	(13.0)	122,823	(17.9)	123,153	(17.9)	121,988	(17.7)
Remaining German rulers	302,146	(44.0)	235,628	(34.3)	226,278	(32.9)	217,653	(31.7)
Total	687,338		687,338		687,338		687,338	

NB: The losses from the Burgundian Kreis to France (1668, 1679) and of Lorraine (1738) have been discounted in the Reich totals.

Table 8.2　Growth of the Habsburg monarchy

Date	In Reich	Outside*	Total
pre-1683	225,390	90,000	315,390
1700	225,390	287,430	512,820
1714–18	251,185	404,508	655,693
1718–20	251,185	487,078	738,263
1720–35	251,185	488,320	739,505
1735–40	251,185	359,700	610,885
1745–8	213,785	359,700	573,485
1748–71	213,785	353,667	567,452
1772–4	213,785	437,432	651,217
1775–8	213,785	447,432	661,217
1779–94	215,875	447,432	663,307
1795	215,875	494,432	710,307

* Includes the following lands under the nominal jurisdiction of Imperial Italy (*Reichsitalien*):

1714–35	16,115
1735–8	22,148
1738–48	47,000
1748	34,667

All figures are in km^2

structure. Ferdinand III already signalled the way by a more cautious approach in his dealings with the important princes and institutions. Leopold I developed this after 1658, avoiding measures that could stir opposition and result in further public humiliations. Instead, he advanced his objectives incrementally through preparatory negotiations before declaring his hand in the Reichstag. Habsburg diplomats would drop controversial measures, or shift discussions to other, potentially more favourable arenas, such as the Kreis assemblies. Simultaneously, Habsburg patronage was expanded to smooth the way both in the Reich and in the hereditary lands.

Humiliating though it was, the loss of Alsace had not substantially reduced the size of the Habsburg possessions, which remained far larger than those of any other German prince. Despite the destruction, which had been severe in Bohemia, the Habsburgs still governed around 7 million subjects. Moreover, their domestic position had improved during the war with the defeat of the Bohemian and Austrian Estates. At Westphalia, they secured important concessions that effectively exempted

Table 8.3   Overview of gains and losses of the Habsburgs

Date	Gains	Losses
(1683–)1699	Hungary, Transylvania	–
(1707–)1714	Netherlands, Sardinia, Milan, Novarra, Naples, Mantua, Castiglione, Solferino	
1718	Serbia, Banat	–
1720	Sicily	Sardinia
1735	Parma, Piacenza	Naples, Sicily
1738/9	Tuscany, Falkenstein	Serbia (part)
1740/45	–	Silesia
1748	–	Parma, Piacenza
1772	Galicia	–
1775	Bukowina	–
1779	Innviertel	–
1795	Little Poland	–

their lands from many of the checks and balances of the imperial constitution, reinforcing their autonomy within the Reich. Ferdinand II had already separated Habsburg and imperial government in his reorganisation of the *Reichshofrat*. The latter remained one of the two supreme courts, but no longer had a major role in advising on dynastic policy. Habsburg administrative institutions were detached from the imperial chancellery (*Reichskanzlei*), which now dealt only with formal business with imperial institutions and princes.

Leopold I felt sufficiently strong to resume violent confessionalisation in Hungary after 1660, intending to reduce this kingdom to the same level of obedience as Austria and Bohemia. He met stiff resistance from the Hungarian aristocracy, who feared for their privileges and rose in revolt after 1671. Military repression failed and Leopold was repeatedly forced to make concessions. Habsburg rule was firmly associated with high taxes, German-speaking military occupation and suppression of local religious and political freedoms. However, the aristocrats hesitated

Table 8.4   Population of the Habsburg monarchy

Region	1618	1648	1700	1726	1740	1754	1790
Austria	2.0	1.92	2.5	3.0	3.71	3.9	4,291,700
Bohemia	4.0	2.38	2.5	4.06	3.64	3.07	4,463,500
Hungary	2.7	2.7	3.2	4.1	5.36	6.16	8,555,800
Galicia	–	–	–	–	–	–	3,435,000
Netherlands	–	–	–	0.9	1.0	1.2	1,888,000
Italian lands	–	–	–	5.93	2.24	1.84	1,840,000
Total	8.7	7.0	8.2	17.99	15.95	16.17	24,474,000

NB: Totals in millions, except that for 1790, which is in full. The acquisition of Little Poland in 1795 added another 1.5 million subjects.

to mobilise wider support for fear that this might rebound on their intensification of the manorial economy. Many Hungarians also feared the Ottomans more than the Habsburgs and some collaborated in return for rewards and patronage. Ottoman defeat by 1699 removed the main external sponsor of Hungarian opposition and paved the way for a partial reorganisation of the aristocracy along the lines pursued earlier in Bohemia and Austria. The Hungarian diet abandoned its claims for elective monarchy and accepted the Habsburgs as hereditary rulers after 1687. Conquest of Transylvania also removed that principality as a potential trouble spot by 1696.

Continued opposition to the often heavy-handed rule from Vienna erupted in the Rákóczi revolt of 1703–11, which came close to reversing this process. Military superiority, combined with well-timed concessions from Joseph I, defused the situation, paving the way for improved relations after 1715. Having recognised the dynasty's control of Hungarian armed forces in that year, the diet also approved the Pragmatic Sanction in 1723, acknowledging a fundamental change in Habsburg inheritance law to ensure that the monarchy could be inherited through the female as well as the male line. The relative success of Habsburg policy in Hungary was demonstrated by the diet's loyalty in the crisis of 1740 when much of Europe chose to dispute the validity of the new law, in the War of the Austrian Succession (see section 8.2).

That war revealed the inadequacy of Habsburg administration, encouraging Haugwitz's reform programme after 1744, which rested primarily on renegotiating tax grants with the provincial Estates. The Hungarian diet voted additional funding in 1751, while tariff reform three years later further integrated the kingdom within the monarchy as a whole, though at some cost to its own economy. The creation of the Council of State in 1761 improved central coordination, though Hungary retained considerable autonomy, along with its dependencies in Croatia, Transylvania and the Military Frontier. Maria Theresa's attempts to force the Hungarians to increase their contribution to central expenses failed in 1765 and no further diet was called for 35 years.

The monarchy had been transformed in the meantime. By 1699, the reconquest of Hungary gave the dynasty more land outside the Reich than inside it for the first time since Charles V. Further gains consolidated this by 1720, when Habsburg possessions were larger than the entire Reich, and though defeats in international conflicts reduced this between 1733 and 1748, it was clear that Austria had now emerged as a distinct great power in its own right (see Tables 8.2 and 8.3).

Ultimately, Austria's growth made the Reich less important, but more immediately it increased Habsburg imperial influence, adding more resources and widening the scope for patronage. Dynastic revival was reflected in the magnificence of the Viennese court, which outshone all its central European rivals and matched others further afield (see section 6.2). For Habsburg service it was worthwhile renouncing religious convictions, and 31 of the 130 imperial councillors serving between 1600 and 1674 were Lutherans and Calvinists who had converted to Catholicism to work in Vienna.[3] The monarchy's diplomatic service expanded rapidly in the 1650s so that it was represented in a dozen German courts, as well as key imperial cities and major European capitals. Its presence within the Reich far exceeded that of France and was heightened by the emperor's formal representation in all key imperial institutions. Better information and extensive personal contacts made it easier to manage imperial politics.

The imperial title retained considerable symbolic importance and practical influence, despite the constitutional revisions imposed at Westphalia. Uncertainty over the Habsburgs' retention of the title slowed their recovery until after 1658. Ferdinand III's eldest son was elected as Ferdinand IV, King of the Romans, in 1653, but died after only thirteen months, opening the prospect of renewed dynastic and imperial crisis. Matters were not resolved before Ferdinand III's death on 2 April 1657, leading to an interregnum of fifteen months during which French influence increased, with the formation of the anti-Habsburg Rhenish Alliance (see section 5.3). Eventually, Ferdinand's younger son Leopold persuaded his relatives to back him, and won the support of the electors, to be elected next emperor in July 1658. His 47-year reign provided the necessary stability for the imperial recovery to gather momentum, while his natural caution suited him to the role he had to play.[4]

The Habsburgs vigorously defended their imperial prerogatives, but were forced to recognise the existence of other imperial titles for the Ottomans (1606), the Russians (1721) and eventually Napoleon (1804). The latter prompted them to create a distinct Austrian hereditary title, which subsumed much of the imagery and symbolism of the old Holy Roman one. By clinging to their status as Europe's premier monarchy, the dynasty was swimming against the tide that was pushing the continent towards a system of independent sovereign states. However, this process was gradual, and its outcome far from clear in the decades following 1648. The growth of their hereditary lands after 1683 offset the declining international prestige of the imperial title. The latter was still crucial in the Reich, which remained a feudal hierarchy. Princes held their lands as imperial fiefs and required the emperor's confirmation before they could formally assume office. No electors and only a few princes appeared in person to request this after the 1560s, yet still they sent written notification to Vienna and paid the necessary feudal dues. Frederick II wrung special concessions from Charles VII in 1742, emphasising his pre-eminence above all other German rulers, and fuelling demands for similar privileges amongst the other electors. Yet, the lesser rulers continued to observe etiquette that emphasised their lack of full sovereignty and even Frederick II formally acknowledged Hohenzollern subordination to imperial authority and paid the fees to be enfiefed with his later acquisitions.[5]

Though the emperor's powers to create new imperial princes were made dependent on the Reichstag's agreement after 1654, he retained considerable influence through his authority over lesser ennoblement (see 6.2). His influence in the imperial church and over the knights and cities gave him further patronage opportunities, while his role as supreme judge enabled him to assert his authority whilst binding the weaker territories to the Reich's hierarchy by resolving their problems. Imperial and dynastic interests remained in harmony, since the Habsburgs won support for their dynastic goals by stabilising the Reich

The revival of the Reichstag

This can be seen most clearly through their new attitude to the Reichstag. The Reichstag had proved a useful forum through which to rally support during the later sixteenth century when it had voted large sums for Rudolfine imperial defence. As it proved more troublesome after 1608, the Habsburgs restricted consultation to the electors, hoping this small elite would be easier to manage. The Reichstag re-emerged after 1641 as the imperial estates sought access to the peace negotiations. Obliged to summon it again within six months of Westphalia, Ferdinand III eventually opened a new session in Regensburg in 1653. This meeting failed to resolve all the unfinished business of the Westphalian negotiations and its final recess of 1654 included important concessions to the princes over debts and taxation. However, careful stage-management enabled Ferdinand to project a new image of Habsburg power and he defeated attempts to curtail his prerogatives.[6]

He played on the electors' corporate elitism to ensure they backed his decision not to summon the full Reichstag again. The elector of Mainz, Johann Philipp von Schönborn, was permitted to convene the ordinary imperial deputation (*Ordentliche Reichsdeputation*), a constitutional device created in 1555, which had a permanent membership selected to ensure representation from all 10 Kreise and each category of imperial Estate. The deputation could act as a substitute Reichstag, overseeing justice, coinage regulation, defence and other matters when the full assembly was not in session. Its efficiency had been impaired by the electors' desire to maintain their corporate distinctiveness and in 1564 it split into two colleges, replicating the Reichstag's potential for deadlock. It shared that institution's fate amidst the escalating tensions and did not meet at all between 1600 and 1643. However, Schönborn's new spirit of bi-partisan politics offered the chance for it to re-emerge as a more convenient forum for managing the Reich, and it remained in session from 1653.

Both Ferdinand and Schönborn were mistaken since the deputation was dominated by powerful princes who proved difficult. The emergency of a new Turkish War forced Leopold I to reconvene the Reichstag in Regensburg in 1663 and it remained permanently open thereafter.[7] The Great Elector led calls from some armed princes to close the meeting, but Leopold soon realised that working with the Reichstag lent greater legitimacy to Habsburg policy. One important example is his choice to involve it in formal declarations of war in 1689 and 1702, though this was not necessary to activate imperial defence. Federal tendencies were checked by the presence of the multitude of lesser territories, who naturally clustered as imperial clientele and counterbalanced the more independently-minded electors and powerful princes. Though the emperor could not dictate policy, he could rally sufficient consensus for limited common action and contain those rulers who might otherwise oppose him.

The extent of the recovery

The imperial recovery was greatest in the south and west, which contained the majority of weaker territories and were also closest to Austria. Habsburg patronage further cemented common bonds by giving imperial nobles property within the hereditary lands, whilst furthering the careers of Austrian and Bohemian nobles in cathedral chapters and as imperial knights. Growing French belligerence encouraged closer collaboration over defence, though it also stimulated the Kreis Association movement, which wished to keep the Reich out of European conflicts (see section 5.3).

The emperor faced greater difficulties in the north and east, where his influence had traditionally been weaker. Leopold I joined the Northern War (1655–60) after 1658, despatching a small army to assist Brandenburg against Sweden, but this failed to re-establish the commanding imperial position in the north that had briefly existed under Wallenstein in the 1620s. The emperor also aided Brandenburg after the Swedes attacked in 1675 during the Dutch War. As in 1658, the imperial military presence was as much to keep an eye on the Great Elector as to fight the Swedes. This time, Brandenburg overran Sweden's German possessions, but had to return most of them in 1679 following French pressure. Hohenzollern resentment at Leopold's failure to do more only made Brandenburg harder to handle. Leopold began a dangerous policy of divide and rule, sponsoring Hanoverian ambitions, to counterbalance those of Brandenburg. This brought immediate returns in the form of political loyalty and military assistance, but at the expense of damaging concessions. Protests at Hanover's new electoral title made trouble in the Reichstag after 1692, while Habsburg ministers already acknowledged by 1705 that it had been a mistake to allow Elector Frederick III to call himself 'king in Prussia' as this had only fuelled Hohenzollern ambitions.[8] Hanover remained a relatively trustworthy partner into the mid-eighteenth century, but the relationship was transformed by its dynasty's personal union with Britain after 1714 so that there were now two north German kings to deal with. Austria's acquisition of the Spanish Netherlands gave it control of the Burgundian Kreis, reviving the

imperial presence in the north-west and allowing the emperor to check
Prussian influence in Westphalia by promoting his clients amongst the
counts and bishops. Improved relations with Saxony offered a further
counterweight against the Hohenzollerns, but could not obscure the
fact that the north was becoming harder to manage by the 1720s, particularly as Sweden's defeat in the Great Northern War (1700–21)
removed it as an active check on Prussian and Hanoverian influence.

However, Bavaria proved the main focal point for anti-Habsburg discontent. Austro-Bavarian relations swung between uneasy cooperation
and outright hostility. Though Ferdinand III honoured the concessions made by his predecessor, he kept the new electorate at arm's
length. Louis XIV deliberately encouraged Bavarian ambitions, recognising the electorate's potential as the chief check on revived Habsburg
influence. Though Bavaria did not follow Münster and Cologne in
openly joining France during the Dutch War, it refused to support the
imperial war effort and maintained a menacing military stance funded
by French subsidies. Leopold contained this threat by cultivating good
relations with the ambitious Max Emanuel, who became elector in
1679. Though Max Emanuel promised undying loyalty, he won significant concessions, including marriage to Leopold's daughter, Maria
Antonia in 1685, which provided the basis for a later Bavarian claim to
the entire Austrian inheritance. Leopold also promised to give the elector the Spanish Netherlands should these pass to Austria. Max Emanuel
provided substantial assistance in reconquering Hungary after 1683,
becoming known to the Ottomans as the 'blue king' on account of
the sky-blue uniforms of the Bavarian troops. He also rebuffed French
attempts to win him over in 1687–8, not least because Louis XIV made
the mistake of simultaneously opposing the election of his brother Joseph
Clemens as elector of Cologne. This ensured the continued loyalty of
both Wittelsbachs during the Nine Years War of 1688–97.[9]

However, Max Emanuel's royal ambitions increasingly conflicted
with Leopold's plans to recover all the Spanish inheritance for Austria
on the death of the last Spanish Habsburg, Carlos II, in 1700. After considerable prevarication, Max Emanuel opted for a French alliance,
taking his brother with him as both declared against Leopold in 1702.[10]
Leopold was already prepared, having carefully cultivated the support of the rival Palatine Wittelsbachs since 1685, when the Catholic
Pfalz-Neuburg line succeeded the defunct Protestant branch. Leopold
backed the Pfalz-Neuburg succession against French opposition during
the Nine Years War and won the firm support of Elector Johann Wilhelm

(r.1690–1716), who provided substantial assistance in defending the Rhine throughout the subsequent War of the Spanish Succession. Habsburg diplomacy furthered the careers of the elector's many children in the imperial church, and encouraged his hopes that he, not Max Emanuel, might receive the Spanish Netherlands.[11] The Habsburgs outwitted both Wittelsbachs, neither of whom gained their coveted royal crown, while Spain's Italian possessions, along with the Netherlands, passed to Austria in 1714.

The emperor's position in Italy improved steadily after 1648 as Spain became more dependent on Austrian assistance, reversing the earlier relationship between the two Habsburg branches. In return for covert aid in the ongoing war against France, Spain abandoned its efforts to detach its northern Italian possessions from the emperor's feudal jurisdiction. Leopold consolidated his position as Spain called on his help to defend its possessions against later French attacks. He established a permanent diplomatic presence in imperial Italy in 1687 and intensified his feudal jurisdiction over the area during the Nine Years War, insisting that, as his vassals, the north Italian rulers pay war taxes and assist in the struggle against France. Imperial and dynastic interests were in harmony, as the German princes were keen to see the Italians share some of the burden of collective security, while Leopold's growing influence reinforced his claims to inherit Spain's possessions. Italy was his first priority when war broke out in 1701 and, thanks to Anglo-Dutch support, the imperial army defeated the French-backed Bourbon forces at the battle of Turin in 1706.[12]

There is some debate as to whether the imperial recovery peaked under Leopold or continued under his successor, Joseph I.[13] Though Joseph has been portrayed as pursuing exclusively dynastic goals, it is clear that he only achieved these by paying attention to wider imperial interests. The high point came between 1704 and 1708. Bavaria's defeat at Blenheim paved the way for the resolution of German problems in the emperor's favour. The fugitive Bavarian and Cologne electors were placed under the ban and their lands were occupied by Habsburg troops. The same process occurred in Italy following the battle of Turin as Austria not only seized Spain's possessions, including Naples and Sicily, but also confiscated the lands of the Italian princes who had sided with the Bourbons. The German settlement was accepted by the Reichstag in 1708, which recognised the validity of the bans on Bavaria and Cologne, as well as Joseph's skilful solution to the controversy over the Hanoverian electoral title (see section 2.2). A short campaign in

1708–9 was sufficient to compel the pope to acknowledge Austria's new position in Italy.

The recovery falters

These favourable settlements began to unravel after Joseph's unexpected death in 1711. The reasons were partly international. Britain and the Dutch Republic only backed Austria's claims to the Spanish Succession after 1701 on the condition that the two Habsburg empires would not be united under one ruler. As Leopold had two sons, this seemed an acceptable solution, since Joseph could continue the Austrian line, while Charles became the new king of Spain. Joseph's death left Charles as the sole male Habsburg. Tired of war, Britain and the Dutch accepted France's candidate instead on the same terms agreed originally with Leopold, recognising the Bourbon Philip V as Spanish king on the condition that Spain and France could never be combined. Austria was to be compensated by being permitted to retain the Netherlands and Italian lands. Having agreed this at Utrecht in 1713, Britain and the Dutch left the war, leaving Charles to fight on alone. Though elected Emperor Charles VI, he was unable to maintain his position either in Spain or against France and was obliged to accept the Anglo-Dutch settlement in 1714.

Charles's continuation of the war after 1711 was a mistake, alienating the traditional Habsburg clientele, who thought he was sacrificing the Reich to his dynastic interests. The 1714 peace disappointed German hopes of improving security along the Rhine, and obliged Charles to restore the outlawed Bavarian and Cologne electors to their lands and titles. The setbacks were initially offset by the gains in the Netherlands and Italy, followed by successful intervention in the Venetian–Ottoman war after 1716. Imperial forces won spectacular victories over the Ottomans, capturing Belgrade and bringing Serbia under Habsburg control by 1718. Meanwhile, Spanish attempts to recover the lost Italian possessions were rebuffed with Anglo-Dutch support.

By 1720 Charles ruled lands that were 44 per cent larger than those held by Leopold (see Tables 8.2, 8.3 and 8.4). However, this only reinforced the trend since 1683 of shifting Habsburg interests southeastwards, and the emperor now held nearly twice as much land outside the Reich as within it. The new acquisitions greatly complicated Habsburg security, particularly the Italian possessions, which were difficult to defend without Anglo-Dutch naval support. By 1702 Leopold had been obliged to grant the duke of Savoy a royal crown in return for his assistance in blocking the Alpine passes to French troops. Savoy also received Sicily as its share of the Spanish succession in 1714, though Charles compelled it to accept the less prosperous island of Sardinia in exchange six years later. The result was an Italian equivalent of Prussia that proved equally difficult to contain.

Distracted by these external problems, Charles mishandled imperial politics, losing some of the ground recovered under his two predecessors. He lost sympathy by appearing to favour Catholics during the religious disputes in the Palatinate and Salzburg. He asserted his role as supreme judge by imposing settlements in the disputes between ruler and Estates in East Frisia and Mecklenburg, but only at the expense of growing Prussian influence in both territories.[14] Throughout, dynastic weakness curtailed Charles's freedom of action since he was convinced he needed German recognition for the Pragmatic Sanction to ensure his daughter could inherit his lands on his death. He made a series of contradictory promises of future concessions to win over key princes, before securing the Reichstag's agreement in 1732.[15]

This might have proved more than empty promises, had Charles not lost vital support and resources in two further wars after 1733. The first was the War of the Polish Succession, fought initially to place a Saxon rather than a French candidate as king of Poland. Most of the fighting took place on the Rhine and in Italy, where Sardinia sided with France and Spain to seize Austria's possessions. Like his two predecessors, Charles managed to convince the Reichstag to accept essentially Habsburg objectives as imperial ones. The Reich mobilised a large army, which halted French attacks on the Rhine. The armed princes provided additional auxiliaries to assist the Austrian army, which grew to an unprecedented 200,000 men. Ominously, Bavaria refused to cooperate, though its ambitious elector, Carl Albrecht, wisely refrained from openly declaring for France. Austrian forces were routed in Italy and the situation only stabilised when Russia sent 13,000 troops through Poland to the Rhine in 1735.[16]

Charles was forced to accept an unsatisfactory settlement, which was eventually ratified as the Peace of Vienna in 1738. Naples and Sicily were surrendered to Spain, while Sardinia received a small part of Milan. Austria was compensated by being allowed to annex Tuscany, whose ruling dukes conveniently died out. The Saxon candidate was accepted as king of Poland, but his French-backed rival, Stanislaus

Leszczynski, was given the duchy of Lorraine and its dependencies, which now left the Reich. On his death in 1766 these lands were formally annexed by France and were not retaken by Germany until 1871. The former duke of Lorraine, Francis Stephen, married Charles's daughter Maria Theresa in 1736 and so became the prospective Habsburg candidate to succeed him as emperor. All parties formally recognised the validity of the Pragmatic Sanction.

This complex settlement was typical of eighteenth-century diplomacy, which tried to resolve international conflict by readjusting the equilibrium between the leading European dynasties. It could not disguise the fact that the Habsburgs had suffered a major reverse; something that became considerably worse with the complications arising from Russia's military assistance. In return for its aid, Russia insisted Austria join it in a new assault on the Ottoman empire, which began in 1735. The Ottomans were expected to collapse as rapidly as in 1716–18. Charles had no desire for additional Balkan territory, but felt that Russia might displace Habsburg influence if it alone made new gains and so agreed to participate].[17] The war was a disaster. The Ottomans not only repelled all Russian and Austrian attacks, but recovered much of the land lost in the last war, including the strategic city of Belgrade. Having lost the war, Habsburg diplomats were outwitted by the French, who mediated a peace settlement entirely in the Ottomans' favour in 1739.

The accumulative effect of these two wars reduced Habsburg territory by over a fifth, and left the monarchy bankrupt. It proved impossible to pay the army, even though it was drastically reduced by 1740, while most of the senior generals were imprisoned on charges of corruption and mismanagement. The Habsburgs were unable to pay for the auxiliaries supplied by German princes since 1733, let alone deliver the political concessions Charles had so rashly promised. Charles's death on 20 October 1740 made an already vulnerable position extremely precarious.

8.2   The Rise of Prussia

Explanations of Prussian growth

Prussia was the beneficiary of Austria's woes. Nine days after Charles's death, Frederick II, himself only king since May, ordered his generals to prepare an invasion of Silesia. This began on 16 December and met only token resistance. An Austrian counter-attack was routed at Mollwitz in April 1741 and Maria Theresa was compelled to acknowledge Prussian possession of Silesia and the neighbouring county of Glatz the following year. This First Silesian War was the start of open Austro-Prussian rivalry that made the Hohenzollern monarchy a European great power.

Explanations for Prussia's emergence diverge in two general directions. One perspective stresses the primacy of foreign policy, arguing that Prussia's exposed position and scattered territory forced it to develop its 'great power' potential, or go under. This approach often reads as a tale of triumph over adversity, as Prussia overcame its material disadvantages as 'the sand box of the Reich', to defeat Sweden and Poland in the seventeenth century, and Austria, Russia and France in the next. In the more overtly nationalist Borussian variant, this was necessary to push German history forward towards unification by 1871. However, this perspective can also be read as an illegitimate expansionist drive to dominate and exploit neighbouring countries. The alternative view emphasises the primacy of domestic policy, in a tale of collaboration between crown and nobles at the expense of Prussian serfs and burghers. Their 'historic compromise' is often seen as laying the foundation of later problems, notably the militarisation of state and society, pushing German development down its supposed authoritarian 'special path' (see Chapter 1).

Cutting across these two perspectives are four other factors that are given various degrees of emphasis. The first is the Hohenzollern dynasty itself, which avoided the succession crises of other European monarchies by producing an unbroken line of healthy, adult male rulers. Those governing between 1640 and 1786 were unquestionably men of exceptional ability, though most historians have, rather unfairly, excepted Frederick III/I from such praise. Even if the calibre of monarchs declined somewhat with Frederick II's death in 1786, there were numerous reforming ministers and able generals to step into the vacuum. These figures have been seen by Borussophile historians as making history, rather than merely responding to events, and they generally feature prominently in explanations that stress the primacy of foreign policy. It often seems appropriate to take this 'top–down' approach to the history of a state that is widely considered a pre-eminent example of absolute monarchy.

Secondly, Prussia's military and administrative development features in both perspectives as providing the means, either to defeat external enemies, or to sustain the internal compromise between crown and nobility. What Hanna Schissler terms the 'military–agrarian complex' is a third factor widely recognised as both a prerequisite and a consequence of Prussia's expansion.[18] By tailoring its recruitment to suit the needs of the manorial economy, Prussia reconciled the demands of a large army with the socio-economic interests of the landed elite. Finally, the dynasty is regarded as having provided a limited focal point for a common identity, linking the scattered lands and peoples. There is far more to this cultural dimension than stock references to Prussian blind obedience and subservience. However, most see it as a process of acculturation whereby the monarchy imposed its values on the population, which either accepted assimilation, or resisted, like the Silesian and Polish Catholics.

The recent research reviewed in the earlier chapters of this book has extended our view of Prussian administration, economy and military–civil relations, but contributed comparatively little to explaining Prussia's emergence as a great power. When shorn of earlier nationalist or ideological excesses, the earlier perspectives remain as a series of useful points, but it is doubtful whether they amount to a full explanation.

Why Prussia?

Prussia's growth is best explained by addressing the question of why it, rather than any other German territory, emerged as a second great power alongside the Habsburg monarchy. The general literature rightly stresses Prussia's vulnerability during the seventeenth century, noting the numerous dangers looming, on the Great Elector's accession in 1640.[19] However, Prussia's growth during this period already set it apart from the other German lands and provided a basis for its future greatness.

Acquisition of Ducal Prussia in 1618 had given the Hohenzollerns twice as much land as any of their rivals; a lead that increased by a further 100 per cent once the territorial redistribution agreed at Westphalia had been completed by 1680 (see Tables 8.1, 8.5, 8.6 and 8.7). However, it was Ducal Prussia that made the Hohenzollerns truly exceptional as the only dynasty other than the Habsburgs to hold significant territory outside imperial jurisdiction. This gave them a head start over other German rulers, who struggled to define their international position after 1648 when it was unclear whether they were simply the Reich's aristocracy, or the equal partners of European royalty. The

Table 8.5   Growth of the Hohenzollern monarchy

Date	In Reich	Outside	Total
1600	36,520	–	36,520
1618	42,816*	36,960	79,776
1648	70,469**	36,960	107,429
1680	75,914	36,960	112,874
1702	77,290	36,960	114,250
1707	77,702	37,730	115,432
1715	79,022	37,730	116,752
1720	83,422	37,730	121,152
1742	120,822	37,730	158,552
1744	124,122	37,730	161,852
1772	124,122	71,830	195,952
1795	131,822	177,925	309,747

* Including Cleves, Mark and Ravensberg, the possession of which was
  disputed until 1666.
** Including the western half of Kammin, which was not surrendered by
  Sweden until 1679.
All figures are in km^2.

Hohenzollerns pulled ahead by securing full sovereignty for Ducal
Prussia following their duplicitous involvement in the Northern War.
This provided the platform for their royal title in 1700, since it was
clear the Habsburgs would not tolerate another king within the Reich.
Recognised internationally in the Peace of Utrecht (1713), the new
title assisted the Hohenzollerns' internal consolidation by extending
their scope for ennoblement and patronage. Meanwhile, their Saxon
and Bavarian rivals exhausted themselves trying to catch up through
their costly involvement in European warfare after 1697.

Despite the geographical location of their new title, the Hohenzollerns remained a German dynasty, in contrast to those other families
associated with foreign crowns (see section 2.1). In each case, the original German land either became an adjunct of the new kingdom, or was
detached from it entirely. The same would have occurred if the Bavarian
and Palatine Wittelsbachs had achieved their royal ambitions, since
their German lands were also too small to be the major partner. In Prussia's case, the German dog firmly wagged the royal tail. The eastern
Prussian kingdom supported the Hohenzollerns' German powerbase,
and subsequent acquisitions were absorbed by a fully-developed central

Table 8.6 Overview of Hohenzollern gains

1609/66	Cleves, Mark, Ravensberg
1618	Ducal (eastern) Prussia
1648	Minden, Halberstadt, Hinterpommern, Kammin (1648/79), Klettenberg
1680	Magdeburg (1666/80), Mansfeld (1680/1780)
1702	Lingen, Mors
1707	Tecklenburg, Neuchâtel
1715	Obergeldern
1720	Vorpommern
1740/5	Silesia, Glatz
1772	Royal (western) Prussia (First Partition)
1792	Ansbach, Bayreuth
1793	Polish lands (Second Partition)
1795	Polish lands (Third Partition)

Table 8.7 Hohenzollern lands and peoples

Date	In Reich		Outside		Total	
	Land	Population	Land	Population	Land	Population
1648	70,469	620,000	36,960	250,000	107,429	870,000
1688	75,914	882,655	36,960	405,000	112,874	1,287,655
1713	77,702	1,430,988	37,730	300,000	115,432	1,730,988
1740	83,422	1,777,866	37,730	603,834	121,152	2,381,700
1756	124,122	3,350,000	37,730	650,000	161,852	4,000,000
1772	124,122	3,470,911	71,830	1,289,608	195,952	4,760,519
1795	131,822	4,550,182	177,925	3,660,000	309,747	8,210,182

NB: The table uses the population figures from 1776 in the 1772 column.

European power. Here, Hohenzollern development mirrors the basic pattern of the Habsburg monarchy in that it grew out of the Reich.

Prussia thus remained a *central* rather than an *eastern* European power until 1772 and its expansion came at the expense of other German dynasties. The gains at Westphalia were all lands within the Reich, pushing the proportion there to over half of all Hohenzollern possessions. The conquest of additional slices of Pomerania (1679, 1715), as well as the inheritance of further enclaves in Westphalia reduced the area outside imperial jurisdiction to a third of the total by 1720. Acquisition of Silesia and East Frisia cut it to a quarter. Moreover, the importance of the western and central lands was often greater than their relative size might suggest. The Westphalian enclaves were much smaller than Ducal Prussia, but had roughly the same population and produced as much tax.

Throughout, Brandenburg remained the main base. Hohenzollern rule here dated from 1415. That in Ducal Prussia only started in 1525 and was characterised by a history of mental illness, a perennial shortage of money, continued Polish overlordship and powerful Estates prior to its inheritance by the main branch. The key political and military institutions developed in Brandenburg and the Berlin–Potsdam axis remained the cultural and economic centre. Ducal Prussia was used as a bolt hole in times of invasion. The royal coronation of 1701 took place there simply because of the Prussian basis of the new title, and Berlin, not Königsberg, remained the political centre.

Expansion within the Reich extended Hohenzollern resources and influence. The Reich offered a limited protective framework against Sweden and Poland in the seventeenth century. More importantly, Prussia could use its rights in imperial institutions to draw on the resources of the unarmed territories in the name of collective defence (see section 5.1). Though this became harder after 1714, it was difficult for the lesser territories to ignore Prussian requests for recruits. Hohenzollern expansion forced the other electors into second rank. None of the

Table 8.8 The Hohenzollern monarchy as a proportion of total 'German' power

Aspect	1648		1714		1748		1792	
Territory (km²)								
Hohenzollerns	107,429	(13.2)	115,432	(10.2)	161,852	(15.0)	203,652	(16.9)
Total	814,298		1,129,576		1,078,735		1,206,600	
Population (millions)								
Hohenzollerns	0.87	(4.3)	1.73	(7.1)	3.48	(11.0)	5.67	(12.9)
Total	20.15		24.5		31.77		43.84	
Army								
Hohenzollerns	700	(1.4)	46,100	(15.2)	135,000	(27.7)	195,000	(24.4)
Total	48,750		303,400		488,000		798,700	

NB: The 1792 figure for military strength is distorted by the Habsburg mobilisation for the Turkish War. If their establishment for 1787 is used (221,600), Prussia maintained 37.3% of a total 'German' establishment of 522,600 in the late 1780s.

other four secular electorates acquired additional land after 1715. Whereas their combined possessions still exceeded those of the Hohenzollerns in that year, they fell to the equivalent of a third of Prussia by the 1790s (see Tables 8.8 and 8.9). While Prussia could not dictate imperial politics, it had sufficient influence to frustrate any measure it disliked. Inheritance of Ansbach and Bayreuth in 1792 gave Prussia a presence in Franconia, as well as the three northern Kreise. Far more importantly, the conversion of the Saxon elector to Catholicism in 1697 allowed the Hohenzollerns to assume informal leadership of the German Protestants in the *corpus evangelicorum* (see section 4.4).

Geography also favoured the Hohenzollerns. Though their northeastern location placed them close to Sweden and Poland, these were destined to decline, whereas dynasties to the west faced a growing threat from France. Brandenburg had a vacuum into which it could expand, not only outwards into Poland, but also within the Reich. It benefited

Table 8.9   Strength of the other secular electors

	Territory	*Population*	*Revenue*	*Army*
Bavaria 1700	42,900	1.3	1.7	20,000
Palatinate 1700	18,418	0.945	1.3	23,100
Pfalz-Bayern (1792)	59,558	2.2	7.0	15,750
Saxony 1700	35,970	2.0	3.3	20,000
1792	35,970	1.8	7.5	22,874
Hanover 1715	25,535	0.7	1.66	17,380
1792	26,460	0.857	4.0	17,836
Totals 1715	122,823	4,945	7.96	80,480
1792	121,988	4,857	18.5	56,460

Notes:
Territory in km^2, population in millions, revenue in millions of florins.
Hanover maintained around 11,000 troops in 1700.

Overview of gains and losses:
Hanover (gains): Wildenhausen (1700), Celle, Hoya, Sachsen-Lauenburg (all 1705), Bremen, Verden (both 1714), Bentheim (1752).
Bavaria (gains): Hohenwaldeck, Sulzburg, Prybaum (all 1734/40); (losses): Innviertel (to Austria 1779).
Palatinate: united with Bavaria after 1777.

from the extinction of neighbouring dynasties, notably in Pomerania, East Frisia and Westphalia, beating both Saxony and Hanover to these lands. With the exception of Hanover, its main rivals were located closer to the Habsburg heartlands of the south and west. They enjoyed considerable autonomy, but limited opportunities for expansion in their immediate vicinity. The Habsburgs regarded Bavaria as a greater danger, and were more willing to promote more distant lands like Brandenburg or Hanover as potential allies.

Prussia's expansion thus progressed through three stages. The Hohenzollerns secured a powerful central European base during the seventeenth century. This was consolidated by further acquisitions between 1702 and 1744, whilst the dynasty developed its sovereign status in Prussia itself with the acquisition of the royal title and its international recognition. Prussia's victories over Austria in 1740–5 signalled its arrival as a German great power, but it only joined the European premier league with the seizure of large parts of Poland after 1772.

Austro-Prussian rivalry

The 1740s proved a turning point in German political history. Open Austro-Prussian conflict coincided with the end of the imperial recovery and the disastrous reign of Charles VII, the only early modern emperor who was not a Habsburg. This inner-German conflict was prolonged by the wider War of the Austrian Succession and inflicted lasting damage on the Reich.[20]

By acting swiftly in 1740, Frederick II secured a decisive advantage over both Bavaria and Saxony, which also claimed shares of Maria Theresa's inheritance. Frederick revived some old Hohenzollern rights to Silesia to give his invasion a veil of legitimacy, but his actions were driven by ruthless calculation. Silesia was not only a large and partially industrialised province, but its seizure was essential to stop Saxony eclipsing Prussia. The Saxon electors had been kings of Poland since 1697, but were prevented by that country's aristocratic constitution from asserting full authority over their new kingdom. Acquisition of Silesia would link the two countries and could well tip the balance of Polish politics in the elector's favour. By seizing Silesia, Frederick forestalled Saxon ambitions, and though the elector joined the war against Austria, he was unable to make any gains, because Bavaria claimed Bohemia for itself. Saxony changed sides in 1742, but was punished by a Prussian invasion during the Second Silesian War (1744–5). Frederick launched this from fear that Austria's improved position elsewhere would encourage Maria Theresa's hopes of recovering Silesia. His initial attack on Bohemia in 1744 ended in ignominious retreat, but a series of spectacular victories the following year compelled both Saxony and Austria to make peace and accept Prussia's hold on Silesia.

Meanwhile, Bavaria had been conclusively defeated. Carl Albrecht received French backing for his bid to annex Austria and Bohemia. Spain joined in, hoping to take Milan, while the Netherlands would go to France, leaving Maria Theresa with only Hungary. The War of the Spanish Succession had seriously weakened Bavaria, and even with substantial French assistance it was not ready until 1741, long after Frederick had made his move. As Franco-Bavarian forces seized Upper Austria and Bohemia, including Prague, the Habsburg monarchy appeared on the point of total collapse. Carl Albrecht was elected emperor in 1742, defeating his rival, Francis Stephen.

The brief Wittelsbach rule did lasting damage to imperial institutions. The new emperor was initially popular, particularly among the lesser rulers and those left disillusioned by the failures of Charles VI's last years. However, few were prepared to back him in his personal feud with Austria, which the Reichstag refused to regard as an imperial war. Imperial prestige was tarnished by the emperor's obvious dependence on French and Prussian support. Attempts to win backing from medium-sized territories like Hessen-Kassel and the Palatinate only cost him further sympathy as it became clear these had demanded far-reaching concessions. Charles's forces were driven back into Bavaria during 1742 and he was forced to flee to Frankfurt. Prussia's resumption of war in 1744 provided temporary respite, but the Austrians returned at the start of 1745. Charles VII died a broken man in January 1745, and his successor was forced to change sides three moths later.[21]

Austria's victory paved the way for Maria Theresa's husband's election as Francis I later in 1745. Though the Habsburgs had recovered the imperial title, it no longer held its previous allure. The dynasty regarded the Germans' failure to support them in their hour of need as a betrayal. This persisted as the lesser territories used the Kreis structure to maintain armed neutrality for the remainder of the war. Peace in 1748 obliged Austria to recognise Prussia's possession of Silesia and to make further concessions in Italy. Overall, the monarchy lost another $43,000 \text{ km}^2$, but none the less survived with its main possessions intact. This feat alone diminished the Reich's significance in Habsburg dynastic planning. It still remained important, but the monarchy's own interests had been thrown more sharply into focus. Germans also now regarded the monarchy more clearly as a separate entity distinct from the Reich.

Prussia emerged as Austria's primary enemy, completely eclipsing Bavaria within the Reich. France acknowledged this by making Frederick II its main German partner after 1745. This situation changed dramatically with the 'diplomatic revolution' of 1756, reversing the 'old system' of European alliances established in 1689.[22] Maria Theresa was determined to neutralise Prussia and restore Habsburg prestige by recovering Silesia and so accepted Kaunitz's advice to ally with France. Skilful diplomacy widened this to include Sweden and Russia by 1757. Meanwhile, Britain feared that it could never defeat France in any colonial contest so long as the French could seize Hanover as a bargaining chip. Fighting had already started in North America in 1754, prompting Britain to sign the defensive Convention of Westminster with Prussia, which promised to protect Hanover. The earlier combinations could not be sustained. Traditional Anglo-Austrian cooperation collapsed, while France and Prussia drifted apart.

Fearing that something was afoot, Frederick II attacked Saxony in August 1756 to use it as a forward base in the coming war. This clear breach of the public peace played into Kaunitz's hands as he sought to mobilise the Reich against Prussia. It helped that both guarantors of the IPO, France and Sweden, were now Austria's allies, enabling Kaunitz to present the war as a police action to restore order in the Reich. In fact, he planned nothing less than the dismemberment of the Hohenzollern monarchy and the complete destruction of its military capability. The participation of Protestant Sweden did little to improve Austria's military position, but did blunt Frederick's propaganda that this was a religious war. None the less, it proved impossible to convince the Reichstag of the complete validity of Kaunitz's interpretation of the conflict. The war was a disaster for the medium and lesser territories, as the new Franco-Austrian combination narrowed their room for manoeuvre. They could no longer play these two great powers against each other to extract concessions, or preserve their neutrality. Geo-politics restricted their choice still further, since Prussia and Hanover dominated the north, while France and Austria could intervene in the south. The resulting Seven Years War thus became a German civil war as the larger northern principalities were sucked into the Anglo-Prussian camp, while the rest reluctantly supported the official imperial war effort.[23]

While France and Britain fought in India and North America, the European war split into two main theatres, both in the Reich. A British expeditionary force, backed by subsidised north German auxiliaries, defended Hanover against the French, while further east, Prussia fended off attacks from Austria, Russia and Sweden. The allies failed to coordinate their operations, enabling Frederick to shuttle his dwindling forces to confront each threat in turn. Having captured Saxony in 1756, Frederick invaded Bohemia the following year, but was defeated and driven out. The imperial army mobilised through the Kreise slowly assembled in Franconia. Reinforced by a large French contingent, it advanced to liberate Saxony, but was decisively defeated by Frederick at Rossbach on 5 November 1757. More than any other event, Rossbach has come to symbolise the apparent impotency of the post-1648 Reich, whilst making Frederick a national hero for having defeated the French. In fact, only a small portion of the imperial army was present at the battle. The Kreis contingents were reassembled and continued to serve with some success in Saxony until 1762. The Russians occupied Ducal Prussia from 1757 and defeated Frederick at Kunnersdorf two years later. With his enemies closing in, Frederick contemplated suicide, but was again saved by his opponents' inability to coordinate their operations. Russia temporarily changed sides in 1762 and then withdrew from the war. Since its own armies had failed to retake Silesia, while France was also exhausted, Austria had no choice but to make peace at Hubertusburg in February 1763 on the basis of the pre-war territorial status quo.

Though not matching the scale of the Thirty Years War, the Seven Years War had a major impact. Large parts of northern Germany had been badly affected, leaving most territories heavily in debt. Lasting damage was done to imperial political culture, and in contrast to 1648, the Peace of Hubertusburg was settled by the great powers and made no provision for reforming the Reich's constitution. The southern territories were disillusioned by Austria's blatant manipulation of the constitution to legitimise its war of revenge and had already withdrawn their contingents from the imperial army before the end of 1762. There was a growing sense of impotence as Prussian and Austrian political and military growth dwarfed even the once-powerful secular electorates. Saxony had been devastated by Frederick, who ruthlessly exploited it to sustain his own war effort. The electors were sinking into the mass of smaller territories, as a 'third Germany' between the two great central

European powers. Combined with financial expediency, this induced most rulers to reduce their armies after 1763, further widening the gap.

None the less, it would be wrong to characterise the later eighteenth century as an era of Austro-Prussian dualism, because this implies that German politics were now exclusively dictated by the two great powers. Imperial institutions remained intact and capable of revival if the will was there. The third Germany still had collective weight, accounting for around half the Reich's surface area. Moreover, the war had damaged both German powers. Prussia lost over 410,000 people, or around a tenth of its population. Mere survival against such formidable odds demonstrated Prussian potential, but the experience left Frederick anxious for the future. He was greatly concerned about Russia, a country he had previously seriously underestimated, and he wanted to prevent another Austro-Russian combination. In addition to international alliances and his own army, he saw the Reich as a third line of defence. The imperial constitution could be manipulated to emasculate the Habsburgs and prevent them mobilising the still considerable resources of the third Germany.

Austria's position was also uncertain. Its new French alliance had proved insufficient to break Prussia. On the contrary, France now withdrew from active involvement in the Reich, distracted by its own mounting domestic problems. Russia, governed by Catherine II from 1762, increased its influence in Poland and the Balkans, treading on traditional Habsburg interests. With the accession of Joseph II as emperor in 1765, Austria moved to rebuild its position in the Reich, restore prestige and counter Prussian influence.

The other German rulers withdrew from European politics. The era of Saxon rule in Poland ended in 1763, while the Hanoverians were now clearly more British than German and no longer visited their electorate. While third-rank princes like those in Württemberg and Hessen-Kassel had not abandoned their ambitions, they also concentrated on maintaining their German position. Enthusiasm for the Reich grew as it appeared the only way of restraining Austria and Prussia.

Its importance was highlighted after 1767 as Joseph affected a temporary rapprochement with Frederick, leading to their joint collaboration with Russia in the First Partition of Poland, in 1772. German rulers were greatly alarmed that this might presage a similar carve-up of central Europe. However, neither Austria nor Prussia felt fully confident about its own position and feared alienating their German allies. Joseph was also personally overconfident, believing he could achieve

Habsburg objectives without further Prussian help. Recovery of Silesia remained an goal, but now took second place to finding alternative security against Prussia through redistributing land within the Reich. Joseph wanted to persuade the Wittelsbachs to exchange Bavaria for the Netherlands, and contemplated lesser swaps involving church land (see section 5.4).

The extinction of the Bavarian Wittelsbach line in 1777 offered an opportunity to realise these plans and Joseph pressured Carl Theodore of the Palatinate to accept the exchange, which would greatly improve Habsburg security. The roles of 1756 were now reversed, as Frederick posed as the defender of the imperial constitution. Having persuaded Saxony to support him, he invaded Bohemia in 1778, beginning the War of the Bavarian Succession. There was little actual fighting as both sides experienced considerable problems feeding their forces, giving rise to the conflict's other name – the 'Potato War'. None the less, it was sufficient to force Joseph to back down and accept the Peace of Teschen, brokered by Russia in 1779. Austria retained a small slice of Bavaria, known as the Innviertel, to save face, but otherwise permitted Carl Theodore to inherit the electorate.

The Peace of Teschen effectively made Russia a guarantor of the imperial constitution. Russian influence was consolidated through permanent diplomatic presence at key courts and a growing web of dynastic alliances with major princely families. It initially favoured Austria, because Joseph had reached a new understanding with Catherine by 1781, raising fears that he might still be able to implement his exchange plans. Frederick countered by hi-jacking the reform movement amongst the middling princes and using their *Fürstenbund* as a front to block Habsburg designs after 1785 (see section 5.4). The *Fürstenbund* collapsed in 1790 as the weaker princes refused to follow Prussia any further. Prussian involvement frustrated its reform programme, but the movement none the less demonstrated the genuine support for the imperial constitution. Joseph's reform of the *Reichskammergericht* after 1767 also indicated what could be achieved when the emperor was willing to work with existing institutions. The imperial title remained important to Habsburg prestige, despite the growth of the monarchy's own empire. Prussia paid more than lip service to constitutional convention, since it still refrained from violent or open interference in the affairs of its smaller neighbours. Politics remained within the boundaries set by the Reich's legalistic culture, which survived despite the use of violence in mid-century. While Austro-Prussian rivalry had strained the Reich, it alone did not bring about its eventual collapse. As the next two sections will show, this only came about as renewed tension between the two German powers coincided with a new danger in the form of external war, rather than popular revolution.

8.3   Germany and the French Revolution

Germany in 1789

Germany in 1789 was a land of great social inequality. The nobility only numbered 1 per cent of the total population, yet owned at least a third of the land. Between a quarter and a half of all Germans lived on the social and economic margins, making just enough to survive in a good year. Crop failure or an economic downturn could spell disaster for many families, who might be forced to join the thousands who already lived rough on the roads. There were disturbing indications that things were getting worse for many people. The rising population was showing signs of outstripping the growth in employment opportunities, while the slowly accelerating processes of industrialisation and urbanisation were dislocating traditional social and economic structures. Many people were neither materially nor emotionally equipped to cope with these changes and were fearful of the future and resentful of those who appeared to be succeeding at their expense.

It would be natural to conclude from this brief survey that Germany was on the brink of revolution. There were some signs that popular protest was growing inexorably towards mass revolutionary action. Serfs reacted angrily to their landlords' demands for more work, by staging strikes or even armed risings. Silesia and other Prussian provinces were badly affected in the mid-eighteenth century, but the situation was even more extreme in the Habsburg lands, where the Bohemian serfs revolted in 1775, to be followed by those in Hungary and Transylvania. Discontent seemed to be growing even in areas without serfdom. The Austrian Netherlands rebelled against the Habsburg monarchy after 1787, followed by the bishopric of Liège two years later.

Yet, all of these disturbances occurred outside the core German and Austrian parts of the Reich. When the French stormed the Bastille in July 1789, Germans remained quiet. They continued to remain quiet while their neighbours across the Rhine swept away the power of their king, nobles and church and proclaimed a new society based on liberty, equality and fraternity. Other than the rising of the Saxon peasants in 1790, there were no large-scale protests within the Reich.

Why there was no German Revolution

This lack of a genuine popular revolution has long puzzled historians, who have advanced a number of explanations, not all of them entirely convincing. Some have argued that German rulers were too well armed to be challenged. Even small counties possessed their own regular armies, officered by noblemen, whom many historians identify as the princes' natural allies against the people. However, a comparison with France indicates that this argument does not work. The French king, Louis XVI (ruled 1774–93), had the largest army in western Europe, yet this failed to save him from revolution and many of those who stormed the Bastille were in fact soldiers from his royal guards.

Others believe that the answer lies in a different comparison between the two countries, arguing that Germany lacked the social and economic conditions thought responsible for the revolution in France. Changes have been identified in the French economy that suggest it was moving away from reliance on traditional agriculture and towards new ways of making money, from commerce and heavy industry. These changes are said to have benefited the French bourgeoisie, who became richer, while the aristocracy grew poorer because they depended on land for their wealth. In this interpretation, the revolution occurred when the bourgeoisie challenged the continued political dominance of the nobility with the help of the French peasants. This did not happen across the Rhine, because the slower pace of economic development left the German bourgeoisie enfeebled and unable to contest the continued power of the nobles and princes. Though persuasive, this argument lacks evidence to support it. New research reveals that the picture in France was considerably more complicated than once thought, and many now doubt that the French bourgeoisie can be credited with having 'made' the Revolution, which was the result of the monarchy's own weakness, as much as of any other factor. In fact, more Germans could be labelled 'bourgeois' than could French people, but like their French counterparts, they rarely conformed to the model of the thrusting, impatient entrepreneur. Most were the privileged inhabitants of the numerous small German towns, and many were employed by princes, as lawyers and officials in their administrations.

More convincing arguments can be found when conditions in the French countryside are compared with those in Germany. On the surface, the situation appears even worse in Germany than in France. French peasants, at least, directly owned around 35% of the farmland, whereas their German counterparts had as little as 4% of the total in some regions, with the rest owned by the princes, nobles and church.[24] However, German landlords leased their land to peasants on relatively favourable conditions. In return for paying rent, German peasants were free to sell their crops and to pass their farms to their children. Thus, even though they did not own it outright, they still had direct access to about 90% of the land west of the Elbe. Conditions east of that river were different, but not necessarily intolerable and even here serfs still had access to 80% of the land and were protected by their monarchs (see section 3.3). In contrast, French peasants were often more at their lord's mercy. The French nobility, clergy and bourgeoisie collectively owned 65% of the country, which they leased on highly unfavourable conditions to the peasants, who were almost permanently in debt to them. Moreover, the lords owned the best land, restricting peasant ownership to the least fertile areas. Hatred of these unfair conditions lay behind the violence in the French countryside in 1789 as peasants stormed their lords' chateaux and burnt their rent contracts.

While this helps explain why the French were more prepared to risk their lives to improve their conditions, it does not tell us why Germans did not embrace the new ideals of liberty, equality and fraternity after 1789. French ideas reached Germany in three ways. About a third of the 160,000 émigrés who fled France after 1792 arrived in the Reich. Many of these were rich aristocrats, but they also included some peasants from border areas like Alsace. German rulers were nervous of diplomatic repercussions and only Trier and Hohenlohe gave them a cautious welcome. Five thousand émigrés collected in Koblenz joining a local population of only 8,000. Their arrogance and excess soon disillusioned their reluctant hosts and contributed to a swell of anti-aristocratic sentiment in the Rhineland.[25]

Other news from France travelled more indirectly through rumours, the press and travellers' reports. German rulers had removed censorship from ecclesiastical supervision and centralised it under secular control during the later eighteenth century, but simultaneously permitted greater freedom of discussion. There was some feeling that these freedoms were being abused before 1789, leading to new restrictions intended to shift responsibility from printers to authors. Leopold II ordered all territories to stiffen their laws in 1791 to counteract French propaganda, but the response was mixed. Prussia tightened censorship, but mainly after 1808, while Bavaria dismantled most of its system in 1803.[26] Territorial fragmentation always made it hard to restrict the circulation of information within the Reich, and French ideas filtered across the Rhine despite tougher laws. The rhetoric of liberty, fraternity and equality clearly influenced German debate, reinforcing the existing trend towards discussing politics in abstract terms.

Popular protests adopted some French slogans and symbols, such as liberty caps and trees, but it is difficult to establish a direct connection between ideology and action. Some areas experienced new protests. Riots broke out in Stuttgart in May 1794 after the authorities tried to punish guildsmen for illegal assembly. The army moved in, shutting down guild lodges and forcing local newspapers to print an official version of events, blaming the disturbances on isolated agitators. However, most imperial cities remained quiet. The presence of Austrian troops in south-west Germany after war started in 1792 may have intimidated some action, but there is little to suggest that the protests were not a continuation of existing disputes, expressed in new language. There was little support for full, abstract equality, which would have necessitated the abolition of deeply-rooted corporate privileges. Popular action remained the defence of the common good, in which the authorities were expected to play their part. The unrest sweeping the duchy of Berg in 1795–8 provides a good example. The inhabitants complained about government corruption and the failure to punish wayward officials and soldiers. Much of this reflected long-standing resentment at the dominance of a few local families, but it was intensified by the current crisis of war and a dysentery epidemic. In short, the authorities were attacked for failing to fulfil their side of the bargain and protect the population in a time of need. The over-hasty evacuation of Düsseldorf was widely resented and villagers refused to accommodate the retreating Bavarians, accusing them of abandoning them to the French invaders in 1795. By the following year, the region stopped paying taxes on the grounds that the government could not defend it.[27]

This case also illustrates the third form of French influence, arriving on the point of the bayonet. As the French crossed the Rhine, they hoped to establish friendly regimes with German sympathisers. A republic was set up in the city of Mainz in 1792, but found little popular support. The French briefly considered repeating the experiment in Franconia in 1795, but then gave up and relied on deals struck with German princes.

By this point, revolutionary ideals had been discredited by the Terror in France and the behaviour of French armies in Germany. The Revolutionary government had inherited the monarchy's catastrophic finances and saw war as a way out of its domestic crisis. Confiscation of ecclesiastical and aristocratic land was driven as much by practical necessity as by ideology, and was continued outside France as the revolutionary armies advanced. French war-making echoed that of Wallenstein in that it was parasitic, using ruthless requisitioning both to sustain its forces and to deny resources to its enemies. The emphasis shifted with the end of the radical Jacobin regime and its replacement by the more conservative Directory in 1795. Alliance with the common people was abandoned in favour of more practical agreements with established governments, leading ultimately to Napoleon's system of satellite and allied states.[28]

It is not surprising that, after some initial enthusiasm, most Germans rejected the French ideals. However, this does not explain why they did not come up with some of their own. The later eighteenth century saw the spread of new ways of thinking associated with rational, Enlightened philosophy, with its radical notions of utility (see section 7.1). Such ideas circulated throughout Europe, but were expressed in very different ways by diverse groups of people. Enlightened thought in France tended to be favoured by those outside the inner circle of political power around the king. Though some French ministers did believe in the need for radical reform, the monarchy was reluctant to put itself at the head of a movement for change. Its critics increasingly saw it as a barrier to necessary, rational development. Moreover, the country's centralised character focused discontent against Louis XVI, implying that all monarchs must be equally wrong.

By contrast, Enlightened ideas in Germany tended to be expressed by princes and their immediate servants. Individual princes might be criticised as tyrants, but their neighbours were often praised as model rulers. The Reich's decentralised character made revolutionary action more difficult, since there was no obvious centre of power to capture. Rather than an obstacle, the state was seen as the motor for progressive reform to improve social and economic well-being. Government remained authoritarian, but it retained its legitimacy by being able to address genuine grievances through limited, local reforms, such as abolishing the use of torture by law courts, curbing the powers of landlords to demand unpaid labour service, or introducing elementary schooling. Unlike France, where many aristocrats remained suspicious of their king, German nobles served relatively willingly in princely armies and administrations and often subscribed to the same reform principles as their ruler.

Thus, far from viewing protest as a direct threat to their continued rule, German monarchs saw it as an unwelcome disruption of their own progressive reform programmes. They interpreted the events in France after 1789 as a vindication of their own style of government. They believed Louis XVI had been overthrown because he had failed to modernise the French monarchy, thus leaving no alternative but revolution. Reform had made this unnecessary in their own lands. Events in France only became dangerous with the start of the Revolutionary Wars, which threatened to disrupt the German reform programmes and divert scarce resources into unproductive warfare.

These arguments explain why the German elite remained hostile to revolution; but the lack of popular radicalism requires further discussion. Government remained guided by the Reich's fundamental laws safeguarding corporate rights and privileges. It was very difficult to tamper with these rights, because of the numerous opportunities to invoke legal and administrative protection (see section 7.2). Though the French were denied such opportunities by their legal system, it would be wrong to conclude that the results were necessarily beneficial to Germans in the long run. The ability to seek legal redress through the courts or by government reform disinclined Germans to fight for political rights. The state became associated with the rule of law, which seemed to offer sufficient protection for life and property, making parliamentary representation less necessary.

German radicals only found wider support after 1806 when the surviving monarchs lined up with Napoleon to promote further reforms in the interests of practical efficiency. This Reform Era had diverse roots, including enlightened absolutism, as well as French influence, and reaction, in Prussia's case, to military defeat. The content and impact of the new measures varied greatly, but everywhere they accelerated the erosion of corporate society by removing local and social privileges. People were treated as individuals, cast off from the protective framework of guilds, communities, manorial estates and other corporations at a time of renewed warfare and rapid socio-economic change.

Radicals hoped the widespread anxiety would make people more receptive to their message, especially as this was now presented in the language of national liberation from the French yoke, rather than popular emancipation. Nationalist fervour found expression in the volunteer rifle battalions of 1813 and in student agitation, but discontent increasingly focused on the restored governments that reappeared after Napoleon's defeat, particularly in Nassau and Hessen-Darmstadt. The new German Confederation coordinated a crackdown in 1819, submerging protest until 1830–4 and 1848–9.[29] These later outbreaks were more obviously inspired by French examples, but still mixed the defence of fading corporate rights with more radical hopes for a better future. German governments rode out these storms after 1789 by broadening earlier reform programmes. Absolutism, in the form of direct personal rule, was dismantled, completing the transition to the impersonal state, without losing its essentially monarchical character. The old Reich disappeared in the process, rather more swiftly than the corporate society it had sustained.

8.4   The End of the Old Reich

The Austro-Prussian rapprochement, 1790–5

The German response to the new French challenge was conditioned by existing power politics, not ideology. The events in Paris coincided with renewed Austro-Prussian tension, another Balkan war, and Poland's final collapse. These eastern European pressures produced what has been called the 'second diplomatic revolution' as Austria joined Prussia in the Convention of Reichenbach on 27 July 1790.[30] This has been portrayed as Europe's crowned heads sinking their differences in the face of a common revolutionary threat. In reality, Austria and Prussia wished to avoid fighting each other so that they could settle their respective Balkan and Polish problems.

After the loss of Silesia, Austria aimed constantly to isolate Prussia. Kaunitz achieved this first by the French alliance in 1756 and then by a secret agreement with Russia in 1781 to balance that country's earlier treaty with Prussia. The Habsburgs only accepted the First Partition of Poland, in 1772, in the hope this would absorb Russian and Prussian expansionist ambitions. They had no desire for further Balkan land and hoped that the Ottomans would survive to contain Russia to the east. The French Revolution upset this delicate balance, since France was no longer able to offer Austria any assistance. As in 1737, the new agreement with Russia dragged Austria into another Turkish War after 1787 for fear of losing its remaining ally. Joseph merely wanted to restrict

Russia's potential gains, but was pushed towards more offensive action by Prussia's attitude. Prussia had become increasingly aggressive since Frederick William II's accession in 1786 and proposed that Austria return the land it took from Poland in 1772 so that Prussia could take Danzig and Thorn. Austria was expected to capture its own compensation from the Ottomans. Joseph II's death on 20 February 1790 gave his successor an opportunity to extract Austria from its new war, which had gone badly from the start. He reversed course, compromising with Prussia by 1790, and confirming a policy of peace without annexations.

Prussia came out of this decidedly better than Austria. First, the emperor recognised Prussia's claims to Ansbach and Bayreuth, permitting it to inherit these lands in 1792, and giving it a presence in the traditional Habsburg preserve of southern Germany. Austria also stood by as Prussia and Russia partitioned Poland a second time, in 1793, partly to mollify Russia for having abandoned it in the Turkish War. Though Austria participated in the third and final Partition, in 1795, this was essentially unwelcome since it removed Poland as a buffer between the three powers. Meanwhile, Habsburg hopes of implementing the exchange plan were dealt a final blow when France invaded the Austrian Netherlands, initiating the Revolutionary Wars in April 1792. Prussian concern to be allowed to digest its new gains prompted it to cooperate in an Austrian counter-attack in the summer of 1792. Though the advance was accompanied by declarations against the revolution, its principal objective was to recover Alsace and Lorraine as compensation for Austria. It failed as the Prussian army turned back after meeting unexpectedly strong French resistance at Valmy in September.

The subsequent French offensive brought the war into the Reich. Many minor German rulers owned land west of the Rhine that fell under French jurisdiction during the later seventeenth century. They protested when the revolutionaries abolished feudal rights and expropriated property, but hoped these difficulties could be resolved peacefully. The western Kreise mobilised to defend the Rhine in 1792, but there was no intention to attack France, or crush its revolution. However, Prussia backed Austria's demands for offensive operations in the hope that these would recover enough land to satisfy the Habsburgs. The Reichstag was persuaded to declare war in 1793, but operations went badly, not least because Prussia was distracted by a Polish insurrection after 1794 and withdrew most of its troops.

The minor territories mobilised unprecedented numbers of troops and armed their peasants to defend the Black Forest against the invaders.

However, many became disillusioned with Austria's lacklustre military performance and the increasingly high-handed attitude of Habsburg generals, who treated some areas like occupied land. Attempts to
reform collective security were blocked by Austria and Prussia, who
saw the existing arrangements as a convenient way to draw on German
resources to sustain their own operations.[31]

The Beginning of the End, 1795–1803

Austro-Prussian collaboration collapsed in April 1795 as the Hohenzollern monarchy left the war by way of the separate Peace of Basel with
France. It had proved impossible to fight on two fronts, and Prussia
pulled out to avoid possible internal collapse. Its withdrawal effectively
partitioned the Reich, because the remaining northern territories were
in no position to defend their sector alone, and, led by Hessen-Kassel,
opted out as well, creating a Prussian-policed neutrality zone that
lasted until 1806. As there was no chance of victory, the southern territories faced a tough choice. Joining the north was the least attractive
option, since geography placed them closer to potential Austrian repri-
sals, while they also had no desire to fall under Prussian domination. The
possibility of reorganising the rump Reich along federal lines was hotly
debated, but stood little chance. This left separate deals with France as
the only realistic choice. Now under the Directory, France seemed a
more reliable partner, as it could offer protection and held out the prospect of future territorial redistribution in favour of the middling
princes. Starting in August 1796, Baden, Württemberg, Bavaria and
other armed territories made their own agreements with France and
left the war.

Not surprisingly, Austria and the remaining minor territories were
defeated and the emperor accepted the Peace of Campo Formio in
1797. The Habsburgs secretly recognised French possession of the Rhineland, in return for the promise of Salzburg and Venice as compensation. The clause concerning Salzburg represented the first step to full
secularisation of the imperial church, but was not yet enacted, because
France was distracted by Napoleon's invasion of Egypt the following
year, bringing temporary respite to central Europe. Pressure from Britain and Russia pushed the emperor into renewing the war in 1799, but
without northern German backing there was no hope of success and the
imperial armies were again defeated.

The French victory at Marengo in 1800 brought imperial Italy under their control and opened the way for an assault on the Habsburg hereditary lands from both the south and west. Francis II, emperor since 1792, made peace at Lunéville in March 1801, agreeing a more radical version of the 1797 settlement. Austria now publicly accepted French possession of the Rhineland, effectively ceding Burgundy and most of the Electoral and Upper Rhenish Kreise. In return, both France and Austria stated that German rulers who had lost land were to be compensated within the Reich at the expense of the imperial church and cities, while the Habsburgs could take Salzburg and eastern Bavaria. The emperor had abandoned his traditional clients to save his hereditary lands.

The pope accepted secularisation in July, hoping to restrict its scope. The task of organising the redistribution was entrusted to a special deputation of the Reichstag. This faced an impossible task. The constitutional dam holding back princely ambition had been broken and the more aggressively minded were determined to secure their share of the spoils. France was free to concentrate on Germany, having made peace with Britain in 1802, while Russia insisted on being involved through its rights as guarantor of the Peace of Teschen. Princes used their dynastic connections to Russia and bilateral agreements with France to back their claims. Once assured of foreign support, they seized neighbouring territories in advance of the imperial deputation's final decision (*Reichsdeputationshauptbeschluß*) of 27 April 1803. The entire imperial church and most cities disappeared.[32] A row of new principalities were created from enlarged counties, but the real beneficiaries were medium territories like Württemberg, Baden, Bavaria and Hessen-Darmstadt. Prussia, which was not supposed to be compensated at all, seized large parts of Westphalia and went on to occupy Hanover.

The final phase

The deputation's decision essentially recognised a *fait accompli*. It reorganised German territory, but did nothing to bolster common institutions. These were not yet entirely meaningless: the Habsburgs considered plans to revive the Reichstag, while the Swabian Kreis continued to function. However, removal of the imperial church and most cities profoundly changed the Reich's character. Protestants now held a majority in the Reichstag, which was dominated by Austria, Prussia, and a few, enlarged principalities. The imperial knights were spared during the reorganisation, but now found there was no one willing to protect them. Württemberg and others that had long regarded the knights' enclaves as an irritating obstacle to their jurisdiction, now seized their possessions, dragging away in chains those who resisted.

Few now trusted either Austria or Prussia, whereas France, under the stable rule of a new Napoleonic empire after 1804, appeared a more acceptable partner. A number of the enlarged principalities helped Napoleon in his attack on Austria in 1805, which pre-empted any reversal of the new arrangements. These allies left the Reich and joined a new French-sponsored Confederation of the Rhine in July 1806, enabling Napoleon to claim the Reich no longer existed. Francis acknowledged this with his abdication on 6 August 1806, having already adopted the hereditary Austrian imperial title two years earlier. Prussia failed to intervene and was now isolated. It joined the European coalition against France, but was defeated by Napoleon and his new German allies in 1806–7. The brief era of French domination in Germany had begun.

Conclusion

The events of 1801–6 swept away a political structure that had existed for a thousand years, radically transforming the map of central Europe. It was a revolution, but primarily a political, rather than a social or economic one. It was made from above, by princes, their advisors and foreign allies, but not simply imposed on an unwilling or hostile population. The mediatisation of over 100 territories and 1,500 feudal lordships represented something more than redrawing frontiers. Removal of the entire imperial hierarchy paved the way for a renegotiation of state–societal relations to broaden the base of the new sovereign states. These remained monarchies, except for four surviving free cities, but the personal and patrimonial aspects of absolutism had been seriously reduced, pushing politics firmly towards the impersonal state. Governments had more uniform authority over their inhabitants and clearer claims to their resources, legitimised by new ideals of patriotic duty and citizenship. This process had many victims, but not all were from the poorer sections of society. A host of lesser princes and lords lost their rights, while aristocratic privileges were curbed generally.

These changes were fundamental, but not entirely sudden. They represented the culmination of trends already present in earlier cameralist and enlightened reforms. The state expanded from mere wardship over society to radical interference in everyday life. Private and public spheres became more distinct as state institutions displaced the clergy, guilds, communes and other corporate groups from political management. Reciprocal feudal ties and patronage were replaced by more uniform relationships of individuals to the state. Officials became bureaucrats serving impersonal institutions. Gender relations also changed as the ideal of bourgeois domesticity redefined the household as the home, confining women to the private world of family and children.

343

This process was accompanied by unrest, but not popular revolution. Protests expressed longstanding discontent with the social and economic dislocation accompanying the accelerating population growth and commercialisation since the 1730s. It was fuelled by the imposition of new fiscal and military burdens from 1792 following thirty years of peace and largely stable taxation. Popular pressure forced governments to remain responsive to broader concerns during the political reorganisation after 1801. However, discontent only became fully politicised long after the Reich had collapsed. The new sovereign states rode out the storms of international war until 1815, but failed to find satisfactory solutions to the underlying social and economic problems. Growing frustration and anxiety made Germans more receptive to new philosophies of liberalism and nationalism, which assumed more definite shape, particularly with further revolutions elsewhere in Europe after 1820.

Broader social reforms were enacted after 1830, abolishing the remnants of lordly jurisdiction and serfdom by 1848 across central Europe. Unlike the 1790s, the pace of change was now clearly driven by popular action, particularly in the revolutionary years of 1848–9, which were accompanied by widespread disorder and bloodshed. This experience left a far deeper impression on German politics than the French Revolution of 1789, spreading fear of the masses amongst the propertied and privileged. The authorities now acted more consciously to shore up established elites, defusing and deflecting popular pressures by reform from above and other diversionary strategies.

However, this conservative reaction had deeper roots in the past, suggesting that recent studies of the old Reich are in danger of exaggerating its modernity and progressive character. The origins of later German conservatism are to be found not only in Prussian militarism and authoritarian traditions, but in a broader political culture that placed the collective good above individual liberty. Ironically, the very vibrancy of the Reich contributed to this by encouraging the rule of law as the basis of state–societal relations. The juridification of imperial politics preserved the Reich's territorial diversity and the corporate society upon which it was based. It slowed, but did not prevent the growth of integrated markets and commercialisation. Courts intervened to sustain corporate privileges, whilst minimising the disruptive consequences of these restrictive practices. The territorial states assumed these conservative characteristics, asserting themselves as arbitrators of social and economic problems. Groups and individuals could achieve modest improvements, without recourse to violence. The complex, multilayered social and political hierarchy prevented sharp divisions along class or confessional lines, particularly after 1648. These attitudes persisted even as cameralist and enlightened reforms began dismantling corporate society. Liberties and privileges were replaced by more uniform rights, but these remained enshrined in law, and political legitimacy continued to rest on respect for those laws, not on representative forms of government. This legacy conditioned the response to the renewed socio-economic change wrought by rapid industrialisation and urbanisation in Germany after 1850.

Glossary

Abschied   *See* **recess**.

Amt   Dual meaning as either a public post held by an official, or an administrative district within a territory.

Armed estate   A territory possessing a permanent military establishment beyond that required to fulfil imperial obligations.

Communalism   Collective political action through communal institutions embodying the associative principle binding neighbours together.

Confessionalisation   The demarcation of religious belief according to confessional orthodoxy, identifying an area and its inhabitants firmly with one variety of Christianity.

Dienstherrschaft   The feudal right to claim labour service from dependent peasants.

Electoral capitulation   Or *Wahlkapitulation*. Agreements between an emperor, or spiritual prince, and the electors made prior to the final confirmation of their election, confirming corporate rights and privileges.

Electors   The princes entitled to participate in the selection of each emperor. Their privileges were codified by the Golden Bull (q.v.).

Estates   A set of complex terms related to the corporate structure of early modern society, which was divided into privileged orders of clergy,

346

nobility and commons. Each of these orders was considered an Estate (*Stand*), as were the recognised subgroups within them. Representative institutions drawing on these groups were also called Estates. Territorial Estates (*Landstände*) were composed of representatives of the corporate groups from a particular territory. As constituent elements of the Reich, each territory (with certain exceptions) was both an 'imperial Estate' (*Reichsstand*) with a place in the Reichstag, and a *Kreisstand* with a seat in the relevant Kreis assembly (q.v.).

Gerichtsherrschaft   The right of feudal jurisdiction over a given area.

Gesindedienst   Also *Gesindezwangsdient*. Labour service performed by the younger sons of dependent peasants for their lord, with little or no remuneration.

Golden Bull   The imperial decree of 1356 codifying the privileges of the electors, or *Kurfürsten*, who chose each emperor. These rights included the indivisibility of the electorates and their exemption from some forms of imperial jurisdiction.

Grundherrschaft   The form of landownership whereby tenants rented plots from their feudal lord.

Gutswirtschaft   The manorial economy characterising the area east of the Elbe, where lordly estates were worked by dependent serfs and hired labourers producing bulk crops traded on the international market.

Immediacy   The status of *Reichsunmittelbarkeit*, indicating a relationship to the emperor that was direct and not mediated by any intermediate authority or lord.

Imperial church   The collective term for the *Reichskirche*, or ecclesiastical territories.

Imperial city   A city, or *Reichsstadt*, with the status of immediacy (q.v.), as distinct from a territorial town. The same applied to other derivatives of the term: imperial knights, imperial counts, imperial prelates.

Imperial Italy   The part of northern Italy under the emperor's feudal jurisdiction, which included Milan, Savoy, Genoa, Parma, Tuscany, Mantua, Solferino and other smaller principalities.

Itio in partes   The constitutional amendment introduced by the Peace of Westphalia in 1648 that permitted the imperial estates assembled in the Reichstag to discuss contentious religious issues in two separate confessional blocks, or *corpora*.

Kreis   Formally *Reichskreis*, or 'imperial circle'. One of the ten regional subdivisions of the Reich into which most territories were grouped.

Kreis assembly   Or *Kreistag*, containing the members of that Kreis, meeting to debate common concerns.

Kreis Association   A formal alliance between two or more Kreise that had been ratified by the assemblies.

Kreis convenor   Or *Kreisausschreibender Fürst*, who coordinated the meetings of the Kreis assembly and dealt with formal correspondence with the emperor and imperial institutions.

Kurfürsten   *See* **electors**.

Land   *See* **territory**.

Landeshoheit   *See* **territorial sovereignty**.

Landschaft   A form of Estates where commoners predominated.

Landtag   Territorial diet, or plenary meeting of the Estates.

Latest Imperial Recess   The last concluding document issued by the Reichstag session of 1653–4. The next meeting of 1663 remained in permanent session and issued legislation as necessary.

Leibeigenschaft   The status of personal serfdom.

Matricular system   The system for distributing fiscal and military burdens to the territories based on a list (*Matrikel*) recording their obligations.

Mediatisation   The loss of the status of immediacy (q.v.), usually through annexation by another territory.

Police regulation   Or *Polizei*, originally spelt *Policey*. Normative legislation issued by established authorities to sustain corporate society by guiding behaviour and addressing social and economic problems.

Privilege of not appealing   The *privilegium de non appellando* exempted territories from the jurisdiction of the two imperial courts. It was usually granted in limited form, though the electors acquired greater exemption.

Public peace   The *Landfrieden*, declared permanent in 1495, that required all territories to renounce violence and submit disputes to arbitration through the imperial courts. Further legislation, especially between 1555 and 1570, strengthened these arrangements.

Recess   The concluding document of an assembly, which listed all agreements and legislation decided at that session.

Reich   As a prefix, denoted 'imperial', as in *Reichsfürst* or 'imperial prince'.

Reichsdeputation   The imperial deputation, or special standing committee, selected by the Reichstag to discuss important business. The ordinary (*ordentliche*) imperial deputation was established by the public peace legislation to oversee the operation of imperial justice and other measures when the Reichstag was not in session. It was effectively superseded once the Reichstag remained in permanent session after 1663. Extraordinary deputations could still be selected to discuss other business, such as the territorial redistribution of 1801–3.

Reichshofrat   The imperial aulic, or count, council, established in 1498 to safeguard the emperor's prerogatives. It developed after 1558 as a second supreme court alongside the *Reichskammergericht*.

Reichskammergericht   The imperial cameral court, created in 1495 and charged with upholding the public peace and acting as a supreme court of appeal. Its judges were mainly appointed by the imperial estates through the Kreis structure.

Reichstag   The imperial diet, or assembly of the emperor and imperial Estates.

Roman month   The unit of account measuring the financial contributions from the territories, paid according to the matricular system (q.v.) for common purposes, usually defence. The term came from the monthly wage bill of the troops intended to escort the emperor to his coronation in Rome.

Romans, King of the   The title *Römischer König* was given to the successor designate chosen by the electors to succeed an incumbent emperor on his death.

Schollenpflichtigkeit   The legal restriction tying rural inhabitants to a specific area and lordly jurisdiction. A key element of serfdom.

Social discipline   The interpretation suggesting that society was transformed by state regulation, encouraging individuals to behave as obedient, thrifty subjects.

Stand, Stände   *See* **Estates**.

Territorial sovereignty   Or *Landeshoheit*, denoting the powers accumulated and developed by the imperial Estates (q.v.) to act on their own initiative in territorial and imperial politics. These powers rested on imperial law and included the right to reform religion, maintain troops, negotiate with foreign governments and issue legislation within the relevant territory, provided these actions were not directed against the integrity and well-being of the emperor and Reich.

Territorialisation   The process of identifying political power and representation in imperial institutions with a given area.

Territory   A constituent part of the Reich, recognised as an imperial Estate.

Appendix 1: Major rulers

Emperors

Note: All were from the Habsburg dynasty till 1740 and simultaneously rulers of the Habsburg monarchy, including Hungary and Bohemia. Francis I was formerly duke of Lorraine and married to the Austrian archduchess and queen of Hungary, Maria Theresa, who was co-regent and ruler of the Habsburg monarchy from 1740. After her death, her son Emperor Joseph II became sole ruler of the monarchy, as were his successors.

1519–56	Charles V
1556–64	Ferdinand I
1564–76	Maximilian II
1576–1612	Rudolf II
1612–19	Matthias
1619–37	Ferdinand II
1637–57	Ferdinand III
1657–8	interregnum
1658–1705	Leopold I
1705–11	Joseph I
1711–40	Charles VI
1740–2	interregnum
1742–5	Charles VII (the Wittelsbach Carl Albrecht of Bavaria)
1745–65	Francis I
1765–90	Joseph II
1790–2	Leopold II
1792–1806	Francis II (assumed a distinct Austrian imperial title in 1804 and ruled till 1835)

Ecclesiastical Electors

Mainz

1545–55	Sebastian von Heußenstamm
1555–82	Daniel Brendel aus Homburg
1582–1601	Wolfgang von Dalberg
1601–4	Johann Adam von Bicken
1604–26	Johann III Schweikard von Kronberg
1626–9	Georg Friedrich von Greiffenklau zu Vollraths
1629–47	Anselm Kasimir Wambold von Umstädt
1647–73	Johann Philipp von Schönborn
1673–5	Lothar Friedrich von Metternich
1675–8	Damian Hartard von der Leyen
1679	Carl Heinrich von Metternich
1679–95	Anselm Franz von Ingelheim
1695–1729	Lothar Franz von Schönborn
1729–32	Franz Ludwig von Pfalz-Neuburg
1732–43	Philipp Carl von Eltz
1743–63	Johann Friedrich Carl von Ostein
1763–74	Emreich Carl Joseph von Breidbach zu Bürresheim
1774–1802	Friedrich Carl Joseph zu Erthal
1802–3	Carl Theodor von Dalberg

Cologne

1515–46	Hermann V, count of Wied (converted to Protestantism, forced from office)
1546–56	Adolf III, count of Schauenburg
1556–8	Anton, count of Schauenburg
1558–62	Johann Gebhard I, count of Mansfeld
1562–7	Friedrich IV, count of Wied (died 1568)
1567–77	Valentin, count of Isenburg (died 1610)
1577–83	Gebhard II, Truchseß of Waldburg (forced from office)
1583–1612	Ernst, duke of Bavaria
1612–50	Ferdinand, duke of Bavaria
1650–88	Maximilian Heinrich, duke of Bavaria
1688–1723	Joseph Clemens, duke of Bavaria
1723–61	Clemens August, duke of Bavaria

1761–84	Maximilian Friedrich von Königsegg-Rothenfels
1784–1801	Maximilian Franz, archduke of Austria
1801–2	Anton Viktor, archduke of Austria (prevented from taking office by the secularisation)

Trier

1556–67	Johann VI von der Leyern
1567–81	Jakob III von Eltz
1581–99	Johann VII von Schönburg
1599–1623	Lothar von Metternich
1623–52	Philip Christoph von Sötern
1652–76	Carl Kaspar von der Leyen
1676–1711	Johann Hugo von Orsbeck
1711–15	Carl Joseph, duke of Lorraine
1716–29	Franz Ludwig von Pfalz-Neuburg
1729–56	Franz Georg von Schönborn
1756–68	Johann Philipp von Walderdorf
1768–1802	Clemens August, prince of Saxony

Secular Electors

Brandenburg-Prussia (Hohenzollern dynasty)

Note: The rulers of Brandenburg-Prussia took their titles from their electorate of Brandenburg until 1701 when their sovereign duchy of East Prussia was raised to a kingdom and they assumed a royal title.

Brandenburg

1535–71	Joachim II
1571–98	Johann George
1598–1608	Joachim Frederick
1608–19	Johann Sigismund
1619–40	George William
1640–88	Frederick William, the Great Elector
1688–1713	Frederick III, from 18 Jan. 1701 King Frederick I
1713–40	Frederick William I, the Soldier King
1740–86	Frederick II, the Great

1786–97   Frederick William II
1797–1840   Frederick William III

Ducal Prussia
1525–68   Albrecht
1568–1618   Albrecht Friedrich
1618   To Brandenburg

Bavaria (Wittelsbach dynasty)

Note: Bavaria was a duchy till 1623 when it was raised to an electorate.

1550–79   Albrecht V
1579–98   Wilhelm V the Pious (abdicated; died 1626)
1598–1651   Maximilian I (elector from 1623)
1651–79   Ferdinand Maria
1679–1726   Max II Emanuel
1726–45   Carl Albrecht (Emperor Charles VII 1742–5)
1745–77   Max III Joseph

Passed to the Palatinate (q.v.).

The Palatinate (Wittelsbach dynasty)

Note: An electorate, joined to Bavaria in 1777. Raised as the kingdom of Bavaria in 1805.

1544–56   Friedrich II the Wise
1556–9   Otto Heinrich
1559–76   Friedrich III the Pious (from the Pfalz-Simmern line)
1576–83   Ludwig IV
1583–1610   Friedrich IV
1610–23   Friedrich V (died 1632)
1623–48   under Bavarian rule
1648–80   Carl Ludwig
1680–5   Carl (the last of the Simmern line of the Palatine
               Wittelsbachs)
1685–90   Philipp Wilhelm (Pfalz-Neuburg line)

1690–1716	Johann Wilhelm
1716–42	Carl Philipp (last of the Pfalf-Neuburg line)
1742–99	Carl Theodor (Sulzbach line, inherited Bavaria in 1777)
1799–1825	Maximilian IV Joseph (Birkenfeld line, king from Dec. 1805)

Saxony (Wettin dynasty)

Note: An electorate, linked by dynastic union to the kingdom of Poland 1697–1763. Raised to a kingdom in 1806.

1532–47	Johann Friedrich (last Ernestine elector, deprived of his title 1547)
1547–53	Moritz (first Albertine elector)
1553–86	August
1586–91	Christian I
1591–1611	Christian II
1611–56	Johann Georg I
1656–80	Johann Georg II
1680–91	Johann Georg III
1691–4	Johann Georg IV
1694–1733	Friedrich August I (Augustus II 'the Strong' of Poland from 1697)
1733–63	Friedrich August II (Augustus III of Poland)
1763	Friedrich Christian
1763–1827	Friedrich August III (king from 1806)

Hanover (Guelph dynasty)

Note: Originally the duchy of Calenberg, but raised to an electorate in 1692 and known generally as Hanover. Its rulers became kings of Great Britain 1714–1837.

1569–92	Wilhelm V the Younger
1592–1611	Ernst II
1611–33	Christian
1633–6	August I

1636–41	Georg I
1641–8	Christian Ludwig
1648–65	Georg II Wilhelm (became duke of Celle)
1665–79	Johann Friedrich
1679–98	Ernst August (also prince-bishop of Osnabrück since 1662; elector from 1692)
1698–1727	Georg Ludwig (King George I of Great Britain from 1714)
1727–60	George II
1760–1802	George III (died 1820)

Main Ecclesiastical Principalities

Bamberg

1556–61	Georg IV Fuchs von Rügheim
1561–77	Veit II von Würzburg
1577–80	Johann Georg I Zobel von Giebelstadt
1580–3	Martin von Eyb
1583–91	Ernst von Mengersdorf
1591–8	Nithard von Thüngen
1598–1609	Johann Philipp von Gebsattel
1609–22	Johann Gottfried von Aschhausen
1622–33	Johann Georg II Fuchs von Dornheim
1633–42	Franz, Count of Hatzfeld
1642–53	Melchior Otto Voit von Salzburg
1653–72	Philipp Valentin Voit von Rieneck
1672–83	Peter Philipp von Dernbach (bishop of Würzburg from 1675)
1683–93	Marquard Sebastian Schenk von Stauffenberg
1693–1729	Lothar Franz von Schönborn (elector of Mainz from 1695)
1729–46	Friedrich Carl von Schönborn (bishop of Würzburg)
1746–53	Johann Philipp Anton von Frankenstein
1753–7	Franz Lonrad von Stadion-Thannhausen
1757–79	Adam Friedrich von Seinsheim (bishop of Würzburg)
1779–95	Franz Ludwig von Erthal (bishop of Würzburg)
1795–1802	Christoph Franz von Buseck

Münster

1557–66	Bernhard von Räsfeld
1566–74	Johann IV, count of Hoya
1574–85	Johann Wilhelm, duke of Jülich-Cleves (died 1609)
1585–1612	Ernst, duke of Bavaria (elector of Cologne)
1612–50	Ferdinand I (elector of Cologne, bishop of Paderborn from 1618)
1650–78	Christoph Bernhard von Galen, Bomber Bernard the Cannon Bishop
1678–83	Ferdinand II von Fürstenberg
1683–8	Max Heinrich (elector of Cologne)
1688–1706	Friedrich Christian von Plettenberg-Lenhausen
1706–18	Franz Arnold Josef Wolf von Metternich (bishop of Paderborn)
1719–61	Clemens August (elector of Cologne)
1761–84	Maximilian Friedrich zu Königsegg-Rothenfels (elector of Cologne)
1784–1801	Maximilian Franz (elector of Cologne)

Osnabrück

Ruled alternately by Catholic bishops and Guelph dukes after 1648.

1553–74	Johann IV, count of Hoya (also bishop of Münster and Paderborn)
1574–85	Heinrich III, duke of Sachsen-Lauenburg (Protestant administrator, also in Osnabrück)
1585	Wilhelm von Schenking
1585–91	Bernhard II, count of Waldeck (Protestant administrator)
1591–1623	Philipp Sigismund, Guelph duke of Lüneburg (Protestant administrator)
1623–5	Eitel Friedrich, count of Hohenzollern (Protestant administrator)
1625–34	Franz Wilhelm von Wartenberg (Catholic bishop)
1634–48	Gustav Gustavson, count of Vasaburg (Swedish administrator)
1648–61	Franz Wilhelm von Wartenberg (reappointed Catholic bishop)

1662–98	Ernst August I (Guelph duke, ruled Hanover from 1679)
1698–1715	Carl Joseph Ignaz, duke of Lorraine (Catholic bishop, elector of Trier from 1711)
1716–28	Ernst August II (Guelph duke)
1728–61	Clemens August (Catholic bishop, elector of Cologne)
1761–4	Duke Georg, Guelph administrator
1764–1802	Frederick, duke of York (Guelph duke)

Paderborn

1547–68	Rembert von Kerßenbroich
1568–74	Johann II, count of Hoya (also bishop of Münster and Osnabrück)
1574–7	Salentin, count of Isenburg
1577–85	Heinrich IV, duke of Sachsen-Lauenburg (also in Osnabrück)
1585–1618	Theodor, baron of Fürstenberg
1618–50	Ferdinand I (elector of Cologne, bishop of Münster)
1650–61	Theodor Adolf von der Recke
1661–83	Ferdinand II von Fürstenberg (bishop of Münster from 1678)
1683–1704	Hermann Werner Wolf von Metternich
1704–18	Franz Arnold Wolf von Metternich (bishop of Münster from 1706)
1719–61	Clemens August (elector of Cologne)
1761–3	interregnum
1763–82	Wilhelm Anton von der Asseburg
1782–9	Friedrich Wilhelm von Westphalen
1789–1802	Franz Egon von Fürstenberg

Würzburg

1558–73	Friedrich von Wirsberg
1573–1617	Julius Echter von Merpelsbrunn
1617–22	Johann Gottfried I von Aschhausen
1623–31	Philipp Adolf von Ehrenberg
1631–42	Franz, Count of Hatzfeld and Gleichen
1642–73	Johann Philipp I von Schönborn (elector of Mainz from 1647)

1673–5	Johann Hartmann von Rosenbach
1675–83	Peter Philipp von Dernbach (bishop of Bamberg)
1683–4	Konrad Wilhelm von Wernau
1684–98	Johann Gottfried II von Guttenberg
1699–1719	Johann Philipp II von Greiffenklau zu Vollraths
1719–24	Johann Philipp III Franz von Schönborn
1724–9	Christoph Franz von Hutten-Stolzenberg
1729–46	Friedrich Carl von Schönborn
1746–9	Anselm Franz von Ingelheim
1749–54	Carl Philipp Heinrich von Greiffenklau zu Vollraths
1755–79	Adam Friedrich von Seinsheim (bishop of Bamberg from 1757)
1779–95	Franz Ludwig von Erthal (bishop of Bamberg)
1795–1802	Georg Carl von Fechenbach (died 1808)
1802–6	Secularised and transferred to Bavaria
1806–14	Ferdinand of Tuscany (as elector)

Main Secular Principalities

Celle (Guelph dukes)

Detached from Calenberg in 1641.

1641–8	Friedrich
1648–65	Christian Ludwig (became ruler of Hanover)
1665–1705	Georg II Wilhelm (previously ruled Hanover)

Passed to Hanover (Calenberg).

East Frisia (Ostfriesland) (Cirksena dynasty)

1540–99	Edzard II
1599–1625	Enno III
1625–8	Rudolf Christian
1628–48	Ulrich III
1648–60	Enno Ludwig
1660–5	Georg Christian
1665–1708	Christian Eberhard

1708–34   Georg Albrecht
1734–44   Carl Edzard

To Prussia.

Gotha (Ernestine Saxons)

1554–66   Johann Friedrich II
1566–1640   shared with other Ernestine dukes
1640–75   Ernst I, the Pious
1675–91   Friedrich I
1691–1732   Friedrich II
1732–1772   Friedrich III
1772–1804   Ernst II
1804–22   August Emil Leopold

Hessen-Darmstadt

Detached from Hessen in the partition of 1567.

1567–96   Georg I
1596–1626   Ludwig V
1626–61   Georg II
1661–78   Ludwig VI
1678   Ludwig VII
1678–1739   Ernst August
1739–68   Ludwig VIII
1768–90   Ludwig IX
1790–1830   Ludwig X (grand duke from 1806)

Hessen-Kassel

Partitioned in 1567, creating separate Kassel and Darmstadt lines.

1509–67   Philipp
1567–92   Wilhelm IV
1592–1627   Moritz (died 1632)

1627–37	Wilhelm V
1637–63	Wilhelm VI
1663–70	Wilhelm VII
1670–1730	Carl
1730–51	Friedrich I (king of Sweden since 1720, territory ruled in his absence by Wilhelm VIII)
1751–60	Wilhelm VIII
1760–85	Friedrich II
1785–1806	Wilhelm IX (elector from 1803)

Holstein-Gottorp

1533–86	Adolf
1586–7	Friedrich II
1587–90	Philipp
1590–1616	Johann Adolf (archbishop of Bremen 1585–96, bishop of Lübeck 1586–1607)
1616–59	Friedrich III (sovereign in Schleswig after 1658)
1659–94	Christian Albrecht (territory under Danish occupation 1675–9, 1684–9)
1694–1702	Friedrich IV
1702–21	Christian August von Holstein-Eutin, regent
1721–39	Carl Friedrich
1739–45	Adolf Friedrich, regent
1745–62	Carl Ulrich, called Peter from 1741; became Tsar Peter III of Russia in 1762

Lorraine

1545–1608	Charles II
1608–24	Henry the Good
1624–5	Francis II (died 1639)
1625–75	Charles IV (land occupied by France 1670–97)
1675–90	Charles V
1697–1729	Leopold
1729–36	Francis (husband of Maria Theresa, emperor from 1745)
1736–66	Stanislaw Leszczynski (former king of Poland)

To France.

Mecklenburg-Schwerin

1552–76	Johann Albrecht I
1576–92	Johann VII
1592–1658	Adolf Friedrich I (co-duke with Johann Albrecht II till 1610)
1658–92	Christian (Louis)
1692–1713	Friedrich Wilhelm (Grabow line)
1713–28	Carl Leopold (deposed, died 1747)
1747–56	Christian Ludwig (adminstrator since 1728)
1756–85	Friedrich II
1785–1837	Friedrich Franz I

Pfalz-Neuburg (Wittelsbach dynasty)

Created by a partition of Zweibrücken in 1569.

1569–1614	Philipp Ludwig
1614–53	Wolfgang Wilhelm
1653–90	Philipp Wilhelm (elector Palatine from 1685)

United with the Palatinate in 1685.

Weimar (Ernestine Saxons)

1554–73	Johann Wilhelm
1573–1605	Johann
1605–40	co-rule of 8 brothers
1640–62	Wilhelm
1662–83	Johann Ernst I
1683–1728	Wilhelm Ernst
1728–48	Ernst August
1748–58	Ernst August Constantin
1758–75	Anna Amalia von Wolfenbüttel, regent
1775–1828	Carl August

Wolfenbüttel (Guelph dukes)

Re-established 1569 through dynastic partition.

1569–98	Heinrich X
1598–1666	August II
1666–1704	Rudolf August ⎫
1666–1714	Anton-Ulrich ⎭ co-rulers
1714–31	August Wilhelm
1731–5	Ludwig Rudolf
1735	Ferdinand Albrecht
1735–80	Carl I
1780–1806	Carl Wilhelm Ferdinand

Württemberg

Note: A duchy until 1803, when it became an electorate, and then a kingdom from 1806.

1550–68	Christoph
1568–93	Ludwig the Pious
1593–1608	Friedrich I
1608–28	Johann Friedrich
1628–74	Eberhard III (under Austrian occupation 1634–48)
1674–7	Wilhelm Ludwig
1677–93	Friedrich Carl, regent
1693–1733	Eberhard Ludwig
1733–7	Carl Alexander
1737–8	Carl Rudolph, regent
1738–44	Carl Friedrich, regent
1744–93	Carl Eugen
1793–5	Ludwig Eugen
1795–7	Friedrich Eugen
1797–1816	Friedrich (elector from 1803, king from 1806)

Appendix 2: Territories, by Kreise, c.1800

Note: all recognised territories (imperial and Kreis Estates) are listed with their titles and owners in parentheses. Where no owner is listed, the land was owned by its native ruler.

Territory	Size (km^2)	Population
Austrian		
Secular		
Austrian lands	113,850	4,291,668
Tarasp (lordship)	82.5	
Ecclesiastical		
Trent (bishopric)	4,125	155,000
Brixen (bishopric)	935	30,000
Total	**118,992.5**	**4,476,668**
Burgundian		
Secular		
Habsburg lands	25,795	1,888,000
Bavarian		
Secular		
Bavaria		
Bavaria (electorate)	32,450	982,505
Upper Palatinate	7,040	165,933
Leuchtenberg (landgraviate)	220	incl. in Bav.
Haag (county)	440	incl. in Bav.

Territory	Size (km²)	Population
Breiteneck (lordship)	110	incl. in Bav.
Hohenwaldeck (lordship)	220	incl. in Bav.
Sulzburg and Prybaum	110 3,000	
Neuburg (and Ehrenfels) (principality)	(40,590)	(1,151,438)
	2,860	90,000
Sulzbach (principality)	1,100	42,000
Sternstein (county, to Prince Lobkowitz)	110	3,140
Ortenburg (county)	110	1,800
Total	*44,770*	*1,288,378*
Ecclesiastical		
Salzburg (archbishopric)	10,450	220,000
Passau (bishopric)	1,100	24,000
Freising (bishopric)	825	25,000
Regensburg (bishopric)	330	10,000
Berchtesgaden (prince-priory)	770	18,000
St Emmeran (abbey)	no land	
Niedermünster (abbey)	no land	
Obermüster (abbey)	no land	
Total	*13,475*	*297,000*
Civic		
Regensburg	27.5	21,000
Total	**58,272.5**	**1,606,378**

Franconian

Secular

Ansbach (margraviate) (to Prussia since 1792)	3,740	215,000
Bayreuth (margraviate) (to Prussia since 1792)	3,960	185,000
Hohenlohe-Neuenstein (principality)*	1,210 ⎱	
Hohenlohe-Waldenburg (principality)**	660 ⎰	100,000
Wertheim (county) (to Prince Löwenstein-Wertheim)	660	16,000
Erbach (county)	577.5	24,000
Schwarzenberg (incl. Seinsheim) (principality)	715	10,000
Castell (county)	440	5,000
Rieneck (county) split between		
Count Nostitz	440 ⎱	
Mainz	220 ⎰	12,000
Limpurg and Speckfeld (split between 6 owners incl. Prussia)	484	14,000
Wiesentheid (lordship) (to Count Schönborn)	93.5	3,000

Territory	Size (km^2)	Population
Welzheim (lordship) (to Württemberg)	55	3,011
Hennenberg (county) split between:		
Electoral Saxony	467.5	22,000
Weimar	291.5	15,000
Meiningen & Römhild	709.5	34,000
Coburg-Saalfeld	148.5	7,600
Gotha	33	1,800
Hildburghausen	41.25	1,800
Hessen-Kassel	374	19,900
Total	*15,320.25*	*689,111*
Ecclesiastical		
Würzburg (bishopric)	4,950	268,000
Bamberg (bishopric)	3,575	180,000
Eichstätt (bishopric)	1,265	62,000
Teutonic Order	550	32,000
Total	*10,340*	*542,000*
Civic		
Nuremberg	1,650	70,000
Rothenburg	275	24,000
Schweinsfurt	110	6,000
Windsheim	55	4,000
Weissenburg	55	6,500
Total	*2,145*	*110,500*
Total	**27,805.25**	**1,341,611**

* Split between the Öhringen, Langenburg, Ingelfingen, and Kirchberg lines.
** Split between the Bartenstein and Schillingsfürst lines.

Swabian

Secular		
Württemberg (duchy)	8,800	620,000
Baden (margraviate)		
Baden-Baden	1,760 ⎫	
Eberstein	330 ⎬	190,000
Baden-Durlach	1,485 ⎪	
Hochberg	990 ⎭	
Hohenzollern-Hechingen (principality)	247.5	12,000
Hohenzollern-Sigmaringen (principality)	165	7,000
Fürstenberg (principality)*	1,842.5	85,000

Territory	Size (km^2)	Population
Öttingen-Wallerstein (principality)	880	40,000
Öttingen-Spielberg (principality)	440	20,000
Vaduz (county) and Schellenburg (lordship) (to Liechtenstein)	165	5,000
Klettgau (landgraviate) (to Schwarzenberg)	302.5	9,000
Tettnang and Argen (lordships) (to Austria since 1780)	330	13,000
Wiesensteig and Mindelheim (lordships) (to Bavaria)	550	19,220
Waldburg-Wolfegg-Waldsee (county)	412.5	14,000
Waldburg-Zeil and Waldburg-Wurzach (counties)	302.5	10,000
Königsegg-Aulendorf and Konigsegg-Rothenfels (counties)	881.1	43,300
Fugger **	1,155	25,000
Hohenems (county) (to Count Harrach)	192.5	4,000
Eglofs (lordship) (to Count Traun und Abensberg)	110	2,000
Thengen (county) (to Prince Auersperg)	82.5	822
Friedberg-Scheer (county) and Eglingen (lordship) (to Prince Thurn und Taxis)	192.5	9,000
Hohengeroldseck (county) (to Count v.d. Leyen)	126.5	4,000
Thannhausen (lordship) (to Count Stadion)	5.5	200
Total	*21,748.1*	*1,132,542*

Ecclesiastical

Augsburg (bishopric)	2,475	92,000
Kempten (bishopric)	880	50,000
Ellwangen (bishopric)	374	20,000
Constance (bishopric)	275	14,000
Baindt (convent)	no land	195
St Blasien*** (abbey) (holding the county of Bonndorf)	192.5	8,000
Buchau*** (convent)	110	3,600
Elchingen (abbey)	137.5	4,000
Gengenbach (abbey)	no land	1,500
Guttenzell (convent)	82.5	1,500
Heggbach (convent)	82.5	3,000
Irsee (abbey)	110	4,400
Kaysersheim (abbey)	165	7,000
Lindau*** (convent)	no land	360
Marchtal (abbey)	165	7,000
Neresheim (abbey) (member since 1764)	82.5	5,000
Ochsenhausen (abbey)	192.5	9,000
Ottobeuren (abbey) (member since 1710, but no vote)	181.5	12,000

Territory	Size (km^2)	Population
Petershausen (abbey)	137.5	3,500
Roggenburg (abbey)	137.5	4,000
Rottenmünster (convent)	55	3,000
Roth an der Roth (abbey)	82.5	2,900
Salmanseiler (also called Salem) (abbey)	330	9,000
Schüssenried (abbey)	143	3,400
Ursberg (abbey)	99	3,600
Weingarten (abbey)	330	14,000
Weissenau (abbey) (member since 1760)	27.5	1,500
Wettenhausen (abbey)	110	5,000
Zwiefalten (abbey) (an imperial estate since 1750)	181.5	4,781
Total	*7,139*	*297,236*
Civic		
Aalen	44	2,300
Augsburg	55	36,000
Biberach	110	7,651
Bopfingen	44	2,000
Buchau	16.5	1,000
Buchhorn	27.5	770
Dinkelsbühl	55	8,000
Esslingen	82.5	10,706
Gengenbach	110	2,000
Giengen	27.5	1,486
Heilbronn	55	9,400
Isny	27.5	1,500
Kaufbeuren	110	7,000
Kempten	44	4,000
Leutkirch	27.5	1,750
Lindau	82.5	7,000
Memmingen	110	12,000
Nördlingen	82.5	8,000
Offenburg	16.5	2,000
Pfullendorf	110	4,000
Ravensburg	137.5	5,000
Reutlingen	38.5	10,500
Rottweil	220	13,333
Schwäbisch-Gmünd	165	15,000
Schwäbisch-Hall	330	16,000
Überlingen	247.5	5,415
Ulm	935	38,000

Territory	Size (km²)	Population
Wangen	82.5	4,000
Weil der Stadt	22	1,800
Wimpfen	33	3,000
Zell am Hammersbach	110	3,000
Total	*3,558.5*	*243,611*
Total	**32,445.6**	**1,672,389**

Other

Neuravensburg (lordship) (to the Abbot of St Gallen)	27.5	900

(part of the Kreis, but without a vote in the assembly)

St Ulrich und Afra   no land

(abbey in the city of Augsburg. Not in the Kreis assembly, but had a vote in the Rhenish prelates bench at the Reichstag since 1577)

* Including Baar (landgraviate), Stühlingen (landgraviate), Heiligenberg (county), Mößkirch (lordship), Gundelfingen (barony).

** Split into six lines: Nordendorf, Glött, Mückhausen, Kirchheim, Babenhausen, Wasserburg.

*** Despite being ruled by clerics, these areas were represented on the secular lords' bench in the assembly.

Upper Rhenish

Secular

Palatine lands (to Palatine-Bavaria)

	Size (km²)	Population
Simmern (principality)	770 ⎫	
Lautern (principality)	1,375 ⎬	83,200
Veldenz (principality)	275 ⎭	
Zweibrücken (principality)	1,980	60,000
Sponheim (half) (county)	440	25,500
	(4,840)	(168,200)

Hessen-Darmstadt

	Size (km²)	Population
H.-Darmstadt (landgraviate)	3,850	180,000
Hanau-Lichtenberg (county)	275	15,000
	(4,125)	(195,000)

Hessen-Kassel

	Size (km²)	Population
H.-Kassel (landgraviate)	7,497.05	335,307
Hersfeld (principality)	481.25	19,434
Hanau-Münzenberg (county)	1,540	60,427
	(9,518.3)	(415,168)

Nassau (counts and princes)

	Size (km²)	Population
Weilburg	770	20,000
Usingen (incl. Wiesbaden)	880	30,000

Territory	Size (km^2)	Population
Idstein (to N.-Usingen)	275	12,000
Ottweiler (to N.-Usingen)	275	12,000
Saarbrücken	770	14,000
	(2,970)	(88,000)
Sponheim (half) (county) (to Baden-Baden)	440	25,500
Salm-Salm (county)	440	16,000
Salm-Kyrburg (county)	110	6,000
Solms (counts)		
Braunfels	385 ⎫	
Hohensolms	220 ⎬ 40,000	
Rödelheim	165	
Laubach	165 ⎭	
Waldeck (principality)	1,045	46,000
Königstein (half) (county) (to Mainz)	220	7,500
Königstein (half) (county) (to Stolberg)	220	7,500
Isenburg (princes)		
Offenbach and Birstein	385	22,500
Büdingen	192.5	10,500
Wächtersbach	110	6,000
Meerholz	82.5	1,500
Grumbach (counts)		
Grumbach (lordship)	330	17,000
Rheingrafenstein (county)	220	11,000
Leiningen (counts)		
Hartenberg	192.5 ⎫ 20,000	
Westerburg	137.5 ⎭	
Wittgenstein (counts)		
Sayn-Wittgenstein-Berleburg	192.5	7,027
Sayn-Wittgenstein	275	8,993
Falkenstein (county) (to Austria)	137.5	4,000
Reipoltskirchen (lordship)*	110	3,000
Kriechingen (to Wied-Runkel since 1726)	110	4,000
Bretzenheim (county, but its ruler had the title of prince)	82.5	3,000
Wartenberg (county)	165	2,800
Dachstuhl (lordship) (Öttingen till 1798, then Princess Colloredo)	110	6,000
Ollbrück (lordship) (to Count Waldbott-Bassenheim-Bornheim)	82.5	1,600
Total	27,778.3	1,143,788

Territory	Size (km²)	Population
Ecclesiastical		
Worms (bishopric)	440	12,000
Speyer (bishopric)	1,540	50,000
Fulda (prince-abbey)	1,815	90,000
Basel (bishopric)	1,045	16,000
Strasbourg (bishopric)	357.5	20,000
Heitersheim (commandery of the knights of St John)	220 ⎫	
Prüm (prince-abbey) (to Trier)	220 ⎬	12,000
Odenheim (priory)	55 ⎭	
Total	*5,692.5*	*200,000*
Civic		
Frankfurt/Main	122	46,000
Worms	city only	6,000
Speyer	55	6,000
Friedberg	city only	2,000
Wetzlar	13.75	6,000
Total	*190.75*	*66,000*
Total	**33,661.55**	**1,410,288**
Lands formerly belonging to the Upper Rhenish Kreis		
Lorraine (duchy) (to France)	18,040	800,000
Savoy (duchy) (to Sardinia)	10,786	350,000

* One-quarter to Count Löwenhaupt-Manderscheid, three-quarters to Count
Hillesheim

Electoral Rhenish

Secular		
Palatinate (electorate)	4,303	228,000
Arenberg (principality)	220	2,900
Beilstein (lordship) (to Nassau)	275	10,000
Niederisenburg (county) split between Trier	110	incl. under Trier
Wied (both lines)	82.5	3,500
Rheineck (burgraviate) (to Prince Sinzendorf)	27.5	1,600
Thurn und Taxis (prince)	(personal member with no land)	
Total	*5,018*	*246,000*

Territory	Size (km^2)	Population
Ecclesiastical		
Mainz (electorate) (incl. Erfurt and Eichsfeld)	6,875	336,000
Cologne (electorate) (incl. Westpahlia and Recklinghausen)	7,480	230,000
Trier (electorate)	7,150	215,000
Koblenz (bailiwick) (Teutonic Order)	–	
Total	*21,505*	*781,000*
Total	**26,523**	**1,027,000**

Westphalian (also called Lower Rhenish)

Territory	Size (km^2)	Population
Secular		
Prussian lands		
Cleves (duchy)	2,750	85,000
Mark (county)	2,631	131,860
Ravensberg (county)	915.03	89,938
Minden (principality: ex-bishopric)	1,198.02	70,363
Tecklenburg (county)	412.37	19,000
Lingen (county)	730.04	25,021
Mörs (principality)	646	25,000
Obergeldern (duchy)	1,320	48,000
East Frisia (principality) (since 1744)	3,300	110,000
	(13,902.46)	(604,182)
Palatine lands		
Jülich (duchy)	4,218	180,000
Berg (duchy)	3,077	261,000
Hanoverian lands		
Verden (principality)	1,320	20,000
Diepholz (county)	495	
Hoya (county)	2,475	60,000
Spiegelberg (county)	71.5	
Nassau-Dietz (house of Orange)		
Dietz (county)	825	
Dillenburg (county)	440	97,000
Hadamar (county)	385	
Siegen (county)	440	
Hessen-Kassel lands		
Schaumburg (part) (county)	467.5	
'Hoya' (former county of Bruchausen)	275	33,755
Auburg (lordship)	110	

Territory	Size (km²)	Population
Oldenburg (duke)		
Oldenburg (duchy)	1,650 ⎫	
Delmenhorst (county)	660 ⎭	95,000
Lippe-Detmold (principality)	1,209	71,000
Schaumburg (part) (Count of Schaumburg-Lippe)	340	20,000
Gemen (lordship) (Baron Bömelberg)	21	1,100
Schleiden (county) and Saffenburg (lordship)		
(duchess of Aremberg)	275	10,000
Gimborn and Neustadt (lordships) (Count Wallmoden)	275	18,000
Gronsfeld (county) (Count Törring-Jettenbach)	55	1,900
Kerpen-Lommerstein (county) (Count Schäsberg)	75	3,000
Mylendonk (lordship) (Count Ostein)	44	1,600
Reckheim (county) (Count Aspremont-Linden)	82.5	3,000
Reichenstein (lordship) (Count Nesselrode)	1 village	
Reifferscheidt (county incl. Dyck)		
(Count Salm-Reifferscheidt)	200	9,100
Virneburg (county) (Count Löwenstein-Wertheim)	84	2,600
Wickerad and Schwanenberg (lordships) (Count Quardt)	84	2,000
Winneburg (lordship)		
(Count Metternich-Winneburg-Beilstein)	140	6,400
Wittem, Eiß and Schlenachen (lordships)		
(Count Plettenberg)	82.5	2,700
Hallermund (county) (Count Platen-Hallermund)	55	1,650
Sayn-Altenkirchen (former county)		
(Ansbach, i.e. Prussia)	165 ⎫	
Sayn-Hachenburg (former county) (Nassau-Weilburg)	110 ⎭	12,000
Bentheim (county) (Counts B.-Bentheim		
and B.-Tecklenburg)	935	22,000
Steinfurt (county) (Count Bentheim-Steinfurt)	65	3,400
Wied-Runkel, and W.-Neuwied (counties)	330	20,000
Anholt (lordship) (Prince Salm-Salm)	55	1,100
Manderscheid lands (Countess Sternberg)*	420	19,000
Fagnolles (county) (Prince de Ligne)	27.5	500
Holzapfel (county) (prince of Anhalt-Bernberg)	165	4,950
Prymont (county) (to Waldeck)	82.5	4,500
Rietberg (county) (Prince Kaunitz)	216	12,000
Total	*36,404.46*	*1,604,437*
Ecclesiastical		
Münster (bishopric)	10,500	311,341
Paderborn (bishopric)	2,970	124,000

Territory	Size (km²)	Population
Liège (bishopric)	5,775	286,000
Osnabrück (bishopric)	2,025	126,000
Stablo and Malmedy (prince-abbeys)	935	10,000
Corvey (prince-abbey)	275	9,000
Werden (abbey)	137.5	1,500
Korneleimünster (abbey)	137.5	1,500
Essen (convent)	155	1,900
Thorn (convent)	82.5	1,000
Herford (convent)	no land	2,000
Total	*22,992.5*	*874,241*
Civic		
Cologne	no land	54,000
Aachen	82.5	30,000
Dortmund	126.5	6,000
Total	*209*	*90,000*
Total	**59,605.96**	**2,568,678**

* Counties of Manderscheid, Blankenheim, Gerolstein; lordships of
Dollendorf, and Junkerath.

Lower Saxon

Secular

Hanover (electorate)		
Calenberg (duchy)	2,640 ⎫	
Grubenhagen (principality)	715 ⎬	260,000
Wildeshausen (lordship)	126.5 ⎭	
Sachsen-Lauenburg (duchy) and Hadeln		
(lordship)	1,457.5	33,000
Celle (Lüneburg) (principality)	11,000	304,000
Bremen (principality: ex-archbishopric)	5,170	180,000
	(21,109)	(777,000)
Brunswick-Wolfenbüttel (duke)		
Wolfenbüttel (principality)	3,190 ⎫	160,000
Blankenburg (principality)	473 ⎭	
Mecklenburg-Schwerin (duke)		
Schwerin (duchy: former duchy of		
Mecklenburg)	7,095	147,000
Güstrow [part] (duchy)	4,400	128,000
Schwerin (principality)	770	25,000

Territory	Size (km^2)	Population
Mecklenburg-Strelitz (duke)		
Güstrow [part] and Stargard (lordship)	2,310	46,000
Ratzeburg (principality)	374	10,000
Prussian lands		
Halberstadt (ex-bishopric)	1,705	96,000
Magdeburg (ex-archbishopric)	5,005	269,000
Danish lands		
Holstein-Glückstadt (duchy)	3,850 ⎫	
Rantzau (county)	247.5 ⎬	150,000
Holstein-Gottorp (duchy) (held since 1773)	3,850	150,000
Swedish lands		
Wismar (part of duchy of Güstrow)	181.5	9,600
Total	*54,560*	*1,967,600*
Ecclesiastical		
Hildesheim (bishopric)	1,760	100,000
Lübeck (bishopric)	522.5	22,000
Total	*2,282.5*	*122,000*
Civic		
Hamburg	412.5	150,000
Lübeck	275	45,000
Bremen	192.5	50,000
Mühlhausen	220	13,000
Nordhausen	55	7,800
Goslar	city only	9,000
Total	*1,155*	*274,800*
Total	**57,997.5**	**2,364,400**
Upper Saxon		
Secular		
Prussian lands		
Brandenburg (electorate)	36,520	980,000
Hinterpommern [Pomerania] (duchy)	22,000	420,000
Vorderpommern (duchy)	4,400	60,000
Cammin (principality: ex-bishopric)	2,365	(incl. with Pomerania)
Mansfeld (county) (two-fifths share)	440	(incl. with Magdeburg)
Klettenberg (lordship)	385	(incl. with Halberstadt)
	(66,110)	(1,460,000)

Territory	Size (km^2)	Population
Saxon lands		
Sachsen-Wittenberg (electorate) ⎫		
Thuringia (landgraviate)		
Meissen (ex-bishopric) ⎬	24,750	1,350,000
Merseburg (ex-bishopric)		
Naumburg-Zeitz (ex-bishopric) ⎭		
Querfurt (principality)	825 ⎫	
Barby (county)	110 ⎬	80,000
Mansfeld (county) (three-fifths share)	660 ⎭	
	(26,345)	(1,430,000)*
Anhalt (princes) **		
Dessau	1,100	53,000
Köthen	880	28,800
Bernberg	880 ⎫	
ex-abbey of Gernrode (to Bernberg)	110 ⎭	35,000
	(2,970)	(116,800)
Saxon duchies (Ernestine Wettins)		
Gotha	1,540	82,000
Altenburg (to Gotha)	1,430	104,000
Saalfeld (principality)		
(to Sachsen-Coburg-Saalfeld)	495	22,000
Weimar	1,320	64,000
Coburg***	1,265	75,000
Eisenach (to Weimar)	440	30,000
	(6,490)	(377,000)
Vorderpommern (incl. Rügen island) (to Sweden)	4,400	104,748
Reuss (princes)†	1,595	77,000
Hartenstein (county) ⎫		
(to Prince Schönburg-Waldenburg) ⎬	1,375	68,000
Glauchau (lordship)		
(to Prince Schönburg-Glauchau) ⎭		
Gleichen (county), Kranichfeld and Blankenhayn		
(lordships) (to Mainz)	137.5	6,000
Schwarzburg-Sondershausen (principality)	880	44,000
Schwarzburg-Rudolstadt (principality)	990	50,000
Stolberg (counties)‡	825	41,000
Hohenstein (county) (to Lüneburg,		
i.e. Hanover)	55	2,000
Walkenried (ex-abbey) (to Wolfenbüttel)	165	8,000
Total	*112,337.5*	*3,784,548*

Territory	Size (km^2)	Population
Ecclesiastical		
Quedlinburg (convent)	110	2,000
Total	**112,447.5**	**3,786,548**

 * Plus outside the Kreis structure: Upper and
  Lower Lausitz   9,625   369,185
 ** Incorporating the Zerbst line that died out in 1793.
*** Split between Meiningen, Coburg-Saalfeld, and Hildburghausen.
 † Split into 5 lines: Greiz, Gera, Schleiz, Lobenstein, Ebersdorf.
 ‡ Split into 5 parts shared by 3 lines: Roßla, Stolberg, Wernigerode.

Lands outside the Kreise

Territory	Size (km^2)	Population
Imperial Knights		
Swabian	3,855	160,000
Franconian	4,400	200,000
Rhenish	2,200	90,000
	(10,455)	(450,000)
Free commune Hammersbach	82.5	2,000
Upper and Lower Lausitz (to Saxony)	9,625	369,185
Silesia (to Prussia)	37,400	1,776,000
Bohemia, Moravia and Austrian Silesia	76,230	4,496,864
Total in Kreise	552,546.36	22,141,960
Total Reich	687,338.86	29,236,009

Appendix 3: The imperial cities, c.1800

City	Kreis	Population Within walls	Outside	Territory (km²)	Religion	Army
Aachen	Westf.	15,000	10,000	110	RC	100
Aalen	Swab.	1,932	368	44	Prot	–
Augsburg	Swab.	36,300		110	Bi-	250
Biberach	Swab.	4,651	3,000	138	Bi-	–
Bopfingen	Swab.	2,000	–	44	Prot.	–
Bremen	Low. Sax.	50,000		193	Prot.	560
Buchau	Swab.	860	–	17	RC	–
Buchhorn	Swab.	470	300	28	RC	–
Cologne	Westf.	54,000	–	city only	RC	258
Dinkelsbühl	Swab.	8,000	–	55	Bi-	–
Dortmund	Westf.	4,500	1,500	127	Prot.	100
Esslingen	Swab.	11,000	–	83	Prot.	–
Frankfurt	Up. Rh.	46,000	–	122	Prot.	600
Friedberg	Up. Rh.	2,000	–	city only	Prot.	19
Gelnhausen	Up. Rh.	[status disputed]				
Gengenbach	Swab.	500	1,500	110	RC	–
Giengen	Swab.	1,700	–	28	Prot.	–
Goslar	Low. Sax.	9,000	–	city only	Prot.	60
Hamburg	Low. Sax.	130,000	20,000	413	Prot.	1,770
Heilbronn	Swab.	5,869	3,375	55	Prot.	100
Isny	Swab.	1,300	–	28	Prot.	–
Kaufbeuren	Swab.	4,100	2,900	110	Bi-	–
Kempten	Swab.	4,000	–	44	Prot.	–
Leutkirch	Swab.	1,750	–	28	Prot.	–
Lindau	Swab.	2,800	4,200	83	Prot.	–
Lübeck	Low. Sax.	45,000		275	Prot.	500

City	Kreis	Population		Territory (km²)	Religion	Army
		Within walls	Outside			
Memmingen	Swab.	6,000	6,000	110	Prot.	–
Mühlhausen	Low. Sax.	13,000		220	Prot.	100
Nordhausen	Low. Sax.	7,800	–	55	Prot.	100
Nördlingen	Swab.	8,000	8,000	83	Prot.	–
Nuremberg	Franc.	30,000	40,000	1,650	Prot.	1,000
Offenburg	Swab.	1,800	–	17	RC	–
Pfullendorf	Swab.	4,000	–	55	Prot.	–
Ravensburg	Swab.	3,300	1,700	138	Bi-	–
Regensburg	Bav.	20,000	–	26	RC	200
Reutlingen	Swab.	7,986	2,514	39	Prot.	–
Rothenburg	Franc.	24,000		275	Prot.	–
Rottweil	Swab.	2,695	10,638	220	RC	300
Schwäbisch-Gmünd	Swab.	5,600	9,400	165	RC	–
Schwäbisch-Hall	Swab.	4,958	9,792	330	Prot.	
Schweinfurt	Franc.	6,000	6,000	110	Prot.	–
Speyer	Up. Rh.	6,000	–	55	Prot.	20
Überlingen	Swab.	2,645	2,770	248	RC	–
Ulm	Swab.	15,000	23,000	930	Prot.	388
Wangen	Swab.	1,800	2,200	83	RC	–
Weissenburg	Franc.	3,000	3,500	55	Prot.	–
Weil der Stadt	Swab.	1,790	–	22	RC	–
Wetzlar	Up. Rh.	6,000	–	14	Prot.	20
Wimpfen	Swab.	3,000		55	Prot.	–
Windsheim	Franc.	4,000	–	55	Prot.	–
Worms	Up. Rh.	6,000	–	city only	Prot.	34
Zell	Swab.	3,000	2,000	110	RC	–

Total
  population: 814,763
Total territory   7,365 km²

Appendix 4: The Ecclesiastical Territories, 1792

	Territory (km²)	Population	Revenue (fl)	Army
Electorates				
Mainz	9,927	336,000	2,250,000	3,082
Cologne	7,480	238,000	1,500,000	1,100
Trier	7,150	240,000	840,000	1,200
Archbishoprics, Bishoprics and Prince-Priories				
Augsburg	2,475	92,000	300,000	350
Bamberg	3,575	192,000	834,000	700
Basel	1,045	16,000	?	–
Berchtesgaden	770	18,000	69,000	paid Bavaria
Brixen	935	30,000	?	–
Constance	275	14,000	?	100
Eichstätt	1,100	62,000	225,000	200
Ellwangen	374	20,000	120,000	60
Freising	825	25,000	170,000	paid Bavaria
Fulda	1,815	90,000	?	200
Hildesheim	2,530	100,000	750,000	100
Kempten	880	50,000	100,000	–
Liege	5,775	286,000	1,185,340	1,000
Lübeck	522	22,000	?	–
Münster	10,500	350,000	1,200,000	1,800
Osnabrück	2,750	125,000	200,000	–
Paderborn	2,750	120,000	150,000	200
Passau	825	24,000	20,000	200
Regensburg	330	10,000	111,380	paid Bavaria
Salzburg	10,450	200,000	1,200,000	1,000
Speyer	1,540	50,000	?	200
St John	220	?	?	?

	Territory (km²)	Population	Revenue (fl)	Army
Archbishoprics, Bishoprics and Prince-Priories (continued)				
Strasbourg	358	20,000	?	–
Teutonic Order	743*	130,000	895,000	–
Trent	4,125	155,000	?	–
Worms	220	12,000	18,000	60
Würzburg	4,950	262,000	1,291,450	3,700
Prelates				
25 Swabian	3,135	54,681	?	?
2 Upper Rhenish	275	6,800	?	?
7 Westphalian	1,722.5	26,900	?	?
1 Upper Saxon	110	2,000		
3 Bavarian	no lands		?	–

* Only 275 was sovereign

Guide to Further Reading

There are few books in English that survey German history between 1558 and 1806. Michael Hughes presents a fairly positive picture of the old Reich in *Early Modern Germany, 1477–1806* (Basingstoke, 1992), while J. Gagliardo offers a more traditional perspective in *Germany under the Old Regime, 1600–1790* (London, 1991). The early seventeenth century is well covered by R. G. Asch, *The Thirty Years War: The Holy Roman Empire and Europe, 1618–48* (Basingstoke, 1997), while the period thereafter is given uneven treatment in R. Vierhaus, *Germany in the Age of Absolutism* (Cambridge, 1989). The later part of the period is rather better covered by J. J. Sheehan, *German History, 1770–1866* (Oxford, 1989), and B. Simms, *The Struggle for Mastery in Germany, 1775–1850* (Basingstoke, 1998).

The literature on the Reich and its institutions is discussed by P. H. Wilson, *The Holy Roman Empire, 1495–1806* (Basingstoke, 1999), while the same author's *German Armies: War and German Politics 1648–1806* (London, 1998) provides extensive further references on imperial politics and military affairs. The debate on the imperial constitution is covered by P. Schroeder, 'The Constitution of the Holy Roman Empire after 1648', *HJ*, 42 (1999), 961–83, and J. Gagliardo, *Reich and Nation: The Holy Roman Empire as Myth and Reality, 1763–1906* (Bloomington, 1980). Important historiographical essays include V. Press, 'The Holy Roman Empire in German History', in E. I. Kouri and T. Scott (eds), *Politics and Society in Reformation Europe* (Basingstoke, 1987), pp. 51–77; T. C. W. Blanning, 'Empire and State in Germany, 1648–1848', *GH*, 12 (1994), 220–36; and the excellent collection of articles in the special issue of the *JMH*, supplement vol. 58 (1986). Derek Croxton makes an important reappraisal of the Peace of Westphalia in 'The Peace of Westphalia of 1648 and the Origins of Sovereignty', *IHR*, 21 (1999), 569–91, and also jointly edits a survey of the wide literature on the topic with A. Tischer, *The Peace of Westphalia: A Historical Dictionary* (Westport, 2002).

Little is yet available in English on the processes of law and conflict resolution, though there is an important study of the *Reichshofrat* by M. Hughes, *Law and Politics in 18th Century Germany* (Woodbridge, 1988). The internal workings of popular protest are brilliantly illuminated by D. M. Leubke, *His Majesty's Rebels: Communities, Factions and Rural Revolt in the Black Forest, 1725–1745* (Ithaca, 1997), while the wider debate on this topic is surveyed by T. Scott. 'Peasant Revolts in Early Modern Germany', *HJ*, 28 (1985), 455–68. Important works on political culture include R. von Friedeberg, *Self Defence and Religious Strife in Early Modern Europe: England and Germany, 1530–1680* (Aldershot, 2002); J. C. Wolfart, *Religion, Government and Political Culture in Early Modern Germany: Lindau, 1520–1628* (Basingstoke, 2002); M. Walker, *German Home Towns: Community, Estate and General Estate 1648–1871* (Ithaca, 1973); and E. Hellmuth (ed.), *The Transformation of Political Culture* (Oxford, 1990). Three other works offer some insights into the Kreise: J. A. Vann, *The Swabian Kreis. Institutional Growth in the Holy Roman Empire, 1648–1715* (Brussels, 1975); R. Wines, 'The Imperial Circles, Princely Diplomacy and Imperial Reform, 1681–1714', *JMH*, 39 (1967), 1–29; R. H. Thompson, *Lothar Franz von Schönborn and the Diplomacy of the Electorate of Mainz* (The Hague, 1974). There are biographies of individual emperors, though these generally focus on their role as Habsburg monarchs: P. S. Fichtner, *Emperor Maxmilian II* (New Haven, 2001); R. J. W. Evans, *Rudolf II and his World* (2nd edn; London, 1997); J. P. Spielman, *Leopold I of Austria* (London, 1977); C. Ingrao, *In Quest and Crisis: Emperor Joseph I and the Habsburg Monarchy* (West Lafayette, 1974); T. C. W. Blanning, *Joseph II* (Harlow, 1994); D. Beales, *Joseph II* (Cambridge, 1986).

The individual territories are rather better covered. Charles Ingrao's *The Habsburg Monarchy, 1618–1815* (2nd edn; Cambridge, 2000), and P. S. Fichtner, *The Habsburg Monarchy, 1490–1848* (Basingstoke, 2003), are the best starting points on this subject and have extensive references to other works in English. Jean Berenger offers a fuller account in *A History of the Habsburg Empire, 1273–1918* (2 vols; Harlow, 1994–7). For the earlier period, R. J. W. Evans, *The Making of the Habsburg Monarchy, 1550–1700* (Oxford, 1977), remains fundamental, while the later part is given detailed coverage in R. Okey, *The Habsburg Monarchy, 1765–1918* (Basingstoke, 2001). Important detailed studies include K. J. MacHardy, *War, Religion and Court Patronage in Habsburg Austria: The Social and Cultural Dimensions of Political Interaction, 1521–1622* (Basingstoke, 2003); P. G. M.

Dickson, *Finance and Government under Maria Theresia, 1740–1780* (2 vols; Oxford, 1987); and F. A. J. Szabo, *Kaunitz and Enlightened Absolutism, 1753–1780* (Cambridge, 1994). Recent research on Prussia is summarised in P. Dwyer (ed.), *The Rise of Prussia: Rethinking Prussian History, 1700–1830* (Harlow, 2000), while the older perspective is presented by H. W. Koch, *A History of Prussia* (London, 1978). Prussian administration and its impact are covered by W. Hubatsch, *Frederick the Great: Absolutism and Administration* (London, 1975), and H. Johnson, *Frederick the Great and his Officials* (New Haven, 1975). Of the numerous biographies of the Prussian rulers, a few stand out: D. McKay, *The Great Elector* (Harlow, 2001); T. Schieder, *Frederick the Great* (Harlow, 1999).

English-language coverage of the smaller territories is patchy. Despite its title, G. Benecke's *Society and Politics in Germany, 1500–1750* (London, 1974) is actually a useful study of the lesser Westphalian territories. Works on the ecclesiastical territories include T. C. W. Blanning, *Reform and Revolution in Mainz, 1743–1803* (Cambridge, 1974); G. Benecke, 'The German Reichskirche', in W. J. Callahan and D. Higgs (eds), *Church and Society in Catholic Europe of the 18th Century* (Cambridge, 1979); J. B. Knudsen, *Justus Moser and the German Enlightenment* (Cambridge, 1986), which has some information on Osnabrück. The special issue of *GH*, vol. 20 (2000), has good articles on the electorates, while other monographs explore the varied experience of the medium territories: J. A. Vann, *The Making of a State: Württemberg, 1593–1793* (Ithaca, 1984); P. H. Wilson, *War, State and Society in Württemberg, 1677–1793* (Cambridge, 1995); C. Ingrao, *The Hessian Mercenary State: Ideas, Institutions and Reform under Frederick II, 1760–85* (Cambridge, 1985); P. K. Taylor, *Indentured to Liberty: Peasant Life and the Hessian Military State, 1688–1815* (Ithaca, 1994); T. Robisheaux, *Rural Society and the Search for Order in Early Modern Germany* (Cambridge, 1989) [on Hohenlohe]. The last two titles are particularly useful for state–societal relations, as is Karl Wegert's excellent *Popular Culture, Crime and Social Control in 18th Century Württemberg* (Wiesbaden, 1994). Some insight into the minor territories is provided by M. J. Legates, 'The Knights and the Problem of Political Organisation in Sixteenth-century Germany', *CEH*, 7 (1974), 99–136; T. J. Glas-Hoschstetter, 'The Imperial Knights in Post-Westphalian Mainz', *CEH*, 11 (1978), 131–49; W. Jannen Jr, '"Das liebe Teutschland" in the 17th Century – Count George Frederick of Waldeck', *European Studies Review*, 6 (1976), 165–95.

Some of the key works on German political development and its impact are now available in translation: O. Brunner, *Land and Lordship: Structures of Government in Medieval Austria* (Philadelphia, 1992); G. Oestreich, *Neo-stoicism and the Early Modern State* (Cambridge, 1982); O. Büsch, *Military Life and Social System in Old Regime Prussia, 1713–1807* (Atlantic Highlands, 1997). Some interesting comparisons are drawn with British history by the articles in J. Brewer and E. Hellmuth (eds), *Rethinking Leviathan* (Oxford, 1999), while the debate on absolutism, its institutions and impact is explored by P. H. Wilson, *Absolutism in Central Europe* (London, 2000), which offers further references. For the Estates, F. L. Carsten, *Princes and Parliaments in Germany* (Oxford, 1959) remains indispensable as a source of information and a powerful liberal argument. More recent perspectives are offered in the excellent collection edited by R. J. W Evans and T. V. Thomas, *Crown, Church and Estates* (New York, 1991).

The older literature on social discipline and confessionalisation is summarised by R. Po-Chia Hsia, *Social Discipline in the Reformation: Central Europe, 1550–1750* (London, 1989), while important German contributions are available in translation in K. V. Greyerz (ed.), *Religion and Society in Early Modern Europe, 1500–1800* (London, 1984). For the debate on confessionalisation, see J. Harrington and H. Walser Smith, 'Confessionalisation, Community and State Building in Germany, 1555–1870', *JMH*, 69 (1997), 77–101, and the important recent contribution by M. R. Forster, *Catholic Renewal in the Age of the Baroque* (New York, 2001), which includes extensive references. The traditional perspective is offered by F. Eyck, *Religion and Politics in German History* (Basingstoke, 1998), while Protestantism's impact is covered by N. Hope, *German and Scandinavian Protestantism, 1700–1918* (Oxford, 1995); B. Nischan, *Prince, People and Confession: The Second Reformation in Brandenburg* (Philadelphia, 1994); and M. Fulbrook, *Piety and Politics: Religion and the Rise of Absolutism in England, Württemberg and Prussia* (Cambridge, 1983).

The best starting points in English for social and economic history are T. Scott, *Society and Economy in Germany, 1300–1600* (Basingstoke, 2002), and S. Ogilvie and R. Scribner (eds), *Germany: A New Social and Economic History* (2 vols; London, 1996), both of which contain extensive further references. William Hagen offers an important reappraisal of East Elbian agrarian society in *Ordinary Prussians: Brandenburg Junkers and Villages, 1500–1840* (Cambridge, 2002), which can be supplemented by the useful shorter articles by the contributors to T. Scott (ed.), *The Peasantries of Europe* (London, 1998), and H. M. Scott (ed.), *The European Nobilities in the 17th and 18th Centuries*, vol. II (Harlow, 1994). The world of the village is explored by J. C. Theibault, *German Villages in Crisis: Rural Life in Hesse-Kassel and the Thirty Years War, 1580–1720* (Atlantic Highlands, 1995), while its political importance is discussed by the prolific Peter Blickle, whose ideas are most accessible through his *Obedient Germans? A Rebuttal* (Charlottesville, 1997) and 'Communalism, parliamentarianism and Republicanism', *Parliaments, Estates and Representation*, 8 (1986), 1–13.

Important examples of the modern approach to cultural history include K. Stuart, *Defiled Trades and Social Outcasts* (Cambridge, 1999); N. Schindler, *Rebellion, Community and Custom in Early Modern Germany* (Cambridge, 2002); and those by D. W. Sabean, *The Power in the Blood: Popular Culture and Village Discourse in Early Modern Germany* (Cambridge, 1984); *Property, Production and Family in Neckarhausen, 1700–1870* (Cambridge, 1990); *Kinship in Neckarhausen, 1700–1870* (Cambridge, 1997). The literature on gender is now extensive. Heide Wunder, *He is the Sun, She is the Moon: Women in Early Modern Germany* (Cambridge, Mass., 1998), and M. E. Wiesner, *Gender, Church and State in Early Modern Germany* (London, 1998), offer good recent introductions. Important specialist studies include J. M. Harrington, *Reordering Marriage and Society in Reformation Germany* (Cambridge, 1995); U. Rublack, *The Crimes of Women in Early Modern Germany* (Oxford, 1999), and her edited collection *Gender in Early Modern German History* (Cambridge, 2002).

German involvement in international conflicts is dealt with by I. Parvev, *Habsburgs and Ottomans: Between Vienna and Belgrade (1683–1739)* (Boulder, 1995); J. Lynn, *The Wars of Louis XIV, 1667–1714* (Harlow, 1999); D. E. Showalter, *The Wars of Frederick the Great* (Harlow, 1996); H. M. Scott, *The Emergence of the Eastern Powers, 1756–1775* (Cambridge, 2001); P. W. Schroeder, *The Transformation of European Politics, 1763–1848* (Oxford, 1994). The varied responses of the lesser territories can be gauged from J. T. O'Connor, *Negotiator Out of Season* (Athens, Geo., 1975); M. Umbach, *Federalism and Enlightenment in Germany, 1740–1806* (London, 2000). The impact of the French Revolution is critically analysed by T. C. W. Blanning, *The Origins of the French Revolutionary Wars* (London, 1986), and his *The French Revolution in Germany: Occupation and Resistance in the Rhineland, 1792–1802* (Oxford, 1983). Further coverage is provided by K. A. Roider, *Baron Thugut and Austria's Response to the French Revolution* (Princeton, 1987), and P. P. Bernard, *From the Enlightenment to the Police State* (Urbana, 1991). The subsequent reorganisation is briefly surveyed by M. Rowe, 'Napoleon and State Formation in Central Europe', in P. G. Dwyer (ed.), *Napoleon and Europe* (Harlow, 2001), pp. 204–24, which offers useful suggestions for further reading, as do the contributions by A. Fahrmeir and J. Breuilly, in M. Rowe (ed.), *Collaboration and Resistance in Napoleonic Europe* (Basingstoke, 2003).

Notes

Chapter 1: The Pecularities of German History

1. For further discussion regarding the implications for early modern German history, see W. Hagen, 'Descent of the Sonderweg: Hans Rosenberg's History of Old-regime Prussia', *CEH*, 24 (1991), 24–50; T. A. Brady, *Communities, Politics and Reformation in Early Modern Europe* (Leiden, 1998); S. Skalweit, 'Preußen als historisches Problem', *Jahrbuch für die Geschichte Mittel- und Ostdeutschlands*, 3 (1954), 189–210.
2. P. C. Hartmann, *Kulturgeschichte des Heiligen Römischen Reiches 1648 bis 1806* (Vienna, 2001).
3. G. Schmidt, *Geschichte des alten Reiches. Staat und Nation in der frühen Neuzeit 1495–1806* (Munich, 1999).
4. G. Benecke, *Society and Politics in Germany 1500–1750* (London, 1974); W. Fühnrohr, *Der Immerwährende Reichstag zu Regensburg. Das Parlament des alten Reiches* (2nd edn; Regensburg, 1987); D. Langewiesche/G. Schmidt (eds), *Föderative Nation. Deutschland Konzepte von der Reformation bis zum Ersten Weltkrieg* (Munich, 2000). For a critical survey, see A. Kohler, 'Das Heilige Römische Reich – ein Föderativsystem?', in T. Fröschl (ed.), *Föderationsmodelle und Unionsstrukturen* (Munich, 1994), pp. 118–26, and M. Umbach (ed.), *German Federalism. Past, Present and Future* (Basingstoke, 2002).
5. E. W. Böckenförde, 'Der Westfälische Friede und das Bündnisrecht der Reichsstände', *Der Staat*, 8 (1969), 449–78.
6. T. A. Brady, *Turning Swiss: Cities and Empire, 1450–1550* (Cambridge, 1985). See also sections 3.4 and 6.3.

Chapter 2: Reich and Territories

1. R. Collins, *Charlemagne* (Basingstoke, 1998), pp. 144–59; H. K. Schulze, *Vom Reich der Franken zum Land der Deutschen* (Berlin, 1998), pp. 188–95.

2. Recent overviews include H. K. Schulze, *Hegemoniales Kaisertum: Ottonen und Salier* (Berlin, 1998); H. Boockmann, *Stauferzeit und spätes Mittelalter in Deutschland 1125–1517* (Berlin, 1998).

3. H. Weisert, 'Der Reichstitel bis 1806', *Archiv für Diplomatik*, 40 (1994), 441–513.

4. W. Hermkes, *Das Reichsvikariat in Deutschland. Reichsvikare nach dem Tode des Kaisers von der Goldenen Bulle bis zum Ende des Reiches* (Bonn, 1968).

5. For good overviews of the individual territories, see G. Köbler, *Historisches Lexikon der deutschen Länder* (5th edn; Munich, 1995); G.W. Sante (ed.), *Geschichte der deutschen Länder*, vol.1 (Würzburg, 1964). See Appendix 2 for a full list of territories. For the Rhineland and Hessen, see M. Braubach, *Rheinische Geschichte*, vol.1 (Düsseldorf, 1976); W. Dotzauer, 'Das Rheinland in der zweiten Hälfte des 17. Jahrhunderts', *Jahrbuch für westdeutsche Landesgeschichte*, 2 (1976), 195–209; K. E. Demandt, *Geschichte des Landes Hessen* (Kassel, 1980).

6. W. Kohl (ed.), *Westfälische Geschichte*, vol.1 (Düsseldorf, 1983).

7. *Das Land Baden-Württemberg* (issued by the Staatliche Archivverwaltung Baden-Württembergs, Stuttgart, 1974), vol. I; K. S. Bader, *Der deutsche Südwesten in seiner territorialstaatlichen Entwicklung* (2nd edn; Sigmaringen, 1978).

8. E. Weis, 'Das Haus Wittelsbach in der europäischen Politik der Neuzeit', *ZBLG*, 44 (1981), 211–31; M. Spindler (ed.), *Handbuch der bayerischen Geschichte* (2nd edn, 2 vols; Munich, 1988).

9. H. Patze and W. Schlesinger (eds), *Geschichte Thüringens* (5 vols; Cologne, 1982).

10. See the two useful pieces by J. Pánek, 'Der böhmische Staat und das Reich in der frühen Neuzeit', in V. Press (ed.), *Alternativen zur Reichsverfassung in der frühen Neuzeit?* (Munich, 1995), pp. 169–78; and 'Das politische system des böhmischen Staates im ersten Jahrhundert der Habsburgischen Herrschaft (1526–1620)', *MIÖG*, 92 (1989), 53–82.

11. J. Berenger, *A History of the Habsburg Monarchy 1273–1918* (2 vols; Harlow, 1994–7). Additional references are given in the Guide to Further Reading.

12. N. Mout, 'Die Niederlande und das Reich im 16. Jahrhundert (1512–1609)', in Press (ed.), *Alternativen*, pp. 143–68; J. Israel, *The Dutch Republic: Its Rise, Greatness and Fall, 1477–1806* (Oxford, 1995).

13. J. Lukowski, *Liberty's Folly: The Polish-Lithuanian Commonwealth in the Eighteenth Century, 1697–1795* (London, 1991); T. Sharp, *Pleasure and Ambition: The Life, Loves and Wars of Augustus the Strong* (London, 2001).

14. A. M. Birke and K. Kluxen (eds), *England und Hannover, Hanover and England* (Munich, 1986); U. Dann, *Hanover and Great Britain 1740–1760* (Leicester, 1991).

15. For her German connections, see C. Scharf, *Katharina II: Deutschland und die Deutschen* (Mainz, 1995).

16. W. Carr, *Schleswig-Holstein 1815–1848. A Study in National Conflict* (Manchester, 1963); L. Steefel, *The Schleswig-Holstein Question* (Cambridge, Mass., 1932).

17. More detail can be found in the useful series of books by B. Arnold, *Princes and Territories in Medieval Germany* (Cambridge, 1991); *German Knighthood, 1050–1300* (Oxford, 1985); *Medieval Germany, 500–1300* (Basingtoke, 1997). For the transition to the sixteenth century, see E. Schubert, 'Die Umformung spätmittelalterlicher Fürstenherrschaft im 16. Jahrhundert', *Rheinische Vierteljahresblätter*, 63 (1999), 204–63.

18. For Charles V and his religious policies, see the recent overviews in H. Soly (ed.), *Charles V, 1500–1558* (Antwerp, 1998); W. Blockmans, *Emperor Charles V, 1500–1558* (London, 2002); W. Maltby, *The Reign of Charles V* (Basingstoke, 2002).

19. E. W. Zeeden, 'Grundlagen und Wege der Konfessionsbildung in Deutschland im Zeitalter der Glaubenskämpfe', *HZ*, 185 (1958), 249–99; H. Schilling, *Religion, Political Culture and the Emergence of Early Modern Society* (Leiden, 1992), pp. 247–301; W. Reinhard, 'Pressures towards Confessionalisation? Prolegomena to a Theory of the Confessional Age', in C. S. Dixon (ed.), *The German Reformation* (Oxford, 1999), pp. 169–92. For a comprehensive survey of all territories, see A. Schindling and W. Ziegler (eds), *Die Territorien des Reiches im Zeitalter der Reformation in der Konfessionalisierung* (7 vols; Munich, 1989–97).

20. P. Moraw, 'Versuch über die Entstehung des Reichstages', in H. Weber (ed.), *Politische Ordnungen und soziale Kräfte im alten Reich* (Wiesbaden, 1980), pp. 1–36. For its subsequent development and operation, see A. Schindling, *Die Anfänge des immerwährenden Reichstags zu Regensburg* (Mainz, 1991); K. Härter, *Reichstag und Revolution 1789–1806* (Göttingen, 1994).

21. K. Schlaich, 'Die Mehrheitsabstimmung im Reichstag zwischen 1495 und 1613', *ZHF*, 10 (1983), 299–340.

22. G. Schmidt, 'Die "deutsche Freiheit" und der Westfälische Friede', in R. G. Asch et al. (eds), *Frieden und Krieg in der frühen Neuzeit* (Munich, 2001), pp. 323–47.

23. A. Gotthard, *Säulen des Reiches. Die Kurfürsten im frühneuzeitlichen Reichsverband* (Husum, 1999).

24. L. Pelizaeus, *Der Aufstiegs Württembergs und Hessens zur Kurwürde 1692–1806* (Frankfurt, 2000). Though Salzburg and Würzburg were originally church lands, they were transformed into secular territories in 1803.

25. Reichstag meetings took place in 1559, 1566, 1567, 1570, 1576, 1582, 1594, 1597–8, 1603, 1608 and 1613. There were no more until 1641. The electoral congress met in 1608, 1611, 1620, 1627, 1630, 1636–7, 1640, 1645, 1652 and 1657–8.

26. M. J. Legates, 'The Knights and the Problem of Political Organisation in Sixteenth-century Germany', *CEH*, 7 (1974), 99–136; V. Press, 'Kaiser und Reichsritterschaft', in R. Endres (ed.), *Adel in der Frühneuzeit* (Cologne, 1991), pp. 163–94.

27. Kulenkampff, 'Einungen und Reichsstandschaft fränkischer Grafen und Herren 1402–1641', *Württembergisch Franken*, 55 (1971), 16–41; J. Arndt,

Das Niederrheinisch-westfälische Reichsgrafenkollegium und seine Mitglieder (1653–1806) (Mainz, 1991); E. Böhme, *Das fränkische Reichsgrafenkollegium im 16. und 17. Jahrhundert* (Stuttgart, 1989).

28. Halberstadt, Verden, Minden, Schwerin, Kammin and Ratzeburg.

29. Meißen, Naumburg and Merseburg went to electoral Saxony. Lebus, Brandenburg and Havelburg went to Brandenburg, which was already well on the way to incorporating them within its territory before the Reformation.

30. Gurk, Sekkau and Lavant.

31. The following were secularised: Hersfeld, Saalfeld, Walkenried, Maulbronn, Herrenalb, Königsbronn and the convent of Kaufingen. The three Protestant convents were Quedlinburg, Gernrode and Gandersheim.

32. The bishoprics of Wallis, Geneva and Lausanne; the abbeys of St Gallen, Kreuzlingen, Beckenried, Stein am Rhein, Schaffhausen and Einsiedeln.

33. Nine abbots: Fulda, Kempten, Weißenburg, Ellwangen, Murbach-Lüders, Corvey, Stablo, Berchtesgaden, Prüm. Plus the grandmasters of the Teutonic Order (1529) and knights of St John (1548). Though the Teutonic Order lost its lands in Prussia and Livonia, it retained small territories in southern Germany.

34. Important examples include Fürstenberg, Schwarzenberg, Schwarzburg, East Frisia, Waldeck, Solms, Nassau, Arenberg, and the Catholic branch of the Hohenzollerns.

35. Eggenberg, Dietrichstein, Auersperg, Thurn und Taxis, Lobkowitz, Liechtenstein and Kaunitz.

36. Khevenhüller, Colloredo, Windischgrätz, Starhemberg, Wurmbrand, Pückler, Harrach and Neipperg.

37. T. Klein, 'Die Erhebungen in der weltlichen Reichsfürstenstand 1550–1806', *BDLG*, 122 (1986), 137–92.

38. Brandenburg (8 votes), Hanover (6), Palatinate (6), Saxony (5), Bohemia (3), Bavaria (2).

39. O. F. Winter, 'Österreichische Pläne zur Neuformierung des Reichstages 1801–1806', *MÖSA*, 15 (1962), 261–335.

40. G. Kleinheyer, *Die Kaiserlichen Wahlkapitulationen* (Karlsruhe, 1968).

41. H. M. Empell, 'De eligendo regis vivente imperatore. Die Regelung in der Beständigen Wahlkapitulation und ihre Interpretation in der Staatsrechtsliteratur des 18. Jahrhunderts', *ZNRG*, 16 (1994), 11–24.

42. C. Kampmann, *Reichsrebellion und kaiserliche Acht. Politische Strafjustiz im Dreißigjährigen Krieg und das Verfahren gegen Wallenstein 1634* (Münster, 1992), and his '"Der Leib des Römischen Reiches ist der Stände Eigentum und nicht des Kaisers". Zur Entstehung der Konkurrenz zwischen Kaiserhof und Reichstag beim Achtverfahren', in W. Sellert (ed.), *Reichshofrat und Reichskammergericht* (Cologne, 1999), pp. 169–98.

43. W. Troßbach, 'Fürstenabsetzungen im 18. Jahrhundert', *ZHF*, 13 (1986), 425–54.

44. See esp. C. Kampmann, 'Reichstag und Reichskriegserklärung im Zeitalter Ludwigs XIV', *Historische Jahrbuch*, 113 (1993), 41–59, revising the earlier interpretation expressed in K. Müller, 'Zur Reichskriegserklärung im 17. und 18. Jahrhundert', *ZSRG GA*, 90 (1973), 246–59.

Chapter 3: Fundamentals

1. H. Schultz, 'Social Differences in Mortality in the 18th Century: An Analysis of Berlin Church Registers', *International Review of Social History*, 36 (1991), 232–48 at 241. See also H. Wunder, *He is the Sun, She is the Moon* (Cambridge, Mass., 1998), pp. 17–21, 114–18; and W. W. Hagen, *Ordinary Prussians: Brandenburg Junkers and Villagers, 1500–1840* (Cambridge, 2002), pp. 262–78.
2. Fuller discussion can be found in C. Dipper, *Deutsche Geschichte 1648–1789* (Frankfurt, 1991), pp. 66–75.
3. J. F. Harrington, *Reordering Marriage and Society in Reformation Germany* (Cambridge, 1995).
4. I owe these insights to Dr David Lederer's paper at the Workshop on Early Modern German History, held at the German Historical Institute, London, May 2002.
5. This paragraph derives in part from new research by Dr Eve Rosenhaft presented at the Second Workshop on Early Modern German History at the German Historical Institute, London, October 2003. See also the useful articles by B. Wunder on the development of state welfare, 'Die Institutionalisierung der Invaliden-, Alters- und Hinterbliebenenversorgung der Staatsbediensteten in Österreich (1748–1790)', *MIÖG*, 92 (1984), 341–406; and 'Pfarrwitwenkassen und Beamtenwitwen-Anstalten vom 16.–19. Jahrhundert: Die Entstehung der staatlichen Hinterbliebenenversorgung in Deutschland', *ZHF*, 12 (1985), 429–98.
6. B. Lundt, 'Konzepte für eine (Zu-)Ordnung der Geschlechte zu Krieg und Frieden (9. bis 15. Jahrhundert', in K. Garber et al. (eds), *Erfahrung und Deutung von Krieg und Frieden* (Munich, 2001), pp. 335–56; P.H. Wilson, 'German Women and War, 1500–1800', *War in History*, 3 (1996), 127–60; B. Engelen, 'Die Soldatenfrauen der preußischen Armee im späten 17. und im 18. Jahrhundert' (PhD, Potsdam, 2003). See also H. Wunder, 'What Made a Man a Man? Sixteenth- and Seventeenth-century Findings', in U. Rublack (ed.), *Gender in Early Modern German History* (Cambridge, 2002), pp. 21–48.
7. S. C. Ogilvie, 'Women and Proto-industrialisation in a Corporate Society: Württemberg Woollen Weaving, 1590–1760', in P. Hudson and W. R. Lee (eds), *Women's Work and the Family Economy in Historical Perspective* (Manchester, 1990), pp. 76–103; and her 'Coming of Age in a Corporate Society: Capitalism, Pietism and Family Authority in Rural Württemberg', *Continuity and Change*, 1 (1986), 279–331.

8. U. Gleixner, 'Frauen, Justiznutzung und dörfliche Rechtskultur', in Garber et al. (eds), *Erfahrung*, pp. 435–61.

9. U. Rublack, *The Crimes of Women in Early Modern Germany* (Oxford, 1999).

10. Wunder, *He is the Sun*, pp. 193–201.

11. M. E. Wiesner, *Gender, Church and State in Early Modern Germany* (Harlow, 1998), esp. pp. 124–5.

12. T. McIntosh, *Urban Decline in Early Modern Germany: Schwäbisch Hall and its Region, 1650–1750* (Chapel Hill, 1997); S. L. Hochstadt, 'Migration in Pre-industrial Germany', *CEH*, 16 (1983), 195–224.

13. M. Walker, *German Home Towns: Community, State and General Estate, 1648–1871* (Ithaca, 1971).

14. A. Gestreich, *Absolutismus und Öffentlichkeit. Politische Kommunikation in Deutschland zu Beginn des 18. Jahrhunderts* (Göttingen, 1994). See also T. C. W. Blanning, *The Culture of Power and the Power of Culture: Old Regime Europe, 1660–1789* (Oxford, 2002); and J. V. H. Melton, *The Rise of the Public in Enlightenment Europe* (Cambridge, 2001).

15. W. H. Bruford, *Culture and Society in Classical Weimar, 1775–1806* (Cambridge, 1962), p. 61. For the Strasbourg ordinance, see F. L. Ford, *Strasbourg in Transition, 1648–1789* (Cambridge, 1958), pp. 15–16.

16. Further discussion with reference to the wider literature can be found in L. Gall, *Von der ständischen zur bürgerlichen Gesellschaft* (Munich, 1993).

17. A. Flügel, *Bürgerliche Rittergüter. Sozialer Wandel und politische Reform in Kursachsen (1680–1844)* (Göttingen, 2000).

18. H. Schissler, 'The Social and Political Power of the Prussian Junkers', in R. Gibson and M. Blinkhorn (eds), *Landownership and Power in Modern Europe* (London, 1991), pp. 99–110 at 104.

19. J. G. Gagliardo, *From Pariah to Patriot: The Changing Image of the German Peasant, 1770–1840* (Lexington, 1969), p. 29.

20. J. de Vries, *European Urbanisation, 1500–1800* (Cambridge, Mass., 1984); H. T. Gräf, 'Small Towns in Early Modern Germany: The Case of Hesse, 1500–1800', in P. Clark (ed.), *Small Towns in Early Modern Europe* (Cambridge, 1995), pp. 184–205.

21. C. R. Friedrichs, 'Capitalism, Mobility and Class Formation in the Early Modern German City', *P&P*, 69 (1975), 24–49; McIntosh, *Urban Decline*, pp. 76–103.

22. Gestreich, *Absolutismus und Öffentlichkeit*, p. 102.

23. W. von Hippel, *Armut, Unterschichten, Randgruppen in der frühen Neuzeit* (Munich, 1995).

24. W. O. McCagg Jr, *A History of Habsburg Jews, 1670–1918* (Bloomington, 1989).

25. C. Küther, *Menschen auf der Straße. Vagierende Unterschichten in Bayern, Franken und Schwaben in der zweiten Hälfte des 18. Jahrhunderts* (Göttingen, 1983); E. Schubert, *Arme Leute, Bettler und Gauner im Franken des Jahrhunderts* (Neustadt/Aisch, 1983).

26. J. G. Gagliardo, *Germany under the Old Regime, 1600–1790* (Harlow, 1991), p. 128. For fuller coverage, see T. Scott, *Society and Economy in Germany, 1300–1600* (Basingstoke, 2002); S. Ogilivie and R. Scribner (eds), *Germany: A New Social and Economic History* (2 vols; London, 1996).

27. Very useful discussion can be found in Dipper, *Deutsche Geschichte*, pp. 29–41.

28. See W. Kohl (ed.), *Westfälische Geschichte*, vol. I (Düsseldorf, 1983), pp. 658–9. See also P. Blickle, 'Untertanen in der Frühneuzeit. Zur Rekonstruktion der politischen Kultur und der sozialen Wirklichkeit Deutschlands im 17. Jahrhundert', *VSWG*, 70 (1983), 483–522.

29. The recent literature is reviewed by H. Kaak, 'Brandenburgische Bauern im 18. Jahrhundert', in R. Pröve and B. Kölling (eds), *Leben und Arbeiten auf märkischen Sand* (Bielefeld, 1999), pp. 120–48. Important recent contributions include Hagen, *Ordinary Prussians*, and the two collections edited by J. Peters, *Konflikt und Kontrolle in Gutsherrschaftsgesellschaften* (Göttingen, 1995) and *Gutsherrschaft als soziales Modell* (Munich, 1995).

30. Schissler, 'Social and Political; Power of the Prussian Junkers', p. 104.

31. D. M. Luebke, 'Serfdom and Honour in Eighteenth-century Germany', *Social History*, 18 (1993), 141–61; W. Dotzauer, 'Der kurpfälzische Wildfangstreit und seine Auswirkungen im rheinhessisch-pfälzischen Raum', *Geschichtliche Landeskunde*, 25 (1984), 81–105.

32. M. Hochedlinger, 'Rekrutierung – Militarisierung – Modernisierung. Militär und ländliche Gesellschaft in der Habsburgermonarchie im Zeitalter des aufgeklärten Absolutismus', in S. Kroll and K. Krüger (eds), *Militär und ländliche Gesellschaft in der frühen Neuzeit* (Hamburg, 2000), pp. 327–75. See generally, F. A. J. Szabo, *Kaunitz and Enlightened Absolutism, 1753–1780* (Cambridge, 1994), pp. 154–80.

33. L. Enders, 'Die Landgemeinde in Brandenburg. Grundzüge ihrer Funktion und Wirkungsweise vom 13. bis zum 18. Jahrhundert', *BDLG*, 129 (1993), 195–256; H. Harnisch, 'Der preußische Absolutismus und die Bauern. Sozialkonservative Gesellschaftspolitik und Vorleistung zur Modernisierung', *Jahrbuch für Wirtschaftsgechichte*, 2 (1994), 1–32. For a representative example of the older view, see G. Corni, 'Absolutistische Agrarpolitik und Agrargesellschaft in Preussen', *ZHF*, 13 (1987), 285–313.

34. C. Hinrichs, *Friedrich Wilhelm I* (Hamburg, 1941), pp. 468–82.

35. Flügel, *Bürgerliche Rittergüter*, pp. 222–3. See also G. W. Pedlow, *The Survival of the Hessian Nobility, 1770–1870* (Princeton, 1988).

36. P. Wick, *Versuche zur Errichtung des Absolutismus im Mecklenburg in der ersten Hälfte des 18. Jahrhunderts* (Berlin, 1964); M. Hughes, 'Die Strafpreussen: Mecklenburg und der Bund der deutschen absolutischen Fürsten, 1648–1719', *Parliaments, Estates and Representation*, 3 (1984), 101–13.

37. H. Weisert, *Geschichte der Stadt Sindelfingen 1500–1807* (Sindelfingen, 1963); P. Sauer, *Affalterbach 972–1972* (Affalterbach, 1972); and his *Tamm. Geschichte einer Gemeinde* (Ulm, 1980).

38. K. S. Bader, *Studien zur Rechtsgeschichte des mittelalterlichen Dorfes* (3 vols; Vienna, 1957–73); H. Wunder, 'Peasant Communities in Medieval and Early Modern Germany', *Recueils de la Société Jean Bodin pour l'histoire comparative des institutions*, 44 (1987), 9–52.

39. For Peter Blickle's ideas, see his *Obedient Germans? A Rebuttal* (Charlottesville, 1997); 'Communalism, Parliamentarism, Republicanism', *Parliaments, Estates and Representation*, 8 (1986), 1–13; and (ed.), *Communalism, Representation and Resistance* (Oxford, 1997).

40. R. Scribner, 'Communalism: Universal Category or Ideological Construct? A Debate in the Historiography of Early Modern Germany and Switzerland', *HJ*, 37 (1994), 199–207; R. von Friedeberg, ' "Kommunalismus" und "Republikanismus" in der frühe Neuzeit?', *ZHF*, 21 (1994), 65–91.

41. See the excellent discussion by R. Scribner, 'Communities and the Nature of Power', in Ogilvie and Scribner (eds), *Germany*, I, pp. 291–326.

42. L. Roper, ' "The Common Man", "the Common Good", "Common Women"': Gender and Meaning in the German Reformation Commune', *Social History*, 12 (1987), 1–21.

43. D. M. Luebke, *His Majesty's Rebels. Communities, Factions and Rural Revolt in the Black Forest, 1725–1745* (Ithaca, 1997); H. Rebel, *Peasant Classes. The Bureaucratisation of Property and Family Relations under Early Habsburg Administration, 1511–1636* (Princeton, 1983); T. Robisheaux, *Rural Society and the Search for Order in Early Modern Germany* (Cambridge, 1989).

44. P. Warde, 'Law, the "Commune", and the Distribution of Resources in Early Modern German State Formation', *Continuity and Change*, 17 (2002), 183–211. See also section 7.2 below, for further discussion.

Chapter 4: The Great War (1618–48)

1. The debates are analysed by J. Burkhardt, *Der Dreißigjährige Krieg* (Frankfurt, 1992). For the events, see R. G. Asch, *The Thirty Years War: the Holy Roman Empire and Europe, 1618–1648* (London, 1997); and G. Barudio, *Der Teutsche Krieg 1618–1648* (2nd edn; Berlin, 1998).

2. For example, S. H. Steinberg, *The Thirty Years War and The Conflict for European Hegemony 1600–1660* (London, 1966); N. M. Sutherland, 'The Origins of the Thirty Years War and the Structures of European Politics', *EHR*, 107 (1992), 587–625. A more moderate version is expressed in G. Parker (ed.), *The Thirty Years War* (London, 1987).

3. K. Repgen, 'Noch einmal zum Begriff 'Dreißigjähriger Krieg', *ZHF*, 9 (1982), 347–52.

4. G. Parker and L. M. Smith (eds), *The General Crisis of the 17th Century* (London, 1997); G. Parker, *Europe in Crisis, 1598–1648* (London, 1979); T. K. Rabb, *The Struggle for Stability in Early Modern Europe* (New York, 1975); H. Langer, *The Thirty Years War* (Poole, 1980).

5. R. Bireley, 'The Thirty Years War as Germany's Religious War', in K. Repgen (ed.), *Krieg und Politik 1618–1648* (Munich, 1984), pp. 85–106.

6. H. Lutz, 'Friedensideen und Friedensprobleme in der frühen Neuzeit', in G. Heiss and H. Lutz (eds), *Friedensbewegungen, Bedingungen und Wirkungen* (Munich, 1984), pp. 28–54.

7. M. Heckel, 'Automonia und pacis compositio', *ZSRG KA*, 45 (1959), 141–248; and his 'Die Religionsprozesse des Reichskammergerichts im konfessionell gespaltenen Reichskirchenrecht', *ZSRG KA*, 77 (1991), 283–350; H. Rabe, *Deutsche Geschichte 1500–1600* (Munich, 1991).

8. B. Ruthmann, 'Das Richterliche Personal am Reichskammergericht und seine politischen Verbindungen um 1600', in W. Sellert (ed.), *Reichshofrat und Reichskammergericht* (Cologne, 1999), pp. 1–26.

9. W. Schulze, *Reich und Türkengefahr im späten 16. Jahrhundert* (Munich, 1978); A. P. Luttenberger, *Kurfürsten, Kaiser und Reich. Politische Führung und Friedenssicherung unter Ferdinand I. und Maximilian II* (Mainz, 1994); P. S. Fichtner, *Emperor Maximilian II* (New Haven, 2001).

10. H. Gabel, 'Glaube – Individium – Reichsrecht. Toleranzdenken im Reich von Augsburg bis Münster', in H. Lademacher and S. Groenveld (eds), *Krieg und Kultur. Die Rezeption von Krieg und Frieden in der Niederländischen Republik und im Deutschen Reich 1568–1648* (Münster, 1998), pp. 157–77; H. Louthan, *The Quest for Compromise: Peacemaking in Counter-Reformation Vienna* (Cambridge, 1997).

11. H. Sturmberger, *Land ob der Enns und Österreich* (Linz, 1979), pp. 32–75. For the individual emperors, see A. Schindling and W. Ziegler (eds), *Die Kaiser der Neuzeit 1519–1918* (Munich, 1990); R. J. W. Evans, *Rudolf II and his World* (2nd edn; London, 1997); B. Rill, *Kaiser Matthias. Bruderzwist und Glaubenskampf* (Graz, 1999).

12. K. Repgen (ed.), *Das Herrscherbild im 17. Jahrhundert* (Münster, 1991). For the debate on Ferdinand's objectives, see A. Wandruska, 'Zum "Absolutismus" Ferdinands II.', *Mitteilungen des oberösterreichischen Landesarchivs*, 14 (1984), 261–8.

13. D. Albrecht, *Maximilian I. von Bayern 1573–1651* (Munich, 1998), pp. 394–405.

14. A. Gotthard, 'Protestantische "Union" und Katholische "Liga" – subsidiäre Strukturelemente oder Alternativentwürfe?', in V. Press (ed.), *Alternativen zur Reichsverfassung* (Munich, 1995), pp. 81–112.

15. H. Smolinsky, 'Formen und Motive konfessioneller Koexistenz in den Niederlanden und am Niederrhein', in K. Garber et al. (eds), *Erfahrung und Deutung von Krieg und Frieden* (Munich, 2001), pp. 287–300.

16. The founder members were the Palatinate, Württemberg, Baden-Durlach, Ansbach, Kulmbach and Pfalz-Neuburg. Over the next two years they were joined by Hessen-Kassel, Zweibrücken, Brandenburg and 16 imperial cities including Nuremberg, Ulm and Strasbourg. Pfalz-Neuburg left when its ruler converted to Catholicism.

17. J. Müller, 'Die Vermittlungspolitik Klesls von 1613 bis 1616', *MIÖG*, supplement 5 (1896/1903), 609–90; S. Ehrenpreis, 'Die Tätigkeit des Reichshofrats um 1600 in der protestantischen Kritik', in Sellert (ed.), *Reichshofrat und Reichskammergericht*, pp. 27–46

18. P. Broucek, 'Feldmarschall Bucquoy als Armeekommandant 1618–1620', in *Der Dreißigjährige Krieg* (issued by the Heeresgeschichtliches Museum, Vienna, 1976), pp. 25–57.

19. J. Bahlcke, 'Die böhmische Krone zwischen staatsrechtlicher Integrität, monarchischer Union und ständischen Föderalismus', in T. Fröschl (ed.), *Föderationsmodelle und Unionsstrukturen* (Munich, 1994), pp. 83–103; R. R. Heinisch, 'Habsburg, die Pforte und der böhmische Aufstand (1618–1620)', *Südost Forschungen*, 33 (1974), 125–65, and 34 (1975), 79–124.

20. M. Kaiser, *Politik und Kriegführung. Maximilian von Bayern, Tilly und die Katholische Liga im Dreißigjährigen Krieg* (Münster, 1999); D. Albrecht, *Die auswärtige Politik Maximilians von Bayern 1618–1635* (Göttingen, 1962); A. Kraus, *Maximilian I. Bayerns großer Kurfürst* (Graz, 1990).

21. M. Kaiser, 'Ständebund und Verfahrensordnung. Das Beispiel der Katholischen Liga (1619–1631)', in B. Stollberg-Rillinger (ed.), *Vormoderne politische Verfahren* (Berlin, 2001), pp. 331–415; F. Stieve, 'Das "Contobuch" der Deutschen Liga', *Deutsche Zeitschrift für Geschichtswissenschaft*, 10 (1893), 97–106; W. Goetz, 'Die Kriegskosten Bayerns und die Ligastände im Dreißigjährigen Krieg', *Forschungen zur Geschichte Bayerns*, 12 (1904), 109–25.

22. F. Müller, *Kursachsen und der böhmische Aufstand 1618–1622* (Münster, 1997).

23. Military operations are summarised by W. Guthrie, *Battles of the Thirty Years War* (2 vols; Westport, 2002–3).

24. R. von Friedeburg, *Self-defence and Religious Strife in Early Modern Europe. England and Germany, 1530–1680* (Aldershot, 2002).

25. I. Hiller, 'Ungarn als Grenzland des christlichen Europa im 16. und 17. Jahrhundert', in R. G. Asch et al. (eds), *Frieden und Krieg in der frühen Neuzeit* (Munich, 2001), pp. 561–76.

26. P. D. Lockhart, *Denmark in the Thirty Years War, 1618–1648* (Selinsgrove, 1996).

27. F. Redlich, 'Contributions in the Thirty Years War', *Economic History Review*, 2nd series, 12 (1959/60), 247–54; S. Adams, 'Tactics or Politics? "The Military Revolution" and the Hapsburg Hegemony, 1525–1648', in J. A. Lynn (ed.), *Tools of War* (Urbana, 1990), pp. 28–52.

28. G. Mann, *Wallenstein* (Frankfurt, 1971); H. Diwald, *Wallenstein. Eine Biographie* (Munich, 1981).

29. H. Ernst, *Madrid und Wien 1632–1637* (Münster, 1991), p. 311.

30. P. Piirmie, 'Just War in Theory and Practice. The Legitimation of Sweden's Intervention in the Thirty Years War', *HJ*, 45 (2002), 499–523; M. Roberts, *Gustavus Adolphus* (2 vols; London, 1953), I, 227–8.

31. G. Barudio, *Gustav Adolf der Große* (Frankfurt, 1982); H. Duchhardt, *Protestantisches Kaisertum und altes Reich* (Wiesbaden, 1977). For subsequent

developments, see H. Langer, 'Der Heilbronner Bund (1633–35)', in Press (ed.), *Alternativen*, pp. 113–22; M. Roberts, 'Oxenstierna in Germany, 1633–1636', *Scandia*, 58 (1982), 61–105.

32. K. Repgen, 'Ferdinand III. (1637–1657)', in Schindling and Ziegler (eds), *Die Kaiser der Neuzeit*, pp. 142–67 at 157.

33. C. Kampmann, *Reichsrebellion und kaiserliche Acht. Politische Strafjustiz im Dreißigjährigen Krieg und das Verfahren gegen Wallenstein 1634* (Münster, 1992).

34. J. H. Elliott, *Count Duke Olivares* (New Haven, 1986).

35. K. Abmeier, *Der Trierer Kurfürst Philipp Christoph von Sötern und der Westfälische Friede* (Münster, 1986).

36. H. Haan, 'Kaiser Ferdinand II. und das Problem des Reichsabsolutismus. Die Prager Heeresreform von 1635', *HZ*, 207 (1968), 297–345; C. Kapser, *Die bayerische Kriegsorganisation in der zweiten Hälfte des Dreißigjährigen Krieges 1635–1648/49* (Münster, 1997).

37. H. Wunder, ' "dan man wiess wohl wass ein hessischer Kopf ist". Frauen in der Friedenspolitik', in Garber et al. (eds), *Erfahrung*, pp. 495–506.

38. M. Bregnsbo, 'Denmark and the Westphalian Peace', in H. Duchhardt (ed.), *Der Westfälische Friede* (Munich, 1998), pp. 361–7.

39. The negotiations are succinctly summarised by K. Repgen, 'Die Hauptprobleme der Westfälische Friedensverhandlungen von 1648 und ihre Lösungen', *ZBLG*, 62 (1999), 399–438.

40. F. Dickmann, *Der Westfälische Frieden* (5th edn; Münster, 1985), p. 187.

41. D. Croxton, 'The Peace of Westphalia of 1648 and the Origins of Sovereignty', *IHR*, 21 (1999), 569–91.

42. G. Schmid, 'Konfessionspolitik und Staatsräson bei den Verhandlungen des Westfälischen Friedenskongresses über die Gravamina Ecclesiastica', *Archiv für Reformationsgeschichte*, 44 (1953), 203–23; F. Jürgensmeier, 'Johann Philipp von Schönborn', *Fränkische Lebensbilder*, 6 (1975), 161–84.

43. F. Jürgensmeier, 'Bikonfessionalität in geistlichen Territorien', in Garber et al. (eds), *Erfahrung*, pp. 261–85; K. Schlaich, 'Majoritas – protestatio – itio in partes – corpus evangelicorum', *ZSRG KA*, 107 (1977), 264–99; and *ZSRG KA*, 108 (1978), 139–79; G. May, 'Die Entstehung der hauptsächlichen Bestimmungen über das ius emigrandi auf dem Westfälischen Friedenskongreß', *ZSRG KA*, 74 (1988), 436–94.

44. This occurred in 1680. Brandenburg had already seized the city of Magdeburg in 1666.

45. G. Treasure, *Mazarin: The Crisis of Absolutism in France* (London, 1995).

46. K. R. Böhme, 'Die Krone Schweden als Reichsstand 1648 bis 1720', in H. Duchhardt (ed.), *Europas Mitte* (Bonn, 1988), pp. 33–9, W. Buchholz, 'Schwedisch-Pommern als Territorium des deutschen Reiches 1648–1806', *ZNRG*, 12 (1990), 14–33; B. C. Fiedler, 'Schwedisch oder Deutsch? Die Herzogtümer Bremen und Verden in der Schwedenzeit (1645–1712)', *Niedersächsisches Jahrbuch für Landesgeschichte*, 67 (1995), 43–57.

47. P. Hoyos, 'Die kaiserliche Armee 1648–1650', in *Der Dreißigjährige Krieg*, pp. 169–232; A. Oschmann, *Der Nürnberger Exekutionstag 1649–1650. Das Ende der Dreißigjährigen Krieges in Deutschland* (Münster, 1991).

48. E. François and C. Gantet, 'Vergangenheitsbewältigung im Dienst des Friedens in der konfessionellen Identität. Die Friedensfeste in Süddeutschland nach 1648', in J. Burkhardt (ed.), *Krieg und Frieden in der historischen Gedächtniskultur* (Munich, 2000), pp. 103–23.

49. H. Medick, 'Historical Event and Contemporary Experience: The Capture and Destruction of Magdeburg', *History Workshop Journal*, 52 (2001), 23–48. For an account by a participant, see J. Peters (ed.), *Ein Söldnerleben im Dreißigjährigen Krieg* (Berlin, 1993). For the debate, see J. Theibault, 'The Rhetoric of Death and Destruction in the Thirty Years War', *Journal of Social History*, 27 (1993), 271–90.

50. G. Franz, *Der Dreißigjährige Krieg und das deutsche Volk* (4th edn, Stuttgart, 1979; 1st edn, 1941).

51. For the debate, see J. Theibault, 'The Demography of the Thirty Years War Revisited: Günther Franz and his Critics', *GH*, 15 (1997), 1–21. See also Table 3.1.

52. J. A. Lynn, 'How War Fed War: the Tax of Violence and Contributions during the *Grand Siècle*', *JMH*, 65 (1993), 286–310. For violence, see also R. G. Asch, ' "Wo der soldat hinkömbt, da ist alles sein": Military Violence and Atrocities in the Thirty Years War', *GH*, 18 (2000), 291–309.

53. M. Kaiser, 'Inmitten des Kriegstheaters: Die Bevölkerung als militärischer Faktor und Kriegsteilnehmer im Dreißigjährigen Krieg', in B. R. Kroener and R. Pröve (eds), *Krieg und Frieden. Militär und Gesellschaft in der frühen Neuzeit* (Paderborn, 1996), pp. 281–303; F. Kleinehagenbrock, 'Die Verwaltung im Dreißigjährigen Krieg. Lokalbeamte in der Grafschaft Hohenlohe zwischen Herrschaft, Untertanen und Militär', in S. Kroll and K. Krüger (eds), *Militär und ländliche Gesellschaft in der frühe Neuzeit* (Hamburg, 2000), pp. 121–42.

54. B. Roeck, 'Der Dreißigjährige Krieg und die Menschen im Reich. Überlegungen zu den Formen psychischer Krisenbewältigung in der ersten Hälfte des 17. Jahrhunderts', in Kroener and Pröve (eds), *Krieg und Frieden*, pp. 265–79.

55. A. V. Berkis, *The Reign of Duke James in Courland, 1638–1682* (Lincoln, Neb., 1960).

56. J. de Vries, *European Urbanisation, 1500–1800* (Cambridge, Mass., 1984).

57. *Herzog Karl Eugen und seine Zeit* (issued by the Württembergische Geschichts- und Altertumsverein, 2 vols; Esslingen, 1907–9), I, p. 363.

58. G. Haug-Moritz, 'Kaisertum und Parität. Reichspolitik und Konfession nach dem Westfälischen Frieden', *ZHF*, 19 (1992), 445–82; D. Stievermann, 'Politik und Konfession im 18. Jahrhundert', *ZHF*, 18 (1991), 177–99; J. Luh, *Unheiliges Römisches Reich. Der konfessionelle Gegensatz 1648 bis 1806* (Potsdam, 1995).

59. M. Schaab, 'Die Wiederherstellung des Katholizismus in der Kurpfalz im 17. und 18. Jahrhundert', *ZGO*, 114 (1966), 147–205.

60. H. Tuechle, *Die Kirchenpolitik des Herzogs Karl Alexander von Württemberg 1733–1737* (Würzburg, 1937); J. Vötsch, 'Die Hohenloher Religionsstreitigkeiten in der Mitte des 18. Jahrhunderts', *Württembergisch Franken*, 77 (1993), 361–400. For the following, see also J. Vötsch, *Kursachsen, das Reich und der mitteldeutsche Raum zu Beginn des 18. Jahrhunderts* (Frankfurt, 2003).

61. D. Freist, 'Zwischen Glaubensfreiheit und Geswissenszwang: Reichsrecht und Misehen nach 1648', in Asch (ed.), *Frieden und Krieg*, pp. 293–322; and her 'One Body, Two Confessions: Mixed Marriages in Germany', in U. Rublack (ed.), *Gender in Early Modern German History* (Cambridge, 2002), pp. 275–304.

62. E. François, *Die unsichtbare Grenze. Protestanten und Katholiken in Augsburg 1648–1806* (Sigmaringen, 1991). For Catholic identity, see M. R. Forster's numerous studies: *The Counter-Reformation in the Villages: Religion and Reform in the Bishopric of Speyer, 1560–1720* (Ithaca, 1992); *Catholic Revival in the Age of the Baroque: Religious Identity in Southwest Germany, 1550–1750* (Cambridge, 2001); 'With and Without Confessionalization: Varieties of Early Modern German Catholicism', *Journal of Early Modern History*, 1 (1998), 315–43.

63. Cited in A. Fauchier-Magnan, *The Small German Courts in the Eighteenth Century* (London, 1958), pp. 31–2. This work is a good example of the traditional perspective emphasising French cultural predominance.

64. Useful introduction by P. C. Hartmann, *Kulturgeschichte des Heiligen Römischen Reiches 1648 bis 1806* (Vienna, 2001). There is good coverage of German music in G. J. Buelow (ed.), *The Late Baroque Era from the 1680s to 1740* (Engelwood Cliffs, 1994).

65. H. Watanabe O'Kelly, *Court Culture in Dresden from Renaissance to Baroque* (Basingstoke, 2002).

Chapter 5: The Reich in Action

1. K. Müller, 'Das "Reichscamerale" im 18. Jahrhundert', in E. Springer and L. Kammerhofer (eds), *Weiner Beiträge zur Geschichte der Neuzeit*, vol. XX (Vienna, 1993), pp. 152–77; E. Isenmann, 'The Holy Roman Empire in the Middle Ages', in R. Bonney (ed.), *The Rise of the Fiscal State in Europe, c.1200–1815* (Oxford, 1999), pp. 243–80; and his 'Reichsfinanzen und Reichssteuern im 15. Jahrhundert', *ZHF*, 7 (1980), 1–76, 129–218.

2. W. Steglich, 'Die Reichstürkenhilfe in der Zeit Karls V.', *Militärgeschichtliche Mitteilungen*, 11 (1972), 7–55.

3. P. Moraw, 'Der "Gemeine Pfennig". Neue Steuern und die Einheit des Reiches im 15. und 16. Jahrhundert', in U. Schultz (ed.), *Mit dem Zehnten fing es an* (Munich, 1986), pp. 130–42; K. Krüger, 'Kriegsfinanzen und

Reichsrecht im 16. und 17. Jahrhundert', in B. R. Kroener and R. Pröve (eds), *Krieg und Frieden* (Paderborn, 1996), pp. 47–57.

4. W. Schulze, 'Die Erträge der Reichssteuern zwischen 1576 und 1606', *JGMOD*, 27 (1978), 169–85.

5. M. Jähns, 'Zur Geschichte der Kriegsverfassung des Deutschen Reiches', *Preußischer Jahrbücher*, 39 (1877), 1–28, 114–40, 443–90; H. Weigel, *Die Kriegsverfassung des alten Deutschen Reiches von der Wormser Matrikel bis zur Auflösung* (Bamberg, 1912).

6. G. E. Rothenberg, *The Austrian Military Border in Croatia, 1522–1747* (Urbana, 1960); and his *The Military Border in Croatia, 1740–1881* (Chicago, 1966).

7. E. Heischmann, *Die Anfänge des stehenden Heeres in Österreich* (Vienna, 1925).

8. C. W. Bracewell, *The Uskoks of Senj: Piracy, Banditry and Holy War in the Sixteenth-century Adriatic* (Ithaca, 1992).

9. A. Kohler, 'Die Sicherung des Landfriedens im Reich. Das Ringen um eine Exekutionsordnung des Landfriedens 1554/55', *MÖSA*, 24 (1971), 140–68; M. Lanzinner, 'Friedenssicherung und Zentralisierung der Reichsgewalt. Ein Reformversuch auf dem Reichstag zu Speyer 1570', *ZHF*, 12 (1985), 287–310.

10. D. Götschmann, 'Das Jus Armorum. Ausformung und politische Bedeutung der reichsständischen Militärhoheit bis zu ihrer definitiven Anerkennung im Westfälischen Frieden', *BDLG*, 129 (1993), 257–76. The militias are covered by H. Schnitter, *Volk und Landesdefension* (Berlin, 1977).

11. H. Ehlert, 'Ursprünge des modernen Militärwesens. Die nassau-oransichen Heeresreformen', *Militärgeschichtliche Mitteilungen*, 38 (1985), 27–56; W. Reinhard, 'Humanismus und Militärismus. Antike Rezeption und Kriegshandwerk in der oranischen Heeresreform', in F. J. Worstbrock (ed.), *Krieg und Frieden im Horizont des Renaissancehumanismus* (Weinheim, 1985), pp. 185–204.

12. P. H. Wilson, 'War in German Thought from the Peace of Westphalia to Napoleon', *European History Quarterly*, 28 (1998), 5–50.

13. Heischmann, *Die Angfänge*, pp. 115–19, 189–98.

14. K. Peball, *Die Schlacht bei St-Gotthard-Mogendorf 1664* (Vienna, 1964). For the following, see also P. H. Wilson, *German Armies: War and German Politics, 1648–1806* (London, 1998) and the sources cited there.

15. H. Angermeier, 'Die Reichskriegsverfassung in der Politik der Jahre 1679–1681', *ZSRG GA*, 82 (1965), 190–222.

16. M. Plassmann, *Krieg und Defension am Oberrhein. Die vorderen Reichskreise und Markgraf Ludwig Wilhelm von Baden (1693–1706)* (Berlin, 2000).

17. W. Schulze, 'Die veränderte Bedeutung sozialer Konflikte im 16. und 17. Jahrhundert', in H. U. Wehler (ed.), *Der deutsche Bauernkrieg 1524–1526* (Göttingen, 1976), pp. 277–302; and his *Bäuerlicher Widerstand und feudale Herrschaft in der frühen Neuzeit* (Stuttgart, 1980).

18. B. Diestelkamp, *Rechtsfälle aus dem alten Reich. Denkwürdige Prozesse vor dem Reichskammergericht* (Munich, 1995).

19. B. Ruthmann, 'Das richterliche Personal am Reichskammergericht und seine politischen Verbindungen um 1600', in W. Sellert (ed.), *Reichshofrat und Reichskammergericht* (Cologne, 1999), pp. 1–26; W. Sellert, 'Das Verhältnis von Reichskammergerichts- und Reichshofratsordnungen am Beispiel der Regelungen über die Visitation', in B. Diestelkamp (ed.), *Das Reichskammergericht in der deutschen Geschichte* (Cologne, 1990), pp. 111–28; S. Jahns, 'Brandenburg-Preussen im System der Reichskammergerichts-Präsentationen 1648–1806', in H. Weber (ed.), *Politische Ordnungen und soziale Kräfte im alten Reich* (Wiesbaden, 1980), pp. 169–202. The elector of Mainz had special responsibility for appointing the administrative staff: H. Duchhardt, 'Kurmainz und das Reichskammergericht', *BDLG*, 110 (1974), 181–217.

20. J. Weitzel, 'Zur Zuständigkeit des Reichskammergerichts als Appellationsgericht', *ZSRG GA*, 90 (1973), 213–45. H. Gabel, 'Beobachtungen zur territorialen Innanspruchnahme des Reichskammergerichts im Bereich des Niederrheinisch-Westfälischen Kreises', in Diestelkamp (ed.), *Das Reichskammergericht*, pp. 143–72.

21. J. Q. Whitman, *The Legacy of Roman Law in the German Romantic Era* (Princeton, 1990); H. Weill, *Frederick the Great and Samuel von Cocceji. A Study in the Reform of the Prussian Judicial Administration, 1740–1755* (Madison, 1961), pp. 52–4.

22. E. Ortlieb, 'Reichshofrat und kaiserliche Kommissionen in der Regierungszeit Kaiser Ferdinands III. (1637–1657)', in Sellert (ed.), *Reichshofrat und Reichskammergericht*, pp. 47–81. See also section 4.2.

23. J. W. von Goethe, *Collected Works* (12 vols, ed. T. P. Saine and J. L. Sammons; Princeton, 1987), vol. IV, *From My Life: Poetry and Truth*, pp. 388–91.

24. K. O. Freiherr von Aretin, 'Kaiser Joseph II und die Reichskammergerichtsvisitation, 1766–1776', *ZNRG*, 13 (1991), 129–44.

25. G. Schmidt von Rhein, 'Das Reichskammergericht in Wetzlar', *Nassauischer Annalen*, 100 (1989), 127–40. The formal establishment of judges was raised to 27 in 1775. The *Reichshofrat* had 12–18 judges before 1648 and 18–34 thereafter.

26. Goethe, *From My Life*, p. 389.

27. S. Westphal, 'Der politische Einfluss von Reichsgerichtsbarkeit am Beispiel der Thüringischen Kleinstaaten (1648–1806)', in Sellert (ed.), *Reichshofrat und Reichskammergericht*, pp. 83–109; A. von Witzleben, *Der Wasunger Krieg zwischen Sachsen-Gotha-Altenburg und Sachsen-Meiningen (1747 bis 1748)* (Gotha, 1855).

28. M. Fimpel, *Reichsjustiz und Territorialstaat. Württemberg als Kommissar von Kaiser und Reich im Schwäbischen Kreis (1648–1806)* (Tübingen, 1999); R. J. Weber, 'Die kaiserlichen Kommission des Hauses Württembergs in der Neuzeit', *ZWLG*, 43 (1984), 205–36.

29. T. Hartwig, *Der Überfall der Grafschaft Schaumburg-Lippe durch Landgraf Wilhelm IX. von Hessen-Kassel* (Hanover, 1911).

30. M. Hughes, *Law and Politics in Eighteenth-century Germany* (Woodbridge, 1988).

31. W. Dotzauer, *Die deutschen Reichskreise (1383–1806)* (Stuttgart, 1998) with extensive references. See also section 2.1.

32. A. K. Mally, 'Der Österreichische Reichskreise. Seine Bedeutung für die habsburgische Erbländer', in W. Wüst (ed.), *Reichskreis und Territorium. Die Herrschaft über die Herrschaft?* (Stuttgart, 2000), pp. 313–31.

33. P. Casser, 'Der Niederrheinisch-Westfälische Reichskreis', in H. Aubin and E. Schulte (eds), *Der Raum Westfalen*, vol. II (Berlin, 1934), pp. 35–72; A. Schindling, 'Kurbrandenburg im System des Reiches während der zweiten Hälfte des 17. Jahrhunderts', in O. Hauser (ed.), *Preußen, Europa und das Reich* (Cologne, 1987), pp. 33–46.

34. P. C. Hartmann, 'Die Kreistage des Heiligen Römischen Reiches – eine Vorform des Parlamentarismus?' *ZHF*, 19 (1991), 29–47.

35. H. Philippi, *Landgraf Karl I. von Hessen-Kassel* (Marburg, 1976); G. A. Süss, 'Geschichte des oberrheinischen Kreises und der Kreisassoziationen in der Zeit des spanischen Erbfolgekrieges (1697–1714)', *ZGO*, 103 (1955), 317–425; and 104 (1956), 10–224.

36. P. C. Storm, *Der Schwäbische Kreis als Feldherr* (Berlin, 1974); B. Sicken, *Der Fränkische Reichskreis* (Würzburg, 1970).

37. F. Magen, 'Die Reichskreise in der Epoche des Dreißigjährigen Krieges', *ZHF*, 9 (1982), 408–60.

38. H. Salm, *Armeefinanzierung im Dreißigjährigen Krieg. Der Niederrheinisch-Westfälische Reichskreis* (Münster, 1990).

39. R. Schnur, *Der Rheinbund von 1658* (Bonn, 1958); A. Schindling, 'Der erste Rheinbund und das Reich', in V. Press (ed.), *Alternativen zur Reichsverfassung in der frühen Neuzeit?*, (Munich, 1995), pp. 123–9.

40. K. Decker, *Frankreich und die Reichsstände 1672–1675* (Bonn, 1975); K. O. Freiherr von Aretin (ed.), *Der Kurfürst von Mainz und die Kreisassoziationen, 1648–1748* (Wiesbaden, 1975).

41. R. Gebauer, *Die Außenpolitik der Schwäbischen Reichskreises vor Ausbruch des Spanischen Erbfolgekrieges (1697–1702)* (Marburg, 1969); Plassmann, *Krieg und Defension*, pp. 348–89.

42. I. Bog, *Der Reichsmerkantilismus* (Stuttgart, 1959); F. Blaich, 'Die Bedeutung der Reichstage auf dem Gebiet der öffentlichen Finanzen im Spannungsfeld zwischen Kaiser, Territorialstaaten und Reichsstädten (1495–1670)', in A. de Maddalena and H. Kellenbenz (eds), *Finanzen und Staatsräson* (Berlin, 1991), pp. 79–111.

43. Dotzauer, *Die deutshcen Reichskreise*, pp. 441–55.

44. O. Volckart, 'Politische Zersplitterung und Wirtschaftswachstum im alten Reich, c.1650–1800', *VSWG*, 86 (1999), 1–38.

45. J. W. Bernhardt, *Itinerant Kingship and Royal Monasteries in Early Medieval Germany, c.936–1075* (Cambridge, 1993). See generally G. Christ, *Studien zur Reichskirche der Frühneuzeit* (Stuttgart, 1989); H. E. Feine, *Die Besetzung der Reichsbistümer vom Westfälischen Frieden bis zur Säkularisation 1648–1803* (Stuttgart, 1921); L. Hüttl, 'Geistlicher Fürst und geistliche Fürstentümer

im Barock und Rokoko', *ZBLG*, 37 (1974), 3–48. K. Andermann, 'Die geistlichen Staaten an Ende des alten Reiches', *HZ*, 271 (2000), 593–619.

46. E. J. Greipl, 'Zur weltlichen Herrschaft der Fürstbischöfe in der Zeit vom Westfälischen Frieden bis zur Säkularisation', *Römische Quartalschrift*, 83 (1988), 252–69, estimates a combined revenue of 18.15 million fl. in 1800. See section 2.2 for their Reichstag representation. See also Appendix 4.

47. Madgeburg, Bremen, Verden, Brandenburg, Havelberg, Schwerin, Ratzeburg, Cammin, Naumburg, Merseburg, Meissen, Minden and Halberstadt. The last two retained some posts for Catholic canons as well.

48. J. J. Schmid, *Alexander Sigismund von Pfalz-Neuburg, Fürstbischof von Augsburg 1690–1737* (Weißenhorn, 1999); K. Jaitner, 'Reichskirchenpolitik und Rombeziehungen Philipp Wilhelms von Pfalz-Neuburg von 1662 bis 1690', *Annalen des Historischen Vereins für den Niederrhein*, 178 (1976), 91–144; R. Reinhardt, 'Zur Reichskirchenpolitik der Pfalz-Neuburger Dynastie', *HJb*, 84 (1964), 118–28.

49. H. Wolf, *Die Reichskirchenpolitik des Hauses Lothringen (1680–1715). Eine Habsburger Sekundogenitur im Reich?* (Stuttgart, 1994).

50. A. Schröcker, 'Heer, Finanzen und Verwaltung. Kurmainz im Pfälzer Krieg 1689 bis 1697', *Archiv für Hessische Geschichte*, NF 31 (1971), 98–114.

51. T. Heiler, 'Die Finanzen des Hochstifts Würzburg im 18. Jahrhundert', *Würzburger Diozesangeschichtsblätter*, 47 (1985), 159–89. See also H. Caspary, *Staat, Finanzen, Wirtschaft und Heerwesen im Hochstift Bamberg (1672–1693)* (Bamberg, 1976). P. Hersche, 'Intendierte Rückständigkeit. Zur Charakteristik des geistlichen Staates im alten Reich', in G. Schmidt (ed.), *Stände und Gesellschaft im alten Reich* (Stuttgart, 1989), pp. 133–49, greatly underestimates the pressures of war on the ecclesiastical territories.

52. G. Bönisch, *Clemens August. Der schillerndste Erzbischof seiner Zeit* (Bergisch Gladbach, 2000).

53. P. Anderson, *Lineages of the Absolutist State* (London, 1974), p. 251.

54. W. von Hoffmann, 'Das Säkularisationsproject von 1743. Kaiser Karl VII. und die römische Kurie', in *Riezler Festschrift: Beiträge zur bayerische Geschichte* (Gotha, 1913), pp. 213–59.

55. K. O. Freiherr von Aretin, *Heiliges Römisches Reich 1776–1806* (2 vols; Wiesbaden, 1967), I, pp. 372–452.

56. A. Kohler, 'Das Reich im Spannungsfeld des preussisch-österreichischen Gegensatzes. Die Fürstenbundbestrebungen 1783–1785', in F. Engel-Janosi et al. (eds), *Fürst, Bürger, Mensch* (Munich, 1975), pp. 71–96; D. Stievermann, 'Der Fürstenbund von 1785 und das Reich', in V. Press (ed.), *Alternativen zur Reichsverfassung in der frühen Neuzeit?*, pp. 209–26; M. Umbach, 'The Politics of Sentimentality and the German *Fürstenbund*, 1775–1785', *HJ*, 41 (1998), 679–704.

57. K. Maier, 'Das Ende der Reichskirche nach dem Frieden von Lunéville 1801', *ZWLG*, 61 (2002), 273–84.

Chapter 6: Territorial Absolutism

1. N. Henshall, *The myth of Absolutism* (Harlow, 1992); R. G. Asch and H. Duch-hardt (eds), *Der Absolutismus – Ein Mythos?* (Cologne, 1996). For discussion of the debates, see P. H. Wilson, *Absolutism in Central Europe* (London, 2000).

2. A. Fauchier-Magnan, *The Small German Courts in the Eighteenth Century* (London, 1958), p. 21. See also, K. Epstein, *The Genesis of German Conservatism* (Princeton, 1966), pp. 256–8.

3. R. Bireley, 'Antimachiavellianism, the Baroque and Maximilian of Bavaria', *Archivum historicum societatis Jesu*, 103 (1984), 137–59; H. Münkler, *Im Namen des Staates. Die Begründung der Staatsraison in der frühen Neuzeit* (Frankfurt, 1987).

4. Cited in T. C. W. Blanning, 'Frederick the Great and Enlightened Absolutism', in H. M. Scott (ed.), *Enlightened Absolutism* (Basingstoke, 1990), pp. 265–88 at 277.

5. R. R. Ergang, *The Potsdam Führer: Frederick William I* (New York, 1941), p. 45.

6. H. Dreitzel, *Monarchiebegriff in der Fürstengesellschaft. Semantik und Theorie der Einherrschaft in Deutschland von der Reformation bis zum Vormärz* (2 vols; Cologne, 1991); and his *Absolutismus und ständische Verfassung in Deutschland* (Mainz, 1992).

7. K. Repgen (ed.), *Das Herrscherbild im 17. Jahrhundert* (Münster, 1991).

8. J. Arndt, 'Der Große Kurfürst. Ein Herrscher des Absolutismus?', in Asch and Duchhardt (eds), *Absolutismus – Ein Mythos?*, pp. 249–73; G. Menk, 'Absolutismus und Regierungsform in Waldeck. Der Zugriff Graf Georg Friedrichs und seines Kanzlers Johann Viëtor auf Staat und Stände 1665–1676', *Hessisches Jahrbuch für Landesgeschichte*, 35 (1985), 69–135.

9. For examples stressing war, see J. Kunisch, *Absolutismus. Europäische Geschichte vom Westfälischen Frieden bis zur Krise des Ancien Régime* (Göttingen, 1986), esp. pp. 186–7; B. M. Downing, *The Military Revolution and Political Change in Early Modern Europe* (Princeton, 1991); T. Ertman, *Birth of the Leviathan* (Cambridge, 1997).

10. Fuller discussion can be found in P. H. Wilson, 'European Warfare 1450–1815', in J. Black (ed.), *War in the Early Modern World, 1450–1815* (London, 1999), pp. 177–206.

11. Marxist perspectives are surveyed in Wilson, *Absolutism*, pp. 22–9, and A. Dorpalen, *German History in Marxist Perspective. The East German Approach* (London, 1985), pp. 138–57.

12. For example, W. te Brake, *Shaping History: Ordinary People in European Politics, 1500–1700* (Berkeley, 1998); and Peter Blickle's works, cited in Chapter 3, note 39 above.

13. R. J. W. Evans, *The Making of the Habsburg Monarchy, 1550–1700* (Oxford, 1979); G. Heilingsetzer, 'The Austrian Nobility, 1600–1650', in R. J. W. Evans and T. V. Thomas (eds), *Crown, Church and Estates* (New York, 1991), pp. 245–60; R. Pörtner, *The Counter-Reformation in Central Europe: Styria, 1580–1630* (Oxford, 2001); K. J. MacHardy, *War, Religion and Court Patronage*

*in Habsburg Austria: The Social and Cultural Dimensions of Political Interaction,
1521–1622* (Basingstoke, 2003).

14. W. W. Hagen, 'Seventeeth-century Crisis in Brandenburg: The Thirty
Years War, the Destabilization of Serfdom, and the Rise of Absolutism',
AHR, 94 (1989), 302–35.

15. E. Melton, 'The Prussian Junkers 1600–1786', in H. M. Scott (ed.), *The
European Nobilities* (2 vols; London, 1995), II, pp. 71–109; P. M. Hahn,
'Aristokratisierung und Professionalisierung. Der Aufstieg der Obristen zu
einer militärischen und höfischen Elite in Brandenburg-Preußen von 1650–
1720', *FBPG*, NF 1 (1991), 161–206; E. Stockinger, 'Vorbildung, Herkunft
und Werdegang militärischer Führer in Deutschlands von 1730–1813',
Wehrkunde, 24 (1975), 592–7.

16. R. Schlögl, 'Absolutismus im 17. Jahrhundert – Bayerischer Adel zwischen
Disziplinierung und Intergration', *ZHF*, 15 (1988), 151–86.

17. J. Duindam, *Myths of Power* (Amsterdam, 1995). For a critique, see Wilson,
Absolutism, pp. 62–80.

18. R. Wagner-Rieger, 'Gedanken zum fürstlichen Schlossbau des Absolutismus', in F. Engel-Janosi (ed.), *Fürst, Bürger, Mensch* (Munich, 1975),
pp. 45–70; C. Mukerji, *Territorial Ambitions and the Gardens of Versailles* (Cambridge, 1997).

19. A. Mączak, 'From Aristocratic Household to Princely Court: Restructuring Patronage in the Sixteenth and Seventeenth Centuries', in R. G. Asch
and A. M. Birke (eds), *Princes, Patronage and the Nobility* (Oxford, 1991),
pp. 315–27. See generally, W.Reinhard (ed.), *Power Elites and State Building*
(Oxford, 1996).

20. M. Golobeva, *The Glorification of Emperor Leopold I in Image, Spectacle and Text*
(Mainz, 2000); F. Matschke, *Die Kunst im Dienst der Staatsidee. Kaiser Karl VI*
(2 vols; Berlin, 1981).

21. See the useful entries on individual courts in J. Adamson (ed.), *The Princely
Courts of Europe, 1500–1750* (London, 1999).

22. W. Ribbe (ed.), *Geschichte Berlins* (2 vols; Munich, 1988).

23. O. Krauske (ed.), 'Aus einer geschriebenen Berliner Zeitung vom Jahre
1713', *Schriften des Vereins für die Geschichte Berlins*, 30 (1893), 97–129 at 127;
C. Hinrichs, 'Die Regierungsantritt Friedrich Wilhelms I', *JGMOD*, 5
(1956), 181–225.

24. W. Neugebauer, 'Staatsverwaltung, Manufaktur und Garnison. Die poly-
funktionale Residenzlandschaft von Berlin-Potsdam-Wusterhausen zur
Zeit Friedrich Wilhelms I', *FBPG*, NF 7 (1997), 233–57; and his 'Hof und
politisches System in Brandenburg-Preußen', *JGMOD*, 46 (2000), 139–69.

25. J. Burkhardt, *Der Dreißigjährige Krieg* (Frankfurt, 1992), pp. 213–24.

26. F. Redlich, *The German Military Enterprizer and his Workforce* (2 vols; Wiesbaden, 1964–5), vol. II.

27. B. R. Kroener, 'Soldat oder Soldateska? Programmatischer Aufriß einer
Sozialgeschichte militärischer Unterschichten in der ersten Hälfte des 17.

Jahrhunderts', in M. Messerschmidt (ed.), *Militärgeschichte. Probleme, Thesen, Wege* (Stuttgart, 1982), pp. 100–23.

28. W. Tettau, 'Erfurts Unterwerfung unter die Mainzische Landeshoheit', *Neujahrsblätter herausgegeben von der Historische Kommission der Provinz Sachsen*, 11 (1887), 3–56; H. Querfurth, *Die Unterwerfung der Stadt Braunschweig im Jahre 1671* (Brunswick, 1953); W. Kohl, *Christoph Bernhard von Galen* (Münster, 1964); J. Mallek, 'Eine andersartige Lösung. Absolutistischer Staatsreich in Preußen im Jahre 1663', *Parliaments, Estates and Representation*, 10 (1990), 177–87.

29. M. Hughes, 'Die Strafpreussen: Mecklenburg und der Bund der deutschen absolutistischen Fürsten, 1648–1719', *Parliaments, Estates and Representation*, 3 (1983), 101–13.

30. T. von Moerner (ed.), *Kurbrandenburgische Staatsverträge von 1601–1700* (Berlin, 1867), pp. 343–4, 696–701.

31. F. Willax, 'Das Verteidigungswesen Nürnbergs im 17. und 18. Jahrhundert', *Mitteilungen des Vereins für Geschichte der Stadt Nürnberg*, 66 (1979), 192–247; T. Schwark, *Lübecks Stadtmilitär im 17. und 18. Jahrhundert* (Lübeck, 1990); J. Ehlers, *Die Wehrverfassung der Stadt Hamburg im 17. und 18. Jahrhundert* (Boppard, 1966); J. Kraus, *Das Militärwesen der Reichsstadt Augsburg, 1548–1806* (Augsburg, 1980). See Appendix 3 for the strength of civic forces.

32. For examples, see P. H. Wilson, *War, State and Society in Württemberg, 1677–1793* (Cambridge, 1995).

33. M. Sikora, *Disziplin und Desertion. Strukturprobleme militärischer Organisation im 18. Jahrhundert* (Berlin, 1996).

34. P. H. Wilson, 'The Politics of Military Recruitment in Eighteenth-century Germany', *EHR*, 117 (2002), 536–68.

35. O. Büsch, *Military System and Social Life in Old Regime Prussia, 1713–1807: The Beginnings of the Social Militarisation of Prusso-German Society* (Atlantic Highlands, 1997). For an extended critique, see P. H. Wilson, 'Social Militarisation in Eighteenth-century Germany', *GH*, 18 (2000), 1–39.

36. D. Showalter, 'Hubertusburg to Auerstädt: The Prussian Army in Decline', *GH*, 12 (1994), 308–33.

37. For example, H. Duchhardt, *Deutsche Verfassungsgeschichte, 1495–1806* (Stuttgart, 1991), pp. 183–4.

38. M. Mann, *The Sources of Social Power* (2 vols; Cambridge, 1986–93), II, pp. 444, 453.

39. H. M. Scott, 'The Rise of the First Minister in Eighteenth-century Europe', in T. C. W. Blanning and D. Cannadine (eds), *History and Biography. Essays in Honour of Derek Beales* (Cambridge, 1996), pp. 21–52; J. H. Elliott and L. W. B. Brockliss (eds), *The World of the Favourite* (New Haven, 1999); M. Kaiser and A. Pecar (eds), *Der zweite Mann im Staat. Oberster Amsträger und Favoriten im Umkreis der Reichsfürsten in der frühen Neuzeit* (Berlin, 2003). Lack of space precludes discussion of women and political power. For this topic, see the forthcoming volume edited by C. Campbell-Orr, which contains

several essays on the German territories: *Queenship in Europe, 1660–1815: The Role of the Consort* (Cambridge, 2004).

40. K. Gutkas, 'Die führenden Persönlichkeiten der habsburgischen Monarchie von 1683 bis 1740', in K. Gutkas (ed.), *Prinz Eugen und das barocke Österreich* (Salzburg, 1985), pp. 73–86; D. McKay, *Prince Eugene of Savoy* (London, 1977).

41. G. Haug-Moritz, 'Friedrich Samuel Graf Montmartin als württembergischen Staatsmann (1756–1766/73)', *ZWLG*, 53 (1994), 205–26.

42. S. Mörz, *Aufgeklärter Absolutismus in der Kurpfalz während der Mannheimer Regierungszeit des Kurfürsten Karl Theodor (1742–1777)* (Stuttgart, 1991), pp. 142, 169–98.

43. C. Dipper, *Deutsche Geschichte 1648–1789* (Frankfurt, 1991), p. 229. See also H. M. Scott, 'Prussia's Royal Foreign Minister: Frederick the Great and the Administration of Prussian Diplomacy', in R. Oresko et al. (eds), *Royal and Republican Sovereignty in Early Modern Europe* (Cambridge, 1997), pp. 500–26.

44. H. Johnson, *Frederick the Great and his Officials* (New Haven, 1975).

45. For Joseph's government, see D. Beales, *Joseph II in the Shadow of Maria Theresa* (Cambridge, 1987). There are good biographies of the key figures: F. A. J. Szabo, *Kaunitz and Enlightened Absolutism, 1753–1780* (Cambridge, 1994); K. A. Roider Jr, *Baron Thugut and Austria's Response to the French Revolution* (Princeton, 1987); P. P. Bernard, *From the Enlightenment to the Police State: The Public Life of Johann Anton Pergen* (Urbana, 1991).

46. K. H. Marcus, *The Politics of Power: Elites of an Early Modern German State* (Mainz, 2000).

47. B. Wunder, 'Die Sozialstruktur der Geheimratskollegien in den süddeutschen, protestantischen Fürstentümer (1660–1720)', *VSWG*, 58 (1971), 145–220. Further detail in J. A. Vann, *The Making of a State: Württemberg, 1593–1793* (Ithaca, 1984), esp. pp. 116–24, 195–201; and W. Metz, 'Zur Sozialgeschichte des Beamtentums in der Zentralverwaltung der Landgrafschaft Hessen-Kassel bis zum 18. Jahrhundert', *Zeitschrft des Vereins für Hessische Geschichte und Landeskunde*, 67 (1956), 138–48.

48. Mörz, *Aufgeklärter Absolutismus*, pp. 145–56; N. von Preradowich, *Die Führungsschichten in Österreich und Preussen (1804–1918)* (Wiesbaden, 1955).

49. B. Dölemeyer, *Frankfurter Juristen im 17. und 18. Jahrhundert* (Frankfurt, 1993).

50. B. Wunder, *Privilegierung und Disziplinierung. Die Entstehung des Berufsbeamtentums in Bayern und Württemberg, 1780–1825* (Munich, 1978).

51. V. Press, 'The System of Estates in the Austrian Hereditary Lands and in the Holy Roman Empire: A Comparison', in R. J. W. Evans and T. V. Thomas (eds), *Crown, Church and Estates*, pp. 1–22. For individual territories, see D. Gerhard (ed.), *Ständische Vertretungen im 17. und 18. Jahrhundert* (Göttingen, 1969); P. Baumgart (ed.), *Ständetum und Staatsbildung in Brandenburg-Preußen* (Berlin, 1983); R. Freiin von Oer, 'Estates and Diets in Ecclesiastical Principalities of the Holy Roman Empire', in *Liber memorialis George de Lagarde* (Louvain, 1970), pp. 259–81.

52. Mainz, Regensburg, Freising, Augsburg, Constanz, Worms and Speyer. See also section 5.4 above.

53. Catholic examples include Bavaria, the Upper Palatinate, Salzburg, Basel, Cologne, Liège, Breisgau, Sundgau, Münster, Paderborn and Osnabrück. Protestant examples include Hessen-Darmstadt, Brunswick-Wolfenbüttel, Saxony and the Ernestine Saxon duchies. See also C. Römer, 'Die braunschweigischen Landstände im Zeitalter der Aufklärung bis 1789', *Niedersächische Jahrbuch für Landesgeschichte*, 63 (1991), 59–71.

54. Protestant Württemberg, Ansbach and Bayreuth, and Catholic Würzburg, Bamberg, Trier and Fulda.

55. Saxony, Brandenburg, Ducal Prussia, Moravia, Silesia and Bohemia.

56. Königsberg in Ducal Prussia, and Paderborn, Osnabrück and Münster in their respective bishoprics.

57. A. Flügel, *Bürgerliche Rittergüter. Soziale Wandel und politische Reform in Kursachsen (1680–1844)* (Göttingen, 2000), offers a detailed case study.

58. B. Kappelhoff, *Absolutistisches Regiment oder Ständeherrschaft? Landesherr und Landstände in Ostfriesland im ersten Drittel des 8. Jahrhunderts* (Hildesheim, 1982); W. Grube, 'Dorfgemeinde und Amtsversammlung in Altwürttemberg', *ZWLG*, 13 (1954), 194–219. Other examples include Basel, Chur, Salzburg, Sitten, Baden, Trier, Voralberg and Alsace.

59. Constance, Hohenzollern-Hechingen, Hohenzollern-Haigerloch, all four parts of Waldburg, Hohenems, Fürstenberg, Königsegg, Hohenlohe, Öttingen, Eberstein, Zweibrücken, the Lower Palatinate, and the imperial cities of Rottweil, Ravensburg, Überlingen, Lindau and Biberach.

60. F. L. Carsten, *Princes and Parliaments in Germany from the Fifteenth to the Eighteenth Century* (Oxford, 1959); W. Grube, *Der Stuttgarter Landtag 1457–1957* (Stuttgart, 1957).

61. K. Vetter, 'Die Stände im absolutistischen Preußen', *Zeitschrift für Geschichte*, 24 (1976), 1290–1306.

62. See his works cited in Chap.3 n.39.

63. R. von Friedeburg, '"Kommunalismus" und "Republikanismus" in der frühen Neuzeit?', *ZHF*, 21 (1994), 65–91, and his '"Reiche", "Geringe Leute" und "Beampte"*: Landesherrschaft, dörfliche "Factionen" und gemeindliche Partizipation 1648–1806', *ZHF*, 23 (1996), 219–65. Alhusius' key work is available in English: *Politica* (Indianapolis, 1995).

64. There are examples in H. Gabel and W. Schulze, 'Peasant Resistance and Politicization in Germany in the Eighteenth Century', in E. Hellmuth (ed.), *The Transformation of Political Culture* (Oxford, 1990), pp. 119–46.

65. P. Stadtler, 'Die Schweiz und das Reich in der frühen Neuzeit', in V. Press (ed.), *Alternativen zur Reichsverfassung* (Munich, 1995), pp. 131–41.

66. Dreitzel, *Absolutismus*, pp. 100–37; V. Press, 'Landtage im alten Reich und im Deutschen Bund', *ZWLG*, 39 (1980), 100–40.

67. E. L. Petersen, 'From Domain State to Tax State: Synthesis and Interpretation', *Scandinavian Economic History Review*, 23 (1975), 116–48. This idea has

been applied to German history by Kersten Krüger, who provides an English summary of his work in 'Public Finance and Modernisation: The Change from Domain State to Tax State in Hesse in the Sixteenth and Seventeenth Centuries', in P. C. Witt (ed.), *Wealth and Taxation in Central Europe* (Leamington Spa, 1987), pp.49–62.

68. P. C. Hartmann, *Das Steuersystem der europäischen Staaten am Ende des Ancien Régime* (Munich, 1979).

69. W. A. Boelcke, 'Die "sanftmütige Accise": Zur Bedeutung und Problematik der "indirekten Verbrauchsbesteuerung" in der Finanzwirtschaft der deutschen Territorialstaaten während der frühen Neuzeit', *JGMOD*, 21 (1971), 93–139.

70. J. Brewer, *The Sinews of Power: War, Money and the English State, 1688–1783* (New York, 1989); M. C. t'Hart, *The Making of a Bourgeois State: War, Politics and Finance during the Dutch Revolt* (Manchester, 1993).

71. P. T. Hoffman and K. Norberg (eds), *Fiscal Crises, Liberty and Representative Government* (Stanford, 1994).

72. P. Blickle, 'Untertanen in der Frühneuzeit', *VSWG*, 70 (1983), 483–522 at 510.

73. Carsten, *Princes and Parliaments*, pp. 12–54.

74. H. Schlechte (ed.), *Das Geheime politische Tagebuch des Kurprinzen Friedrich Christian 1751–1757* (Weimar, 1992), p. 34.

75. G. Otruba, 'Das österreichische Wirtschaftssystem im Zeitalter des Prinz Eugen', in J. Kunisch (ed.), *Prinz Eugen und seiner Zeit* (Freiburg, 1986), pp. 57–90; B. Holl, *Hofkammerpräsident Gundaker Thomas Graf Starhemberg und die österreichische Finanzpolitik der Barockzeit (1703–1715)* (Vienna, 1976).

76. A. Schmid, *Max III. Josef und die europäischen Mächte. Die Außenpolitik des Kurfürstentums Bayerns 1745–1765* (Munich, 1987), pp. 256, 268–71; A. F. v.d. Asseburg, *Denkwürdigkeiten des Achatz Ferdinand von der Asseburg* (Berlin, 1842), p. 226 n. 1; F. Wintterlin, *Geschichte der Behördenorganisation in Württemberg* (2 vols; Stuttgart, 1904–6), I, pp. 95–6.

77. R. Koser, 'Der preussische Staatsschatz von 1740', *FBPG*, 4 (1891), 529–51; and his 'Die preußischen Finanzen im Siebenjährigen Kriege', *FBPG*, 13 (1900), 153–217, 329–75.

78. W. Real, 'Die preußischen Staatsfinanzen und die Anbahnung des Sonderfriedens von Basel 1795', *FBPG*, NF 1 (1991), 53–100.

79. P. G. M. Dickson, *Finance and government under Maria Theresia, 1740–1780* (2 vols; Oxford, 1987), II, pp. 74–7, 375; *Krieg gegen die Französischen Revolution 1792–7* (2 vols; issued by the Austrian Kriegsarchiv, Vienna, 1905), I, pp. 182–97.

80. H. P. Ullmann, 'The Emergence of Modern Public Debts in Bavaria and Baden between 1780 and 1820', in Witt (ed.), *Wealth and Taxation*, pp. 63–79.

81. H. L. Mikoletzky, 'Die große Anliehe von 1706', *MÖSA*, 7 (1954), 268–93.

Chapter 7: State and Society

1. G. Oestreich, *Neostoicism and the Early Modern State* (Cambridge, 1982); W. Schulze, 'Gerhard Oestreichs Begriff "Soziale Disziplinierung in der frühen Neizeit"', *ZHF*, 14 (1987), 265–302.

2. M. Raeff, *The Well-ordered Police State: Social and Institutional Change through Law in the Germanies and Russia 1600–1800* (New Haven, 1983), p. 176.

3. For a variety of critiques, see H. Rebel, 'Reimagining the *oikos*. Austrian Cameralism in its Social Formation', in J. O'Brien and W. Rosenberry (eds), *Golden Ages, Dark Ages: Reimagining the Past* (Berkeley, 1991), pp. 48–80; G. Lottes, 'Disziplin und Emanzipation. Das Sozialdisziplinierungskonzept und die Interpretation der frühneuzeitlichen Geschichte', *Westfälische Forschungen*, 42 (1992), 63–74; A. Landwehr, '"Normendurchsetzung" in der frühen Neuzeit? Kritik eines Begriffs', *Zeitschrift für Geschichtswissenschaft*, 48 (2000), 146–62. Good introductions to the alternatives are in S. Breuer, 'Sozialdisziplinierung. Probleme und Problemverlagerung eines Konzepts bei Max Weber, Gerhard Oestreich und Michel Foucault', in C. Sachße and F. Tennstedt (eds), *Soziale Sicherheit und soziale Disziplinierung* (Frankfurt, 1986), pp. 45–69; M. Ludwig-Mayerhofer, 'Disziplin oder Distinktion? Zur Interpretation der Theorie des Zivilisationsprozesses von Norbert Elias', *Kölner Zeitschrift für Soziologie und Sozialpsychologie*, 50 (1998), 217–37.

4. M. Stolleis (ed.), *Policey im Europa der frühen Neuzeit* (Frankfurt, 1996); and his *Geschichte des öffentlichen Rechts in Deutschland*, vol. I, *Reichspublizistik und Policeywissenschaft 1600–1800* (Munich, 1988); K. G. A. Jeserich et al. (eds), *Deutsche Verwaltungsgeschichte*, vol. I (Stuttgart, 1983), pp. 389–91, 398.

5. P. Nitschke, *Verbrechensbekämpfung und Verwaltung. Die Entstehung der Polizei in der Grafschaft Lippe 1700–1814* (Münster, 1990), pp. 112–13.

6. P. Münch, 'Die "Obrigkeit im Vaterstand": Zu Definition und Kritik des "Landesvaters" während der frühen Neuzeit', *Daphnis*, 11 (1982), 15–40.

7. R. Po-Chia Hsia, *Social Discipline in the Reformation: Central Europe, 1550–1750* (London, 1989), pp. 146–7.

8. U. Gleixner, 'Frauen, Justiznutzung und dörfliche Rechtskultur', in K. Garber et al. (ed.), *Erfahrung und Deutung von Krieg und Frieden* (Munich, 2001), pp. 453–61.

9. J. Nowosadtko, 'Die policierte Fauna in Theorie und Praxis. Frühneuzeitliche Tierhaltung, Seuchen- und Schädlingsbekämpfung im Spiegel der Policeyvorschriften', in K. Härter (ed.), *Policey und frühneuzeitliche Gesellschaft* (Frankfurt, 2000), pp. 297–340.

10. Good introductions in R. Sandgruber, '"Österreich über alles". Programmatik und Realität der Wirtschaft zur Zeit Prinz Eugens', in E. Zöllner and K. Gutkas (eds), *Österreich und die Osmanen − Prinz Eugen und seine Zeit* (Vienna, 1988), pp. 153–71; P. H. Smith, *The Business of Alchemy: Science and Culture in the Holy Roman Empire* (Princeton, 1994).

11. K. Schwieger, 'Militär und Bürgertum. Zur gesellschaftlichen Prägekraft des preußischen Militärsystems im 18. Jahrhundert', in D. Blasius (ed.), *Preußen in der deutsche Geschichte* (Königstein, 1980), pp. 179–200 at 197.
12. For suggestions along these lines, see I. Mittenzwei and E. Herzfeld, *Brandenburg-Preußen 1648–1789* (Cologne, 1987), p. 351; and P. Bachmann and K. Zeisler, *Der deutsche Militärismus vom 17. Jahrhundert bis 1917* (2nd edn; Cologne, 1986).
13. T. C. W. Blanning, *Reform and Revolution in Mainz, 1743–1803* (Cambridge, 1974), pp. 75, 82–4.
14. A. Jakob, *Die Neustadt Erlangen* (Erlangen, 1986).
15. M. Walker, *The Salzburg Transaction: Expulsion and Redemption in Eighteenth-century Germany* (Ithaca, 1992).
16. M. Fulbrook, *Peity and Politics: Religion and the Rise of Absolutism in England, Württemberg and Prussia* (Cambridge, 1983); R. L. Gawthrop, *Pietism and the Making of Eighteenth-century Prussia* (Cambridge, 1993); C. Hinrichs, *Preußentum und Pietismus. Der Pietismus in Brandenburg-Preußen als religiös-soziale Reformbewegung* (Göttingen, 1971).
17. Cited in Nitschke, *Verbrechensbekämpfung*, p. 43. See also C. Dipper, *Deutsche Geschichte 1648–1789* (Frankfurt, 1991), pp. 189–99.
18. R. A. Dorwart, *The Prussian Welfare State before 1740* (Cambridge, Mass., 1971). For the Mainz measures, see Blanning, *Reform and Revolution*, pp. 188–90.
19. S. Kroll, 'Kursächsisches Militär und ländliche Randgruppen im 18. Jahrhundert', in S. Kroll and K. Krüger (eds), *Militär und ländliche Gesellschaft* (Hamburg, 2000), pp. 275–95.
20. M. Foucault, *Discipline and Punish: The Birth of the Prison* (Harmondsworth, 1979). For the European perspective, see K. H. Metz, 'Staatsraison und Menschenfreundlichkeit. Formen und Wandlungen der Armenpflege im Ancien Régime Frankreichs, Deutschlands und Großbritanniens', *VSWG*, 72 (1985), 1–26.
21. F. Wintterlin, 'Zur Geschichte des herzoglichen Kommerzienrats', *Württembergische Vierteljahreshefte für Landesgeschichte*, NF 20 (1911), 310–27; W. Söll, *Die staatliche Wirtschaftspolitik in Württemberg im 17. und 18. Jahrhundert* (Tübingen, 1934), pp. 87–90, 98–100, 115–20.
22. P. H. Wilson, 'Johann Jakob Moser und die württembergische Politik', in A. Gestrich and R. Lächle (eds), *Johann Jakob Moser* (Stuttgart, 2002), pp. 1–25; and his 'Der Favorit als Sündenbock. Joseph Süß Oppenheimer (1698–1738)', in M. Kaiser and A. Pecar (eds), *Der zweite Mann im Staat* (Berlin, 2003), pp. 155–76.
23. The debate is discussed further in P. H. Wilson, *Absolutism in Central Europe* (London, 2000), pp. 108–20.
24. P. G. M. Dickson, *Finance and Government under Maria Theresia 1740–1780* (2 vols; Oxford, 1987), II, pp. 398–9.

25. F. A. J. Szabo, *Kaunitz and Enlightened Absolutism, 1753–1780* (Cambridge, 1994).

26. See C. Ingrao, 'The Smaller German States', in H. M. Scott (ed.), *Enlightened Absolutism* (Basingstoke, 1990), pp. 221–43; and his edited collection *Imperial Principalities on the Eve of Revolution: The Lay Electorates*, special issue of *GH*, 20 (2002).

27. C. Ingrao, *The Hessian Mercenary State. Ideas, Institutions and Reform under Frederick II, 1760–1785* (Cambridge, 1987); G. Fischer, 'Die Subsidienverträge des Markgrafen Alexander von Ansbach-Bayreuth', *Archiv für die Geschichte und Altertumskunde von Oberfranken*, 30 (1927), 68–87; E. Städter, *Die Ansbach-Bayreuther Truppen im amerikanischen Unabhängigkeitskrieg 1777–1783* (Neustadt/Aisch, 1955); W. Deeters, 'Das erste Jahrzehnt des braunschweigischen Finanzkollegs 1773 bis 1785', *Braunschweigisches Jahrbuch*, 56 (1975), 101–19.

28. For the debate, see P. H. Wilson, 'The German "Soldier Trade" of the Seventeenth and Eighteenth Centuries. A Reassessment', *IHR*, 18 (1996), 757–92.

29. M. Umbach, *Federalism and Enlightenment in Germany, 1740–1806* (London, 2000); J. B. Knudsen, *Justus Möser and the German Enlightenment* (Cambridge, 1986).

30. G. Fertig, 'Balancing, Networking and the Causes of Emigration: Early German Transatlantic Migration in a Local Perspective, 1700–1754', *Continuity and Change*, 13 (1998), 419–42.

31. H. Möller, *Fürstenstaat oder Bürgernation: Deutschland 1763–1815* (Berlin, 1989), p. 82; P. J. Hauben, 'The First Decade of an Agrarian Experiment in Bourbon Spain: The "New Towns" of Sierra Morena and Andalusia, 1766–75', *Agricultural History*, 39 (1965), 34–40.

32. B. Wunder, 'Das Kaiserliche Emigrationspatent von 1768', in W. Wüst (ed.), *Reichskreis und Territorium* (Stuttgart, 2000), pp. 111–22.

33. Toleration edicts were issued for all Christians in Hamburg (1785), Prussia (1788), Bavaria (1803), Württemberg (1803), Baden (1818), Hessen (1831) and Saxony (1841).

34. P. C. Hartmann, *Kulturgeschichte des Heiligen Römischen Reiches 1648 bis 1806* (Vienna, 2001), pp. 331–7; B. Tolley, *Pastors and Parishioners in Württemberg during the Late Reformation, 1581–1621* (Stanford, 1995), pp. 130–1.

35. B. Wunder, *Geschichte der Bürokratie in Deutschland* (Frankfurt, 1986), pp. 55–6.

36. Cited in Blanning, *Reform and Revolution*, pp. 164–5. See also J. V. H. Melton, *Absolutism and the Eighteenth-century Origins of Compulsory Schooling in Prussia and Austria* (Cambridge, 1988); G. Heiß, 'Erziehung der Waisen zur Manufakturarbeit. Pädagogische Zielvorstellungen und ökonomische Interessen der maria-theresianischen Verwaltung', *MIÖG*, 85 (1977), 316–31.

37. E. J. Hobsbawm, *Bandits* (Manchester, 1959); C. Küther, *Räuber und Gauner in Deutschland* (2nd edn; Göttingen, 1987).

38. U. Danker, *Räuberbandedn im alten Reich um 1700* (Frankfurt, 1988).

39. O. Ulbricht, 'The World of a Beggar around 1775: Johann Gottfried Kästner', *CEH*, 27 (1994), 153–84.
40. Nitschke, *Verbrechensbekämpfung*, p. 48. See also section 3.2 above.
41. R. J. Evans, *Rituals of Retribution: Capital Punishment in Germany, 1600–1987* (London, 1996), pp. 43–4.
42. H. Weill, *Frederick the Great and Samuel von Cocceji* (Madison, Wisconsin, 1961), pp. 102–5.
43. A. Gestreich, *Absolutismus und Öffentlichkeit* (Göttingen, 1994), pp. 120–4. See also R. van Dülmen, *Theatre of Horror: Crime and Punishment in Early Modern Germany* (Cambridge, 1990).
44. I. Mittenzwei, *Friedrich II. von Preußen* (4th edn; Berlin, 1986), pp. 97–100; T. C. W. Blanning, *Joseph II* (Harlow, 1994), p. 82.
45. M. Spindler (ed.), *Handbuch der bayerischen Geschichte* (2nd edn, 2 vols; Munich, 1988), II, pp. 1248–52; H. E. Strakosch, *State Absolutism and the Rule of Law: The Struggle for the Codification of Civil Law in Austria, 1753–1811* (Sydney, 1967).
46. K. Wegert, *Popular Culture, Crime and Social Control in 18th Century Württemberg* (Stuttgart, 1994), pp. 212–13. See also K. Härter, 'Soziale Disziplinierung durch Strafe? Intentionen frühneuzeitlichen Policeyordnungen und staatlichen Sanktionspraxis', *ZHF*, 26 (1999), 365–79.
47. U. Rublack, 'State-formation, gender and the experience of governance in early modern Württemberg', in U. Rublack (ed.), *Gender in Early Modern German History* (Cambridge, 2002), pp. 200–17.
48. J. Schlumbohm, 'Gesetze, die nicht durchgesetzt werden – Ein Strukturmerkmal des frühneuzeitlichen Staates?', *Geschichte und Gesellschaft*, 23 (1997), 647–63.
49. For the debate, see T. Scott, 'Peasant Revolts in Early Modern Germany', *HJ*, 28 (1985), 455–68.
50. W. Troßbach, 'Bauernbewegungen in deutschen Kleinterritorien zwischen 1648 und 1789', in W. Schulze (ed.), *Aufstände, Revolten, Prozesse* (Stuttgart, 1983), pp. 233–60; and his 'Bäuerlicher Widerstand in deutschen Kleinterritorien zwischen Bauernkrieg und Französischen Revolution', *Zeitschrift für Agrargeschichte und Agrarsoziologie*, 35 (1988), 1–16.
51. V. Press, 'Von den Bauernrevolten des 16. zur konstitutionellen Verfassung des 19. Jahrunderts. Die Untertanenkonflikte in Hohenzollern-Hechingen und ihre Lösungen', in H. Weber (ed.), *Politische Ordnungen und soziale Kräfte im alten Reich* (Wiesbaden, 1980), pp. 85–112.
52. J. J. Moser, *Neues teutsches Staatsrecht* (20 vols; Frankfurt, 1766–75), vol. XV, pp. 820–1.
53. W. Trossbach, 'Widerstand als Normalfall: Bauernunruhen in der Grafschaft Sayn-Wittgenstein-Wittgenstein 1696–1806', *Westfälische Zeitschrift*, 135 (1985), 25–111; G. Benecke, *Politics and Society in Germany, 1500–1750* (London, 1974), p. 187.
54. C. R. Friedrichs, 'Urban Politics and Urban Social Structures in Seventeenth-century Germany', *European History Quarterly*, 22 (1992), 187–216.

55. G. L. Soliday, *A Community in Conflict: Frankfurt Society in the 17th and 18th Centuries* (Hanover, New Hampshire, 1974).
56. D. M. Luebke, *His Majesty's Rebels: Communities, Factions and Rural Revolts in the Black Forest, 1725–1745* (Ithaca, 1997). See also, the sources in Chapter 5, n. 17, above.
57. For a good example, see R. Blickle, 'Peasant Protest and the Language of Women's Petitions', in Rublack (ed.), *Gender in Early Modern German History*, pp. 177–99.
58. F. Hertz, 'Die Rechtsprechung der höchsten Reichsgerichte im römisch-deutschen Reich und ihre politische Bedeutung', *MIÖG*, 69 (1961), 331–58; R. Sailer, *Untertanenprozesse vor dem Reichskammergericht* (Cologne, 1999).
59. Examples can be found in S. Herrmann, 'Die Durchführung von Schuldenverfahren im Rahmen kaiserlicher Debitkommissionen im 18. Jahrhundert am Beispiel des Debitwesens der Grafen von Montfort', in W. Sellert (ed.), *Reichshofrat und Reichskammergericht* (Cologne, 1999), pp. 111–27.
60. V. Press, 'Die Reichsstadt in der altständischen Gesellschaft', in J. Kunisch (ed.), *Neue Studien zur frühneuzeitlichen Geschichte* (Berlin, 1987), pp. 9–42, and his 'Reichsstadt und Revolution', in B. Kirchgässner and E. Naujoks (eds), *Stadt und wirtschaftliche Selbstverwaltung* (Sigmaringen, 1987), pp. 9–57.
61. K. E. Demandt, *Geschichte des Landes Hessen* (Kassel, 1980), pp. 306–11.
62. Rublack, 'State-formation', p. 212.

Chapter 8: Imperial and European Politics

1. P. Schroeder, 'The Constitution of the Holy Roman Empire after 1648', *HJ*, 42 (1999), 961–83; S. Pufendorf, *Die Verfassung des deutschen Reiches*, transl. and ed, H. Denzer (Stuttgart, 1994).
2. H. E. Feine, 'Zur Verfassungsentwicklung des Heiligen Römischen Reiches seit dem Westfälischen Frieden', *ZSRG GA*, 52 (1932), 65–133. The best recent study of the period after 1648 is K. O. Freiherr von Aretin, *Das alte Reich 1648–1806* (3 vols; Stuttgart, 1993–7).
3. H. F. Schwarz, *The Imperial Privy Council in the Seventeenth Century* (Cambridge, Mass., 1943), p. 403.
4. There is no adequate modern biography of Leopold I, one of the most important emperors. For a starting point, see J. P. Spielman, *Leopold I of Austria* (London, 1977), which offers insight into his personal character.
5. J. J. Noël, 'Zur Geschichte der Reichsbelehnungen im 18. Jahrhundert', *MÖSA*, 21 (1968), 106–22.
6. A. Müller, *Der Regensburger Reichstag von 1653/54* (Frankfurt, 1992).
7. M. Schnettger, *Der Reichsdeputationstag 1655–1663* (Münster, 1996).
8. V. Press, 'Kurhannover im System des alten Reiches 1692–1806', in A. M. Birke and K. Kluxen (eds), *England und Hannover* (Munich, 1986), pp. 53–79;

G. Schnath, *Geschichte Hannovers im Zeitalter der neunten Kur und der englischen Sukzession 1674–1714* (5 vols; Hildesheim, 1938–82); L. & M. Frey, *A Question of Empire: Leopold I and the War of Spanish Succession, 1701–1705* (New York, 1983); A Berney, *König Friedrich I und das Haus Habsburg (1701–1707)* (Munich, 1927).

9. L. Hüttl, *Max Emanuel. Der Blaue Kurfürst 1679–1726* (Munich, 1976); R. Place, 'Bavaria and the Collapse of Louis XIV's German Policy', *JMH*, 49 (1977), 369–93.

10. K. O. Freiherr von Aretin, *Das Reich. Friedensordnung und europäische Gleichgewicht 1648–1806* (Stuttgart, 1992), pp. 221–32; R. de Schryver, *Max II. Emanuel von Bayern und das spanische Erbe* (Mainz, 1996).

11. K. Müller, 'Kurfürst Johann Wilhelm und die europäische Politik seiner Zeit', *Düsseldorfer Jahrbuch*, 60 (1986), 1–23; G. W. Sante, 'Die kurpfälzische Politik des Kurfürsten Johann Wilhelm', *HJb*, 44 (1924), 19–64; M. Braubach, 'Johann Wilhelm. Kurfürst von der Pfalz, Herzog von Jülich und Berg (1658–1716)', *Rheinische Lebensbilder*, 1 (1961), 83–101.

12. L. Auer, 'Zur Rolle Italiens in der österreichischen Politik um das spanischen Erbe', *MÖSA*, 31 (1978), 52–72.

13. V. Press, 'Josef I (1705–1711)', in R. Melville et al. (eds), *Deutschland und Europa in der Neuzeit* (Wiesbaden, 1988), pp. 277–97, presents a balanced view.

14. B. Rill, *Karl VI. Habsburg als barocke Großmacht* (Graz, 1992).

15. H. von Zwiedineck-Südenhorst, 'Die Anerkennung der pragmatische Sanktion Karls VI. durch das deutsche Reich', *MIÖG*, 16 (1895), 276–341. For Habsburg diplomacy in this period, see the detailed account by M. Braubach, *Prinz Eugen von Savoyen* (5 vols; Munich, 1963–5).

16. J. L. Sutton, *The King's Honour and the King's Cardinal: The War of the Polish Succession* (Lexington, 1980); P. H. Wilson, *German Armies: War and German Politics, 1648–1806* (London, 1998), pp. 226–34 and the sources cited there.

17. K. A. Roider Jr, *The Reluctant Ally: Austria's Policy in the Austro-Turkish War, 1737–1739* (Baton Rouge, 1972); Wilson, *German Armies*, pp. 234–41.

18. H. Schissler, 'The Social and Political Power of the Prussian Junkers', in R. Gibson and M. Blinkhorn (eds), *Landownership and Power* (London, 1991), pp. 99–110. See also section 3.3.

19. The best recent survey is D. McKay, *The Great Elector* (Harlow, 2001).

20. For a sympathetic portrait of the embattled Charles VII, see P. C. Hartmann, *Karl Albrecht, Karl VII* (Regensburg, 1985). For Prussia's wars, see D. E. Showalter, *The Wars of Frederick the Great* (London, 1996).

21. A. Schmid, *Max III. Joseph und die europäischen Mächte* (Munich, 1987).

22. E. Buddruss, *Die französische Deutschlandpolitik 1756–1789* (Mainz, 1995); L. Schilling, *Kaunitz und das Renversement des Alliances* (Berlin, 1994).

23. For this and the following, see Wilson, *German Armies*, pp. 260–97.

24. E. Weis, 'Ergebnisse eines Vergleiches der grundherrschaftlichen Strukturen Deutschlands und Frankreichs', *VSWG*, 57 (1970), 1–14.

25. J. Smets, 'Von der "Dorfidylle" zur preußischen Nation. Sozialdisziplinierung der linksrheinischen Bevölkerung durch die Franzosen am Beispiel der allgemeinen Wehrpflicht (1802–1814)', *HZ*, 262 (1996), 695–738.

26. P. E, Selwyn, *Everyday Life in the German Booktrade* (Pennsylvania, 2000).

27. K. Müller, 'Bürgerproteste und Handwerkerunruhen im Herzogtum Berg in der Zeit der Französischen Revolution', in H. Berding (ed.), *Soziale Unruhen in Deutschland* (Göttingen, 1988), pp. 92–110.

28. T. C. W. Blanning, *The French Revolution in Germany: Occupation and Resistance in the Rhineland, 1792–1802* (Oxford, 1983).

29. K. H. Wegert, *German Radicals Confront the Common People: Revolutionary Politics and Popular Politics, 1789–1849* (Mainz, 1992).

30. M. Hochedlinger, *Krise und Wiederherstellung: Österreichische Großmachtpolitik zwischen Türkenkrieg und 'zweiter Diplomatischer Revolution' 1789–91* (Berlin, 2000); J. Lukowski, *The Partitions of Poland: 1772, 1793, 1795* (Harlow, 1999).

31. K. Härter, *Reichstag und Revolution 1789–1806* (Göttingen, 1992); S. S. Biro, *The German Policy of Revolutionary France* (Cambridge, Mass., 1957).

32. D. Hohrath et al. (eds), *Das Ende reichsstädtischer Freiheit 1802* (Ulm, 2002). Six imperial cities remained after 1803: Augsburg, Nuremberg, Frankfurt, Bremen, Lübeck and Hamburg.

Index

Aachen, imperial city, 79, 301
absolutism
  conservative legacy, 337–8, 343–5
  contemporary views, 274, 336–7
  decline, 262, 338
  economic impact, 264, 288–9
  emergence, 209, 212–17, 228–30, 243,
    254, 288
  enlightened, 91, 210, 278–85, 288,
    336–7, 343
  fiscal impact, 257
  imperial, 8, 11, 110, 116, 209
  interpretations, 175, 208–9, 212–14,
    235, 265, 278, 320
  limits, 210–12, 229, 236, 246–7, 252,
    280, 296
  military power, 208, 226, 228
  personal character, 253–4, 262, 338,
    343
  political impact, 157, 253
  and public sphere, 61, 156, 218, 221,
    226
  social impact, 264, 288–9, 337–8, 343–5
  theory, 209–12, 236, 251, 274, 288, 302
Adami, Adam (1610–63), abbot of
    Murrhardt from 1628, 138–9
administrators, Protestant, 43, 124, 200
Adriatic Sea, 80, 147, 164–5
Africa, 147
agrarian depression, 14th century, 86, 148,
    264
agrarian reform, 54, 91–6, 284, 344
  impact, 90, 336

agriculture, 51, 78, 82–90, 97
  crops, 51, 86, 92
  limitations , 256
  see manorial economy
Aktenversendung, 179
Albrecht (1397–1439), German king and
    emperor from 1438, 20
Albrecht von Hohenzollern (1498–
    1568), Teutonic grand master
    (1510–25) and duke of Prussia
    from 1525, 27
alchemy, 260
Allgäu region, 102
alliance rights, 12–13, 34, 190
Alsace, landgraviate
  and France, 44, 140, 170, 174, 334
  and Habsburgs, 26–7, 140, 339
  composition, 23, 38
Althann, Michael Johann Count
    (1679–1722), Habsburg courtier,
    236
Althusius, Johannes (1557–1638), political
    theorist, 211, 250
Allgemeine Deutsche Bibliothek, 62
Amalia, Elisabeth von Solms (1602–51),
    regent of Hessen-Kassel (1637–50),
    134
America, emigration to, 283
Anhalt, principalities, 24, 29, 87
Anhalt-Bernberg, principality, 298
Anhalt-Dessau, principality, 205, 282
Anna Petrovna (1708–28), duchess of
    Holstein-Gottorp, 29

Ansbach, margraviate
  finance, 259, 282,
  imperial politics, 184, 189, 194
  and Prussia, 323–4, 339
  society, 77
  territory, 24
anti-clericalism, 284–5, 299
anti-Semitism, 76–8, 154, 278, 291, 299,
  301
Anton Ulrich (1633–1714), duke of
  Wolfenbüttel from 1666, 193
armed princes, 169–70, 173–4, 192–4,
  202, 346
armies
  cost, 125–7, 143, 160, 163, 165, 167–8,
    231, 234, 258–62
  economic impact, 94, 104, 225, 232, 234,
    256, 270–1, 276, 278
  interpretations, 208, 225
  permanent, 171, 175, 208, 231, 270
  purpose, 225, 275
  officers, 214, 216, 231–4
  origins, 125, 143, 157, 169, 225, 228
  size, 118, 120, 125, 170, 172–2, 225–8,
    231, 258, 318, 323–4, 378–81
  social impact, 73, 92, 270
  structure, 171–2, 174, 225–6, 230–2, 239,
    training, 225, 231, 233,
  used for repression, 96, 110, 151, 191,
    214–15, 228–30, 270, 275, 302–3,
    309–10,
Auersperg, Johann Weickard Prince von
  (1615–77), Habsburg minister, 235–6
Augsburg, bishopric, 199–200
Augsburg, Confession (1530), 31
Augsburg, imperial city, 61, 72, 148–9
Augsburg, League (1686), 192
  see also Nine Years War
Augsburg, Peace (1555)
  implementation, 105–6, 114, 140
  interpretations , 104, 108
  modifications to, 127, 133–4, 139
  terms, 42–3, 116, 149
August Wilhelm (1722–58), prince of
  Prussia, 224
Augustus II 'the Strong' (1670–1733),
  elector of Saxony (1694) and king of
  Poland (1697), 233

Augustus III (1693–1733), elector of
  Saxony and king of Poland from 1733,
  200
Austria, archduchy
  Bavarian invasion, 327
  confessionalisation, 110, 123, 267–8
  economy, 83, 88, 93, 270, 277
  Estates, 16, 109, 111–13, 115, 118,
    122–3, 308
  nobility, 88, 113, 121, 199, 214–15,
    243–4, 314
  relationship to Reich, 26, 40, 46, 159,
    163–4, 171, 185–6
  religion, 66, 107, 109–13, 123
  revolt (1595–7), 121, 299
  see Habsburg monarchy
Austrian Kreis, 173, 184–6, 193–4, 199
Austro-Prussian rivalry
  confessional element, 149, 151–3, 325,
    338
  constitutional impact, 183, 197
  events, 203–5, 319–31, 338–41
  impact on Reich, 9, 175, 195, 203–5,
    327–32, 339–40
  impact on territories, 92, 284
Avignon, 206

Bach, Johann Sebastian (1685–1750),
  composer, 156
Baden, margraviates, 69, 83, 87, 89, 95
Baden-Baden, margraviate, 24, 45–6, 158,
  219
Baden-Durlach, margraviate
  army, 167
  electoral status, 40
  Estates, 251
  expansion, 207
  finances, 261
  government, 247
  imperial politics, 126, 205, 261, 340–1
  influence, 24, 45–6,141, 189, 219
  legal system, 294
  relationship to Reich, 178
Balthasar, 'Krummfinger', bandit, 291
Baltic Sea, 80, 104, 147–8
Baltic tolls, 124, 129
Bamberg, bishopric, 24, 77, 184, 190, 193,
  199, 286

bandits, 290–2, 296
banks, 94, 259, 262, 281
Bartenstein, Johann Christoph Baron von (1685–1750), Habsburg minister, 236
Basel, bishopric, 199, 241, 286
Basel, city, 38, 80
Basel, Peace (1795), 234, 261, 340
Bauernlegen, 86–7
Bauernschütz, 91–5
Bavaria, electorate
  ally of Habsburgs, 114–17, 120, 136, 315
  army, 114, 120, 123, 217, 225, 231–2, 291, 315, 325, 225
  censorship, 335
  crime, 290–2
  economy, 54, 79, 82–4, 217, 282
  education, 286
  electoral status, 39, 41, 120, 132, 134, 141, 315
  Estates, 217, 251, 260
  exchange plans, 204, 331
  finance, 223, 256–7, 325, 335, 259–62
  government, 120, 217, 238–9, 241
  French alliance, 133, 135, 170, 194, 215, 327, 340
  imperial ambitions, 13, 40, 195, 223, 322, 326
  influence, 24, 229, 328, 341
  legal system, 294–6
  mortality, 53
  nobility, 199, 217, 243–4
  opposes the Habsburgs, 48, 175, 22–3, 315–18, 326–7
  population, 54, 188, 325
  religion, 66
  revolts, 230, 299, 302–3
  size, 8, 188, 325
  society, 56, 97
Bavarian Kreis, 24, 184, 188, 192–3, 197, 199
Bayreuth, margraviate
  imperial politics, 184, 190, 194
  and Prussia, 323–4, 339
  society, 77, 271–2
  territory, 24
Beccaria, Cesare (1738–94), legal reformer, 294

Becher, Johann Joachim (1625–82), cameralist, 286
begging, 73, 78, 274, 277, 290
Belgiojoso, Jacopo, imperial general, 111
Belgrade, city, 317, 319
Below, Georg von, historian, 83
Benedictines, 286
Berchtesgaden, princely priory, 199, 204, 273
Berg, duchy, 24, 45, 108, 139, 335
Berlin, city
  crime, 291
  economy, 79–80, 94, 270, 324
  and Hohenzollern institutions, 219, 223–5, 273, 276
  population, 271
  religion, 274
  society, 53, 73
  taxes, 257
Bernadotte, Jean-Baptiste (1763–1844), marshal of France and (as Charles XIV) king of Sweden, 28
Bernhard (1604–39), duke of Weimar, 130, 134
Besançon, imperial city, 38
Biberach, imperial city, 149
birth control, 52, 58
birth rate, 52–4
Bischoffwerder, Johann Rudolf von (1741–1803), Prussian minister, 225
Bismarck, Otto von (1815–98), Prussian statesman, 2, 4, 6
Black Death, 50, 86, 96
Black Forest, 90, 97, 339
Blasius, Julie (b.1781), bandit, 291
Blenheim, battle (1704), 175, 316
Blickle, Peter, historian, 98–9, 250
Bocskay, Stephen (1557–1606), prince of Transylvania (1605), 110–11
Bodin, Jean (1530–96), political theorist, 33, 105, 305
Bohemia, kingdom
  Bavarian invasion, 326–7
  crime, 291
  economy, 25, 79, 83, 88, 92–3, 148, 283
  Estates, 15, 111–13, 115–17, 121–3, 130, 252–3, 308

Bohemia, kingdom (*continued*)
  monarchy, 111, 113, 118, 122–3
  nobility, 92–3, 123, 214–15, 324
  Prussian invasions, 77–8, 329, 331
  relationship to Reich, 22, 25–6, 39, 145,
      159, 163, 185
  religion, 77–8, 112, 117, 123, 273
  revised constitution (1627), 122–3
  Swedish invasion, 135
  unrest, 92–3, 299, 332
Bohemian Revolt (1618)
  causes, 16, 103–4, 111, 117–20, 251
  consequences, 88, 122–3, 214–15,
      250
  failure, 121–3
Boitzenburg, manorial estate, 88
Book of Concord (1580), 31, 107, 273
Bonn, town, 219
Borussian historiography, 4–6, 320
Brakel, town, 38
Brandenburg, electorate,
  armed forces, 167, 170
  economy, 83, 86–9, 91, 93–4, 147,
      270
  education, 286
  Estates, 90, 216, 251
  finances, 257
  government, 236, 239, 273
  imperial politics, 114, 134–5, 229,
      313–14, 326
  influence, 25, 27, 39, 46
  population, 53
  religion, 25, 41, 66, 107, 212, 273–4
  society, 70, 98
  unrest, 216, 270, 299
  see also Prussia
Brandenburg African Company, 147
Brandenburg Recess (1653), 90, 216
Breisach, fortress, 140
Breisgau, landgraviate, 26, 261
Breitenfeld, first battle (1631), 128
Breitenfeld, second battle (1642), 135
Bremen, archbishopric, 124, 127, 142, 184,
      186
Bremen, imperial city, 25, 37, 77, 143
Brenner, Martin (d.1618), bishop of
      Seckau from 1585, 110
Breslau, city, 80

Britain,
  economy, 3, 80, 147, 257
  education, 245
  finance, 257, 259, 263
  and German princes, 231, 281, 329
  government, 160, 208–9, 254
  and Habsburgs, 165, 194, 316–18,
      340–1
  and Hanover, 28, 223, 314, 328–30
  legal system, 241, 294–5
  parliament, 121–2, 249–50, 257
  and Prussia, 328–9
  and Reich, 115, 137, 194, 272
  religion, 285
Brixen, bishopric, 199
'Brothers' Quarrel', 109–13, 118
Brunswick, city, 38, 156, 229
Brunswick, duchies
  army, 167
  crime, 291
  imperial politics, 114, 129, 184, 186–7,
      193
  partitions, 25
  see Guelphs; Wolfenbüttel
Brussels, city, 27
Buchau, imperial city, 301
Bückler, Johannes (1780–1803), bandit,
      291
Bucquoy, Charles Bonaventura de
      Longueval Baron de (1571–1621),
      imperial general, 118
Buda, city, 123
Budweis, town, 118
bureaucracy
  efficiency, 242, 247
  ethos, 242, 245–7, 343
  interpretations, 208, 234–5, 242, 247
  lower echelons, 76, 238, 240–3, 266, 275,
      291
  municipal, 72, 98, 101
  size, 216, 241
  social composition, 66, 214, 216–17,
      242–4, 311, 333
  structure, 235–42
  see ministers *and* individual territories
burghers
  careers, 243–7, 277–8
  life expectancy, 53

landownership, 94–5
numbers, 71
political representation, 15, 72, 249, 254, 300–1
social transformation, 65, 74–5
status, 65, 71–3
wealth, 72, 301
Burgundian Kreis
Austrian acquisition, 27, 314, 316
Kreis Association, 193
population, 50
relationship to Reich, 119, 131–2, 137, 143, 163, 171, 184–6, 341
and Spain, 26–7, 108–9, 119, 131–2, 159, 166
Burgundian Treaty (1548), 27, 131, 187
Burgundy, duchy, 23, 26–7
Büsching, Anton Friedrich (1727–93), geographer, 279
Buxtehude, Dietrich (1637–1707), composer, 156

Calenberg, duchy, 25, 39
Calvinism
clergy, 65–6
constitutional recognition , 134, 139, 141
princely conversion to, 41, 66, 107–8, 212
theology, 107, 273
see religion
Calwer Company, 81–2
Cambrai, bishopric, 43
Cambrai, imperial city, 38
cameralism
influence, 245–6, 280, 288–9, 343
measures, 271–2, 289–90
theory, 240, 243, 268–70, 274–5, 277, 284
Campo Formio, Peace (1797), 340–1
canons, see cathedral chapters
canton system, 92, 233–4, 321
capitalism
agrarian, 86, 91, 254
analytical model, 64
spread, 70, 79–80, 104, 213, 264, 288
Capuchins, 123
Carinthia, duchy, 26, 93

Carl Albrecht, see Charles VII
Carl Alexander (1684–1737), duke of Württemberg from 1733, 150, 252, 278
Carl Eugen (1728–93), duke of Württemberg from 1737, 252, 278, 303
Carl Friedrich (1700–39), duke of Holstein-Gottorp from 1703, 28
Carl Leopold (d.1747), duke of Mecklenburg-Schwerin from 1713, 48, 96, 303
Carl Philipp (1661–1742), elector Palatine from 1716, 150
Carl Theodor (1724–99), elector Palatine from 1742, 206, 223, 237, 244, 331
Carlos II (1661–1700), king of Spain from 1665, 315
Carnioloa, duchy, 26, 93
Carolina law code, 59, 179
cathedral and abbey chapters, 15, 21, 198–202, 238, 248, 314
Catherine II the Great (1729–96), Russian empress from 1762, 29, 283, 330
Catholicism, 31–2
princely conversions to, 150–1, 252
see religion
Catholic League, see Liga
Catholic Renewal Movement, 204–7, 286
Celle, duchy, 25, 169, 291
censorship, 334–5
Cernin family, 122
Charlemagne (742–814), emperor from 800, 18, 20, 29
Charles V (1500–58), emperor from 1519, abdication, 40
coronation, 21
dynastic empire, 26–7, 34
and imperial cities, 72
and imperial constitution, 8, 32, 39, 47, 159, 185
and religion, 13, 32, 105
wars, 163, 166, 168
Charles VI (1685–1740), emperor from 1711
government, 236
Habsburg succession, 53, 195, 318–19, 327

Charles VI (1685–1740) (*continued*)
  Reich, 48, 151, 158, 180, 232, 272,
    317–18
  as king of Spain, 317
Charles VII (Carl Albrecht) (1697–1745),
    emperor from 1742
  as elector of Bavaria, 223, 318
  considers secularisation, 203, 282
  election, 20, 40, 195, 326–7
  weakens imperial constitution, 48, 195,
    312, 327
Charles II (1540–90), archduke of Styria
    from 1564, 110
Chemnitz, battle (1639), 135
Chemnitz, Bogislaw Philipp von
    (1605–78), propagandist, 305–6
Chiemsee, bishopric, 43
child labour, 276, 287
childhood, 54–5, 58, 69, 267–8
Christian IV (1577–1648), king of
    Denmark from 1588, 124–5
Christian Prince von Anhalt Bernberg
    (1568–1630), Protestant general, 115
church
  territorial, 31, 198, 249
  structure, 31–2, 65–7, 95–6, 239, 273
  see clergy; confessionalisation; imperial
    church; religion
citizenship, 60, 65, 71, 75, 300, 343
class formation, 64, 74–5
class struggle, 249–50, 290–1, 297, 300,
    304, 345
Clemens August of Bavaria (1700–61),
    elector of Cologne (1723), bishop of
    Münster (1719), Paderborn (1719),
    Hildesheim (1724), and Teutonic
    grand master (1732), 203
Clemens Wenzeslaus of Saxony
    (1739–1812), elector of Trier
    (1768–1802), bishop of Freising
    (1763–8), Regensburg (1763–8) and
    Augsburg (1768–1802), 200, 205–6
clergy
  life expectancy, 53
  marriage, 56
  political representation, 15, 248–9, 254
  social composition, 65–7, 72, 82,
    199–202, 244

  social role, 56
  status, 63, 70
  supervision of, 31–2, 65–7, 205, 239,
    285
  training, 67, 107–8, 243
  welfare, 56, 207, 285
Cleves, duchy
  dispute over, 45, 108, 112, 115, 182
  education, 286
  Estates , 228
  government, 241
  Prussian rule, 184, 323
  religion, 115, 139
  territory, 24
Cleves, town, 223
climate, 51, 54, 82, 104, 148
co-adjutors, 202
Coburg, duchy, 182, 290, 294
Collegium Germanicum, 107
Cologne, electorate
  cathedral chapter, 199
  dispute election (1583), 108
  economy, 80
  Estates, 178
  and France, 170
  imperial politics, 48, 120, 134, 183,
    204–5, 315
  influence, 23, 39–40, 184
  possession of , 108, 200, 203, 315
  relationship to Reich, 39–40, 178
  society, 77
  territory, 23, 187–8
Cologne, imperial city, 108, 219, 229,
    271
  peace talks in (1637), 136
colonies, 3, 26, 80, 132, 148, 283–4
  German, 147
common good, 12, 63, 99–100, 211, 266,
    269, 274, 335
Common Penny, 160–1, 177, 254
communal government
  divisions within, 72–3, 100, 300–2
  limitations, 264
  structure, 15–17, 84, 97–8, 100–2, 238
  urban, 30, 34, 37, 60, 72, 97–8, 249,
    300–1
  see imperial cities; residence towns;
    settlement

communalism, 98–102, 250–1, 298, 346
  and 'turning Swiss', 17, 38, 44
concubinage, 55–6
Confederatio Bohemica (1618), 118
Confederation of the Rhine (1806–13), 11,
  342
Confessio Bohemica (1575), 112
confessionalisation
  confessional state, 152, 239, 267, 273,
    288, 294
  decline of, 149–54, 203, 271–3, 288,
    294
  defined, 32, 346
  Habsburg, 110, 123, 139, 214–16
  as process, 30–2, 105–8, 110, 112, 115,
    123, 139, 267–8, 299
  political impact, 31, 212, 242, 266
Conring, Hermann (1606–81), political
  theorist, 211
consistories, 31, 239, 243, 271
Constance, bishopric, 184, 199–200, 206
Constance, former imperial city, 38
convents, 200, 203, 285
corporate groups, as political actors, 104,
  209, 249, 254, 266, 282, 300, 343
corporate rights, 9, 30, 58, 63, 74, 197,
  229–30, 247, 250, 267, 335
corpus evangelicorum, 140, 151–2, 325
counts palatine, 243
Courland, duchy, 27, 147
courts (dynastic)
  Bavarian, 155–6, 217, 219–20, 222–4
  cost, 221, 223–5, 271
  criticism of, 154–5, 236–7
  French, 155
  function, 215, 218, 224
  Habsburg, 109, 113, 155, 219–22, 311
  Hanoverian, 219, 223
  Hohenzollern, 217–20, 223–5, 271,
  imperial, 22, 35
  interpretation, 218
  lesser princes, 219–20, 271, 286
  Palatine, 219, 223
  Saxon, 223–4
  size, 217, 220–2
  Spanish, 109
  structure, 238, 242
  Württemberg, 219–20, 277–8

courts (law)
  imperial: case load, 151, 180–1, 299,
    302; effectiveness, 106, 114, 116,
    147, 180–3, 303–4; funding, 177,
    180; jurisdiction, 10, 106, 140, 143,
    176–9, 238; purpose, 106, 181–2;
    staff, 177–8, 180–1, 183; verdicts,
    96, 151, 153, 182–5, 252
  local, 98, 176, 301
  territorial, 55, 59, 90, 93–4, 153, 176,
    179, 181, 336–7
culture
  'high', 154–6
  'home town', 61–71, 99–101, 148–9, 154
  political: imperial, 36, 100, 222, 266,
    303–4, 331, 336–7, 344; territorial,
    210–12, 245–7, 250–1, 264–7
  'popular', 78, 289–93, 298, 335
  religious, 154, 156, 222, 273–4
  see common good; customs, norms
crime, 59, 73, 76, 101, 145–6
  attitudes towards, 292–3, 296
  interpretations, 289–91
  level, 292
Croatia, kingdom, 163–4, 311
currency, 196–7, 254, 261, 313
customs, 51, 55, 153

Danckelmann, Eberhard von
    (1643–1722), Prussian minister, 236
Danzig (Gdansk), city, 339
day labourers, 64, 71, 291
De statu ecclesiae (1763), 204
debt peonage, 84
debts (state), 109, 138, 168, 251, 258–63,
    303
Decapolis, 38
defence reform, 134, 170–5, 192, 231
Defenestration of Prague (1618), 117
Denmark, kingdom, 25
  economy, 83, 92
  encroachment on Reich, 38, 43, 124,
    129, 135
  and German princes, 28–9, 170, 193
  legal system, 294
  religion, 109
Derfflinger, Georg (1606–95),
    Hohenzollern field marshal, 244

Descartes, René (1596–1650),
    philosopher, 279
despotism, 48, 210, 249, 300
deviancy, 264
Dienstherrschaft, 85, 89, 346
Dietrichstein family, 122
diets, *see* Estates, Reichstag
disease, 51–3, 272, 283, 335
Dithmar, Justus Christoph (1676–1745),
    cameralist, 277
Dijon, town, 135
divorce, 55, 59, 285
Dobris, manorial estate, 93
Donauwörth, imperial city, 38, 114, 147,
    182
Dortmund, imperial city, 301
Dresden, city, 223–4
Droysen, Johann Gustav (1808–86),
    historian, 4
dualist model of German politics, 7–9, 34
Düren, town, 38
Durlach, residence town, 73, 219
Düsseldorf, town, 335
Dutch Republic, 16, 43, 80, 115
    and Austria, 165, 194, 316–18
    economy, 147–8, 257
    government, 122, 208, 211, 257
    and Prussia, 216, 260
    relationship to Reich, 137, 186–7
    subsidies to German princes, 170, 231,
        259
Dutch Revolt (1568–1648)
    character, 16, 27, 104, 106
    outcome, 136–7, 208
    and Reich, 103, 126–7, 131–2, 166–7
    support for, 108, 119, 121, 166, 186
Dutch War (1672–9), 169–70, 172, 192,
    230, 314–15
dynasticism, 13, 16–9, 157, 212, 219,
    288

East Frisia, principality, 24, 66, 187
    Estates, 249, 252, 257, 318
    Prussian rule, 324, 326
Eggenburg, Prince Johann Ulrich von
    (1568–1634), Habsburg minister,
    235, 244
'ecclesiastical reservation', 43

economy
    commercialisation, 74, 85–8, 91–4, 254,
        256, 262, 344
    comparison with France, 33–4
    gender, 58
    imperial regulation, 196–8, 344
    markets, 64, 73–4, 79, 83, 88, 92, 101,
        256, 265, 344
    'moral', 277
    overseas trade, 147
    productivity, 78, 83, 86, 92, 94–5, 101,
        213, 269, 332
    protectionism, 196, 198, 269–70, 277
    state regulation, 64, 239
    structure, 78, 80, 82–3, 146, 148
    urban, 301
    working day, 275
    see agriculture; cameralism; factories;
        industrialisation; mining; textile
        industry
education
    clerical, 67, 107–8
    higher, 243, 245–6, 274, 278, 286–7
    legal, 180–1, 245–6
    primary, 140, 274, 284, 286–8, 336
    purpose, 245, 285, 287–8
    regulation of, 267, 273, 284
    and social status, 74
    and state administration, 238, 243, 278
Eichsfeld, principality, 299
Eichstätt, bishopric, 200
Eisenach, duchy, 63
Elbe river, 22, 25, 70, 83, 86, 98–9
electoral capitulation, 47–8, 202, 346
electoral college, 20, 23, 35, 40–1, 128,
    137
Electoral Rhenish Kreis, 23, 184, 188–9,
    191, 193, 195, 197, 341
electors
    ecclesiastical, 23, 39
    influence, 40, 128, 307
    interests, 40, 47, 158, 166
    new titles, 39–40, 44, 120, 123, 132, 134,
        141, 174, 193, 314, 316
    obligations, 169
    powers, 20, 40–1, 47–8, 178, 314, 312,
        346
    secular, 39, 173, 307, 325, 329

Elisabethe, Christine von Braunschweig-Wolfenbüttel (1715–97), queen of Prussia, 224
Elias, Norbert, social theorist, 218
Emden, town, 66, 187
Emigration Patent (1768), 283
emigration, right of, 106, 140, 153, 272, 283
émigrés, French, 334
emperor
  contemporary views of, 100, 305–6
  coronation, 18, 21
  crown lands, 21–2, 157–8
  election, 20–1, 39–40, 119, 129, 134, 311–12
  medieval, 19–20, 25, 29, 37, 176–7, 198, 205
  powers, 10, 22, 33–4, 47–9, 119, 138, 158, 166, 176, 179, 243–4, 312
  role, 22, 108–10, 203, 312
  as supreme judge, 176, 179, 318
  see imperial title, Habsburgs
Enders, Liselott, historian, 83
enlightened thought, 91–2, 279–80, 284–5, 294–5, 336
  see absolutism
enlightenment, popular, 284
ennoblement, 22, 214, 243–4, 312
Erfurt, city, 38, 139, 188, 191, 228–30
Erlangen, town, 148, 271–2
Ernst August (1629–98), duke (1679) and elector (1692) of Hanover, 39, 193
Erthal, Friedrich Carl von (1719–1802), elector of Mainz from 1775, 206
Essen, imperial city, 271
Estates
  assemblies, 15–16, 248, 251–2, 310–11
  decline, 231, 251
  definition, 346–7
  divisions within, 121–2
  in ecclesiastical territories, 201
  emergence, 15, 160, 247–8
  external diplomacy, 111–13, 115, 122
  and imperial courts, 178
  interpretations, 248–51
  powers, 37, 250–1
  ruler-Estate relations, 10, 111, 150, 214, 228–9, 250–1, 318

  structure, 14–16, 96, 201, 248–9, 254
  survival, 201, 208–9, 252–3, 258
  and taxation, 161, 165, 213, 216, 231
  and territorial government, 236, 238, 250, 262
  see Bohemian Revolt; society; and under individual territories
Estonia, 27
Eugene, prince of Savoy (1663–1736), imperial general, 236
European Commission, 7
Extentionists, 229, 231

factories, 63, 79–82, 207, 270
Falkenstein, county, 23
family, see household
favourites, 236–7
Febronism, 204–6
federalism,
  aristocratic, 14, 111–13, 118, 121–2, 250, civic, 37–8,
  and German history, 11–12, 47
  popular, 16–17, 44
  princely, 12–14, 19, 170–1, 185, 193, 306–7, 313, 340
  see communalism
Feine, Erich, historian, 306
Felbinger, Johann Ignaz (1724–88), educationalist, 287
Ferdinand I (1503–64), emperor from 1558, 32, 40, 47, 179
Ferdinand II (1578–1637), emperor from 1619
  as archduke of Styria, 109–10, 165
  character, 109–10, 117, 122, 235
  death, 134
  government, 309
  imperial politics, 39, 48, 118–24, 127–8, 130, 170, 305
  interpretations, 8, 109
  patronage, 122, 244
  and Wallenstein, 41, 126–8, 130–1
Ferdinand III (1608–57), emperor from 1637
  confessionalisation, 123, 139
  election, 134
  government, 235
  imperial politics, 39, 135–42

Ferdinand III (1608–57) (*continued*)
  imperial recovery, 44, 48, 308, 313, 315
  succession, 53, 311–12
Ferdinand IV (1633–54), king of the
    Romans from 1653, 53, 311
Ferdinand of Bavaria (1577–1650), elector
    of Cologne, bishop of Liège,
    Hildesheim, Münster (all from 1612)
    and Paderborn (1618), 120, 134, 190
Fettmilch, Vincenz (d.1616), 76–7
feudal jurisdiction, 84–5, 87–90, 99
financiers, 77, 258, 278
Firmian, Leopold Anton Eleutherius
    Baron von (1679–1744), archbishop
    of Salzburg from 1727, 272
Fontainebleau, treaty of (1631), 133
forestry, 79, 88, 101, 182, 254, 300
Foucault, Michel, social theorist, 276
France
  army, 333, 336
  Austrian alliance (1756), 195, 328–31,
    338
  cultural influence, 62, 154–6, 218, 222,
    335
  economy, 80, 147, 197, 271, 277, 333–4
  education, 245
  encroachment on Reich, 26–7, 43–4,
    119, 140, 170, 186, 195, 206, 306,
    339
  and German princes 40, 133, 135, 170,
    191–2, 194, 201, 231, 259, 315,
    327–8, 335, 340–2
  government, 160, 209, 243, 246–7, 262
  legal system, 294, 337
  nobility, 19, 243, 246, 254, 334, 336
  population, 50, 71
  religion, 106, 132, 150, 204, 271
  and Sweden, 104, 133, 135, 140, 170
  and Thirty Years War, 103–4, 112, 115,
    129, 132–4
  war with Spain (1635–59), 131–2,
    136–7, 143, 191
  wars with the Reich, 47, 49, 148, 150,
    161, 164, 166, 169–70, 174–5,
    189
  see also revolution
Franche Comté, province, 27, 44, 170,
    186

Franconian Kreis
  army, 175, 329,
  assembly, 190
  and Associations, 192–6
  composition, 24, 38, 184, 188–9, 325
  crime, 291,
  economy, 80, 89, 197, 257
  invasions of, 128, 335
  society, 69, 97
Francis I (1708–65), duke of Lorraine,
    emperor from 1745, 319, 327
Francis II (1768–1835), emperor from
    1792, 341–2
Francke, August Hermann (1663–1727),
    theologian and social reformer,
    274
Frankfurt am Main, imperial city
  economy, 61, 79–80, 259
  legal system, 295
  population , 271
  reform, 303
  and Reich, 21, 23, 327
  religion, 76–7, 273
  society, 77, 245
  unrest, 76–7, 301
Frankfurt an der Oder, town, 80, 246,
    278
Franks, dynasty, 18–19, 22–4
Franz Günther, historian, 144
Frederick III/I (1657–1713), elector of
    Brandenburg (1688) and king in
    Prussia (1701), 94, 216, 223, 236
  interpretations, 320
  royal title, 314
Frederick II 'the Great' (1712–86), king of
    Prussia from 1740
  ambitions, 326–7
  character, 224, 237, 320
  court of, 224–5
  finance, 260
  French alliance, 328
  image, 149, 153, 329
  and imperial constitution, 312, 330
  nobility, 216, 242, 244
  opinions, 210, 280
  reforms, 91, 94, 272, 281, 284, 287–8,
    292–5
  war, 5–6, 234, 319–20, 326–31

Frederick V (1598–1632), elector Palatine from 1610, 115–16, 118–24, 132
Frederick of Hessen-Kassel (1676–1751), king of Sweden from 1720, 28
Frederick William (1620–88), the Great Elector of Brandenburg from 1640,
 government, 212, 216, 223, 236
 and Reich, 147, 191, 313
 significance, 208, 321
 toleration, 271,
 uses force, 228
Frederick William I (1688–1740), king in Prussia from 1713
 army, 216, 228
 court of, 223–4
 finances, 260, 271
 opinions, 210
 reforms, 94, 294, 241
 religion, 271–2
Frederick William II (1744–97), king of Prussia from 1786, 224, 339
free masonry, 280
Freising, bishopric, 188, 199–200, 205
French Revolution, see revolution
French Wars of Religion (1562–98), 105–6, 108, 115, 166
Friedland, duchy, 126
Friedrich (1744–1816), duke (1797), elector (1803) and king (1806) of Württemberg, 252
Friedrich II (1720–85), landgrave of Hessen-Kassel from 1760, 281
Friedrich III (d.1659), duke of Holstein-Gottorp from 1616, 147
Fronen, 85
Fugger, county, 298
Fulda, bishopric, 199–200, 286
Fürstenbund, see League of Princes
Fürth, town, 148
Fux, Johann Joseph (1660–1741), composer, 156

Gabor, Bethlen (1580–1629), prince of Transylvania (1613) and king of Hungary (1620) 110, 116, 118, 122
Galen, Christoph Bernhard von (1606–78), bishop of Münster from 1650, 107–8, 191, 228–9

Galicia, principality, 93
Gallicanism, 204
Geitzkoffler, Zacharias (1560–1617), imperial treasurer, 169
Gelehrten, 74–5
Gelnhausen, imperial city, 77
gender
 identity, 57–8
 inheritance, 58–9, 69, 310
 law, 59, 153, 292, 295–6
 literacy, 62
 mortality, 52–4
 politics, 250, 267
 social status, 55–6, 59–60, 63–4, 78, 100, 199, 244, 343
 welfare, 56–7, 274
 work, 58–60
 see households; marriage
General Civil Code, Prussia (1794), 275
Georg Friedrich (1573–1630), margrave of Baden-Durlach from 1604, 124
Georg Friedrich (1620–92), count (1682 prince) of Waldeck from 1664, 212, 236
Georg Wilhelm (1595–1640), elector of Brandenburg from 1619, 236
Gerichtsherrschaft, 85, 347
German Confederation (1815–66), 11, 29, 179, 196, 253, 338
German Liberty, 36, 47, 75, 105, 149, 305
Germany, Federal Republic of, 8, 11–12
Gesindezwangdienst, 87–9, 95, 347
Giengen, imperial city, 301
Gierke, Otto von (1841–1921), historian, 97
Glatz, county, 320, 323
Goethe, Johann Wolfgang von (1749–1832), writer, 180–1
Gold Coast, 147
Golden Bull (1356), 20, 39–40, 47, 178, 347
Goslar, imperial city, 25
Gotha, duchy, 24, 144, 241, 273
Göttingen, town, 38
Gottorp, see Holstein
government, purpose of, 146
 see absolutism; cameralism
Grand Alliance (1689), 193

Graz, town, 26, 80
Great Elector, *see* Frederick William
Great Northern War (1700–21), 315
Great Turkish War (1683–99), 26, 148,
    158, 173–4, 192, 222, 272, 311, 315
Greiz, lordship, 298
Grimmelshausen, Johann Jacob
    (1621–76), novelist, 154
Grundherrschaft, 83–6, 347
Guelph (Welf), dynasty, 25, 28, 45, 134,
    186–7, 191, 200, 229
    see also Brunswick; Wolfenbüttel
guilds, 58, 64, 71–4, 140, 292, 300, 335, 339
Gustavus II Adolphus (1594–1632), king
    of Sweden from 1611, 128–9, 133,
    143, 149
Gutsherrschaft, 83–90, 122
Gutswirtschaft, see manorial economy
gypsies, 76, 290–1

Habsburg dynasty (Austrian)
    ambitions, 307, 309, 315
    'Brothers Quarrel', 107–13
    crisis (1654–8), 53, 311–12
    and imperial church, 199–200, 203–6
    and imperial title, 5, 8, 20, 22, 35, 119,
        129, 134, 311–12, 326–7, 331, 342
    influence in Reich, 17, 39–40, 47–9, 105,
        108, 113–17, 142, 158, 236,
        305–19, 329
    partition (1556–64), 26–7, 109, 113,
        159, 163, 165–6
    prestige, 142, 151, 305–7, 311–12, 331
    see Pragmatic Sanction
Habsburg dynasty (Spanish), 19, 26–7,
    108, 115, 118–19
    extinction, 27, 315
    see Spain
Habsburg monarchy
    army: condition, 168, 225; defeats, 135,
        318–19, 340; maintenance, 126–7,
        134, 158–65, 168–9, 171–3, 194–5;
        recruitment, 92, 118, 232–3, size,
        112, 118, 126, 134, 143, 165, 225–6,
        318; victories, 121, 132, 134–5, 310,
        316–17
    church–state relations, 31, 199–200,
        205–6, 284–5

debts, 109, 138, 168, 258–61, 319
diplomatic network, 311, 316, 319, 328
and Dutch Revolt, 108–9, 127
economy, 80, 91–3, 147, 269
Estates, 16, 109–13, 117–23, 165, 212,
    214–16, 232–3, 252–3, 308
expenditure, 126, 165, 171, 221, 223,
    258–9, 288
French alliance (1756), 195, 328–31
and French Revolutionary Wars, 6,
    338–42
government, 25, 235–41, 244–7, 309,
    311
great power status, 5, 164
legal system, 290, 294–5
nobility, 44, 67, 88, 92–3, 122–3,
    214–16, 244
patronage: in monarchy, 44, 88, 122–3,
    187, 214–16, 221, 243–4, 308, 314;
    in Reich, 44–5, 127, 174, 187,
    192, 198–203, 221, 308, 312–14,
    317–19
population, 50, 272, 285, 308, 310
reform, 91–3, 280, 284–5, 310–11
relationship to Reich, 26, 178, 185–6,
    309, 327–8
religion, 77–8, 109–13, 123, 139, 152,
    272–3, 308–9
revenue, 126, 256–8, 261, 280, 310–11
size, 25–7, 242, 307–8, 311, 317, 319,
    327
    see Austria; Bohemia; Burgundy;
    Hungary
Hagen, William, historian, 83
Halberstadt, bishopric, 25, 124, 127, 141,
    323
Halle, town, 271
Halle University, 246, 274, 287
Hamburg, imperial city,
    culture, 155–6
    legal system, 291, 294
    reform, 303
    relationship to Reich, 25, 37–8
    revenue, 256
    society, 61, 77
    unrest, 301
Hamburg Peace Preliminaries (1641),
    137–8

Hamburgische Allgemeine Versorgungs Anstalt, 57

Hanau, principality, 77, 278

Hanover, duchy, electorate from 1692
annexation, 341
army, 231, 325
and Britain, 28, 223, 244, 314, 328–30
economy, 83, 95
electoral status, 39, 174, 193, 223, 314, 316
Estates, 253
expansion, 25, 28, 169, 184, 186
and Habsburgs, 39, 326
influence, 152, 170, 183, 187, 315
legal system, 294
religion, 66, 200
revenue, 325
society, 69
size, 325

Hansa, 37–8

Harnisch. Helmut, historian, 83

Harz mountains, 78

Hauenstein, district, 90, 95, 298

Haugwitz, Friedrich Wilhelm Count von (1700–65), Habsburg minister, 237, 280, 310

Haugwitz, Heinrich Christian Kurt von (1752–1832), Prussian minister, 225

health, 268
see medicine; mortality; plague

Heidelberg, town, 23, 150, 219, 278

Heidelberg Catechism (1563), 107

Heilbronn League (1633–4), 130, 132, 134

Heinrich (1726–1802), prince of Prussia, 224

Henry IV (1553–1610), king of France from 1589, 115

Herford, town , 38

Hessen-Darmstadt, landgraviate
army, 225
dispute with Kassel, 45, 182
economy, 95
education, 287
expansion, 341
finance, 259, 303
government, 239
influence, 40, 194

relationship to Reich, 178
unrest, 338

Hessen-Homburg, landgraviate, 45

Hessen-Kassel, landgraviate
army, 167, 183, 225, 231, 302
crime, 291
education, 246
Estates, 251
finance, 257, 281–2
influence, 13, 23, 46, 136, 141, 189, 191, 203, 240
partition, 45, 182, 189
population, 54
reforms, 281, 294
religion, 66, 107, 150
and Sweden, 28, 134
unrest, 297

Hessen-Marburg, landgraviate, 45

Hessen-Rheinfels, landgraviate, 45

Hildburghausen, duchy, 303

Hildesheim, bishopric, 25, 199, 200–1, 203, 229

Hobsbawm, Eric, historian, 290

Hofburg, palace, 219, 221–2

Hofkriegsrat, 165, 239–40

Hohenlohe-Langenburg, principality, 95

Hohenlohe-Waldenburg, principality, 150–2, 298, 334

Hohenzollern dynasty, 27, 320
Franconian branch, 45
influence, 46, 141
Prussian branch, 324
religion, 212
see also Ansbach; Bayreuth; Brandenburg; Prussia

Hohenzollern-Hechingen, principality, 297–8

Holstein, duchy, 25, 28–9, 45, 124, 194
economy, 87, 89, 92, 95, 147
education, 287
Estates, 251

Homona, György Drugeth de, Hungarian aristocrat, 122

Honoratioren, 72

honour, 68, 75–6

Hontheim, Nikolaus von , 204–6

Horn, Count Axel (1592–1657), Swedish general, 130

Hörnigk, Philipp Wilhelm von
    (1638–1712), cameralist, 268–9
Horst, Johann Christoph Peter
    (1783–1813), bandit, 291
householders, 58, 69, 98, 100, 176
    tensions amongst, 102
households
    ideal, 59–60, 101, 267, 275, 290, 343
    peasant, 88, 90, 176
    princely, 218, 238, 247
    structure, 58, 61
Höxter, town, 229
Hubertusburg, hunting lodge, 224
Hubertusburg, peace (1763), 329
Huguenots, 132–3, 150, 216, 271
Hungary
    defences, 135, 164–5, 168, 192
    economy, 80, 83, 88, 92–3
    Estates, 15, 111, 113, 117, 123, 249,
        310–11
    monarchy, 15, 310
    nobility, 67, 92–3, 110–13, 122, 309–10
    and Ottomans, 26, 109–11, 215, 310
    population, 283
    reconquest, 26, 174, 272, 311, 315
    relationship to Reich, 26, 159
    religion, 77, 107, 110–11, 113, 123
    revolt (1604–6), 110–12
    revolt (1671–81), 309
    revolt (1703–11), 215–16, 228, 310
    revolt (1784), 93, 299, 332
Hussites, 112, 185
hygiene, 51

Ilgen, Heinrich rüdiger von (1678–1728),
    Hohenzollern minister, 236
illegitimacy, 55
immediacy (Reichsunmittelbarkeit), 30, 67,
    347
immunisation, 52, 54
imperial army, 134, 163
imperial ban, 48–9, 126, 316
imperial church
    armed forces, 202, 380–1
    Estates, 248
    finance, 202, 380–1
    imperial politics, 202–7, 314, 316
    interpretation, 203

jurisdiction, 32, 66, 198, 205, 265, 294
population, 286, 380–1
political structure, 15, 21, 187, 198,
    201–3, 212, 238, 347
reforms, 274–5, 285–6
secularisation, 40, 42–4, 121, 124, 127,
    138–41, 198, 200, 203–7, 282, 285,
    340–1
size, 42–4, 198–9, 380–1
society, 77, 199–201, 244
see cathedral chapters and individual
    territories
imperial circles, see Kreise
imperial cities
    armed forces, 71, 230, 378–9
    college, 35, 37–8
    decline , 73–4, 147–8, 271
    defined, 347–8
    finance, 158, 256, 303, 378–9
    government, 14, 71–2, 139
    mediatisation, 38, 114, 147, 182, 341
    numbers, 37–8, 378–9
    reforms, 303
    relationship to Reich, 72, 158, 169, 171,
        306, 311–12
    religion, 140, 378–9
    unrest, 76–7, 149, 300–1
imperial commissioners, 182–3, 303
imperial constitution, 10, 33, 105–6, 127,
    142, 157, 282, 305–6, 309, 329–30
    see individual elements
imperial counts
    careers, 199
    Estates, 249
    lands, 23, 187, 298–300, 303, 341
    numbers, 43, 45
    and Reich, 14, 42–6, 169, 171, 174
imperial courts, see courts, Reichshofrat,
    Reichskammergericht
imperial defence, 35, 157–75, 191–5, 313,
    329, 340
    mobilisation system, 162, 166–7, 171,
        174–5, 185, 192, 195, 213
imperial deputation, 313, 341, 349
imperial estates, 35, 47, 49, 159, 176, 248,
    299, 313
imperial fiefs, 29–30, 126, 142, 312
Imperial Germany, see Reich, Second

imperial hierarchy, 9–11, 13, 19, 37, 44, 159, 174, 184–5, 197–8, 248, 304, 306, 312

Imperial Italy,
   composition, 23, 308, 348
   Habsburg influence, 127, 131, 137, 316–17
   relationship to Reich, 21, 23, 181, 185, 189, 316

imperial knights
   and emperor, 10, 41–2, 139, 312, 314
   influence, 199–200, 245, 249
   lands, 41–2, 77, 298
   mediatisation , 341–2
   numbers, 41

imperial law, see law
imperial patriotism, 18, 134, 307
imperial police ordinances, 56, 76, 266, 274
imperial prelates, 42–3, 199, 207, 248–9
imperial recovery, 142, 305–19, 326
imperial title, 18, 20–1, 23, 26, 157, 311–12, 327, 331, 342
   Austrian (1804), 312, 342
imperial translation, 20
imperial vicars, 21
imperial war, 49, 313

industrialisation
   advocacy of, 269
   arms industries, 104, 207, 270–1
   development, 80–2, 146, 148, 332
   extractive industries, 74, 78–9
   and German history, 2, 71, 264, 345

infanticide, 54, 59, 295
inflation, 51, 148, 196, 267, 299
inheritance, 56, 84, 93
   disputes, 186
   impartiable, 58, 68–9
   partiable, 69, 86
   see Pragmatic Sanction

Inner Austria, 26
Innsbruck, town, 26
Innviertel, district, 331
Investiture Contest (1076–1122), 198
IPM (instrumentum pacis monasteriense), 137, 186
IPO (instrumentum pacis osnabrugense),
   celebration of, 143–4,
   confirmation of, 48

constitutional terms, 33–4, 138, 140, 142, 157, 182
   guarantees for, 142, 328
   religious terms, 33, 139–40, 149–53, 200, 272, 286
   territorial terms, 140–1, 147
irenicism, 107
Isenburg, counties and principalities, 23, 298
Isny, imperial city, 149
Italy, 81, 118, 155, 327
   see imperial Italy
itio in partes, 140, 149, 152, 348

Jankau, battle (1645), 135
Jena, duchy, 24
Jesuits
   and education, 67, 108, 110
   influence, 32, 123, 286
   suppression (1773), 205, 284
Jews, 76–8, 158, 278, 285, 301,
   bandits, 291
   toleration, 77, 123, 286
Johann Wilhelm (1685–1716), elector Palatine from 1690, 150, 315–16
Johnson, Hubert, historian, 237
Joseph I (1678–1711), emperor from 1705,
   in Hungary, 310
   imperial justice, 180
   imperial recovery, 39, 48, 316–17,
   Saxon alliance, 223
Joseph II (1741–90), emperor from 1765
   agrarian and fiscal reforms, 91–3, 252, 257–8, 260–1, 280–1, 285
   character, 237, 285, 330
   ecclesiastical reforms, 205–6, 285
   education reforms, 286–8
   exchange plans, 204
   foreign policy, 338–9
   and imperial justice, 180, 331
   imperial legislation, 283–4
   and Reich, 158, 205–6, 330–1
journeymen, 53
judiciary, territorial, 55, 176, 238–9, 266, 300
   see courts, lawyers

Jülich, duchy
dispute over, 45, 108, 112, 115, 182, 187
religion, 115, 139
juridification, 175, 301–4, 344
Justi, Heinrich Gottlob (1717–71),
cameralist, 279
justice
attitudes to, 181–2, 293, 296–8, 301–4
criminal, 291–6
see courts; juridification; law

Kaak, Heinrich, historian, 83
Kammerzieler, 177
Kammin, bishopric, 141, 323
Karlsruhe, residence town, 219
Kassa, town, 111
Kaunitz family, 122, 187
Kaunitz, Wenzel Anton Prince von
(1711–94), Habsburg minister, 92–3,
237, 280, 284, 328, 338
Kehl, fortress, 175, 195
Keiser, Reinhard (1674–1739), composer,
156
Kempten, princely abbey, 206, 249, 298
Kepler, Johannes (1571–1630),
astronomer, 110
Khlesl, Cardinal Melchior (1552–1630),
Habsburg minister, 109, 115–17, 235,
244
Kinsky family, 122
Kitzingen, town, 72
Kleinstaaterei, 5, 7, 209, 281, 300
Klettenberg, county, 323
Klostermayer, Matthias (1736–71),
bandit, 291
Knapp, Geor Friedrich, historian, 83
Koblenz, town, 62, 204, 219, 334
Königsberg, town, 223, 228, 324
Königstein, county, 23
Korneleimünster, imperial abbey, 298
Kreis Associations, 190–5, 203, 314, 348
Kreis convenors, 183–7, 189–90, 348
Kreise
assemblies, 46, 159, 174, 183, 185,
187–90, 195–6, 308, 348
composition, 185–90, 364–77
and defence, 159, 166–7, 171–5, 192–6,
329

economic coordination, 196–8
finance, 168
function, 46, 183, 196, 348,
interpretations, 190
public order, 290–1, 302
reform of, 196
relationship to Reich, 184–5, 307, 313
Kreittmayr, Aloyisus Wiguläus Xaverius
Baron von (1705–90), Bavarian
lawyer, 295
Krems, town, 118
Kunnersdorf, battle (1759), 329

land banks, 94, 281
Landeshoheit, see sovereignty
Landfrieden, see public peace
Landschaften, 249–50
landownership, 68, 70, 84, 86–9, 92, 94–5,
300, 334
princely, 95, 254
land reclaimation, 272
language
French, 154
German, 28, 154, 309
and politics, 16, 18, 100, 122, 215, 335
Lausitz, margraviate, 25, 87,
Estates, 112, 118
Saxon acquisition, 121, 123–4, 133,
141
Lautner, Anton, bandit, 291
law
and animals, 268
codification, 64, 89, 101, 176, 179, 238,
295–6
conservative character, 303–4, 337–8,
344–5
criminal, 59, 179, 268, 293–6
customary, 176
feudal, 97
fundamental, 211
imperial, 59, 126–7, 129, 131, 139–40,
162, 167, 177–8, 230, 293, 301
indigenous, 242–3
purpose, 181–2
natural, 211
and religion, 105, 176
Roman, 55, 92, 176
— rule of, 175, 304, 337, 344

territorial, 30, 100–1, 176
written, 101, 265, 293, 298, 301
lawyers, 72, 177, 180, 245–6, 277, 287,
    293, 333
Laxenburg Alliance (1682), 192
League of Corresponding Princes (1692),
    193
League of Princes (1785), 205, 331
legitimacy, political, 36, 211
Leibeigenschaft, 89, 348
Leibherrschaft, 85
Leibniz, Gottfried Wilhelm (1646–1716),
    philosopher, 279
Leiningen, county, 23
Leipzig, city, 62, 68, 79–80, 82, 155–6, 286
Leipzig Convent (1631), 128, 133, 190
Lemgo, town, 38
Leopold I (1640–1705), emperor from
    1658
  character, 312
  confessionalisation, 123
  election, 53, 311–12
  government, 92, 235–6
  image, 222
  imperial church, 202
  imperial constitution, 48–9, 229, 251,
    313
  imperial defence, 169–74, 191–2
  imperial justice, 180
  imperial recovery, 26, 142, 194, 308–10,
    313, 316, 318
Leopold II (1747–92), emperor from 1790,
    93, 253, 258, 334–5
Leopold (1586–1632), bishop of Passau
    (1605–7) and Strasbourg from 1607,
    112–13, 117
Leopold Johann (b.&d.1716), archduke of
    Austria, 53
Letter of Majesty (1608), 112
liberalism, 3, 60, 208, 249–50, 253
liberties, 36, 121, 140, 344–5
  see German Liberty
liberty, as a revolutionary ideology, 334–5
Lieben (Stará Libená), treaty (1608), 112
Liechtenstein, Carl (1567–1627), prince
    (1608), landowner and governor of
    Bohemia, 215
Liechtenstein family, 214

Liège, bishopric, 24, 199, 201, 204–5, 229,
    332
life assurance, 57
life expectancy, 51–4
Liga
  army, 120–1, 124, 126–7
  dissolution, 133–4
  finances, 125–7
  organisation, 115–16, 120, 190, 203
Limnaeus, Johann (1592–1663), political
    theorist, 306
Lingen, county, 323
Lippe-Detmold, principality, 239, 241,
    252, 266, 292, 300
List, Nickel (d.1699), bandit, 291
literacy, 62, 243, 284, 288
Little Ice Age, 51, 104
Lobkovic family, 122
lordship,
  feudal, 15, 297
  territorial, 30, 33–4, 176, 254
  see manorial lordship
Lorraine, duchy
  and France, 44
  and Habsburgs, 108, 131, 200, 319
  and Reich, 23, 189
  religion, 272
Louis, XIV (1638–1715), king of France
    from 1643, 38, 155, 170, 175, 186, 191,
    271, 315
Louis XVI (1754–93), king of France from
    1774, 333, 336–7
Lower Saxon Kreis, 25, 124–5, 143, 184,
    186–7, 191, 197
Lübeck, bishopric, 139, 200
Lübeck, congress (1638), 136–7
Lübeck, imperial city, 25, 37–8
Lübeck, treaty (1629), 124
Luben von Wulffen, Christian Freidrich
    (1666–1721), Prussian treasury
    official, 94
Ludwig VIII (1691–1768), landgrave of
    Hessen-Darmstadt from 1739, 303
Ludwigsburg, residence town, 219
Lunéville, peace (1801), 341
Lutheranism, 31–2
  princely conversions to, 25
  see clergy; religion

Lutter am Barenberge, battle (1627), 134

Lützen, battle (1632), 129–30

Luxembourg, duchy, 23, 27, 119, 121, 170, 175, 186

Luxembourg dynasty, 20, 22

Machiavelli, Nicoló (1469–1527), political theorist, 210

Magdeburg, archbishopric, 25, 80, 114, 127, 141, 184, 200, 323

Magdeburg, city, 128, 144, 228–9, 323

magic, 60

Mainz, city, 271, 335

Mainz, electorate
  cathedral chapter, 200
  constitutional role, 35, 39–40, 178, 180, 184, 199
  dispute with the Palatinate, 90, 182, 188–9
  dispute with Würzburg, 182
  economy, 95
  imperial politics, 120, 134, 190–5, 204–6, 307
  influence, 21, 23, 139, 184, 203, 313
  internal politics, 228–9
  religion, 77, 203, 286
  welfare, 275, 286
  see Erfurt, Schönborn

malnutrition, 51

Mann, Michael, sociologist, 234–5, 242

Mannheim, town, 23, 219

manorial economy, 92, 148, 216, 297, 299, 310, 321
  defined, 86, 347

Mansfeld, Count Ernst (1580–1626), general, 118, 124

Mansfeld, Count Heinrich, landowner, 93

Mansfeld, county, 323

Mantua, marquisate, 127–8

Marengo, battle (1800), 341

Maria Anna (1551–1608), archduchess of Styria, 109

Maria Antonia (1669–92), archduchess of Austria, 315

Maria Theresa (1717–80), empress
  domestic policy, 237, 311
  inheritance of, 53, 318–19, 326–8

reforms, 92–3, 246–7, 284–5
  and Reich, 303

Mark, duchy
  dispute over, 45, 108, 323
  economy, 78
  education, 286
  Estates, 228
  government, 241
  society, 70, 139
  territory, 24

marriage
  age, 53–5, 58–9, 69, 89
  cross-confessional, 152–3
  legal status, 59–60
  regulation of, 55–7, 234, 267, 285
  social status, 64, 102, 244–5
  unmarried mothers, 275

Martinic family, 122

Marx, Karl (1818–83), political economist, 64, 264

matricular list, 35, 38, 44, 162–3, 171, 348

matricular system, 162–4, 168, 177, 348

Mattheson, Johann (1681–1764), composer, 156

Matthias (1557–1619), emperor from 1612, 109–17, 119, 165, 219, 235

Mauritius, 147

Max Franz (1756–1801), elector of Cologne-Münster from 1784, 205

Max Heinrich (1621–88), elector of Cologne, bishop of Hildesheim, Liège and Berchtesgaden from 1650, 229

Maximilian I (1459–1519), emperor from 1493, 21, 177, 179

Maximilian II (1527–76), emperor from 1564, 108

Maximilian (1573–1651), duke (1598), elector (1623) of Bavaria, 109, 114–15, 121
  ambitions, 120, 123, 128, 133, 136

Max Emanuel (1662–1726), elector of Bavaria from 1678, 315–17

Mazarin, Cardinal Jules (1602–61), French statesman, 142, 191

Mecklenburg, duchy
  economy, 87–8, 95–6
  Estates, 96, 252, 257
  foreign occupations, 126, 129, 183

influence, 25, 194
internal politics, 48, 95–6, 303, 318
legal system, 294
population, 144
relationship to Reich, 45–6, 178
mediatisation, 38, 44, 343, 349
medical care, 60, 79, 145, 196, 268, 273–4
see immunisation
Meiningen, duchy, 182
Meissen, bishopric, 121
mentality, *see* culture
Merseberg, bishopric, 121
Metz, bishopric, 38, 43, 140
Metz, imperial city, 38, 140
migration, 60–1, 73, 87, 144–5, 283–4
forced, 123, 271–3, 334
Milan, duchy, 23, 119, 318, 327
militarism, 222, 274, 344
military
conscription, 70, 92, 233–4, 321
recruitment, 15, 61, 84, 144, 160, 167–8,
232–4, 256
technology, 160, 164–5, 167, 212–13,
225–6, 254
see armies; imperial defence; soldiers
Military Frontier, 164–5, 233, 311
'military revolution', 212
militia, 71–2, 97, 125, 164, 167–8, 225–6,
228, 230–3, 339
Minden, bishopric, 139, 141, 323
mining, 74, 78–9, 86, 92, 148, 254
ministers, 225, 235–7, 240
Mittelmayer family, 270
modernisation, 293, 303, 337
Moldavia, principality, 110
monarchism, as trend in imperial politics,
11, 19, 33, 47, 109, 170, 185, 305–7
monarchy
composite, 248
constitutional, 208–10
mixed, 47, 121, 210–11, 213, 250–1
monasteries, 31, 203–4, 285
monopolies, 256–7
Montmartin, Friedrich Samuel Count von
(1712–78), Württemberg minister,
236
Moravia, margraviate, 25, 92–3, 285
Estates, 112, 118, 122

Mors, county, 323
mortality, 51–4, 60
Moser, Friedrich Karl von (1723–98),
government official and writer, 281
Moser, Johann Jacob (1701–85), lawyer,
277–8, 281, 299
Mulhausen (Thuringia), imperial city, 301
Mulhouse (Alsace), imperial city, 38
Munich, city, 206, 269, 292
Munich, treaty (1619), 120
Münster, bishopric
army, 228
economy, 89
education, 287
Estates, 201
influence, 169, 184, 187–8, 194, 202,
315
internal politics, 228–9
possession of, 200, 203, 205,
religion, 107–8
society, 70
Münster, city, 38, 152, 191, 228
peace talks in, 137
Münster, treaty (1648), *see* IPM
Muratori, Ludovico Antonio
(1672–1750), Italian social reformer,
275, 286
music, 155–6, 223, 238

Nantes, edict (1598), 271
Naples, kingdom, 26, 316
Napoleon Bonaparte (1769–1821), 6, 28
defeat, 11, 338
victory over Austria (1805), 46, 234
reorganisation of Germany, 234, 261–2,
336, 340, 342
Nassau, counties and principalities, 23,
107, 178, 272, 338
Nassau-Dillenburg, county, 167
Nassau-Siegen, principality, 151, 298, 303
Nassau-Weilburg, county, 298
nationalism
early expressions of, 70, 154–5, 204, 329,
337–8, 344
and German history, 4–6, 27, 29, 281
as imperial patriotism, 18, 134, 307
Naumburg, bishopric, 121
Nazism, 2, 6, 12, 144

Netherlands
  Austrian rule, 24, 332
  economy, 81
  exchange plans, 204, 315–16, 327, 331,
    338
  population, 50
  see Burgundian Kreis; Dutch Republic
Neuburg, see Pfalz-Neuburg
Neumark, district, 87, 89
Neu Wied, county, 298
Neuchâtel (Neuenburg), principality, 323
Nine Years War (1688–97), 49, 150, 172,
    174, 177, 192–3, 313, 315–16
nobility
  careers, 199–200, 206, 213–14, 216–17,
    231, 238, 242–7, 337
  curbs on privileges, 336, 343–4
  education, 243, 287
  life expectancy, 53
  hatred, 334
  imperial, 30, 41–2, 44
  interests, 91, 104, 121–2, 337
  military obligations, 29, 84, 160, 167
  numbers, 41–2, 67, 215–17, 332
  origins, 29–30
  patronage, 67, 221
  political power, 199–200, 213–14
  political representation, 15, 67–8, 96,
    248–9, 254
  'service nobility', 208
  status, 36, 63, 67–8, 70, 72, 243–4
  territorial, 30, 199–200, 245, 249
  wealth, 68, 88, 91, 95, 216–17, 244,
    257–8, 334
  see ennoblement; imperial knights;
    landownership; manorial economy
Nordhausen, imperial city, 25
Nördlingen Association (1702), 194
Nördlingen, battle (1634), 130, 132–3
Nördlingen, imperial city, 61, 72
Nordstrand island, 147
norms, societal, 59–62, 70, 102
Northern War (1655–60), 148, 191, 216,
    314, 322
nuncios, papal, 204–6
Nuremberg, imperial city, 24, 81, 148, 301
Nuremberg Congress (1649–50), 143
nutrition, 51, 54, 90

Obergeldern, duchy, 323
Oestreich, Gerhard, historian, 264–5,
    268
Oldenburg, duchy, 24, 28–9, 62
Olivares, Gaspar de Guzmán count-duke
    (1585–1645), Spanish minister,
    131–2
Oñate, Iñigo Velez count de (d.1658),
    Spanish ambassador, 118
opera, 154–6
Ortenau, imperial bailiwick, 158
Ostende Company, 147
Oppenheimer, Joseph Süß (1698–1738),
    financier, 277, 296
Oppenheimer, Samuel (1630–1703),
    banker, 258
Orange dynasty, 211, 216, 229
Osnabrück, bishopric, 24, 63, 77, 87, 107,
    139, 199–201
Osnabrück, treaty (1648) see IPO
Ottoman Turks, 22, 76, 106
  and Hungary, 26, 109–11, 159, 215,
    310–1
  imperial title, 312
  and Thirty Years War, 116, 118, 122–3,
    137
  see Turkish Wars
Ottonian dynasty, 19
outcasts, 75–8

Paderborn, bishopric
  economy, 83, 89
  education, 287
  Estates, 201
  possession of, 200, 203
  society, 70, 199, 214
palaces, 218–19, 221–4
Palatinate, electorate
  ambitions, 316, 322, 327
  annexation, 261
  army, 325
  and Bohemia, 118, 121, 211
  dispute with Mainz, 90, 182, 188–9
  electoral status, 39, 41, 120, 132, 134,
    141
  finance, 259, 325
  government, 237, 241

as Habsburg ally, 315–16
Habsburg occupation, 119–21
imperial church, 316
influence, 13, 21, 114–17
legal system, 294–5
relationship to Reich, 178, 184
religion, 41, 66, 77, 107, 123, 139, 150,
   318
size, 325,
papacy,
annexed by France, 206
and German bishops, 198–9, 202–6
and German politics, 18, 20–2, 31–2,
   66–7, 105, 136, 139, 154
war with Habsburgs (1708–9), 316–17
Paragraph 180, 161, 229, 251
Parma, duchy, 23
Passau, bishopric, 66, 112–13, 188,
   199–200, 205, 286
patricians, 72, 74, 300
patriotic societies, 75
patronage, 32, 44–5, 65, 101, 221, 228,
   242–7
see under individual territories
peasants
access to land, 70, 84–9, 94–5, 334
inheritance, 56, 69, 84, 86, 93, 334
life expectancy, 53
literacy, 62
numbers, 69
obligations, 69–70, 84–95, 160–1, 230,
   233–4, 254, 256–8, 299
political representation, 15, 249–51
social mobility, 199, 214, 243–4, 287
status, 63, 69–71
see communalism; protest
Peasants War (1524–6), 79, 101, 160, 176,
   267, 297
pensions, 56–7, 247
Pergen, Johann Anton (1724–1814),
   Habsburg minister, 237, 284
persecution, 76–8, 230, 271–3, 285, 299
Persia, empire, 123
Personalisten, 44–5
Peter III (Carl Peter Ulrich) (1728–62),
   duke of Holstein-Gottorp and tsar, 29
Peters, Jan, historian, 83
petitions, 237

Pfalz-Neuburg, duchy, 115, 182, 184, 187,
   189, 191
army, 228
and imperial church, 200
and the Palatinate, 150, 315
Pfalz-Simmern, duchy, 184, 189
Philip III (1578–1621), king of Spain from
   1598, 119
Philipp (1509–67), landgrave of Hessen
   from 1518, 45
Philippsburg, fortress, 140, 175, 195
physiocrats, 277
Pietism, 273–4
Pirna, treaty (1634), 133
plague, 50–1, 53, 96
Poland, kingdom
decline, 129, 320, 324
and Ducal Prussia, 216, 324
economy, 80, 83
Estates, 249
insurrection (1794–5), 234, 339
monarchy, 28, 151, 318
nobility, 67, 111, 122
partitions, 9, 67, 78, 204, 216, 234,
   260–1, 323, 326, 330, 338–9
and Reich, 27–8
police forces, 302
see armies
police regulation, 63, 69–70,
defined, 349
impact, 73, 265
interpretations, 264–5
motives, 101, 265
see cameralism
political communication, 61–2, 334–5
Pomerania, duchy
economy, 87–9, 216
relationship to Reich, 45, 143
Prussian, 46, 14, 244, 323
size, 25
Swedish, 128, 141, 186, 314
Pöppelmann, Matthäus Daniel
   (1662–1736), architect, 223
population
contemporary theory of, 284
decline, 50, 87, 144–5
growth, 51, 65, 70, 86, 96, 101–2, 213,
   242, 282, 332

population (*continued*)
 recovery, 50, 86, 269
 size, 50–1, 96
 urban, 61, 71, 96–7,144, 148, 271
Portia, Johann Ferdinand Count
  (1606–65), Habsburg minister, 235
Portugal, 131, 147
Potsdam, residence town, 94, 223–4,
  270–1, 324
Pragmatic Sanction (1713), 310, 318–19
Prague, city
 attacks on, 113, 136, 327
 defences, 165
 economy, 80
 imperial court, 22, 109, 112–13, 219
 society, 77–8
 university, 245
Prague, Defenestration (1618), 117–18
Prague, peace (1635), 133–6, 139, 144,
  170, 190
Press, Volker, historian, 303
Pressburg, treaty (1608), 112
Preysing family, 217
Prignitz, district, 90
princes
 aims, 13, 176, 182, 197, 200–1, 211, 213,
   277, 288, 299–300, 341
 alliances, 12–14, 34, 190, 193, 205, 331
 college, 35, 41–6
 creation of, 44–5, 312, 341
 deposition of, 48, 151, 303
 life expectancy, 53
 numbers, 43, 45–6
 patronage, 200–2, 214–17, 228, 242–7
 powers, 12, 30, 32–5, 242–4, 246–7, 256,
   296, 312
 royal titles, 28–9, 118, 151, 174, 223,
   314, 316, 318, 322, 344
 titles, 29–30, 34, 39
 wealth, 254, 262, 300
 workload, 235, 237
Princes Revolt (1552), 32, 159
privy councils, 235, 239–40, 243
proletarians, 60, 64, 71, 73–5, 81–2, 89, 95
propaganda, 62, 129, 305–6, 328, 335
property rights, 36, 75, 79, 83, 89
 see inheritance
prostitution, 56, 58, 76, 100, 276

protest
 attitudes to, 304
 causes, 79, 90, 160–1, 277, 297–301,
   334–5
 consequences, 215
 factionalism, 72, 102, 302
 fear of, 111, 121, 272, 309–10
 incidence, 297–301
 interpretations, 214, 290, 297
 measures against, 106, 176, 267–8, 270,
   272, 288, 301–4
 methods, 90, 102, 216, 230, 237, 297,
   302, 304, 332
 rural, 90, 92–4, 96, 160–1, 216, 230,
   297–300, 332
 sectarian, 76–8, 291, 299, 301
 urban, 76–7, 149, 161, 229, 300–1, 332
 see crime
Protestant Union (1608–22)
 collapse, 124–6, 132,
 formation, 114–15, 190
 tensions within, 13, 116
Prussia, monarchy
 army, 92, 208, 216–17, 225–9, 233–4,
   270, 321, 324
 bureaucracy, 208, 216–17, 235, 237,
   240–3, 246–7
 censorship, 335
 crime, 291
 defeat (1806), 6, 234, 261, 337, 342
 economy, 3, 74, 80–9, 93–5, 270–2,
   324
 education, 246, 274, 286–8
 Estates, 252–3
 finance, 224–5, 260–1, 280
 and French Revolutionary Wars,
   338–40
 and German unification, 4–6, 11–12,
   320
 influence in Reich, 46, 96, 187–8, 194,
   197, 252, 314–15, 329–31
 interpretations, 2–5, 208–9, 224, 235,
   320–1
 legal system, 59, 93, 179, 181, 293–5
 militarism, 274, 344
 nobility, 67–8, 74, 86–9, 94–5, 216–17,
   233–4, 241–4
 population, 50, 217, 323–4, 330

relationship to Reich, 46, 178–80, 184, 312

religion, 77, 149, 152, 271–2

royal title, 174, 223, 244, 314, 322, 324

size, 307, 321–5

society, 59, 73, 77–8, 88, 233–4, 320–1

welfare, 274–5

see Brandenburg

Prussia (Ducal, or East), duchy (1525), kingdom (1701)

economy, 79, 83, 87–8, 94

Estates, 216, 228

finance, 225

government, 241

importance, 321–2, 324

literacy, 62

militia, 167

population, 50–1, 272

relationship to Reich, 27, 145

Russian invasion, 329

sovereignty (1660), 216, 229, 322, 326

Prussia (Royal, or West), 27, 323

public order

concern for, 92

problems, 160, 175

responsibility for, 30, 174, 238, 265, 290, 303

Public Peace,

enforcement, 120–1, 124, 159, 166, 171, 177, 328

legislation, 12, 34, 48, 105–7, 161, 177, 190, 252, 349

public sphere, 61–2, 74–5, 164, 286, 293, 334–7, 343

publishing, 62, 334

Pufendorf, Samuel von (1632–94), political theorist, 306

punishment, 101, 176, 197, 265, 278, 290–6

see workhouses

Rákóczi revolt (1703–11), 215–16, 228, 310

Rantzau, county, 298

Ravensberg, county, 139, 323

reading clubs, 75

Recklinghausen, district, 89

Reform Era (1807–19), 337–8

Reformation, 13, 31–2, 72, 97, 104–5, 150–1, 254

Second, 66, 107

reformation, power of, 32–4, 139

Regensburg, bishopric, 188, 199–200, 205

Regensburg electoral congress (1630), 128

Regensburg, electorate (1803), 40

Regensburg, imperial city, 24, 38, 272

Reibald, Josef Anton (d.1773), Palatine chancellor, 244

Reich

attempted reform of, 47, 205, 282, 303–4, 331, 340–1

collapse, 9, 40, 65, 331–2, 342–4

contemporary views of, 18, 33, 36, 183, 305–6, 330

as feudal system, 29, 142, 312

international position, 11, 13, 18–19, 22, 105, 142–3, 190, 212, 321–2

interpretations, 1–7, 11, 23, 163, 180, 196, 329

population, 50, 54, 71, 96, 144–5, 148, 364–77

reorganisation (1803), 40, 46, 206–7, 341

size, 22–3, 307, 364–77

Reich, Second, 1–2, 4, 6, 11–12, 22, 263

Reichsdeputationshauptbeschluß (1803), 341

Reichshofrat

constitutional position, 10, 114, 140, 349

effectiveness, 114, 116, 180–3, 252, 302–3

establishment, 179

reorganisation, 309

see courts

Reichskammergericht

constitutional position, 10, 114, 140, 349

effectiveness, 106, 114, 116, 127, 177, 180–1, 252, 293, 302

establishment, 106, 177, 183

purpose, 106, 140, 163, 177–9, 197

reform, 180, 331

see courts

Reichskirche, see imperial church

Reichstag

development, 35, 158, 160

economic policy, 196–7

Reichstag (*continued*)
  function, 35, 47–9, 100
  and Habsburgs, 308, 312–14
  interpretations, 36
  and justice, 177–8
  meetings; (1521) , 35, 163; (1608), 114;
    (1613), 116; (1640–1), 136–7;
    (1653–4), 161, 169, 251, 313,
    348
  permanent, 41, 313
  procedure, 35–6, 140, 211, 341
  structure, 10, 37–47, 140, 211, 341
Reinkingk, Dietrich (1590–1664),
    political theorist, 306
religion
  alliances, 13, 115–17, 120, 128–9,
    132–3, 136–42
  Austro-Prussian rivalry, 149, 151–3,
    203–5, 272, 284, 325, 328
  culture, 154, 156, 222, 273–4
  economy, 71, 82, 268–9, 275
  education, 67, 108, 110, 153, 273–4,
    286–8
  human reproduction, 52, 55
  identity, 64, 154, 242
  imperial politics, 5, 13, 32, 39, 41–3, 47,
    105–8, 124–5, 133–4, 140, 149–54,
    318, 341
  international relations, 19, 22, 103–4,
    164, 166–8
  justice, 106, 114, 126, 179–80, 293
  Kreis politics, 184, 188–90
  local politics, 97, 149, 251
  marriage, 55–6, 60, 152–3
  migration, 106, 140, 153, 164, 271–3
  military recruitment, 234
  political stability, 36, 211–12, 272
  popular protest, 106, 299, 301
  social stability, 36, 55, 146, 176, 212,
    264–6
  social status, 60, 63, 67, 70, 76, 242–3,
    245, 311
  territorial politics, 30–3, 106, 109–14,
    122, 149–52, 154, 242, 321
  welfare, 31, 274–7
  see clergy; confessionalisation; imperial
    church
rents, 65, 70, 84–6, 90–3, 217, 300

representative institutions, 7, 14–16,
    121–2, 249–53, 257, 300, 304, 347
  see also communalism; Estates;
    Landschaften; Reichstag
republicanism, 14, 208, 211, 250–1
residence towns, 73, 77, 271–2
Restitution Edict (1629), 127–8, 133–4,
    139
Reunions, French policy, 170
Reuss, principalities, 24, 274
Reversalien, 150
Revolution, French (1789), 59, 75, 99, 206,
    332–8, 344
Revolution, German (1830 & 1848), 65,
    244, 262, 338, 344
  (1918), 29, 96
  absence in late 18th century, 288, 290,
    301–4, 332–40
Revolutionary War, American (1775–83),
    281–4
Revolutionary Wars, French (1792–1802)
  economic impact, 260–1, 292, 335–6
  interpretations, 6, 9, 338
  and Reich, 14, 82, 93, 95, 195, 206, 252,
    337
  and Switzerland, 251
Rhenish Alliance (1658–68), 169, 191–2,
    228–9
Rhineland
  economy, 80–1, 84, 146, 148, 283
  French in, 206, 271, 334–6, 339, 341
  local politics, 21, 23–4, 90, 249
  security, 128, 191–5, 316–18, 339–40
  society, 69, 271
Richelieu, Cardinal and duc Armand
    (1585–1642), French statesman,
    132–3, 136
Riedesel, lordship, 298
Rijswijk, peace (1697), 150–1, 175
Rocroi, battle (1643), 135
Roman Month, 163, 168–9, 350
Romans, king of the, 21, 112, 134, 202,
    311, 350
Romanticism, 75, 279–80
Rossbach, battle (1757), 329
Rostock, town, 95–6
Rothschild, Meyer Amshel (1743–1812),
    banker, 278, 281

'rough music', 101
Rublack, Ulinka, historian, 303
Rudolf II (1552–1612), emperor from 1576, 47, 108–15, 125, 180, 219
  imperial defence, 165, 168, 170–1, 313
Rudolstadt, town, 154
Russia
  army, 234, 318
  as Austrian ally, 318–19, 328–31, 338–40
  economy, 83
  emigration to, 283
  expansion, 11, 27
  imperial title, 312
  influence in Reich, 28–9, 40, 137, 331, 341
  population, 50

Saarburg, town, 38
Salien dynasty, 19
St Bartholomew massacre (1572), 106
St Blasien, imperial abbey, 90, 207
St Gallen, imperial abbey, 95
St Thomas (West Indies), 147
Salzburg, archbishopric,
  electoral status, 40
  influence, 24, 43, 184, 188, 199
  internal politics, 200–1, 272, 318
  secularisation, 40, 204–5, 340–1
Sardinia, kingdom, 26, 318
Savoy, duchy, 21, 23, 189, 230, 271
  royal title, 318
Saxon duchies, see Coburg; Eisenach;
  Gotha; Hildburghausen; Jena;
  Meiningen; Weimar
Saxony, electorate
  army, 167, 231, 258, 325
  economy, 79, 81–3, 87–8, 146, 148, 197
  education, 286–7
  electoral status, 39, 41, 120
  finances, 256, 258, 325
  and German Protestants, 107, 114, 116, 123, 125, 128, 133–4, 141, 150–1, 325
  government, 239
  and imperial church, 121, 200
  influence, 8, 13, 21, 120, 184, 186–7, 315, 322, 325–7

and Lausitz, 121, 123–4, 133, 141
  legal system, 294, 299
  and Poland, 28, 151, 223, 244, 318, 326
  population, 54, 325
  Prussian invasions, 258, 260, 282, 326–9
  relationship to Reich, 21, 178
  religion, 66, 77, 150, 223, 273
  revolt (1790), 299, 304, 333
  size, 8, 25, 325
  society, 68, 70, 77, 98
  Swedish occupation, 135, 141
  see Lower and Upper Saxon Kreise
Sayn, see Wittgenstein
Schaffhausen, town, 38
Schaumburg-Lippe, county, 183, 298
Schiller, Freidrich von (1759–1805), writer, 281, 291
Schinderhannes see Bückler, Johannes
Schissler, Hanna, historian, 321
Schleswig, duchy, 25, 28–9, 43, 88, 92
Schlüchter, Andreas (1659–1714), architect, 223
Schmalkaldic War (1546–7), 13, 120
Schollenpflichtigkeit, 85, 87, 89, 350
Schönborn family, 200
Schönborn, Johann Philipp von (1605–73), bishop of Würzburg (1642), elector of Mainz (1647), 139, 189–92, 203, 228–9, 307, 313
Schönborn, Lothar Franz von (1655–1729), bishop of Bamberg (1694), elector of Mainz (1695), 193–4, 203, 307
Schönburg, county, 298
Schöning, Hans Adam von (1641–96), Hohenzollern general, 236
Schröder, Wilhelm von (1640–88), cameralist, 268–9
Schütz, Heinrich (1585–1672), composer, 155
Schwäbisch-Gmünd, imperial city, 149
Schwäbisch-Hall, imperial city, 61, 72
Schwann, Friedrich (1729–60), bandit, 291
Schwarzburg, principality, 298
Schwarzenberg, Adam Count von (1583–1641), Hohenzollern minister, 236

Schwarzenberg, county, later principality, 24
Schwerin, castle, 96
Schwerin, Otto Count von (1616–79), Hohenzollern minister, 236
Seckendorff, Veit Ludwig von (1626–92), cameralist, 268, 306
secularisation
  in German territories, 31, 127, 134, 204–6, 285
  imperial church, 40, 42–4, 121, 127, 138–41, 198, 200, 203–7, 282, 285, 340–1
  and peace, 105, 149
  and politics, 149–54
Sendlingen massacre (1705), 302–3
Serbia, 317
serfdom, 69–70, 83–95, 112
  abolition, 93–5, 284, 299, 344
settlement patterns, 51, 78, 84, 96–7, 102
Seven Years War (1756–63)
  demographic impact, 283, 330
  destruction, 224, 329
  economic impact, 83, 92, 149, 196, 280
  events, 6, 153, 236, 328–9
  fiscal impact, 258–60, 329–30
  and imperial constitution, 49, 152, 329
  military impact, 92, 234, 329–30
Sicily, kingdom, 26, 316
Sierra Morena, 283–4
Silesia, duchy, 25
  economy, 74, 80, 87–8, 93, 146, 148, 283, 287,
  education, 287
  Estates, 112, 118
  Prussian possession, 320, 324, 326, 338
  religion, 77, 139
  Saxon occupation, 121, 123
Simplicissimus (1669), 154
Simultaneum, 150, 152
Sinelli, Father Emmerich (d.1685), Habsburg court confessor and bishop of Vienna, 236
Sinzendorf, Ludwig Philipp Count von (1871–1752), Habsburg chancellor, 236
Slavata family, 122

slave trade, 147
slavery, 90, 92, 269
Slavonia, principality, 92
Slavs, 22
social discipline, 264–5, 289, 296–7, 304, 350
social militarisation, 233–4
society
  class models , 64, 68, 74–5, 214–15, 290–2, 300–1, 304
  contemporary views of, 63–4, 67, 70–1, 75–7, 265–6, 269
  corporate structure, 15, 58, 63–4, 67–8, 71–2, 96, 156, 162, 248, 337
  groups in, 65–73
  mobility, 64, 73–5, 214, 243–4, 287
  transformation, 64–5, 74–5, 264–5
  see gender; households; marriage
Soest, town, 38
'soldier trade', 281, 283
soldiers
  conditions, 144–6, 168, 231–2, 234
  marriage, 55, 73, 234
  mercenaries, 118, 125, 232
  motivation, 144, 231
  status, 75, 78, 146, 226, 228
  violence, 145–6
  see armies, military
Solms, counties, 23, 298
Sonderweg, 2, 5
Sonnenfels, Joseph von (1733–1817), cameralist, 279, 284
sovereignty
  of Reich, 34, 305–6
  territorial, 12, 30, 33–5, 216, 254, 266, 343, 350
Spain
  and Austria, 119, 126, 131–2, 135–7, 159, 191, 216–18, 327
  and Burgundian Kreis, 314
  economy, 147, 198
  emigration to, 283–4
  and German princes, 108, 231
  government, 160, 246
  nobility, 19, 243, 246, 254
  and Reich, 103, 127, 131–2, 166–7, 170, 184, 186
Spanish Road, 108, 119, 131–2, 140

Spener, Philipp Jacob (1635–1705), theologian, 273–4
Speyer, bishopric, 23, 66
Speyer, imperial city, 76–7, 177
Spinola, Ambrosio di (1659–1630), Spanish general, 121
Spinoza, Benedict (Baruch) (1632–77), radical Dutch philosopher, 279
Sporck, Johann, Habsburg general, 214
Stanislaus Leszcynski (1677–1766), king of Poland, 318–19
Starhemberg, Gundaker Thomas Count, Habsburg finance minister, 236, 259
state
  impersonal, 253–4, 262, 265, 338, 343
  interpretations, 253–6, 276, 289, 296
  see absolutism
States General, Dutch, 122
Staufer dynasty, 19
Stavenow, manorial estate, 90
Steinberg, S. H., historian, 145
Stolberg, county, 24
Stralsund, town, 129
subsidies, 169–70, 232–3, 259, 281, 315
subsistence crises, 51, 277, 283, 300
Strasbourg, bishopric, 23, 112, 201
Strasbourg, imperial city, 38, 63, 170
Stuttgart, residence town, 248, 335
Stuttgart, treaty (1634), 133
Styria, duchy, 26, 109–10, 252
sumptuary laws, 63, 267
Swabian Kreis
  army, 175
  assembly, 196
  Association, 192–6
  economy, 83
  invasions, 128, 170
  mortality, 53
  public order, 291
  society, 42, 70, 97, 199
  vitality, 341
Sweden
  decline, 143, 150, 315, 320, 324
  French alliance, 104, 133, 135
  as imperial estate, 140–3, 186–7, 199, 306–7, 328–9
  influence, 27–8, 38, 48, 136–8, 190, 272

legal system, 294
military intervention, 103, 128–36, 143, 271, 324
propaganda, 129, 305–6
Sybel, Heinrich von (1817–95), historian, 4

tax registers, 275
taxation
  burden, 51, 73, 84–5, 93, 100, 144, 213, 217, 257–8, 299
  emergence, 157–62, 254
  exemptions from, 68, 93, 233
  growth, 15, 91, 96, 101, 125, 248, 256
  imperial, 85, 116, 125, 143, 57–64, 166, 168–9, 177, 299
  methods, 158, 160–2, 177, 254–7, 263
  military, 125, 145, 158, 160–1, 167, 202, 216, 225, 228–31, 251–2
  political implications, 213, 269, 300
  protests against, 96, 102, 160–1, 176, 228–9, 251–2, 297, 299–300, 335
  sources, 91, 254, 270, 272, 300
Tecklenburg, county, 323
Telemann, Georg Philipp (1681–1767), composer, 156
territorialisation, 29–35, 46, 265, 350
Teschen, peace (1779), 331, 341
Teutonic Order, 27, 43, 147, 203, 286
textile industry, 53, 58, 74, 81–2, 92, 270, 277, 287
theatre, 154
'Third Germany', 9, 329–30
Third Party, as force in imperial politics, 128, 190–4
Thirteen Years War (1593–1606), 110–12, 165, 168
Thirty Years War (1618–48)
  causes, 45, 103–17, 169, 182
  cultural impact, 154–5, 222, 273
  demographic impact, 50, 53–4, 96, 144–5, 271
  economic impact, 51, 81, 87, 94, 146–9, 170, 213, 216, 308, 329
  events, 117–36
  fiscal impact, 125–6, 143, 145, 251, 257
  interpretations, 5, 7, 103–5, 144, 149
  military impact, 143, 157, 169, 225, 228, 230–1

Thirty Years War (1618–48) (*continued*)
  political impact, 44, 47, 138–44,
      149–53, 179, 187, 190, 208, 219,
      299, 305–9
  propaganda in, 62, 129, 305–6
  psychological impact, 145–6, 226 268,
      273
  see Westphalia, peace of
Thomasius, Christian (1655–1728),
      cameralist, 277
Thorn, city, 339
Thurgut, Franz Maria Baron von
      (1736–1818), Habsburg minister,
      237
Thuringia, region, 24–5, 144, 188, 291
Thurn, Heinrich Matthias Count von
      (1567–1640), Bohemian general, 113,
      117–18, 122
Tilly, Jean Tserclaus Baron (1559–1632),
      Bavarian general, 120–1, 126–8,
      144
Tirol, county, 26, 97, 233, 249
tithes, 51, 85
toleration
  for Christian dissenters, 109–10, 115,
      164–5, 271–3, 284–6
  imperial law, 152–4, 139–40,
  for Jews, 76–8, 286
  opposition to, 284–5, 289
Törring family, 217
torture
  abolition, 294–5, 336
  judicial, 68, 179, 293
  by soldiers, 145–6
Toul, bishopric, 38, 43, 140
Toul, imperial city, 38, 140
Transylvania, principality, 116, 122, 135,
      159, 215, 229
  conquest, 26, 310
  Habsburg rule in, 311
Trauttmannsdorff, Maximilian Count von
      (1584–1650), Habsburg ambassador,
      135, 138, 140, 235
Treitschke, Heinrich von (1834–96),
      historian, 4
Trent, bishopric, 199, 249
Trent, Council of (1545–63), 32, 107
  decrees, 67, 107, 110, 202

Trier, electorate
  chapter, 200
  Estates, 201
  and France, 132–3, 334
  imperial politics, 120, 191, 204–5
  possession of, 200, 205
  relationship to Reich, 39–40, 178
  society, 77
  territory, 23, 188, 199
Trieste, 80, 147
Tscherneml, Georg Erasmus (1567–1626),
      Upper Austrian Estates' leader from
      1608, 113
Tübingen University, 278
Tugendliche Gesellschaft, 154
Tullian, Lips (d.1715), bandit, 291
Turin, battle (1706), 316
Türkheim, battle (1675), 170
'Turkish Aid', 161
Turkish Wars
  characteristics, 164, 269
  of 16th century, 26, 106, 109–11, 161,
      163–5, 168, 233
  (1662–4), 169, 172, 191, 229, 313
  (1683–99), *see* Great Turkish War
  (1716–18), 173, 317, 319
  (1737–9), 319, 338
  (1787–92), 253, 324, 338–9
  see Ottomans; Thirteen Years War
Tuscany, grand duchy, 23
Twelve Years Truce (1609–21), 119, 131

Uckermark, district, 86–7, 89
Ukraine, 80
Ulm, imperial city, 61, 81, 301
United Provinces *see* Dutch Republic
universities, 96, 243, 245–6, 285–7
Upper Rhenish Kreis, 140, 171, 184–5,
      189, 191, 193, 195, 197, 341
Upper Rhenish Union (1679), 171, 189,
      192
Upper Saxon Kreis, 25, 46, 143, 184,
      186–7, 197
Urban VIII (Maffeo Barberini)
      (1567–1644), pope from 1623, 136
urbanisation, 71
Urbarium decree, 92–3
Uskoks, 165

Utrecht, bishopric, 43
Utrecht, peace (1713), 194, 317, 322

vagrancy, 78, 162, 276, 283, 290–2, 332
Valmy, battle (1792), 339
Valtelline passes, 119, 132
Vasa dynasty, 28
Venice, republic, 23, 119, 165, 173, 305,
    340
  war with the Ottomans (1714–18), 317
Verden, bishopric, 24, 124, 127, 141, 186
Verdun, bishopric, 38, 43, 140
Verdun, imperial city, 38, 140
Verden, town, 38
Versailles, palace, 218–19
Versailles, peace (1919), 104
Vienna, city
  attacks on, 118, 135, 174, 222
  development, 269
  fortifications, 165
  ghetto, 77, 285
  Habsburg court, 26, 113, 179, 219, 221,
      236, 311
  and Passau, 66
  university, 285
Vienna, congress (1814–15), 196
Vienna, treaty (1606), 111–12
Viennese City Bank, 259
Vierklösterstreit, 114
Voltaire, François Marie Arouet de
    (1694–1778), philosopher, 154, 244,
    280
Voralberg, 97

Waldeck, principality, 287
Waldensians, religious minority, 230, 271
Wallachia, principality, 110
Wallenstein, Albrecht Wenzel Eusebius
    von (1583–1634), imperial general
  dismissal, 41, 128, 130–1
  influences, 126–7, 130, 143, 169, 314,
      336
Wallenstein family, 122
Wangen, imperial city, 301
War of the Austrian Succession (1740–8),
  causes, 40, 53, 326
  events, 77–8, 195, 203, 310, 326–7
  impact on Reich, 203, 282, 326–8

War of the Bavarian Succession (1778–9),
    260, 331
War of the Polish Succession (1733–5),
    152, 173, 175, 218–19
War of the Spanish Succession (1701–14),
    48, 150, 152, 158, 173, 175, 192–5,
    313–18, 327
Warburg, town, 38
Warsaw, city, 223
Wartenberg, Franz Wilhelm von
    (1593–1661), bishop of Osnabrück
    (1627), Verden (1630), Minden
    (1631), Regensburg (1649) and
    cardinal (1661), 107, 138–9
Wartenberg, Johann Casimir Kolbe von
    (1643–1712), Hohenzollern minister,
    236
Weber, Max (1864–1920), sociologist, 234
Wegert, Karl, historian, 296
Weimar, duchy, 24, 63, 205, 241, 287, 294
Weimar Republic (1919–33), 12
welfare
  impact, 54, 73, 78
  local, 90
  measures, 56–7, 247, 73–7, 281
  motives, 58, 253, 274–7
  responsibility for, 31, 162
Westphalia, duchy, 188
Westphalia, peace (1648)
  celebration , 143–4, 149
  constitutional changes, 12, 33–4, 138,
      140, 142, 169, 179, 186
  interpretations, 5, 143–4, 153, 306
  negotiations, 48, 103, 136–8, 190, 307,
      313
  political impact, 9, 19, 138–43, 157, 187
  religious terms, 33, 77, 138–40, 149–50,
      308–9
  territorial redistribution, 140–3, 308,
      321, 323
Westphalian Kreis
  army, 194
  assembly, 195
  and Associations, 191, 193
  composition, 24, 169, 184, 186–8, 199,
      326
  economy, 81–3, 148, 197
  Estates, 252

Westphalian Kreis (*continued*)
  invasions , 143, 167, 282
  Prussian influence , 315, 341
  society, 42, 46, 69–70, 244
Wetterau, region, 23
Wettin dynasty
  Albertine branch, 39, 120, 151
  Ernestine branch, 39, 120, 182, 194
  partition, 45
  see Saxon duchies; Saxony
Wetzlar, imperial city, 76–7, 177, 181–2
White mountain, battle (1620), 121, 123
widowhood, 56–7, 75, 274
Wildfang dispute, 90, 182
Wilhelm V (d.1637), landgrave of Hessen-
    Kassel from 1627, 134
Wilhelm IX (1743–1821), landgrave of
    Hessen-Kassel from 1785, 281
Wilhelm Hyacinth (d.1743), prince of
    Nassau-Siegen 1699–1708, 151, 303
Wismar, town, 186
witchcraft, 179, 293, 296
Wittelsbach dynasty, 39–40, 45, 120
  political influence, 46, 188, 200, 206,
    315–17, 331
  see Bavaria; Palatinate; Pfalz-Neuburg
Wittstock, battle (1636), 135
Woellner, Johann Christoph von
    (1732–1800), Prussian minister, 225
Wolfenbüttel, duchy, 25, 69, 251, 286–7,
    294
Wolff, Christian (1679–1754),
    philosopher, 279
workhouses, 68, 275–7, 290, 295
Wörlitz, gardens, 282
Worms, bishopric, 23, 184, 189, 191, 200
Worms, imperial city, 35, 76–7
Württemberg, duchy
  army, 153, 167
  economy, 81–2
  education, 278, 286–7

  electoral status, 39–40
  Estates, 78, 150, 248, 252–3, 257–8, 260,
    273, 278
  finances, 252, 258, 260–1
  government, 236, 239–41, 243, 247,
    277–8
  influence, 126, 141, 184, 207, 261, 340–1
  legal system, 277, 294, 296
  population, 96, 144, 283
  religion, 66, 150, 273
  size, 13, 24, 189
  society, 65, 69, 77–8, 243
  unrest, 335
  welfare, 57, 59
Würzburg, bishopric
  chapter, 200, 202
  dispute with Mainz, 182
  electoral status, 40
  finances, 202
  influence, 139, 190, 202
  militia, 230
  society, 73, 77
  territory, 24, 199
Wusterhausen, palace, 224

Zell, imperial city, 301
Zerotin, Karel (1564–1636), Moravian
    leader, 122
Zincke, Georg Heinrich (1692–1769),
    cameralist, 277
Zinzendorf, Count Ludwig (1721–80),
    Habsburg minister, 260
Zinzendorf, Count Nikolaus (1700–60),
    leader of the Moravian
    fundamentalist movement, 274
Zsitva Torok, treaty (1606), 111, 123
Zúñiga, Don Balthasar (1561–1623),
    Spanish ambassador, 118–19
Zusmarshausen, battle (1648), 135
Zweibrücken-Kleeberg, principality, 28
Zwiefalten, imperial abbey, 207